The Intersection of AI and Student Development in Learning

Robert Zheng
https://orcid.org/0000-0003-0507-3340
University of Utah, USA

IGI Global
Scientific Publishing
Publishing Tomorrow's Research Today

Vice President of Editorial Melissa Wagner
Director of Acquisitions Mikaela Felty
Director of Book Development Jocelynn Hessler
Production Manager Mike Brehm
Cover Design Jose Rosado

Published in the United States of America by
IGI Global Scientific Publishing
701 East Chocolate Avenue
Hershey, PA, 17033, USA
Tel: 717-533-8845 | Fax: 717-533-7115
Website: https://www.igi-global.com E-mail: cust@igi-global.com

Library of Congress Cataloging-in-Publication Data

Names: Zheng, Robert editor http://id.loc.gov/authorities/names/n2007039881 http://id.loc.gov/rwo/agents/n2007039881
Title: The intersection of AI and student development in learning / [edited by] Robert Zheng.
Description: Hershey, PA : IGI Global Scientific Publishing, [2026] | Includes bibliographical references and index. | Summary: "This book aims to examine the relationship between AI technology and cognitive development in education and the untethering the ethical and policy aspects of AI application in education"-- Provided by publisher.
Identifiers: LCCN 2025013486 (print) | LCCN 2025013487 (ebook) | ISBN 9798337329277 hardcover | ISBN 9798337329284 paperback | ISBN 9798337329291 ebook
Subjects: LCSH: Artificial intelligence--Educational applications http://id.loc.gov/authorities/subjects/sh87006783 | Learning http://id.loc.gov/authorities/subjects/sh85075520 | Student growth (Academic achievement) http://id.loc.gov/authorities/subjects/sh2017000303
Classification: LCC LB1028.43 .I686 2026 (print) | LCC LB1028.43 (ebook) | DDC 370.15/23028563--dc23/eng/20250530
LC record available at https://lccn.loc.gov/2025013486
LC ebook record available at https://lccn.loc.gov/2025013487

British Cataloguing in Publication Data
A Cataloguing in Publication record for this book is available from the British Library.

Editorial Advisory Board

Table of Contents

Detailed Table of Contents

Affordances included personalization, automated feedback, and multimodal engagement; challenges were infrastructure, bias, and over-reliance. Teachers generally viewed AI positively but had concerns about its reliability. Most studies used learn-apply-reflect cycles in pre-service contexts. AI improved teaching efficacy and digital skills, but findings relied on self-reports and short-term data. Geographic concentration in Asia and researcher-led initiatives constrain generalizability. The review highlights the need for AI literacy in curricula, institutional support, and more longitudinal research.

This study aims to explore learners' perceptions of AI use in the foreign language learning process and to investigate whether their perceptions differ under specific variables, such as age, gender, grade, department, and proficiency in the target language. This descriptive study administered a background questionnaire and the Perceptions of AI Usage Scale (PAS) to 897 EFL learners. Descriptive statistics, independent samples t-test, ANOVA, and Tamhane were used for data analysis. The study concluded that learners perceive that integrating AI tools and environments contributes to writing and reading skills, and they seem doubtful about the effect of AI on speaking, listening comprehension, pronunciation, and communicative skills. It was also concluded that learners' perceptions of AI usage do not show any difference based on gender, while their perceptions seem to be related to learners' ages, grades, departments, and proficiency levels in the target language.

Teaching and learning a second language have changed considerably over the past several decades with a new paradigm focusing on student proficiency in the target language. Digital technologies have become practical tools for both instructors and students. Among the latest developments is artificial intelligence, which can perform tasks to achieve learning objectives without exhaustive human guidance. ChatGPT's natural language processing abilities appear to hold promise for the provision of corrective written feedback to second language learners. The purpose of the present study was to examine second language learners' perceptions of receiving corrective written feedback from ChatGPT using the IDEE framework (Su & Yang, 2023) as a research lens. Results indicate that there are benefits of using ChatGPT for both language learners and instructors. The study has implications for instructors, world language program coordinators, and educationalists.

The purpose of this chapter is to illustrate how Generative Artificial Intelligence (AI) can be leveraged to support high school students' mathematical reasoning through writing. Specifically, this chapter provides background information related to difficulties high school students with disabilities may experience in mathematics and writing and highlights how AI could be leveraged to address such challenges. In this chapter, we also describe an iterative process our research team used to develop a usable AI browser plugin to facilitate the argument and mathematics learning of high school students with learning challenges and report the preliminary results of studies we conducted to evaluate initial usability and efficacy of an intervention utilizing the AI plugin on students' mathematical reasoning and argumentative mathematical writing. We also discuss implications for practice for teachers, teacher educators, and instructional designers and present recommendations for future research in this area.

Learning occurs as students select, organize, and integrate knowledge into structured networks. Online mathematical discussions offer opportunities for this knowledge building process, yet little is known about how students' social positions within discussion networks relate to their knowledge structures. Using over two million discussion records, we classified students into core, peripheral, and x-peripheral roles based on the breadth and depth of their interactions. Large language models were then used to generate knowledge graphs (KGs), which we analyzed with graph-theoretic metrics. Core students showed broader concept activation, more coherent organization, and deeper integration than x-peripheral students. Participation patterns also predicted knowledge structures differently across roles: tutor replies supported richer and more integrated KGs for core and peripheral students, while x-peripheral students benefited more from self-directed engagement. These results show how participation roles shape mathematical knowledge construction and demonstrate the value of LLM-generated KGs as scalable measures of knowledge structures.

This study explores positive emotional expressions in interdisciplinary distance education (DE) by examining how happiness emerges in relation to group composition through AI-supported emotion detection in multimodal data. Within interdisciplinary educational settings, diverse learner backgrounds give rise to a range of affective responses that shape collaborative experiences. The research focuses on how such emotions unfold in both homogeneous and heterogeneous student groups with different group compositions. Sixteen participants engaged in a 10-week interdisciplinary DE course. By integrating facial emotion recognition with text mining, this study offers a holistic analysis of video- and text-based interactions. Findings revealed that happiness was most frequently linked to three socio-emotional factors: the familiarity effect, the process of establishing oneself, and a sense of ontological security. These insights inform affectively responsive instructional design and support the integration of AI in fostering emotionally attuned learning environments.

The application of Artificial Intelligence (AI) in the educational field is changing the process of learning to offer an individualised learning experience, benefiting students with cognitive and affective needs. This chapter discusses the point of AI and student growth, adaptive learning technologies, intelligent tutoring systems, and emotion-aware intelligent AI models that increase engagement and knowledge retention. Increasing student achievements in academic and socio-emotional development, the AI-driven insights provide teachers with the possibility to develop dynamic curricula and cater to specific learning styles. The chapter further analyses issues of ethical concern, including algorithmic bias and data privacy, and policy systems to implement AI responsibility in education. Case studies and empirical studies help analyse in the chapter the manner in which AI-based personalisation is transforming pedagogical methods to achieve equal access to quality education.

This chapter aims to explore the potential of artificial intelligence (AI)-supported tools in improving learners' complex learning. The chapter is focused on the pedagogical aspects of integrating AI tools by examining the relationship between student learning and the theoretical models of learning that include cognitive load theory, self-determined theory and the ICAP approach. A proof of concept study was conducted by taking into account learners' cognitive and affective behaviors in AI-supported complex learning. It was found that the learners demonstrated differently in terms of their cognitive and affective performance when engaged across a variety of learning activities, i.e., active, constructive, and interactive. The results highlight the importance of pedagogy in implementing AI technology in education. Discussions based on the findings were made pertaining to future research in an effort to provide guidance for professionals (e.g., researchers, practitioners, learners) who are interested in integrating AI in learning.

The rapid integration of artificial intelligence (AI) into education and professional practice has brought about transformative opportunities and pressing ethical challenges. This chapter examines the principles, guidelines, and responsibilities that students must understand and follow when interacting with AI technologies. This chapter examines key topics, including academic integrity, data privacy, algorithmic bias, intellectual property, and the responsible use of generative AI tools such as ChatGPT and GitHub Copilot. Through real-world case studies, theoretical frameworks, and practical scenarios, the chapter fosters critical thinking and ethical reasoning among computer science students. It also provides educators with strategies for promoting ethical awareness and decision-making in AI-assisted learning environments. By grounding technical education in strong ethical foundations, this chapter aims to prepare future programmers and engineers to contribute to a trustworthy and socially responsible AI landscape.

Artificial Intelligence (AI) is revolutionizing education by transforming how students learn, engage, and develop. AI technologies, such as adaptive learning platforms, intelligent tutoring systems, and automated assessment tools, enable personalized learning experiences and provide valuable data-driven insights to enhance academic success. This chapter explores AI's transformative impact on student development, focusing on its role in fostering personalized instruction, increasing student engagement, and improving assessment and feedback practices. It also addresses the ethical concerns, challenges, and future opportunities associated with AI integration in education. By combining AI innovations with human-centred pedagogical approaches, educators can create more inclusive and effective learning environments that cater to diverse student needs, ensuring that AI serves as a tool to empower all learners while preserving essential human interaction in the educational process.

Advancements in AI, such as ChatGPT, have garnered significant interest within higher education. In response, policymakers and practitioners are striving to develop evidence-based strategies for its integration. Generating valid and reliable evidence requires robust tools to explore students' use of ChatGPT in higher education. This paper discusses the development and validation of a questionnaire designed to assess the perceived Knowledge, Will, Skill, Technological Support, and Use (KWSTU) of ChatGPT. The questionnaire was grounded in the theoretical foundation of the Will-Skill-Tool (WST) model and underwent rigorous content and construct validation. Confirmatory Factor Analysis validated five distinct factors comprising 30 items, with statistical evidence indicating good model-fit indices. Moreover, path analysis was employed to investigate the factors influencing ChatGPT use among university students in Pakistan. This study provides a validated instrument and empirical insights that have significant implications for policy, practice, and research to make informed decisions.

Preface

The rapid advancement of artificial intelligence (AI) has brought multiple areas of changes in education. AI is now considered as essential as other literacy skills such as writing and reading (Zhang et al., 2025). As an emerging technology, AI has not only infiltrated into every corner of our quotidian life but also shown potential in improving the condition of education with its unique features in terms of (a) facilitating learner cognitive and affective processes, (b) scaling-up educational assessment and evaluation, and (c) renovating pedagogy to meet the requirements of the 21st century. Research has demonstrated the benefits of AI in learning, leading to changes in learner behavior, motivation and performance (Cosentino et al., 2025; Luo et al., 2025; Xing et al., 2025). In their study on the effect of generative AI in teachable agents, Xing and colleagues find that the teachable agent powered by generative AI aligns well with naturalistic learning and therefore is conducive for creative and innovative mathematical thinking. In a separate study on language teaching with AI, Hong and Guo (2025) reported the improvement of cognitive load, motivation and self-autonomy among students who participated in AI-enhanced learning. The researchers concluded that AI-enhanced environments can significantly improve learners' learning outcomes. They went on to underscore the importance of integrating AI interventions to enhance motivation, manage cognitive load, and foster learner autonomy in teaching and learning. Similar findings were obtained in STEM education research where researchers discovered the positive impacts of AI on students' (a) reflective thinking in STEM learning (Lin et al., 2025), (b) performance through personalized feedback (Villegas-Ch et al., 2025), and (c) abilities to engage in critical thinking and problem solving (Shabalala, 2024). Evidently, like other new educational technologies, AI holds promises for delivering education that champions individual creativity and critical thinking, embraces innovation and creation, and supports personalized learning to bring the learners' potential to their fullest possible.

Benefits of AI in teaching and learning aside, some scholars express their concerns over the use of AI and resultant outcomes in education. Aldawsari and Almohish

(2024) conducted a survey of Saudi Arabian educational technologists ($N = 20$), tapping into their perceptions on the threats and opportunities of integrating AI in higher education. The results show that challenges pertaining to AI integration exist. They include technological infrastructure, pedagogical adaptation, and the need for comprehensive training programs to empower both teachers and learners. Other challenges are human-AI interaction, data security, privacy, and potential risks associated with AI technology in educational institutions. The researchers cautioned the integration of AI in education demands proactive addressing of ethical, pedagogical, and practical considerations to unlock its full potential and ensure the best possible learning outcomes. By examining AI integration in instructional design, Choi et al. (2024) identified the challenges (e.g., unreliable output, inconsistencies) and threats (e.g., quality control) when integrating AI in the process of instructional design. Recognizing the challenges of AI integration in instructional design, the researchers suggested that "it still requires human interventions and moderations to provide more reliable and trustworthy outputs for quality control purposes" (p. 843). Taking a different perspective, Kumar et al. (2024) explore the effects of using ChatGPT in STEM course design. The study interviewed five instructors to glean their thoughts on AI integration. The researchers observed the weaknesses associated with AI integration in STEM course design which include mental fatigue, over-reliance, and AI-generated content reliability. In short, while AI holds the promise to improve education in general, teaching and learning in particular, it is not without challenges. Issues include content reliability, data privacy, mental fatigue, over reliance, and so forth. To better understand the promises of AI and its challenges, the current edited text is called for to further unveil the issues of concern at a deeper level.

Twenty-nine scholars around the world have contributed to the book with essays based on their unwavering hard work and years of research. The first half of the book amasses essays that focus on AI integration in teaching and learning (Chapters 1-5). Topics of this section include AI-human collaboration in K-12 education, research on AI in language learning, and the utilization of AI in STEM for learners with disabilities. The second half of the book presents essays that explore various aspects in AI-powered environment (Chapters 6-12). Topics include relationship between learners' social roles and knowledge structures, research on AI-supported emotion detection in learning, student development in AI-driven personalized learning, learners' complex learning with AI, design of effective AI, student development and learning with AI and assessment development and validation on key factors related to AI use. The following provides a brief introduction to each chapter, which I hope would prepare the readers to better appreciate the content as they peruse the essays in this book.

ORGANIZATION OF THE BOOK

As it was mentioned earlier, the first half of the book consists of essays that focus on AI integration in teaching and learning (Chapters 1-5). Topics of this section include AI-human collaboration in K-12 education, research on AI in language learning, and the utilization of AI in STEM for learners with disabilities.

Chapter 1. Written by Wing Sha Chan, Jinhee Kim, Seongryeong Yu, and Rita K. Detrick of Old Dominion University, the authors explore an important issue in the research of AI: Human-AI Collaboration (HAC) in k-12 education. The chapter covers four essential areas: curriculum design, student and teacher–AI interaction, learning environments, and the evolution of HAC over time. The authors first introduce the concept of HAC in K–12 contexts, highlighting how humans and AI can leverage each other's strengths through co-evolutionary processes that foster mutual learning and collaboration, followed by a review of current HAC practices in schools and discussion on their contributions to both teaching and learning. Finally, the authors recommend future directions for HAC research and practice and discuss the implications for educational policy, AI system design, and instructional design to strengthen human-AI partnerships in education.

Chapter 2. By conducting a systematic review of AI-enhanced professional development in language teacher education, Idil Sayin and Derya Coskun of Suleyman Demirel University investigated the role of artificial intelligence on curriculum related activities like lesson planning and adaptive tutoring. The authors examined the affordances of AI that include personalization, automated feedback, and multimodal engagement and identified the challenges associated with the use of AI, which include infrastructure, bias, and over-reliance. The authors observed teachers generally viewed AI positively but had concerns about its reliability. In their review, the authors came to the conclusion that most studies used learn-apply-reflect cycles in pre-service contexts and that AI as a curriculum assistant tool improved teaching efficacy and digital skills. In reflection, the authors pointed out the findings were relied on self-reports and short-term data and therefore proper caution must be exercised when interpreting the results. The authors concluded by highlighting the need for AI literacy in curricula, institutional support, and more longitudinal research.

Chapter 3. This is a chapter focusing on the effects of AI on English as Foreign Language (EFL) learning. Written by Selami Aydin and Cansu Candemir Ozkan of Istanbul Medeniyet University, the authors explore learners' perceptions of AI use in the foreign language learning process and investigate whether their perceptions differ due to specific variables, such as age, gender, grade, department, and proficiency in the target language. The study reported that learners perceive factors like AI tools and environments contribute to writing and reading skills, however they seem to have reservation in the effect of AI on speaking, listening comprehension, pronunciation, and communicative skills. It was quite interesting the authors observed that learners' perceptions of AI usage do not show any difference based on gender, rather, the factors like ages, grades, departments, and proficiency levels in the target language seem to play a role in their perceptions.

Chapter 4. Pete Swanson and Michael R. Richey of United States Air Force Academy contribute a chapter on the topic of Spanish language learners' perceptions of AI in corrective written feedback in the classroom, which is somewhat along the line of the study in Chapter 3 but charting off to a specific focus: second language learners' perceptions of receiving corrective written feedback from ChatGPT. Teaching and learning a second language have changed considerably over the past several decades with a new paradigm focusing on student proficiency in the target language. Digital technologies have become practical tools for both instructors and students. Among the latest developments is artificial intelligence, which can perform tasks to achieve learning objectives without exhaustive human guidance. ChatGPT's natural language processing abilities appear to hold promise for the provision of corrective written feedback to second language learners. Swanson and Richey examined second language learners' perceptions of receiving corrective written feedback from ChatGPT using the IDEE framework as a research lens. Results indicate that there are benefits of using ChatGPT for both language learners and instructors. The study has implications for instructors, world language program coordinators, and educationalists.

Chapter 5. In this chapter, Bundock of Utah State University, Li, Kiuhara and Zheng of University of Utah examined how Generative Artificial Intelligence (AI) can be leveraged to support high school students' mathematical reasoning through writing. Specifically, this chapter provides background information related to difficulties high school students with disabilities may experience in mathematics and writing and highlights how AI could be leveraged to address such challenges. The authors also describe an iterative process to develop a usable AI browser plugin to facilitate the argument and mathematics learning of high school students with learning challenges. Their studies report the preliminary results of the efficacy of an intervention utilizing the AI plugin on students' mathematical reasoning and argumentative mathematical writing. Discussions were made with reference to the implications for the practice for teachers, teacher educators, and instructional designers with recommendations for future research in this area.

The rest of the book consists of essays that explore various aspects in AI-powered learning environment (Chapters 6-12). Topics include a focus on the relationship between learners' social roles and knowledge structures, research on AI-supported emotion detection, student development in AI-driven personalized learning, learners' complex learning with AI, design of effective AI, student development and learning with AI and assessment development and validation on key factors related to AI use.

Chapter 6. Chenglu Li of University of Utah and Bailing Lyu of Auburn University examined students' mathematical discussions and their knowledge building process in an online environment. Based on over two million discussion records, the authors classified students into core, peripheral, and x-peripheral roles based on the breadth and depth of their interactions. Large language models were used to generate knowledge graphs (KGs) which are further analyzed with graph-theoretic metrics. Core students showed broader concept activation, more coherent organization, and deeper integration than x-peripheral students. Participation patterns also predicted knowledge structures differently across roles: tutor replies supported richer and more integrated KGs for core and peripheral students, while x-peripheral students benefited more from self-directed engagement. The findings of the study suggest participation roles may influence and shape mathematical knowledge construction. Additionally, the study has pioneered a novel approach in research by demonstrating the value of LLM-generated KGs as scalable measures of knowledge structures.

Chapter 7. Tugba Ozturk, Gulgun Afacan Adanir and Bahadırhan Aktas (Ankara University, Cambridge University) explore positive emotional expressions in interdisciplinary distance education (DE) by studying how happiness emerges in relation to group composition through AI-supported emotion detection in multimodal data. Within interdisciplinary educational settings, diverse learner backgrounds give rise to a range of affective responses that shape collaborative experiences. The research focuses on how such emotions unfold in both homogeneous and heterogeneous student groups with different group compositions. By integrating facial emotion recognition with text mining, this study offers a holistic analysis of video- and text-based interactions. Findings revealed that happiness was most frequently linked to three socio-emotional factors: the familiarity effect, the process of establishing oneself, and a sense of ontological security. The findings of the study will help inform the design of affectively responsive instruction and support the integration of AI in fostering emotionally attuned learning environments.

Chapter 8. Rashid Hashmi of Sharda University studied AI-driven personalized learning in an adaptive technology learning environment. The author discusses the point of AI use and student growth, adaptive learning technologies, intelligent tutoring systems, and emotion-aware intelligent AI models that increase engagement and knowledge retention. The author observed the AI-driven tools provide teachers with the possibility to develop dynamic curricula and cater to specific learning styles. The author in his discussion also visits issues of ethical concern, including algorithmic bias and data privacy, and policy systems to implement AI responsibility in education. Case studies and empirical studies help illuminate how AI-based personalization transforms pedagogical methods in achieving equal access for quality education.

Chapter 9. Taking from cognitive and affective perspectives, Zheng, Wallace, Charles, and Soto (University of Utah, Millersville University) explore the potential of artificial intelligence (AI)-supported tools in improving learners' complex learning. The authors base off their research from a theoretical framework that includes cognitive load theory, self-determined theory and the ICAP theory. The proof of concept study was conducted by taking into account learners' cognitive and affective behaviors in AI-supported complex learning. It was found that the learners behaved differently in terms of their cognitive and affective performance when engaged across a variety of learning activities, i.e., active, constructive, and interactive. The results highlight the importance of pedagogy in implementing AI technology in education. Discussions were made with reference to the implications of the findings for teaching and learning. Recommendations were made to provide guidance for professionals (e.g., researchers, practitioners, learners) in their future efforts to integrate AI in teaching and learning.

Chapter 10. In this chapter, Hanh Le of University of the Cumberlands examines the principles, guidelines, and responsibilities that students must understand and follow when interacting with AI technologies. The chapter covers multiple key topics, including academic integrity, data privacy, algorithmic bias, intellectual property, and the responsible use of generative AI tools such as ChatGPT and GitHub Copilot. Through real-world case studies, theoretical frameworks, and practical scenarios, the author discusses how to foster students' critical thinking and ethical reasoning as well as ethical awareness and decision-making in AI-assisted learning environments. By grounding technical education in strong ethical foundations, this chapter provides helpful references for those who prepare future programmers and engineers to contribute to a trustworthy and socially responsible AI landscape.

Chapter 11. This chapter, authored by Sam Ramaila of University of Johannesburg, examines AI's transformative impact on student development, focusing on its role in fostering personalized instruction, increasing student engagement, and improving assessment and feedback practices. It also addresses the ethical concerns, challenges, and future opportunities associated with AI integration in education. The author in his final note points out that by combining AI innovations with human-centred pedagogical approaches, educators can create more inclusive and effective learning environments that cater to diverse student needs, ensuring that AI serves as a tool to empower all learners while preserving essential human interaction in the educational process.

Chapter 12. Aisha Naz Ansari, Sohail Ahmad and Sadia Muzaffar Bhutta of Aga Khan University present in this chapter the development and validation of a questionnaire designed to assess the perceived Knowledge, Will, Skill, Technological Support, and Use (KWSTU) of ChatGPT. The questionnaire was grounded in the theoretical foundation of the Will-Skill-Tool (WST) model and underwent rigorous content and construct validation. Confirmatory Factor Analysis validated five distinct factors comprising 30 items, with statistical evidence indicating good model-fit indices. Moreover, path analysis was employed to investigate the factors influencing ChatGPT use among university students in Pakistan. This study provides a validated instrument and empirical insights that have significant implications for policy makers, practitioners, and researchers to make informed decisions.

CONCLUSION

The current book focuses on the role of AI in education covering a wide range of topics: students' learning, pedagogical practices, cognitive and affective processes, personalization and motivation, and assessment. Although evidence has shown the benefits of AI in learning, research that aims to understand the functional roles of AI at deeper level is lacking, particularly in the areas of AI and knowledge construction, the relations between learning activities and deep processing with AI, the pedagogical and ethical perspectives in AI empowered learning, etc. The chapters in this book fill the gap in the literature of AI research by bringing in unique expertise and research experiences from the authors who represent a wide range of domains from cognitive and social psychology to teacher education, special education, language and mathematics teaching, to psychometric research design, and instructional design. The readers will benefit from reading the essays that offers insights on policy guidance, theoretical frameworks, and pedagogical approaches pertaining to AI integration. In that regard, the current text will serve as a useful companion to teachers, educators, administrators, and policy makers with respect to how to effectively integrate AI in education in general, and teaching and learning in particular.

With the advancement of new technologies, AI being one of them has seen its in-roads into classrooms and schools. Yet, a book that systematically examines roles of AI and their relationships with teaching and learning, represents a timely effort that meets the need of both researchers and practitioners. As such, the current book provides a much-needed resource for those who are interested in effectively applying artificial intelligence to practices in education.

Robert Z. Zheng
University of Utah, USA
December 2025

REFERENCES

Aldawsari, M. M., & Almohish, R. I. (2024). Treats and opportunities of students' use of AI-integrated technology (ChatGPT) in online higher education: Saudi Arabian educational technologists' perspectives. *International Review of Research in Open and Distance Learning*, *25*(3), 19–36. DOI: 10.19173/irrodl.v25i3.7642

Choi, G. W., Kim, S. H., Lee, D., & Moon, J. (2024). Utilizing generative AI for instructional design: Exploring strengths, weaknesses, opportunities, and threats. *TechTrends*, *68*(4), 832–844. DOI: 10.1007/s11528-024-00967-w

Cosentino, G., Anton, J., Sharma, K., Gelsomini, M., Giannakos, M., & Abrahamson, D. (2025). Hybrid teaching intelligence: Lessons learned from an embodied mathematics learning experience. *British Journal of Educational Technology*, *56*(2), 621–649. DOI: 10.1111/bjet.13525

Hong, X. Q., & Guo, L. (2025). Effects of AI-enhanced multi-display language teaching systems on learning motivation, cognitive load management, and learner autonomy. *Education and Information Technologies*, *30*(12), 17155–17189. DOI: 10.1007/s10639-025-13472-1

Kumar, J. A., Zhuang, M., & Thomas, S. (2024). ChatGPT for natural sciences course design: Insights from a strengths, weaknesses, opportunities, and threats analysis. *Natural Sciences Education*, *53*(2), e70003. DOI: 10.1002/nse2.70003

Lin, C. J., Lee, H. Y., Wang, W. S., Huang, Y. M., & Wu, T. T. (2025). Enhancing reflective thinking in STEM education through experiential learning: The role of generative AI as a learning aid. *Education and Information Technologies*, *30*(5), 6315–6337. DOI: 10.1007/s10639-024-13072-5

Luo, L. J., Hu, J. M., Zheng, Y. J., & Li, C. (2025). Human vs. AI: Does AI learning assistant enhance students' innovative behavior? *Education and Information Technologies*, *30*(12), 17483–17530. DOI: 10.1007/s10639-025-13474-z

Shabalala, N. P. (2024). Elevating STEM learning: Unleashing the power of ai in open distance eLearning. *Research om Social Sciences and Technology*, *9*(3), 269–288. DOI: 10.46303/ressat.2024.59

Villegas-Ch, W., Buenano-Fernandez, D., Navarro, A. M., & Mera-Navarrete, A. (2025). Adaptive intelligence tutoring systems for STEM education: Analysis of the learning impact and effectiveness of personalized feedback. *Smart Learning Environments*, *12*(1), 1–31. DOI: 10.1186/s40561-025-00389-y

Xing, W. L., Song, Y., Li, C. L., Liu, Z. F., Zhu, W. D., & Oh, U. (2025). Development of a generative AI-powered teachable agent for middle school mathematics learning: A design-based research study. *British Journal of Educational Technology*, *56*(5), 2043–2077. https://doi-org.ezproxy.lib.utah.edu/10.1111/bjet.13586. DOI: 10.1111/bjet.13586

Zhang, S., Prasad, P. G., & Schroeder, N. L. (2025). Learning about AI: A systematic review of reviews on AI literacy. *Journal of Educational Computing Research*, *6*(5), 1292–1322. DOI: 10.1177/07356331251342081

Acknowledgement

I would like to thank all authors for their hard work who voluntarily spent hundreds of hours putting together a collection of essays that represent the cutting-edge research on artificial intelligence and student development in learning. This book would not have been possible if it were not for their dedicated efforts and support. My appreciation also goes to our reviewers for their expertise assistance, who provided insightful comments and suggestions that hold this book up to highest standard and quality.

I would also like to thank the Publisher, especially Ms. Elizabeth Barrantes at IGI Global, who has demonstrated professionalism with high caliber. Their support and guidance have made the process of editing this column smooth and pleasant.

And last, but not the least, I would like to thank my family for their encouragement, support, and warm reception they gave to my work and for their allowance for my work schedules. I could not have done this without them! Finally, I would like to thank my mother who has always been the inspiration in my life.

Robert Z. Zheng
University of Utah, Salt Lake City, USA

Section 1
Pedagogical Practices and AI Integration

Chapter 1
Learning Design to Advance Human–AI Collaboration in K–12 Education

Wing Sha Chan
https://orcid.org/0009-0008-6549-3009
Old Dominion University, USA

Jinhee Kim
https://orcid.org/0000-0002-3365-7354
Old Dominion University, USA

Seongryeong Yu
https://orcid.org/0000-0003-1087-3713
Old Dominion University, USA

Rita Kay Detrick
http://orcid.org/0009-0000-5610-2864
Old Dominion University, USA

ABSTRACT

This chapter explores key components for designing effective Human-AI Collaboration (HAC) in K–12 education, addressing the current lack of theoretical and conceptual frameworks for structuring and implementing HAC in teaching and learning. It examines four essential areas: curriculum design, student and teacher–AI interaction, learning environments, and the evolution of HAC over time. The chapter introduces the concept of HAC in K–12 contexts, highlighting how humans and AI can leverage each other's strengths through co-evolutionary processes that foster mutual learning

DOI: 10.4018/979-8-3373-2927-7.ch001

and collaboration. It reviews current HAC practices in schools and discusses their contributions to both teaching and learning. Finally, it presents future directions for HAC research and practice, emphasizing implications for educational policy, AI system design, and instructional design to strengthen human-AI partnerships in education.

INTRODUCTION

The rise of generative artificial intelligence (AI) and large language models has driven rapid innovation in educational technology (Yan et al., 2024). AI now supports and collaborates with students across diverse disciplines, including world languages, mathematics, and the arts, by cultivating social connections and offering personalized instruction (Kim & Cho, 2023; Kim, Yu et al., 2025; Song et al., 2025b). Acting as a thought partner, AI guides students through ideation and creative problem-solving by providing adaptive resources and posing reflective questions during design-based learning (Kim & Cho, 2023). AI also functions as a learning companion, deepening conceptual understanding and addressing misconceptions. Through social dialogue and emotional feedback, AI promotes both content mastery and the development of metacognitive skills (Song et al., 2025a).

Alongside Student-AI Collaboration (SAC), Teacher-AI Collaboration (TAC) advances pedagogical innovation and professional growth. Rather than viewing AI as a threat (Koh et al., 2023), educators increasingly regard it as a transformative instructional partner. Kim (2024b) outlined six TAC models: One Teach, One Observe; One Teach, One Assist; Co-teaching in Stations; Parallel Teaching (Online/Offline); Differentiated Teaching; and Team Teaching. These models expand possibilities for structuring instruction and enhancing teaching practice. For example, in a high school English class, an AI co-teacher might provide conversational practice and pronunciation feedback while the teacher focuses on grammatical instruction and leveraging AI's native-like fluency to enhance learning effectiveness (Adeoye & Sabela, 2024; Mujiono, 2023). TAC can also streamline instructional delivery by generating structured information (Fazal, 2025), organizing formative feedback cycles (Cohn et al., 2024), and accommodating diverse learning styles, abilities, and interests (Damasevičius & Sidekerskienė, 2024).

Beyond pedagogical innovation and instructional support, TAC also holds promise for supporting teachers' professional development through data-driven insights and personalized guidance. AI systems can analyze diverse forms of student performance and engagement data, ranging from behavioral interactions and assignment results to emotional cues and sensory inputs. This can help to reveal underlying cognitive structures, learning challenges, and affective states (Zall & Kangavari, 2022). These insights enable teachers to refine their teaching strategies and design personalized learning sequences for individual learners (Nazaretsky et al., 2022).

Despite increasing interest in Human-AI Collaboration (HAC) in education, its effective implementation in K-12 remains complex. AI agents can enhance learning by providing immediate feedback, individualized materials, and automated scaffolding; however, these features can also conflict with principles of self-regulated learning (SRL), a vital component of lifelong learning (Winne, 2013). Research further indicates a nuanced tension between automation and teachers' professional autonomy. Over-automation can encroach on classroom roles teachers wish to maintain, constraining their ability to set instructional goals, whereas under-automation can leave them burdened with repetitive tasks, limiting time for personalized instruction (Kim, 2024a).

Additionally, the lack of theoretically grounded frameworks and an implementation roadmap for AI in Education (AIED) leaves teachers without clear guidance (Mouta et al., 2025). Teachers are expected to integrate AI into an already condensed curriculum without sufficient training or infrastructure. Unlike traditional educational technologies, AI applications function as active agents in the classroom, adaptively engaging with students' learning processes. This shift introduces substantial pedagogical challenges, requiring teachers to design and facilitate student-AI interactions, collaboration, and learning experiences in environments previously characterized by human-only exchanges (Kim et al., 2022).

In response to these challenges, this chapter examines key considerations for designing and implementing HAC in K-12 learning and teaching. It also offers implications for developing theoretically grounded approaches to AI-assisted learning and teaching. The discussion that follows addresses major components of HAC in K-12 education, including learning goals, content, assessment, student-AI interaction, learning environments, and evolution over time.

HUMAN-AI COLLABORATIVE INTERACTION IN K-12 EDUCATION

HAC interaction refers to any form of engagement or communication between humans and AI systems. It emphasizes a synergistic partnership in which humans and AI leverage their respective strengths and skills to achieve shared goals. HAC spans a spectrum of interactions, including cooperative, competitive, and even conflictual dynamics that mirror human interpersonal interactions (Jiang et al., 2024).

In K-12 education, HAC can be understood as a dynamic partnership in which AI systems work alongside educators and students to enhance learning processes and outcomes. This framework moves beyond traditional tool-based uses of technology to position AI as an active participant in educational practice. Thoughtful interaction with AI, through capabilities such as personalization and instant feedback, has the potential to amplify human capacities like creativity and problem-solving. To structure the analysis of HAC in K-12 settings, this chapter draws on the SAC model developed by Kim et al. (2022) as illustrated in Figure 1.

Figure 1. Student-AI Collaboration (SAC) Model (adapted from in Kim et al., 2022)

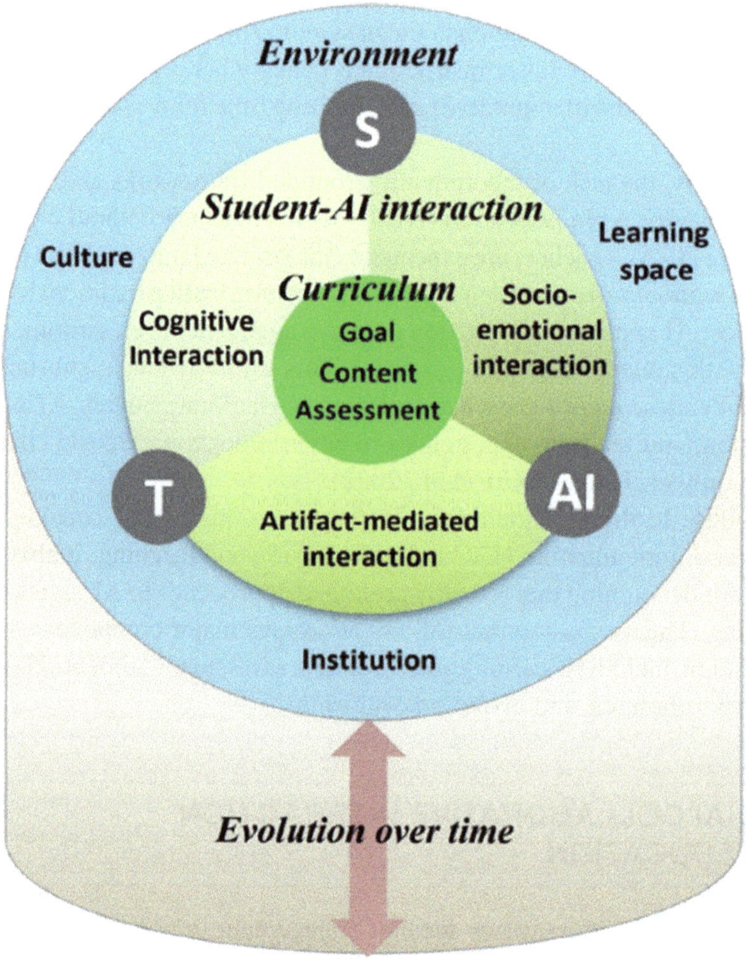

The SAC model provides a comprehensive framework comprising four interrelated dimensions that shape meaningful human-AI partnerships in education: curriculum design and implementation, human–AI interaction types (including cognitive, socio-emotional, and artifact-mediated), the learning environment, and the evolution of these relationships over time.

Curriculum design and implementation addresses how learning objectives, content, and activities are intentionally structured to integrate AI. Human-AI interaction types classify the modes through which students and AI systems communicate and collaborate. The learning environment defines the contextual conditions in which collaboration occurs, while evolution over time reflects how human-AI relationships develop as the human's skills, trust, and critical thinking mature.

The SAC model is grounded in the Backward Design framework (Wiggins & McTighe, 2005), a three-stage approach to curriculum development. The first stage, *Goals*, identifies desired learning outcomes; the second, *Assessment*, determines acceptable evidence of achievement; and the third, *Instruction*, designs learning experiences that equip students for success. Through this structure, the SAC model defines collaboration with AI as purposeful and pedagogically aligned. Scaffolding practices within this model cultivates human agency, positioning humans as creative directors who guide AI as a subordinate collaborator.

Drawing on the SAC model, the following example illustrates how its four dimensions can operate in an educational partnership with AI. The scenario centers on a high school environmental science project titled *Our Watershed's Health*, designed with the principles of Backward Design and integrating AI across all SAC dimensions.

In Stage 1 (Goals), students aim to develop a data-driven, actionable plan to improve an aspect of their local watershed's health. Their final product, a Watershed Restoration Proposal, includes a research summary, analyzed water quality data, and a presentation with persuasive visuals. Using an AI tool, students will generate an initial list of potential pollutants in an urban watershed, which they can verify through primary research.

In Stage 2 (Assessment), representing cognitive interaction, students employ an AI-powered data analysis tool to upload their collected pH and nitrate level readings. They prompt the AI to identify temporal trends and possible causes of pollution spikes. When students encounter difficulties or frustration, social-emotional interaction occurs through AI chatbot tutors that respond with supportive dialogue and reflective prompts. Finally, artifact-mediated interaction takes place as students use an AI image generator to create compelling before-and-after visuals of a restored riverbank for their final presentation.

These collaborative activities unfold within a blended learning environment that supports small-group collaboration and employs vetted AI tools. The teacher acts as a facilitator, guiding inquiry and maintaining oversight through access to AI-generated learning analytics. Over the semester, as students' skills and critical judgment mature, their relationship with AI evolves from reliance on simple prompts to engaging with AI as a subordinate collaborator in their learning process.

Although originally developed to examine student-AI collaboration, the SAC framework is equally applicable to teacher–AI collaboration and instructional design, encompassing both student- and teacher-centered collaborative dynamics. It can guide both students and teachers in engaging with AI through cognitive, socioemotional, and artifact-mediated interactions that enhance learning design and classroom practice (Kim et al., 2022).

Ideally, SAC principles would be embedded throughout the curriculum to align with learning goals, content delivery, and assessment, thereby preparing K-12 students for an AI-driven future. Such alignment occurs when AI is integrated into specific learning tasks such as drawing activities (Kim et al., 2022) or creative math writing (Song et al., 2025b) to support improvisation, stimulate new ideas, and guide learners in recognizing conceptual patterns (Kim & Lee, 2023; Lin et al., 2020). Collaborating with AI also offers teachers opportunities to personalize instruction in environments constrained by class size, time, or limited student data (Fan et al., 2025; Kim, 2024b; Kim & Lee, 2023). For TAC to succeed, institutions must foster supportive conditions through clear policies, reliable infrastructure, and professional development that empower educators to become active partners in Human-AI Collaboration (Kim, 2024a; Kim et al., 2022).

Because effective HAC cannot be understood through a single lens, the SAC model offers a useful framework for examining how HAC can be intentionally designed and implemented in K-12 education. It helps organize inquiry into how human–AI partnerships are structured within curriculum design, shaped by interaction types, situated in school environments, and developed over time. Through this lens, the chapter seeks to identify practical insights and design considerations that promote student growth, teacher agency, and educational equity.

CURRICULUM: LEARNING GOALS, CONTENT, ASSESSMENT

Building on the SAC model (Kim et al., 2022), curriculum design for HAC in K-12 education requires rethinking what, how, and why students learn in partnership with AI. The curriculum should not merely serve as a backdrop for HAC but be intentionally restructured to reflect the distributed agency of human actors (e.g., students and teachers) and AI systems. Effective curriculum design must consider three interconnected dimensions: learning goals, curriculum content, and assessment strategies. Aligning these dimensions fosters meaningful interaction between humans and AI agents, while promoting student autonomy, creativity, and critical thinking in AI-mediated learning environments (see Table 1).

Table 1. Curriculum Dimension and Key Elements of HAC Curriculum Design (Adapted from Kim et al., 2022; Kim, 2024a)

Curriculum Dimension	Key Elements
Learning Goals	Collaborative problem solving with AI, Critical evaluation of AI responses, Ethical and responsible use of AI
Curriculum Content	Contextualized prompts with AI roles (peer/mentor), AI-related epistemic tasks (questioning, critiquing, refining), Integrated modules on AI's capabilities, limitations, and impact
Assessment	Process-oriented assessment (logs, reflections), Collaborative outcome evaluation (co-authored work), AI-literacy assessment (understand, critique, regulate)

In traditional curricula models, learning outcomes have primarily emphasized individual student performance within teacher-directed instruction. In HAC contexts, however, learning outcomes expand to encompass shared engagement and distributed agency between students and AI systems. When students interact with AI as collaborators rather than passive recipients of information, learning objectives must include metacognitive, collaborative, and AI literacy-oriented objectives (Kim et al., 2022).

Research supports this shift; in one study, elementary and middle school students using a generative AI-powered teachable agent in mathematics demonstrated heightened metacognitive awareness (i.e. understanding one's own thought processes) and self-monitoring behaviors as they revised their strategies in response to AI feedback (Song et al., 2025a). Beyond student engagement, HAC curricula can also advance teacher goals, such as differentiating instruction through AI-provided learner analytics or co-developing learning targets using formative data. In Kim's (2024) study of Chinese secondary school teachers, instructors used AI to identify student misconceptions and adjust instruction mid-lesson, creating dynamic, data-informed practices that balanced student needs with teacher autonomy.

To realize these goals, HAC curricula should provide content structures that enable students and teachers to collaborate meaningfully with AI systems. Core objectives include collaborative problem-solving with AI (e.g., design or inquiry-based learning), critical evaluation of AI outputs, and ethical, responsible use of AI tools. Such aims become particularly salient when AI functions as a learning companion or co-designer (Kim, 2024a), supporting students not only in executing tasks but also in managing and monitoring interactions in ways that foster their agency, creativity, and critical thinking (Kim & Cho, 2023).

With respect to content, the HAC curriculum extends beyond disciplinary knowledge to include the competencies necessary for effective human-AI interaction (Kim et al., 2022). A key direction is the integration of AI-related interactive tasks (e.g., questioning, critiquing, and refining AI outputs) as central components of subject-area learning (Kim et al., 2022) (see Table 1). In a drawing-based learning task, Kim and Cho (2023) found that students who perceived AI as a teammate rather than a tool engaged in deeper reflection and iterative idea refinement. Evidence from Kim et al. (2025) further showed that students with higher AI literacy employed more sophisticated prompting strategies in AI-assisted writing tasks, leading to higher-quality outcomes. Together, these studies underscore the need for curriculum content that cultivates epistemic agency in AI-mediated learning.

From the teacher's perspective, curriculum content may include co-instructional materials prepared with AI, such as adaptive lesson plans or real-time content scaffolds, and models of TAC (e.g., *One Teach, One Assist*, or *Parallel Teaching*). In a practical application of these models, a high school English teacher focused on grammar instruction while an AI agent provided students with real-time pronunciation feedback, enabling multimodal content engagement across listening, speaking, and writing (Kim, 2024b).

Across disciplines, curriculum content should also embrace students' embodied, visual, and material engagement with knowledge construction. In art education, Yu et al. (2025) explored how students engaged in multimodal (e.g., visual and spatial) representations, emphasizing learning as co-construction with materials, tools, and others. Extending this to HAC, AI systems can serve not merely as information providers but as creative co-authors of multimodal outputs (e.g., maps, diagrams, or conceptual illustrations) that align with diverse literacy practices and learner identities.

Content that supports HAC may include contextualized prompts positioning AI as a peer or mentor in creative and analytical tasks; activities that foster iterative dialogue with AI (e.g., story generation, hypothesis testing); and integrated modules on AI fundamentals, including its capabilities, limitations, and social implications. In project-based learning scenarios, students might use AI to brainstorm ideas, gather data, or prototype solutions while reflecting on the process and outcomes of these collaborations (Jiang & Pang, 2023). Such content design emphasizes the co-construction process between humans and AI rather than focusing solely on product-oriented outputs as shown in Table 1.

To fully align with this process-oriented approach, a corresponding shift in assessment is essential. Assessment in HAC requires moving beyond traditional summative evaluations to capture the processual and collaborative dimensions of learning. A primary challenge lies in the absence of assessment models that account for both the learner's development and the contribution of AI to that process (Kim, 2024a).

An effective HAC assessment framework should address how students interact with AI over time, what they co-produce, and how well they manage their partnership with AI. Process-oriented assessment can document evolving interactions with AI through reflection journals, version histories, or interaction logs. AI systems can further enhance this by generating real-time feedback timelines that help students and teachers monitor progress and adjust learning strategies accordingly (Cohn et al., 2024). For teachers, such analytics can serve as powerful formative assessment tools, enabling them to identify patterns, detect struggling learners, and personalize feedback at scale.

Assessment must also capture the quality of collaborative outcomes between humans and AI, such as co-authored texts or co-developed designs, highlighting the distributed nature of agency in HAC. This includes examining *how* students use AI in context, not only *what* they produce. In one study, the sophistication of student prompts in AI-assisted writing varied significantly by AI literacy level, ranging from superficial keyword entries to iterative, strategic dialogue (Kim, Yu, Lee et al., 2025). These differences influenced both product quality and reflective depth, suggesting that prompt use itself can serve as a performance indicator.

Finally, the HAC curriculum should include assessments of students' AI literacy, such as their capacity to understand, critique, and regulate AI-supported learning. From this perspective, AI-generated analytics on students' emotional, behavioral, and cognitive engagement can provide rich formative evidence (Nazaretsky et al., 2022). Beyond the individual level, research also highlights the importance of socially shared regulation in AI-supported environments: students collaboratively set goals, negotiate interpretations, and adapt AI responses in group contexts (Kim, Detrick, Yu et al., 2025). Capturing such collective regulatory practices, alongside individual outcomes, is essential for authentic and adaptive assessment. Together, these dimensions underscore the need for assessment systems that are formative, process-based, and responsive to the unique dynamics of human-AI co-learning (Song et al., 2025a) (see Table 1).

HUMAN-AI INTERACTION (HAI): COGNITIVE, SOCIO-EMOTIONAL, AND ARTIFACT-MEDIATED INTERACTION

Cognitive Interaction

Cognitive interaction refers to task-focused engagement with subject matter or learning processes, where understanding develops through thinking, reasoning, and co-constructing knowledge (Dillenbourg et al., 1995; Hmelo-Silver & Barrows, 2008). Within the SAC model (Kim et al., 2022), cognitive interaction emerges when students iteratively exchange and refine domain-specific knowledge through dialogue with AI tools, particularly during scenario-based analysis or structured inquiry tasks. In a geology lesson scenario, students might work with an AI system to discuss rocks characteristics, infer rock types, and apply classification criteria (Kim et al., 2022).

Cognitive interaction enhances thinking, decision-making, and problem-solving skills as students treat AI as both a cognitive tool and intellectual peer. Wang et al. (2024) analyzed K-12 mathematics tutoring dialogues and found that high school students demonstrated stronger reasoning skills and sustained engagement, while primary students also responded positively, albeit with room to strengthen cognitive interactions. Similarly, Kim (2024a) explored K-12 teachers' perspectives on designing SAC and found that they prioritized capacity building, domain knowledge, and authentic, process-oriented assessment indicating a shift from performance optimization toward cognitive transformation.

In this context, AI is not simply a facilitator of efficiency but a co-constructor of knowledge that supports deeper intellectual engagement. AI systems can scaffold meta-cognitive awareness by prompting students to design flawed systems for peers to debug or to reconstruct arguments using incomplete evidence, thereby cultivating evidential reasoning. Such activities promote higher-order thinking by forging conceptual bridges between ideas.

Through these exchanges, AI initiates instructional scaffolding by posing step-by-step questions, personalizing content, and providing real-time feedback. Students, in turn, interpret and evaluate AI outputs, refining their reasoning and solutions. These iterative processes strengthen critical thinking and create psychologically safe spaces for learning through productive failure. Cognitive interaction, therefore, extends beyond completing tasks efficiently to embody a reciprocal partnership in which AI's analytical capabilities and students' judgment coalesce to deepen understanding.

Beyond collaboration with students, AI can also serve as a cognitive partner for teachers in instructional settings. Teachers remain the orchestrating force, blending AI's data-driven diagnostics with their pedagogical expertise. In practice, AI can translate complex analytics into actionable feedback and transform its detailed instructional support into effective learning operations. AI tutoring systems exemplify this partnership: they adapt to individual learners' knowledge gaps, enabling teachers to differentiate instruction and meet students at their current level of understanding (Kim et al., 2022). By providing personalized content and adaptive embedded assessments, AI supports cognitive interaction by addressing challenges posed by diverse abilities within the classroom (Filiz et al., 2025).

As a partner in TAC, AI helps teachers critically analyze their own pedagogical decisions by turning generated content into actionable insights for refining instruction. In practice, teachers can leverage AI systems to analyze classroom audio and video, mapping dialogue patterns between teachers and students. They can then tag student questions by cognitive demand, track wait time, and identify scaffolding strategies aligning with Kim's (2024a) conception of AI as a cognitive scaffolder that supports teachers in fostering high-order thinking. Similarly, when providing feedback after grading, teachers can use AI to shift the grading process from a corrective process to a reasoning-focused approach, cultivating epistemic mindsets that promote reflection and deeper understanding (Kartal et al., 2024). Together, these examples position AI as a coach that guides and extends teachers' cognitive practice.

Designing such systems requires attention to both the artifacts of AI interfaces and the principles underlying their design. Drawing onHutchins' (2000) theory of distributed cognition, cognitive processes can be shared across individuals, artifacts, and time, thereby linking human reasoning with AI capabilities. Effective design should therefore integrate human thought processes with AI functionality, allowing students to engage with tasks without needing to consult external manuals (Kim et al., 2022). Simple drag-and-drop tools, such as those in Google's Teachable Machine (Yim & Su, 2025), demonstrate interfaces that support immediate participation without specialized training.

In addition to ease of use, AI environments should prioritize accessibility and cultural inclusivity. Icons, language, and multimodal interactions through touch, voice, gesture, and visual creation should be universally interpretable (Eguchi et al., 2021). Such responsive interfaces, coupled with real-time feedback and step-by-step scaffolding, promote critical evaluation and iterative learning while providing teachers with aggregated analytics for instructional planning (Kim et al., 2022; Kim, 2024a; Song et al., 2025a). Echoing the principle of distributed cognition, students engage fluidly with AI in learning tasks, while teachers maintain oversight of human-AI activities and guide instruction through shared digital environments.

Social-Emotional Interaction

Research indicates that AI systems engage with human emotions, social cues, and relational dynamics (e.g., Kim et al., 2022; Kim et al., 2024; Kim et al., 2025).. Through features like autonomy, personalization, and reactivity, AI serves as an adaptive collaborator, capable of dynamically tailoring its responses to individual student behaviours and needs. When students perceive AI as a social actor, they can form rapport and experience affective support as the system responds to their psychological and emotional states. These social-emotional interactions are especially effective when scaffolded feedback is provided to reinforce learning.

Evidence from Huang (2025) involving 616 high school students showed that AI chatbots created continuous feedback loops of interaction and feedback. The researcher concluded that this dynamic and continuous exchange between students and the AI system significantly enhanced student engagement and reinforced linguistic construction. Students reported feeling excited and delighted when AI recognized their work and offered recommendations. Consistent with these findings, Hwang et al. (2020) stated that an adaptive learning system incorporating both emotional and cognitive analytics alleviated elementary students' math-related anxiety, and the students improved their math performance.

AI social robots that detect and elicit emotional responses also illustrate the potential of social-emotional interaction. In Berrezueta-Guzman et al.'s (2025) study with 40 preschool children, early exposure to AI-powered robots significantly enhanced children's emotional recognition, collaboration, and social engagement. Parents and teachers reported positive impacts on emotional development and overall classroom dynamics. Similarly, Huang et al. (2024) found that the perceived availability of AI support also favorably promotes students' self-efficacy towards task achievement (Huang et al., 2024).

Beyond classroom learning, AI systems designed as digital companions, such as mental health apps, offer emotional support, personalized feedback, and detect emotional patterns by emulating human interaction. This enhances social connections and improves relationships that are crucial for reducing psychological distress. In a study of 80 female middle school students using two AI mental health apps (i.e.,*GymBuddy* and *Elomia*), Jiang and Yang (2025) found that AI-integrated interventions fostered socio-emotional interaction among students, resulting in significant improvement in psychological distress symptoms.

In TAC, social-emotional interaction centers on combining teachers' empathic and ethical expertise with AI's monitoring and adaptive capabilities to foster holistic student development and create supportive learning environments. Teachers remain irreplaceable in fostering emotional intelligence, empathy, and creativity, while AI contributes by monitoring classroom moods, peer interactions, and engagement. Kim (2024a) described how K-12 teachers envision socio-emotional interaction in TAC as collegial collaboration built on mutual trust, shared responsibilities, and a no-blame culture for improving teaching. These K-12 teachers also expect AI to possess conflict resolution skills, which are crucial for managing school-related issues constructively and enhancing socio-emotional interactions (Kim, 2024a). AI alleviates socio-emotional strain by reducing administrative burdens on grading and data processing. Such a foundation is developed based on complementary roles that AI handles routine tasks, and teachers account for designing tasks with empathy and creativity.

Artifact-Mediated Interaction

Artifact-mediated interaction refers to the use of interactive visualizations and digital tools to support humans' engagement with AI-driven learning activities. Such interaction deepens exploration and representation of knowledge in educational contexts (Kim et al., 2022) . The characteristics of an AI system's interface and how students interact with AI through interfaces significantly impact the learning experience. Building on the earlier discussions of distributed cognition (Hutchins, 2000), Kim et al. (2022) emphasized that cognitive processes extend beyond the individual mind to include external structures such as digital technologies and interfaces. From this perspective, the interface functions as a critical mechanism within the cognitive system, mediating the interplay between human cognition, particularly memory and understanding, and external representations.

Kim et al.'s (2022) findings also showed that teachers strongly emphasized the need for intuitive AI interfaces and hardware. This is particularly crucial for younger students or those without prior AI experience, as the interface itself should serve as a robust medium for expression that allows students to work on tasks without needing additional manuals to understand how the AI system functions. Since much of the AI experience in schools is algorithm-based, the interface acts as a bridge between students and AI. Research indicates that both the design of an AI system's interface and students' interaction patterns with these interfaces significantly influence learning outcomes and student engagement. Park et al. (2022), studying 42 students in grades 3-5, found that visual interfaces for AI planning tasks are engaging and intuitive, though usability challenges such as block deletion and misconceptions about sequence ordering highlighted the importance of thoughtful interface design for effective artifact-mediated interaction.

Emerging technologies such as smart assistants, augmented reality (AR), generative AI tools, and AI-integrated Internet of Things (IoT) devices further expand these interactions between students and AI systems.Thangavel et al. (2025) noted that AR devices like *Microsoft HoloLens* and *Apple Vision Pro* use holographic projections and spatial computing to enhance student engagement with AI-powered interfaces. K-12 students have also managed to work with AI in IoT devices and Generative AI in design tools, such as using *Canva*'s AI to suggest layouts and *MidJourney* to generate images from text (Delello et al., 2024). While these tangible interfaces and dynamics promote artifact-mediated interaction and provide enhanced functionality in educational settings, their high cost and limited classroom adaptability may affect the practicality for widespread use (Thangavel et al., 2025). In AI-powered language learning systems, sustained engagement depends on adaptive responsiveness (Dmello et al., 2024), the cultivation of perseverance through design-thinking frameworks (Rahimi & Sevilla-Pavón, 2025), and accurate speech-recognition capabilities that ensure reliable user interaction (Abbas & Ganesan, 2025). Collectively, these features sustain students' motivation and persistence through artifact-mediated engagement.

Cognitive, socio-emotional, and artifact-mediated interactions operate as a dynamic, interconnected system. Cognitive work is shaped by the affective context as the sensation of support may correlate to more engagement of metacognitive work. Conversely, socio-emotional responses often arise from cognitive challenges. Both dimensions are embodied through artifacts that channel attention, reduce cognitive load, and foster positive affect. In this sense, the three forms of human-AI interaction are dynamically interwoven.

Extending this discussion from SAC to TAC, artifact-mediated interaction also underpins successful teacher-AI collaboration. Within the SAC framework, interfaces function as a critical external structure that integrate human cognition with digital manipulation (Kim et al., 2022). This lens significantly accentuates the interface and functions as a vital bridge to connect teachers with AI systems. As teachers have expressed a strong desire for AI interfaces to offer a rich array of integrated digital tools (Kim, 2024a), teachers can interact with AI-embedded dashboards to monitor student learning and gain insight into individual needs . AI robots equipped with interactive peripherals, such as touch-screen displays, microphones, cameras, and speakers, serve as interfaces that enable multimodal interaction and allow teachers to observe and manage the robot's engagement with students (Berrezueta-Guzman et al., 2025). The effectiveness of these artifacts design directly shapes teachers' trust in the AI and determines their pedagogical utility, reinforcing artifact-mediated interaction as a central mechanism in both student- and teacher-AI collaboration.

Environment: Learning Pace, Institution, And Culture

A well-configured learning space is a prerequisite for the successful implementation of SAC and AI integration in the classroom. This foundational space comprises two essential dimensions: the physical learning environment and the digital learning environment (Kim et al., 2022).

The physical environment should be flexible and adaptable to accommodate emerging learning modes introduced by SAC.Configurable spaces allow teachers to reorient classrooms based on student needs or convert into specialized areas such as computer labs. The design of the physical environment facilitates activities such as working on simulations with AI on laptops in a science lab configuration.

Complementing this, the digital learning environment requires robust infrastructure. Kim et al. (2022) emphasized the importance of secure wireless networks for reliable real-time interaction and data access, as well as a one-to-one ratio of school-owned, portable devices for consistent access. Cloud-based learning platforms are identified as the core component of this digital environment. These platforms can form the operational foundation of AI-enhanced classrooms that actively enable personalized and adaptive learning (Wang & Cheng, 2021). The digital environment centers on AI-powered platforms that allow instructors to analyze student data, provide personalized content, and present ideas via dashboards (Yoon et al., 2024). The software adopted in the digital learning space is another operational consideration. Various types of interactive educational software are augmented by

AI, namely collaborative AI tutors, generative AI, and immersive AI. In China, collaborative AI agents, called *Squirrel AI*, work for SAC and TAC. Students, teachers, and AI systems should integrate seamlessly with existing systems via LMS, digital textbooks, and administration systems to avoid adding repetitive tasks for teachers.

Effective implementation of AI in education requires robust institutional support across three key areas: financial and infrastructure support, curricula and pedagogical development, and legal-ethical governance (Kim et al., 2022). Public education systems frequently encounter substantial challenges in securing sufficient funding and development time for AIED methodologies (Zawacki-Richter et al., 2019). Schools are often constrained by dedicated funding for AI tools, teacher training, and infrastructure upgrades, including high-speed internet and emerging technological devices. Woodruff et al. (2023) conducted a study with 4,528 educators from a range of districts across all 50 states. Findings showed that improving access to technology and infrastructure was essential, specifically mentioning the provision of reliable internet access, hardware, and software. Educators directly express concerns about the cost required to implement AI in their classrooms and the digital divide (Zhang & Zhang, 2024). A primary aspect of this digital divide is the significantly less reliable high-speed internet access for students in rural districts compared to those urban or suburban areas (Woodruff et al., 2023). Insufficient funds create barriers to AI adoption, leading to unequal opportunities for students and educators.

To mitigate these inequalities, low-cost AI tools such as *Teachable Machine*, free-tier generative AI, and affordable robotics kits could be used to align with learning objectives. Wu et al. (2021) suggested a low-cost resource for K-12 schools to access a powerful computational environment. In China, the *Mo* web-based platform is designed as a solution to make K-12 AI education affordable and address the inequitable distribution of AI educational resources. By doing so, it eliminates the need for individual schools to build complex local infrastructure. Karalekas et al. (2023) highlighted the educational value of using low-cost 3D-printed robots, such as the *Arduino Mini Manipulator* and the *SelfLearn* robot, in K-12 contexts. These robots do not require specially designed classrooms or dedicated spaces for movement. They could be easily integrated into any educational environment, which avoids additional infrastructure costs. The implication is that HAC could be introduced and incorporated into K-12 education through classroom-compatible technologies, initiated by institutions without significant infrastructure costs. More importantly, they serve as an essential foundation for enabling AI integration into curriculum development and pedagogical practice.

Institutional support must also extend to curriculum and pedagogical development. Kim et al. (2022) suggested that teachers emphasized that without clear directions and guidelines from upper-level institutions on AI in educational curriculum and pedagogy, schools would find it challenging to adopt the new technology. Specifically, the need for institutional support includes formulating a system-wide vision and strategic priorities at the national level. Teachers suggested that the government should base this vision on an in-depth understanding of students' learning and development, and the impacts that AI will have on learning (Kim et al., 2022). This vision should then be communicated to teachers to enhance their understanding of how to implement SAC and augment student capabilities (An et al., 2020).

Another area of institutional support is the development of a master plan for curriculum design. The plan should clearly define learning objectives across school and grade levels, outline how AI can support personalized resources and outcomes, and detail assessment methods for the multi-dimensional competencies fostered by student-AI interaction. Ultimately, research shows that teachers also expressed a strong need for the government to plan training programs and continuous support to develop teachers' AI knowledge (Kim, 2024a). Such training is essential for educators to stay current with the rapidly evolving field of AI, interpret AI outputs into meaningful feedback, and effectively apply AI in educationally relevant ways.

Finally, the need for institutional safeguards regarding legal and ethical governance issues and equity assurance should be addressed. While the introduction of AI in classrooms raises some legal and ethical issues related to personal information and privacy, institutional safeguards are necessary to protect students from potential disputes. Teachers also noted the importance of AI ethics education for students, aiming to establish their moral sensitivity toward AI (Kim et al., 2022). Moreover, to ensure safe and effective implementation, teachers called for an inter-sectoral governance and coordination mechanism. This mechanism would foster concerted effort and maximize cross-sector collaboration among diverse stakeholders, including students, teachers, parents, policymakers, researchers, and EdTech providers. Kim et al. (2022) reported that a teacher suggested establishing AIED collaboration councils to facilitate circles of collaboration, ensuring that schools' demands and preferences are voiced to external stakeholders. This suggests a need for a central governing board and coordination body for policy implementation (Chiu, 2024). Institutional support is critical to establish effective policies, develop comprehensive curricula, guide pedagogical practices, and ensure adherence to legal and ethical standards.

Beyond infrastructure and policy, school culture is a crucial environmental factor for the effective integration of HAC. AIED can be achieved through the collective efforts of the diverse stakeholders in the educational system, including students, parents and guardians, teachers, policymakers, academicians, and others. Educational stakeholders should strive to establish a deeper understanding of hybrid intelligence, focusing on leveraging the unique strengths of each intelligence type to create a more effective and constructive educational environment, shifting from viewing AI as a threat to embracing AI as a collaborator (Kim et al., 2022; Kim, 2024b).

Teachers should receive AI-specific professional development training to enhance student understanding via AI analytics and improve their reflective practice on teaching methods. By recognizing AI's strengths, students should overcome the initial AI skepticism and create more engaging AI-enhanced activities. Additionally, students should be given more support with respect to foundational AI knowledge and data literacy education, error analysis and debugging guidance with in-depth AI instructional scaffolding, and AI ethics education. They should enhance critical thinking, creative skills, problem-solving abilities, and collaborative skills .

In addition to teachers and students, parents and guardians should be included in governance mechanisms to ensure ethical oversight and clear communication about the role and impact of AI. Parents and guardians should gain a deeper understanding of the purposes, benefits, and ethical considerations of AI-driven courses to better support their children's learning. Finally, policymakers should shape the AIED ecosystem by developing system-wide visions, establishing stakeholder governance, and supporting teacher professional development. They should be taught to make informed decisions on appropriate AI systems, evaluate their capabilities, risks, and ethics, and safeguard learners and teachers.

As school culture is critical for HAC integration to be effective, government-led national initiatives across Asia are fostering such cultural readiness for AI by integrating AI education into K-12 curricula from a top-down approach. Su et al. (2022) described a trend of AI integration across various countries. In 2018, the Singapore government announced the AI Singapore project, which aims to develop students' AI capabilities. The project brought together research institutions, including AI start-ups and companies, to develop AI learning products to grow students' AI knowledge and develop talents to power Singapore's AI efforts. This fosters talents' cultural readiness for a national AI ecosystem. In 2019, the South Korean government announced the National AI Scheme to enhance the country's AI competitiveness by 2030. The Ministry of Education in South Korea had made plans to introduce AI to all high school students in 2021 and further extend AI education to kindergarten, primary, and middle schools by 2025 (Su et al., 2022). Such policy further demonstrates the impact of government-led projects on promoting cultural readiness within the community.

In 2020, the Japanese national curriculum mandated computer science education offerings starting at primary schools (Eguchi et al., 2021). The initiative aimed to prepare K-12 students to be capable of understanding and utilizing AI-enhanced technologies in their future, thereby maintaining Japan's competitiveness as one of the leading countries in the AI-driven world. This not only emphasizes technological citizenship with the embedment of cultural readiness, but it also promotes the awareness and understanding of AI ethics among K-12 students (Eguchi et al., 2021). In 2021, Hong Kong Education City (EdCity) announced the Go AI Scheme, which aims to promote AI Education in Hong Kong through introducing self-paced learning platforms and enhancing teachers' and students' AI knowledge and future-ready skills in the 21st century (Hong Kong Education City, 2021). Overall, national momentum for cultural readiness has been created as cultural catalysts via the implementation of educational schemes.

Building on this momentum, stakeholders and communities should proactively embrace ethical co-creation on cultural readiness. While some argue that this cultural sensitivity in AI design may risk bias in AI algorithms (Solyst et al., 2023), additional auditing, diverse training data, and active student involvement in AI critique could take place as long as the cultural shift is encouraged. Such involvement would take the form of guiding students to engage in critiquing AI outputs and diversifying training data. Transparent governance should be advised for public dialogues on ethics to align AI systems with community values. These active countermeasures could promote cultural readiness. With this systemic alignment that HAC is prioritized in policies, cultural readiness is an add-on of HAC to a societal-normed practice.

Evolution Over Time

AI in education functions have evolved beyond static tools into adaptive learning partners. Students and AI systems have created a reciprocal relationship, wherein both parties learn and adapt through continuous interaction This co-evolutionary process links students' cognitive growth with the refinement of AI algorithms, as systems learn from student responses and performance data (Tan & Cheah, 2021). Three key mechanisms drive this dynamic. First, AI systems continuously update student models and profiles through collected interaction data. Second, AI systems optimize adaptive feedback mechanisms based on learner responses and real-time performance. Finally, AI systems enhance analytical accuracy through sustained use and iterative refinement. Consequently, AI systems have transformed from conventional tools to a dynamic cognitive partner in the learning process where both humans and AI mutually develop through sustained educational interactions (Kim et al., 2022; Song et al., 2024).

Reflecting on these characteristics, the evolution of HAC in K-12 context can be conceptualized in three key stages: Foundational, Intermediate, and Advanced. In the Foundational Stage, AIED focuses on sparking and developing students' curiosity and basic interaction with AI through hands-on experience (George, 2023), playful interaction through storytelling with AI-generated characters and voice assistants are to be designed (Han, 2024), and embodied learning experience with AI (Memarian & Doleck, 2024). Tangible AI experiences could include asking *Alexa* or *Siri* questions, exploring robotics kits, coding robots to navigate mazes, and utilizing AI-powered drawing tools (Chiu, 2024; Jeon, 2023). After gaining

AI experiences, K-5 students are competent in using *DALL·E* to create artifacts (Kammer & Hays, 2023). Along with experiential learning, ethical seeds should be planted by holding simple discussions on potential bias, privacy breaches, algorithmic discrimination, misinformation, and digital divides despite AI's extraordinary capabilities (UNESCO, 2021). It is recommended that teachers should explicitly ask questions about whether AI is a fair tool and why AI robots often provide incorrect or incomprehensible responses to prompts (Chiu, 2024).

In the Intermediate Stage, students develop critical thinking and co-creation skills with AI. Students could develop AI-augmented problem-solving skills by using AI in multidisciplinary subjects. These skills are developed through practical applications, such as using AI to analyze climate data for AI in science and leveraging *ChatGPT* to detail on positive and negative impacts of a debate topic for AI debate club grants students opportunities to interact with AI systems ubiquitously (Kim, 2025). Furthermore, students could experience more hands-on collaboration to train simple machine language models via diverse platforms, for instance, *Google's Teachable Machine* (Yim & Su, 2025). Building on the preliminary ethical development at the foundation stage, students in grades 6 to 8 could engage in case studies examining algorithmic bias and role-playing scenarios for privacy discussions.

In the Advanced Stage, students are equipped with collaboration skills with AI and work on complex, real-world problems to make innovation and a real-world impact. Project-based AI partnerships are encouraged to incorporate SAC into social-good projects (Kim, 2024a). This recommendation reflects a growing international consensus, exemplified by UNESCO (2021) and its exploration of AI's broader contributions and ethical considerations for sustainable development and education. One of UNESCO's perspectives on AI's potential is to support genuine education. UNESCO and other international communities are positioning themselves to ensure AI's role in building inclusive knowledge societies. Specifically, AI is being leveraged to support genuine education by addressing challenges such as promoting students' engagement and inclusion, delivering personalized knowledge, and providing adaptive feedback on the learning process. With respect to quality education, UNESCO (2021) highlights that AI can serve as teachers' aides and enhance instructional design and practice, particularly in designing and delivering personalized learning that might otherwise be unfeasible for individual teachers. This frees up teachers' time and attention for other activities, such as offering socio-emotional support or assisting students who are most in need.

These stages can be operationalized through AI-driven formative assessment techniques. Formative assessment techniques, including interaction logs, prompt strategies, and project work, provide the continuous data between students and AI. In the view of the AI-to-students dimension, AI acts as a dynamic cognitive partner and provides personalized scaffolding and feedback. These AI-Driven formative assessment techniques are shown in Table 2.

Table 2. Synthesis of Concrete Example Techniques for Formative Assessment Using AI

Stage	Primary Focus of Assessment	Concrete AI Formative Assessment Techniques	Example Tools / Activities
Foundational Stage	Engagement and basic interaction	1. Teachers track how often a student asks a voice AI questions and the complexity of those questions with an interactive log. 2. Students use AI educational apps that provide positive and encouraging feedback to build confidence.	1. Voice assistants (e.g. Siri, Alexa) (Chiu, 2024; Jeon, 2023) 2. AI-powered drawing apps (DALL.E) (Kammer & Hays, 2023)
Intermediate Stage	Critical thinking and co-creation	1. Students introduce rubrics to assess the quality of prompts used in AI-assisted writing or research tasks. 2. Students submit the version history of a document co-written with AI with highlights and explanation of their key revisions. 3. Students provide an AI-generated summary of a historical event and identify omissions or biases using primary sources.	1. Generative AI tools (e.g. ChatGPT) (Kim, 2025) 2. Google's Teachable Machine (Yim & Su, 2025)
Advanced Stage	Collaboration and real-world problem solving	1. Students create a portfolio for a project that includes their initial prompts, AI responses, their critiques and refinements, and a final reflective essay on the collaboration. 2. Students are given a dataset and an AI-generated analysis; they must audit the analysis for statistical flaws, ethical biases, and logical consistency. 3. In group projects using AI for data modeling, groups are assessed on their team charter for AI use and their negotiations with the AI tool. 4. AI provides teachers with analytics on classroom discourse patterns via audio analysis to help them refine their questioning techniques and group facilitation.	

Together with SAC, TAC is expected to evolve over time. Kim (2024a) proposed that this evolution progresses from basic augmentation to sophisticated co-orchestration and synergy. Currently, AI is often seen as supporting teachers by reducing administrative burdens, such as grading or attendance checks, or by monitoring student data. The evolution of TAC is envisioned as a more active and collaborative relationship, where teachers and AI are equal team members who co-orchestrate classroom interactions and activities. The goal is to develop human-AI co-orchestration systems that optimize the complementary strengths of human intelligence and AI, allowing the two to behave more intelligently together than the two would separately.

This includes AI systems that can adaptively present educational resources aligned with the teacher's current goals or provide feedback on the quality of the teacher's instruction to help them improve over time. Teachers, in turn, could modify or create new actions for AI systems, establishing a continuous cycle of mutual learning and improvement. However, a significant current challenge lies in the fact that many AI tools are commercially driven and designed without sufficient grounding in educational rationale or pedagogical principles. The future of TAC needs to be guided by long-term educational visions and goals with built-in curriculum systems/structure and pedagogical support.

Hence, the evolution calls for TAC to support students' life-long learning and personalized learning across broader areas of development, including cognitive, social, emotional, and well-being, rather than just rote memorization or factual knowledge. It should enable diverse teaching pedagogies, such as guided discovery, project-based learning, and deep learning, to foster higher-order thinking and critical engagement.

CONCLUSION

The review of current literature offered a clearer understanding of how to design and support HAC across four dimensions identified by Kim et al. (2022): (1) Curriculum, (2) Human-AI interaction, (3) Learning Environment, and (4) HAC evolution over time. This chapter, however, is not intended to rigidly align with existing frameworks, but rather as a prompt to conceptualize new possibilities, raise questions, and propose discussion to more effectively structure HAC.

One of the main conclusions drawn from HAC in the K-12 classroom setting is that educational AI should be developed and used as an educational companion, enabling it to achieve primary educational goals and leverage effective pedagogical strategies. Given that a primary goal of education is to cultivate well-rounded individuals equipped with knowledge, skills, and higher-order thinking abilities to navigate life and contribute to society, existing studies explore the diverse roles and potentials of AI to go beyond improving and measuring student knowledge and skills and optimizing for standardized testing results by spoon-feeding pre-specified content; they expect AI to support multifaceted areas of learning both in the short-and-long term including the development of one's personality among other forms of development. Accordingly, the key motivation and scientific goal of AIED is to "make computationally precise and explicit forms of educational, psychological and social knowledge which are often left implicit" (Self, 1999, p. 1). Achieving this requires 1) understanding and modeling the characteristics and behavior of learners and teachers, 2) effective pedagogical strategies; and 3) the collaborative, social, affective, and meta-cognitive aspects of learning as well as the contexts and settings in which learning occurs (Luckin, 2010; Kim, 2024b). Thus, researchers should not strive for what is technically possible, but rather always consider what makes pedagogical sense and is educationally meaningful and relevant.

In this regard, more research is needed to explore, design, and validate components and architecture for sophisticated AI models, the nature and mechanism of Human-AI Collaboration in the educational domain, and critical analysis and reflection of the relationship among pedagogical, ethical, social, cultural, and technical dimensions of AIED in diverse ranges of subject-specific domains supporting both cognitive and soft skills, such as creativity, critical thinking, communication, collaboration, and self-direction (Fan et al., 2025; Kim, 2024a).

Furthermore, the successful implementation of AIED requires a structured approach, where infrastructure development and governance evolve in tandem while mitigating potential risks and ensuring a positive and equitable learning environment for all. The governance dimension highlights the importance of addressing academic misconduct, data privacy, transparency, and accountability. This ensures that educational stakeholders recognize and respond to the ethical challenges associated with and posed by AI technologies, fostering responsible use and maintaining trust within the K-12 education community. By focusing on governance, K-12 institutions are encouraged to develop and enforce clear policies, guidelines, and procedures that address these concerns, ensuring that AI is used responsibly and ethically to support a learning environment that is fair, equitable, and inclusive.

In addition, effective use of AI in K-12 education depends on the continuous monitoring, evaluation, and implementation of advanced digital infrastructure and AI technologies within K-12 schools. Recent studies (e.g. Kim et al., 2022) highlight the value of creating and supporting a dedicated, well-resourced technical support team that can (a) guide the adoption, management, and maintenance of AI technologies, (b) address emerging technical issues, (c) provide ongoing training for students and teachers, and (d) provide continuous monitoring to identify opportunities for improvements and adaptation to enable schools to iteratively refine their AI integration strategies in response to new insights and changing needs (Kim et al., 2022).

This can ensure that AI technologies are seamlessly integrated into the educational environment, minimizing disruptions and maximizing their potential benefits.

Realizing sustainable AI demands collective action by governments, educators, and the broader community to ensure that digital infrastructure grows in harmony with the learning environment and educational goals. Through these collaborative processes and communication, stakeholders can identify general best practices based on actual usage and feedback of teachers and learners to coordinate policy and guidelines effectively. Collaboration and interaction between stakeholders will be key to creating a common understanding for different stakeholders around AIED in K-12 education and addressing the key challenges effectively to overcome resistance to AIED in K-12 education (Detrick & Kim, in press). The *AI4Future* project involved stakeholders across the Chinese University of Hong Kong, K-12 schools and AI industry local to the university, and the government with the goal of developing an AI literacy test that would inform curricula (Chiu et al., 2024). The project employed a co-creation approach where secondary school principals worked directly with researchers to develop a curriculum that was later endorsed and adopted as the official curriculum by the local government in Hong Kong (Chiu et al., 2024). This sort of cross-sector, multi-stakeholder collaboration will enable the use of AI-powered tools in education as a standard practice rather than an inconsistent trend.

REFERENCES

Abbas, I., & Ganesan, S. (2025, May). Exploring the feasibility of AI-driven educational robots in simulation environments for early childhood learning: A pilot study. In *2025 IEEE International Conference on Electro Information Technology (eIT)* (pp. 1-9). IEEE. DOI: 10.1109/eIT64391.2025.11103623

Adeoye, M. A., & Sabela, W. (2024). Navigating the future of education: Integrating AI and collaborative learning in teacher professional development. *International Journal of Technology. Education and Social Humanities*, *2*(2), 41–60.

An, P., Holstein, K., d'Anjou, B., Eggen, B., & Bakker, S. (2020, April). The TA framework: Designing real-time teaching augmentation for K-12 classrooms. In *Proceedings of the 2020 CHI Conference on Human Factors in Computing Systems* (pp. 1-17). Association for Computing Machinery. DOI: 10.1145/3313831.3376277

Berrezueta-Guzman, S., Dolón-Poza, M., & Wagner, S. (2025). Supporting preschool emotional development with AI-powered robots. In *Proceedings of the 24th Interaction Design and Children* (pp. 1134–1139). arXiv preprint. https://doi.org// DOI: 10.1145/3713043.3731548

Chiu, T. K. (2024). *Empowering K-12 education with AI: Preparing for the future of education and work*. Taylor & Francis. DOI: 10.4324/9781003498377

Chiu, T. K. F., Chen, Y., Yau, K. W., Chai, C., Meng, H., King, I., Wong, S., & Yam, Y. (2024). Developing and validating measures for AI literacy tests: From self-reported to objective measures. *Computers and Education. Artificial Intelligence*, *7*, 100282. DOI: 10.1016/j.caeai.2024.100282

Cohn, C., Snyder, C., & Fonteles, J. H., TS, A., Montenegro, J., & Biswas, G. (2024). A multimodal approach to support teacher, researcher and AI collaboration in STEM+ C learning environments. *British Journal of Educational Technology*, *56*(2), 595–620. DOI: 10.1111/bjet.13518

Delello, J. A., Watters, J. B., & Garcia-Lopez, A. (2024). Artificial intelligence in education: Transforming learning and teaching. In Delello, J. A., & McWhorter, R. R. (Eds.), *Disruptive technologies in education and workforce development* (pp. 1–26). IGI Global. DOI: 10.4018/979-8-3693-3003-6.ch001

Detrick, R., & Kim, J. (in press). Collaborative approaches: Bridging the gap between generative AI developers and educators. In Sabbaghan, S. (Ed.), *Navigating generative AI in higher education: Ethical, theoretical, and practical perspectives*. Edward Elgar. DOI: 10.4337/9781035337873.00018

Dillenbourg, P., Baker, M. J., Blaye, A., & O'Malley, C. (1995). The evolution of research on collaborative learning. In Spada, H., & Reimann, P. (Eds.), *Learning in humans and machine: Towards an interdisciplinary learning science* (pp. 189–211). Elsevier.

Dmello, V. J., Frank, D., Bidi, S. B., & Rajendran, A. (2024). Unlocking the enigma of online learning: How learning styles shape adoption intention? *E-Learning and Digital Media*, *0*(0), 1–16. DOI: 10.1177/20427530241257651

Eguchi, A., Okada, H., & Muto, Y. (2021). Contextualizing AI education for K-12 students to enhance their learning of AI literacy through culturally responsive approaches. *KI- Künstliche Intelligenz, 35*(2), 153–161. DOI: 10.1007/s13218-021-00737-3

Fan, L., Kim, J., Detrick, R., & Li, N. (2025). Developing students' higher-order thinking skills with generative AI insights and strategies from a case study. In El-Sayary, A. (Ed.), *Prompt engineering and generative AI applications for teaching and learning* (pp. 411–428). IGI Global Scientific Publishing. DOI: 10.4018/979-8-3693-7332-3.ch024

Fazal, S. (2025). Attitude towards teacher-AI collaboration in academic writing instruction: Transforming future of English language teaching. In Ali, M. M., Anwar, M. N., Fazal, S., & Ayyaz, S. (Eds.), *AI applications for English language learning* (pp. 15–42). IGI Global Scientific Publishing. DOI: 10.4018/979-8-3693-9077-1.ch002

Filiz, O., Kaya, M. H., & Adiguzel, T. (2025). Teachers and AI: Understanding the factors influencing AI integration in K-12 education. *Education and Information Technologies*, *30*(13), 1–37. DOI: 10.1007/s10639-025-13463-2

George, A. S. (2023). Preparing students for an AI-driven world: Rethinking curriculum and pedagogy in the age of artificial intelligence. *Partners Universal Innovative Research Publication*, *1*(2), 112–136. DOI: 10.5281/zenodo.10245675

Han, A. (2024). *StoryAI: Designing, developing, and evaluating generative AI-Powered story-authoring platform for young learners*. University of California.

Hmelo-Silver, C. E., & Barrows, H. S. (2008). Facilitating collaborative knowledge building. *Cognition and Instruction*, *26*(1), 48–94. DOI: 10.1080/07370000701798495

Hong Kong Education City. (2021). *AI education for future-ready generations.* Go AI Scheme. https://www.edcity.hk/ai/en

Huang, F., Wang, Y., & Zhang, H. (2024). Modelling generative AI acceptance, perceived teachers' enthusiasm and self-efficacy to English as a foreign language learners' well-being in the digital era. *European Journal of Education, 59*(4), e12770. DOI: 10.1111/ejed.12770

Huang, M. (2025). Student engagement and speaking performance in AI-assisted learning environments: A mixed-methods study from Chinese middle schools. *Education and Information Technologies, 30*(6), 7143–7165. DOI: 10.1007/s10639-024-12989-1

Hutchins, E. (2000). Distributed cognition. International encyclopedia of the social and behavioral sciences, 138(1), 1-10. https://arl.human.cornell.edu/linked%20docs/Hutchins_Distributed_Cognition.pdf

Hwang, G. J., Sung, H. Y., Chang, S. C., & Huang, X. C. (2020). A fuzzy expert system-based adaptive learning approach to improving students' learning performances by considering affective and cognitive factors. *Computers and Education: Artificial Intelligence, 1*, 100003. DOI: 10.1016/j.caeai.2020.100003

Jeon, M. (2023). *Developing middle schoolers' artificial intelligence literacy through project-based learning: Investigating cognitive & affective dimensions of learning about AI*. Indiana University.

Jiang, C., & Pang, Y. (2023). Enhancing design thinking in engineering students with project-based learning. *Computer Applications in Engineering Education, 31*(4), 814–830. DOI: 10.1002/cae.22608

Jiang, J., & Yang, Y. (2025). GymBuddy and Elomia, AI-integrated applications, effects on the mental health of the students with psychological disorders. *BMC Psychology, 13*(1), 1–9. DOI: 10.1186/s40359-025-02640-0 PMID: 40200376

Jiang, T., Sun, Z., Fu, S., & Lv, Y. (2024). Human-AI interaction research agenda: A user-centered perspective. *Data and Information Management, 8*(4), 100078. DOI: 10.1016/j.dim.2024.100078

Kammer, J., & Hays, L. (2023). *Digital literacy made simple: Strategies for building skills across the curriculum*. International Society for Technology in Education.

Karalekas, G., Vologiannidis, S., & Kalomiros, J. (2023). Teaching machine learning in K–12 using robotics. *Education Sciences, 13*(1), 67. DOI: 10.3390/educsci13010067

Kartal, O. Y., Yazgan, A. D., Temelli, D., & Yavuz Kartal, M. (2024). The impact of epistemological beliefs and school climate on the sustainability of critical thinking dispositions in middle school students. *Sustainability (Basel), 16*(20), 8786. DOI: 10.3390/su16208786

Kim, J. (2024a). Leading teachers' perspective on teacher-AI collaboration in education. *Education and Information Technologies, 29*(7), 8693–8724. DOI: 10.1007/s10639-023-12109-5

Kim, J. (2024b). Types of teacher-AI collaboration in K-12 classroom instruction: Chinese teachers' perspective. *Education and Information Technologies, 29*(13), 17433–17465. DOI: 10.1007/s10639-024-12523-3

Kim, J. (2025). Artificial intelligence in achieving sustainable development: Expectations of undergraduate students. *TechTrends, 69*(1), 138–148. DOI: 10.1007/s11528-024-01025-1

Kim, J., & Cho, Y. H. (2023). My teammate is AI: Understanding students' perceptions of student-AI collaboration in drawing tasks. *Asia Pacific Journal of Education, 45*(3), 1013–1027. DOI: 10.1080/02188791.2023.2286206

Kim, J., Detrick, R., Yu, S., Song, Y., Bol, L., & Li, N. (2025). Socially shared regulation of learning and artificial intelligence: Opportunities to support socially shared regulation. *Education and Information Technologies, 30*(9), 1–39. DOI: 10.1007/s10639-024-13187-9

Kim, J., Lee, H., & Cho, Y. H. (2022). Learning design to support student-AI collaboration: Perspectives of leading teachers for AI in education. *Education and Information Technologies, 27*(5), 6069–6104. DOI: 10.1007/s10639-021-10831-6

Kim, J., & Lee, S. S. (2023). Are two heads better than one?: The effect of student-AI collaboration on students' learning task performance. *TechTrends, 67*(2), 365–375. DOI: 10.1007/s11528-022-00788-9 PMID: 36258920

Kim, J., Yu, S., Detrick, R., & Li, N. (2025). Exploring students' perspectives on generative AI-assisted academic writing. *Education and Information Technologies, 30*(1), 1265–1300. DOI: 10.1007/s10639-024-12878-7

Kim, J., Yu, S., Lee, S. S., & Detrick, R. (2025). Students' prompt patterns and its effects in AI-assisted academic writing: Focusing on students' level of AI literacy. *Journal of Research on Technology in Education*, 1–18. DOI: 10.1080/15391523.2025.2456043

Koh, J., Cowling, M., Jha, M., & Sim, K. N. (2023). The human teacher, the AI teacher and the AIED-teacher relationship. *Journal of Higher Education Theory and Practice, 23*(17), 199–211. DOI: 10.33423/jhetp.v23i17.6543

Lin, Y., Guo, J., Chen, Y., Yao, C., & Ying, F. (2020). It is your turn: Collaborative ideation with a co-creative robot through sketch. In *Proceedings of the 2020 CHI Conference on Human Factors in Computing Systems* (pp. 1-14). Association for Computing Machinery. DOI: 10.1145/3313831.3376258

Luckin, R. (2010). *Re-designing learning contexts: Technology-rich, learner-centered ecologies*. Routledge. DOI: 10.4324/9780203854754

Memarian, B., & Doleck, T. (2024). Embodied AI in education: A review on the body, environment, and mind. *Education and Information Technologies, 29*(1), 895–916. DOI: 10.1007/s10639-023-12346-8

Mouta, A., Torrecilla-Sánchez, E. M., & Pinto-Llorente, A. M. (2025). Comprehensive professional learning for teacher agency in addressing ethical challenges of AIED: Insights from educational design research. *Education and Information Technologies, 30*(3), 3343–3387. DOI: 10.1007/s10639-024-12946-y

Mujiono, M. (2023). Educational collaboration: Teachers and artificial intelligence. *Jurnal Kependidikan: Jurnal Hasil Penelitian Dan Kajian Kepustakaan Di Bidang Pendidikan. Pengajaran Dan Pembelajaran, 9*(2), 618–632. DOI: 10.33394/jk.v9i2.7801

Nazaretsky, T., Bar, C., Walter, M., & Alexandron, G. (2022, March). Empowering teachers with AI: Co-designing a learning analytics tool for personalized instruction in the science classroom. *In Proceedings of the 12th international learning analytics and knowledge conference* (pp. 1–12). Association for Computing Machinery. DOI: 10.1145/3506860.3506861

Park, K., Mott, B., Lee, S., Gupta, A., Jantaraweragul, K., Glazewski, K., Scribner, J. A., Ottenbreit-Leftwich, A., Hmelo-Silver, C. E., & Lester, J. (2022). Investigating a visual interface for elementary students to formulate AI planning tasks. *Journal of Computer Languages, 73*, 101157. DOI: 10.1016/j.cola.2022.101157

Rahimi, A. R., & Sevilla-Pavón, A. (2025). The role of design thinking skills in artificial-intelligence language learning (DEAILL) in shaping language learners' L2 grit: The mediator and moderator role of artificial intelligence L2 motivational self-system. *Computer Assisted Language Learning*, 1–49. DOI: 10.1080/09588221.2025.2477710

Self, J. (1999). The defining characteristics of intelligent tutoring systems research: ITSs care, precisely. *International Journal of Artificial Intelligence in Education, 10*, 350–364.

Solyst, J., Yang, E., Xie, S., Ogan, A., Hammer, J., & Eslami, M. (2023). The potential of diverse youth as stakeholders in identifying and mitigating algorithmic bias for a future of fairer AI. In *Proceedings of the ACM on Human-Computer Interaction* (pp. 1-27). Association for Computing Machinery. DOI: 10.1145/3610213

Song, C., Shin, S. Y., & Shin, K. S. (2024). Implementing the dynamic feedback-driven learning optimization framework: A machine learning approach to personalize educational pathways. *Applied Sciences (Basel, Switzerland)*, *14*(2), 916. DOI: 10.3390/app14020916

Song, Y., Kim, J., Liu, Z., Li, C., & Xing, W. (2025a). Students' perceived roles, opportunities, and challenges of a generative AI-powered teachable agent: A case of middle school math class. *Journal of Research on Technology in Education*, 1–19. DOI: 10.1080/15391523.2024.2447727

Song, Y., Kim, J., Xing, W., Liu, Z., Li, C., & Oh, H. (2025b). Elementary school students' and teachers' perceptions toward creative mathematical writing with Generative AI. *Journal of Research on Technology in Education*, 1–23. DOI: 10.1080/15391523.2025.2455057

Su, J., Zhong, Y., & Ng, D. T. K. (2022). A meta-review of literature on educational approaches for teaching AI at the K-12 levels in the Asia-Pacific region. *Computers and Education: Artificial Intelligence*, *3*, 100065. DOI: 10.1016/j.caeai.2022.100065

Tan, D. Y., & Cheah, C. W. (2021). Developing a gamified AI-enabled online learning application to improve students' perception of university physics. *Computers and Education: Artificial Intelligence*, *2*, 100032. DOI: 10.1016/j.caeai.2021.100032

Thangavel, S., K, S., & K, S. (2025). Revolutionizing education through augmented reality (AR) and virtual reality (VR): Innovations, challenges and future prospects. *Asian Journal of Interdisciplinary Research*, *8*(1), 1–28. DOI: 10.54392/ajir2511

UNESCO. (2021). *AI and education: Guidance for policymakers.* UNESCO Publishing. https://unesco.org/en/articles/ai-and-education-guidance-policy-makers

Wang, D., Shan, D., Ju, R., Kao, B., Zhang, C., & Chen, G. (2024). Investigating dialogic interaction in K12 online one-on-one mathematics tutoring using AI and sequence mining techniques. *Education and Information Technologies*, *30*(7), 9215–9240. DOI: 10.1007/s10639-024-13195-9

Wang, T., & Cheng, E. C. K. (2021). An investigation of barriers to Hong Kong K-12 schools incorporating Artificial Intelligence in education. *Computers and Education: Artificial Intelligence*, *2*, 100031. DOI: 10.1016/j.caeai.2021.100031

Wiggins, G. P., & McTighe, J. (2005). *Understanding by design*. Ascd.

Winne, P. H. (2013). Self-regulated learning viewed from models of information processing. In Zimmerman, B., & Schunk, D. (Eds.), *Self-regulated learning and academic achievement* (pp. 145–178). Routledge.

Woodruff, K., Hutson, J., & Arnone, K. (2023). Perceptions and barriers to adopting artificial intelligence in K-12 education: A survey of educators in fifty states. *Faculty Scholarship,* 1–28. https://digitalcommons.lindenwood.edu/faculty-research-papers/506.

Wu, , CLi, , YLi, , JZhang, , QWu, , F. (2021, May). Web-based platform for K-12 AI education in China. In *Proceedings of the AAAI Conference on Artificial Intelligence, 35*(17), 15687-15694. DOI: 10.1609/aaai.v35i17.17848

Yan, W., Nakajima, T., & Sawada, R. (2024). Benefits and challenges of collaboration between students and conversational generative artificial intelligence in programming learning: An empirical case study. *Education Sciences, 14*(433), 1–20. DOI: 10.3390/educsci14040433

Yim, I. H. Y., & Su, J. (2025). Artificial intelligence (AI) learning tools in K-12 education: A scoping review. *Journal of Computers in Education, 12*(1), 93–131. DOI: 10.1007/s40692-023-00304-9

Yoon, S., Min, S., & Kang, D. (2024). Comprehensive analysis of AI-based math learning platforms for K-12 education. In C. Bonk & G. Marks (Eds.), *Proceedings of E-Learn: World Conference on E-Learning in Corporate, Government, Healthcare, and Higher Education* (pp. 113-122). Association for the Advancement of Computing in Education.

Yu, S., Han, H., & Ahn, H. (2025). Mapping children's sense of belonging through multimodal composition in the classroom. *Language, Culture and Curriculum, 38*(3), 1–22. DOI: 10.1080/07908318.2025.2534382

Zall, R., & Kangavari, M. R. (2022). Comparative analytical survey on cognitive agents with emotional intelligence. *Cognitive Computation, 14*(4), 1223–1246. DOI: 10.1007/s12559-022-10007-5

Zawacki-Richter, O., Marin, V. I., Bond, M., & Gouverneur, F. (2019). Systematic review of research on artificial intelligence applications in higher education – Where are the educators? *International Journal of Educational Technology in Higher Education, 16*(39), 1–27. DOI: 10.1186/s41239-019-0171-0

Zhang, J., & Zhang, Z. (2024). AI in teacher education: Unlocking new dimensions in teaching support, inclusive learning, and digital literacy. *Journal of Computer Assisted Learning, 40*(4), 1871–1885. DOI: 10.1111/jcal.12988

KEY TERMS AND DEFINITIONS

AI in Education (AIED): AI in Education encompasses the design, development, and application of artificial intelligence technologies to enhance educational processes, teaching effectiveness, and learner outcomes. AIED seeks to model and respond to learners' cognitive, emotional, and behavioral states, thereby promoting personalized, data-informed, and equitable learning environments.

Human-AI Collaboration (HAC): Human-AI collaboration refers to the dynamic partnership between humans and artificial intelligence systems in which both entities contribute their unique strengths to achieve shared goals. In educational contexts, HAC involves leveraging AI's data-processing, adaptability, and personalization capabilities alongside human creativity, critical thinking, and empathy. This collaboration supports teaching and learning by enhancing decision-making, fostering personalized learning experiences, and promoting mutual growth through continuous interaction. Rather than replacing human roles, HAC emphasizes co-evolution—where humans and AI systems learn from and with each other to improve performance, understanding, and problem-solving across diverse educational tasks.

K–12 Education: K–12 education refers to the formal education system that encompasses kindergarten through 12th grade, typically serving students from approximately ages 5 to 18. It represents the foundational stage of a student's academic journey, including primary (elementary), middle, and secondary (high) school levels. K–12 education aims to develop essential knowledge, skills, and social competencies that prepare learners for higher education, careers, and civic life. In many countries, including the United States, K–12 serves as the core framework for general education, integrating academic content, technology, and social-emotional learning to support students' holistic development.

Learning Design: Learning design refers to the systematic process of planning, structuring, and sequencing learning experiences, activities, and assessments to achieve specific learning outcomes. It integrates pedagogical theories, learner needs, technological affordances, and contextual factors to create meaningful and effective educational experiences. Learning design emphasizes intentional decision-making that connects learning goals with appropriate strategies and tools, often represented through models, templates, or design frameworks.

Student–AI Collaboration (SAC): Student–AI collaboration represents the partnership between learners and artificial intelligence systems in co-constructing knowledge, solving problems, or engaging in learning tasks. Rather than functioning merely as a tool, AI acts as a cognitive or creative partner that provides feedback, scaffolding, or adaptive support. Effective student–AI collaboration emphasizes mutual engagement, agency, and shared task ownership to enhance learning processes and outcomes.

Student–AI Interaction (SAI): Student–AI interaction denotes the dynamic exchanges between learners and AI-driven systems (e.g., chatbots, adaptive learning platforms, or virtual tutors) during learning processes. These interactions involve information input, feedback reception, and system adaptation to learner responses. The quality and design of such interactions influence student engagement, motivation, and knowledge construction.

Teacher–AI Collaboration (TAC): Teacher–AI collaboration refers to the cooperative relationship between educators and artificial intelligence systems to design, deliver, and improve teaching and learning experiences. In this partnership, AI supports teachers by offering data-driven insights, automating routine tasks, or generating adaptive learning materials, while teachers contribute pedagogical expertise, ethical judgment, and contextual understanding. The collaboration aims to augment, not replace, teacher capacities, fostering more personalized and inclusive instruction.

Teacher–AI Interaction (TAI): Teacher–AI interaction refers to the communicative and operational exchanges between educators and AI technologies in the context of teaching and learning. This includes teachers' engagement with AI systems for instructional decision-making, assessment, content generation, or classroom management. Effective teacher–AI interaction requires interpretability, trust, and alignment between the system's analytics and the teacher's pedagogical goals.

Chapter 2
AI-Enhanced Professional Development for Language Teachers: A Systematic Review

İdil Sayın
https://orcid.org/0000-0001-5546-2673
Süleyman Demirel University, Turkey

Derya Coşkun
https://orcid.org/0000-0001-6044-6109
Süleyman Demirel University, Turkey

ABSTRACT

This systematic review analyzes AI-enhanced professional development in language teacher education using the Intelligent Technology-Enhanced Language Learning framework. Following PRISMA 2020, 23 empirical studies (2020-2025) from Web of Science and Scopus were reviewed with qualitative content analysis. Findings showed that AI supported lesson planning, AI literacy, and adaptive tutoring. Affordances included personalization, automated feedback, and multimodal engagement; challenges were infrastructure, bias, and over-reliance. Teachers generally viewed AI positively but had concerns about its reliability. Most studies used learn-apply-reflect cycles in pre-service contexts. AI improved teaching efficacy and digital skills, but findings relied on self-reports and short-term data. Geographic concentration in Asia and researcher-led initiatives constrain generalizability. The review highlights the need for AI literacy in curricula, institutional support, and more longitudinal research.

DOI: 10.4018/979-8-3373-2927-7.ch002

INTRODUCTION

The transformative power of artificial intelligence (AI) on teacher education programs has been highlighted in various studies (e.g., Çelik, 2023; Duan & Zhao, 2024; Kohnke, 2024; Lan, 2024; Prilop et al., 2025). To begin with, Kohnke (2024) states that AI is known to have transformed teacher professional development through real-time feedback, personalized learning paths, and adaptive learning environments. Similarly, Lan (2024) refers to the transformative role of AI in teachers' professional identity development and collaborative learning experiences. Prilop et al. (2025) also emphasize that AI has transformed teacher education programs by reshaping teaching and learning practices and traditional learning methods. In this regard, three functions of AI literacy as *AI as a teaching tool*, *AI as teaching content*, and *AI as a learning tool* are underlined. Based on these three domains, both teacher educators and pre-service teachers are expected to utilize AI effectively, reflectively, and ethically by being aware of its potential benefits and limitations. Therefore, designing professional development initiatives such as hands-on experiences, courses, training programs, and community of practices has come to the fore to enhance language teachers' motivation, knowledge, and confidence in using AI tools. In addition to these variables, Guggemos and Seufert (2021) underscore the importance of technological collaboration, knowledge, joint effort, and teacher communities to enhance teachers' professional development process.

AI has contributed not only to the professional development of teachers but also to the academic and personal development of students in different regards. To illustrate, Novawan et al. (2024) report that English language teachers stated AI integration contributed to creating a dynamic and responsive learning environment by enhancing student participation. The teachers also note that AI tools enable students to improve their autonomous learning abilities by motivating them through multiple sources and providing instant feedback and personalized learning opportunities. In line with autonomous learning opportunities, the findings of Mah and Groß's (2024) study reveal that educators in higher education institutions preferred professional development programs to be in the form of digital workshops and self-paced online courses. Hence, it can be concluded that teachers should be supported via AI-focused professional development programs. Accordingly, formal training programs, workshops, and different opportunities should be provided for language teachers to boost their professional development by using AI tools and pedagogical knowledge about how to integrate AI into their classes. In this vein, a number of studies (e.g., Lan, 2024; McGrath et al., 2023) highlight the significance of institutional support and tailored professional development opportunities to enhance university teachers' AI-related knowledge. Along with this, training on AI literacy and the ethical and technical use of AI competencies should be integrated into pre-service teacher education to further promote pre-service teachers' professional development (Kohnke et al., 2025).

The existing literature reveals the lack of opportunities and support to promote teachers' professional development by incorporating AI into language teacher education programs and curricula. For instance, Novawan et al. (2024) found that although language teachers use AI tools to enhance their language skills and design materials, they often lack institutional policies or frameworks to guide AI integration into language teaching programs. In a similar sense, Tan et al. (2025) remark that there is no balance in the studies conducted within the context of AI and professional development, that the effects of AI are explored on teaching processes, while teachers' AI-related professional needs are neglected. Additionally, Mah and Groß (2024) draw attention to the research gap in understanding how teachers' professional development can be effectively fostered with AI. According to the study, educators at higher education show interest in learning and teaching via AI tools; however, there are relatively few studies exploring teachers' preferences, needs, and challenges regarding AI-related professional development. Likewise, Çelik et al. (2022) identify the gap in the literature that teachers' professional development has not been addressed as a central theme in AI-based studies.

Despite AI's potential in language teacher education, a notable gap persists: rapid adoption has not been accompanied by the systematic support for teachers needed to enable effective pedagogical integration. Thus, this review examines three interconnected gaps: (1) an imbalance in research focus, with attention centere2024; Shiing processes and student outcomes rather than language teachers' AI-related professional development needs, even as teachers use AI to design materials without clear policies, frameworks, or professional development to guide principled integration (Novawan et al., 2024; Tan et al., 2025); (2) limited evidence on how to foster teacher professional development with AI, despite strong interest from higher-education educators (Lyu et al., 2025; Mah & Groß, 2024), and the marginal status of professional development as a theme in AI-based studies (Çelik et al., 2022); and (3) framework misalignment, as Technology-Enhanced Language Learning (TELL) framework underrepresents contemporary AI's dynamic capabilities, while emerging needs (e.g., data interpretation, prompt engineering, and ethical decision-making etc.) remain undertheorized in teacher-education contexts (Akinsemolu & Onyeaka, 2025; Huang et al., 2023; Laoha et al., 2025; Novawan et al., 2024; Shi, 2025).

To address these gaps, this systematic review synthesizes existing research on language teachers' professional development in AI-enhanced contexts. The study employs the Intelligent Technology-Enhanced Language Learning (ITELL) framework to examine pre-service and in-service teachers' perceptions, experiences, affordances, and challenges. Given that effective AI integration in language education depends on AI-enhanced teacher professional development, this review aims to establish an evidence base for programs that support teachers in adopting AI while navigating its complexities and ethical considerations. In line with the existing research and aims of the current study, this chapter seeks to answer the following research questions:

1. What purposes does AI serve in language teacher education and professional development programs?
2. What are the primary affordances and challenges associated with integrating AI technologies into language teacher education and professional development programs?
3. In what ways do language teachers perceive and respond to the integration of AI tools into their education and professional development experiences?
4. How are AI-driven technologies being implemented in language teacher education and professional development programs?
5. What evidence exists regarding the effectiveness of AI-supported language teacher education and professional development initiatives?
6. In what educational and institutional contexts is AI being integrated into language teacher education and professional development?

LITERATURE REVIEW

Artificial Intelligence in Language Education

Language education has evolved through several technological shifts, from 1950s language labs to 1990s multimedia software and now AI-powered adaptive learning systems. Early computer-assisted language learning (CALL) was rule-based with limited interactivity, initially focusing on drills, then shifting to language use, and later integrating skills and technology through multimedia networked computers (Warschauer & Healey, 1998). Unlike previous technological tools, contemporary AI tools provide expanded functionality and enable personalized learning experiences, thereby reshaping education beyond merely serving as technological tools (Walter, 2024). Current AI tools for language learning include and move beyond intelligent tutoring systems, chatbots, automated writing evaluation systems, and speech recognition technologies. Intelligent Tutoring Systems (ITS) provide personalized instruction and adaptive learning paths (Anoir et al., 2024; Slavuj et al., 2015; Tafazoli et al., 2019). Automated writing evaluation systems offer instant grammar and style feedback. They also ease the burden of grading student writings for teachers (Huawei & Aryadoust, 2022; Shi & Aryadoust, 2024). Furthermore, speech recognition technologies and chatbots help develop and assess fluency and accuracy (Alenezi & Alenezi, 2025; Jeon et al., 2023; Lyu et al., 2024). Collectively, these AI tools cover a wide range of language skills. This comprehensive coverage is especially useful for foreign language education, where opportunities to practice and use authentic language are often limited to classroom settings.

This extensive history of CALL (Chapelle, 2001; Levy, 1997) has led to the development of robust criteria, such as validity, authenticity, and positive impact, for evaluating technology-mediated tasks. As a result, language education represents a particularly suitable and well-regulated domain for the application of AI technologies. The rapid adoption of AI tools in language education has made it essential to thoroughly evaluate their effectiveness in improving language skills, the challenges educators encounter in implementation, and potential directions for their future development (Zhu & Wang, 2025). Although frameworks such as Technology-Enhanced Language Learning (TELL) outline how technological tools can be used most effectively in language education, TELL is best suited to tools that provide relatively static, predefined learning pathways. In contrast, AI tools, with their unique affordances, help resolve and exceed TELL's boundaries (Huang et al., 2023), making it necessary to broaden the framework. Building on TELL, Intelligent Technology-Enhanced Language Learning (ITELL), also referred to as *TELL with AI*, expands the static resource base and, crucially, introduces dynamic adaptation (Novawan et al., 2024).

The ITELL framework does not specify predefined dimensions but instead identifies core characteristics that distinguish it from TELL. These characteristics include adaptability and personalization, real-time feedback, intelligent tutoring, adaptive assessment and proficiency tracking, advanced Natural Language Processing (NLP) interaction, dynamic content generation, predictive analytics, and multimodal learning (Novawan et al., 2024; pp. 3-4). The framework further categorizes AI tools as either narrow or general AI. Narrow AI, which specializes in specific language learning tasks, currently dominates practical applications in educational contexts. Examples of such tools include automated writing evaluation systems, chatbots, and language translation services, each designed to address particular language learning objectives and challenges. In contrast, general AI represents the potential for developing human-like cognitive capabilities within language teaching systems.

The distinctions established by ITELL are significant. Whereas traditional TELL provides digital resources and approaches that require manual integration by educators, ITELL enables responsive ecosystems that continuously adapt to learner performance, preferences, and proficiency levels (Bahari et al., 2025; Huang et al., 2023; Novawan et al., 2024). This transformation fundamentally alters the pedagogical landscape and necessitates new competencies among educators (Akinsemolu & Onyeaka, 2025; Laoha et al., 2025). In particular, teachers are now required to analyze and act upon data, develop effective instructions or prompts, and conduct assessments in an ethical and transparent manner.

Artificial Intelligence in Language Teacher Education

There is a growing body of literature that recognizes the importance of AI on language teacher education programs. To illustrate, Case et al. (2025) referred to three affordances of AI use in language teacher education programs, which were reducing teacher workload, enhancing learner engagement, and scaffolding pre-service teachers' learning and critical thinking skills. Likewise, pre-service teachers from diverse subject specializations in Kohnke et al.'s (2025) study stated that AI could contribute to personalized learning, lesson-planning, material design, and student assessment. In addition, Moorhouse and Kohnke (2024) explored the effects of generative AI (GenAI) on initial teacher education program and found that teacher educators acknowledged that GenAI would be influential on curriculum, instruction, and assessment. Therefore, they suggested updating teacher training programs, adapting the course contents in line with GenAI, and incorporating critical AI into teacher education programs. Responsible use of AI and modelling techniques were the strategies proposed by the teacher educators to implement AI-related tasks in their teaching contexts.

In response to these benefits, the studies also reported certain difficulties and challenges in integrating AI into language teacher education. For instance, the resistance towards AI, lack of technological infrastructure and institutional support were mentioned as some of the challenges to improving AI literacy (Kohnke et al., 2025; Ng et al., 2021). In another study by Moorhouse and Kohnke (2024), teacher educators had some assessment-related concerns such as detecting AI and plagiarism issues.

Considering all the benefits and challenges of integrating AI into language teacher education programs, some suggestions for further studies have been proposed. To illustrate, Case et al. (2025) noted that pre service language teachers should be trained to keep up with the changing digital future and ongoing research should be conducted to explore how teacher roles evolve with these changes. Teachers' preferences about the use of AI, their shifting roles and responsibilities along with technological developments should be also explored in future studies (Case et al., 2025). Additionally, Kohnke et al. (2025) claimed that teacher training programs should develop guidelines and hand-on practices on AI training to keep up with the technological developments in the field. They also suggested integrating AI literacy into teacher education programs by designing AI-related policies, enhancing institutional support, designing continuous professional development programs, and addressing ethical issues. An inclusive teacher education program should be designed to bridge the gap between the opportunities provided by AI and pre-service teacher training programs. In this sense, it is recommended to equip educators and pre-service teachers with AI literacy and self-directed learning skills (Kohnke et al.,

2025). Lastly, Moorhouse and Kohnke (2024) recommended developing theoretical perspectives and frameworks to explore the connection between language teacher education and AI.

METHODOLOGY

Procedure

The planning, execution, and documentation of this systematic review were guided by the 2020 Preferred Reporting Items for Systematic Reviews and Meta-Analysis (PRISMA) statement (Page et al., 2021). Specifically, the review includes studies that (a) are indexed in Web of Science (WoS) or Scopus, (b) were published between 2020 and 2025, (c) are written in English, (d) present empirical research, and (e) integrate AI as part of or as the focus of a professional development program for language teachers (including both pre-service and in-service contexts). Conversely, studies were excluded if they (a) are not indexed in WoS or Scopus, (b) were published outside the 2020-2025 window or are planned for publication after 2025, (c) are written in languages other than English, (d) lack empirical content (e.g., review articles, theoretical or conceptual papers), or (e) do not explicitly integrate AI in language teacher professional development.

In this systematic review, language teacher education refers to both pre-service and in-service professional development initiatives aimed at preparing and supporting teachers who teach languages other than students' native languages. This encompasses teachers of English as a Foreign Language (EFL), English as a Second Language (ESL), Teaching English to Speakers of Other Languages (TESOL), Teaching English as a Foreign Language (TEFL) and teachers of other second or foreign languages. The scope of language teacher education in this review includes formal degree programs at the undergraduate and graduate levels, certification courses, professional development workshops, and training seminars. It covers preparation for teaching in K-12, higher education, and adult education contexts, across both face-to-face and online modalities. Although most studies reviewed focus on English-language teaching contexts (EFL, ESL, TESOL), educators preparing to teach other languages in multilingual or multicultural environments are also included. Additionally, AI is defined as computational systems and technologies that simulate aspects of human intelligence to support teaching, learning, and professional development processes. This definition includes GenAI tools, which are capable of producing text, lesson plans, and instructional materials; ITS that provide adaptive feedback and personalized learning pathways; chatbots designed for conversational practice and interactive learning; NLP applications that analyze and generate language; machine learning and deep learning algorithms that adapt to user input; and immersive technologies, including AI-enhanced virtual reality (VR) simulations. In accordance with the search strategy, only technologies explicitly identified as AI-powered, AI-driven, or AI-enhanced in the original studies were included. Tools based solely on rule-based automation without adaptive or intelligent capabilities were excluded. AI tools designed primarily for student use without a teacher education component have not been included in this study.

The Scopus and WoS databases were included in the search process due to their broad, peer-reviewed coverage and strict indexing standards. Both databases are strong in education, applied linguistics, and technology, all of which are relevant to the current study's focus. Additionally, their advanced search tools ensured consistent and manageable results. Including more databases risked redundancy and lower efficiency. Furthermore, the 2020-2025 period was selected to reflect current changes in AI-enhanced professional development for language teachers. These years saw the rapid adoption of AI tools, especially after the introduction of transformer-based models and the digital transformation triggered by COVID-19. Studies before 2020 may not capture current technology, teaching methods, or challenges. Focusing on this timeframe ensures findings are up to date and relevant. The database search was conducted on March 28, 2025, using a search string refined through consultation with teacher educators and a review of the literature. The final search string was:

("artificial intelligence" OR "AI" OR "machine learning" OR "deep learning" OR "natural language processing" OR "NLP" OR "chatbot" OR "intelligent tutoring system" OR "ITS" OR "intelligent learning environment") AND ("professional development" OR "teacher training" OR "teacher education" OR "in-service training" OR "continuing professional development" OR "CPD" OR "pre-service training" OR "teacher preparation" OR "teacher development") AND ("language teacher" OR "language instructor" OR "second language teacher" OR "foreign language teacher" OR "language educator" OR "ESL teacher" OR "EFL teacher" OR "ESL" OR "EFL" OR "TESOL" OR "TEFL" OR "TESL").

Figure 1 presents the PRISMA flow diagram (Page et al., 2021) outlining study identification, screening, eligibility assessment, and inclusion in the qualitative synthesis.

Figure 1. PRISMA flow diagram

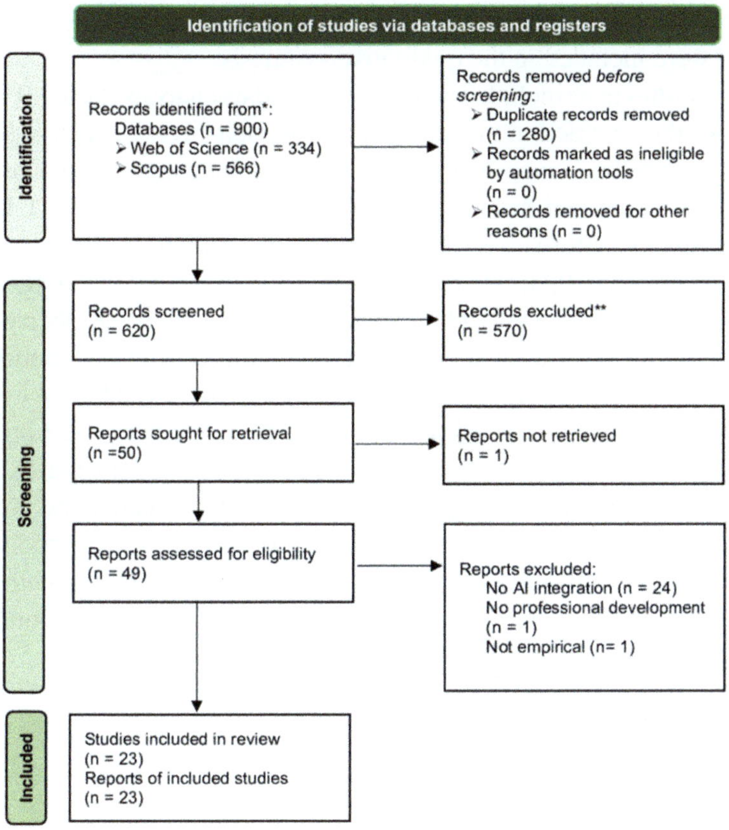

In the identification phase, the search string retrieved 900 records from the databases. After removing 280 duplicate records, 620 unique titles and abstracts remained for screening. In this process, two reviewers independently screened abstracts and titles to determine eligibility, tagging each study as "Eligible" or "Not Eligible". Intercoder reliability was high (Cohen's $\kappa = 0.83$), which exceeded the 0.80 benchmark for excellent agreement (Landis & Koch, 1977). Discrepancies were resolved via consensus meetings guided by the coding framework. When disagreements arose regarding study categorization or thematic coding, both reviewers presented their rationale and supporting evidence from the original texts. Through collaborative discussion and reference to the predefined coding framework, consensus was reached on all disputed items. During title/abstract screening, 570 records were excluded because they did not meet the inclusion criteria, leaving 50 reports for full-text retrieval. One report could not be obtained; therefore, 49 full-text studies were assessed for eligibility. Full-text screening followed the same independent, dual-reviewer process. Out of 49 studies, 26 were excluded for the following reasons: 24 did not involve any AI integration, one did not address professional development, and one was non-empirical. Ultimately, 23 studies met all inclusion criteria and were included in the qualitative synthesis.

Once the studies to be included were identified, data analysis started. Two reviewers conducted data extraction via qualitative content analysis (Miles & Huberman, 1994). To capture the comprehensive use of AI in language teacher professional development, we defined seven coding categories (Purposes of AI Integration (RQ1, category 1), Affordances (category 2) and Challenges (RQ2, category 3), Teachers' Perceptions (RQ3, category 4), Implementation Strategies (RQ4, category 5), Evidence of Effectiveness (RQ5, category 6), and Context (RQ6, category 7)). The purposes of AI integration identify the main aims of studies that utilize AI for professional development. Implementation Strategies describe how AI was woven into training (e.g., hands-on workshops, online modules, peer-coaching sessions, or blended learning designs). Affordances highlight the benefits that AI provides, while challenges present the struggles that AI presents. Teachers' perceptions and responses examine the attitudes and emotional reactions of study participants. Evidence of effectiveness examines how each study measured impact, whether through self-reports, pre- and post-training assessments, or surveys. Finally, context informs whether the study aimed for pre- or in-service teacher training.

RESULTS

Table 1 summarizes the 23 studies by author, year, country, context, language, and keywords. The Appendix contains a comprehensive table detailing author, year, country, purposes, affordances, challenges, teachers' perceptions, implementation strategies, evidence of effectiveness, and context.

Table 1. Overview of Included Studies

Study	*Country*	*Context*	*Language*
Arefian et al. (2024)	Iran	In-service	English (L2)
Belda-Medina & Kokošková (2024)	Spain	Pre-service	English (L2)
Buendgens-Kosten (2024)	Germany	Pre-service	English (L2)
Butler & Jiang (2025)	USA	Pre-service	English (L2)
Chu & Wang (2024)	China	In-service	English (L2)
Davoodi (2024)	USA	In-service	English (L2)

continued on following page

Table 1. Continued

Study	*Country*	*Context*	*Language*
Ghosh (2025)	India	Both (Pre-service & In-service)	Not mentioned
Hieu & Thao (2024)	Vietnam	In-service	English (L2)
Kartal (2024)	Türkiye	Pre-service	English (L2)
Khajavi & Ezhdehakosh (2025)	Iran	Pre-service	English (L2)
Lee et al. (2025a)	South Korea	Pre-service	English (L2)
Lee et al. (2025b)	South Korea	Pre-service	English (L2)
Minnillo et al. (2024)	USA	Both (Pre-service & In-service)	Spanish; German; Chinese; Hindi; Urdu and English (L2)
Mohammadi (2024)	Iran	In-service	English (L2)
Moorhouse et al. (2024)	China	Pre-service	English (L2)
Moorhouse et al. (2025)	China	Pre-service	English (L2)
Pitura et al. (2025)	Poland	Pre-service	English (L2)
Tafazoli (2024)	Iran	In-service	English (L2)
Urazbayeva et al. (2024)	Kazakhstan	In-service	English (L2)
Uysal & Yüksel (2024)	Türkiye	Pre-service	English (L2)
Xin (2024)	China	In-service	English (L2)
Yang & Markauskaite (2025)	Australia	Pre-service	Chinese; Italian; German; and Korean (L2)
Zulianti et al. (2025)	Indonesia	In-service (Novice)	English (L2)

Table 1 shows that the 23 studies are primarily from Asia, particularly China and Iran, with fewer originating from the United States, Europe, and Australia. The majority of these studies focus on pre-service teachers, while a smaller proportion examines in-service cohorts. Nearly all studies are situated in English L2 contexts. Research coverage beyond English as L2 and other languages remains limited.

Purposes of AI in Language Teacher Education and Professional Development

The first research question explores the purposes of the reviewed studies. It was found that the studies aimed to enhance language teacher education and professional development programs by using various methods, integrating different AI tools and procedures. The detailed purposes of these studies are presented in Table 2 below.

Table 2. Purposes of AI Integration Across Selected Studies

Purposes of AI Integration	*Studies*
AI-Supported Teaching Materials and Lesson Planning	Chu & Wang (2024); Lee et al. (2025b); Moorhouse et al. (2025); Tafazoli (2024); Urazbayeva et al. (2024); Xin (2024); Zulianti et al. (2025)
Teacher Professional Development and Competence	Buendgens-Kosten (2024); Davoodi (2024); Minnillo et al. (2024); Moorhouse et al. (2024); Yang & Markauskaite (2025)
AI-Assisted Writing and Language Production	Belda-Medina & Kokošková (2024); Butler & Jiang (2025); Hieu & Thao (2024); Kartal (2024)
Adaptive Tutoring and Assessment Tools	Ghosh (2025); Mohammadi (2024)
Immersive and Simulation-Based AI Learning	Pitura et al. (2025)
Teacher Perceptions, Beliefs, and Reflective Practice	Arefian et al. (2024); Khajavi & Ezhdehakosh (2025); Uysal & Yüksel (2024)
Chatbot Integration for English as a Lingua Franca (ELF) and Interaction	Lee et al. (2025a)

As inferred from Table 2, the studies were conducted for various purposes to support the professional development of pre- and in-service teachers in different aspects. To illustrate, one of the prominent aims of the reviewed studies was to help teachers to design lesson plans and teaching materials to enhance the efficacy of teaching (e.g., Chu & Wang, 2024; Lee et al., 2025b; Moorhouse et al., 2025; Tafazoli, 2024; Urazbayeva et al., 2024; Xin, 2024; Zulianti et al., 2025). Another aim of the reviewed studies was to improve teachers' AI literacy and professional competencies. The findings revealed that using AI contributed to teachers' digital literacy skills, professional development, and instructional competencies (e.g., Buendgens-Kosten, 2024; Davoodi, 2024; Minnillo et al., 2024; Moorhouse et al., 2024; Yang & Markauskaite, 2025). Thus, the reviewed studies revealed that both professional competencies such as engaging in critical reflection and collaborative practices and instructional competencies such as lesson planning, material design, assessment techniques could be improved through AI integration into teacher education and professional development programs.

Furthermore, the studies examined the impact of AI tools and practices on students' language learning skills and teachers' assessment techniques. In this regard, some studies (e.g. Belda-Medina & Kokošková, 2024; Butler & Jiang, 2025; Hieu & Thao, 2024; Kartal, 2024) revealed the positive role of AI-assisted writing on students' writing and language skills, while other studies (e.g., Ghosh, 2025; Mohammadi, 2024) indicated that AI enabled teachers to adapt their teaching strategies with the help of adaptive tutoring systems provided by AI. Additionally, the impact of AI-supported immersive learning environments was explored in one study (e.g.,

Pitura et al., 2025), which found that this learning context provided pre-service teachers with authentic and experiential learning experiences. Similarly, another study (e.g., Lee et al., 2025a) exploring the integration of chatbots in an ELF context revealed that AI enhanced communicative competence and authentic interaction among participants.

Lastly, teachers' perceptions, beliefs, and roles regarding the ethical and responsive use of AI were investigated (e.g., Arefian et al., 2024; Khajavi & Ezhdehakosh, 2025; Uysal & Yüksel, 2024). The studies revealed that while some teachers were willing to learn and use AI, others had some concerns about integrating AI into their lessons

Affordances and Challenges of Integrating AI into Language Teacher Education and Professional Development

The second research question addresses the reported affordances and challenges associated with integrating AI into language teacher education and professional development programs. Accordingly, the findings on the affordances and challenges of AI are presented in Table 3 and Table 4, respectively.

Table 3. Affordances of AI Integration Across Selected Studies

Affordances of AI Integration	*Studies*
Personalization and Adaptivity	Davoodi (2024); Ghosh (2025); Hieu & Thao (2024); Khajavi & Ezhdehakosh (2025); Minnillo et al. (2024); Mohammadi (2024); Tafazoli (2024)
Student Engagement and Motivation	Arefian et al. (2024); Ghosh (2025); Hieu (2024); Khajavi (2025); Lee (2025a); Pitura et al. (2025); Urazbayeva et al. (2024); Uysal & Yüksel (2024)
Reflective Practice and Professional Growth	Arefian et al. (2024); Lee et al. (2025a); Lee et al. (2025b); Minnillo et al. (2024); Moorhouse et al. (2025); Tafazoli (2024); Uysal & Yüksel (2024); Yang & Markauskaite (2025)
Creativity and Brainstorming	Arefian et al. (2024); Belda-Medina & Kokošková (2024); Buendgens-Kosten (2024); Chu (2024); Hieu (2024); Kartal (2024); Moorhouse (2024); Moorhouse (2025); Urazbayeva (2024)
Teaching Efficiency Improvements	Belda-Medina (2024); Buendgens-Kosten (2024); Butler & Jiang (2025); Chu & Wang (2024); Davoodi (2024); Kartal (2024); Khajavi & Ezhdehakosh (2025); Mohammadi (2024); Moorhouse et al. (2024); Moorhouse et al. (2025); Xin (2024); Yang & Markauskaite (2025)
Multimodal and Multilingual Support	Yang & Markauskaite (2025)

As shown in Table 3, AI integration was beneficial for teachers' professional development in terms of instructional, professional, and personal affordances. To begin with instructional affordances, several studies (e.g., Davoodi, 2024; Ghosh, 2025; Hieu, 2024; Khajavi, 2025; Minnillo, 2024; Mohammadi, 2024; Tafazoli, 2024) have identified that teachers could provide differentiated and personalized instruction for the students in mixed ability classes with the help of AI. Another instructional affordance reported by several studies (e.g., Belda-Medina, 2024; Buendgens-Kosten, 2024; Butler, 2025; Chu, 2024; Davoodi, 2024; Kartal, 2024; Khajavi, 2025; Mohammadi, 2024; Moorhouse, 2024; Moorhouse, 2025; Xin, 2024; Yang, 2025) was based on the improvements in teaching efficiency. These studies have found that AI supported instructional effectiveness by providing automated feedback and reducing teacher workload. Further, while some studies (e.g., Arefian, 2024; Ghosh, 2025; Hieu, 2024; Khajavi, 2025; Lee, 2025a; Pitura, 2025; Urazbayeva, 2024; Uysal, 2024) have revealed that AI-aided learning environments created by teachers promoted student engagement and motivation, one study by Yang (2025) indicated the multimodal and multilingual support provided by AI at inclusive and multicultural language learning environments.

As per professional affordances, teachers benefited from AI to design lesson plans and assess the learners while engaging in some professional development and reflective practices (e.g., Arefian, 2024; Lee, 2025a; Lee, 2025b; Minnillo, 2024; Moorhouse, 2025; Tafazoli, 2024; Uysal, 2024; Yang, 2025). Along with professional growth, it has been found that AI integration enhanced teachers' creativity and brainstorming skills (e.g., Arefian, 2024; Belda-Medina, 2024; Buendgens-Kosten, 2024; Chu, 2024; Hieu, 2024; Kartal, 2024; Moorhouse, 2024; Moorhouse, 2025; Urazbayeva, 2024) by providing them with the opportunity to engage with current and experiential teaching methods. Apart from the advantages, the reviewed studies revealed that AI integration also presented some challenges and barriers, as outlined in Table 4 below.

Table 4. Challenges of AI Integration Across Selected Studies

Challenges of AI Integration	*Studies*
Teacher and Student Readiness	Davoodi (2024); Ghosh (2025)
Lack of Interaction or Depth	Belda-Medina & Kokošková (2024); Butler & Jiang (2025); Kartal (2024); Moorhouse et al. (2024); Pitura et al. (2025)
Overreliance on AI	Belda-Medina & Kokošková (2024); Buendgens-Kosten (2024); Moorhouse (2024)
Accuracy and Bias Issues	Belda-Medina (2024); Buendgens-Kosten (2024); Butler & Jiang (2025); Chu & Wang (2024); Kartal (2024); Lee et al. (2025b); Mohammadi (2024); Moorhouse et al. (2024); Moorhouse et al. (2025); Yang & Markauskaite (2025)

continued on following page

Table 4. Continued

Challenges of AI Integration	*Studies*
Tool Limitations and Output Reliability	Belda-Medina & Kokošková (2024); Lee et al. (2025b); Minnillo et al. (2024); Moorhouse et al. (2025); Xin (2024); Yang & Markauskaite (2025)
Technical and Infrastructure Barriers	Arefian et al. (2024); Davoodi (2024); Hieu & Thao (2024); Khajavi & Ezhdehakosh (2025)

Similar to the affordances, challenges can be tackled from three perspectives: instructional, professional, and personal challenges. As Table 4 indicates, the lack of interpersonal interaction and depth (e.g., Belda-Medina, 2024; Butler, 2025; Kartal, 2024; Moorhouse, 2024; Pitura, 2025) provided by AI-supported learning environments was one of the instructional challenges. In this regard, the studies revealed that both pre- and in-service teachers were concerned that the lack of real communication would reduce the cognitive and critical depth. Another instructional challenge was related to the incorrect or biased outputs generated by AI (e.g., Belda-Medina, 2024; Buendgens-Kosten, 2024; Butler, 2025; Chu, 2024; Kartal, 2024; Lee, 2025b; Mohammadi, 2024; Moorhouse, 2024; Moorhouse, 2025; Yang, 2025) were also regarded as a major challenge for integrating AI into language classrooms. Furthermore, participants in some reviewed studies (e.g., Belda-Medina, 2024; Lee, 2025b; Minnillo, 2024; Moorhouse, 2025; Xin, 2024; Yang, 2025) mentioned limitations including irrelevant responses and inconsistent outputs.

The third research question focuses on participants' perceptions and responses regarding the integration of AI into their education and professional development experiences. Based on the analysis, Table 5 presents perceptions and responses to AI integration.

Table 5. Perceptions and Responses to AI Integration Across Selected Studies

Perceptions and Responses	*Studies*
Positive Attitudes Toward AI	Belda-Medina (2024); Buendgens-Kosten (2024); Chu (2024); Ghosh (2025); Hieu & Thao (2024); Mohammadi (2024); Moorhouse (2024); Pitura (2025); Tafazoli (2024); Urazbayeva (2024); Uysal & Yüksel (2024)
Improved Awareness and Competence	Buendgens-Kosten (2024); Chu & Wang (2024); Davoodi (2024); Ghosh (2025); Khajavi & Ezhdehakosh (2025); Lee et al. (2025a); Lee et al. (2025b); Minnillo (2024); Mohammadi (2024); Moorhouse (2024); Pitura et al. (2025); Tafazoli (2024); Urazbayeva et al. (2024); Zulianti et al. (2025)
Engagement and Motivation	Ghosh (2025); Lee et al. (2025b); Mohammadi (2024); Pitura et al. (2025); Zulianti et al. (2025)

continued on following page

Table 5. Continued

Perceptions and Responses	*Studies*
Concerns and Ethical Considerations	Belda-Medina & Kokošková (2024); Buendgens-Kosten (2024); Hieu & Thao (2024); Khajavi & Ezhdehakosh (2025); Lee et al. (2025b); Minnillo et al. (2024); Mohammadi (2024); Moorhouse et al. (2024); Tafazoli (2024); Uysal & Yüksel (2024); Xin (2024); Yang & Markauskaite (2025)
Resistance or Skepticism	Butler & Jiang (2025); Davoodi (2024)

As can be seen in Table 5, several studies (e.g., Belda-Medina, 2024; Buendgens-Kosten, 2024; Chu, 2024; Ghosh, 2025; Hieu, 2024; Mohammadi, 2024; Moorhouse, 2024; Pitura, 2025; Tafazoli, 2024) revealed teachers' positive attitudes towards the use of AI. Moreover, some studies (e.g., Buendgens-Kosten, 2024; Chu, 2024; Davoodi, 2024; Ghosh, 2025; Khajavi, 2025; Lee, 2025a; Lee, 2025b; Minnillo, 2024; Mohammadi, 2024; Moorhouse, 2024; Pitura, 2025; Tafazoli, 2024; Urazbayeva, 2024; Zulianti, 2025) revealed the contribution of AI into teachers' digital literacy skills development and professional growth. Accordingly, both the pre- and in-service teachers noted that they could improve their confidence and awareness about AI tools with the help of AI-integrated programs and platforms. Based on teacher responses, the findings also indicated that AI-integration was influential on increasing student-engagement, motivation, and active participation (e.g., Ghosh, 2025; Lee, 2025b; Mohammadi, 2024; Pitura, 2025; Zulianti, 2025).

Along with all these positive attitudes and responses, some studies referred to concerns and ethical considerations (e.g., Belda-Medina, 2024; Buendgens-Kosten, 2024; Hieu, 2024; Khajavi, 2025; Lee, 2025b; Minnillo, 2024; Mohammadi, 2024; Moorhouse, 2024; Tafazoli, 2024; Uysal, 2024; Xin, 2024; Yang, 2025) and resistance and skepticism (e.g., Butler, 2025; Davoodi, 2024) about the integration of AI.

Implementation of AI in Language Teacher Education and Professional Development

The fourth research question examines how AI is being integrated into language teacher education and professional development programs. Table 6 details the specific tools (e.g., intelligent tutors, simulations) and the ways (e.g., workshops, courses, PD programs) they have been embedded into language teacher education and professional development programs.

Table 6. Implementation strategies of AI-enhanced education into language teacher education

Implementation	*Studies*
AI-Enhanced Lesson Planning & Classroom Practice	Ghosh (2025); Hieu & Thao (2024); Mohammadi (2024); Kartal (2024); Khajavi & Ezhdehakosh (2025); Lee et al. (2025b); Xin (2024); Uysal & Yüksel (2024)
Simulation & Immersive AI-Based Experiences	Pitura et al. (2025); Lee et al. (2025a); Lee et al. (2025b); Yang & Markauskaite (2025)
Prompt Engineering & AI Literacy Development	Arefian et al. (2024); Tafazoli (2024); Urazbayeva et al. (2024); Xin (2024); Uysal & Yüksel (2024)
AI Integration within Formal Teacher Education Courses	Belda-Medina & Kokošková (2024); Butler & Jiang (2025); Chu & Wang (2024); Khajavi & Ezhdehakosh (2025); Minnillo et al. (2024); Moorhouse et al. (2024); Moorhouse et al. (2025)
Short-Term Workshops & Professional Development	Buendgens-Kosten (2024); Davoodi (2024); Minnillo et al. (2024); Tafazoli (2024); Zulianti et al. (2025)
Collaborative Inquiry & Reflective Practice with AI	Arefian et al. (2024); Belda-Medina & Kokošková (2024); Chu & Wang (2024)
AI for Teacher Agency, Ethical Awareness, and Critical Use	Buendgens-Kosten (2024); Butler & Jiang (2025); Khajavi & Ezhdehakosh (2025); Lee et al. (2025b)

As presented in Table 6, the implementation strategies for AI integration in language teacher education and professional development can be organized into seven distinct approaches.

The most prevalent approach, represented by eight studies, focuses on AI-enhanced lesson planning and classroom practice. Studies in this category (e.g., Ghosh, 2025; Hieu & Thao, 2024; Khajavi & Ezhdehakosh, 2025; Mohammadi, 2024) typically followed a learn-apply-reflect cycle in which participants first learned about AI tools and how to utilize them for instructional purposes, then applied them to authentic teaching tasks, and finally engaged in reflective or evaluative activities. For instance, Khajavi and Ezhdehakosh (2025) implemented a 16-week practicum in which pre-service teachers first learned about the use of ChatGPT for instructional purposes, then applied this knowledge in classroom lesson design, and concluded with reflective demonstrations. Similarly, Moorhouse et al. (2024) integrated GenAI tools into an 11-week flipped Master's course. Pre-service teachers were guided through AI-enhanced lesson planning, materials development, and pedagogical reflection. These studies demonstrate that AI is not merely an isolated technical skill but rather an integrated component of broader professional development, encompassing both digital competence and pedagogical thinking.

A second implementation approach, identified in four studies, emphasizes simulation and immersive AI-based experiences. Rather than structured reflection, these studies prioritized experiential immersion through virtual reality and metaverse environments. For example, Pitura et al. (2025) utilized VR-based teaching simulations combined with AI-generated questioning to immerse pre-service teachers in authentic classroom experiences. Likewise, Lee et al. (2025a) utilized metaverse environments with AI chatbots for interactive English teaching simulations to provide pre-service teachers with the opportunity to experience Global Englishes. Yang and Markauskaite (2025) similarly employed GenAI tools for multimodal resource creation across successive training sessions. These implementations are more experiential and exploratory as they focus on the development of digital confidence, classroom communication, and creative pedagogical applications rather than formal reflective practice.

The third category in Table 6, prompt engineering and AI literacy development, was addressed by five studies aiming to equip teachers with the skills to craft precise prompts and critically evaluate AI-generated outputs. For example, Urazbayeva et al. (2024) and Tafazoli (2024) implemented iterative, prompt-driven activities alongside hands-on workshops using ChatGPT. Arefian et al. (2024) organized weekly reflection sessions centered on ChatGPT use, while Xin (2024) and Uysal and Yüksel (2024) focused on developing teachers' critical evaluation skills for AI-generated materials. This suggests that prompt engineering is considered a vital component of effective AI use in language instruction.

Table 6 further reveals that seven studies integrated AI directly within formal teacher education courses, embedding AI as a curricular component rather than treating it as an optional tool. For instance, Butler and Jiang (2025) and Moorhouse et al. (2024) systematically wove AI tools into semester-long university courses, designing assignments and assessments that explicitly require AI for developing instructional materials, planning lessons, and justifying pedagogical choices. Similarly, Chu and Wang (2024), Minnillo et al. (2024), Khajavi and Ezhdehakosh (2025), and Belda-Medina and Kokošková (2024) incorporated AI integration throughout their courses. This illustrates that AI is not simply an enhancement to teacher-training programs, but also an element that has the potential to become a norm.

In contrast to sustained coursework integration, five studies employed short-term workshops and professional development sessions (Table 6). Short-term implementations by Davoodi (2024), Minnillo et al. (2024), Buendgens-Kosten (2024), Zulianti et al. (2025), and Tafazoli (2024) typically aimed to raise initial awareness of AI's pedagogical possibilities through presentations on AI's potential and hands-on exposure to AI tools. For example, Buendgens-Kosten (2024) designed short, interactive interventions to raise pre-service teachers' awareness of AI's capabilities and limitations, while Zulianti et al. (2025) conducted five 16-hour modules focused on TPACK-based AI integration for novice teachers.

The sixth implementation strategy identified in Table 6 emphasizes collaborative inquiry and reflective practice with AI, represented in three studies. For example, Chu and Wang (2024) employed the double-stimulation model to support collaborative material design with AI. In contrast, Arefian et al. (2024) organized weekly reflection sessions centered on the use of AI, and Belda-Medina and Kokošková (2024) conducted a five-stage intervention focused on comparative evaluation of AI versus human-produced texts. These studies move beyond technical skill-building to foster teacher agency, the co-construction of knowledge, and critical thinking about the role of AI in education.

Finally, four studies in Table 6 specifically focused on developing teacher agency, ethical awareness, and critical use of AI. Studies by Butler and Jiang (2025), Buendgens-Kosten (2024), and Lee et al. (2025b) highlight the ethical issues and agency challenges posed by AI, such as plagiarism, over-reliance, and the devaluation of teacher creativity. Khajavi and Ezhdehakosh (2025) similarly emphasized ethical considerations and critical evaluation throughout their 16-week intervention. These implementations recognize that effective AI integration requires not only technical competence but also critical awareness of AI's societal and pedagogical implications.

Evidence of the Effectiveness of AI-Enhanced Teacher Education Initiatives

The fifth research question examines what evidence exists regarding the effectiveness of AI-enhanced language teacher education. The findings are organized into categories reflecting the effects of AI integration in teacher education and professional development, and are presented in Table 7.

Table 7. Evidence of the effectiveness of AI-enhanced language teacher education

Evidence	*Studies*
Enhanced Teaching Efficacy & Learner Outcomes	Ghosh (2025); Mohammadi (2024); Zulianti et al. (2025)
Increased AI Literacy & Competence	Moorhouse et al. (2024); Moorhouse et al. (2025); Lee et al. (2025b); Urazbayeva et al. (2024)
Boosted Confidence, Motivation & Engagement	Davoodi (2024); Hieu & Thao (2024); Pitura et al. (2025); Yang & Markauskaite (2025)
Efficiency & Material Creation Improvements	Chu & Wang (2024); Minnillo et al. (2024); Tafazoli (2024); Uysal & Yüksel (2024); Xin (2024)
Reflective Practice & Professional Agency	Arefian et al. (2024); Belda-Medina & Kokošková (2024); Buendgens-Kosten (2024); Kartal (2024)
Perceptions, Acceptance & Concerns	Butler & Jiang (2025); Khajavi & Ezhdehakosh (2025)
Global Awareness & Authentic Interaction	Lee et al. (2025a)

Studies show that AI-enhanced professional development has significant potential to enhance the education of language teachers. Several studies noted the positive impact of AI-supported professional development on teaching efficacy and, indirectly, on student learning outcomes. For example, Ghosh (2025) used structural equation modeling to investigate factors associated with the effectiveness of ITS and found that pre-service teachers' perceptions of AI's usefulness and ease of use significantly enhanced their teaching efficacy, which, in turn, led to improved student performance. The study also confirmed that these factors had indirect positive effects on learner outcomes, probably through boosting teachers' instructional confidence. Similarly, Zulianti et al.'s (2025) study showed that teachers who participated in TPACK-based AI professional development demonstrated significantly higher knowledge of AI tools, stronger teaching skills, and increased self-efficacy compared to teachers who did not receive a similar professional development. Mohammadi (2024) reported a significant improvement in teachers' Language Assessment Literacy (LAL) after the implementation of AI-assisted assessment training.

Another key piece of evidence supporting AI-enhanced teacher education is the enhancement of teachers' AI literacy, prompt engineering skills, and overall digital pedagogical competence. Urazbayeva et al. (2024) demonstrated that a workshop on ChatGPT for teachers significantly contributed to teachers' technological pedagogical content knowledge, which in turn empowered them to integrate AI tools into lesson planning, assessment design, and material creation. Similarly, Moorhouse et al. (2024) found that professional development training on GenAI increased pre-service teachers' competence and familiarity with AI tools, along with enhanced awareness of prompt engineering and the ethical use of AI. In another study, Moorhouse et al. (2025) observed that working with large language models enabled pre-service teachers to develop and apply several prompting strategies while refining their pedagogical decisions based on the output. Likewise, Lee et al. (2025b) reported that when pre-service teachers engaged in GenAI-supported lesson design projects, they not only improved GenAI literacy but also maintained pedagogical agency by critically evaluating and adapting AI outputs.

The evidence also reveals that AI-enhanced professional development enhances language teachers' confidence, motivation, and willingness to integrate technology into their instructional practices. Pitura et al. (2025) found that pre-service teachers who participated in virtual reality (VR)-AI simulations reported greater confidence in teaching complex grammar points and demonstrated an increased capacity for reflective practice. Similarly, Hieu and Thao (2024) demonstrated that the use of ChatGPT in creative writing tasks promoted both teacher and student creativity, increased engagement, and enhanced teachers' comfort with integrating technology. Davoodi (2024) further supported these findings by documenting how a Connectivist professional development model on AI training improved teachers' attitudes toward

AI use, with positive perceptions rising from 26% to 78%. Participants also reported greater feelings of empowerment, collaboration, and professional agency. Yang and Markauskaite (2025) provided additional evidence that AI integration fostered expansive professional agency, with teachers increasingly engaging in creative, reflective, and proactive pedagogical behaviors across successive training sessions.

Several studies have highlighted the improvements in material creation that AI-enhanced teacher education offers. Tafazoli (2024) illustrated how pre-service teachers utilized Gen-AI to create inclusive and engaging lesson materials that fostered critical thinking and student engagement. Chu and Wang (2024) showed that teachers who integrated AI into their lesson planning reported significant time savings and greater willingness to experiment with new approaches. Xin (2024) further highlighted that AI tools such as ChatPDF helped teachers create differentiated and learner-centered reading materials. However, the selective adoption of AI outputs is also mentioned as critical. Similarly, Uysal and Yüksel (2024) observed that while AI-generated lesson plans scored highly for engagement and structure, pre-service teachers identified weaknesses in differentiation, assessment, and feedback, which also underscores the need for human oversight. Finally, Minnillo et al. (2024) reported how AI-supported PD to pre- and in-service language teachers enhanced both the material design process and teachers' prompt-writing competence.

Another finding reported in studies is the effect of AI-enhanced teacher education in fostering reflective practice and professional agency. Arefian et al. (2024) demonstrated that ChatGPT-driven reflective practice enabled teachers to deepen their self-analysis and enhance their lesson planning. In their study, teachers also emphasized the importance of critical analysis and reflection through their professional judgment, in response to technical limitations, cultural mismatches, and the risks of over-reliance on AI-generated suggestions. Similarly, Belda-Medina and Kokošková (2024) found that collaborative writing tasks using AI not only improved idea generation and engagement but also encouraged pre-service teachers to reflect on AI's limitations and affordances critically. Kartal (2024) highlighted that AI integration encouraged critical thinking and creativity and required pre-service teachers to analyze AI-generated content consciously and critically. Buendgens-Kosten (2024) noted that working with large language models enhanced pre-service teachers' critical awareness of digital texts and AI's potential limitations, thereby fostering more informed and ethical decision-making.

The evidence also suggests that AI tools, particularly chatbots and immersive simulations, can enhance teachers' global awareness and intercultural communication skills. Lee et al. (2025a) conducted a quasi-experimental study demonstrating that AI chatbot interactions in 3D metaverse environments significantly increased pre-service teachers' Global Englishes Awareness and confidence in English as a lingua franca for communication.

Alongside the growing acceptance of AI and the several affordances that AI tools provide to language teacher education, studies also reveal important concerns regarding AI tools, such as over-reliance, ethical risks, and changes to traditional teaching roles. Butler and Jiang (2025) found that while high-performing teachers critically evaluated AI's limitations, lower-performing teachers tended to over-rely on AI for academic writing tasks. Similarly, Khajavi and Ezhdehakosh (2025) found that although pre-service teachers acknowledged AI's interactivity and feedback capabilities, they also voiced concerns about potential erosion of the teacher's role and the risk of over-reliance on AI.

Educational and Institutional Contexts for AI-Enhanced Language Teacher Education and Professional Development

The sixth research question investigates the educational and institutional contexts in which AI is integrated into language teacher education. Table 8 outlines the range of contexts and study groups.

Table 8. Context of AI-enhanced language teacher education

Context	*Study*
PD for 8 EFL teachers (mix of novice and experienced).	Arefian et al. (2024)
Undergraduate EFL pre-service teachers.	Belda-Medina & Kokošková (2024)
Undergraduate/graduate TEFL teacher education seminars (Germany); digital pedagogy focus.	Buendgens-Kosten (2024)
Graduate-level TESOL pre-service teachers (international).	Butler & Jiang (2025)
Professional Development (PD) for EAP instructors in universities; AI integration focus.	Chu & Wang (2024)
PD for in-service bilingual/ESL elementary teachers and administrators.	Davoodi (2024)
Mixed: Pre-service in formal education; in-service in active classrooms.	Ghosh (2025)
Tertiary-level EFL classrooms (creative writing/AI); not strictly teacher training.	Hieu & Thao (2024)
Undergraduate (senior) pre-service EFL teacher training.	Kartal (2024)
Undergraduate (senior) pre-service EFL teacher training.	Khajavi & Ezhdehakosh (2025)
Undergraduate pre-service English teachers (97 participants).	Lee et al. (2025a)
Undergraduate (3rd-year) pre-service ELT majors (18 participants).	Lee et al. (2025b)
Mixed group: language faculty, graduate TAs, undergrads, and instructional technologists.	Minnillo et al. (2024)

continued on following page

Table 8. Continued

Context	*Study*
PD for 261 EFL teachers (adult education); AI-driven assessment literacy and practice.	Mohammadi (2024)
Master's level (Master of Education (MEd) ELT) pre-service teachers; 'Grammar for Teaching' course.	Moorhouse et al. (2024)
Master's level (MEd ELT) pre-service teachers at a university.	Moorhouse et al. (2025)
Graduate level (Master of Arts in TEFL); 17 female pre-service EFL teachers.	Pitura et al. (2025)
Professional development for 23 English language teachers.	Tafazoli (2024)
In-service EFL teacher training for 24 teachers.	Urazbayeva et al. (2024)
Undergraduate (3rd-year) pre-service EFL teacher training.	Uysal & Yüksel (2024)
PD for three full-time EFL teachers.	Xin (2024)
Undergraduate multi-language teacher education (Chinese; Italian; German; and Korean).	Yang & Markauskaite (2025)
Novice English teachers (early-career).	Zulianti et al. (2025)

Across the 23 studies, AI-enhanced language teacher education appears in a variety of formal and informal institutional settings, spanning both pre- and in-service contexts. Pre-service context (12 studies) consists of both undergraduate groups, such as pre-service EFL teachers in Spain (Belda-Medina & Kokošková, 2024), third-year undergraduates in Türkiye (Uysal & Yüksel, 2024; Kartal, 2024), senior undergraduates in Iran (Khajavi & Ezhdehakosh, 2025), multi-language undergraduates in Australia (Yang & Markauskaite, 2025), and undergraduates in South Korea (Lee et al., 2025a,b), and graduate groups, including an MA in TEFL in Poland (Pitura et al., 2025), MEd ELT courses in Hong Kong (Moorhouse et al., 2024, 2025), and international TESOL groups in the U.S. (Butler & Jiang, 2025). In-service context (9 studies) ranges from small PD workshops for 3-24 practicing EFL instructors in Iran (Tafazoli, 2024; Arefian et al., 2024; Mohammadi, 2024), Kazakhstan (Urazbayeva et al., 2024), China (Chu & Wang, 2024; Xin, 2024), Vietnam (Hieu & Thao, 2024), and Indonesia (Zulianti et al., 2025), to larger-scale programs for 261 adult-education teachers in Iran (Mohammadi, 2024) and bilingual/ESL elementary teachers in Texas (Davoodi, 2024). Only two studies (Ghosh, 2025; Minnillo et al., 2024) included both pre-service and in-service language teachers.

DISCUSSION

Regarding the first research question, the findings of this review showed that studies have been conducted for various purposes to contribute to both pre- and in-service teachers' professional development. One of those purposes was to enhance teaching efficacy by using AI. When analyzed through the ITELL framework, this purpose aligns primarily with the framework's emphasis on adaptability and personalization, as teachers utilized AI's capacity to generate tailored lesson plans and differentiated materials responsive to diverse learner needs. In line with this finding, Kohnke et al. (2025) found that pre-service teachers designed and adapted their lesson plans by using the feedback and suggestions provided by AI. The study also revealed that teachers could engage with critical and reflective teaching practices with the help of AI while planning lessons and designing materials. This capacity for real-time feedback, a core ITELL characteristic, enabled iterative refinement of instructional materials, allowing teachers to receive immediate suggestions for improvement rather than waiting for delayed peer or supervisor review. However, Kohnke et al. (2025) also specify that teachers should not rely solely on AI to prepare their lesson plans, and they should be aware of the capabilities and limitations of AI while designing their lessons and materials.

The studies also aimed to enhance teachers' digital literacy skills and professional development through institutional support and teacher training programs. Similarly, Kohnke et al. (2025) stated that future teachers should be trained on AI literacy to support their professional development needs. This also aligns with the prerequisites of ITELL emphasizing teacher adaptability and readiness to enhance ethical and responsive use of AI in language teacher education. On the other hand, Prilop et al.'s (2025) study revealed that AI literacy among teacher educators was underdeveloped, and this literacy should not be restricted to using AI tools. Therefore, the reviewed studies indicated that AI training was beneficial not only for students but also for teachers in terms of guiding them on how to integrate AI into their classes to support students' language learning abilities. In this vein, ITELL also supports dynamic and adaptive learning environments in which teachers could enhance their AI literacy, pedagogical competencies, and professional learning. Therefore, future studies can explore the possible effects of ITELL models on teachers' autonomy, agency, and readiness. Concerning the studies exploring teacher beliefs, the findings confirm that AI has played a transformative role in enabling teachers to engage in reflective practices, question their teaching methods, and enhance learner autonomy in the classroom. Likewise, previous studies (e.g., Lan, 2024; Prilop et al., 2025) have identified that AI has reshaped instructional plans and teaching practices in language classrooms. Accordingly, the use of AI in teacher education enabled teachers to question the traditional teaching and assessment methods and to enhance their AI literacy. Thus, the studies concluded that teacher education and professional development programs should foster the ethical, reflective, and critical use of AI tools. These results broadly support ethical and reflective dimensions of ITELL, which aims to guide teachers to ethically use and critically evaluate AI tools in language teaching by addressing fairness and integrity issues.

Considering all these purposes, AI had a supportive role in promoting both pre- and in-service teachers' professional development by guiding them on how to keep up with the advanced technology and adapting their teaching methods. As a result, AI tools and technologies were used to enhance teachers' professional and autonomous learning skills. In this regard, Mah and Groß (2024) found that integrating AI-supported teachers' professional development and instructional decision-making processes by facilitating self-reflection, personalized lesson planning, and pedagogical skills.

The second research question explored the affordances and challenges of AI integration into language teacher education and PD programs. To begin with affordances, the findings revealed that AI could promote learner autonomy, which was in line with the previous study (Novawan et al., 2024) supporting the contribution of AI integration into student autonomy and learning, which also accords with multimodal and interactive learning aspects of ITELL enhancing collaborative learning and active engagement. In accordance with the present results, previous studies have demonstrated that AI integration promoted teacher professional development. To illustrate, Duan and Zhao's (2024) study indicated that AI enhanced teacher autonomy and professional growth by reducing the workload and digital burnout. In line with these findings, ITELL framework also supports teacher agency and reflective practice by positioning teachers as co-constructors of AI tools rather than passive users. In this vein, Çelik (2023) emphasized the importance of training teachers on the affordances of AI tools to facilitate the effective integration of AI into English teacher education contexts.

As for challenges, institutional, instructional, and technical limitations were some of the problems and barriers to implement AI in language teacher education programs. In response to these current challenges, participants in Novawan et al.'s (2024) study expressed similar concerns about the lack of educational policies regarding the ethical use of AI, which could lead to plagiarism, biased responses, and learning difficulties. Similarly, pre-service teachers in Kohnke et al.'s (2025) study reported that incorrect or superficial responses, student misuse of AI tools, and a lack of policies could be some challenges regarding the use of AI in schools. Some studies (e.g., Arefian, 2024; Davoodi, 2024; Hieu, 2024; Khajavi, 2025) touched upon another instructional challenge, which was the technical and infrastructure barriers such as limited access to AI tools or lack of technical assistance or training that affects the use of AI in English language teaching programs.

Regarding professional and personal challenges, it could be stated that the two challenges were interconnected. For example, one of the professional challenges of AI integration was related to teacher and student readiness (e.g., Davoodi, 2024;

Ghosh, 2025), indicating a lack of training and confidence in using AI in teacher education. However, these professional challenges could stem from personal issues, such as teacher roles, competencies, and perceptions regarding the use of AI. Another challenge, overdependence on AI (e.g., Belda-Medina, 2024; Buendgens-Kosten, 2024; Moorhouse, 2024), could also be regarded as both a professional and a personal challenge, which could have negative impacts on critical thinking, language learning, and teaching skills. All these challenges and barriers raise some crucial questions about the efficient and ethical use of AI tools. In this regard, Duan and Zhao (2024) emphasized that data privacy and the ethical use of AI are significant points to consider enhancing the efficiency of teaching through AI-supported implementations. As for the ways of overcoming these challenges, Novawan et al. (2024) note that ITELL should be integrated into language education and successful implementation of this framework depends on teachers' ethical awareness, adaptive mindset, and professional abilities.

The third research question focused on teacher perceptions and responses about AI integration into language teacher education and professional development programs. The findings revealed teachers had positive attitudes towards AI, which was also consistent with a previous study (Prilop et al., 2025) revealing teacher educators' excitement about potentials and opportunities provided by AI. In this sense, ITELL does not aim to replace AI with human capabilities and intelligence; instead, it views AI as a supportive component in language teaching to enhance creativity and engagement. Further, Guggemos and Seufert (2021) stressed the significance of positive attitudes and high self-efficacy for the efficient integration of AI into teacher training programs. The participants in these studies reported the benefits of AI integration into student learning, instructional planning, and teacher workload. In addition, teachers had some concerns about use of AI in language teacher education. This finding corroborated the study of McGrath et al. (2023), who found that teachers were skeptical about the use of AI or trusting the sources provided by AI. In a similar sense, teacher educators in Prilop et al.'s (2025) study expressed concerns that AI reduces the quality of education, while Kohnke et al. (2025) reported that AI could support instructional creativity when it is used by having critical literacy and ethical awareness. Hence, Çelik (2023) suggested promoting teachers' ethical understanding of the effective use and integration of AI tools to address ethical dilemmas and problems. Concerning ethical issues and concerns, ITELL aims to foster ethical AI literacy and balanced use of AI tools by differentiating between human intelligence and algorithmic assistance. As a result, Novawan et al. (2024) suggest that ITELL provides a comprehensive understanding towards the responsible, reflective, and ethical integration of AI into teacher education programs.

Within the scope of fourth research question, the implementation strategies of AI-driven technologies are examined. It was found that implementation strategies are highly diverse in terms of duration, methods, and focus. The prevalence of the learn-apply-reflect cycle across multiple studies (e.g., Khajavi & Ezhdehakosh, 2025; Moorhouse et al., 2024) suggests there is broad agreement that effective AI integration requires more than just technical skill or awareness. It shows AI tools are not only complementary technologies but also shape pedagogical decision-making. This supports ITELL's focus on adaptable, context-sensitive learning and marks a shift from transfer-based professional development models. However, the comprehensiveness of the cycle may depend on its duration, depth, and institutional support, which vary across studies. Khajavi and Ezhdehakosh's (2025) 16-week internship provided ample time for experimentation and reflection, whereas shorter initiations may have offered teachers only surface-level experience. This may not be enough for teachers to gain the skills they need to use AI tools within the ITELL framework. Integrating AI directly into semester-long courses (Butler & Jiang, 2025; Chu & Wang, 2024; Moorhouse et al., 2024) could provide an opportunity to offer a more integrated and interconnected teacher education experience by making AI a part of the teacher education curriculum rather than an optional enhancement. This approach is useful for developing the complex competencies demanded by ITELL.

The focus on prompt engineering and AI literacy in various studies (Arefian et al., 2024; Tafazoli, 2024; Urazbayeva et al., 2024) reflects the growing recognition that effective AI use requires understanding how to communicate with and critically evaluate these tools. This competency aligns with the advanced NLP interaction feature of ITELL and further emphasizes the need for teachers to learn how to achieve desired outcomes from AI tools. However, framing AI literacy primarily through the technical skill of prompt engineering may be an underestimation. While developing effective prompts is critical for creating effective, personalized, and needs-based educational outputs, it can lead teachers to perceive themselves solely as technicians optimizing the performance of these tools rather than developing critical perspectives that question the relevance, biases, and impact of AI on learning. To address this, several studies have explicitly addressed ethical awareness, teacher agency, and critical engagement with AI (Buendgens-Kosten, 2024; Butler & Jiang, 2025; Khajavi & Ezhdehakosh, 2025; Lee et al., 2025b). These practices acknowledge concerns that have profound implications for educational integrity and professional identity, such as plagiarism, over-reliance, bias, and the potential devaluation of teacher creativity. Consequently, this aligns with calls for responsible AI use and critical AI literacy (Kohnke et al., 2025; Moorhouse & Kohnke, 2024).

The use of VR simulations, metaverses, and AI chatbots (Lee et al., 2025a; Pitura et al., 2025; Yang & Markauskaite, 2025) demonstrates ITELL's multimodal learning and intelligent tutoring characteristics. These tools have the potential to bridge the preparation gap by providing pre-service teachers with practice in realistic but low-risk environments, building confidence and experience before entering real classrooms. The only drawback is that tools like VR simulations and metaverses are expensive and comparatively hard to access. In contrast, chatbots have overcome this accessibility problem by becoming widespread and accessible tools in recent years.

Overall, most implementation strategies involve research-oriented or independently initiated courses, workshops, or interventions led by researchers, rather than systematic, institutionally mandated programs. As a result, teachers lack clear policies for AI integration (Novawan et al., 2024), and professional development remains fragmented rather than coherent (Tan et al., 2025).

The evidence reviewed regarding the fifth research question on the effectiveness of AI-enhanced teacher education demonstrates positive outcomes while also identifying areas that require further investigation. Although evidence of effectiveness aligns with specific ITELL characteristics, further research is needed to address the remaining characteristics. For instance, adaptability and personalization are indirectly supported by studies reporting improvements in teaching effectiveness and student outcomes (Ghosh, 2025; Zulianti et al., 2025). Teachers who develop proficiency with AI tools that adapt to student needs are better able to differentiate instruction and address individual student profiles. Additionally, evidence of enhanced AI literacy and prompt engineering skills (Moorhouse et al., 2024, 2025; Urazbayeva et al., 2024) indicates that teachers can acquire the technical competencies required to utilize ITELL's advanced NLP interaction capabilities. Some ITELL characteristics are largely absent from current effectiveness research. There is limited evidence that AI-enhanced teacher training improves teachers' abilities in adaptive assessment, proficiency tracking, predictive analytics to anticipate student challenges, or in designing multimodal learning experiences through AI. Although VR and metaverse-based multimodal learning are used in teacher professional development, no studies have examined the development of teachers' competencies to design such experiences for instructional purposes (see Lee et al., 2025a; Pitura et al., 2025). This gap is notable because these dimensions may represent the most significant advantages of AI over previous educational technologies.

Additionally, examination of effectiveness measures reveals a predominance of self-reported outcomes, including perceptions, confidence, attitudes, and motivation. These findings may be influenced by a novelty effect (Elston, 2021). Consequently, longitudinal, mixed-methods research is required to track teachers from professional development through to classroom instruction, measuring not only intentions or perceptions but also implemented practices and resulting student learning.

Furthermore, many studies equate AI's effectiveness with efficiency through faster planning, rapid material generation, and easier differentiation (Chu & Wang, 2024; Minnillo et al., 2024; Tafazoli, 2024; Xin, 2024). However, this efficiency framing warrants careful examination. AI outputs require human oversight to address weaknesses in differentiation, assessment, and feedback, and to manage technical limitations, cultural mismatches, and risks of over-reliance (Arefian et al., 2024; Uysal & Yüksel, 2024). Such oversight can consume the time AI appears to save, creating a false sense of efficiency and shifting teachers' roles from teaching to reviewing algorithms and algorithmic outputs.

Evidence also indicates that AI-enhanced teacher education provides greater benefits to experienced teachers, who gain more from AI-assisted assessment training and demonstrate higher levels of critical AI competence. In contrast, less prepared teachers are at risk of over-reliance and inadequate evaluation of AI-generated outcomes (Butler & Jiang, 2025; Mohammadi, 2024). These findings suggest that AI-enhanced language teacher education should be differentiated according to teachers' experience levels.

For the last research question, contexts were examined. Pre-service contexts (12 studies) predominate over in-service contexts (9 studies). This may be because incorporating AI into university courses is easier than fitting it into in-service teachers' schedules and school rules. However, focusing AI-enhanced teacher education (studies) on pre-service teachers, who lack the classroom experience to contextualize AI's possibilities and limitations, may not be fully meaningful. Furthermore, pre-service teachers lack the classroom experience needed to assess when AI's affordances are useful, when they should be ignored, and how to adapt them to real-world students (as expected by the ITELL framework). Finally, few studies consider both groups together (only two studies). Bringing novice and experienced teachers together can be effective, as experienced teachers bring pedagogical wisdom, while novices bring technology fluency. Keeping them separate misses this interaction and could widen the gap in teacher education.

Most studies are small, short-term studies led by researchers rather than institutions, which suggest experimental initiatives rather than systemic adoption. Even the larger Mohammadi (2024, n=261) study remains a discrete professional development. Notably, there is a lack of longitudinal evidence of sustainable institutional change in this field. Geographically, contexts cluster heavily in Asia (China, South Korea, Iran, Türkiye, Kazakhstan, Vietnam, Indonesia, and Poland), with representation from the U.S., Australia, Germany, and Spain. In terms of research focus, EFL/ESL dominates, while few multilingual studies exist (e.g., Yang & Markauskaite, 2025), reinforcing the prevalence of English-centric tools. Furthermore, institutional support is weak (limited policies, funding, and technical support), resulting in self-selected participation and fragile sustainability (Novawan et al., 2024). Graduate-level settings predominate, thereby skewing access toward privileged programs. The concentration in 2024-2025 reflects an emerging field. Overall, moving beyond longitudinal studies will require policy commitments, sustainable funding, infrastructure, and equity-focused design.

CONCLUSION

The aim of the present study was to examine AI-enhanced language teacher education and professional development programs by providing a comprehensive overview of the existing research landscape. Within this scope, 23 related studies were analyzed in terms of their purposes, affordances, challenges, teachers' perceptions, implementation strategies, evidence of effectiveness, and context.

The findings illustrate that AI serves multifaceted purposes in language teacher education and professional development programs. Researchers have employed AI to support lesson planning and the design of teaching materials, enhance language teachers' AI literacy and digital competencies, facilitate adaptive tutoring and assessment, create immersive simulation experiences, and foster reflective and ethical practices. Across various contexts, including undergraduate and graduate pre-service programs, as well as short-term in-service workshops, AI tools (e.g., ITS, chatbots, VR simulations) are most often embedded within a learn-apply-reflect cycle. However, some implementations foreground experiential immersion or critical analysis of AI-generated versus human-generated texts.

The affordances of AI integration are reflected in several studies as personalization and adaptivity enable differentiated instruction, automated feedback and content generation improve teaching efficiency and creativity, and multimodal supports boost student engagement and teacher motivation. However, these gains coexist with persistent challenges, including technical and infrastructure barriers, tool limitations and bias, the risk of over-reliance on AI, and uneven teacher and student readiness. Teachers' perceptions tend to be positive, showing increased confidence, competence, and professional agency, but they also voiced ethical concerns, skepticism about AI's reliability, and the need for critical oversight. Empirical evidence suggests that AI-enhanced professional development can significantly enhance teaching efficacy, assessment literacy, material creation, and global and intercultural awareness. However, the risks of diminished human agency and the potential for biased, superficial, or unreliable outputs remain pertinent.

Through the perspective of the ITELL framework (Novawan et al., 2024), reviewed studies manifest its several core characteristics. Adaptability and personalization emerge as AI-driven customization that enables tailored lesson planning and differentiated instruction (Davoodi, 2024; Ghosh, 2025; Hieu & Thao, 2024; Khajavi & Ezhdehakosh, 2025; Minnillo et al., 2024; Mohammadi, 2024; Tafazoli, 2024). Feedback mechanisms are evidenced by real-time automated feedback systems that guided material refinement and reflective planning (Belda-Medina & Kokošková, 2024; Kartal, 2024; Xin, 2024). ITS and adaptive assessment tools supported diagnostic feedback and in-the-moment strategy adjustments (Ghosh, 2025; Mohammadi, 2024). Assessment and proficiency tracking tools enhanced language assessment literacy and provided nuanced performance insights (Mohammadi, 2024). Although the use of chatbots is evident in one of the studies reviewed (Lee et al., 2025a), it did not utilize NLP. However, the study noted that chatbot integration in ELF and metaverse simulations facilitated authentic communicative practice and intercultural confidence. Dynamic content generation reduced material creation burdens and heightened creativity through AI-supported lesson planning and writing prompts (Chu & Wang, 2024; Lee et al., 2025b; Tafazoli, 2024; Urazbayeva et al., 2024; Xin, 2024). Finally, multimodal learning was addressed via immersive VR and simulation-based AI environments that fostered experiential engagement and reflective decision-making (Pitura et al., 2025).

Consequently, although studies demonstrate AI's capabilities for personalization, feedback, and immersive simulations, none yet utilize predictive analytics to forecast teacher development trajectories, and only one investigates chatbots, without an NLP-driven chatbot (Lee et al., 2025a). Likewise, the predominance of short-term implementations (Minnillo et al., 2024; Tafazoli, 2024) calls for longitudinal, cross-cultural efficacy studies. Despite widespread concerns about biased or unethical outputs, no research has tested structured bias-mitigation or data-privacy frameworks (Buendgens-Kosten, 2024). Additionally, the reviewed studies demonstrate geographic concentration in Asia. There is limited representation of multilingual teacher education contexts. The research predominantly focuses on pre-service rather than in-service contexts. Furthermore, most implementations remain researcher-led initiatives, not institutionally integrated programs. This indicates challenges in achieving sustainable and scalable outcomes.

To address these gaps, future initiatives should develop AI-based predictive models for early identification of teacher support needs; design NLP-powered conversational agents for authentic discourse practice; implement comprehensive AI-literacy curricula (with the integration of prompt engineering and ethical reflection) (Ghosh, 2025; Urazbayeva et al., 2024); establish institutional AI governance units to provide infrastructure, technical assistance, and policy guidance (Arefian et al., 2024; Davoodi, 2024); and foster cross-institutional communities of practice, open repositories of annotated AI-generated lesson materials, and targeted prompt-engineering workshops to strengthen teachers' critical engagement with AI outputs. Therefore, providing training for teachers on AI literacy with some initiatives, collaborative discussions, and hands-on experience have been suggested in some studies (e.g., Case et al., 2025; Kohnke et al., 2025; Prilop et al., 2025). In addition, future studies should explore designing AI-related policies and frameworks to enhance critical and ethical use of AI. Additionally, these policies could be improved after comparing and analyzing national and international policies on integration of AI into language teacher education and professional development programs. Future research should also prioritize longitudinal studies that track teachers from professional development through classroom implementation, examining sustained impact on teaching practices and student learning outcomes. Comparative studies across diverse geographic, linguistic, and institutional contexts are also necessary to understand how cultural and systemic factors influence AI integration. Moreover, research should investigate the development of differentiated professional development models that account for teachers' varying experience levels, technological readiness, and pedagogical contexts. Finally, hands-on practices and mentoring models on use of AI in teacher training programs could be designed and then the effects of these practices and models could be explored through longitudinal and intervention studies.

For language teacher educators and professional development coordinators, the findings suggest several implications. First, AI integration should shift from one-time workshops to ongoing, cyclical professional development. This process should blend technical training, pedagogical reflection, and ethical reasoning. The learn-apply-reflect cycle, shown in multiple studies, provides a practical model to build competence and critical awareness. Second, teacher education programs should embed prompt engineering and AI literacy in their curricula. This ensures that pre- and in-service teachers develop skills to critically evaluate and contextualize AI-generated outputs. Third, institutions must set clear AI policies and ethical guidelines to address concerns about plagiarism, bias, privacy, and over-reliance. Fourth, professional development should align with teachers' experience levels, as research shows that novices and experienced teachers use AI tools differently and need tailored support. Finally, institutions should invest in sustainable infrastructure and ongoing technical support, as persistent access issues and lack of support remain challenges. Addressing these areas enables responsible, effective AI integration that supports, not replaces, teacher expertise.

Lastly, this systematic review has several methodological limitations. First, limiting the search to Scopus and WoS for 2020-2025 may have excluded relevant research from other databases or languages. Second, most studies relied on self-reported outcomes, such as perceptions, confidence, and attitudes, which may reflect novelty effects instead of sustained pedagogical change and limit claims about long-term effectiveness. Third, most interventions were small-scale and short-term, so findings may not apply to larger, sustained implementations. Fourth, the studies' focus on Asia may limit understanding of AI integration across diverse institutional and resource settings. Finally, publication bias may have skewed findings toward positive outcomes, as null or negative results are often unpublished.

REFERENCES

Akinsemolu, A. A., & Onyeaka, H. (2025). The role of artificial intelligence in transforming language learning: Opportunities and ethical considerations. *Journal of Language and Education, 11*(1), 148–152. DOI: 10.17323/jle.2025.22118

Alenezi, A., & Alenezi, A. (2025). Evaluating the effectiveness of chatbot-assisted learning in enhancing English conversational skills among secondary school students. *Education Sciences, 15*(9), 1–15. DOI: 10.3390/educsci15091136

Anoir, L., Khaldi, M., & Erradi, M. (2024). Intelligent tutor systems and the personalization of pedagogical objects in adaptive e-Learning. In *Interactive media with next-gen technologies and their usability evaluation* (1st ed., pp. 185–196). Chapman and Hall/CRC. DOI: 10.1201/9781032664828-14

Arefian, M. H., Çomoğlu, I., & Dikilitaş, K. (2024). Understanding EFL teachers' experiences of ChatGPT-driven collaborative reflective practice through a community of practice lens. *Innovation in Language Learning and Teaching*, 1–16. DOI: 10.1080/17501229.2024.2412769

Bahari, A., Han, F., & Strzelecki, A. (2025). Integrating CALL and AIALL for an interactive pedagogical model of language learning. *Education and Information Technologies, 30*(10), 14305–14333. Advance online publication. DOI: 10.1007/s10639-025-13388-w

Belda-Medina, J., & Kokošková, V. (2024). ChatGPT for language learning: Assessing teacher candidates' skills and perceptions using the Technology Acceptance Model (TAM). *Innovation in Language Learning and Teaching*, 1–16. DOI: 10.1080/17501229.2024.2435900

Buendgens-Kosten, J. (2024). "Just a pocket knife, not a machete": Large language models in TEFL teacher education & digital text sovereignty. *Technology in Language Teaching & Learning, 6*(1), 1192–1192. DOI: 10.29140/tltl.v6n1.1192

Butler, Y. G., & Jiang, S. (2025). How do pre-service language teachers perceive generative AIs' affordance?: A case of ChatGPT. *System, 129*, 1–17. DOI: 10.1016/j.system.2025.103606

Case, R., Liu, L., & Mintz, J. (2025). Integrating AI technology into language teacher education: Challenges, potentials, and assumptions. *Computers in the Schools, 42*(2), 93–99. DOI: 10.1080/07380569.2025.2458950

Celik, I. (2023). Towards Intelligent-TPACK: An empirical study on teachers' professional knowledge to ethically integrate artificial intelligence (AI)-based tools into education. *Computers in Human Behavior*, *138*, 1–12. DOI: 10.1016/j.chb.2022.107468

Celik, I., Dindar, M., Muukkonen, H., & Järvelä, S. (2022). The promises and challenges of artificial intelligence for teachers: A systematic review of research. *TechTrends*, *66*(4), 616–630. DOI: 10.1007/s11528-022-00715-y

Chapelle, C. A. (2001). *Computer Applications in Second Language Acquisition*. Cambridge University Press. DOI: 10.1017/CBO9781139524681

Chu, T., & Wang, W. (2024). Exploring EFL teachers' epistemic agency and its influencing factors in an AI-integrated context through the double stimulation model. *The Asia-Pacific Education Researcher*, *34*, 1–9. DOI: 10.1007/s40299-024-00940-4

Davoodi, A. (2024). Crafting innovative paths in non-linear professional learning for bilingual education: The role of connectivism in the age of AI. *Professional Development in Education*, *51*(3), 434–450. DOI: 10.1080/19415257.2024.2421492

Duan, H., & Zhao, W. (2024). The effects of educational artificial intelligence-powered applications on teachers' perceived autonomy, professional development for online teaching, and digital burnout. *International Review of Research in Open and Distance Learning*, *25*(3), 57–76. DOI: 10.19173/irrodl.v25i3.7659

Elston, D. M. (2021). The novelty effect. *Journal of the American Academy of Dermatology*, *85*(3), 565–566. DOI: 10.1016/j.jaad.2021.06.846 PMID: 34153390

Fitas, R. (2025). Inclusive education with AI: Supporting special needs and tackling language barriers. *AI and Ethics*, *5*(6), 5729–5757. DOI: 10.1007/s43681-025-00824-3

Ghosh, S. S. (2025). Assessing the efficacy of intelligent tutoring systems in language teacher education: A quantitative study. *Computers in the Schools*, *42*(2), 121–144. DOI: 10.1080/07380569.2024.2435308

Guggemos, J., & Seufert, S. (2021). Teaching with and teaching about technology - Evidence for professional development of in-service teachers. *Computers in Human Behavior*, *115*, 1–11. DOI: 10.1016/j.chb.2020.106613

Hieu, H. H., & Thao, L. T. (2024). Exploring the impact of AI in language education: Vietnamese EFL teachers' views on using ChatGPT for fairy tale retelling tasks. *International Journal of Learning. Teaching and Educational Research*, *23*(3), 486–503. DOI: 10.26803/ijlter.23.3.24

Huang, X., Zou, D., Cheng, G., Chen, X., & Xie, H. (2023). Trends, research issues and applications of artificial intelligence in language education. *Journal of Educational Technology & Society*, *26*(1), 112–131.

Huawei, S., & Aryadoust, V. (2022). A systematic review of automated writing evaluation systems. *Education and Information Technologies*, *28*(1), 771–795. DOI: 10.1007/s10639-022-11200-7

Jeon, J., Lee, S., & Choi, S. (2023). A systematic review of research on speech-recognition chatbots for language learning: Implications for future directions in the era of large language models. *Interactive Learning Environments*, *32*(8), 4613–4631. DOI: 10.1080/10494820.2023.2204343

Kartal, G. (2024). The influence of ChatGPT on thinking skills and creativity of EFL student teachers: A narrative inquiry. *Journal of Education for Teaching*, *50*(4), 627–642. DOI: 10.1080/02607476.2024.2326502

Khajavi, Y., & Ezhdehakosh, M. (2025). Enhancing language teacher education: Exploring the integration of AI-powered tools in preservice teacher education. *Journal of Research in Applied Linguistics*, *16*(1), 174–191. DOI: 10.22055/RALS.2024.48226.3405

Kohnke, L. (2024). Enhancing teacher professional development with AI. In Kohnke, L. (Ed.), *Optimizing digital competence through microlearning: Flexible approaches to teacher professional development* (pp. 55–66). Springer Nature Singapore., DOI: 10.1007/978-981-97-8839-2_6

Kohnke, L., Zou, D., Ou, A. W., & Gu, M. M. (2025). Preparing future educators for AI enhanced classrooms: Insights into AI literacy and integration. *Computers and Education: Artificial Intelligence*, *8*, 1–9. DOI: 10.1016/j.caeai.2025.100398

Lan, Y. (2024). Through tensions to identity-based motivations: Exploring teacher professional identity in Artificial Intelligence-enhanced teacher training. *Teaching and Teacher Education*, *151*, 1–15. DOI: 10.1016/j.tate.2024.104736

Landis, J. R., & Koch, G. G. (1977). The Measurement of Observer Agreement for Categorical Data. *Biometrics*, *33*(1), 159–174. DOI: 10.2307/2529310 PMID: 843571

Laoha, R., Chomthong, W., & Pongpanich, W. (2025). Artificial intelligence and English as a foreign language (EFL) teachers' competency: A systematic review. *Higher Education Studies*, *15*(3), 262. DOI: 10.5539/hes.v15n3p262

Lee, S., Jeon, J., & Choe, H. (2025a). Enhancing pre-service teachers' global Englishes awareness with technology: A focus on AI chatbots in 3D metaverse environments. *TESOL Quarterly*, *59*(1), 49–74. DOI: 10.1002/tesq.3300

Lee, S., Jeon, J., & Choe, H. (2025b). Generative AI (GenAI) and pre-service teacher agency in ELT. *ELT Journal*, *79*(2), 287–296. DOI: 10.1093/elt/ccaf005

Levy, M. (1997). *CALL: Context and conceptualization*. Oxford University Press.

Lyu, B., Lai, C., & Guo, J. (2024). Effectiveness of chatbots in improving language learning: A meta-analysis of comparative studies. *International Journal of Applied Linguistics*, *35*(2), 834–851. DOI: 10.1111/ijal.12668

Lyu, W., Zhang, S., Chung, T., Sun, Y., & Zhang, Y. (2025). Understanding the practices, perceptions, and (dis)trust of generative AI among instructors: A mixed-methods study in the U.S. higher education. *Computers and Education: Artificial Intelligence*, *8*, 100383. DOI: 10.1016/j.caeai.2025.100383

Mah, D. K., & Groß, N. (2024). Artificial intelligence in higher education: Exploring faculty use, self-efficacy, distinct profiles, and professional development needs. *International Journal of Educational Technology in Higher Education*, *21*(1), 1–17. DOI: 10.1186/s41239-024-00490-1

McGrath, C., Pargman, T. C., Juth, N., & Palmgren, P. J. (2023). University teachers' perceptions of responsibility and artificial intelligence in higher education-An experimental philosophical study. *Computers and Education: Artificial Intelligence*, *4*, 1–9. DOI: 10.1016/j.caeai.2023.100139

Miles, M. B., & Huberman, A. M. (1994). Qualitative data analysis: An expanded sourcebook. *Sage (Atlanta, Ga.)*.

Minnillo, S., Jones, L., & García, S. (2024). AI in the L2 classroom: Serving language educators through professional development. *Journal of Linguistics and Language Teaching*, *16*(1), 1–14. DOI: 10.5070/L2.21198

Mohammadi, M. (2024). Language teachers' assessment literacy in AI-aided adaptive learning environments. *Journal of Research in Applied Linguistics*, *15*(2), 73–88. DOI: 10.22055/rals.2024.46120.3235

Moorhouse, B. L., Ho, T. Y., Wu, C., & Wan, Y. (2025). Pre-service language teachers' task-specific Large Language Model prompting practices. *RELC Journal*, 1–22. DOI: 10.1177/00336882251313701

Moorhouse, B. L., & Kohnke, L. (2024). The effects of generative AI on initial language teacher education: The perceptions of teacher educators. *System*, *122*, 1–10. DOI: 10.1016/j.system.2024.103290

Moorhouse, B. L., Wan, Y., Wu, C., Kohnke, L., Ho, T. Y., & Kwong, T. (2024). Developing language teachers' professional generative AI competence: An intervention study in an initial language teacher education course. *System*, *125*, 1–13. DOI: 10.1016/j.system.2024.103399

Ng, D. T., Leung, J. K., Chu, S. K., & Qiao, M. S. (2021). Conceptualizing AI literacy: An exploratory review. *Computers and Education: Artificial Intelligence*, *2*, 100041. DOI: 10.1016/j.caeai.2021.100041

Novawan, A., Walker, S. A., & Ikeda, O. (2024). The new face of technology-enhanced language learning (TELL) with artificial intelligence (AI): Teacher perspectives, practices, and challenges. *Journal of English in Academic and Professional Communication*, *10*(1), 1–18. DOI: 10.25047/jeapco.v9i1.3754

Page, M. J., McKenzie, J. E., Bossuyt, P. M., Boutron, I., Hoffmann, T. C., Mulrow, C. D., Shamseer, L., Tetzlaff, J. M., Akl, E. A., Brennan, S. E., Chou, R., Glanville, J., Grimshaw, J. M., Hróbjartsson, A., Lalu, M. M., Li, T., Loder, E. W., Mayo-Wilson, E., McDonald, S., & Moher, D. (2021). The PRISMA 2020 statement: An updated guideline for reporting systematic reviews. *BMJ (Clinical Research Ed.)*, *372*(71), n71. Advance online publication. DOI: 10.1136/bmj.n71 PMID: 33782057

Pitura, J., Kaplan-Rakowski, R., & Asotska-Wierzba, Y. (2025). The VR-AI–Assisted simulation for content knowledge application in pre-service EFL teacher training. *TechTrends*, *69*(1), 100–110. DOI: 10.1007/s11528-024-01022-4

Prilop, C. N., Mah, D. K., Jacobsen, L. J., Hansen, R. R., & Elena, K. (2025). Generative AI in teacher education: Using AI-enhanced methods to explore teacher educators' perceptions. *Institute for Vocational Training and Lifelong Learning, 3*, 5390-6092. https://doi.org/DOI: 10.31219/osf.io/szcwb

Shi, H., & Aryadoust, V. (2024). A systematic review of AI-based automated written feedback research. *ReCALL*, *36*(2), 187–209. DOI: 10.1017/S0958344023000265

Shi, L. (2025). Assessing teachers' generative artificial intelligence competencies: Instrument development and validation. *Education and Information Technologies*, *30*(16), 23365–23384. Advance online publication. DOI: 10.1007/s10639-025-13684-5

Slavuj, V., Kovačić, B., & Jugo, I. (2015, May). Intelligent tutoring systems for language learning. In *2015 38th International Convention on Information and Communication Technology, Electronics and Microelectronics (MIPRO)* (pp. 814-819). IEEE. DOI: 10.1109/MIPRO.2015.7160383

Tafazoli, D. (2024). Exploring the potential of generative AI in democratizing English language education. *Computers and Education: Artificial Intelligence*, *7*, 1–12. DOI: 10.1016/j.caeai.2024.100275

Tafazoli, D., María, E. G., & Abril, C. A. (2019). Intelligent language tutoring system: Integrating intelligent computer-assisted language learning into language education. [IJICTE]. *International Journal of Information and Communication Technology Education*, *15*(3), 60–74. DOI: 10.4018/IJICTE.2019070105

Tan, X., Cheng, G., & Ling, M. H. (2025). Artificial intelligence in teaching and teacher professional development: A systematic review. *Computers and Education: Artificial Intelligence*, *8*, 1–19. DOI: 10.1016/j.caeai.2024.100355

Urazbayeva, G., Kussainova, R., Aibergen, A., Kaliyeva, A., & Kantayeva, G. (2024). Innovation off the bat: Bridging the ChatGPT gap in digital competence among english as a foreign language teachers. *Education Sciences*, *14*(9), 1–15. DOI: 10.3390/educsci14090946

Uysal, B. Ç. B., & Yüksel, İ. (2024). AI-powered lesson planning: Insights from future EFL teachers. In Pan, F. (Ed.), *AI in Language Teaching, Learning, and Assessment* (pp. 101–132). IGI Global Scientific Publishing., DOI: 10.4018/979-8-3693-0872-1.ch006

Walter, Y. (2024). Embracing the future of artificial intelligence in the classroom: The relevance of AI literacy, prompt engineering, and critical thinking in modern education. *International Journal of Educational Technology in Higher Education*, *21*(1), 15. Advance online publication. DOI: 10.1186/s41239-024-00448-3

Warschauer, M., & Healey, D. (1998). Computers and language learning: An overview. *Language Teaching*, *31*(2), 57–71. DOI: 10.1017/S0261444800012970

Xin, J. J. (2024). Investigating EFL teachers' use of generative AI to develop reading materials: A practice and perception study. *Language Teaching Research*, *0*(0), 1–30. DOI: 10.1177/13621688241303321

Yang, H., & Markauskaite, L. (2025). Fostering language student teachers' transformative agency for embracing GenAI: A formative intervention. *Teaching and Teacher Education*, *159*, 1–20. DOI: 10.1016/j.tate.2025.104980

Zhu, M., & Wang, C. (2025). A systematic review of research on AI in language education: Current status and future implications. *Language Learning & Technology*, *29*(1), 1–29. DOI: 10.64152/10125/73606

Zulianti, H., Hastuti, H., Nurchurifiani, E., Hastomo, T., Maximilian, A., & Ajeng, G. D. (2025). Enhancing novice EFL teachers' competency in AI-powered tools through a TPACK-based professional development program. *World Journal of English Language*, *15*(3), 117–117. DOI: 10.5430/wjel.v15n3p117

KEY TERMS AND DEFINITIONS

AI Literacy: The knowledge, skills, and critical awareness necessary to effectively, reflectively, and ethically utilize AI tools in educational contexts (Ng et al., 2021).

Artificial Intelligence (AI): Computational systems and technologies that simulate aspects of human intelligence to support teaching, learning, and professional development processes.

Generative AI: AI systems capable of creating new content, including text, images, lesson plans, and instructional materials based on user prompts (Moorhouse & Kohnke, 2024).

Intelligent Technology-Enhanced Language Learning (ITELL): A framework that extends Technology-Enhanced Language Learning (TELL) and emphasizes dynamic adaptation, personalization, real-time feedback, and intelligent tutoring capabilities (Novawan et al., 2024).

Intelligent Tutoring Systems (ITS): AI-driven learning systems that deliver personalized instruction, adjust learning paths, and provide diagnostic feedback tailored to each learner's skills and progress (Anoir et al., 2024; Fitas, 2025).

Language Teacher Education and Professional Development: Both pre-service and in-service educational initiatives designed to prepare and support educators who teach languages other than students' native languages. This encompasses formal degree programs, certification courses, workshops, and training seminars across K-12, higher education, and adult education contexts in face-to-face and online modalities.

Pre-service Teachers: Teacher candidates enrolled in formal teacher education programs at undergraduate or graduate levels who are preparing to enter the teaching profession.

Prompt Engineering: The skill of crafting effective instructions or queries to AI systems to achieve desired pedagogical outcomes (Moorhouse et al., 2024; Urazbayeva et al., 2024; Tafazoli, 2024).

APPENDIX

Table 9. Data extracted from studies

Study	Arefian et al. (2024)
Country	Iran
Purpose of AI Integration	To explore novice and experienced Iranian EFL teachers' individual and collective reflection experiences with ChatGPT-driven Collaborative Reflective Practice (CRP) and how this contributes to their professional development
Affordances	Scaffolding reflection through AI as a mentor, peer, or educator Deepening reflection by connecting theory with practice through iterative planning Boosting motivation, creativity, and confidence through emotional support Building community cohesion via collaborative interpretation of AI outputs
Challenges	Struggling with low digital literacy and weak infrastructure Encountering AI suggestions that conflict with cultural or ideological norms Navigating ethical concerns over privacy and data misuse
Perceptions	Using ChatGPT as a reflective partner to deepen teacher reflection
Implementation Strategies	Intro workshop: 1-hour on ALACT model and collaborative reflective practice (CRP) process Individual-Collaborative cycle: teachers share detailed prompts with ChatGPT before/during/after lessons, then meet in 2 novice + 2 experienced teams for 60 minutes weekly CRP (in-person & via WhatsApp/Skype) over a 12-week semester
Evidence of Effectiveness	• Findings indicate enhanced lesson planning, deeper reflection, innovation, flexibility, increased noticing skills, professional confidence, peer collaboration, and stronger collaboration among teachers. • Teachers described ChatGPT as empowering, particularly where access to mentors was limited. • Collective reflection helped contextualize AI advice, resulting in more authentic, practical teaching decisions.
Context	In-service: PD for 8 EFL teachers (mix of novice and experienced).
Study	Belda-Medina & Kokošková (2024)
Country	Spain
Purpose of AI Integration	To explore pre-service EFL teachers' critical skills and perceptions of ChatGPT use in collaborative language learning tasks (writing and text refinement) • To investigate their perceptions and acceptance of ChatGPT as a tool for language learning and teaching • To raise awareness of AI tools and encourage reflective thinking about their educational use
Affordances	Supporting idea generation and overcoming writer's block Saving time by reducing the effort spent on searching for ideas and corrections Enhancing vocabulary use through synonym suggestions and improved word choice Improving writing structure with better organization and logical flow Increasing academic productivity by speeding up assignment and test completion

continued on following page

Table 9. Continued

Challenges	Over-relying on ChatGPT, reducing learner independence Weakening critical thinking and creativity due to copy-paste habits Dealing with outdated or inaccurate AI content Increasing risk of plagiarism and reduced learning ownership Failing to distinguish between AI and human-generated texts
Perceptions	Increasing perceived usefulness and confidence in ChatGPT Strengthening behavioral intention for future use Expressing concerns about over-reliance and harm to critical thinking
Implementation Strategies	Five-stage mixed-method intervention over four months (Feb–May 2023): Pre-survey & AI intro Two sessions of human-only text production & refinement tasks Evaluation of anonymized human vs. ChatGPT-4 samples using Text Inspector Hands-on LLM workshop (ChatGPT-4, ChatSonic, Quillbot) & post-survey Delayed survey & focus-group interviews
Evidence of Effectiveness	Statistically significant improvement in Perceived Usefulness (PU2, PU7 $p < .001$), Attitude (ATT1, ATT2 $p < .000$), Behavioral Intention (BI1, BI4 $p < .001$) in the Technology Acceptance Model (regarding the use of ChatGPT). Focus-group theme frequencies: brainstorming (69.8%), time-saving (64.2%), vocabulary expansion (62.5%); critical-thinking concerns (65.7%), accuracy (62.3%), over-reliance (60.2%), plagiarism (58.6%). Text-analysis misattribution patterns (e.g., 31% GPT identification in L2 task) Delayed survey results showed stronger positive change than the immediate post-survey which suggests growing long-term adoption. Interview data confirmed improved writing skills, idea generation, and learning engagement after using ChatGPT.
Context	Pre-service: Undergraduate EFL pre-service teachers.
Study	Buendgens-Kosten (2024)
Country	Germany
Purpose of AI Integration	To explore how pre-service TEFL teachers engage with and evaluate LLMs (e.g., ChatGPT) in the context of English language teaching. To develop participants' digital text literacy, including awareness of AI's limitations and pedagogical risks. To encourage critical reflection on AI-assisted teaching and material design.
Affordances	Saving time in grammar exercise creation and lesson planning Supporting grammar correction and error identification Facilitating vocabulary brainstorming and writing prompts Assisting novice teachers with pedagogical task design
Challenges	Over-relying on AI-generated content Losing teacher agency and creativity Producing pedagogically flawed or linguistically inappropriate content Facing ethical dilemmas around control, authorship, and originality
Perceptions	Viewing LLMs as tools requiring teacher control Maintaining ethical and pedagogical awareness Expressing cautious optimism toward AI integration

continued on following page

Table 9. Continued

Implementation Strategies	90-minute interactive intervention embedded in three TEFL seminars, comprising: Introduction to LLMs/ChatGPT; Group discussion on digital writing purposes; Station-based tasks (ranking ChatGPT's capabilities; comparing human vs. AI texts; designing "cheat-proof" assignments); Reflection and a 500-word essay homework.
Evidence of Effectiveness	Qualitative findings suggest: Increased critical awareness of AI's role in language education. Growth in digital text literacy, especially in recognizing AI limitations. Development of professional decision-making regarding AI use in future teaching.
Context	Pre-service: Undergraduate/graduate TEFL teacher education seminars (Germany); digital pedagogy focus.
Study	Butler & Jiang (2025)
Country	USA
Purpose of AI Integration	To investigate how pre-service language teachers perceive the affordances and limitations of ChatGPT in academic writing To examine how perceptions relate to their writing performance and self-assessed writing confidence
Affordances	Enhancing time efficiency by quickly generating content for writing tasks Ensuring clear structure through logical paragraphing and subheadings Improving language accuracy with strong grammar and precise vocabulary Summarizing academic content clearly and concisely Covering a broad range of viewpoints and sources when properly prompted Supporting lower-confidence writers by modeling academic language and structure
Challenges	Generating shallow arguments that lack depth Failing to maintain coherence across ideas and sources Including inaccurate, fabricated, or outdated information Using vague and overgeneralized language Producing citation issues or insufficient referencing Relying on prompt quality to determine output strength Ignoring or misinterpreting task instructions (e.g., formatting, word count)
Perceptions	Expressing mixed views on ChatGPT Critiquing AI quality, coherence, and appropriateness (high performers) Appreciating structure and grammar support (lower performers) Aligning self-assessments with their AI attitudes
Implementation Strategies	Embedded ChatGPT tasks in a semester long applied linguistics course (Prompt Design and Reporting; Classroom Discussions and Activities) Four-step assignment: write original essay, opinion statement, ChatGPT generated essay, critical reflection
Evidence of Effectiveness	High-performing pre-service language teachers critically assessed ChatGPT's weaknesses. Low-performing pre-service language teachers praised its assistance with language and structure. Epistemic Network Analysis showed significant differences in how these groups conceptualized affordances ($p < .001$).
Context	Pre-service: Graduate-level TESOL pre-service teachers (international).

continued on following page

Table 9. Continued

Study	Chu & Wang (2024)
Country	China
Purpose of AI Integration	To support knowledge creation among EFL teachers (e.g., lesson plans, teaching materials) To enhance teaching efficiency and reduce workload To explore how AI can foster innovation through collective inquiry
Affordances	Reducing preparation time for tasks like lesson planning and quiz creation Encouraging creative teaching methods and idea generation Enhancing convenience through user-friendly AI tools Promoting collaboration through shared practices and collective inquiry
Challenges	Encountering unreliable or inaccurate content Addressing ethical and legal concerns like plagiarism and copyright Fearing diminished human creativity through overuse Feeling burdened by the fast pace of AI advancements
Perceptions	Demonstrating growing confidence in AI's utility over time Viewing AI as a helpful tool that complements teacher input Recognizing limitations while supporting innovation
Implementation Strategies	Monthly collective inquiries (four sessions over the academic year), structured by the double-stimulation model: conflict awareness, second-stimulus interaction, collaborative knowledge creation. Task design: GPT prompts used to generate EAP course materials-lesson plans, slides, quizzes, interactive tasks. Facilitation: Led by team leaders and researchers, with follow-up semi-structured interviews of the three most active participants.
Evidence of Effectiveness	Teachers reported time saved in material preparation. Willingness to experiment with AI tools was increased. Macro-level factors (policies, systemic reforms) had minimal perceived impact, whereas micro-level drivers such as peer AI-adoption trends, supportive school AI atmospheres, and positive beliefs in AI's efficiency and creativity, consistently shaped teachers' knowledge-creation actions and epistemic agency during PD activities. Teachers created new knowledge and improved teaching strategies with AI. Teachers actively explored AI strategies (e.g., prompt shortcuts on Reddit), collaboratively evaluated and adapted GenAI outputs, and integrated AI tools into problem-solving discussions which signs an enhanced agency, reflective practice, and co-construction of professional knowledge.
Context	In-service: PD for EAP instructors in universities; AI integration focus.
Study	Davoodi (2024)
Country	USA
Purpose of AI Integration	To examine how a Connectivist PD program enhances AI literacy among bilingual/ ESL teachers, transforms their perceptions and attitudes toward AI integration, and fosters collaborative, non-linear professional learning networks

continued on following page

Table 9. Continued

Affordances	Acting as an adaptive knowledge source for real-time feedback and content creation Enabling personalized lessons and differentiated instruction Automating routine tasks (e.g., grading) to free up teacher time Bridging resource gaps (e.g., language support for ELLs)
Challenges	Beginning with low AI confidence and foundational skills Experiencing emotional barriers like job insecurity Lacking infrastructure and long-term institutional training Balancing pedagogical ethics with AI tool integration
Perceptions	Replacing initial fear with trust after PD Seeing AI as a pedagogical support tool Gaining confidence, AI literacy, and reflective teaching skills
Implementation Strategies	Phase 1 (in-person): one-day workshop with hands-on GPT-4 sessions, collaborative lesson-design activities Phase 2 (asynchronous): video tutorials on AI tools, reflective assignments
Evidence of Effectiveness	Survey data showed significant improvement in positive attitudes towards AI (teachers: from 26% to 78%). Increased confidence and efficiency in using AI for teaching and administrative tasks. Teachers and administrators reported feeling more empowered, collaborative, and informed. AI seen as beneficial for equity and personalization but with recognition of the need for teacher oversight.
Context	In-service: PD for in-service bilingual/ESL elementary teachers and administrators.
Study	Ghosh (2025)
Country	India
Purpose of AI Integration	To determine factors influencing the effectiveness of Intelligent Tutoring Systems (ITS) in teacher education To explore the impact of ITS on the instructional practices of language teachers To assess ITS effects on student learning outcomes
Affordances	Providing immediate feedback on tasks and performance Offering adaptive learning paths aligned with learner progress Enhancing learner engagement and autonomy Supporting content retention and practical teaching knowledge development Enabling self-regulated learning and differentiated instruction
Challenges	Facing a learning curve with ITS tools Lacking prior AI exposure Missing instructor interaction Adapting to self-paced learning Encountering institutional integration barriers
Perceptions	Expressing overall positive attitudes toward ITS Finding TutorMate basic but helpful (pre-service teachers) Reporting strong benefits of Cognitive Tutor (in-service teachers) Gaining confidence with increased familiarity Noting a need for support in using ITS easily Experiencing more engagement and better tracking Appreciating self-paced and reflective learning Missing teacher interaction and recommending blended support Feeling more confident using educational technology after intervention

continued on following page

Table 9. Continued

Implementation Strategies	ITS tools tailored by experience level: Pre-service: TutorMate (used in university labs, semester-long, weekly 2-hour) In-service: Cognitive Tutor (week-long PD workshop, advanced analytics) ITS integrated via structured training modules with emphasis on data-driven teaching
Evidence of Effectiveness	Structural Equation Modeling (SEM): Perceived usefulness → teaching efficacy ($\beta = 0.45$, $p < .001$); perceived ease of use → teaching efficacy ($\beta = 0.32$, $p < .01$); teaching efficacy → student performance ($\beta = 0.50$, $p < .001$) Indirect effects of perceived usefulness and perceived ease of use on student performance are also significant ($\beta = 0.22$, $p < .01$; $\beta = 0.18$, $p < .05$) Confirmatory Factor Analysis (CFA) & SEM fit indices all within good-fit thresholds ($CFI \geq .95$; $RMSEA \leq .05$)
Context	Both (Pre-service & In-service): Pre-service in formal education; in-service in active classrooms.
Study	Hieu & Thao (2024)
Country	Vietnam
Purpose of AI Integration	To support creative writing (fairy tale retelling) To explore teachers' perceptions of ChatGPT integration in EFL writing tasks
Affordances	Increasing student engagement and personalization of learning Improving language proficiency and reducing teacher workload Promoting technology adoption and creative thinking Stimulating teacher reflection and professional growth
Challenges	Over-relying on AI for instruction or content Experiencing cultural or contextual mismatches Facing challenges in integrating AI into current teaching practices Using AI at inappropriate complexity levels Suppressing student creativity and initiative Coping with technical limitations and ethical risks (e.g., data privacy)
Perceptions	Appreciating ChatGPT's benefits while raising concerns Questioning contextual fit and student dependence
Implementation Strategies	In-class storytelling sessions: ChatGPT was embedded directly into fairy-tale retelling activities, with students generating and then refining narratives. Differentiated task design: Teachers used ChatGPT to adjust prompt complexity and scaffolding according to each learner's proficiency. Pedagogical experimentation: Educators iteratively adapted lesson plans based on AI output quality, exploring new classroom workflows
Evidence of Effectiveness	ChatGPT integration broadly supported teacher growth across career stages as professional development benefits were identified by seven of nine participants (all three novice, two mid-career, two near-end-career teachers). Anecdotal evidence based on teacher observations: Increased engagement, improved vocabulary and grammar, more creativity, more tech comfort for teachers.
Context	In-service: Tertiary-level EFL classrooms (creative writing/AI); not strictly teacher training.
Study	Kartal (2024)
Country	Türkiye

continued on following page

Table 9. Continued

Purpose of AI Integration	To explore pre-service English teachers' perceptions of ChatGPT's impact on their thinking skills and creativity To identify benefits and challenges experienced when using ChatGPT for academic assignments and classroom discussions To understand strategies they employ to balance AI-generated content with independent critical analysis.
Affordances	Accessing relevant information rapidly through AI tools Enhancing learning efficiency via quick content generation Clarifying complex concepts and exploring diverse perspectives Boosting creativity and productivity in assignments and lesson design Stimulating critical thinking during instructional preparation
Challenges	Producing simplistic or inauthentic classroom content Over-relying on AI tools instead of original thought Losing autonomy and difficulty distinguishing AI input from personal ideas
Perceptions	Accepting ChatGPT enthusiastically Noticing gains in creativity, efficiency, and critical thinking Collaborating with peers to improve AI outputs Emphasizing the need for content validation
Implementation Strategies	Embedded ChatGPT into lesson planning and classroom tasks (lesson planning, material creation, and classroom activities) during a 14-week practicum Weekly written narratives documenting ChatGPT use Weekly online group interviews and end-of-semester individual interviews for reflective analysis
Evidence of Effectiveness	Thematic analysis showed six major themes (Benefits, Challenges, Co-creation, Critical Analysis, Collaboration, Recommendations).
Context	Pre-service: Undergraduate (senior) pre-service EFL teacher training.
Study	Khajavi & Ezhdehakosh (2025)
Country	Iran
Purpose of AI Integration	To investigate preservice teachers' perceptions of AI tools' effectiveness in enhancing teaching practices To identify concerns about AI's implications for educator roles To understand how these perceptions may influence future teaching practices.
Affordances	Personalizing learning experiences based on individual learner needs Delivering immediate feedback through automated evaluation systems Improving resource efficiency by automating grading and routine tasks Enhancing conversational practice through AI chatbot interaction
Challenges	Coping with poor technical infrastructure (e.g., VPN blocks, internet speed) Facing training gaps and low AI confidence Risking overuse and reliance on AI tools Dealing with hallucinations and misinformation Navigating ethical/privacy concerns and technology access inequalities
Perceptions	Showing high acceptance and digital fluency Reporting enhanced planning efficiency and confidence Cautioning against teacher replacement Highlighting ethical awareness and privacy concerns

continued on following page

Table 9. Continued

Implementation Strategies	16-week practicum with a 5-week AI module (fundamentals of ChatGPT, Copilot, Pi, Sider) followed by classroom application Activities: in-class practice, collaborative lesson planning, microteaching video using AI tools
Evidence of Effectiveness	Thematic analysis of interviews showed high acceptance of AI's affordances (interactivity, feedback) alongside articulated concerns about teaching roles; participants recommended more hands-on AI modules in teacher education.
Context	Pre-service: Undergraduate (senior) pre-service English teacher training.
Study	Lee et al. (2025a)
Country	South Korea
Purpose of AI Integration	To investigate the potential of English as a lingua franca (ELF) interactions with AI chatbots in raising GE awareness To explore the feasibility of a computer-assisted GELT (CA-GELT) approach
Affordances	Raising awareness of Global Englishes through meaningful tasks Recognizing and appreciating diverse English varieties Exposing learners to authentic, real-world conversational input Encouraging critical reflection on linguistic authenticity and identity Promoting task-based, immersive, and low-pressure practice environments Stimulating interest in ELF and GELT integration in curricula
Challenges	Designing custom AI chatbots to avoid native-speaker bias
Perceptions	Accepting English variety and ELF exposure via chatbots Strengthening confidence and reducing communication anxiety Appreciating chatbot capabilities like accent recognition
Implementation Strategies	Three-stage chatbot intervention (EG2): Weeks 3–6: interaction with text-based chatbots through information-gap tasks in metaverse. Weeks 7–10: Speech-recognition dialogues with AI-avatar avatars. Weeks 11–14: Daily-conversation topics via Wizard-of-Oz avatars
Evidence of Effectiveness	Statistical analysis showed that AI Chatbot activities on Global Englishes increased Global Englishes Awareness of pre-service language teachers ($p < .001$). Thematic analysis demonstrated that AI chatbots are beneficial for increasing pre-service teachers' awareness of diverse English, offering authentic experiences, helping them to acknowledge the authenticity of their own English, and alleviating fears of communicating with real people.
Context	Pre-service: Undergraduate pre-service English teachers (97 participants).
Study	Lee et al. (2025b)
Country	South Korea
Purpose of AI Integration	To explore how pre-service English teachers engage with and utilize AI tools in an instructional context To investigate pre-service teachers' perceptions of participating in a GenAI-enhanced lesson design project

continued on following page

Table 9. Continued

Affordances	Fostering teacher-AI collaboration and shared agency in educational tasks Applying GenAI tools for instructional planning and content creation Enhancing digital literacy and pedagogical competence via PD Promoting ethical and responsible use of AI through critical reflection
Challenges	Struggling with output reliability and contextual appropriateness Addressing academic dishonesty and potential misuse Lacking GenAI literacy and prompt-crafting skills Failing to meet complex pedagogical demands with current tools Calling for institutional training and ethical implementation support
Perceptions	Collaborating actively with GenAI in teaching processes Forming strategic teacher–AI partnerships Generating and refining materials through prompt engineering Enhancing student engagement and creative lesson design Improving GenAI literacy and technical skills Emphasizing ELT expertise for validating AI output Engaging in peer scaffolding to improve quality Facing challenges like misinformation, prompt difficulty, and ethical concerns Calling for formal GenAI training and classroom use guidelines
Implementation Strategies	4-week, 3-stage lesson design (intro, creation, refinement) Tools: ChatGPT, Copilot, DALL-E3 Peer collaboration to compensate for individual gaps in GenAI skills
Evidence of Effectiveness	Participants reported increased GenAI literacy, self-efficacy, and reflective practice. GenAI-supported lesson designs were described as more engaging, creative, and structured. Teachers maintained pedagogical agency by adapting and refining outputs. Peer scaffolding enhanced output quality and technological confidence. Some developed ethical guidelines for responsible AI use in future classrooms.
Context	Pre-service: Undergraduate (3rd-year) pre-service ELT majors (18 participants).
Study	Minnillo et al. (2024)
Country	USA
Purpose of AI Integration	To provide hands-on training for L2 educators on AI-mediated pedagogy, practice effective prompt-writing, and interaction with AI tools
Affordances	Developing effective prompt-writing skills through guided practice Enabling pedagogical innovation using AI for conversations and personalized feedback
Challenges	Receiving inconsistent AI responses that fail to follow prompts Losing hands-on training time due to session overruns Addressing equity and data privacy concerns Calling for context-sensitive institutional AI policies
Perceptions	Questioning AI's role critically Viewing AI as supportive of—not replacing—teacher expertise Raising concerns about equity, bias, and academic integrity

continued on following page

Table 9. Continued

Implementation Strategies	1.5-hour hybrid workshop (Feb 2024) at Davis Language Center with: Panel presentations by diverse L2 educators (25-30 min) Q&A (10 min) Interactive hands-on tasks with teacher/student scenarios and guided handouts (20-30 min) Show-and-tell & reflections
Evidence of Effectiveness	Qualitative insights from participant reflections and Q&A indicated enhanced awareness of AI's pedagogical potentials, improved prompt-writing skills, and critical engagement.
Context	Both (Pre-service & In-service): Mixed group: language faculty, graduate TAs, undergrads, and instructional technologists.
Study	Mohammadi (2024)
Country	Iran
Purpose of AI Integration	To develop Language Assessment Literacy (LAL) among teachers. To enhance Teaching Quality (TQ) in AI-aided Adaptive Learning Environments (ALEs). To evaluate the impact of AI-supported ALEs on teachers' assessment skills and classroom practices.
Affordances	Enhancing assessment precision with data-driven tools Providing individualized learning paths and real-time adaptive feedback Aligning curriculum dynamically with student needs Supporting strategic customization of materials and feedback delivery Enabling personalized professional development Increasing technological literacy and pedagogical reflection
Challenges	Spending extra time implementing AI tools Handling increased workload during AI transition Adapting to structured AI-driven instructional paths Questioning fairness and transparency of AI-assisted assessment Struggling with navigation and security in digital systems Experiencing difficulty among experienced teachers in adopting AI
Perceptions	Acknowledging AI's contributions to efficiency, engagement, and growth Valuing feedback and support (novice teachers) Prioritizing customization and reflection (senior teachers) Expressing skepticism and fairness concerns (experienced teachers)
Implementation Strategies	Pre-test administration 50-hour training program (10 hours theory + 40 hours practice) Use of AI tools: Magic School and/or EdApp during 16 classroom teaching sessions Post-test administration Semi-structured interviews with a sample of participants
Evidence of Effectiveness	After AI-assisted language assessment interventions, preand post-test analysis showed: Language Assessment Literacy (LAL) pre ($M=128.97$) vs. post ($M=211.04$), $t(260)=93.684$, $p<.001$. Senior LAL > Novice ($p=.011$); Experienced Teaching Quality > others ($p<.001$) (Senior teachers outperformed others in LAL). Qualitative thematic analysis: 17 advantage themes & 10 challenge themes from 45 interviewees.
Context	In-service: PD for 261 EFL teachers (adult education); AI-driven assessment literacy and practice.

continued on following page

Table 9. Continued

Study	Moorhouse et al. (2024)
Country	China
Purpose of AI Integration	To develop pre-service teachers' Professional GenAI Competence (P-GenAI-C) across five domains: To enable effective and responsible use of GenAI tools in English language teaching
Affordances	Increasing efficiency in lesson planning, material creation, and feedback delivery Supporting creativity through the generation of engaging, context-rich activities Enhancing lesson design with ideas for differentiated instruction Assisting in language error analysis and grammar explanation Developing prompt engineering skills for effective AI use Promoting student-centered thinking by tailoring lessons to learner needs Aiding in material development, including texts, tables, exercises, quizzes, and visuals
Challenges	Over-relying on AI, risking reduced creativity and critical thinking Encountering inaccurate or generic outputs Failing to personalize tasks to student proficiency Managing ethical risks such as cheating or plagiarism Struggling with student or parent acceptance of AI-assisted teaching Lacking preparedness to teach students responsible GenAI use
Perceptions	Demonstrating limited awareness and narrow AI use before intervention Raising concerns about ethical risks and misuse Developing critical awareness and recognizing AI's pedagogical potential Asserting teacher agency and professional responsibility in AI use Embracing AI as a supportive tool rather than a replacement
Implementation Strategies	11-week flipped-course intervention integrating GenAI into 'Grammar for Teaching' MEd (ELT) course GenAI integrated into 8 of 11 sessions, each aligned with one or more P-GenAI-C aspects Tools: ChatGPT & hotpot.ai (sessions 1–6), Alayna.us & magicschool.ai (session 10), Quillbot (sessions 10–11) Experiential group tasks: iterative prompt design, lesson-plan refinement, materials creation Assignments requiring GenAI use: planning, material creation, reflection Assignments 2–3 required GenAI-usage logs, pedagogical rationales & reflections
Evidence of Effectiveness	Paired-samples t-tests showed significant pre-post gains in competency (t(53)=3.582, d=0.487) and familiarity (t(53)=8.235, d=1.121) in GenAI tools. Thematic analysis revealed increased frequency of all professional GenAI competence themes and emergence of four new themes post-intervention: prompt engineering, professional reflection, teachers' responsibilities, stakeholder acceptance.
Context	Pre-service: Master's level (MEd ELT) pre-service teachers; 'Grammar for Teaching' course.
Study	Moorhouse et al. (2025)
Country	China

continued on following page

Table 9. Continued

Purpose of AI Integration	To assist pre-service teachers in improving grammar lesson plans To develop task-specific prompting practices and enhance their ability to use LLMs effectively in teaching To simulate real-world professional practices where teachers may use AI tools (e.g., brainstorming, lesson adaptation)
Affordances	Enhancing lesson quality by refining objectives, materials, and scaffolding strategies Saving time in lesson development and brainstorming Iterating and fine-tuning lesson elements through instant AI feedback Developing prompt literacy to craft effective AI queries Cross-checking outputs from multiple LLMs to select the most suitable response
Challenges	Receiving irrelevant, incorrect, or overly complex responses Refining prompts multiple times to improve answer quality Struggling with nuanced or pedagogically sound content generation Abandoning AI use due to frustration with poor results Requiring high pedagogical content knowledge and AI literacy
Perceptions	Encountering irrelevant or overly complex AI outputs Refining prompts repeatedly to get acceptable responses Noticing difficulties with nuance and pedagogical soundness Abandoning AI use due to frustration in some cases Requiring high pedagogical content knowledge and AI literacy
Implementation Strategies	11-week flipped 'Grammar for Teaching' course integrating GenAI Group creation of lesson plans followed by individual LLM-assisted revisions Use of institutional LLM and third-party LLMs (ChatGPT-3.5, GPT-4 via Poe) Collection of interaction logs, reflections, and pedagogical rationales
Evidence of Effectiveness	Reflections and logs showed that pre-service language teachers could refine lesson plans meaningfully with AI assistance. Pre-service language teachers demonstrated growth in prompting skills, pedagogical content knowledge, and AI tool use awareness.
Context	Pre-service: Master's level (MEd ELT) pre-service teachers at a university.
Study	Pitura, et al. (2025)
Country	Poland
Purpose of AI Integration	To investigate how pre-service EFL teachers experience and interpret the VR-AI–assisted simulation designed to facilitate their content (grammar) knowledge application
Affordances	Creating a safe, immersive environment for experimentation without classroom pressure Enabling practice with realistic, AI-generated, thought-provoking student questions Promoting self-reflection, knowledge reinforcement, and increased confidence Providing opportunities for practical rehearsal of complex grammar instruction
Challenges	Lacking real interaction or feedback in VR Experiencing technological issues (e.g., VR headset, virtual board) Coping with psychological discomfort in unfamiliar VR settings Using pre-programmed AI responses that feel artificial

continued on following page

Table 9. Continued

Perceptions	Valuing simulation for revision, confidence-building, and preparation Considering AI questions useful for deeper thinking and strategy reflection Expressing skepticism about transferability to real classrooms Preferring traditional teaching environments despite novelty
Implementation Strategies	10–15 min VR sessions via Oculus Quest 2 + Virtual Speech app Role-play scenario: teach present perfect, answer AI-generated questions Pre-brief online: study website orientation Post-simulation e-questionnaire capturing reflections
Evidence of Effectiveness	Thematic analysis showed improvement in; Confidence in teaching the present perfect. Ability to reflect on knowledge and teaching methods. Awareness of weaknesses and need for better preparation.
Context	Pre-service: Graduate level (MA in TEFL); 17 female pre-service EFL teachers.
Study	Tafazoli (2024)
Country	Iran
Purpose of AI Integration	To explore how GenAI can help English language teachers overcome educational challenges To provide personalized professional development opportunities To promote digital literacy and technological confidence among teachers To demonstrate the potential of GenAI for creating and adapting learning materials
Affordances	Generating updated, affordable, and customizable learning materials Creating supplementary readings, quizzes, and tasks using AI tools Providing personalized feedback and support aligned with teachers' professional needs Offering tailored professional development for contexts lacking localized training Presenting ideologically neutral content that promotes diverse cultural viewpoints Encouraging critical thinking and open dialogue in the classroom Ensuring accessibility through user-friendly design, even for those with limited digital literacy Operating smoothly on low-end devices via browser-based platforms Simulating conversations with global personas to enhance communicative competence Fostering cross-cultural awareness, language proficiency, and global connectedness
Challenges	Not addressing AI challenges explicitly in the findings
Perceptions	Viewing ChatGPT as accessible, adaptable, and supportive Overcoming initial skepticism and gaining confidence Perceiving GenAI as a solution to systemic issues
Implementation Strategies	3×120 min webinars via Zoom & Focusky Live ChatGPT demos & hands-on prompt practice (on the use of Q&A and follow-up reflective essays & interviews
Evidence of Effectiveness	Thematic analysis uncovered that; Teachers successfully created and used AI-generated resources. GenAI helped improve student engagement, access, and critical thinking. Teachers reported feeling more motivated and capable after GenAI use. Teachers acknowledged GenAI's transformative potential across access, personalization, tech barriers, and global engagement.

continued on following page

Table 9. Continued

Context	In-service: Professional development for 23 English language teachers.
Study	Urazbayeva et al. (2024)
Country	Kazakhstan
Purpose of AI Integration	Enhancing instructional creativity through diverse lesson idea generation Reducing cognitive load during assessment via automated support Increasing cost-efficiency by eliminating the need for paid materials Supporting lesson and assessment planning through motivational assistance
Affordances	Enhancing instructional creativity through diverse lesson idea generation Reducing cognitive load during assessment via automated support Increasing cost-efficiency by eliminating the need for paid materials Supporting lesson and assessment planning through motivational assistance
Challenges	Verifying and editing AI-generated outputs for accuracy Manually digitizing handwritten student work Repeating prompts due to generic or overly repetitive AI content
Perceptions	Seeing ChatGPT as a creative, supportive assistant Valuing grading and idea-generation features Acknowledging current limitations while expecting future enhancements Appreciating AI's potential to personalize teaching
Implementation Strategies	Eight-week, researcher-guided, prompt-driven intervention with one complex prompt per week Introductory hands-on workshop on prompt-engineering Digital distribution of eight piloted prompts (lesson plans, explanations, vocab lists, worksheets, tech integration, quizzes, writing feedback, speaking activities) Weekly email reminders and peer support mechanisms
Evidence of Effectiveness	Pre- and post-test analysis of the ChatGPT Integration Proficiency Assessment showed significant pre-post gains in Technological Content Knowledge ($p < .001$), Technological Pedagogical Knowledge ($p < .001$), and Technological Pedagogical Content Knowledge ($p = .002$), and total score ($p < .001$). Qualitative reflections report boosted AI literacy, pedagogical creativity, and reduced grading burden.
Context	In-service: In-service EFL teacher training for 24 teachers.
Study	Uysal & Yüksel (2024)
Country	Türkiye
Purpose of AI Integration	To explore how pre-service teachers assess AI-powered lesson plans for 5th-grade writing lessons To identify pedagogical strengths, areas for improvement, and enhancement strategies To investigate teachers' beliefs about integrating AI into their teaching and professional development
Affordances	Promoting student interaction and lesson coherence Clarifying learning outcomes and enriching content resources Supporting effective time management and reflective practices
Challenges	Providing insufficient differentiation, adaptation, and feedback Needing detailed rubrics, explicit assessment criteria, and time optimization

continued on following page

Table 9. Continued

Perceptions	Viewing AI-based plans as engaging and creativity-enhancing Emphasizing the importance of pedagogical expertise Advocating formal training and ethical guidelines
Implementation Strategies	Three-step procedure: Generate lesson plans through a fixed ChatGPT prompt; Evaluate them using an AI-generated rubric reviewed by researchers; Provide qualitative justifications and reflect on future AI use through open-ended prompts
Evidence of Effectiveness	Teachers evaluated AI-powered lesson plans (ChatGPT) using rubrics. Mean rubric score: 3.54 out of 5, indicating generally positive evaluations. High scores for engagement (M = 4.11), appropriateness (M = 4.05), and lesson structure (M = 3.89). Lower scores for differentiation (M = 2.71) and assessment/feedback (M = 2.98). Qualitative data confirmed that AI can inspire creativity and structure but lacks depth in differentiation and evaluation design.
Context	Pre-service: Undergraduate (3rd-year) pre-service EFL teacher training.
Study	Xin (2024)
Country	China
Purpose of AI Integration	To evaluate or modify reading texts, to design reading tasks, and to obtain pedagogical suggestions via ChatPDF
Affordances	Modifying text and designing tasks rapidly using AI Offering pedagogical suggestions and rationales Supporting learner centered and differentiated material creation Providing opportunities for professional development
Challenges	Failing to interpret or evaluate multimodal content Dealing with hallucinations and inconsistent reliability Needing critical teacher evaluation of AI content Facing contextual limitations such as large classes and limited time
Perceptions	Noting AI's pedagogical insights and efficiency Recognizing limitations such as evaluation burden and multimodal constraints Identifying opportunities for PD and learner-centered design
Implementation Strategies	Teachers uploaded existing reading-lesson PDFs to ChatPDF and engaged in iterative dialogue following a D-R-E-A-M cycle (Determine needs → Render prompts → Evaluate suggestions → Adjust prompts → Make final decision)
Evidence of Effectiveness	Teachers reported improved efficiency in materials creation. Produced learner-centred, differentiated materials. Fostered reflective practice and pedagogical growth, especially for less experienced teachers. Acceptance of AI-generated content (ChatPDF) rates varied (T1: 10%, T2: 50%, T3: 62.5%), reflecting selective adoption based on context and reliability.
Context	In-service: PD for three full-time EFL teachers.
Study	Yang & Markauskaite (2025)
Country	Australia

continued on following page

Table 9. Continued

Purpose of AI Integration	To enhance student language teachers' capabilities in using GenAI tools for teaching purposes To develop their transformative agency through a formative intervention focused on GenAI engagement To integrate GenAI with pedagogical and content knowledge in language teacher education
Affordances	Supporting multilingual and multimodal material creation using GenAI tools Enabling rapid content generation through prompt-based lesson material creation Addressing inclusivity by tailoring outputs to language-specific needs Integrating professional knowledge by aligning GenAI use with audience, pedagogy, and context Encouraging critical thinking through reflection on teaching, ethics, and technology Enhancing pronunciation instruction with AI-generated voice-over tools
Challenges	Receiving culturally biased or stereotypical outputs (e.g., image generation) Aligning AI content poorly with pedagogical goals Spending time on repeated prompt revisions to meet teaching needs Fearing teacher replacement or devaluation of teaching roles Questioning AI reliability, trust, and ethical use Worrying about managing student misuse of AI in the classroom
Perceptions	Starting with skepticism, discomfort, and low trust Shifting toward more positive, agentive views during sessions Ending with recognition of GenAI as a partner under ethical use Emphasizing the need for teacher monitoring and formal training
Implementation Strategies	Non-Change-Lab formative intervention over four weeks: three 20–35 min hands-on GenAI sessions followed by a 60 min reflective discussion. Task progression: Text → multimodal resources → AI-generated audio → group reflection. Tool ensemble: ChatGPT 3.5 for text, Bing Image for visuals, EaseUS voice-over for audio. Collaborative design: Small groups negotiated prompts, shared domain knowledge, and co-constructed lesson materials
Evidence of Effectiveness	Analysis demonstrated that teachers spent more time doing "expansive" activities (like creating, analyzing, reflecting) with the AI (basic in session 1 to more sophisticated, independent actions by session 4). Across all four sessions, there were 277 expansive actions versus 132 routine ones, and agentive (self-directed) actions rose from 40 to 36 expanded-agency moves. The intervention really helped teachers become more confident and proactive in using GenAI.
Context	Pre-service: Undergraduate multi-language teacher education (German, Korean, Italian).
Study	Zulianti et al. (2025)
Country	Indonesia
Purpose of AI Integration	To improve novice EFL teachers' competency in using AI-powered tools in ELT through a TPACK-based professional development (PD) program To evaluate the effectiveness of a TPACK-based professional development (PD) program focused on AI use in ELT

continued on following page

Table 9. Continued

Affordances	Increasing familiarity with AI-powered tools such as grammar checkers and writing assistants Strengthening skills in designing and delivering AI-supported lessons Enhancing self-efficacy in using AI tools through professional development Creating effective lesson plans that integrate AI tools into ELT instruction
Challenges	Adapting AI tools designed for business to educational contexts Struggling to identify suitable points in the curriculum for AI integration Lacking project-based learning in AI-supported lesson plans Starting with limited AI knowledge and experience
Perceptions	Reporting positive experiences with AI tools post-training Expressing increased confidence and motivation to use AI Requesting institutional support and showing willingness to innovate
Implementation Strategies	Quasi-experimental design with experimental (PD) and control groups Five 16-hour modules on CKAI, TCKAI, PCKAI, TPKAI, TPACKAI (online and face-to-face) Activities included workshops, lesson-plan creation, hands-on tool exploration, and peer collaboration
Evidence of Effectiveness	Knowledge (of AI-tools) test: Experimental M = 85.25 vs Control M = 68.15; $p < .001$) Teaching skills (using AI-tools): Experimental M = 87.25 vs Control M = 64.40; $p < .001$) Self-efficacy (with teaching AI-tools): Experimental M = 81.05 vs Control M = 70.95; $p < .001$) Interview data: All 5 participants reported gains in AI-tools knowledge (14 mentions); 4 noted enhanced teaching-efficacy skills using AI-tools (12 mentions) and increased self-efficacy with teaching AI tools (8 mentions)
Context	In-service (Novice): Novice English teachers (early-career).

Chapter 3
How Do EFL Learners Perceive Using Artificial Intelligence?

Selami Aydin
https://orcid.org/0000-0003-1614-874X
Istanbul Medeniyet University, Turkey

Cansu Candemir Özkan
https://orcid.org/0000-0001-7876-7402
Istanbul Medeniyet University, Turkey

ABSTRACT

This study aims to explore learners' perceptions of AI use in the foreign language learning process and to investigate whether their perceptions differ under specific variables, such as age, gender, grade, department, and proficiency in the target language. This descriptive study administered a background questionnaire and the Perceptions of AI Usage Scale (PAS) to 897 EFL learners. Descriptive statistics, independent samples t-test, ANOVA, and Tamhane were used for data analysis. The study concluded that learners perceive that integrating AI tools and environments contributes to writing and reading skills, and they seem doubtful about the effect of AI on speaking, listening comprehension, pronunciation, and communicative skills. It was also concluded that learners' perceptions of AI usage do not show any difference based on gender, while their perceptions seem to be related to learners' ages, grades, departments, and proficiency levels in the target language.

DOI: 10.4018/979-8-3373-2927-7.ch003

INTRODUCTION

EFL learning facilitates interaction and communication on an international scale, as English is the predominant language in various domains, including education, science, technology, tourism, and aviation. Thus, proficiency in English enhances employment prospects both domestically and internationally (Rumsey, 2024). Therefore, basic English language skills are essential for global educational opportunities at schools and universities. Its dominance on the internet, constituting 59% of all web content (Statista, 2024), requires English proficiency to access vast amounts of information. Additionally, familiarity with English is beneficial for engaging with films, television shows, and books prevalent in popular culture (Harmer, 2003). From the learners' perspective, EFL learning presents distinct advantages. For instance, it promotes opportunities for interaction and communication across diverse contexts (Verga & Kotz, 2013), enhances intercultural awareness (Byram, 2012), and fosters the development of problem-solving and critical thinking skills (W. Liang & Fung, 2021). Moreover, EFL learning improves cognitive and affective functions (Kennedy, 2006). To this end, these multifaceted benefits constitute the critical role of EFL learning in today's interconnected world.

On the other hand, while proficiency in the target language offers distinct advantages, the EFL learning process is often characterized by various challenges. Notably, the absence of authentic and contextual materials, limited practice opportunities, and an over-dependence on the first language during the learning process are significant impediments to effective learning (Savran Çelik & Aydın, 2018). These issues deprive learners of comprehensible input and output, resulting in inadequate knowledge of grammar and vocabulary, as well as deficient basic language skills (Krashen, 1982). Consequently, these barriers may lead to affective issues such as lack of motivation, demotivation, anxiety, and low self-confidence among EFL learners. The lack of vocabulary, grammar, pronunciation, and speaking ability may lead to psychological issues, including low self-confidence, nervousness, and shyness (Rukiati et al., 2023). These challenges can foster negative perceptions and attitudes toward learning a new language, ultimately leading to failure (Aydın, 2020; Aydın & Tekin, 2023). AI applications can potentially address the aforementioned challenges encountered in the EFL learning process (Sayici & Aydın, 2025). For example, AI can facilitate translation between the native and target languages within cross-cultural learning contexts (Shadiev et al., 2018), as well as identify and correct errors in written and oral language (Altınay & Aydın, 2025; Kanero et al., 2018). With the aid of AI technology, students can practice public speaking while receiving immediate feedback on their intonation and pronunciation (Ballıdağ & Aydın, 2025; Hazaymeh et al., 2024). Additionally, AI applications can serve as collaborative and autonomous learning tools, providing environments where learners can engage and communicate in the target language (Hoşer & Aydın, 2026; Kannan & Munday, 2018). These tools also provide access to authentic and contextual materials, which are crucial for developing basic language skills and knowledge areas, such as grammar and vocabulary (Könez & Aydin, 2026; Yılmaz & Aydın, 2025). Consequently, learners can benefit from adaptive and personalized learning experiences tailored to their individual needs, expectations, performance, and proficiency levels (Berk & Aydın, 2025). However, the effective utilization of AI in language learning largely depends on EFL learners' perceptions of AI tools and environments (Aydın & Zeinolabedini, 2024). Learners' perceptions of AI usage may influence their success in learning the target language. Despite its importance, there is a considerable lack of research on learners' perceptions of AI-based tools and environments in the EFL learning process, as seen in the research synthesis below.

THEORETICAL BACKGROUND

AI, an interdisciplinary fusion of computer science and linguistics, can multitask, including understanding, learning, and acquiring knowledge. AI leverages its ability to use creative language by reactivating existing knowledge (Aydın & Altınay, 2026; Korteling et al., 2021; Sarker, 2022). The application of AI in foreign language learning aligns with *Activity Theory*, which examines the mental capabilities of learners as they utilize the cultural and technical aspects of human actions (Bertelsen & Bødker, 2003). This socio-technical system encompasses elements such as actors, social context, concepts, tool mediation, division of labor, and rules (Bryant et al., 2005), blending cultural context with technical aspects of learning (Woolf et al., 2013). AI also supports self-regulated and self-directed learning within the framework of autonomous learning, rooted in Bandura's (1986) Social Cognitive Theory. This theory defines such learning as an agentive activity characterized by initiative, resourcefulness, and persistence (Aydın, 2023; Ponton & Rhea, 2006). *Learner-centeredness*, which involves engagement in activities and tasks (Dang, 2006), is well-suited to AI applications that foster active participation. Moreover, AI tools facilitate technologically connected *interaction* (Anderson & Elloumi, 2004), providing learners with comprehensible input and opportunities for negotiating meaning (Ellis, 2009). The theoretical underpinnings of AI usage in language learning are further supported by concepts such as *active learning*, which emphasizes student-centered teaching (Meyers, 1993); *blended learning,* which integrates technology with face-to-face components (Hockly, 2018); and *flipped learning*, which incorporates interactive activities in both traditional and technological environments (Ercan & Aydın, 2022; Romero et al., 2019). Additionally, *constructivism*, which forms the foundation for learning outcomes (Wood et al., 1976), positions AI as a facilitator of action-taking during activities. This is complemented by *scaffolding*, a process of organizing tasks and activities according to learners' intellectual readiness (Vygotsky, 1978).

Perception is defined as the organization and interpretation of sensory information to comprehend environmental stimuli (Schacter et al., 2009) and is influenced by the learner's attention, expectations, memory, and learning (Bernstein et al., 2008). Bruner's (1957) model outlines three phases in the perceptual process. Initially, when learners encounter an unfamiliar target, they are open to new information based on perception. If the information is insufficient, the learner seeks additional cues to clarify their understanding. Finally, the learner gathers more cues to confirm the categorization of the target. The Social Cognitive Theory, which posits that cognitive processes and the environment influence human behaviors, suggests that agency is shaped by beliefs, attitudes, and perceptions, which can directly impact behavior (Aydın, 2022; Fishbein & Ajzen, 1975). From a constructive viewpoint, perception is the outcome of the interaction between stimuli and the learner's knowledge and expectations. On the other hand, from a computational perspective, perception operates through simple mechanical rules applicable to unconscious entities rather than through conscious intentionality or motivation (Gregory, 2015). This implies that perception may rely on algorithms designed to mimic human perceptual processes without involving conscious or sentient experiences (Démuth, 2013). The term 'unconscious entities' does not refer to human learners, but rather to computational systems, such as algorithms and machine-learning models, that process data and generate responses without awareness or intentionality. For example, image-recognition algorithms and natural language processing models can detect patterns and respond to stimuli mechanically without conscious processing (LeCun et al., 2015). In educational contexts, such computational perceptions can still facilitate pedagogical procedures by analyzing input, providing corrective feedback, and generating adaptive responses for learners (Zawacki-Richter et al., 2019). This distinction explains how computational perception remains mechanical yet supports learning processes in ways that complement human, constructivist perceptions.

Previous Research

From a general perspective, research shows conflicting results regarding the use of AI in the EFL learning process. To begin with, research indicates that AI has a positive impact on EFL, facilitating both pedagogical and learning procedures (Alhalangy & AbdAlgane, 2023). For instance, AI tools provide opportunities for meaningful conversations and collaborative learning (Tafazoli et al., 2019). Moussalli and Cardoso (2020) found that AI usage was beneficial for comprehension in basic language skills, grammar, and vocabulary learning. Similar positive effects were reported regarding reading comprehension, speaking performance (Yin et al., 2021), and writing quality (Fitria, 2021). In this way, integrating AI applications into EFL teaching practices could support student learning and help improve language skills in the classroom (Hazaymeh et al., 2024). The potential benefits of technology use in language education include providing personalized feedback and support, engaging and motivating learners, and supporting the development of language skills (Baskara, 2023). For instance, Liang et al. (2023) reported that AI utilization enhanced self-confidence and motivation, while also decreasing anxiety. On the other hand, research demonstrated certain negative conclusions. For example, Wang et al. (2022) found that learners had unsatisfactory experiences due to the lack of teachers' input and subject-specific teaching (Alrajhi, 2023). Learners also found the feedback provided by AI tools too technical (Yu et al., 2022). Moreover, AI tools have increased plagiarism in students' assignments, failed to facilitate complicated reasoning (Perkins, 2023), debilitated problem-solving and critical thinking skills in the writing context (Nguyen, 2023), and ultimately produced decontextualized content (Wilson et al., 2021). Rukiati et al. (2023) noted that privacy and the potential reduction of the role of human teachers in the learning process were among the concerns associated with the use of AI in language education.

While the studies mentioned primarily examine AI-based experimental environments, focusing on the use of AI tools for teaching basic language skills and knowledge areas, a notable gap exists in research regarding learners' perceptions of AI-based language learning (An et al., 2023). In a recent study, An et al. (2023) investigated the perceptions of 524 high school students regarding AI-based language learning. Using survey data, they discovered that cultural interest, performance expectancy, and instrumental promotion could predict learners' behavioral intentions to use AI tools. Zou et al. (2020) explored university students' attitudes toward developing speaking skills with AI-assisted mobile applications. They found that students favored AI tools due to the limited feedback provided by teachers. However, this study focused on attitudes and speaking skills rather than overall perceptions of language learning. Amin (2024) found that participants had positive perceptions of using AI applications for learning pronunciation, largely due to their positive pedagogical effects. In another study, Persulessy et al. (2024) examined engineering students' perceptions of AI in vocabulary learning, concluding that learners had positive views on using AI tools. Similarly, Phan (2023) conducted a mixed-method study with 100 learners, finding positive perceptions of AI-powered writing tools regarding their simplicity, adaptability, and accessibility in the EFL writing context. Lee et al. (2024) found that AI-based writing tools could improve English language learners' writing skills, but excessive use could interfere with learners' English writing process. Ibrahim et al. (2023) conducted a global survey comparing the performance of ChatGPT among students in 32 university-level courses across five countries. They found a consensus among learners regarding its use, although it did not specifically address language learning. Likewise, Demir and Güraksın (2022) analyzed middle school students' perceptions of AI through metaphors, finding generally positive views, though not explicitly related to foreign language learning. Additionally, Al-Badi et al. (2022) reported that both university students and teachers held positive perceptions of AI in personalized learning, although they did not specifically focus on foreign language learners. However, Baskara (2023) stated that ChatGPT's ability to generate human-like text based on input was a potentially helpful tool for supporting students in their writing practice. In addition, Darwin et al. (2024) noted that AI could be a valuable asset in developing critical thinking skills.

OVERVIEW OF THE STUDY

As previously stated, EFL learning has paramount significance due to multiple factors. However, while proficiency in the target language brings unique advantages, the EFL learning process is often fraught with several challenges, such as the absence of authentic and contextual materials, limited practice opportunities, and an over-dependence on the first language. From this perspective, AI applications may hold the potential to address the aforementioned challenges encountered in the EFL learning process. However, the benefits are confined to how EFL learners perceive AI in the EFL learning process. In the research context, conflicting results exist regarding the use of AI in the EFL learning process. For instance, while AI usage has a positive impact on EFL in terms of facilitating pedagogical and learning procedures, collaborative learning, comprehension in basic language skills, grammar and vocabulary learning, reading comprehension, speaking performance, and writing quality, while research demonstrates certain negative conclusions such as unsatisfactory experiences, technical problems, plagiarism, uncomplicated reasoning, debilitation of problem-solving and critical thinking skills in the writing context; production of decontextualized content, privacy, and the possibility of reducing the role of teachers. Moreover, the number of studies on EFL learners' perceptions of AI usage appears to be scarce. Specifically, while several studies focus on learners' perceptions of AI usage in speaking, pronunciation, and writing skills, as well as vocabulary learning within an overall language context, other studies concentrate on AI usage in personalized learning, AI use through metaphors, and critical thinking skills, rather than specifically addressing language learning. With these concerns in mind, the current study aims to explore learners' perceptions of AI use in the foreign language learning process and to determine whether their perceptions differ according to specific variables, such as age, gender, grade level, department, and proficiency in the target language. Within this scope, the study seeks answers to the following research questions:

- How do learners perceive the use of AI in the EFL learning process?
- Do their perceptions of using AI differ in accordance with their ages, gender, grades, departments, and proficiency levels in the target language?

METHOD

Research Context

This study employed an analytical approach and a deductive objective, aiming to gain further insight into EFL learners' perceptions of AI tools in language learning. Since the study focused on how learners perceive AI tools and environments in learning, a questionnaire and a scale seemed appropriate to gather data on the variables. The rationale behind preferring a descriptive research design was that collecting data from participants' points of view without any intervention in a natural context was important. Thus, a descriptive research design was the most appropriate to fulfill the aims of the study (Seliger & Shohamy, 1989).

Participants

The study sample group consisted of 897 participants. The mean score for their age was 20.98 (SD = 1.95), within the range of 18 to 29. The group consisted of 612 female students (68.2%) and 285 male students (31.8%). The participants were preparatory (n = 69, 7.7%), first-grade (n = 195, 21.7%), second-grade (n = 195, 21.7%), third-grade (n = 154, 17.2%), and fourth-grade (n = 210, 23.4%) students. They were intermediate (B1) (n = 34, 3.8%), upper-intermediate (B2) (n = 163, 18.2%), and advanced (C1) (n = 700, 78.0%) learners of English, according to the Common European Framework of Reference (CEFR) standards. Of the participants, 728 (81.2%) were students enrolled in the Department of English Language Teaching (ELT), whereas 99 (11.0%) were from the Department of English Language and Literature (ELL). Finally, 70 (7.8) students enrolled in the Department of Translation and Interpretation (TI) (English), as shown in Table 1. The participants were selected among EFL learners enrolled in English-medium departments to ensure relevance to the focus of AI use in language learning. Their diversity in academic level, department, and proficiency allowed a comprehensive examination of how these variables influence learners' perceptions.

Table 1. Descriptives for the participants (n=897)

		Mean	Std. Dev.
Age		**20.98**	**1.95**
		N	%
Gender	Female	612	68.2
	Male	285	31.8
Grade	Preparation	69	7.7
	1	269	30.0
	2	195	21.7
	3	154	17.2
	4	210	23.4
Proficiency	B1	34	3.8
	B2	163	18.2
	C1	700	78.0
Department	ELT	728	81.2
	ELL	99	11.0
	TI	70	7.8

Instrumentation

Two research instruments were adopted in the study. First, a background questionnaire was used to gather information on the participants' ages, genders, grades, departments, and proficiency levels in the target language. Second, the PAS developed by Aydın (2024) was used to measure the participants' perceptions of AI usage in the foreign language learning process. The PAS consisted of 17 items, divided into two constructs: the contributions of AI to language learning and concerns about AI usage. The items were scored on a scale of one to five (1 = strongly disagree, 2 = disagree, 3 = undecided, 4 = agree, and 5 = strongly agree). The reliability of the scale, as measured by Cronbach's alpha, was found to be 0.88, indicating high internal consistency. The validity of the scale was supported by the explained variance of 70%, demonstrating an acceptable level of construct validity.

Procedure

After approval from the ethics committee of a state university, participants were invited to respond to the online version of the research instruments, prepared via Google Forms, through Google Classroom posts and emails. A text was added before the tools to inform participants about the purpose of the study, the voluntariness of their participation, and the confidentiality of their responses. The participants were informed that they were free to withdraw from the research at any time without consequences and that the data collected would be used for scientific purposes, accessed only by the researchers, and kept confidential. The form was kept online for one month.

Analysis

IBM SPSS Version 21 was used to analyze the data collected. The analysis was conducted in three main steps, which consisted of observing reliability and validity, calculating descriptive statistics, and conducting inferential analyses. First, the reliability coefficients and % of variances were also calculated for the scale. The reliability coefficient in Cronbach's alpha was .87 for the scale. Regarding validity, the value for the percentage of variance was 69.54 for the scale. The values for reliability and % of variance, along with the reliability coefficient, indicated acceptable reliability and validity of the scale used in the study. This step indicated that the scale was appropriate for measuring learners' perceptions of AI use in EFL learning, which is the main construct of the study. The construct subsumes concepts such as perceived benefits, perceived limitations, and challenges. Second, descriptive data, including mean scores, frequencies, percentages, and standard deviations, were calculated for each item in the scale, as it was necessary to describe and organize the characteristics of the measured items (Fisher & Marshall, 2009). This analysis provided an overall picture of learners' perceptions and directly addressed the first research question of the study. Third and last, the independent samples t-test and ANOVA were used to see whether the participants' perceptions differed regarding age, age interval, gender, grade, department, and proficiency level in the target language (Sarstedt & Mooi, 2019). These inferential tests were chosen because they enable comparison across demographic groups, which aligns with the second research question. When significant differences were found, post-hoc tests (Tamhane) were used to determine where the differences occurred. This ensured that the analyses were both statistically sound and directly tied to answering research questions asked in the study.

RESULTS

Perceptions of AI Usage

The values in Table 2 indicate that EFL learners' perceptions of AI usage in language learning seem to be conflicting. For example, EFL learners agreed that the integration of AI tools and environments contributed to personalized ($\bar{x}$=3.91), autonomous ($\bar{x}$=3.85), and adaptive learning ($\bar{x}$=3.82). They also believed that AI tools had positively influenced the writing quality of their products ($\bar{x}$=3.85), writing skills ($\bar{x}$=3.83), and reading skills ($\bar{x}$=3.58). On the other hand, EFL learners seemed undecided regarding speaking performance ($\bar{x}$=2.94), listening comprehension ($\bar{x}$=3.07), and pronunciation skills ($\bar{x}$=3.09). Similarly, they were undecided about the positive effects of AI tools and environments on increasing classroom participation ($\bar{x}$ = 2.94), emotional support in language learning ($\bar{x}$ = 2.58), and anxiety levels ($\bar{x}$ = 3.08). They also seemed undecided about AI's effectiveness compared to traditional methods ($\bar{x}$=3.27). Interestingly, EFL learners were unsure whether AI tools enhanced their communicative skills ($\bar{x}$=3.47). Lastly, while EFL learners complained that the use of AI debilitated their problem-solving abilities ($\bar{x}$ = 3.49), they did not seem aware of unnatural language content ($\bar{x}$ = 3.26) and inappropriate language content ($\bar{x}$ = 2.85).

Table 2. Descriptives for learners' perceptions of AI usage (n=897)

Factors	Items		Strongly disagree	Disagree	Undecided	Agree	Strongly agree	Mean	Std. Deviation
Contributions	I believe that AI-supported learning is more effective than traditional methods.	%	9.5	15.6	32.6	23.6	18.7	3.27	1.20
		N	85	140	292	212	168		
	AI tools can enhance my communication skills.	%	5.8	14.4	27.4	31.5	20.8	3.47	1.14
		N	52	129	246	283	187		
	The integration of AI tools into language classes contributes to autonomous learning.	%	2.8	5.5	21.5	44.8	25.4	3.85	.96
		N	25	49	193	402	228		
	The integration of AI tools in language classes contributes to personalized learning.	%	2.5	6.0	18.7	44.1	28.7	3.91	.96
		N	22	54	168	396	257		
	The integration of AI tools in language classes contributes to adaptive learning.	%	2.0	6.0	24.7	42.3	25.0	3.82	.94
		N	18	54	222	379	224		
	AI tools provide emotional support in language learning.	%	23.4	29.2	22.3	15.7	9.4	2.58	1.26
		N	210	262	200	141	84		
	AI tools help to reduce my anxiety level.	%	14.8	17.9	27.8	23.7	15.7	3.08	1.28
		N	133	161	249	213	141		
	I find AI tools helpful in practicing my pronunciation skills.	%	16.4	18.7	22.3	25.1	17.5	3.09	1.34
		N	147	168	200	225	157		
	AI tools enhance my listening comprehension.	%	16.5	17.4	25.0	24.4	16.7	3.07	1.32
		N	148	156	224	219	150		
	I think that AI tools positively impact my reading comprehension.	%	5.0	10.6	27.3	35.9	21.2	3.58	1.09
		N	45	95	235	322	190		
	I find that AI tools enhance my speaking performance.	%	15.4	22.4	28.1	21.2	12.9	2.94	1.25
		N	138	201	252	190	116		
	I believe that AI tools can positively influence my writing skills.	%	4.1	7.8	19.5	38.4	20.2	3.83	1.07
		N	37	70	175	344	271		
	I believe that AI tools positively influence writing quality.	%	3.5	7.1	21.1	38.0	30.3	3.85	1.04
		N	31	64	189	341	272		
	My participation in classroom activities has increased after I started using AI tools.	%	16.1	20.8	30.3	18.7	14.0	2.94	1.26
		N	144	187	272	168	126		
Concerns	I think the use of AI debilitates my problem-solving abilities.	%	5.8	10.9	33.3	28.8	21.2	3.50	1.11
		N	52	98	299	258	190		
	I think that AI tools produce unnatural language content.	%	6.0	20.8	31.3	24.7	17.1	3.26	1.15
		N	54	187	281	222	153		
	AI tools produce inappropriate language content.	%	14.2	28.1	28.3	17.7	11.7	2.85	1.21
		N	127	252	254	159	105		

Age, Gender, Grade, Department, And Proficiency

EFL learners' perceptions of AI utilization regarding pronunciation and listening skills significantly differ in age intervals. According to the values in Tables 3 and 4, participants in the 18-19 interval found AI tools more helpful in practicing pronunciation (p =.00) and enhancing listening comprehension (p =.00) than those in the 22-23 interval.

Table 3. Age and perceptions of AI usage (ANOVA)

Items	Age Intervals	N	Mean	Std. Deviation	F	Sig.
I find AI tools helpful in practicing my pronunciation skills.	18-19	223	3.28	1.33	4.77	.00
	20-21	326	3.10	1.32		
	22-23	284	2.87	1.33		
	24-+	64	3.33	1.37		
AI tools enhance my listening comprehension.	18-19	223	3.27	1.31	5.13	.00
	20-21	326	3.12	1.30		
	22-23	284	2.84	1.30		
	24-+	64	3.20	1.42		

Table 4. Multiple comparisons for age and perceptions of AI usage (Tamhane)

Dependent Variable	(I) Intervals for Age	(J) Intervals for Age	Mean Difference (I-J)	Std. Error	Sig.
I find AI tools helpful in practicing my pronunciation skills.	18-19	22-23	.41*	.12	.00
AI tools enhance my listening comprehension.	18-19	22-23	.44*	.12	.00
	20-21	22-23	.28*	.11	.05

*. The mean difference is significant at the 0.05 level.

Only one item significantly differs regarding their perceptions of AI usage and grade. According to the values in Tables 5 and 6, first-grade students had stronger beliefs that AI-supported learning was more effective than the traditional methods in classroom settings than fourth-grade students did (p=.00). It should also be noted that the level of perceptions of AI usage as an alternative to traditional methods gradually decreased from higher to lower grades.

Table 5. Grade and perceptions of AI usage (ANOVA)

Items	Grade	N	Mean	Std. Deviation	F	Sig.
I believe that AI-supported learning is more effective than traditional methods.	Preparation	69	3.30	1.13	2.59	.04
	1	269	3.38	1.29		
	2	195	3.32	1.14		
	3	154	3.30	1.18		
	4	210	3.04	1.17		

Table 6. Multiple comparisons for grade and perceptions of AI usage (Tamhane)

Dependent Variable	(I) Intervals for Grade	(J) Intervals for Grade	Mean Difference (I-J)	Std. Error	Sig.
I believe that AI-supported learning is more effective than traditional methods.	1	4	.34*	.11	.03

*. The mean difference is significant at the 0.05 level.

The values presented in Tables 7 and 8 indicate that participants in the departments of English Language Teaching and English Language and Literature have more positive perceptions of AI usage regarding autonomous ($p = .04$) and adaptive learning ($p = .02$) compared to those in the department of Translation and Interpretation. Within this scope, those who studied English Language and Literature stated that the integration of AI tools in language classes contributed more to autonomous learning than those who enrolled in the Department of Translation and Interpretation. Similarly, the students in the Department of English Language Teaching believed that integrating AI tools in language classes contributed more to adaptive learning than the students in the Department of Translation and Interpretation.

Table 7. Departments and perceptions of AI usage (ANOVA)

Items	Departments	N	Mean	Std. Deviation	F	Sig.
The integration of AI tools into language classes contributes to autonomous learning.	English Language Teaching	728	3.28	1.20	3.23	.04
	English Language and Literature	99	3.25	1.15		
	Translation and Interpretation	70	3.13	1.30		
The integration of AI tools in language classes contributes to adaptive learning.	English Language Teaching	728	3.86	.96	4.12	.02
	English Language and Literature	99	3.95	.87		
	Translation and Interpretation	70	3.59	1.06		

Table 8. Multiple comparisons for departments and perceptions of AI usage (Tamhane)

Dependent Variable	(I) Department	(J) Department	Mean Difference (I-J)	Std. Error	Sig.
The integration of AI tools into language classes contributes to autonomous learning.	English Language and Literature	Translation and Interpretation	.36*	.15	.05
The integration of AI tools in language classes contributes to adaptive learning.	English Language Teaching	Translation and Interpretation	.34*	.13	.03

*. The mean difference is significant at the 0.05 level.

The proficiency levels of the participants in the target language seem significantly related to their perceptions of AI usage regarding enhancing communicative skills (p=.02) and inappropriateness of language content produced by AI tools (p=.01). According to the values in Tables 9 and 10, the students who were at B2 and C1 levels believed that AI tools could enhance more communicative skills than the ones who were at the level of B1. Similarly, those at the C1 level had a higher level of awareness of inappropriate language content than those at the B2 level.

Table 9. Proficiency levels in the target language and perceptions of AI usage (ANOVA)

Items	Proficiency	N	Mean	Std. Deviation	F	Sig.
AI tools can enhance my communicative skills.	B1	34	2.94	.98	3.98	.02
	B2	163	3.45	1.17		
	C1	700	3.50	1.14		
AI tools produce inappropriate language content.	B1	34	3.00	1.10	4.61	.01
	B2	163	3.09	1.19		
	C1	700	2.78	1.22		

Table 10. Multiple comparisons for proficiency levels and perceptions of AI usage (Tamhane)

Dependent Variable	(I) Proficiency	(J) Proficiency	Mean Difference (I-J)	Std. Error	Sig.
AI tools can enhance my communication skills.	B1	B2	-.51*	.19	.03
		C1	-.56*	.17	.01
AI tools produce inappropriate language content.	C1	B2	-.31*	.10	.01

* The mean difference is significant at the 0.05 level.

In summary, the findings revealed that learners' perceptions of AI usage varied significantly across age intervals, grades, departments, and proficiency levels, as illustrated in Figure 1. The differences regarding their perceptions were confined to inappropriate content, communicative skills, adaptive and autonomous learning, the effectiveness of AI use, and listening and pronunciation skills. On the other hand, gender does not appear to be a significant variable in learners' perceptions of AI usage in the language learning process.

Figure 1. Multiple analyses of the factors

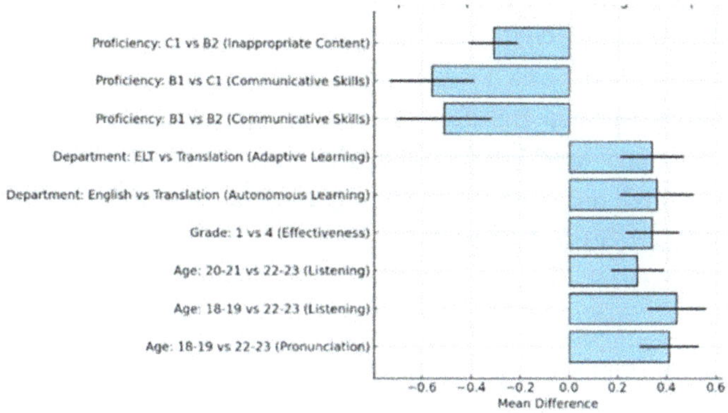

CONCLUSIONS AND DISCUSSION

The findings of this study, which aim to explore learners' perceptions of AI use in the foreign language learning process and to determine whether their perceptions differ in accordance with certain variables, such as age, gender, grade, department, and proficiency in the target language, reveal two main conclusions. The first conclusion is that while EFL learners perceive that the integration of AI tools and environments contributes to personalized, autonomous, adaptive learning, writing, and reading skills, they seem doubtful about AI's effect on speaking performance, listening comprehension, pronunciation skills, their communicative skills, classroom participation, emotional support, anxiety levels, and traditional methods used in classroom settings. In addition, while EFL learners are aware that AI usage can hinder their problem-solving abilities, they seem undecided about the inappropriate language content that AI tools produce. The second conclusion is that while learners' perceptions of AI usage do not show any difference regarding gender, they appear to be related to learners' ages, grades, departments, and proficiency levels in the target language. For instance, younger learners prefer AI to help develop their pronunciation and listening skills, whereas lower-grade students have a more positive perception of AI as an alternative to traditional language learning methods. In addition, students who study literature and language teaching are more aware that integrating AI into language classes contributes to autonomous and adaptive learning than students of translation and interpretation. Finally, proficient learners are more aware of the impact of AI on communication skills and the inappropriate language content it generates.

Pedagogical Implications

The comparison between the conclusions of this study and those reached in previous research is provided below. First, the study confirms the positive impact of AI tools on personalized, autonomous, and adaptive learning, particularly in the areas of writing and reading skills. It also aligns with findings that AI supports pedagogical and learning procedures, engaging and motivating learners (Alhalangy & AbdAlgane, 2023; Baskara, 2023; Hazaymeh et al., 2024). However, this study finds that EFL learners express doubts about AI's effectiveness in enhancing speaking performance, listening comprehension, pronunciation skills, communicative abilities, classroom participation, emotional support, anxiety levels, and traditional classroom methods, while previous studies report positive effects of AI on speaking performance and pronunciation (Amin, 2024; Yin et al., 2021; Zou et al., 2020). This discrepancy suggests that while AI tools are recognized for their potential benefits, learners may still harbor reservations about their effectiveness in certain skill areas, particularly those requiring nuanced human interaction and feedback. Second, the current study highlights learners' awareness of the potential negative impacts of AI, such as the debilitation of problem-solving abilities and indecision about inappropriate language content produced by AI tools. This finding is consistent with research that reports negative aspects of AI usage, including the weakening of problem-solving and critical thinking skills (Nguyen, 2023), the production of decontextualized content (Wilson et al., 2021), and concerns about technical feedback and plagiarism (Perkins, 2023; Yu et al., 2022). Third, in terms of demographic influences, the study finds that learners' perceptions of AI usage vary by age, grade, department, and proficiency levels, though not by gender. This finding is supported by An et al. (2023), who note that cultural interest, performance expectancy, and instrumental promotion predict learners' behavioral intentions to use AI tools. Nevertheless, prior studies do not extensively address demographic differences in perceptions of AI.

The results of the current study seem significant for several reasons. While previous research has mainly focused on the overall efficacy of AI tools in enhancing specific language skills such as reading, writing, and pronunciation (Amin, 2024; Fitria, 2021; Yin et al., 2021), this study deals with the nuanced perceptions of EFL learners regarding AI integration across a broader point of view. Unlike the studies that predominantly highlight positive outcomes (Hazaymeh et al., 2024; Moussalli & Cardoso, 2020), this study addresses the learners' reservations about the impact of AI on speaking performance, listening comprehension, communicative skills, classroom participation, and emotional support. This comprehensive approach reveals a more balanced perspective, acknowledging both the advantages and potential drawbacks. Moreover, this research uniquely explores demographic variables, including age, grade, department, and proficiency levels, offering insights into how these factors influence learners' perceptions of AI usage. This finding regarding demographic analysis is not extensively covered in prior studies and often overlooks the diversity of learner experiences and preferences (An et al., 2023). Additionally, the current research highlights learners' awareness of the limitations of AI usage, particularly its potential to weaken problem-solving abilities and produce inappropriate language content. These concerns are crucial for developing more effective AI tools and ensuring they are used responsibly within language learning settings.

Practical Recommendations

In light of the findings, some practical recommendations can be noted. First, it is essential to raise EFL learners' awareness of the nature of AI technologies, including both their potential contributions and possible limitations within language learning contexts. Within this scope, learners should be instructed on how to use AI to facilitate personalized, autonomous, and adaptive learning experiences, while also being informed about the challenges associated with overreliance on AI, such as weakened problem-solving skills or exposure to inappropriate language content. In this regard, structured training sessions can be designed to enhance learners' skills in effectively utilizing AI tools to support the development of fundamental language skills, including reading, writing, listening, and speaking, as well as linguistic knowledge areas such as grammar, vocabulary, and pronunciation. As part of this process, practical classroom applications can include the use of AI-based writing assistants to support drafting and revision skills, speech recognition tools to aid pronunciation practice, and adaptive reading platforms to personalize vocabulary and comprehension exercises. Comparisons of such tools can also be introduced to help learners critically evaluate their strengths and limitations. Furthermore, learners should be equipped with the necessary competencies to use AI to foster autonomous learning habits, engage in adaptive learning paths, and enhance critical thinking and evaluative skills, especially in verifying AI-generated content.

Second, considering that teachers' perspectives are central to the successful integration of AI in EFL classrooms, and they determine not only how technologies are adopted but also how learners experience them, they should play a pivotal role in balancing the benefits of AI with the irreplaceable value of human interaction, emotional support, and context-sensitive instruction. To achieve this, EFL teachers should have structured opportunities for professional development that address both technical and pedagogical competencies, as well as the ethical implications of AI use. Examples may include case studies in which teachers experiment with AI-supported feedback tools, compare them with traditional approaches, and reflect on their effectiveness in promoting learner engagement and achievement.

Third, continuous professional development opportunities should be made available for EFL teachers to ensure they are prepared to integrate AI technologies into their instructional practices in pedagogically sound and ethical ways. Teacher education programs, both pre-service and in-service, should include modules focused on the pedagogical, technical, and ethical aspects of AI use in EFL teaching. Teachers should also be encouraged to adopt a balanced instructional approach, in which AI is used to supplement rather than replace human interaction. This approach should emphasize the importance of maintaining emotional support for learners, providing content that is both meaningful and contextually relevant, and offering personalized and constructive feedback. Such balanced integration can mitigate the limitations of AI while maximizing its educational value. Fourth, the successful implementation of these strategies requires institutional and systemic support. Pre-service teacher education curricula and in-service training frameworks should be revised to explicitly address the integration of AI in language education, encompassing both theoretical knowledge and practical applications. These programs should also include case studies, practical workshops, and reflective practices to help educators critically engage with AI technologies. Additionally, showcasing institutional case studies where AI integration has been successfully implemented can provide models for best practices, offering policymakers and administrators concrete guidance for future planning. Finally, educational policymakers play a pivotal role in guiding the ethical and equitable implementation of AI in language learning environments. Policymakers should strive to develop comprehensive policies that promote the integration of AI tools alongside traditional methods, ensuring this integration enhances rather than disrupts pedagogical coherence. This includes setting clear standards and guidelines for the use of AI in language classrooms, ensuring data privacy and ethical use, and establishing monitoring mechanisms for AI-generated content. Moreover, ensuring equal access to AI tools and infrastructure across various educational settings is crucial to preventing digital inequality and promoting inclusive education. In addition to these pedagogical aspects, it is equally important to consider the ethical and equity dimensions of AI integration, which are critical for ensuring its responsible and sustainable use in EFL contexts, as clarified below.

Ethical and Equity Considerations

The ethical and equity dimensions of AI integration in the EFL teaching and learning contexts also require explicit attention. The first A is *data privacy*, as learners' personal information and usage patterns may be collected and processed by AI systems. Thus, institutions should adopt transparent policies and adhere to strict privacy regulations to ensure responsible data management (Aydın, 2025). The second critical issue involves *academic integrity*. With the growing sophistication of AI tools, learners may be tempted to rely on them in ways that undermine originality, authenticity, and fair assessment practices. Thus, there is a strong necessity for clear guidelines, awareness-raising initiatives, and teacher support, which are essential to promote responsible use and safeguard integrity (Aydın & Zeinolabedini, 2024; Sayici & Aydın, 2025). Last, equity of access is a pressing challenge. While technologically advanced schools and learners can benefit from AI-supported platforms, those in under-resourced contexts may face barriers due to limited digital infrastructure or socioeconomic constraints (Hammerschmidt et al., 2025). In conclusion, policymakers and institutions should prioritize inclusive strategies that ensure equal access to AI technologies across various educational settings, as guaranteeing equitable opportunities for all learners is fundamental to the fair and sustainable integration of AI in language education.

FUTURE TRENDS

The integration of AI into EFL learning is expected to evolve in several promising directions. To begin with, advances in generative AI and natural language processing will likely produce more sophisticated systems capable of providing context-sensitive feedback, nuanced conversational practice, and adaptive support across diverse learner profiles (Yildiz Durak & Onan, 2025). Moreover, personalized learning will become increasingly refined through real-time data analysis, enabling learners to receive tailored instruction that adapts dynamically to their progress, preferences, and challenges (Mahmoud & Sørensen, 2024). At the same time, multimodal AI tools that integrate text, speech, and visual recognition are anticipated to enhance language learning by creating more immersive and interactive experiences (Alcivar et al., 2024). Furthermore, affective computing may allow AI systems to recognize and respond to learners' emotional states, potentially offering motivational support and reducing foreign language anxiety (Vistorte et al., 2024). Finally, as ethical awareness and digital equity gain greater attention, future trends will emphasize responsible innovation by embedding privacy safeguards, academic integrity standards, and equal access measures into AI-supported language education (Compagnoni et al., 2025). The above-mentioned issues collectively suggest that AI will not simply supplement language teaching but will gradually reshape EFL learning environments toward more personalized, interactive, and inclusive experiences.

Limitations and Recommendations for Further Research

The study is not without limitations. The study sample group was limited to 897 EFL learners enrolled in undergraduate programs. The data collected was confined to a background questionnaire and the PAS developed by Aydın (2024). The data collected were limited to a descriptive research design. Thus, the data analysis was confined to descriptive statistics, independent samples t-tests, ANOVA, and Tamhane's T2 test. Finally, it should be noted that the data included in the current study were limited to EFL learners' overall perceptions of AI usage in EFL learning, but not their actual use of AI.

Further research on EFL learners' perceptions of AI usage in EFL learning is warranted. For this purpose, longitudinal, qualitative, and experimental studies should be conducted to gain a deeper understanding of learners' perceptions. In addition to certain variables such as age, gender, grade, department, and proficiency levels, cultural, social, emotional, psychological, and individual factors should be investigated in various research settings and contexts. Research should also focus on learners' awareness of content accuracy and appropriateness.

REFERENCES

Al-Badi, A., Khan, A., & Eid-Alotaibi, . (2022). Perceptions of learners and instructors towards artificial intelligence in personalized learning. *Procedia Computer Science, 201*, 445–451. DOI: 10.1016/j.procs.2022.03.058

Alcivar, D., Macias, M., & Vera, A. (2024). *Integration of artificial intelligence in English teaching*. CID - Centro de Investigación y Desarrollo., DOI: 10.37811/cli_w1046

Alhalangy, A., & AbdAlgane, M. (2023). Exploring the impact of AI on the EFL context: A case study of Saudi universities. *Journal of Intercultural Communication*, 41–49. DOI: 10.36923/jicc.v23i2.125

Alrajhi, A. S. (2023). Genre effect on Google Translate–assisted L2 writing output quality. *ReCALL, 35*(3), 305–320. DOI: 10.1017/S0958344022000143

Altınay, G., & Aydın, S. (2025). Automated feedback effect on foreign language writing motivation and anxiety. In *AI's Role in Language Learning and Communication* (pp. 27–64). IGI Global Publishing., DOI: 10.4018/979-8-3373-5681-5.ch002

Amin, E. (2024). EFL students' perception of using AI text-to-speech apps in learning pronunciation. SSRN *Electronic Journal, 21*(3), 887–903. DOI: 10.2139/ssrn.4746800

An, X., Chai, C., Li, Y., Zhou, Y., & Yang, B. (2023). Modeling students' perceptions of artificial intelligence assisted language learning. *Computer Assisted Language Learning*, •••, 1–22. DOI: 10.1080/09588221.2023.2246519

Anderson, T., & Elloumi, F. (2004). *Theory and practice of online learning*. Athabasca University.

Aydın, S. (2020). Affective states and learning outcomes in EFL education. In Celik, S. (Ed.), *Preparing teachers for a changing world: Contemporary issues in EFL education* (pp. 153–164). Vizetek.

Aydın, S. (2022). The Metaverse in foreign language learning: A theoretical framework. *Innovational Research in ELT, 3*(2), 12–19. DOI: 10.29329/irelt.2022.505.2

Aydın, S. (2023). Teachers' perceptions of the use of the Metaverse in foreign language teaching and learning. In G. Durak & S. ÇAnkaya (Eds.), *Shaping the Future of Online Learning: Education in the Metaverse* (pp. 201–219). DOI: 10.4018/978-1-6684-6513-4.ch011

Aydın, S. (2024). Construction and validation of the Perceptions of AI Usage Scale in a foreign language learning context. *Unpublished Research Paper.*

Aydın, S. (2025). Using AI in foreign language teaching. *Paper Presented at GLO-TECH 2025: Redefining Language Learning and Translation in the Digital Age.*

Aydın, S., & Altınay, G. (2026). Artificial intelligence in education: An evaluation of four decades. In Bozkurt, A. (Ed.), *Rethinking Education and Agency in the Age of Human-Generative AI Interaction* (pp. 19–94). IGI Global Scientific Publishing., DOI: 10.4018/979-8-3373-1195-1.ch002

Aydın, S., & Tekin, I. (2023). Positive psychology and language learning: A systematic scoping review. *Review of Education, 11*(3), 1–27. DOI: 10.1002/rev3.3420

Aydın, S., & Zeinolabedini, M. (2024). Integrating artificial intelligence into foreign language learning: Learners' perspectives. *11th EJER Congress.*

Ballıdağ, M., & Aydın, S. (2025). *A comparison of the effects of AI-based chatbots and peer interactions on speaking anxiety among EFL learners.* Future in Educational Research., DOI: 10.1002/fer3.70005

Baskara, F. R. (2023). Integrating ChatGPT into EFL writing instruction: Benefits and challenges. *International Journal on E-Learning, 5*(1), 44–55. DOI: 10.31763/ijele.v5i1.858

Berk, E. H., & Aydın, S. (2025). The impact of artificial intelligence-powered writing assistance systems on metacognitive writing strategies. In *Transformations in Digital Learning and Educational Technologies* (pp. 241–274). IGI Global., DOI: 10.4018/979-8-3373-3678-7.ch011

Bernstein, D., Nash, P., Clarke-Stewart, A., Penner, L., & Roy, E. (2008). *Essentials of psychology* (4th ed.). Houghton Mifflin Company.

Bertelsen, O., & Bødker, S. (2003). Activity Theory. In Carroll, C. (Ed.), *HCI models, theories, and frameworks: Toward a multidisciplinary science* (pp. 291–324). Elsevier., DOI: 10.1016/B978-155860808-5/50011-3

Bruner, J. (1957). On perceptual readiness. *Psychological Review, 64*(2), 123–152. DOI: 10.1037/h0043805 PMID: 13420288

Bryant, S., Forte, A., & Bruckman, A. (2005). Becoming Wikipedian. *Proceedings of the 2005 International ACM SIGGROUP Conference on Supporting Group Work - GROUP '05*, 1–10. DOI: 10.1145/1099203.1099205

Byram, M. (2012). Language awareness and (critical) cultural awareness – relationships, comparisons and contrasts. *Language Awareness*, *21*(1–2), 5–13. DOI: 10.1080/09658416.2011.639887

Compagnoni, I., Oguilve, V., & Wen, W. (2025). Ethical frontiers of AI in language pedagogy: Navigating transparency, accountability, and equity. *International Journal of Linguistics*, *17*(4), 1–25. DOI: 10.5296/ijl.v17i4.22768

Dang, H. (2006). Learner-centeredness and EFL instruction in Vietnam: A case study. *International Education Journal*, *7*(4), 598–610.

Darwin, R., Rusdin, D., Mukminatien, N., Suryati, N., Laksmi, E. D., & Marzuki, . (2024). Critical thinking in the AI era: An exploration of EFL students' perceptions, benefits, and limitations. *Cogent Education*, *11*(1), 1–18. DOI: 10.1080/2331186X.2023.2290342

Demir, K., & Güraksın, G. (2022). Determining middle school students' perceptions of the concept of artificial intelligence: A metaphor analysis. *Participatory Educational Research*, *9*(2), 297–312. DOI: 10.17275/per.22.41.9.2

Démuth, A. (2013). *Perception theories*. Trnava University.

Ellis, R. (2009). Corrective feedback and teacher development. *Journal of Linguistics and Language Teaching*, *1*(1), 3–18. DOI: 10.5070/L2.V1I1.9054

Ercan, G. E., & Aydın, S. (2022). Flipped learning in the English as a foreign language learning context: A theoretical framework. In *The new normal of online language education* (pp. 161–180). Eğiten.

Fishbein, M., & Ajzen, I. (1975). *Belief, attitude, intention, and behavior: An introduction to theory and research*. Addison-Wesley Publishing Company.

Fisher, M., & Marshall, A. (2009). Understanding descriptive statistics. *Australian Critical Care*, *22*(2), 93–97. DOI: 10.1016/j.aucc.2008.11.003 PMID: 19150245

Fitria, T. (2021). Grammarly as AI-powered English writing assistant: Students' alternative for writing English. *Metathesis: Journal of English Language, Literature, and Teaching*, *5*(1), 65–78. DOI: 10.31002/metathesis.v5i1.3519

Gregory, R. (2015). *Eye and brain: The psychology of seeing*. Princeton University Press. DOI: 10.2307/j.ctvc77h66

Hammerschmidt, T., Stolz, K., & Posegga, O. (2025). Bridging the gap: Inequalities that divide those who can and cannot create sustainable outcomes with AI. *Behaviour & Information Technology*, •••, 1–30. DOI: 10.1080/0144929X.2025.2500451

Harmer, J. (2003). Popular culture, methods, and context. *ELT Journal*, *57*(3), 288–294. DOI: 10.1093/elt/57.3.288

Hazaymeh, W., Bouzenoun, A., & Remache, A. (2024). EFL instructors' perspective on using AI applications in English as a foreign language teaching and learning. *Emerging Science Journal*, *8*, 73–87. DOI: 10.28991/ESJ-2024-SIED1-05

Hockly, N. (2018). Blended learning. *ELT Journal*, *72*(1), 97–101. DOI: 10.1093/elt/ccx058

Hoşer, S., & Aydın, S. (2026). The impact of AI-enhanced gamification on vocabulary learning in a foreign language context. In *AI-Powered Solutions for Bilingual Proficiency and Communication* (pp. 249–278). IGI Global Scientific Publishing., DOI: 10.4018/979-8-3373-0275-1.ch008

Ibrahim, H., Liu, F., Asim, R., Battu, B., Benabderrahmane, S., Alhafni, B., Adnan, W., Alhanai, T., AlShebli, B., Baghdadi, R., Bélanger, J., Beretta, E., Celik, K., Chaqfeh, M., Daqaq, M., Bernoussi, Z., Fougnie, D., Garcia de Soto, B., Gandolfi, A., & Zaki, Y. (2023). Perception, performance, and detectability of conversational artificial intelligence across 32 university courses. *Scientific Reports*, *13*(1), 1–13. DOI: 10.1038/s41598-023-38964-3 PMID: 36593249

Kanero, J., Geçkin, V., Oranç, C., Mamus, E., Küntay, A., & Göksun, T. (2018). Social robots for early language learning: Current evidence and future directions. *Child Development Perspectives*, *12*(3), 146–151. DOI: 10.1111/cdep.12277

Kannan, J., & Munday, P. (2018). New trends in second language learning and teaching through the lens of ICT, networked learning, and artificial intelligence. *Círculo de Lingüística Aplicada a la Comunicación*, *76*, 13–30. DOI: 10.5209/CLAC.62495

Kennedy, T. (2006). Language learning and its impact on the brain: Connecting language learning with the mind through content-based instruction. *Foreign Language Annals*, *39*(3), 471–486. DOI: 10.1111/j.1944-9720.2006.tb02900.x

Könez, S., & Aydin, S. (2026). Empowering learner autonomy for developing writing skills through AI-enhanced reflective journals. In *Harnessing AI's Potential to Support Student Success and Teaching Excellence* (pp. 217–244). DOI: 10.4018/979-8-3373-1122-7.ch008

Korteling, J., van de Boer-Visschedijk, G., Blankendaal, R., Boonekamp, R., & Eikelboom, A. (2021). Human- versus artificial intelligence. *Frontiers in Artificial Intelligence*, *4*, 622364. Advance online publication. DOI: 10.3389/frai.2021.622364 PMID: 33981990

Krashen, S. D. (1982). *Principles and practice in second language acquisition*. Pergamon Press.

LeCun, Y., Bengio, Y., & Hinton, G. (2015). Deep learning. *Nature*, *521*(7553), 436–444. DOI: 10.1038/nature14539 PMID: 26017442

Lee, Y., Davis, R., & Lee, S. (2024). University students' perceptions of artificial intelligence-based tools for English writing courses. *Online Journal of Communication and Media Technologies*, *14*(1), e202412. Advance online publication. DOI: 10.30935/ojcmt/14195

Liang, J., Hwang, G., Chen, M., & Darmawansah, D. (2023). Roles and research foci of artificial intelligence in language education: An integrated bibliographic analysis and systematic review approach. *Interactive Learning Environments*, *31*(7), 4270–4296. DOI: 10.1080/10494820.2021.1958348

Liang, W., & Fung, D. (2021). Fostering critical thinking in English-as-a-second-language classrooms: Challenges and opportunities. *Thinking Skills and Creativity*, *39*, 1–12. DOI: 10.1016/j.tsc.2020.100769

Mahmoud, C., & Sørensen, J. (2024). Artificial intelligence in personalized learning with a focus on current developments and future prospects. *Research and Advances in Education*, *3*(8), 25–31. DOI: 10.56397/RAE.2024.08.04

Meyers, M. (1993). *Teaching to diversity: Teaching and learning in the multi-ethnic classroom*. Addison-Wesley Publishing Company.

Moussalli, S., & Cardoso, W. (2020). Intelligent personal assistants: Can they understand and be understood by accented L2 learners? *Computer Assisted Language Learning*, *33*(8), 865–890. DOI: 10.1080/09588221.2019.1595664

Nguyen, T. (2023). EFL teachers' perspectives toward the use of ChatGPT in writing classes: A case study at Van Lang University. *International Journal of Language Instruction*, *2*(3), 1–47. DOI: 10.54855/ijli.23231

Perkins, M. (2023). Academic integrity considerations of AI Large Language Models in the post-pandemic era: ChatGPT and beyond. *Journal of University Teaching & Learning Practice*, *20*(2). Advance online publication. DOI: 10.53761/1.20.02.07

Persulessy, S., Nikijuluw, R., & Jakob, J. C. (2024). Utilizing artificial intelligence in language learning: What about engineering students' perception? *Journal of English Education Program*, *5*(1), 48–58. DOI: 10.26418/jeep.v5i1.71159

Phan, T. (2023). Students' perceptions of the AI technology application in English writing classes. *Proceedings of the AsiaCALL International Conference, 4*, 45–62. DOI: 10.54855/paic.2344

Ponton, M., & Rhea, N. (2006). Autonomous Learning from a Social Cognitive Perspective. *New Horizons in Adult Education and Human Resource Development, 20*(2), 38–49. DOI: 10.1002/nha3.10250

Romero, M., Buzón-García, O., & Touron, J. (2019). The flipped learning model in online based education for secondary teachers. *Journal of Technology and Science Education, 9*(2), 109. DOI: 10.3926/jotse.435

Rukiati, E., Wicaksono, J., Taufan, G., & Suharsono, D. (2023). AI on learning English: Application, benefit, and threat. *Journal of Language, Communication, and Tourism, 1*(2), 32–40. DOI: 10.25047/jlct.v1i2.3967

Rumsey, C. (2024). *Why it's important to learn English*. Studio Cambridge. https://www.studiocambridge.co.uk/why-it-is-important-to-learn-english/

Sarker, I. (2022). AI-based modeling: Techniques, applications and research issues towards automation, intelligent and smart systems. *SN Computer Science, 3*(2), 1–20. DOI: 10.1007/s42979-022-01043-x PMID: 35194580

Sarstedt, M., & Mooi, E. (2019). *Regression Analysis*. Springer., DOI: 10.1007/978-3-662-56707-4_7

Savran Çelik, Ş., & Aydın, S. (2018). A review of research on the use of native language in EFL classes. *The Literacy Trek, 4*(2), 1–14.

Sayici, S., & Aydın, S. (2025). Using artificial intelligence in foreign language teaching: Teachers' perspectives. *Proceedings of The World Conference on Education and Teaching, 4*(1), 1–10. DOI: 10.33422/etconf.v4i1.1016

Schacter, D., Gilbert, D., & Wegner, D. (2009). *Introducing psychology*. Macmillan.

Seliger, H. W., & Shohamy, E. (1989). *Second language research methods*. Oxford University Press.

Shadiev, R., Wu, T., Sun, A., & Huang, Y. (2018). Applications of speech-to-text recognition and computer-aided translation for facilitating cross-cultural learning through a learning activity: Issues and their solutions. *Educational Technology Research and Development, 66*(1), 191–214. DOI: 10.1007/s11423-017-9556-8

Statista. (2024). *Languages most frequently used for web content as of January 2024, by share of websites*. https://www.statista.com/statistics/262946/most-common-languages-on-the-internet/

Tafazoli, D., María, E., & Abril, C. (2019). Intelligent language tutoring system. *International Journal of Information and Communication Technology Education*, *15*(3), 60–74. DOI: 10.4018/IJICTE.2019070105

Verga, L., & Kotz, S. (2013). How relevant is social interaction in second language learning? *Frontiers in Human Neuroscience*, *7*, 1–7. DOI: 10.3389/fnhum.2013.00550 PMID: 24027521

Vistorte, A., Deroncele-Acosta, A., Ayala, J., Barrasa, A., López-Granero, C., & Martí-González, M. (2024). Integrating artificial intelligence to assess emotions in learning environments: A systematic literature review. *Frontiers in Psychology*, *15*, 1387089. Advance online publication. DOI: 10.3389/fpsyg.2024.1387089 PMID: 38966729

Vygotsky, L. (1978). Interaction between learning and development. In Cole, M., Steiner, V. J., Scribner, S., & Souberman, E. (Eds.), *Mind in society* (pp. 79–91). Harvard University Press.

Wilson, J., Ahrendt, C., Fudge, E., Raiche, A., Beard, G., & MacArthur, C. (2021). Elementary teachers' perceptions of automated feedback and automated scoring: Transforming the teaching and learning of writing using automated writing evaluation. *Computers & Education*, *168*, 104208. DOI: 10.1016/j.compedu.2021.104208

Wood, D., Bruner, J., & Ross, G. (1976). The role of tutoring in problem solving. *Journal of Child Psychology and Psychiatry, and Allied Disciplines*, *17*(2), 89–100. DOI: 10.1111/j.1469-7610.1976.tb00381.x PMID: 932126

Woolf, B., Lane, H., Chaudhri, V., & Kolodner, J. (2013). AI grand challenges for education. *AI Magazine*, *34*(4), 66–84. DOI: 10.1609/aimag.v34i4.2490

Yildiz Durak, H., & Onan, A. (2025). A systematic review of AI-based feedback in educational settings. *Journal of Computational Social Science*, *8*(96), 1–40. DOI: 10.1007/s42001-025-00428-1

Yılmaz, Ö. K., & Aydın, S. (2025). The impact of the use of artificial intelligence-generated materials on reading motivation among EFL learners. *Reading Research Quarterly*, *60*(3), e70016. DOI: 10.1002/rrq.70016

Yin, J., Goh, T., Yang, B., & Xiaobin, Y. (2021). Conversation technology with micro-learning: The impact of chatbot-based learning on students' learning motivation and performance. *Journal of Educational Computing Research*, *59*(1), 154–177. DOI: 10.1177/0735633120952067

Yu, D., Zhou, Y., Li, Y., Shen, X., Tian, M., Yang, B., Su, J., & Sun, Y. (2022). A survey of English learning softwares based on TPACK framework. *The 17th Academic Annual Conference of the Information Technology Education Professional Committee of China Educational Technology Association*, 1–9.

Zawacki-Richter, O., Marín, V., Bond, M., & Gouverneur, F. (2019). Systematic review of research on artificial intelligence applications in higher education – where are the educators? *International Journal of Educational Technology in Higher Education, 16*(1), 1–27. DOI: 10.1186/s41239-019-0171-0

Zou, B., Liviero, S., Hao, M., & Wei, C. (2020). Artificial intelligence technology for EAP speaking skills: Student perceptions of opportunities and challenges. In N. Freiermuth, M., Zarrinabadi (Ed.), *Technology and the Psychology of Second Language Learners and Users. New Language Learning and Teaching Environments* (pp. 433–463). Palgrave Macmillan. DOI: 10.1007/978-3-030-34212-8_17

KEY TERMS AND DEFINITIONS

Adaptive learning: It is an instructional approach that utilizes AI algorithms to tailor content, difficulty, and feedback to learners' individual needs, abilities, and performance levels. It ensures that each learner receives customized support aligned with their progress and proficiency.

Artificial intelligence: Artificial intelligence refers to computer systems that perform tasks requiring human-like intelligence, such as understanding language, analyzing data, and providing feedback. In the context of EFL learning, AI supports activities such as pronunciation correction, writing assistance, and adaptive feedback, making the learning process more interactive, individualized, and data-driven.

Autonomous learning: Autonomous learning is a process in which learners take control of their own learning by setting goals, selecting effective strategies, and evaluating their own progress. AI technologies facilitate autonomy by providing feedback, tracking performance, and allowing learners to make independent decisions about their learning paths.

Communicative skills: Communicative skills refer to learners' ability to use language appropriately and effectively in real-life communication, including speaking, listening, reading, and writing. AI tools enhance these skills by offering interactive dialogues, pronunciation evaluation, and contextualized language practice.

English as a foreign language learning: It is the process of learning English in contexts where it is not the native language of the learner. It often relies on formal education and digital technologies, including AI-based tools, to develop learners' linguistic competence, communicative ability, and intercultural awareness.

Language proficiency: denotes a learner's overall competence and fluency in using the target language accurately and effectively. It includes mastery of grammar, vocabulary, pronunciation, and discourse, and it is commonly evaluated through frameworks such as the Common European Framework of Reference for Languages.

Perception: It refers to learners' interpretations, beliefs, and attitudes toward the usefulness, effectiveness, and limitations of AI in language learning. These perceptions influence how learners engage with AI tools and shape their motivation, confidence, and acceptance of technology in educational settings.

Personalized learning: Personalized learning is a learner-centered approach that tailors the educational experience to each individual's goals, preferences, and learning styles. Through data analysis and continuous monitoring, AI personalizes materials, recommendations, and assessments to enhance engagement and achievement.

Chapter 4
Students' Perceptions of Using ChatGPT for Corrective Written Feedback in the Spanish Classroom

Pete Swanson
https://orcid.org/0000-0001-5543-2845
United States Air Force Academy, USA

Michael Ryan Richey
United States Air Force Academy, USA

ABSTRACT

Teaching and learning a second language have changed considerably over the past several decades with a new paradigm focusing on student proficiency in the target language. Digital technologies have become practical tools for both instructors and students. Among the latest developments is artificial intelligence, which can perform tasks to achieve learning objectives without exhaustive human guidance. ChatGPT's natural language processing abilities appear to hold promise for the provision of corrective written feedback to second language learners. The purpose of the present study was to examine second language learners' perceptions of receiving corrective written feedback from ChatGPT using the IDEE framework (Su & Yang, 2023) as a research lens. Results indicate that there are benefits of using ChatGPT for both language learners and instructors. The study has implications for instructors, world language program coordinators, and educationalists.

DOI: 10.4018/979-8-3373-2927-7.ch004

INTRODUCTION

Instructor feedback is an important part of second language acquisition, and there is potential for feedback to be bolstered by generative artificial intelligence (AI). Feedback is commonly recognized as offering significant learning advantages, giving second language learners understanding of their strengths and areas for improvement (Hyland, 2016). With technological advancements to aid in the provision of feedback, computer-generated feedback is becoming popular in second language writing (Kurt & Kurt, 2024). The implementation of generative AI is not new nor a future technology in educational contexts (Gašević et al., 2023) and is "particularly effective in improving student outcomes" (Fuchs, 2023, p. 1). By providing quality constructive criticism to language learners about what skillful writing in the target language looks like and how to improve on subsequent performances, meaningful feedback can lead to enhancement of writing skills (Graham et al., 2015). AI has been shown to give teachers the ability to provide more personalized feedback to students as well as providing a more engaging learning experience for students (Su & Yang, 2023). However, more research is needed due to the continued evolution of the technology. The present study focuses on the use of ChatGPT as a tool for instructors to give students written corrective feedback on writing assignments in the Spanish classroom and language learners' perceptions of such feedback.

BACKGROUND

AI's growing attractiveness and utility are undeniable (Pazzanese, 2020). Global business spending on AI was expected to hit $110 billion annually by 2024 (Business Wire, 2020). Industries such as retail and banking spend heavily on AI, and it is expected that AI will be "the disrupting influence changing entire industries over the next decade" (Pazzanese, 2020, p. 1). It is predicted that the United States spend more than half of all AI spending led by the retail and banking industries (Business Wire, 2020). Western Europe will be the second largest geographic region while China is expected to be the third largest region (Business Wire, 2020). Its potential to revolutionize various aspects of human life such as providing breakthroughs in healthcare, education, and environmental sustainability may be impressive. Companies that use AI will have the ability to synthesize information by converting data into information and subsequently into knowledge. Additionally, AI is learning how to understand relationships between knowledge and apply that learning to solve business problems. Further, AI is able to deliver insights at scale, which will support decision-making (Business Wire, 2020). The United Nations Environment Programme (2024) stated that a substantial benefit of AI is that it can detect patterns in data (i.e., anomalies and similarities), and use historic knowledge to accurately predict future outcomes, which could make AI invaluable for monitoring the environment, and assist businesses, governments, and individuals make more planet-friendly decisions.

However, AI poses serious issues in the areas of the cost of innovation, issues of consent, personal data misuse, criminal and malicious use, freedom and autonomy loss, unemployment, and the decision-making loss of humans, among others (Stahl, A. 2021; Stahl, B.C., 2021). Additionally, most large-scale AI deployments are housed in data centers, which can be environmentally problematic. For example, in order to generate AI models, incredible quantities of electricity are required to train AI tools such as ChatGPT. Prentice (2025) reported that "training GPT-4 took 300 times more energy (60 million kWh) than training GPT-3" (p. 4). It is expected that GPT-5 will require considerably more energy than that. Nevertheless, "AI is already at work all around us, impacting everything from our search results to our online dating prospects, to the way we shop" (Stahl, A. 2021, p. 2). Interestingly, the vast majority of Fortune 500 companies with AI initiatives have yet to show a return on investment regarding this technology (Estrada, 2025), suggesting that AI's effectiveness is nascent.

AI and Education

Research has shown that AI's use in education has contributed to technological advances and theoretical innovations as well as having positive pedagogical impact (Roll & Wylie, 2016) in areas such as intelligent tutors for content delivery, feedback provision, and progress supervision (Bayne, 2015). While AI has gained attention in education recently, the development of AI-supported learning models began in the 1960s, which can be considered the golden age of Computer-Assisted Learning applications (Ilkka, 2018). An early development in the 1970s called Intelligent Tutoring Systems was the first educational software containing an artificial intelligence component that monitored students' work, provided feedback, and offered hints (Shute & Zapata-Rivera, 2010). A decade later a deep learning technique was developed (Hopfield, 1982) that allowed computers to use previously stored or used information in new experiences. In the 1990s, artificial neural networks such as those proposed by Hopfield advanced the field by imitating the human brain. At the turn of the century, widespread research on and use of distance education increased with the use of virtual reality (Ilkka, 2018).

Research in general education suggests that AI can have significant benefits. For example, Su and Yang (2023) suggested that AI tools can be used to make a significant contribution by personalizing student learning, which can lead to improved teacher effectiveness and student engagement (Chaudhri et al., 2013) if students are properly guided by their teacher (Klimova et al., 2024). Chatbots—a software application or web interface designed to have textual or spoken conversations—can be considered among the most important emerging AI developments in language learning that can assist students in developing their speaking, reading, writing, and listening skills, among other language-related talents (Gayed et al., 2022). Among the many chatbots, ChatGPT has become a very sophisticated and popular one that educationalists have embraced.

In the field of teaching and learning world languages, Baskara and Mukarto (2023) advanced the notion that teachers can use ChatGPT for multiple tasks such as tailoring lesson plans and materials to individual learners' needs and interests as well as to creating personalized practice exercises (e.g., fill in the blank) and authentic language materials (e.g., dialogues, readings). By doing so, such materials can reflect language learners' proficiency levels, interests, and goals, which can enhance teacher effectiveness and learner motivation. Current research has focused on the effectiveness of various tools and techniques that can promote second language acquisition (e.g., Hoi, 2020; Shadiev & Yang, 2020). For example, Kim et al. (2019) explored using chatbots and virtual assistants to support second language learners. Sandberg et al. (2014) investigated gamification in the classroom showing that participants learned more vocabulary in less time and demonstrated stronger effectiveness than those who did not use games. However, Steinkuehler and Squire (2014) have cautioned that such success playing a game is closely linked to the exact conditions under which the game is played.

As summarized above, the literature suggests that AI can be effective in providing feedback to students in the world language classroom. The present study advances the field's understanding of students' perceptions of AI-driven feedback by examining students' opinions during an AI related classroom activity, filling an important gap in the literature.

Second Language Writing and Possibilities for Feedback

Writing is a crucial skill for second language learners and is considered more challenging than other skills because the student must express thoughts into words (Shang, 2022) and then assemble them in a precise manner to effectively communicate meaning (Farida & Rosyidi, 2019). Within the Communication goal area of the *World-Readiness Standards for Learning Languages* (The National Standards Collaborative Board, 2015) is the presentational standard that states that language learners need to learn how to "present information, concepts, and ideas to inform, explain, persuade, and narrate on a variety of topics"... [while] adapting to various audiences of listeners, readers, or viewers (p. 59). Developing presentational communication in written texts differs from developing oral proficiency. As Glisan and

Donato (2021) noted, "gone are the days when anyone would suggest that language could be taught on its own as only discrete grammar points" (p. 66). At the turn of the century, the field moved from teaching world languages via the four skills (i.e., listening, reading, speaking, writing) to the three modes of communication (interpretive, interpersonal, presentational). The three modes describe how learners use and interact with language in real-world contexts by interpreting messages (e.g., written, oral, visual) without any active negotiation of meaning. It is in the interpersonal mode where language learners engage in two-way oral or written communication to share information, feelings, and opinions. The presentational mode focuses on rehearsed language where students present spoken or written information which they prepare for an audience. Using today's paradigm of teaching and learning a second language, students are able to comprehend and produce written texts in addition to developing speaking proficiency.

It is important to note that during the language acquisition process making errors is natural and can provide evidence that learners are progressing in their language development (Lightbown & Spada, 2013). Researchers (Bitchener, 2012; Hyland & Hyland, 2006; Wirantaka, 2022) exploring the effectiveness of corrective written feedback have reported that focused feedback, which targets errors of a specific type, is more effective and valuable for learners than unfocused feedback, which addresses all types of errors. Such an approach to written corrective feedback can catch student attention and encourage them to concentrate on correcting specific errors. Wirantaka (2022) advanced the notion that written corrective feedback should be understandable, focused, and direct. That is, the feedback should be clear and easy to respond to. Furthermore, it should address specific types of errors and stipulate specific guidance to correct mistakes.

With respect to the area of world language teaching and learning, AI platforms such as ChatGPT can support language teachers by assisting teachers in the development of educational materials (e.g., lesson plans, assessments) that are more engaging and interactive, and even gamify learning activities (Çobanoğullari, 2024). Additionally, teachers can employ AI tools to provide corrective written feedback on students' writing samples. When learning a new language, practice and focus on function—learners being able to understand and demonstrate how a second language is used for specific purposes (Hildebrandt & Swanson, 2016)—play a crucial and decisive role. However, with large class sizes and varying levels of proficiency in classes, traditional teacher-provided written corrective feedback faces certain challenges like cognitive overload, inconsistency, and time constraints (Williams, 2024).

However, research has shown that AI tools like ChatGPT can help overcome such limitations by providing immediate and comprehensive feedback to students, which can free teachers so they can have more time to attend to curricular issues (e.g., course content). Zhang (2024) reported that corrective written feedback from

ChatGPT can provide students personalized solutions, explanations, and suggestions for improvement in writing, which can help students at different proficiency levels as well as those who have different learning needs (Guo & Wang, 2023). Researchers (e.g., Kurt & Kurt,2024; Schmidt & Strasser, 2022) reported that AI's educational use to enhance the written corrective feedback process has been positive as it can support students and challenge them to achieve specific language learning goals in a self-directed manner. However, Kellogg and Raulerson (2007) caution that learners must have frequent opportunities to write and to receive timely, focused feedback on their writing.

While developing and working with AI tools such as ChatGPT to provide corrective written feedback for students has been shown to be a tremendous tool, acting on the feedback is critical when acquiring a new language. Researchers (Ebadi & Amini, 2022; Wilson et al., 2024) reported that students generally viewed written corrective feedback from ChatGPT positively regardless of level of proficiency. Yan (2023) reported that ChatGPT can be requested to comment on student tone asking for either an academic or a more casual tone, which can lead to familiarization of different linguistic features associated with various genres of writing. Additionally, language learners were found to regard ChatGPT as a highly usable yet lowly intrusive means of receiving written corrective feedback on (Huang et al., 2022) because of ChatGPT's straightforward interface. Furthermore, students find that such instant feedback leads to writing improvements on the spot. Research has shown that students receiving such feedback improved not only their grammar, lexical density, syntax, and vocabulary but also the overall quality of their writing (Yan, 2023; Zou & Huang, 2023). In addition to the identification of errors, students reported that such feedback enhances their comprehension because it is comprehensive and explained well (Zhang, 2024) and enhances their engagement in writing in the target language (Cheng et al., 2023). Overall, researchers report that students find such feedback helpful, motivating, and even preferable over other feedback types (Fong & Schallert, 2023; Graham et al., 2015).

While ChatGPT has yielded positive results for language learners such as practicality, interactivity, and adaptability (Kurt & Kurt, 2024), its use is not perfect. It can be fallible by producing occasional inconsistencies while dependent on the quality of teacher-created prompts as well as misleading or inaccurate responses (Hua et al., 2024). Nevertheless, AI tools such as ChatGPT have considerable educational benefits. However, large language models like ChatGPT in higher education language learning require further investigation with respect to written corrective feedback for language learners.

Conceptual Framework

Given the disruptive nature of AI technology and its current status of development in the educational community, it is prudent to employ deliberately a theoretical framework to structure efforts and enable outcomes with clarity. The IDEE framework contains a four-part structure where researchers (1) identify desired outcomes, (2) determine the appropriate level of automation, (3) ensure ethical considerations, and (4) evaluate effectiveness (Su & Yang, 2023). With respect to using the framework to evaluate the effectiveness of using ChatGPT for written corrective feedback in the second language teaching and learning, each part of the framework is presented below.

Identify desired outcomes

Before using ChatGPT for educational purposes, it is important to identify the objectives of the application. From a backwards design curricular approach (Wiggins & McTighe, 2005), it is crucial to know what knowledge is worth being familiar with, what knowledge and skills should be mastered, and which understandings can be considered enduring—information that is important to remember once they have completed a course. This guarantees that the use of technology aligns with the desired outcomes. With respect to the present study, the objective was to provide undergraduate Spanish language learners with targeted and timely feedback on their writing assignments in order to improve the quality of their written communication.

Determine the appropriate level of automation

Su and Yang (2023) noted that "depending on the objectives, it may be appropriate to fully automate the teaching or learning experience using educative AI or to use it as a supplement to traditional teaching methods" (p. 4). Thus, instructors can use ChatGPT to generate student feedback in a variety of ways (e.g., based on observations during class). Such feedback can be customized to the individual needs that can provide highly tailored and efficient feedback. In the case of the present study, the researchers requested that ChatGPT's feedback should be in English and provide feedback on specific grammatical structures, vocabulary, and verb tenses.

Ensure ethical considerations

"The ethical implications of using educative AI must be carefully considered" (p. 4) as not all technologies impact all users in similar fashion. Gašević et al. (2023) caution that some student populations might be at greater risk of harm than others because the data used to train AI have bias embedded within them or within the process of creating algorithms. This bias can then produce results that can be seen as problematic or even harmful to certain populations. Thus, ethics, bias, and fairness are central to AI's growing influence. Su and Yang (2023) proposed that it is important to ensure that ChatGPT's feedback is free from bias and based on objective observations. Additionally, they posit that ChatGPT should not replace the important role of human coaches in providing support and guidance to instructors. With respect to the present study, the researchers acknowledged that the ChatGPT large language model continues to mature yet can create bias. Furthermore, the researchers monitored the feedback and worked directly with the participants regarding the feedback provided.

Evaluate effectiveness

Finally, the evaluation of the effectiveness of ChatGPT in achieving the desired outcomes is essential. Effectiveness can be measured by analyzing the impact of feedback on the students, teaching practices, and the instructors. Su and Yang (2023) advanced the notion that effectiveness can be achieved via teacher evaluations, feedback surveys, and other assessment tools. The researchers developed a participant questionnaire and requested student feedback regarding the use of ChatGPT for written corrective feedback.

RESEARCH QUESTIONS

The present study is guided by the following research questions with respect to the IDEE framework:

1. Was the objective of providing the participants with targeted and timely feedback on their writing assignments in order to improve the quality of their written communication met through the utilization of ChatGPT?
2. Did the instructor-created prompt provide the appropriate level of automation with respect to feedback to the participants on specific grammatical structures, vocabulary, and verb tenses (i.e., time and quality at desire levels)?
3. What were the participants' perceptions of the ethical and environmental concerns of using ChatGPT for corrective written feedback?
4. What were the participants' perceptions of the effectiveness of using ChatGPT for corrective written feedback?

THE STUDY

Rationale

Generative AI offers manifold opportunities in the field of education for its capability to process rapidly large volumes of student data (e.g., writing samples) and to produce precisely guided analysis for a personalized learning experiences (Çobanoğullari, 2024; Su & Yang, 2023). The researchers recognize generative AI's potential to ingest student writing assignment submissions written in a different language (i.e., Spanish), identify errors, and provide individualized feedback, all in a fraction of the time required of a human to perform one of those functions. The purpose of this study was to assess the ability of generative AI to reduce instructors' time invested in error identification in student writing assignments and to increase the volume of impactful, personalized feedback available to students.

Artificial Platform

ChatGPT—Generative Pre-trained Transformer—is a robust, online large language model AI chatbot that lets users enter prompts to receive humanlike text, images, or even videos that are created by AI (OpenAI, 2022). The model functions using a transformer architecture that "utilizes unsupervised learning to generate human-like text across various domains" (Baskara & Mukarto, 2023, p. 347). The basic ChatGPT platform is free of charge but does require that the user establish an account. ChatGPT has additional features such as attachment upload and voice production, and it can read a variety of world language scripts. The most recent version of the model, GPT-3, contains an extraordinary number of parameters, estimated to be around 175 billion (Benbya et al., 2020). Such power allows ChatGPT to produce coherent and contextually appropriate responses to various prompts such as prompts, questions, and text completions. Additionally, ChatGPT is able to understand natural language queries and provide answers and summaries at amazing speed. A particular facet of ChatGPT is that it can communicate in the text between different languages. Such features hold significant potential for world language teachers and second language learners as they can provide personalized and interactive learning experiences (Baskara & Mukarto, 2023). However, ChatGPT is fallible as it can occasionally produce incorrect answers (OpenAI, 2022) as the accuracy of the system depends heavily on the complexity, diversity, and quality of the training data, as well as the quality of the student input (Fuchs, 2022). Language is a human endeavor, and ChatGPT might struggle to understand the nuances and complexities of human language as input by second language learners, leading to misunderstandings and incorrect responses.

Procedures

Following IRB approval in February 2025, participants in second-year Spanish classes (*N*= 49) at the United States Air Force Academy turned in writing samples (~200 words) in the target language in a *Word* document and responded to instructor-created prompts regarding themes (e.g., shopping, professional life) the class was studying. Participants were not allowed to use spell check or grammar check, nor were they permitted to use online translators. The writing sample was their original work. Data from proficiency testing indicated that the participants' proficiency level in Spanish ranged from Novice-High to Intermediate-Mid on the ACTFL Proficiency Scale (2024). Course outcomes included articulating and sharing opinions, reacting to authentic readings and videos, narrating in varying verb tenses regarding textbook themes (e.g., professional life, health and the human body).

The researchers created and pilot tested the prompt ChatGPT used to generate feedback to the participants' short essays with prior writing samples. The prompt was revised twice in order to focus specifically on grammar points and vocabulary about which the participants would write. In order to analyze the writing samples for the writing prompts, the researchers input the prompt into ChatGPT based on Lima and Wallace's (2024) recommendations. The prompt informs ChatGPT to identify errors and provide feedback. It also provides information about the class context and participants' background as well as the role it should play as a university-level Spanish teacher. Finally, it tells ChatGPT the linguistic aspects to which it should limit itself and those which it should ignore. Specifically, the prompt requested feedback on grammar (e.g., verb tenses, object pronouns) and informed the model that the participants were second year Spanish students and had three to four years of prior instruction in Spanish. Additionally, the prompt requested that the model act as a university-level Spanish teacher with 15 years of classroom experience (i.e., a native speaker of American English with a bachelor's degree in Spanish, having lived eight years in Spain). Finally, the prompt requested that the model provide a copy of the original writing with errors in strike-though font, a one sentence explanation of each error and an explanation of how to correct it. The prompt requested that ChatGPT not provide feedback regarding formality of vocabulary nor make suggestions for idiomatic language.

For each of the participants' writing samples, the researchers entered the prompt into ChatGPT. Then, the researchers input the students' writing submission into ChatGPT, and output was provided very quickly. ChatGPT provided the participants' writing sample with errors identified by the strike through test (e.g., un grande problema). For each of the identified errors, an explanation was provided below the writing sample (e.g., un grande problema "Grande" goes after the noun, and "un" should be "un problema grande." The researchers reviewed the ChatGPT output and determined if the feedback items were accurate, useful, adequate, redundant, repetitive, or irrelevant. The revised ChatGPT output was copied and pasted below each original submission and then returned to the participants via email. Ethical considerations were mitigated as the researchers did not input personal identifiable information to adhere to IRB regulations. Finally, the researchers evaluated the effectiveness of using ChatGPT for feedback by measuring time invested in human evaluation versus AI evaluation of the same writing response. Near the end of the study, the researchers developed a questionnaire asking the participants about their opinions receiving feedback from ChatGPT.

Questionnaire

In order to create a questionnaire regarding participants' perceptions of ChatGPT for corrective written feedback, the researchers reviewed the literature on using AI for educational purposes. Next, the researchers met with other faculty members in the Department of Languages and Cultures to talk about their perceptions of using AI for corrective written feedback on writing assessments. Afterward, the researchers developed a questionnaire using a 6-point Likert scale (1 — Strongly Disagree to 6 —Strongly Agree) with a participant demographic sheet. The instrument was designed to measure participants' perceptions of four dependent variables related to using ChatGPT for written corrective feedback: (1) ChatGPT's Effectiveness, (2) Environmental Concern, (3) Learner Privacy and Bias, and (4) Learner Motivation. The researchers field tested the questionnaire with four colleagues using *Google Forms* to test its functionality as well as its content validity and reliability. Afterward, the researchers emailed the participants with a link to the questionnaire. Data collection concluded in May 2025. Following data collection, the researchers used *SPSS 27.0* to analyze the participants' ratings to the statements on the questionnaire as well as the demographic variables. The reliability coefficient for the questionnaire was high (.86), indicating that (1) the respondents' answers to the statements were consistent and that (2) the coefficient shows satisfactory consistency for research purposes (Henson, 2001).

Participants

Of the 49 Spanish language learner participants, 32 (65%) self-reported as male. Nearly seven out of 10 reported their ethnicity as White/Caucasian (69%) with seven (14%) reporting as Latino/a and six (12%) as multiracial. Two self-reported as either African American or Pacific Islander. Participant median age was 19.78 (SD=0.91) and the majority (n=42) were in their second year at the United States

Air Force Academy. The participant demographics are similar to those of the cadet wing (United States Air Force Academy, 2025).

THE SIGNIFICANCE OF THE STUDY

As noted earlier, AI's use for educational purposes can have positive pedagogical impacts (Roll & Wylie, 2016) for a variety of purposes (Bayne, 2015), as discussed below. Given the small sample size, the data are reported in frequencies regarding the four dependent variables of interest: (1) ChatGPT's Effectiveness, (2) Environmental Concern, (3) Learner Privacy and Bias, and (4) Learner Motivation. Participant responses from the 6-point Likert scale: (1) Strongly Disagree, (2) Disagree, (3) Slightly Disagree, (4) Slightly Agree, (5) Agree, and (6) Strongly Agree) were collapsed to reflect disagreement and agreement to the questionnaire statements.

While the present study is exploratory regarding use of ChatGPT for providing corrective written feedback to students learning Spanish, initial findings suggest that using ChatGPT holds potential for its use in evaluating second language learners' writing sample and providing quality feedback that can help increase proficiency in the target language (i.e., Spanish). With respect to the first research question representing the first pillar of the IDEE framework (Su & Yang, 2023), the objective of providing the participants with targeted and timely feedback on their writing assignments in order to improve the quality of their written communication was met. That is, a large volume of corrective written feedback was provided to the participants; however, that feedback was tainted by hallucinations (i.e., incorrect responses generated by the predictive nature of AI) that are part of this technology presently. When determining the level of automation as outlined by the IDEE framework, instructors and course designers must take into account not only the time saved by using AI but also the time instructors must spend reviewing the AI generated feedback for hallucinations. The instructors developed, tested, and then refined the prompt several times prior to data collection because ChatGPT can be fallible, producing inconsistencies because a poorly developed prompt can lead to misleading or inaccurate responses (Hua et al., 2024). Its ability to have instructors request certain types of feedback (e.g., grammar errors) while ignoring other types helps instructors achieve the desired outcome of provision of corrective written feedback to second language learners. Results from the questionnaire showed that ChatGPT can identify writing errors rapidly and make a variety of feedback suggestions for improving the written artifact per the instructor-created prompt. Data analysis showed that three quarters of the participants (n=36) agreed that using ChatGPT for writing assessments was effective for achieving the course outcomes.

As Wiggins and McTighe (2005) noted, teachers should consider their long-term performance goal, which is the bottom-line goal of education is transfer.

Turning to the second research question regarding the determination of the appropriate level of automation with respect to feedback to the participants on specific grammatical structures, vocabulary, and verb tenses, ChatGPT generated appropriate feedback for the task, which saved instructor time and energy. Results from the study indicated that 69% of the participants agreed that using ChatGPT for corrective written feedback helped improve their writing in Spanish. Furthermore, 75% of the participants agreed that using ChatGPT for corrective written feedback during revisions of writing assignments was appropriate for grading the final draft of the short essay, which suggests that the instructor-created prompt focused on error correction and was at the appropriate level for the participants (see Appendix A). ChatGPT identified students' writing errors rapidly and provided a variety of feedback ideas (e.g., incorrect verb tense use, word choice) for improving the written artifact per the instructor-created prompt (see Appendix A). Its ability to have instructors request certain types of feedback (e.g., grammar errors) while ignoring other types was deemed helpful in meeting the desired outcome. ChatGPT feedback can be customized to individual needs, which can provide highly tailored and effective feedback.

With respect to the penultimate research question about the participants' perceptions of the ethical concerns (i.e., learner privacy and bias) of using ChatGPT for corrective written feedback, most of the participants (n=37, 75%) agreed that it was appropriate to have their data (i.e., the essay they wrote) stored and shared as part of the AI language model dataset. Sixty-five percent of the participants agreed that students should be aware of the output from AI models given the quantity of data the AI model receives (e.g., language, demographics), which corroborates Hua et al.'s (2024) assertion that ChatGPT generated textual hallucinations. That is, the text can look semantically or grammatically correct, yet it is actually unfaithful and meaningless, which leads to the risk of spreading misinformation. Thus, given the inherent bias in these systems, language learners should be mindful because these AI models can provide inaccurate, misleading, and unethical information. Turning to the second part of the research question, the environmental concerns of using ChatGPT for corrective written feedback, the majority of the participants (n=34, 69%) agreed that the large amount of energy used to power AI applications was worth its use with only 15 participants in disagreement to various degrees (see Figure 1).

Figure 1. The Large Amount of Energy Used to Power AI Applications Is Worth Its Use.

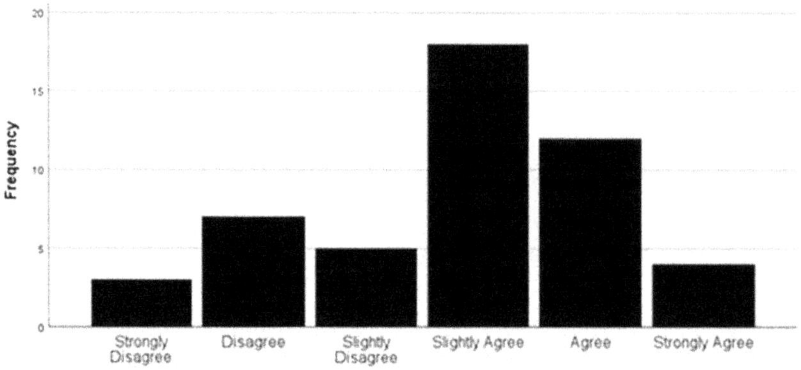

Turning to the final research question about the participants' perception of ChatGPT's effectiveness for providing corrective written feedback, as shown in Figure 2, almost three quarters of the participants (*n*=36) agreed that using ChatGPT for writing assessments was effective for achieving the course outcomes (e.g., articulating and sharing opinions, reacting to authentic readings and videos). A similar finding was found when asked if teachers' use of ChatGPT for corrective written feedback improved their ability to write in Spanish where 69% of the sample (*n*=34) expressed agreement. When asked if ChatGPT should be used more for corrective written feedback, 65.5% of the sample (*n*=32) agreed. Seventy-five percent of the participants (*n*=37) expressed agreement that using ChatGPT for corrective written feedback during revisions of writing assignments was appropriate for grading the final draft of the short essay. Nine out of 10 participants (*n*=45) expressed that there are advantages and disadvantages to using ChatGPT for corrective written feedback.

Figure 2. Using ChatGPT for Writing Assessments Was Effective for Achieving the Course Outcomes.

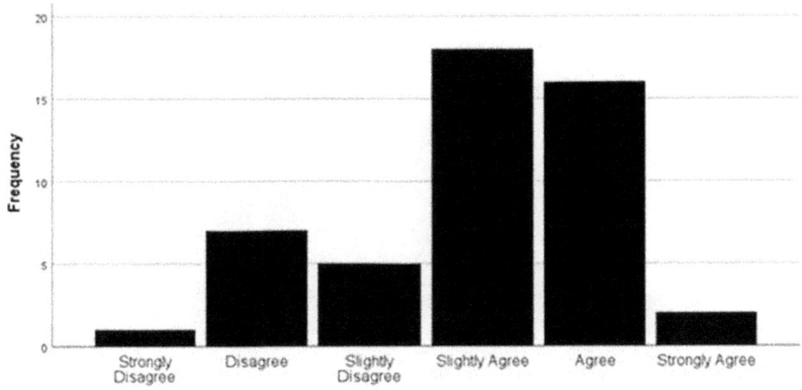

Interestingly, approximately half of the sample (*n*=27) agreed that the feedback they received from ChatGPT increased their confidence to acquire Spanish while 87.7% of the participants (*n*=43) agreed that they preferred the traditional method of receiving corrective written feedback. That is, instructors mark up the short essay showing errors with comments before returning it to the participants for revision. In similar fashion, slightly more than half of the participants agreed (55%), with the majority of the responses in the slightly disagree / slightly agree options, that using ChatGPT for corrective written feedback increased their motivation to learn Spanish (see Figure 3). Such a finding contradicts earlier research in general regarding ChatGPT's use in education (Fong & Schallert, 2023; Graham et al., 2015).

Figure 3. Using ChatGPT for Corrective Written Feedback Increased Participant Motivation to Learn Spanish.

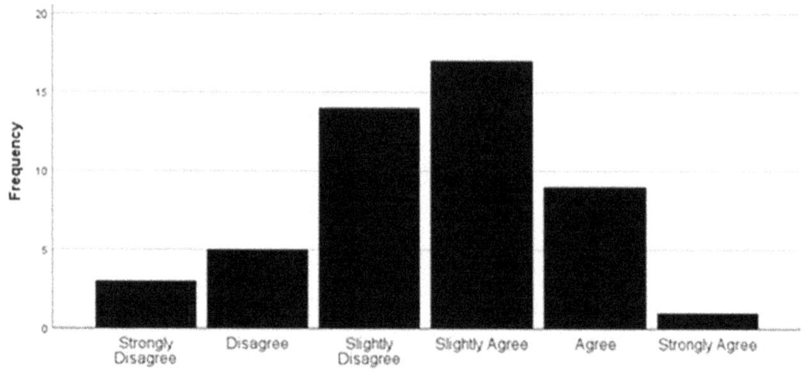

FUTURE RESEARCH DIRECTIONS AND CONCLUSION

This pilot study explored the use of ChatGPT as a tool for instructors to give students written corrective feedback on writing assignments in the Spanish classroom. Overall, the data showed that the participants acknowledged that were benefits for using ChatGPT for writing assignments. Of the findings, several of importance warrant discussion. First, most of the participants expressed agreement that ChatGPT was effective for achieving the course outcomes as it provided quality feedback to help them improve their learning of the Spanish language. Additionally, they recognized that there are inherent biases with using ChatGPT. Moreover, the majority agreed that using ChatGPT helped improve their writing in the target language. However, 87.7% of the participants (n=43) reported that they preferred the traditional method of receiving corrective written feedback even though they felt that using ChatGPT helped improve their writing. Such a finding may suggest that they prefer a more human touch to evaluation of their academic work. Interestingly, approximately half of the sample thought that its use increased their motivation or confidence to write in the target language. Confidence (i.e., one's sense of efficacy) in language learning is critical as one's self-efficacy not only affects expectations of failure or success but also influences motivation and setting goals. Efficacy beliefs —— "people's judgments of their capabilities to organize and execute courses of action required to attain designated types of performances" (Bandura, 1986, p. 391) —— provide a base of human motivation, personal accomplishment, and well-being because, unless people believe that their actions can produce desired outcomes, they have little incentive to act or to persevere when confronted with difficulties. Acquiring a second language is difficult for adults (Hartshorne et al., 2018) and having a strong sense of efficacy is critical.

While this study has its limitations (e.g., small sample size, unique institution of higher education), the data provide evidence that using ChatGPT for corrective written feedback in a world language can provide multiple benefits such as the provision of more personalized learning experiences, saving precious time and energy for instructors, the improvement of assessment systems, and offering useful suggestions for teachers (Su & Yang, 2023), which may create a new ecology of education.

Avenues for further research include conducting qualitative studies with second language learners to determine their suggestions for using ChatGPT to accelerate one's proficiency in the target language. Additionally, research on how second language learners are using generative AI to acquire a new language would benefit language instructors regardless of target language. Furthermore, research investigating instructors' perceptions when using other AI platforms for corrective written feedback in other languages would be informative. Finally, it would be helpful to evaluate the effectiveness of ChatGPT via quasi-experimental empirical studies having control and experimental groups studying the same language at the same level. Comparison between the two groups could help identify the advantages and disadvantages of using ChatGPT for educational purposes. Viewed collectively, as Baskara and Mukarto (2023) suggested, the ethical and social ramifications of utilizing ChatGPT in language learning must be included. Large language models like ChatGPT provide benefits for second language learning and the authors call for further research.

Distribution Statement A: Approved for public release: distribution unlimited.

Disclaimer: The views expressed in this article are those of the author and do not necessarily reflect the official policy or position of the United States Air Force Academy, the Air Force, the Department of Defense, or the U.S. Government. USAFA-DF-2025-661

REFERENCES

American Council on the Teaching of Foreign Languages. (2024). ACTFL proficiency guidelines. https://www.actfl.org/uploads/files/general/Resources-Publications/ACTFL_Proficiency_Guidelines_2024.pdf

Bandura, A. (1986). *Social foundations of thought and action: A social cognitive theory*. Prentice-Hall.

Baskara, R., & Mukarto, M. (2023). Exploring the implications of ChatGPT for language learning in higher education. *Indonesian Journal of English Language Teaching and Applied Linguistics*, *7*(2), 343–358. DOI: 10.21093/ijeltal.v7i2.1387

Bayne, S. (2015). Posthumanism and research in digital education. In Haythornthwaite, C., Andrews, R., Fransman, J., & Meyers, E. M. (Eds.), *SAGE handbook of e-learning research* (pp. 82–89). SAGE.

Benbya, H., Davenport, T. H., & Pachidi, S. (2020). Artificial intelligence in organizations: Current state and future opportunities. *MIS Quarterly Executive*, *19*(4), 9–21.

Bitchener, J. (2012). A reflection on 'the language learning potential of written corrective feedback. *Journal of Second Language Writing*, *21*(4), 348–363. DOI: 10.1016/j.jslw.2012.09.006

Business Wire. (2020, August 25). Worldwide spending on artificial intelligence is expected to double in four years, reaching $110 billion in 2024. https://www.businesswire.com/news/home/20200825005099/en/Worldwide-Spending-on-Artificial-Intelligence-Is-Expected-to-Double-in-Four-Years-Reaching-%24110-Billion-in-2024-According-to-New-IDC-Spending-Guide

Chaudhri, V. K. H., Lane, C., Gunning, D., & Roschelle, J. (2013). Applications of artificial intelligence to contemporary and emerging educational challenges. *Artificial Intelligence Magazine*, *34*(3), 10–12.

Cheng, X., Liu, Y., & Wang, C. (2023). Understanding student engagement with teacher and peer feedback in L2 writing. *System*, *119*, 103176. DOI: 10.1016/j.system.2023.103176

Çobanoğullari, F. (2024). Learning and teaching with ChatGPT: Potentials and applications in education. *The EuroCALL Review*, *31*(1), 4–15. DOI: 10.4995/eurocall.2024.19957

Ebadi, S., & Amini, A. (2022). Examining the roles of social presence and human-likeness on Iranian EFL learners' motivation using artificial intelligence technology: A case of CSIEC chatbot. *Interactive Learning Environments*, •••, 1–19. DOI: 10.1080/10494820.2022.2096638

Estrada, S. (2025, August 18). MIT report: 95% of generative AI pilots at companies are failing. *Fortune*. https://fortune.com/2025/08/18/mit-report-95-percent-generative-ai-pilots-at-companies-failing-cfo/

Farida, A. N., & Rosyidi, M. I. (2019). Students' writing quality: Its coherence and cohesion. Language Circle. *Journal of Language and Literature*, *14*(1), 121–129. DOI: 10.15294/lc.v14i1.21505

Fong, C. J., & Schallert, D. L. (2023). Feedback to the future: Advancing motivational and emotional perspectives in feedback research. *Educational Psychologist*, *58*(3), 146–161. DOI: 10.1080/00461520.2022.2134135

Fuchs, K. (2023). Exploring the opportunities and challenges of NLP models in higher education: Is Chat GPT a blessing or a curse? *Frontiers in Education*, *8*, 1–4. DOI: 10.3389/feduc.2023.1166682

Gašević, D., Siemens, G., & Sadiq, S. (2023). Empowering learners for the age of artificial intelligence. *Computers and Education: Artificial Intelligence*, *4*, 100130. DOI: 10.1016/j.caeai.2023.100130

Gayed, J. M., Carlon, M. K. J., Oriola, A. M., & Cross, J. S. (2022). Exploring an ai-based writing assistant's impact on English language learners. *Computer Education: Artificial Intelligence*, *3*, 100055. DOI: 10.1016/j.caeai.2022.100055

Glisan, E. W., & Donato, R. (2021). *Enacting the work of language instruction: High-leverage teaching practices* (Vol. 2). ACTFL.

Graham, S., Hebert, M., & Harris, K. R. (2015). Formative assessment and writing: A meta-analysis. *The Elementary School Journal*, *115*(4), 523–547. DOI: 10.1086/681947

Guo, K., & Wang, D. (2023). To resist it or to embrace it? Examining ChatGPT's potential to support teacher feedback in EFL writing. *Education and Information Technologies*, *29*(7), 8435–8463. DOI: 10.1007/s10639-023-12146-0

Hartshorne, J. K., Tenenbaum, J. B., & Pinker, S. (2018). A critical period for second language acquisition: Evidence from 2/3 million English speakers. *Cognition, 177*, 263–277. DOI: 10.1016/j.cognition.2018.04.007 PMID: 29729947

Henson, R. K. (2001). Understanding internal consistency reliability estimates: A conceptual primer on coefficient alpha. *Measurement & Evaluation in Counseling & Development, 34*(3), 177–189. DOI: 10.1080/07481756.2002.12069034

Hildebrandt, S. A., & Swanson, P. (2016). *Understanding the world language edTPA: Research-based policy and practice*. Information Age Publishing.

Hoi, V. N. (2020). Understanding higher education learners' acceptance and use of mobile devices for language learning: A Rasch-based path modeling approach. *Computers & Education, 146*, 103761. DOI: 10.1016/j.compedu.2019.103761

Hopfield, J. J. (1982). Neural networks and physical systems with emergent collective computational abilities. *Proceedings of the National Academy of Sciences*. DOI: 10.1073/pnas.79.8.2554

Hua, S., Jin, S., & Jiang, S. (2024). The limitations and ethical considerations of ChatGPT. *Data Intelligence, 6*(1), 201–239. DOI: 10.1162/dint_a_00243

Huang, W., Hew, K. F., & Fryer, L. K. (2022). Chatbots for language learning—Are they really useful? A systematic review of chatbot-supported language learning. *Journal of Computer Assisted Learning, 38*(1), 237–257. DOI: 10.1111/jcal.12610

Hyland, K. (2016). Teaching and researching writing. (2017). *Journal of Writing Research, 8*(3), 531–533. DOI: 10.17239/jowr-2017.08.03.05

Hyland, K., & Hyland, F. (Eds.). (2006). *Feedback in second language writing: Contexts and issues*. Cambridge University Press. DOI: 10.1017/CBO9781139524742

Ilkka, T. (2018). The impact of artificial intelligence on learning, teaching, and education. *European Union*.

Kellogg, R. T., & Raulerson, B. A. (2007). Improving the writing skills of college students. *Psychonomic Bulletin & Review, 14*(2), 237–242. DOI: 10.3758/BF03194058 PMID: 17694907

Kim, H., Shin, D., Yang, H., & Lee, J. H. (2019). A study of AI chatbot as an assistant tool for school English curriculum. *Korean Association for Learner-Centered Curriculum and Instruction, 19*(1), 89–110. DOI: 10.22251/jlcci.2019.19.1.89

Klimova, B., Pikhart, M., & Al-Obaydi, L. H. (2024). Exploring the potential of ChatGPT for foreign language education at the university level. *Frontiers in Psychology, 15*, 1269319. DOI: 10.3389/fpsyg.2024.1269319 PMID: 38655215

Kurt, G., & Kurt, Y. (2024). Enhancing L2 writing skills: ChatGPT as an automated feedback tool. *Journal of Information Technology Education, 23*(24), 2–17. DOI: 10.28945/5370

Lightbown, P. M., & Spada, N. (2013). *How languages are learned* (4th ed.). Oxford University Press.

Lima, E. F., & Wallace, L. (2024, September 12). Technology innovation: Using ChatGPT to elevate pronunciation pedagogy [Conference teaching workshop]. PSLLT 2024 Conference, Ames, IA, United States. https://drive.google.com/file/d/1YS_SXSJuOMcUm_k4GZwXGsA9ozDLjYWt/edit

Open A.I. (2022). *What is ChatGPT? Commonly asked questions about ChatGPT.* https://help.openai.com/en/articles/6783457-what-is-chatgpt

Pazzanese (2020, October 26). Great promise but potential for peril. Harvard Gazette. https://news.harvard.edu/gazette/story/2020/10/ethical-concerns-mount-as-ai-takes-bigger-decision-making-role/

Prentice, R. (2025, April 22). Ai and the energy issue. *Ethics Unwrapped.* https://ethicsunwrapped.utexas.edu/ai-and-the-energy-issue

Roll, I., & Wylie, R. (2016). Evolution and revolution in artificial intelligence in education. *International Journal of Artificial Intelligence in Education, 26*(2), 582–599. DOI: 10.1007/s40593-016-0110-3

Sandberg, J., Maris, M., & Hoogendoorn, P. (2014). The added value of a gaming context and intelligent adaptation for a mobile learning application for vocabulary learning. *Computers & Education, 76*, 119–130. DOI: 10.1016/j.compedu.2014.03.006

Schmidt, T., & Strasser, T. (2022). Artificial intelligence in foreign language learning and teaching: A call for intelligent practice. *Anglistik: International Journal of English Studies, 33*(1), 165–184. DOI: 10.33675/ANGL/2022/1/14

Shadiev, R., & Yang, M. (2020). Review of studies on technology-enhanced language learning and teaching. *Sustainability (Basel), 12*(2), 524. DOI: 10.3390/su12020524

Shang, H. F. (2022). Exploring online peer feedback and automated corrective feedback on efl writing performance. *Interactive Learning Environments, 30*(1), 4–16. DOI: 10.1080/10494820.2019.1629601

Shute, V. J., & Zapata-Rivera, D. (2010). Intelligent systems. In E. Baker, P. Peterson, & B. McGaw (Eds.), Third edition of the Formative and Stealth Assessment international encyclopedia of education (pp. 75–80). Elsevier. DOI: 10.1016/B978-0-08-044894-7.00247-5

Stahl, A. (2021, March 10). How ai will impact the future of work and life. *Forbes*. https://www.forbes.com/sites/ashleystahl/2021/03/10/how-ai-will-impact-the-future-of-work-and-life/?sh=3c5c1a5279a3

Stahl, B. C. (2021). *Artificial intelligence for a better future*. Springer. DOI: 10.1007/978-3-030-69978-9

Steinkuehler, C. A., & Squire, K. (2014). Videogames and learning. In Sawyer, K. (Ed.), *Cambridge handbook of the learning sciences* (pp. 377–394). Cambridge University Press. DOI: 10.1017/CBO9781139519526.023

Su, J., & Yang, W. (2023). Unlocking the power of ChatGPT: A framework for applying generative ai in education. *ECNU Review of Education,* 1-12. *Doi:* DOI: 10.1177/20965311231168423

The National Standards Collaborative Board. (2015). *World-readiness standards for learning. languages*. ACTFL.

United Nations Environment Programme. (2024). *AI has an environmental problem. Here's what the world can do about that.* https://www.unep.org/news-and-stories/story/ai-has-environmental-problem-heres-what-world-can-do-about

United States Air Force Academy. (2025). *About.* https://datausa.io/profile/geo/air-force-academy-co?redirect=true#:~:text=The%205%20largest%20ethnic%20groups,(Hispanic)%20(3.66%25)

Wiggins, G., & McTighe, J. (2005). *Understanding by design* (2nd ed.). ASCD.

Williams, A. (2024). Delivering effective student feedback in higher education: An evaluation of the challenges and best practice. *International Journal of Research in Education and Science, 10*(2), 473–501. DOI: 10.46328/ijres.3404

Wilson, J., Palermo, C., & Wibowo, A. (2024). Elementary English learners' engagement with automated feedback. *Learning and Instruction, 91*, 101890. DOI: 10.1016/j.learninstruc.2024.101890

Wirantaka, A. (2022). Effective written corrective feedback on efl students' academic writing. *Eralingua: Jurnal Pendidikan Bahasa Asing dan Sastra,* 6(2), 387-399.

Yan, D. A. (2023). Impact of ChatGPT on learners in a l2 writing practicum: An exploratory investigation. *Education and Information Technologies*, *28*(11), 1–25. DOI: 10.1007/s10639-023-11742-4 PMID: 37361815

Zhang, Y. (2024). Incorporating ChatGPT as an automated written corrective feedback tool into L2 writing class. *Tydskrif vir Taalonderrig*, *4*(4), 22–34. DOI: 10.54475/jlt.2024.024

Zou, M., & Huang, L. (2023). The impact of ChatGPT on L2 writing and expected responses: Voice from doctoral students. *Education and Information Technologies*, *29*(11), 13201–13219. DOI: 10.1007/s10639-023-12397-x

KEY TERMS AND DEFINITIONS

Artificial intelligence: A broad term used to describe a collection of technologies that can solve problems and perform tasks to achieve defined objectives without explicit human guidance.

ChatGPT: ChatGPT—Generative Pre-trained Transformer—is an online large language artificial intelligence model chatbot developed by OpenAI that permits users enter prompts to receive humanlike text, images, or even videos that are created by AI.

Corrective Written Feedback: Instructor-given feedback to a student in order to help them identify and correct errors in their writing.

Second Language Acquisition: The process of learning a language other than one's native language. It's an educational field that studies how humans learn and use additional languages after acquiring their first language.

APPENDIX

Para el proyecto, mis amigos y yo vamos a ayudar la comunidad local en Colorado Springs con los veteranos locales. Vamos a aportarlos con comida (si tienes hambre), con refugio y un lugar para dormir y usar el baño, y lo mas importante es ayudarlos con la salud mental. Vamos a contratar algunos psicólogos para hablar con estos veteranos quien tienen dolores de la cabeza como PTSD o algo otro.

Esto es una buena idea para muchas razones. Primero, si hiciéramos este proyecto, podríamos levantar mucho dinero para ayudar la comunidad aquí en Colorado Springs. También si obtuviéramos mucha atención del público, podríamos hablar más sobre los problemas sistémicos con los veteranos en Los Estados Unidos.

Segundo, si hiciéramos este proyecto en Colorado Springs, podríamos atracar mas soportar porque Colorado Springs tiene muchos veteranos de USAFA, West Point, la academia de Navy y mucha mas veteranos. Recomiendo que enviemos un mensaje al todos los postgrados quien quiere ayudar a nosotros con este proyecto.

Finalmente, recomiendo que las personas quien trabajen en este proyecto conmigo tengan cuidado. Veteranos han visto mucho, mucho malas imágenes durante las guerrillas y la mayoría del tiempo son muy impredecibles. Por esta razón, cuando estamos ayudando los veteranos tenemos que ser muy muy gracioso, paciente, y también tenemos que conocer que estos veteranos puede ser peligros para nosotros.

En total, mi idea para ayudar los veteranos locales de Colorado Springs tiene mucho potencial para ser un grande proyecto. Si levantamos mucho dinero y mucha personas quieren ayudar a nosotros, podamos ayudar a muchas personas.

Original Text with Errors in Strikethrough

Para el proyecto, mis amigos y yo vamos a ayudar ~~la~~comunidad local en Colorado Springs con los veteranos locales. Vamos a ~~aportarlos~~ con comida (si ~~tienes~~ hambre), con refugio y un lugar para dormir y usar el baño, y ~~lo mas~~ importante es ~~ayudarlos~~ con ~~la salud~~ ~~mental~~. Vamos a contratar algunos psicólogos para hablar con estos veteranos ~~quien~~ tienen dolores de la cabeza como PTSD o ~~algo otro~~.

Esto es una buena idea para muchas razones. Primero, si ~~hiciéramos~~ este proyecto, podríamos levantar mucho dinero para ayudar la comunidad aquí en Colorado Springs. También si ~~obtuviéramos~~ mucha atención del público, podríamos hablar más sobre los problemas sistémicos con los veteranos en ~~los Estados Unidos~~.

Segundo, si ~~hiciéramos~~ este proyecto en Colorado Springs, podríamos ~~atracar mas soportar~~ porque Colorado Springs tiene muchos veteranos de USAFA, West Point, la academia de Navy y ~~mucha mas~~ veteranos. Recomiendo que enviemos un mensaje ~~al todos~~ los postgrados ~~quien~~ quiere ayudar ~~a nosotros~~ con este proyecto.

Finalmente, recomiendo que las personas en este proyecto conmigo tengan cuidado. ~~Veteranos han visto~~ mucho, ~~mucho malas imágenes~~ durante las guerrillas y la mayoría del tiempo son muy impredecibles. Por esta razón, cuando estamos ayudando ~~los veteranos~~ tenemos que ser ~~muy muy gracioso~~, paciente, y también tenemos que conocer que estos veteranos ~~puede ser peligros~~ para nosotros.
En total, mi idea para ayudar ~~los veteranos~~ locales de Colorado Springs tiene mucho potencial para ser ~~un grande~~ proyecto. Si levantamos mucho dinero y ~~mucha personas~~ quieren ayudar, ayudar ~~a nosotros~~, ~~podamos~~ ayudar a muchas personas.

Explanations of Each Error

1. **"ayudar la comunidad"**

"Ayudar" requires the personal "a" before people. This should be "ayudar a la comunidad".

2. **"aportarlos"**

"Aportar" is not used with a direct object pronoun like "los" when referring to what is being given; it means "to contribute" something, not "to provide to them". A verb like "proveer" or "darles" would be more appropriate.

3. **"si tienes hambre"**

In this context, "si" introduces a general condition, and it should use the third person singular ("tiene") or an impersonal form rather than second person.

4. **“ lo mas importante”**

The phrase is missing the accent on “más” and needs the definite article to agree with a neuter subject: “lo más importante”.

5. **“ayudarlos con la salud mental”**

While understandable, “salud mental” would benefit from a definite article — “la salud mental” — to specify the known issue. Also, this phrase is somewhat awkward with “ayudarlos”; a better verb or phrasing is typically needed to convey assistance with an abstract concept.

6. **“veteranos quien tienen”**

“Quien” refers to people but only in restrictive clauses introduced with a preposition or as a subject in non-restrictive clauses. Here, “que” is appropriate as a restrictive relative pronoun.

7. **“PTSD o algo otro”**

The correct phrase is “otra cosa” or similar. “Algo otro” is incorrect — “otro” cannot follow “algo”.

8. **“si hiciéramos este proyecto” (x2)**

“Hiciéramos” is the imperfect subjunctive, which is used in contrary-to-fact “if” clauses. However, this condition appears more hypothetical than contrary-to-fact, so depending on the intended meaning, the indicative or future could be more appropriate. Still, if the intent is purely speculative, “hiciéramos” is correct; just watch consistency.

9. **“obtuviéramos mucha atención”**

This is correct in terms of structure for a hypothetical conditional. No change needed here — included for context with other “if” clauses.

10. **“Los Estados Unidos”**

“Los” should not be capitalized mid-sentence. Only “Estados Unidos” is capitalized.

11. **"atracar mas soportar"**

This phrase does not make sense. "Atracar" means to dock or to rob, and "soportar" means to endure. Likely the intended meaning was to gain more support — "recibir más apoyo".

12. **" mucha mas veteranos"**

"Mucha" should agree in gender and number with "veteranos" → "muchos más".

13. **"al todos los postgrados"**

"Al" is incorrect before "todos". It should just be "a todos los postgrados".

14. **"postgrados quien quiere ayudar a nosotros"**

As above, "que" should be used to refer to people in restrictive relative clauses without a preceding preposition.

15. **"ayudar a nosotros "**

This is not the correct placement or form of the indirect object pronoun. It should be "ayudarnos" if attached to the verb or "nos" before the verb.

16. **"personas quien trabajen"**

In a restrictive clause referring to people without a preposition, use "que," not "quien." Also, "trabajen" is correct subjunctive after "recomiendo que".

17. **"Veteranos han visto mucho"**

"Veteranos" needs the definite article ("Los veteranos"). Also, consider tense consistency: depending on narrative flow, past perfect or preterite might be better.

18. **"mucho malas imágenes"**

"Mucho" modifies a singular or non-count noun. Since "imágenes" is plural, it should be "muchas imágenes malas." Word order also needs attention.

19. **"ayudando los veteranos"**

This needs the personal “a” — “ayudando a los veteranos”.

20. **“ser muy muy gracioso, paciente...”**

“Gracioso” means “funny,” not “kind” or “nice.” Possibly a vocabulary error. Also, adjective agreement is needed: “gracioso” doesn’t agree with “tenemos que ser” if referring to a mixed or female group.

21. **“ temenos que conocer estos veteranos”**

“Conocer” is used for people or places, not for facts or concepts. “Saber” would be the correct verb here.

22. **“puede ser peligros”**

“Peligros” is a noun, but “ser peligroso” is the correct adjective form.

23. **“ayudar los veteranos “**

Needs the personal “a” → “ayudar a los veteranos”.

24. **“ un grande proyecto”**

Adjectives of quantity or size like “grande” precede the noun and take the short form “gran” before a singular noun.

25. **“mucha personas”**

“Personas” is feminine plural, so the adjective should be “muchas”.

26. **“ayudar a nosotros”**

Same issue as earlier — incorrect placement and form. Should use “nos”.

27. **“ podamos ayudar”**

This is the present subjunctive, but in a conditional sentence like “si X, Y,” the result clause needs the conditional tense: “podríamos”.

Chapter 5
Leveraging AI to Support High School Students' Mathematical Reasoning Through Writing

Kaitlin Bundock
https://orcid.org/0000-0002-2698-6432
Utah State University, USA

Chenglu Li
https://orcid.org/0000-0002-1782-0457
University of Utah, USA

Sharlene A. Kiuhara
https://orcid.org/0000-0003-3541-5495
University of Utah, USA

Robert Zheng
https://orcid.org/0000-0003-0507-3340
University of Utah, USA

ABSTRACT

The purpose of this chapter is to illustrate how Generative Artificial Intelligence (AI) can be leveraged to support high school students' mathematical reasoning through writing. Specifically, this chapter provides background information related to difficulties high school students with disabilities may experience in mathematics and writing and highlights how AI could be leveraged to address such challenges. In this chapter, we also describe an iterative process our research team used to develop a usable AI browser plugin to facilitate the argument and mathematics learning of

DOI: 10.4018/979-8-3373-2927-7.ch005

high school students with learning challenges and report the preliminary results of studies we conducted to evaluate initial usability and efficacy of an intervention utilizing the AI plugin on students' mathematical reasoning and argumentative mathematical writing. We also discuss implications for practice for teachers, teacher educators, and instructional designers and present recommendations for future research in this area.

INTRODUCTION

Generative Artificial Intelligence (AI) is increasingly a topic of interest for educators working with school-aged children (in the U.S., ages 5-18). While much of the conversation about generative AI among educators focuses on ways to guide students in using AI ethically and in ways to supplement their own independent work (i.e., preventing plagiarism that includes the use of AI), some educators are enthusiastically embracing AI as a learning tool to support their students. This may be especially relevant to teachers of students with disabilities (in the U.S., special education teachers) and related service personnel (e.g., school psychologists, speech-language pathologists, behavior analysts) who work with students with disabilities to maximize their learning and life outcomes.

One particular group of students with disabilities who may stand to benefit from the incorporation of AI in education are students with mathematics learning disabilities (MLD). Students with MLD are students who have been identified as having a specific learning disability that affects them in the area of mathematics, meaning that their mathematics performance in the areas of calculation or concepts and applications is lower than that expected for their grade level and same age peers (Geary, 2011; Hott et al., 2020). Other definitions of MLD characterize students who consistently score below the 10th percentile in mathematics as students with MLD (Geary, 2011). Such students typically receive specially designed instruction to support their mathematics learning. An estimated 5-7% of school-aged children in the U.S. are categorized as having an MLD (Geary, 2011; Hott et al., 2020). It is important to note that many other students (around 10% in any given year) may score below the 10th percentile in mathematics (Geary, 2011), and that mathematics is a persistently challenging academic area in which many students may benefit from AI learning supports. However, in this chapter we focus on students with MLD as a starting point for the development of AI tools built to support students' mathematics learning because this particular population is in need of specialized support; if AI tools can be effectively built and utilized to support the learning of students with MLD, other students who are low-achieving in mathematics would also likely benefit.

An important consideration when working with students with MLD is to recognize that these students may also face additional learning challenges. Empirical evidence supports the comorbidity of MLD with reading comprehension and spelling difficulties (Korhonen et al., 2012; Krowka & Fuchs, 2017). These additional challenges can create further learning barriers when solving word problems (Schleppegrell, 2007). During mathematics instruction, mathematical concepts are presented in a language-rich context. Therefore, it is essential to support students' language development alongside their mathematical learning because mathematical understanding and reasoning often require the integration of both numerical and linguistic ability. Educators must consider strategies that address both aspects to ensure a comprehensive and effective learning experience for students with MLD.

Given the complex mathematics and language challenges students with MLD may have, the use of AI may be one way to efficiently and effectively support learners with MLD. The purpose of this chapter is to illustrate how Generative Artificial Intelligence (AI) can be leveraged to support high school students' mathematical reasoning and justification through writing. Specifically, this chapter will provide background information related to difficulties high school students with disabilities may experience in mathematics and writing, highlight how AI could be leveraged to address such challenges, and describe an iterative process our research team used to develop a usable AI browser plugin to facilitate the argument and mathematics learning of high school students with learning challenges. Our research team used an exploratory methodology, in which we conducted multiple iterative research cycles to develop, refine, and evaluate the AI browser plugin and intervention. In this chapter, we report the results of studies we conducted to evaluate the effectiveness of an intervention utilizing the AI plugin on students' mathematical reasoning and argumentative mathematical writing. We will also discuss implications for practice for teachers, teacher educators, and instructional designers. Finally, we will present recommendations for future research in this area.

Academic Difficulties High School Students with Disabilities May Experience

High school students with learning disabilities may experience challenges with a variety of academic demands, in part due to increased complexity of content at the high school level combined with increased expectations for independence in navigating educational contexts in schools. Mathematics and writing are two areas in which high school students with learning disabilities may encounter difficulties. Mathematics and writing proficiency remain areas of persistent difficulty for secondary students in U.S. public schools, especially for students with disabilities (NAEP Mathematics, 2013; NAEP Writing, 2011). However, there is evidence indicating that it may be powerful to address these difficulties together through interventions targeting both mathematics and writing. Constructing written arguments to learn mathematics is shown to be an empirically effective instructional practice to enhance students' mathematics learning in K-12 classrooms (Bangert-Drowns et al., 2004; Graham et al., 2020). Additionally, research indicates that systematic and explicit instruction is effective for using writing to develop elementary and secondary students' conceptual and procedural understanding of mathematics (Bundock et al., 2021; Hacker et al., 2019; Kiuhara et al., 2020, Kiuhara et al., 2023). Approaches that combine both mathematics and writing may be especially appealing for use in a high school context, in which time is limited as students must complete coursework required for graduation while balancing extracurricular activities, career and technical education courses, along with increased responsibilities outside of school such as a job or family obligations.

Implications for Incorporating AI to Support High School Students with Mathematics Learning Disabilities

There is great potential for AI to address several common challenges that students with MLD may experience when learning mathematics or writing. Specifically, students with MLD may often experience cognitive and/or behavioral challenges that impede learning (Geary, 2004; Geary et al., 2008; Hallet et al., 2010). For example, these students may exhibit delays in language and vocabulary development (Desoete, 2015; Forsyth & Powell, 2017; Krowka & Fuchs, 2017). Korhonen et al. (2012) examined high school students' language ability based on their performance on a mathematics test and found students who scored in the lowest percentile on the mathematics test also performed the lowest on the three language measures for word comprehension, reading comprehension, and spelling. Additionally, research findings suggest students with MLD may exhibit difficulties with working memory capacity that may impact step sequencing and interpretation of mathematical concepts (Geary, 2004; Swanson & Fung, 2016), and difficulty self-regulating learning processes and attention during learning (Graham & Harris, 2018).

Generative AI stands to address these challenges when used as an innovative learning support, as evidenced in a review by Kasneci and colleagues (2023). Using generative AI may enrich and deepen students' learning and increase self-regulation of their mathematics and writing learning in particular. Embedding AI in a learning platform may allow the AI to identify gaps in a student's understanding and adapt responses to students' prompts using real-time feedback and targeted support. However, given limitations and ethical concerns related to AI, it is important for researchers and teachers to systematically develop and apply these powerful technologies to benefit students' learning, especially for high school students with MLD.

In the context of enhancing students' algebraic reasoning through writing, generative AI powered by large language models (LLMs) offers a promising educational tool for providing effective, automated, and personalized support to students on a large scale. Previous implementations of AI in education have demonstrated its potential to guide, enhance, and evaluate students' writing in areas such as online discourse analysis, language acquisition, and real-time support in STEM learning (Du & Qian, 2022; MacNeil et al., 2023). However, it is important to explore how generative AI can specifically support students with MLD based on prior research.

Zhai et al. (2024) compared the cognitive load and problem-solving abilities of ChatGPT and GPT-4 with the performance of 4th, 8th, and 12th grade students on the National Assessment of Educational Progress (NAEP) Science assessments, using Sweller's (2011) cognitive load theory. While the study found that large language models (LLMs) can respond with a high degree of accuracy to the inherent difficulty of tasks as the cognitive demands increase, the LLMs were not sensitive to the application of knowledge in novel contexts, particularly in the 8th and 12th grade assessments. The middle and high school science items required students to demonstrate creativity and advanced cognitive skills compared to the 4th grade assessment items, such as critical thinking and analytical abilities requiring the application of cognitive and metacognitive strategies, to achieve higher scores; the LLMs were not adept at handling these aspects.

Taub and Azevedo (2019) investigated how students' prior domain knowledge influenced their use of cognitive and metacognitive strategies and self-regulated learning processes when engaging in learning platforms using an AI-powered intelligent tutoring system. Specifically, they explored whether differences existed in students' ability to comprehend tasks, set goals, create plans, employ taught learning strategies, and adapt their goals, plans, and strategies accordingly based on having high prior knowledge and low prior knowledge. While both student groups employed cognitive and metacognitive strategies, the participants with low prior knowledge demonstrated lower frequencies of strategies application, likely because they were also having to learn new material. These findings highlight how varying levels of students' prior knowledge may influence their ability to navigate and process information within a tutoring system enhanced by generative AI.

A shift towards AI-driven instruction shows promise in enhancing student outcomes, increasing teacher efficiency, and promoting greater inclusion and accessibility in K-12 settings. The evidence gained from AI applications can help inform and shape educational practices and policies specific to AI and special education. Yet, research has shown that widely adopted AI tools can produce disparate effects on students based on their prior knowledge, cognitive, and metacognitive skills (Shirah & Sidney, 2023; Shoufan, 2023; Taub & Azevedo, 2019; Vanbecelaere et al., 2020), underscoring the need for thoughtful and equitable design—particularly when developing AI tools for students receiving specialized instruction. However, few studies have investigated LLMs to extend our understanding of using AI to promote higher-order thinking (e.g., critical thinking) and rhetorical text structure (e.g., argumentation) targeted for using argumentative writing to develop students' problem solving and mathematical reasoning, specifically for developing algebraic reasoning for high school students with MLD.

Recent advances in AI are enabling the development of personalized learning systems, intelligent tutoring platforms, and adaptive assessments that cater to individual students' strengths, challenges, and learning characteristics. Moreover, the integration of AI in K-12 special education has the potential to enhance the way students eligible to receive special education services learn and interact with mathematics content, and how their teachers leverage AI in their implementation of services. However, given the limitations and ethical concerns related to AI, it is important for researchers and teachers to systematically develop and apply these powerful technologies to benefit students' learning, especially for students with learning challenges.

THEORETICAL FOUNDATION FOR THE USE OF AI TO SUPPORT STUDENT LEARNING

When building interventions that incorporate AI, it is important to draw from existing research and theory regarding how students learn and what strategies have been demonstrated through research to be effective at address learning challenges. In this section, we provide a brief description of some of the theoretical and research foundations that inform our intervention development work.

Effects of Cognitive Load on Complex Learning

One of the challenges facing students in complex learning, particularly students with MLD, is the amount of cognitive load imposed on learners during their learning. Cognitive load is also described as the mental load associated with the process of specific learning materials. For example, a learner who has learnt addition and subtraction in arithmetic would feel challenged and subsequently experience new levels of mental load as he/she spends efforts to learn multiplication and division. However, not all types of cognitive loads are detrimental to learning. Some are healthy and beneficial to learning such as learners' mental efforts to learn and discover new knowledge; others can slow and even hamper learners' learning which include high level content difficulty and occasionally inappropriate ways of content delivery that may tax extra cognitive resources in memory. Sweller and colleagues

(Sweller, 1988; Sweller et al., 1998) proposed that three types of cognitive load that can significantly affect learners' learning. They are intrinsic, extraneous and germane cognitive load. Intrinsic cognitive load refers to the load associated with the difficulty of the content materials. Sweller (1988) asserts that content difficulty can be explained by the level of element interactivity. For example, when a learner learns 26 alphabets, the level of element interactivity remains at a low level, i.e., his/her processing effort (cognitive load) is limited to individual alphabets. If the learner learns a sentence "the train runs on the tracks," the level of element interactivity becomes higher as it involves both alphabets and syntax (e.g., subject, verb, adverbial phrase). Subsequently, the learner is likely to experience a higher level of mental load (i.e., cognitive load) when learning the content at syntax level. Research suggests that intrinsic cognitive load may be bypassed and alleviated using effective instructional strategies like prior-knowledge training, just-in-time knowledge support, etc. (Zheng & Gardner, 2020). The authors in the current study employed an AI tool to provide just-in-time support to students' mathematical learning in an effort to alleviate their intrinsic cognitive load during their complex learning.

The second type of cognitive load includes extraneous cognitive load which is considered impertinent to learning. According to Sweller (1988), extraneous cognitive load refers to the cognitive load caused by the format and manner in which information is presented. For example, teachers may unwittingly increase learners' extraneous cognitive load by presenting materials that require students to mentally integrate mutually referring, disparate sources of information. Examples include (1) placing corresponding diagrams and texts on separate pages instead of next to each other – a violation of Spatial Contiguity Principle (See Mayer's Cognitive Theory of Multimedia Learning, 2001), or (2) presenting the content with video, caption and audio simultaneously – a violation of Modality Principle (Mayer, 2001). Both examples represent bad practices in content delivery which can impose extraneous cognitive load on learners as they deal with the content.

The third type of cognitive load refers to germane cognitive load. Germane cognitive load is related to the mental effort associated with problem solving or new knowledge acquisition during learning (Sweller et al., 1998). Therefore, germane cognitive load needs to be encouraged and nurtured while engaging in learning. Importantly, research has shown that germane cognitive load is positively correlated with learners' motivation and interest which are critical in explaining learners' success in learning (Fehrmann, 2025; Gupta & Zheng, 2020). In their study on students' math problem solving, Gupta and Zheng (2020) noticed that germane cognitive load and motivation were positively correlated, leading to higher achievement outcomes in math problem solving. Similar findings were obtained showing positive relationship between germane cognitive effort and motivation (Woo, 2014; Zeithofer et al., 2024).

Cognitive scientists have been trying to unveil the relationship between three types of cognitive load and specifically how they collectively affect learners' learning (Greenberg & Zheng, 2023; Sweller, 1988; 2018; Sweller et al., 1998). Drawing from the theory of cognitive architecture in working memory (Baddeley, 2012), Sweller and colleagues noted that since the working memory is limited, three types of cognitive load, when added together, should constitute the overall cognitive load in working memory. They also added three types of cognitive load are additive to each other and therefore cannot exceed the overall capacity of working memory in any learning situation.

Due to working memory limitation and the additive nature of cognitive load, Sweller (2018) proposed that when designing an instruction, one must keep the extraneous cognitive load low if the intrinsic cognitive load is high in order to allow sufficient cognitive resources for germane cognitive load to process the difficult content in working memory. In complex learning like mathematics both intrinsic and extraneous cognitive loads cannot be high at the same time as they can hurt the learner's learning. Zheng and Greenberg (2018) explained when both intrinsic and extraneous loads are high, there will be hardly any cognitive resources left for the learner to engage in an effortful learning which is often measured as germane cognitive load in cognitive load theory.

Mathematics Intervention Research

One of the main targets of our intervention work is to develop an intervention that supports students' mathematical reasoning and argumentation. Addressing these skills through word-problem solving is advantageous, given that students often face challenges related to word problems because word problems require students to read and interpret text. Additionally, word problem skills facilitate overall mathematics achievement (Stevens & Powell, 2016; Wang et al., 2016), enable the application of mathematics to real word problems (Verschaffel et al., 2000), foster critical thinking (Dolapcioglu & Doğanay, 2022), and are an important prerequisite to higher level science and mathematics courses and careers (Seo et al., 2018).

However, word problems are challenging for many students (Daroczy et al., 2015). Successfully solving word problems requires students to integrate multiple skills, including effective reading to extract information, attention to detail to avoid copying errors, knowledge of mathematical symbols and notations, and a conceptual understanding of mathematics in order to enable problem deconstruction and the development of solution plans. Additionally, students must complete computations accurately and interpret the results of the problem in context correctly (Pongsakdi et al., 2020; Powell et al., 2020). Given the complexity of word problems and their incorporation of linguistic and mathematic skills, word problems are an appropriate form of mathematics problems through which to help students build mathematical reasoning and argumentation.

The focus area of our intervention work in the current sequence of studies is the concept of rate of change (i.e., slope), which is defined as a unit per unit change or comparison (Confrey & Smith, 1994). Rate of change is a core mathematical concept that is foundational to higher-level mathematics and is also found in everyday life (e.g., calculating average miles per gallon, creating budgets, determining appropriate quantities when converting recipes). Rate of change problems can pose particular challenges for students because they require students to understand the structure of linear equations conceptually, interpret each variable in a linear equation, set up and solve algebraic equations, represent rate with tables, and graph linear equations. Approximately 60% of high school students struggle to understand rate of change problems (Edson & Sedaghat, 2015). Despite the significant challenges students may have with rate of change problems, it is crucial for students to understand rate of change because the concept of rate of change is a building block for more advanced mathematics (i.e., algebra and higher-level mathematics; Hattikudor et al., 2012; Teuscher et al., 2010; Teuscher & Reys, 2012).

Research conducted on mathematics interventions indicates that several strategies are effective at helping students improve their mathematics performance. These strategies include teaching problem-solving strategies, instilling multiple ways to conceptualize problems, and developing self-regulating learning skills to support strategy use and motivation (Elia, 2020; Hwang & Riccomini, 2016; Cleary et al., 2017). In the context of strategy instruction, mathematics educators often emphasize heuristic strategies that break down the problem-solving process into more manageable steps (Hwang & Riccomini, 2016). Teaching students heuristic strategies supports a variety of students with and without disabilities (Hacker et al., 2019; Jitendra et al., 2017; Montague, 2014). Research has also examined the impact of heuristic strategies on students' academic performance in other areas, including writing. Heuristic strategies may therefore be a powerful way to help students improve their mathematical reasoning as well as their written mathematics argumentation.

Mathematical Writing Intervention Research

It is becoming more and more common for students to be expected to explain and justify their mathematical reasoning through writing (Hughes & Lee, 2020; Powell et al., 2017). However, expressing mathematical reasoning through writing can be very challenging for students; only 2% of 8th graders scored at the advanced level for persuading, explaining, and conveying experiences (National Assessment of Educational Progress for Writing [NAEP], 2011) and only 7% of 8th graders scored at the advanced level for mathematics, in which they are asked to justify a mathematical concept or relationship (NAEP for Mathematics, 2022). Due to the challenges this can pose for both students and teachers, there is a need to develop and evaluate the effectiveness of interventions that target students' mathematical reasoning and written argumentation. Despite this need, there have so far been few interventions developed to specifically help students, including students with disabilities, improve their mathematical writing. Research conducted on mathematical writing indicates several benefits to students improving their mathematical writing. Targeting students mathematical writing is an effective way to help students improve not only their writing abilities (Arsenault et al., 2022; Hughes et al., 2020; Kiuhara et al., 2020; Kiuhara et al., 2023), but also their mathematics understanding, reasoning, and proficiency (Graham et al., 2020; Hebert et al., 2019; Hughes et al., 2020; Hughes & Lee, 2020; Powell et al., 2017).

Research that has been conducted on mathematical writing indicates that mathematical writing instruction should include specific elements, such as planning, editing, revising, and sharing writing with peers (Powell et al., 2017; Kiuhara et al., 2020). Students, especially those with disabilities or who may have other academic challenges, may benefit from additional instructional supports and scaffolds (Kiuhara et al., 2020; Powell et al., 2017; Riccomini et al., 2024). Studies focused on helping students with learning challenges improve their mathematical writing have incorporated supports such as sentence starters, sentence strips, word banks, and talk frames (Braxton & Terrell, 2024; Cohen et al., 2015; Riccomini et al., 2024), as well as visual representations of mathematics concepts (Hughes & Lee, 2020; Kiuhara et al., 2020; Riccomini et al., 2024) and graphic organizers (Graham et al., 2020). AI could be leveraged to provide these and similar additional scaffolds to support the communication of higher-level or more complex reasoning, understanding and using mathematical symbols in writing, and using specific mathematics vocabulary (Jitendra et al., 2021; Powell et al., 2017; Riccomini et al., 2024).

We considered this research base when developing our intervention, with the goal of creating an intervention that would be effective for helping students improve their mathematical reasoning and argumentation while also being feasible to implement in busy secondary school settings.

Research on AI Chatbots to Support Mathematics and Writing

There is a small but emerging research base related to the use of AI Chatbots to support students' learning in the areas of mathematics and writing. Much of the publications on this topic are currently articles written with the purpose of providing guidance for how to use AI Chatbots to support teachers' practice and students' learning (e.g., Guo et al., 2022; Smith et al., 2024) or to describe design processes (e.g., Laksana & Fiangga, 2022; Nguyen et al., 2019), rather than presenting research conducted on the effectiveness of using AI Chatbots to support students' learning. Additionally, while Smith and colleagues (2024) provide guidance about using AI Chatbots to generate mathematical writing examples to support students with learning disabilities specifically, there are currently no published studies evaluating the effectiveness of using AI Chatbot technology on improving students' learning.

Research examining the effectiveness of AI Chatbot technology of students' writing and students' mathematics separately indicates mixed results (Cheng et al., 2024; Duong & Chen, 2025; Lee and Yeo, 2022). Lee and Yeo (2022) conducted a study to examine whether an AI Chatbot was effective at helping pre-service teachers develop questioning strategies in an open-ended mathematics context. They found that some design features could lead to PSTs exhibiting improved questioning strategies to support mathematics learning. Cheng and colleagues (2024) developed an AI Chatbot that included scaffolding and social-emotional considerations, embedded within an online mathematics learning platform. Cheng and colleagues (2024) examined the mathematics learning of middle and high school students across the AI condition and a more traditional online learning condition and found no significant differences between conditions. Duong and Chen (2025) developed and examined the effectiveness of an AI chatbot designed to support Vietnamese high school students with their English writing practice at home. They included higher and lower proficiency students in their mixed-method approach and found that the chatbot improved all elements of students' writing, including content, organization, vocabulary, language use, and mechanics. Additional research is needed to more fully examine the range of possible applications and effectiveness of AI chatbot technology within educational contexts. In particular, there is currently no published research examining the use of AI chatbots to support the mathematical writing of students with learning disabilities.

CASE EXAMPLE – DEVELOPING AN AI BROWSER PLUGIN TO SUPPORT STUDENT LEARNING

Our research team used an exploratory design to engage in an iterative process to develop an AI browser plugin using GPT-4o (Hurst et al., 2024) embedded within the Canvas© Learning Management System (LMS). Our goal was to develop an intervention, with embedded AI, to help high school students with disabilities improve their mastery of algebraic concepts through constructing written arguments. Given that our main goal was to develop the intervention with an embedded AI, an exploratory design allowed us to employ an iterative process across multiple stages as we designed, tested, refined, and piloted the intervention. In this section, we first describe the intervention focus. Next, we describe our development process and briefly present findings related to student outcomes. A brief description of each stage of our development process is provided below.

Intervention Focus: FACT + RRCC

Our instructional approach for teaching both rate of change and mathematical reasoning through writing centered around the a self-regulated instructional framework, Self-Regulated Strategy Development (SRSD, a teacher-implemented evidence-based instructional approach shown to be effective in over 100 studies with elementary, secondary, and college students who may or may not need additional instructional supports (Graham & Harris, 2018; Harris & Graham, 2009). Additionally, students learned to address affective processes, such as beliefs and attitudes about learning and writing, and to manage behaviors that might hinder their learning, such as starting a task, maintaining focus, or completing a task (Graham & Harris, 2018). SRSD is a well-established learning strategies approach for enhancing students' genre knowledge, writing quality, and their ability to set individual learning goals and monitor progress toward these goals (Gillespie & Graham, 2014; Graham et al., 2014; Graham et al., 2012).

The SRSD framework consists of six instructional stages: Developing Background Knowledge, Discuss It, Model It, Memorize It, Support It, and Independent Performance (Harris et al., 2008). During these stages, the teacher guides students to become self-regulated learners. Kiuhara and colleagues extended the SRSD framework to develop elementary students' mathematical reasoning of fractions through argumentative writing using two learning strategies: FACT + RRCC (Hacker et al., 2019; Kiuhara et al., 2020). Each letter of FACT represents steps to engage students in the mathematical problem-solving process: **F** = Figure it out; **A** = Act on it; **C** = Compare your reasoning with a peer; **T** = Tie it up in an argument. The "T" in FACT represents the letters to construct a written argument justifying the student's answer providing an opportunity for students to begin articulating their mathematical reasoning: **R** = Restate the task; **R** = Provide reasons; **C** = Present the counterclaim; and **C** = Conclude the paragraph, The researchers found that FACT + RRCC strategies helped students with and without MLD meet the cognitive demands of mindful planning of writing and the cognitive processes of mathematical reasoning. Compared to students in the control condition who received regular instruction, students who received FACT and RRCC made meaningful gains ($g = .60$) and showed significant and substantial improvement in their mathematical language and quality of mathematical reasoning ($g = 1.82$); number of argumentative writing elements ($g = 3.20$) and total words written ($g = 1.92$). Notably, the students with MLD who received FACT + RRCC demonstrated statistically significant gains in their fraction knowledge compared to their same-aged peers without MLD ($g =

1.04). These results suggest that the evidence-based principles embedded in FACT benefited students with MLD. Based on these findings, we adapted FACT + RRCC from a teacher-facilitated instruction to an asynchronous learning platform using AI to enhance algebraic reasoning to high school students with MLD.

Development Process

Our multidisciplinary research team is composed of individuals with expertise in special education, writing, mathematics, cognition and learning technologies, and the use of AI models in teaching and learning. To develop the intervention with an embedded AI browser plugin, we engaged in multiple stages of iterative design and development. Stage 1 included preparation and design, Stage 2 involved a usability test with one learning module, Stage 3 consisted of pilot testing three learning modules with one high school student for usability and feedback, and Stage 4 entailed refining the intervention in preparation of a pilot test of seven learning modules using single-case design with 8 high school students with MLD. We provide more information about each of these stages below.

Stage 1: Preparation and Design

In the first stage, we engaged in discussions to determine the overall set-up of the intervention (modality and features in the Canvas© LMS), desired functionality of the embedded AI browser plugin, scope of the content to include in the intervention, and specific intervention objectives. Since our project involved several research studies, we also discussed how we would measure a variety of outcomes at different stages of our studies. We used OpenAI's GPT-4o as the foundation model to develop a conversational AI that guides student learning through the FACT + RRCC framework. To support this, we employed LangGraph, an open-source framework for building agentic AI, to construct an agentic workflow that tracks and responds to the learner's current stage within the FACT + RRCC process. Similar to traditional chatbots that rely on a state machine to manage conversational flow, our system (Swoop AI) used the agentic workflow to dynamically determine and transition between states (e.g., identifying whether the student is in the "F" or "A" phase), based on the LLM's own reasoning instead of intent classification (e.g., a separate classifier to identify the current state that often does not generalize well). Once the system identified the learner's current state, it provided relevant contextual information, such as definitions (e.g., *Figure it out!*) and exemplar activities, to Swoop AI to support in-context learning. To further enhance students' argumentative thinking within the FACT + RRCC framework, we implemented a chain-of-thought prompting strategy, encouraging the AI to break down student prompts and respond with detailed reasoning.

To ensure the developed AI is portable across diverse learning environments, including any learning management system such as Canvas©, we developed it as a browser extension using React.js and CRXJS. This packaging enables seamless integration into any webpage across devices (e.g., laptops, tablets, and mobile phones). As a browser extension, the AI can also access the content of the current webpage upon students' agreement, enabling augmented interactions such as transforming plain text into interactive hypertext that triggers the AI, thereby enhancing usability and accessibility. Figure 1 shows the integrated AI into a Canvas course.

In the initial development of the intervention, we prioritized feasible implementation in school contexts. We used Canvas© as the LMS for our intervention because many secondary schools and universities use Canvas© in the area where we are located. We structured the intervention as a course in Canvas©. The lessons were structured as pages with textual and visual information with integrated prompts for students to interact with our chatbot, Swoop, who was depicted as a red-tailed hawk that is the university mascot. We also designed the intervention so that students had access to both a virtual notebook as well as a paper notebook to record their notes. An important component of the intervention was teaching students how to monitor and track progress and regulate their learning. To support use of this component, the intervention included paper folders that included tracking sheets for students to record the number of RRCC steps, writing words, and mathematics vocabulary words used in their written mathematical arguments.

Figure 1. The Integrated AI into a Canvas Course

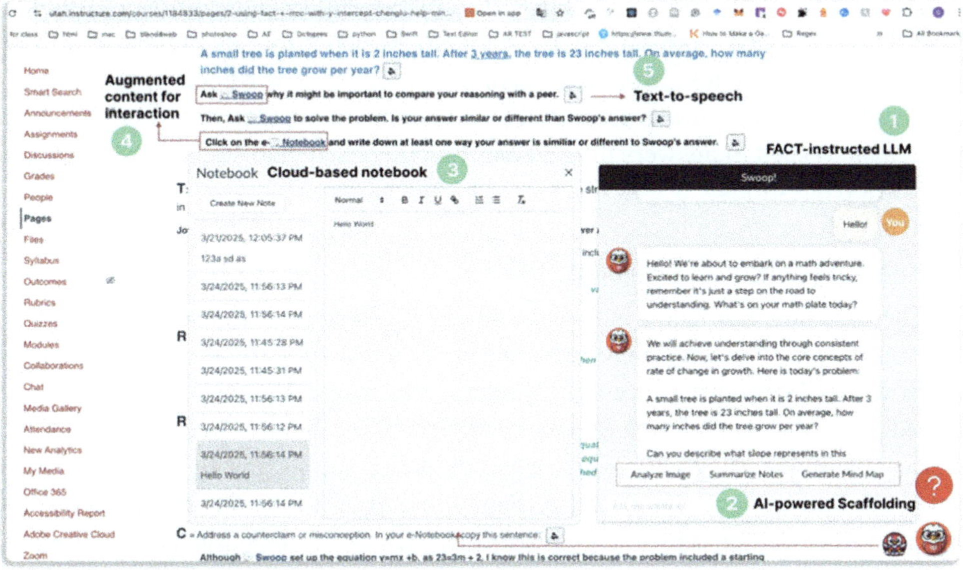

Note. Essential components of the developed AI: (1) an LLM-based conversational agent powered by agentic workflow; (2) AI-powered scaffolding that allows multimodal interaction; (3) a cloud-based notebook; (4) interaction in Canvas page; and (5) accessibility features (e.g., text-to-speech, speech-to-text).

The first learning module focused on reviewing foundational skills needed for understanding slope and linear equations and included word problems with y-intercepts greater than zero (e.g., $y = mx + b$; $140 = 35x + 70$). The second module introduced students to the FACT + RRCC strategy in the context of problems that included y-intercepts greater than zero. The third learning module was formatted as a Canvas "quiz" to engage the student in interactive practice solving word problems (e.g., *Amy sells necklaces. She starts with $3. After she sold 2 necklaces, she had $7. After she sold 4 necklaces, she had $11. How much does she sell each necklace for?)* While the Canvas© LMS labels this particular feature as a "quiz", we conceptualized this as a practice opportunity rather than an assessment.

After this design and development stage, we conducted a usability test in preparation for a pilot study, both of which are described more below. The focus of the usability test was to evaluate the usability of the AI system (Swoop chatbot) using one learning module and the intervention as constructed in the Canvas© LMS.

Stage 2: Usability Test

In the second stage, we tested the usability of the AI system (Swoop chatbot that consisted of an abbreviated version of the intervention with one lesson only) that included a no-AI condition and an AI-only condition. Each condition presented information about the FACT + RRCC strategy and explained how to use it to solve rate of change word problems. In the no-AI condition, this information was presented as written text, similar to reading a webpage or textbook. In the AI condition, this information was presented by Swoop in an interactive format, in which participants typed in answers to questions Swoop posed, and students were able to ask Swoop questions.

Methods for Stage 2: Usability Test

The experimental study included 240 U.S. college students with and without learning disabilities who were recruited from a crowd-sourcing platform called Prolific. Prolific has been successfully adopted for research across diverse domains, including business, health, and education (Palan and Schitter, 2018; Song et al., 2025; Stanton et al., 2022), with strong evidence supporting the validity of the data collected through the platform (Peer et al., 2022). One distinct advantage of Prolific over other crowdsourcing platforms, such as Amazon Mechanical Turk, is its robust prescreening process for participant pool building and its large, verified base of undergraduate student participants. Of the participants, 188 completed both pre- and post-surveys on usability (15 items adapted from the validated scale on technology acceptance by Sezer & Yilmaz, 2019) and formative learning outcomes (two items) related to mathematics and writing. To further ensure the quality of the collected responses, we included three attention check questions, items that explicitly instructed participants to select a specific option (Kung et al., 2018). After keeping participants who passed the attention checks, there were 179 responses (n_{exp}=74, n_{ctrl}=105). Specifically, we ran the study in the following order (see Figure 2):

1. We first set up screening criteria on Prolific by including only U.S.-based undergraduate/graduate students who were actively enrolled and self-reported with learning disabilities. 1,046 were eligible and were invited to participate in the study.
2. 240 participants opened our web portal through the invitation link to go through the consent form, study overview, and pre-test on their demographics and high school level linear equation knowledge items.
3. Participants were randomly assigned to different groups and instructed to engage with the intervention. To encourage active engagement with the intervention, a 15-minute time requirement was implemented before participants could proceed to the post-test. Students in the control group did not have access to AI and instead used text-only instruction to learn and apply the FACT+RRCC framework. In contrast, students in the experimental group did not receive the text-based instruction but interacted with the AI to learn the same framework

for math problem-solving. During the intervention, clickstream data were collected from all participants. For those in the experimental group, we also captured their eye-tracking data and interactions with the AI. However, due to the exploratory nature of this study and space limitations, we do not report analyses of participants' logs, messages, or eye-tracking data in this chapter.

4. Finally, participants proceeded to the post-test page to answer questions on math problems and usability, after which they were shown a code to redeem compensation on Prolific ($8 each for ~30 minutes).

Figure 2. Experimental Setup of the Usability Study

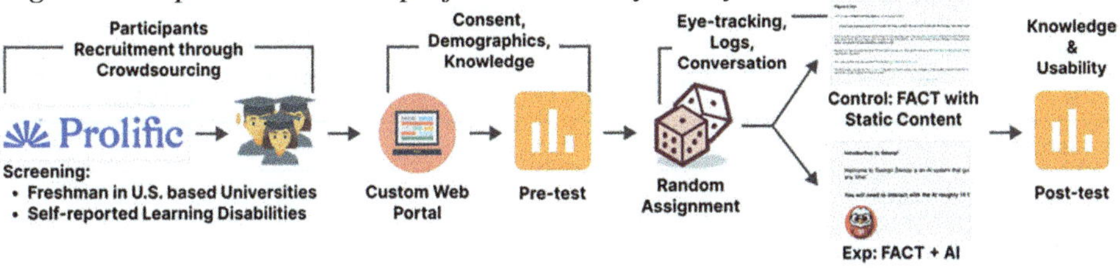

Results for Stage 2: Usability Test

Table 1 presents descriptive data on participants' gender, race, learning disability, enrolled institution, and academic program. A Chi-square goodness-of-fit test was conducted to compare the demographics between the experimental and control groups. No statistically significant differences were found, supporting the validity of the random assignment. Table 2 shows the usability results and statistical test for comparison for the groups (see Appendix A for detailed usability questions). Overall, participants in the experimental group perceived the intervention (AI vs. no-AI) as more useful, effective, and usable, as reflected by a statistically significant difference on the overall usability responses ($t(149) = 1.98$, $p = 0.049$, $d = 0.30$). Further analysis of individual usability items revealed that the experimental group rated the intervention as significantly more comfortable to use ($t(159) = 2.05$, $p = 0.042$, $d = 0.31$), easier to adopt ($t(172) = 2.31$, $p = 0.022$, $d = 0.35$), easier to master ($t(169) = 2.94$, $p = 0.004$, $d = 0.45$), more flexible ($t(165) = 3.34$, $p = 0.001$, $d = 0.51$), and more satisfying in meeting their needs ($t(159) = 2.03$, $p = 0.044$, $d = 0.31$). Although participants made descriptive gains from pre- to post-test on their math knowledge, we found no significant difference in math knowledge items between the groups.

Table 1. Descriptives of Participants' Self-reported Demographics

Characteristic	Exp (n=74)	Ctrl (n=105)
Gender		
Female	39 (52.7%)	55 (52.4%)
Male	29 (39.2%)	43 (41.0%)
Other	6 (8.1%)	7 (6.7%)
Race/Ethnicity		
White	44 (59.5%)	64 (61.0%)
Black/African American	9 (12.2%)	21 (20.0%)
Asian	7 (9.5%)	3 (2.9%)
Other/Multiracial	14 (18.9%)	17 (16.2%)
Learning Disability		
	41 (55%)	52 (50%)
Institution Type		
4-year college or university	52 (70.3%)	72 (68.6%)
Community college	21 (28.4%)	33 (31.4%)
Student Level		
Undergraduate student	65 (87.8%)	95 (90.5%)
Graduate student	8 (10.8%)	10 (9.5%)
Other	1 (1.4%)	0 (0.0%)

Table 2. Usability Responses' Descriptive and Inferential Statistics by Participating Groups

Question	Exp Mean (SD)	Ctrl Mean (SD)	t-test, p-value
Usefulness	4.32 (1.07)	4.04 (1.09)	t(157) = 1.68, p=0.094
Enhances learning	4.15 (1.12)	4.05 (1.07)	t(153) = 0.61, p=0.542
Feel comfortable using	**4.32 (1.00)**	**3.99 (1.07)**	**t(159) =2 .05, p=0.042***
Productivity	4.04 (1.18)	3.70 (1.19)	t(156) = 1.91, p=0.058
Easy to use	**4.41 (0.92)**	**4.04 (1.12)**	**t(172) = 2.31, p=0.022***
Skillful use	**4.38 (0.87)**	**3.95 (1.01)**	**t(169) = 2.94, p=0.004****
Flexible	**4.28 (1.00)**	**3.75 (1.09)**	**t(165) = 3.34, p=0.001****
Sufficient info	4.32 (0.86)	4.19 (0.86)	t(157) = 1.03, p=0.306
Would use again	4.12 (1.19)	3.85 (1.06)	t(145) = 1.62, p=0.107
Usage intention	3.93 (1.27)	3.81 (1.07)	t(139) = 0.70, p=0.485

continued on following page

Table 2. Continued

Question	Exp Mean (SD)	Ctrl Mean (SD)	t-test, p-value
Satisfied	4.27 (1.12)	4.10 (1.00)	t(143) = 1.06, p=0.292
Needs met	**4.26 (1.07)**	**3.92 (1.09)**	**t(159) = 2.03, p=0.044***
More info needed	2.97 (1.52)	2.79 (1.49)	t(156) = 0.81, p=0.416
Use strategies	3.23 (1.38)	3.25 (1.28)	t(150) = -0.09, p=0.929
Writing help	3.78 (1.26)	3.67 (1.24)	t(155) = 0.62, p=0.537
Overall	**4.05 (0.86)**	**3.81 (0.79)**	**t(149) = 1.98, p=0.049***

Note. Statistically significant results were bolded. * suggests p-value < 0.05 and ** means p-value < 0.01.

Stage 3: Pilot Test

In the third stage, we conducted a pilot test with one high school student to evaluate the acceptability of the AI system (Swoop chatbot) and the broader intervention embedded in the Canvas© LMS., which consisted of three learning modules. Similar to the usability test, the learning modules were structured as pages with textual and visual information with integrated prompts for students to interact with Swoop, who was depicted as a red-tailed hawk that is the university mascot. We included a virtual notebook as well as a paper notebook for the student to record their notes. An important component of the intervention and central to SRSD was teaching students how to monitor and track progress and regulate their learning. To support the student's self-regulation, the intervention included a booklet with tracking sheets for students to record the number of RRCC steps, writing words, and mathematics vocabulary words used in their written mathematical arguments. The first module of the intervention focused on reviewing foundational skills needed for understanding slope and linear equations and included problems that included y-intercepts greater than zero (e.g., $y = mx + b$; $140 = 35x + 70$). The second module introduced the FACT + RRCC strategy in the context of word problems that included y-intercepts greater than zero. The third learning module, as noted earlier, allowed the student to practice solving word problems and applying the FACT + RRCC strategies with activities for the student to check their work and set learning goals.

Also at Stage 3, we adjusted the embedded AI browser plugin and intervention based on information we gained during the Stage 2 through the Canvas© LMS with the AI browser plugin. The student did not have a learning disability but was at a comparable age of our intended intervention participants. The student completed the modules and provided our research team with feedback about the usability of the modules and the embedded AI. The feedback from the student allowed the team to further fine tune the intervention

Stage 4: Intervention Refinement for Research Study

In Stage 4 and in preparation for our research study with high school students with MLD, we adjusted the embedded AI browser plugin and intervention based on information we gained during Stage 3 In Stage 4, we adjusted the intervention so the sequence of instruction consisted of 7 learning modules. Learning Module 1 reviewed foundational concepts and language for rate of change problems with y-intercepts greater than zero. Learning Module 2 introduced the FACT + RRCC learning strategies. Learning Module 3 was formatted as a Canvas quiz, which included one word problem broken down into 15 different questions or steps, designed to prompt the student through the various stages of the FACT + RRCC strategy. Learning Module 4 focused on checking work and setting learning goals.

Learning Modules 5 to 7 were each formatted as a Canvas quiz to further scaffold interactive practice with opportunities to apply FACT + RRCC. Reflective questions were added to direct the student to count the RRCC steps used in their writing, number of math words used in their writing, and number of writing words used in their writing; questions asking the student to describe how they will continue practicing their use of the strategies). Learning Module 5 included one problem broken down into 19 different questions or steps. The questions prompted students to recall components of the FACT + RRCC strategy to help facilitate memorization. Learning Module 6 included one problem, broken into 17 questions or steps, and was designed for the student to take on more independence for solving the word problem. Finally, Module 7 included the least scaffolds; it included one problem broken into 5 different questions. Each of the quizzes included reflective questions (e.g., prompts to direct the student to count the RRCC steps used in their writing, number of math words used in their writing, and number of writing words used in their writing; questions asking the student to describe how they will continue practicing their use of the strategies, etc.).

Additionally, universal design features were added to the modules to support the learning and support needs of students with MLD. These additions included text-to-speech for students who have difficulty with reading comprehension, accessible buttons to activate Swoop, and providing speech-to-text as an e-Notebook for who may find typing difficult due to limited fine-motor skill development for typing on a keyboard.

Methods for Stage 4: Research Study

We employed a single-case two-sample randomization design (Hwang & Levin, 2022) to evaluate the impact of the FACT + RRCC intervention on the mathematics and mathematical reasoning outcomes of high school students with disabilities (Kiuhara et al., 2025). Eight high school students with disabilities were randomly placed in FACT+AI and FACT only conditions. Single-case designs are experimental and are used by researchers interested in examining functional relationships between independent and dependent variables in contexts in which it is desired or only feasible to include a small number of participants (Horner et al., 2005). Analysis of single-case design results focuses on patterns within participants as well as across participants to determine the likelihood of a functional relationship existing between the intervention and outcome variables. Because our study concluded at the end of May 2025 and analysis is ongoing, in this chapter we report only preliminary findings on the intervention's effects on cognitive load and a student's mathematical reasoning based on their written responses on an algebra test asking the student to solve a word problem and explain their reasoning.

Preliminary Results for Stage 4: Research Study

Impact on Cognitive Load. Given the different roles each cognitive load plays in learners' learning, the current study zeros in on the relationship between three types of cognitive load in AI-supported learning. The participants were asked to learn and solve the linear equation problems. During the learning and problem solving they were provided with an AI support tool named Swoop. The participants searched for information with Swoop to understand the concepts, the use of equation, and the related outcomes. It was predicted that with the support of Swoop, the learners would be able to (a) access the relevant knowledge (e.g., slope) immediately, which may help address the concerns related to lacking proper prior knowledge/schemata in the subject area. The support of AI (Swoop) is conceived as an instructional effort that may (a) alleviate learners' intrinsic cognitive load through a rebuilt of their prior knowledge (Zheng & Gardner, 2020), and (b) free cognitive resources without holding simultaneously sundry information in their working memory. We thus anticipated that the benefits of AI-supported learning would include (a) alleviating intrinsic cognitive load by making relevant knowledge readily available to learners, thus reducing the stress on their lacking proper schemata in learning, and (b) reducing extraneous cognitive load through an optimization in instructional design, i.e., freeing cognitive resources for robust learning with just-in-time knowledge support.

Results showed no significant differences were found between control and experiment groups in terms of intrinsic, extraneous, and germane cognitive load ($p > .01$). Nor was there any difference in performance ($p > .01$). A correlation was run for the three types of cognitive and performance scores. As expected, no differences were found among them. We posit that the non-significance is the self-reported cognitive load measure was administered at the end of the study, after the learning occurred, which may cause inaccuracy in self-reporting on the cognitive load experienced by the learners. Ayres (2018) proposes a multiple cognitive load measurement approach for self-reported measurement to capture the variation and changes of learners' cognitive load during the learning. It is recommended that future research take into consideration the multiple cognitive load measurements to better describe the learners' cognitive processes in terms of the mental load experienced at time points during the intervention.

Effects on Mathematical Reasoning: A Case Example. Mathematical reasoning represents the concepts and skills needed to draw conclusions based on evidence or assumptions and to generalize, model, and analyze mathematical symbols and equations to solve problems (NCTM, 2000). Students may increase their understanding of mathematical concepts through the process of reasoning and sense making through explanation and application (Martin, 2009). One of the intended goals of the intervention was to support students with MLD in developing mathematical reasoning and sense making. Because the content of our intervention focused on operations and algebraic thinking with rate of change, we modified an existing mathematical reasoning rubric used to measure the quality of mathematical reasoning developed by Kiuhara and colleagues to holistically assess both procedural reasoning (i.e., interpreting symbols and equations) and conceptual reasoning. We drew from Kieran (2004) to emphasize a shift from merely calculating the answer using rote procedures to reasoning through a problem-solving process using both conceptual and procedural knowledge and skills. In the context of rate of change word problems, one component that indicates conceptual understanding is correctly representing the variables in the word problem in an equation because doing so requires understanding the underlying relationships in the word problem.

To evaluate students' mathematical reasoning, we administered a writing prompt asking students to justify their answer to a word problem. Figure 3 presents an example of a student's algebraic thinking before and after completing the intervention. We scored students' responses using a 12-point (0-11) mathematical reasoning rubric, the student's pre-intervention response to the prompt received a score of 1. In the pre-intervention example, the student provided a description of the steps they used to approach the problem (*"in the calculator, I put 20 times 10"*) and states what they determined the answer to be (*"in 10 days he can make 20 per day"*). However, the response included unclear reasoning (*"it said there were 10 completed, and if it took Alexander 10 days to make 30"*), showing little understanding of the underlying concepts in the word problem. The student also did not provide a description of how they checked their answer and reasoning in this response. The answer they determined for the problem is also not correct (correct answer is 17 pieces per day).

The student's post-intervention response to the prompt received a score of 7. In the post-intervention example, the student included a position (*"My task was to find out how many pounds Jack needed to harvest in the next 10 days"*) and an accurate step-by-step description of a solution strategy (*"used the values they gave me"*, *"used the y=mx+b equation"*, *"entered values into the equation"*). The student also wraps up their explanation with a concluding sentence (*"Therefore, I got my answer"*). The student also provided the correct answer to this problem in a prior question on the assessment.

When the student's pre- and post-intervention writing is compared, there are a few elements that indicate potential growth in algebraic thinking. First, the student did not refer to an equation in their pre-intervention writing but referred to the correct equation in their post-intervention writing. The post-intervention written response also indicates that the student recognizes the need to identify and use an equation that is aligned with the problem, and that the values and information in the problem can be represented in an equation. The student did not determine the correct answer to the problem in the pre-intervention prompt, but they did determine the correct answer to the problem in the post-intervention prompt, demonstrating accuracy in setting up and solving the equation. There is still additional room for growth in the student's post-intervention writing. Specifically, they would have received a higher score on the post-intervention response had they included specific numbers or labels in their writing, as well as a description of how they checked their answer and reasoning.

Figure 3. Pre-Post Example of a Student's Algebraic Thinking

Pre Example	Post Example
Prompt: Alexander is completing a puzzle. He has already completed 30 pieces and needs to complete a total of 200 pieces. How many pieces should he complete per day to finish in the next 10 days? *(correct answer: 17 pieces per day)*	Prompt: Jack is working on a farm. He has already harvested 50 pounds of tomatoes and needs to harvest a total of 200 pounds. How many pounds should he harvest per day to finish in the next 10 days? *(correct answer: 15 pounds per day)*
Student's Response: In the calculator, I put 20 times 10 because in the problem it said that there were 10 completed, and if it took Alexander 10 days to make 30, then in 10 days he can make 20 per day.	Student's Response: My task was to find out how many pounds Jack needed to harvest in the next 10 days. So I used the values they gave me. I used the y=mx+b equation to find my answer. Then, after knowing what equation I was gonna use, I entered my values in the equation. Therefore, I got my answer. *(provided correct answer to this problem in prior question on assessment)*

DISCUSSION

In this chapter we describe considerations and research relevant to the design and implementation of AI to support the mathematical writing of students with learning disabilities. We view this work as adding to the emerging research base on the use of AI to students' academics. Building from the guidance provided by Smith and colleagues (2024), we present implications for practice in this section of the chapter. In consideration of research studies examining the impact of AI chatbots on students' writing (Duong & Chen, 2025) and students' mathematics (Cheng et al., 2024), we also present suggested directions for future research.

Implications for Practice

The use of AI in educational settings holds great promise for improving accessibility and support options for students with disabilities. However, because research on the effectiveness of AI in supporting learners is still emerging, it is important for educational professionals to stay up to date with recommendations for practice stemming from research. In our iterative development of the intervention to develop students' procedural and conceptual understanding of rate of change leveraging AI, we identify areas for educators to keep in mind when planning how to incorporate AI into their teaching.

First, it is important for educators to attend to cognitive load. With many technological innovations, it can be tempting to try out a lot of different things at the same time, or attempt complex implementations of the technology just to see how much the technology might be able to do. However, when learners are working on acquiring new knowledge and skills, it is recommended to keep extraneous cognitive load low to allow for germane cognitive load to be encouraged. Germane cognitive load is associated with higher motivation and higher achievement outcomes in math problem solving (Fehrmann, 2025; Gupta & Zheng, 2020; Sweller et al., 1998; Woo, 2014; Zeithofer et al., 2024). Essentially, this means it is important to limit distracting information or the need for additional processing so students can focus on the complex academic task at hand (in this case, mathematics word problems). When considered in the context of AI, educators can limit extraneous cognitive load by ensuring that whatever AI system they are implementing is easy to use, so that learners can focus on using the AI to support their learning instead of having to spend extra cognitive load on figuring out how to access and use the AI. We recommend that educators interested in implementing AI learning supports start small and focus on accessibility from the beginning, and increase use of AI learning supports as their experience increases and students gain familiarity and comfortability with the technology.

Second, in our intervention research with our AI system, we found that there were some features that made more sense to keep in hard-copy form, rather than building into the AI system. For example, some of the students who we worked with preferred being able to work through mathematics problems on paper, rather than on the electronic notebook we built into the Canvas(c) LMS. Additionally, our team felt that having students keep a written record of writing elements they were tracking (FACT + RRCC components, writing words, mathematics words) was better than building this into the AI system because the written record was easier for students to work with and provided a visual reminder of progress for the students. Building from our experiences, we recommend that educators consider what hard-copy supplements may be needed or preferred alongside the AI system they are implementing. When considering what hard-copy supplements may be useful, it is important for educators to prioritize students' learning goals and consider what specific hard-copy supports can enhance students' experience and learning.

Third, when using an AI system it is integral to check for accuracy. This is a point highlighted by Smith and colleagues (2024) as well. In our projects, we used ChatGPT to help generate mathematics word problems and possible solutions (for multiple choice questions). There were numerous instances in this process in which ChatGPT provided mathematically inaccurate information, as well as mathematics word problems that did not make sense contextually. It was essential for us to review the information provided through ChatGPT and the AI system we developed for this intervention to ensure that students were provided with accurate information and mathematics word problems that made sense (i.e., didn't include odd information not well aligned to rate contexts, in this case). However, we would also recommend that educators consider how to incorporate this weakness of AI into their instruction. For example, in the context of mathematics it is crucial for students to learn how to check their work and evaluate the reasonableness of answers. It may be possible to leverage AI to help students learn and practice this skill; students could be shown the importance of checking the reasonableness of answers through evaluating answers provided by AI.

The implications for practice we describe here should be considered by educators as well as individuals working on developing technology or AI based products or interventions for use in schools. In addition to these recommendations, we also strongly encourage developers to conduct usability and pilot tests with the individuals who are the targeted consumers of their products (in this case, teachers and/or students) to ensure that products are designed to meet areas of need, are easy to implement, and are accessible and usable by people with a broad range of abilities.

RECOMMENDATIONS FOR FURTHER RESEARCH

While the results of the research we present in this chapter are preliminary (our analysis is on-going at the time of the writing of this chapter), there are several potential areas of future research that may be promising related to the use of AI to support student learning. First additional research is needed regarding the impact of

AI supported interventions on student outcomes, including cognitive load, mathematical writing, and algebraic thinking. First, the preliminary results of the research study conducted in Stage 4 indicated no significant differences were found between the control and experimental groups in terms of intrinsic, extraneous, and germane cognitive load nor performance. We recommend that future research incorporate measures of cognitive load at multiple time points during intervention to better describe variation and changes in learners' cognitive processes in terms of mental load (Ayers, 2018).

Second, while analysis of full mathematical writing and mathematics achievement is ongoing for the study conducted in Stage 4, we recommend that additional research examines the impact of AI supported interventions on the algebraic thinking of secondary students with MLD. This study evaluated students' algebraic thinking in a narrow context (rate of change word problems); additional research should examine other aspects of algebraic reasoning – both content that is prerequisite to rate of change (e.g., translating between linguistic depictions of problems/variable relationships and algebraic depictions of problems/variable relationships), and that builds from rate of change (e.g., describing features of graphed lines in the context of different kinds of equations). Additionally, researchers should consider and evaluate the impact of measuring algebraic reasoning in different ways, given the limited research on the impact of interventions on complex mathematics outcomes (such as algebraic reasoning). In this study, we evaluated algebraic reasoning based on students' written explanations. Researchers should consider evaluating algebraic reasoning based on students' written explanations in addition to or compared with visual representations or spoken descriptions. Research on both intervention and assessment related to algebraic reasoning would provide practitioners with insights into ways to best help students with MLD struggling with advanced mathematical reasoning.

In the research studies presented in this chapter, we focus specifically on how AI can support the mathematical writing of students with disabilities. The results of our research cannot be generalized to other contexts. Additional research should be conducted related to academic learning targets in other content areas (e.g., English Language Arts, science, social studies) as well as other mathematics topics. The learning targets (mathematical writing and solving rate of change word problems) in our studies are complex, requiring students to integrate conceptual mathematical understanding, procedural mathematics skills, reading textual information, and generating written text to present their reasoning. Future research should examine the utility and effectiveness of using AI to support students' learning of simpler, more discrete skills (e.g., solving a series of multiplication problems that are not word problems, learning a set of vocabulary words). Researchers could also conduct studies comparing the utility and effectiveness of AI to support students' learning for discrete versus complex skills. Such information would provide useful information to help educational professionals identify where or how incorporating AI in educational context may be most impactful.

While AI technologies are growing quickly, it is important to recognize that building AI systems that target specific areas or aspects of learning can be time and resource intensive. Given the rapid growth of publicly accessible AI technologies, researchers should consider exploring whether existing publicly accessible AI technologies can be effective at supporting students academically, especially in the natural educational environments in which teachers may implement them. In particular, it is important to examine teachers' perspectives related to the use of AI in educational contexts, including what aspects of their teaching they feel could be best supported through AI. Lee and Yeo (2022) found that pre-service teachers expressed favorable ratings of using AI chatbots to help them develop mathematics questioning strategies, but additional research should be conducted with in-service teachers and to examine a broader range of AI applications. Additionally, researchers should investigate what training or supports teachers feel they need in order to best leverage AI in order to implement it effectively in educational contexts.

In the research presented in this chapter, we focused on an AI-supported intervention delivered through an LMS. We designed the intervention for students to work through individually, with guidance as needed from a tutor. The tutor provided only technological guidance (no mathematics or writing instruction), but all research sessions were conducted one-on-one, with an individual student working through the intervention modules without any peers in the same location. Researchers should investigate whether AI supported interventions can be implemented in a full classroom context. Such research could examine the effectiveness of an AI supported intervention in the context of a whole class working through the same content at the same pace. Additionally, research should examine the effectiveness and feasibility of an AI supported intervention in the context of a differentiated classroom, in which students may or may not be working through the same content at varying paces. This is similar to the research conducted by Cheng and colleagues (2024), in which they examined the impact of an AI chatbot in an online learning platform. Online learning platforms can be used outside of traditional classrooms or within traditional classrooms. Cheng and colleagues found mixed results in their study, in that there were no significant differences in mathematics performance between students in the AI and control conditions, but students expressed positive attitudes towards the chatbots. Given that AI chatbot technology in a mathematics context appears to be acceptable to students, and AI chatbot technology can improve students' writing performance (Duong and Chen, 2025), researchers should continue to examine the effectiveness of AI chatbots for improving students' mathematical writing performance. An AI supported intervention that is effective and feasible in a range of educational contexts may increase accessibility and inclusion of students with disabilities.

CONCLUSION

In this chapter, we presented information about the design and development process we used to develop an AI supported intervention with the goal of helping students with disabilities improve their mathematical writing and mathematics achievement. AI supported interventions have the potential to boost the learning of students with disabilities, based on the positive initial results we found in our evaluation of the usability and effectiveness of the AI system embedded within the FACT + RRCC strategy in the context of rate of change word problems. Based on our initial results, we presented recommendations for practice for educational professionals to consider, along with suggestions for advancing research in this area. When developers and researchers attend to accessibility, usability, and feasibility when considering implementation of AI learning supports in educational contexts, there is great potential for this technology to create more accessible and inclusive learning environments for students with disabilities.

REFERENCES

Arsenault, T. L., Powell, S. R., Hebert, M. A., King, S. G., Lin, X., & Lang, D. (2022). Influence of writing ability and computation skills on mathematics. *Reading and Writing*, *36*, 2025–2053. DOI: 10.1007/s11145-022-10375-2

Ayres, P. (2018). Subjective measures of cognitive load: What can they reliably measure? In Zheng, R. (Ed.), *Cognitive load measurement and application: A theoretical framework for meaningful research and practice* (pp. 9–28). Routledge.

Baddeley, A. (2012). Working memory: Theories, models, and controversies. *Annual Review of Psychology*, *63*(1), 1–29. DOI: 10.1146/annurev-psych-120710-100422 PMID: 21961947

Bangert-Drowns, R. L., Hurley, M. M., & Wilkinson, B. (2004). The effects of school-based writing-to-learn interventions on academic achievement: A meta-analysis. *Review of Educational Research*, *74*(1), 29–58. DOI: 10.3102/00346543074001029

Bundock, K., Hawken, L. S., Kiuhara, S. A., O'Keeffe, B. V., O'Neill, R. E., & Cummings, M. B. (2021). Teaching rate of change and problem solving to high school students with high incidence disabilities at tier 3. *Learning Disability Quarterly*, *44*(1), 35–49. DOI: 10.1177/0731948719887341

Cheng, L., Croteau, E., Baral, S., Heffernan, C., & Heffernan, N. (2024). Facilitating student learning with a chatbot in an online math learning platform. *Journal of Educational Computing Research*, *62*(4), 687–717. https://doi-org.dist.lib.usu.edu/10.1177/07356331241226592. DOI: 10.1177/07356331241226592

Cleary, T. J., & Callan, G. L. (2017). Assessing self-regulated learning using microanalytic methods. In Schunk, D. H., & Greene, J. (Eds.), *Handbook of Self-Regulation of Learning and Performance* (2nd ed., pp. 338–351). Routledge. DOI: 10.4324/9781315697048-22

Confrey, J., & Smith, E. (1994). Exponential functions, rates of change, and the multiplicative unit. *Learning Mathematics,* 31–60. DOI: 10.1007/978-94-017-2057-1_2

Daroczy, G., Wolska, M., Meurers, W. D., & Nuerk, H.-C. (2015). Word problems: A review of linguistic and numerical factors contributing to their difficulty. *Frontiers in Psychology*, *6*. Advance online publication. DOI: 10.3389/fpsyg.2015.00348 PMID: 25883575

Desoete, A. (2015). Language and math. In P. Aunio, R. Mononen, & A. Laine, Mathematical learning difficulties—snapshots of current European research. *LUMAT,* *5*, 647–674.

Dolapcioglu, S., & Doğanay, A. (2022). Development of critical thinking in mathematics classes via authentic learning: An action research. *International Journal of Mathematical Education in Science and Technology*, *53*(6), 1363–1386. DOI: 10.1080/0020739X.2020.1819573

Du, M., & Qian, Y. (2022). Application of massive open online course to grammar teaching for English majors based on deep learning. *Frontiers in Psychology*, *12*, 755043. Advance online publication. DOI: 10.3389/fpsyg.2021.755043 PMID: 35069332

Duong, T., & Chen, H. (2025). An AI chatbot for EFL writing: Students' usage tendencies, writing performance, and perceptions. *Journal of Educational Computing Research*, *63*(2), 406–430. https://doi-org.dist.lib.usu.edu/10.1177/073456331241312363. DOI: 10.1177/07356331241312363

Edson, A. J., & Sedaghat, S. (2015). Using learning progressions as a design tool for task development: The case of rate of change. *The Journal of Mathematical Behavior*, *39*, 87–100.

Elia, I. (2020). Word problem solving and pictorial representations: Insights from an exploratory study in kindergarten. *ZDM Mathematics Education*, *52*(1), 17–31. DOI: 10.1007/s11858-019-01113-0

Fehrmann, R. (2025). Implementing augmented reality models in the classroom environment using merge cubes: A quantitative study of the effects on students' cognitive load and motivation. *Education Sciences*, *15*(4), 414–432. DOI: 10.3390/educsci15040414

Forsyth, S. R., & Powell, S. R. (2017). Differences in the mathematics vocabulary knowledge of fifth-grade students with and without learning difficulties. *Learning Disabilities Research & Practice*, *32*(4), 231–245. DOI: 10.1111/ldrp.12144

Geary, D. C. (2004). Mathematics and learning disabilities. *Journal of Learning Disabilities*, *37*(1), 4–15. DOI: 10.1177/00222194040370010201 PMID: 15493463

Geary, D. C. (2011). Consequences, characteristics, and causes of mathematical learning disabilities and persistent low achievement in mathematics. *Journal of Developmental and Behavioral Pediatrics*, *32*(3), 250–263. DOI: 10.1097/DBP.0b013e318209edef PMID: 21285895

Geary, D. C., Boykin, A. W., Embretson, S., Reyna, V., Siegler, R., Berch, D. B., & Graban, J. (2008). Chapter 4: Report of the task group on learning processes. In U.S. Department of Education (Ed.), *The final report of the National Mathematics Advisory Panel* (pp. 4-xi–4-221). Washington, DC: U.S. Department of Education. http://www.ed.gov/ about/bdscomm/list/mathpanel/report/learning-processes.pdf

Gillespie, A., & Graham, S. (2014). A meta-analysis of writing interventions for students with learning disabilities. *Exceptional Children*, *80*(4), 454–473. DOI: 10.1177/0014402914527238

Graham, S., & Harris, K. R. (2018). An examination of the design principles underlying a self-regulated strategy development study. *Journal of Writing Research*, *10*(2), 139–187. DOI: 10.17239/jowr-2018.10.02.02

Graham, S., Harris, K. R., & McKeown, D. (2014). The writing of students with learning disabilities, meta-analysis of self-regulated strategy development writing intervention studies, and future directions: Redux. In Swanson, H. L., Harris, K. R., & Graham, S. (Eds.), *Handbook of learning disabilities* (2nd ed., pp. 405–438). The Guilford Press.

Graham, S., Kiuhara, S. A., & MacKay, M. (2020). The effects of writing on learning in science, social studies, and mathematics: A meta-analysis. *Review of Educational Research*, *90*(2), 179–226. DOI: 10.3102/0034654320914744

Graham, S., McKeown, D., Kiuhara, S. A., & Harris, K. R. (2012). A meta-analysis of writing instruction for students in the elementary grades. *Journal of Educational Psychology*, *104*(4), 879–896. DOI: 10.1037/a0029185

Greenberg, K., & Zheng, R. (2023). Revisiting the debate on germane cognitive load versus germane resources. *Journal of Cognitive Psychology*, *35*(3), 295–314. DOI: 10.1080/20445911.2022.2159416

Guo, K., Wang, J., & Chu, S. K. W. (2022). Using chatbots to scaffold EFL students' argumentative writing. *Assessing Writing*, *54*, 100666. DOI: 10.1016/j.asw.2022.100666

Gupta, U., & Zheng, R. (2020). Cognitive load in solving mathematics problems: Validating the role of motivation and the interaction among worked examples, task difficulty, and prior knowledge. *European Journal of STEM Education, 5*(1), 05.

Hacker, D. J., Kiuhara, S. A., & Levin, J. R. (2019). A metacognitive intervention for teaching fractions to students with or at-risk for learning disabilities in mathematics. Special issue on metacognition in mathematics education. *ZDM Mathematics Education*, *51*(4), 601–612. DOI: 10.1007/s11858-019-01040-0

Hallet, D., Nunes, T., & Bryant, P. (2010). Individual differences in conceptual and procedural knowledge when learning fractions. *Journal of Educational Psychology*, *102*(2), 395–406. DOI: 10.1037/a0017486

Harris, K. R., & Graham, S. (2009). Self-regulated strategy development in writing: Premises, evolution, and the future. *British Journal of Educational Psychology* Monograph Series II: No. 6. Teaching and Learning Writing (pp. 113–135). *British Psychological Society., 422542*. Advance online publication. DOI: 10. 1348/978185409X

Harris, K. R., Graham, S., Mason, L., & Friedlander, B. (2008). *Powerful writing strategies for all students*. Brookes.

Hattikudor, S., Alibali, M. W., Prather, R. W., Knuth, E. J., Asquith, P., & Nathan, M. (2012). Constructing graphical representations: Middle schoolers' intuitions and developing knowledge about slope and y-intercept. *School Science and Mathematics*, *112*(4), 230–240. DOI: 10.1111/j.1949-8594.2012.00138.x

Hebert, M. A., Bohaty, J., Roehling, J., & Powell, S. R. (2019). Piloting a mathematics-writing intervention with late elementary students at-risk for learning difficulties. *Learning Disabilities Research & Practice*, *34*(3), 144–157. DOI: 10.1111/ldrp.12202

Horner, R. H., Carr, E. G., McGee, G., Odom, S., & Wolery, M. (2005). The use of single-subject research to identify evidence-based practice in special education. *Exceptional Children*, *71*(2), 165–179. DOI: 10.1177/001440290507100203

Hott, B. L., Morano, S., Peltier, C., Pulos, J., & Peltier, T. (2020). Are students with mathematics learning disabilities receiving FAPE?: Insights from a descriptive review of Individualized Education Programs. *Learning Disabilities Research & Practice*, *35*(4), 170–179. DOI: 10.1111/ldrp.12231

Hughes, E. M., & Lee, J. (2020). Effects of a mathematical writing intervention on middle school students' performance. *Reading & Writing Quarterly*, *36*(2), 176–192. DOI: 10.1080/10573569.2019.1677537

Hughes, E. M., Riccomini, P. J., & Lee, J. (2020). Investigating written expressions of mathematical reasoning for students with learning disabilities. *The Journal of Mathematical Behavior*, *58*, 1–14. DOI: 10.1016/j.jmathb.2020.100775

Hurst, A., Lerer, A., Goucher, A. P., Perelman, A., Ramesh, A., Clark, A., . . . Kivlichan, I. (2024). *Gpt-4o system card. arXiv.* https://doi.org//arXiv.2410.21276DOI: 10.48550

Hwang, J., & Riccomini, P. J. (2016). Enhancing mathematical problem solving for secondary students with or at risk of learning disabilities: A literature review. *Learning Disabilities Research & Practice*, *31*(3), 169–181. DOI: 10.1111/ldrp.12105

Hwang, Y., & Levin, J. R. (2022). Demonstration of single-case two-sample randomization-test procedures: Underperforming children's implementation of an effective memory strategy. *Journal of Education for Students Placed at Risk*, *28*(3), 294–305. DOI: 10.1080/10824669.2022.2081167

Jitendra, A. K., Harwell, M. R., Dupuis, D. N., & Karl, S. R. (2017). A randomized trial of the effects of schema-based instruction on proportional problem-solving for students with mathematics problem-solving difficulties. *Journal of Learning Disabilities*, *50*(3), 322–336. DOI: 10.1177/0022219416629646 PMID: 26968809

Kasneci, E., Seßler, K., Küchemann, S., Bannert, M., Dementieva, D., Fischer, F., Gasser, U., Groh, G., Günnemann, S., Hüllermeier, E., Krusche, S., Kutyniok, G., Michaeli, T., Nerdel, C., Pfeffer, J., Poquet, O., Sailer, M., Schmidt, A., Seidel, T., & Kasneci, G. (2023). ChatGPT for good? On opportunities and challenges of large language models for education. *Learning and Individual Differences*, *103*, 102274. Advance online publication. DOI: 10.1016/j.lindif.2023.102274

Kieran, C. (2004). Algebraic thinking in the early grades: What is it? *The Mathematics Educator*, *8*, 139–151.

Kiuhara, S. A., Gillespie Rouse, A., Dai, T., Witzel, B., Morphy, P., & Unker, B. (2020). Constructing Written Arguments to Develop Fraction Knowledge. *Journal of Educational Psychology*, *112*(3), 584–607. DOI: 10.1037/edu0000391

Kiuhara, S. A., Levin, J. R., Tolbert, M., O'Keeffe, B. V., O'Neill, R. E., & Jameson, M. J. (2023). Teaching argument writing in math class: Challenges and solutions to improve the performance of 4th and 5th graders with disabilities. Special issue on teaching writing. *Reading and Writing*. Advance online publication. DOI: 10.1007/s11145-023-10459-7 PMID: 37359030

Kiuhara, S. A., Li, C., Bundock, K., Levin, J. R., Smith, S., & Zheng, R. (2025). SRSD and AI? Effects of algebraic thinking through writing for high school students with a mathematics learning disability [Manuscript in preparation]. Department of Special Education, University of Utah

Korhonen, J., Linnanmaki, K., & Aunio, P. (2012). Language and mathematical performance: A comparison of lower secondary school students with different level of mathematical skills. *Scandinavian Journal of Educational Research*, *56*(3), 333–334. DOI: 10.1080/00313831.2011.599423

Krowka, S. K., & Fuchs, L. S. (2017). Cognitive profiles associated with responsiveness to fraction intervention. *Learning Disabilities Research & Practice*, *32*(4), 216–230. DOI: 10.1111/ldrp.12146 PMID: 29123333

Kung, F. Y., Kwok, N., & Brown, D. J. (2018). Are attention check questions a threat to scale validity? *Applied Psychology*, *67*(2), 264–283. DOI: 10.1111/apps.12108

Laksana, F. S., & Fiangga, S. (2022). The development of web-based chatbot as a mathematics learning media on system of linear equations in three variables. *Jurnal Mathedunesa*, *11*(1), 145–154. DOI: 10.26740/mathedunesa.v11n1.p145-154

Lee, D., & Yeo, S. (2022). Developing an AI-based chatbot for practicing responsive teaching in mathematics. *Computers & Education*, *191*, 104646. Advance online publication. DOI: 10.1016/j.compedu.2022.104646

MacNeil, S., Tran, A., Hellas, A., Kim, J., Sarsa, S., Denny, P., & Leinonen, J. (2023). Experiences from using code explanations generated by large language models in a web software development e-book. *SIGCSE 2023: Proceedings of the 54th ACM Technical Symposium on Computer Science Education* V. 1, 931-937. https://doi.org/DOI: 10.1145/3545945.3569785

Martin, G. (2009). *Focus in high school mathematics: Reasoning and sense making*. NCTM.

Mayer, R. (2001). *Multimedia learning*. Cambridge Press. DOI: 10.1017/CBO9781139164603

Montague, M., Krawec, J., Enders, C., & Dietz, S. (2014). The effects cognitive strategy instruction on math problem solving of middle-school students of varying ability. *Journal of Educational Psychology*, *106*(2), 469–481. DOI: 10.1037/a0035176

National Center for Education Statistics. (2022). [NAEP mathematics report card: National achievement-level results]. The Nation's Report Card. Retrieved from https://www.nationsreportcard.gov/mathematics/nation/achievement/?grade=8

National Center for Education Statistics. (2022). [NAEP writing report card: National achievement-level results]. The Nation's Report Card. https://nces.ed.gov/nationsreportcard/pubs/main2007/2008468.aspx

National Council of Teachers of Mathematics. (2000). *Principles and standards for school mathematics*. NCTM.

Nguyen, H. D., Pham, V. T., Tran, D. A., & Le, T. T. (2019). Intelligent tutoring chatbot for solving mathematical problems in high-school. *2019 11th International Conference on Knowledge and Systems Engineering (KSE),* Da Nang, Vietnam, 2019. Pp. 1-6, DOI: 10.1109/KSE.2019.8919396

Palan, S., & Schitter, C. (2018). Prolific. ac—A subject pool for online experiments. *Journal of Behavioral and Experimental Finance*, *17*, 22–27. DOI: 10.1016/j.jbef.2017.12.004

Peer, E., Rothschild, D., Gordon, A., Evernden, Z., & Damer, E. (2022). Data quality of platforms and panels for online behavioral research. *Behavior Research Methods*, *54*(4), 1643–1662. DOI: 10.3758/s13428-021-01694-3 PMID: 34590289

Pongsakdi, N., Kajamies, A., Veermans, K., Lertola, K., Vauras, M., & Lehtinen, E. (2020). What makes mathematical word problem solving challenging? Exploring the roles of word problem characteristics, text comprehension, and arithmetic skills. *ZDM Mathematics Education*, *52*(1), 33–44. DOI: 10.1007/s11858-019-01118-9

Powell, S. R., Berry, K. A., & Benz, S. A. (2020). Analyzing the word-problem performance and strategies of students. *The Journal of Mathematical Behavior*, *58*, 100759. DOI: 10.1016/j.jmathb.2020.100759

Powell, S.R., Hebert, M.A., Cohen, J.A., Casa, T.M., & Firmender, J.M. (2017). A synthesis of mathematics writing: Assessments, interventions, and surveys. *Journal of Writing Research, 8*(3), 493-526. doi:: DOI: 10.17239/jowr-2017.08.03.04

Riccomini, P. J., Hughes, E. E., Deshpande, D., Lee, J., Fiveash, L., & Lin, T. (2024). Teaching fifth-grade students with specific learning disabilities to explain their mathematical reasoning through written expression. *Learning Disability Quarterly*, *47*(2), 124–136. DOI: 10.1177/07319487241235148

Schleppegrell, M. J. (2007). The linguistics challenges of mathematics teaching and learning: A research review. *Reading & Writing Quarterly*, *23*(2), 139–159. DOI: 10.1080/10573560601158461

Seo, E., Shen, Y., & Alfaro, E. C. (2018). Adolescents' beliefs about math ability and their relations to STEM career attainment: Joint consideration of race/ethnicity and gender. *Journal of Youth and Adolescence*, *48*(2), 306–325. DOI: 10.1007/s10964-018-0911-9 PMID: 30141096

Sezer, B., & Yilmaz, R. (2019). Learning management system acceptance scale (LMSAS): A validity and reliability study. *Australasian Journal of Educational Technology*, *35*(3), 15–30. DOI: 10.14742/ajet.3959

Shirah, J. F., & Sidney, P. G. (2023). Computer-based feedback matters when relevant prior knowledge is not activated. *Learning and Instruction*, *87*, 101796. DOI: 10.1016/j.learninstruc.2023.101796

Shoufan, A. (2023). Exploring students' perceptions of ChatGPT: Thematic analysis and follow-up survey. *IEEE Access : Practical Innovations, Open Solutions*, *11*, 38805–38818. DOI: 10.1109/ACCESS.2023.3268224

Smith, R. A., Smith, E., & Price, M. (2024). Utilizing emergent AI chatbot technology to generate mathematical writing models for elementary students with learning disabilities. *Intervention in School and Clinic*, *59*(5), 339–346. https://doi-org.dist.lib.usu.edu/10.1177/10534512241233512. DOI: 10.1177/10534512241233512

Song, Y., Li, C., Xing, W., Lyu, B., & Zhu, W. (2025). Investigating perceived fairness of AI prediction system for math learning: A mixed-methods study with college students. *The Internet and Higher Education*, *65*, 101000. DOI: 10.1016/j.iheduc.2025.101000

Stanton, K., Carpenter, R. W., Nance, M., Sturgeon, T., & Villalongo Andino, M. (2022). A multisample demonstration of using the prolific platform for repeated assessment and psychometric substance use research. *Experimental and Clinical Psychopharmacology*, *30*(4), 432–443.. DOI: 10.1037/pha0000545 PMID: 35025585

Stevens, E. A., & Powell, S. R. (2016). Unpacking word problems for diverse learners: A guide to using schemas. *Childhood Education*, *92*, 86–91. DOI: 10.1080/00094056.2016.1134253

Swanson, H. L., & Fung, W. (2016). Working memory components and problem-solving accuracy: Are there multiple pathways? *Journal of Educational Psychology*, *108*(8), 1153–1177. DOI: 10.1037/edu0000116

Sweller, J. (1988). Cognitive load during problem solving: Effects of on learning. *Cognitive Science*, *12*(2), 257–285. DOI: 10.1207/s15516709cog1202_4

Sweller, J. (2011). Cognitive load theory. In Mestre, J. P., & Ross, B. H. (Eds.), *The Psychology of Learning and Motivation: Cognition in Education* (pp. 37–76). Elsevier Academic Press., DOI: 10.1016/B978-0-12-387691-1.00002-8

Sweller, J. (2018). The role of independent measures of load in cognitive load theory. In Zheng, R. (Ed.), *Cognitive load measurement and application: A theoretical framework for meaningful research and practice* (pp. 3–8). Routledge.

Sweller, J., van Merrienboer, J. J., & Paas, F. (1998). Cognitive architecture and instructional design. *Educational Psychology Review*, *10*(3), 251–296. DOI: 10.1023/A:1022193728205

Taub, M., & Azevedo, R. (2019). How does prior knowledge influence eye fixations and sequences of cognitive and metacognitive SRL processes during learning with an Intelligent Tutoring System? *International Journal of Artificial Intelligence in Education*, *29*(1), 1–28. DOI: 10.1007/s40593-018-0165-4

Teuscher, D., & Reys, R. E. (2012). Rate of change: AP calculus students' understandings and misconceptions after completing different curricular paths. *School Science and Mathematics*, *112*(6), 359–376. DOI: 10.1111/j.1949-8594.2012.00150.x

Teuscher, D., Reys, R. E., Evitts, T. A., & Heinz, K. (2010). Slope, rate of change, and steepness: Do students understand these concepts? *Mathematics Teacher*, *103*(7), 519–524. DOI: 10.5951/MT.103.7.0519

Verschaffel, L., Greer, B., & De Corte, E. (2000). *Making sense of word problems*. Swets & Zeitlinger.

Wang, A. Y., Fuchs, L. S., & Fuchs, D. (2016). Cognitive and linguistic predictors of mathematical word problems with and without irrelevant information. *Learning and Individual Differences*, *52*, 79–87. DOI: 10.1016/j.lindif.2016.10.015 PMID: 28190942

Woo, J.-C. (2014). Digital game-based learning supports student motivation, cognitive success, and performance outcomes. *Journal of Educational Technology & Society*, *17*(3), 291–307.

Zeithofer, I., Zumbach, J., Schweppe, J. (2024). Complexity affects performance, cognitive load, and awareness. Learning & Instruction, 94, pN.PAG-N.PAG. Doi:-DOI: 10.1016/j.learninstruc.2024.102001

Zhai, X., Nyaaba, M., & Ma, W. (2024). Can generative AI and ChatGPT outperform humans on cognitive-demanding problem-solving tasks in science? *Science & Education*, •••, 1–22.

Zheng, R., & Gardner, M. (2020). *Memory in education*. Routledge/Taylor & Francis Group.

Zheng, R., & Greenberg, K. (2018). Effective design in human and machine learning: A cognitive perspective. In: Zhou, J., Chen, F. (Eds), *Human and Machine Learning*. Human – Computer Interaction Series. Springer, Cham. https://doi.org/ DOI: 10.1007/978-3-319-90403-0_4

KEY TERMS AND DEFINITIONS

Cognitive load: cognitive load is described as the mental load associated with the process of specific learning materials. Sweller and colleagues' model of cognitive load includes three types of cognitive load: intrinsic, extraneous, and germane (Sweller, 1988; Sweller et al., 1998).

Generative Artificial Intelligence (AI): generative artificial intelligence is artificial intelligence that produces original content in response to prompts provided by a human. Generative AI can produce text, images, or other media.

Large Language Models (LLM): large language models (LLM) are a type of AI designed to generate human-like language in response to prompts or directions (e.g., answer questions, generate novel writing, translate or summarize text, etc.). LLMs draw from large data sets consisting of written material, such as information found in published works or online.

Mathematical reasoning: mathematical reasoning represents the concepts and skills needed to draw conclusions based on evidence or assumptions and to generalize, model, and analyze mathematical symbols and equations to solve problems (NCTM, 2000).

Mathematical writing: mathematical writing is writing (words, phrases, sentences) produced to express mathematical concepts, explanations, arguments, or other information. Mathematical writing is typically considered to include four genres: exploratory, informative/explanatory, creative, argumentative.

Mathematics Learning Disability (MLD): mathematics learning disabilities (MLD) are disabilities that impact students in the area of mathematics. Students with MLD are students who have been identified as having a specific learning disability that impacts them in mathematics, meaning that their mathematics performance in the areas of calculation or concepts and applications is lower than expected for their grade level and same age peers (often characterized as scoring below the 10th percentile in mathematics).

Rate of change: rate of change (i.e., slope) is defined as a unit per unit change or comparison (Confrey & Smith, 1994). Rate of change is a core mathematical concept foundational to higher-level mathematics.

Self-Regulated Strategy Development (SRSD): SRSD is a well-established learning strategies approach for enhancing students' genre knowledge, writing quality, and their ability to set individual learning goals and monitor progress toward these goals. The SRSD framework consists of six stages: developing background knowledge, discuss it, model it, memorize it, support it, and independent performance (Harris et al., 2008).

APPENDIX

Figure 4. Usability Questions – Control: Q6: Please select the choice that best describes your experience navigating through the online math course

	Strongly disagree	Somewhat disagree	Neither agree nor disagree	Somewhat agree	Strongly agree
I found the written explanations in the online math course to be useful.	○	○	○	○	○
Using the written explanations in a math course enhances the effectiveness of my learning.	○	○	○	○	○
I feel comfortable using the written explanations about the math concepts.	○	○	○	○	○
Using written explanations like this in math learning would enhance my productivity.	○	○	○	○	○
I found the online math lesson to be easy to use.	○	○	○	○	○
This is an attention check. Please select "Somewhat disagree"	○	○	○	○	○
It would be easy for me to become skillful at understanding and using the information provided in the online mathematics lesson.	○	○	○	○	○
I found the online math lesson flexible to work with.	○	○	○	○	○
I have the required information to make effective use of the online math lesson.	○	○	○	○	○
Given that I had access to the online math lesson in math learning, I predict that I would use it.	○	○	○	○	○
I intend to use the online math lesson and tools provided as often as needed.	○	○	○	○	○
I was satisfied with the online math lesson.	○	○	○	○	○
I feel that the online math lesson served my needs well.	○	○	○	○	○
I found I needed more information about the math concepts in order to solve the math problem.	○	○	○	○	○
After learning about the two strategies (FACT + RRCC), I predict that I would use them.	○	○	○	○	○
I found writing about my mathematical reasoning helped me understand the math concept.	○	○	○	○	○

Figure 5. Usability Questions – Experiment: Q5: Please select the choice that best describes your experience with the Chatbot

	Strongly disagree	Somewhat disagree	Neither agree nor disagree	Somewhat agree	Strongly agree
I find using the Chatbot in a math course useful.	○	○	○	○	○
Using the Chatbot in a math course enhances the effectiveness of my learning.	○	○	○	○	○
I feel comfortable when using the Chatbot.	○	○	○	○	○
Using the Chatbot in math learning would enhance my productivity.	○	○	○	○	○
I find the Chatbot easy to use.	○	○	○	○	○
This is an attention check. Please select "Somewhat disagree"	○	○	○	○	○
It would be easy for me to become skillful at using the Chatbot.	○	○	○	○	○
I find the Chatbot flexible to work with.	○	○	○	○	○
I have the required information to make effective use of the Chatbot.	○	○	○	○	○
Given that I had access to the Chatbot in math learning, I predict that I would use it.	○	○	○	○	○
I intend to use the Chatbot in math learning as often as needed.	○	○	○	○	○
I was satisfied with the Chatbot.	○	○	○	○	○
I feel that the Chatbot served my needs well.	○	○	○	○	○
I found I needed more information about the math concepts in order to solve the math problem.	○	○	○	○	○
After learning about the two strategies (FACT + RRCC), I predict that I would use them.	○	○	○	○	○
I found writing about my mathematical reasoning helped me understand the math concept.	○	○	○	○	○

Section 2
AI and Learner Development

Chapter 6
Examining the Relationship Between Social Roles and Knowledge Structures in Online Math Discussions:
An LLM-Powered Knowledge Graph Approach

Chenglu Li
https://orcid.org/0000-0002-1782-0457
University of Utah, USA

Bailing Lyu
https://orcid.org/0000-0002-6964-9081
University of Utah, USA & Auburn University, USA

ABSTRACT

Learning occurs as students select, organize, and integrate knowledge into structured networks. Online mathematical discussions offer opportunities for this knowledge building process, yet little is known about how students' social positions within discussion networks relate to their knowledge structures. Using over two million discussion records, we classified students into core, peripheral, and x-peripheral roles based on the breadth and depth of their interactions. Large language models were then used to generate knowledge graphs (KGs), which we analyzed with graph-theoretic metrics. Core students showed broader concept activation, more coherent organization, and deeper integration than x-peripheral students. Participation

DOI: 10.4018/979-8-3373-2927-7.ch006

patterns also predicted knowledge structures differently across roles: tutor replies supported richer and more integrated KGs for core and peripheral students, while x-peripheral students benefited more from self-directed engagement. These results show how participation roles shape mathematical knowledge construction and demonstrate the value of LLM-generated KGs as scalable measures of knowledge structures.

INTRODUCTION

Learning theories emphasize the importance of knowledge structure, defined as "the structure of interrelationships between elements, concepts, and procedures in a particular domain, organized into a unified body of knowledge," in student learning (Koubek et al., 1994; Piaget, 1952; Reif & Heller, 1982). The role of knowledge structure is grounded in the cognitive framework of knowledge schemas that illustrate how individuals organize and interpret information. Knowledge schemas are mental structures that evolve with experience and enable learners to integrate new information into existing cognitive frameworks more efficiently (Anderson, 1984; Rumelhart et al., 1986). They serve as scaffolding for understanding, facilitating both the encoding and retrieval of knowledge by connecting new ideas to prior knowledge. The richer and more interconnected these schemas are, the more capable learners become at transferring knowledge across contexts, solving problems, and developing expertise (Bransford et al., 2000). In mathematics, effective learning requires students to select, activate, and integrate mathematical knowledge units (e.g., situated properties of inequalities for problem-solving) into a coherent and structured framework, facilitating deeper understanding. Analyzing and assessing students' knowledge structures thus provides valuable insights into their learning processes and contributes to the development of effective educational strategies.

A well-established approach to evaluate students' knowledge structures involves asking students to construct knowledge graphs (KGs), also referred to as concept maps in cognitive science, which represent semantic networks of relationships between knowledge entities (Pan et al., 2024). In STEM disciplines, knowledge can often be represented hierarchically in a connected manner. KGs help students organize such complex relationships,such as mathematical dependencies, causal mechanisms in science, or feedback loops in engineering systems, into coherent, intuitive, and visual formats (O'Donnell et al., 2002). Educational literature highlights how KGs serve as powerful tools for supporting STEM education by making students' cognitive structures explicit and enhancing metacognitive engagement, where these visual representations enable learners to externalize and reflect on the connections among concepts, promoting diagnostic self-assessment and real-world connections with content knowledge (Ifenthaler, 2010; Nesbit & Adesope, 2006; Novak & Cañas, 2006). For example, Ifenthaler et al. (2011) developed a framework to analyze students' KGs through relational, structural, and semantic dimensions, enabling precise comparisons with expert models. Their study demonstrated that such analysis can reveal misconceptions, track learning progress, and support individualized feedback in STEM education. Although traditional KG construction has provided valuable insights by having students manually create KGs and compare them to expert models, it presents significant challenges at scale. These include the substantial resources needed for reliable and valid scoring, limited coverage of subject-specific terms, and variability in how students construct concept maps.

Recent studies have sought to construct students' KGs with automatic methods to provide actionable insights for teaching and learning by using natural language processing (NLP) and traditional machine learning models. For example, Li et al. (2022) developed an educational KG extraction pipeline by integrating multimodal data sources, including textual, visual, and relational. In their study, the researchers trained deep learning models and leveraged NLP techniques such as entity recognition and dependency parsing to enable more personalized and context-aware learning environments. In another example, Albreiki et al. (2024) used machine learning-based clustering and entity-relation modeling to build student KGs, identifying at-risk learners by mapping their engagement and performance data into interpretable graph-based profiles. Also, Zheng et al. (2023) developed a KG-based automated assessment and feedback system that analyzes online collaborative discussion data using deep learning and rule-based analytics to deliver real-time evaluation of students' knowledge-building processes and to provide personalized guidance to support online collaborative learning. While promising, the existing automated approaches in education often rely on extensive volumes of training data, typically thousands of entries if not more, which require substantial content expertise and intensive manual effort to prepare. Recent advancements in large language models (LLMs) offer promising directions to address these limitations. Leveraging their few-shot learning and small sample finetuning capabilities, LLMs can automatically and accurately extract knowledge entities and their relationships from students' learning data, such as online discussions, to generate KGs that represent students' knowledge structures. This study proposes using LLM-generated KGs as a scalable and standardized method to assess students' knowledge structures in online mathematical discussions, where students iteratively share, refine, and transform knowledge. To the best of our knowledge, although preliminary studies have explored LLM-powered KG construction in domains like material chemistry, medicine, and language (Dagdelen et al., 2024; Hu et al., 2024), this study is among the first to systematically apply this novel and well-suited approach in an educational context.

Specifically, this study examines how students' participation in online mathematical discussions relates to their knowledge structures, as assessed through LLM-generated KGs, to deepen understanding of how online mathematical discussions influence learning. According to situated learning theory, learning occurs as learners progressively move from peripheral participation toward fuller participation in communities of practice (Lave & Wenger, 1991), which, in the context of online discussions, underscores the importance of active and central participation for supporting student learning. Previous empirical research has demonstrated a positive relationship between student participation in online mathematical discussions and mathematics learning, with the effectiveness of these discussions depending on the level of student participation (Lee & Recker, 2022; Lyu et al., 2024). In particular, both the breadth (e.g., the number of peers students engage with) and depth (e.g., the length of discussion threads) of students' social interactions in online discussions have been strongly associated with their learning outcomes. However, limited research has examined how participation roles, such as peripheral or core participants, as conceptualized in situated learning theory (Lave & Wenger, 1991) and determined by students' breadth and depth of interaction in discussions, relate to students' mathematical knowledge structures. To address this gap, we employed a core-periphery framework to classify students as core, peripheral, or x-peripheral (Introne et al., 2016) based on the breadth and depth of their social interactions across more than two million discussion records. We then generated students' KGs using LLMs to represent students' mathematical knowledge structures derived from their discussion content. Mayer's Selection-Organization-Integration (SOI) framework (Mayer, 1996) was applied to identify and quantify key features of students' knowledge selection, organization, and integration within the KGs, providing a structured assessment of their knowledge structures. Finally, regression analyses were conducted to examine the relationships between students' core-periphery roles, discussion participation patterns (i.e., initiated posts and replies), and knowledge structures. This study addresses three research questions:

1. How do core, peripheral, and x-peripheral students differ in their participation patterns in discussions?
2. How do students' core-periphery roles and participation patterns predict their knowledge structures?
3. How are students' participation patterns associated with their knowledge structures within core, peripheral, and x-peripheral students?

BACKGROUND

Online Mathematical Discussions

Online mathematical discussions, grounded in Vygotsky's social constructivist theory (Vygotsky, 1978), are recognized as an effective strategy for supporting the construction of mathematical knowledge structures. These discussions enable students to share, elaborate on, and critically engage with mathematical ideas, fostering knowledge building (Smith & Stein, 2018). Studies have demonstrated a positive correlation between students' participation in online mathematical discussions and their mathematics learning. These studies have examined mathematics learning through a range of analytical approaches. One common method involves coding students' discussion comments to identify underlying cognitive processes, such as asking clarifying questions, articulating problems, and negotiating mathematical meanings, which reflect active engagement in meaning-making (e.g., Luebeck & Bice, 2005; Lyu et al., 2024; Song et al., 2025). Another approach focuses on detecting markers of mathematical proficiency by analyzing the presence of conceptual understanding, procedural fluency, and strategic competence within students' contributions during discussions, thereby capturing the depth and accuracy of their mathematical reasoning in real time (e.g., Lyu et al., 2026; Saleem et al., 2021; Sudiarta et al., 2018). A third line of research evaluates students' mathematical knowledge by measuring learning outcomes through tests, quizzes, or course performance data collected after online discussions, linking participation patterns with academic achievement (e.g., Lee & Recker, 2022; Leite et al., 2024).

Although these approaches provide important insights into the relationship between online participation and mathematics learning, as well as the cognitive processes involved, they have not directly assessed student learning through the evaluation of their mathematical knowledge structures. This gap underscores the need for a deeper theoretical and methodological lens on learning, one that moves beyond participation metrics and explores how students organize and restructure mathematical ideas. While online discussions facilitate the co-construction of meaning, theoretical perspectives, such as schema theory (Anderson, 1984) and conceptual change frameworks (DiSessa & Sherin, 1998), highlight that learning involves the integration of new ideas into existing mental frameworks. These frameworks emphasize not only the accumulation of knowledge, but also its reorganization of how learners link, refine, and reconcile mathematical concepts in light of new experiences. Analyzing the coherence and connectivity within students' knowledge structures can potentially offer a deeper and more nuanced understanding by illuminating how students' thinking evolves throughout online discussions and identifying fragmentation of understanding that may not be visible through traditional performance-based assessments alone. Accordingly, the present study uses LLMs to generate students' KGs and examines quantitative features of these KGs to directly assess their mathematical knowledge structures and investigate how participation in online discussions shapes these structures.

Social Roles and Knowledge Structures in Online Discussions

Research in online mathematics discussions has highlighted the significance of students' social roles in shaping their learning opportunities and outcomes. Studies have identified a variety of roles based on participants' functioning, such as initiators, elaborators, critics, and facilitators, which emerge in collaborative discourse and influence how mathematical concepts are explored, negotiated, and extended (Kizilcec et al., 2013; Wise et al., 2017). Students who take on more epistemically productive roles, namely those who question, explain, or connect ideas, tend to demonstrate deeper conceptual understanding and contribute more meaningfully to group learning (Lin & Chan, 2018; Siqin & Chu, 2021). At the same time, roles such as social supporters, though potentially less directly engaged with mathematical content or active participation, can still play a valuable role in fostering group cohesion and maintaining a supportive learning environment (Cheng & Hill, 2022). However, despite growing interest in social role dynamics in online discussions, much of the existing research has focused on categorizing roles based on functional behaviors or discourse patterns, with comparatively less attention paid to their relational and positional dimensions within the broader interaction network.

Network-oriented perspectives on learning, such as social network theory (Liu et al., 2017; Zou et al., 2021) and connectivism (Siemens, 2006), conceptualize individuals and information resources within a learning community as interconnected entities whose connections form a network through which learning can be facilitated. In the context of online mathematical discussions, students' interaction patterns naturally position them as distinct nodes within the communication network, and these structural positions can reflect meaningful participation roles, such as core or peripheral contributors. Situated learning theory offers a complementary sociocultural lens for interpreting these positional differences. According to this perspective, learning is a situated activity defined by legitimate peripheral participation, through which learners gradually move from peripheral toward fuller participation as they acquire expertise within a community of practice (Lave & Wenger, 1991). Applied to online mathematical discussions, students' social roles, manifested through patterns of peripheral or central participation, may therefore play a critical role in shaping their learning opportunities and knowledge-construction processes. This theoretical alignment underscores the importance of examining how such roles influence students' participation patterns and the development of their mathematical knowledge structures in collaborative learning environments. Moreover, prior research has shown that participation often clusters around a small subset of highly active individuals, while many others remain at the margins, rarely initiating contributions or influencing the direction of discourse (Wilkerson, 2016). These empirical patterns further highlight the need to move beyond traditional role typologies and investigate how roles are distributed across the discourse network and what this distribution reveals about the development, flow, and organization of mathematical knowledge. As such, this study examines how different social roles, specifically core, peripheral, and x-peripheral participation roles, established through analyses of the structure and distribution of students' social ties within the interaction network (see Methods for details), relate to students' mathematical knowledge structures in online learning environments.

Knowledge Structures and Selection-Organization-Integration Model

Theoretical frameworks in learning science underscore the pivotal role of knowledge structures in guiding how learners interpret, integrate, and apply new information. Cognitive constructivism posits that learning occurs by assimilating new information into existing knowledge structures (Piaget, 1952), and schema theory suggests that knowledge is stored as organized and interconnected "nodes" in long-term memory, which are selectively activated during learning tasks (Anderson, 1984). Social constructivism further asserts that learning takes place through interactions with others, integrating both personal and shared knowledge (Vygotsky, 1978). Conceptual change theory adds that meaningful learning often requires reorganizing prior knowledge when new information conflicts with existing conceptions, making the examination of learners' conceptual networks crucial for identifying how their understanding shifts over time (DiSessa & Sherin, 1998). Although these perspectives differ in emphasis, they converge on two insights central to this study: first, that students' mathematical knowledge can be represented as interconnected networks of concepts, emphasizing the importance of knowledge structures and making KGs a promising analytic approach for assessing these structures; and second, that effective learning requires learners to select, organize, and integrate information, a process that aligns closely with the Selection-Organization-Integration (SOI) framework (Mayer, 1996). These two points suggest the value of operationalizing students' KGs using metrics that reflect how their mathematical ideas are selected, organized, and interconnected, thereby enabling the assessment of their knowledge structures.

According to the SOI framework, students construct knowledge from diverse resources by engaging in three core cognitive processes: selection, organization, and integration (Mayer, 1996). Selection entails identifying relevant or important information, organization involves restructuring and linking selected information into a coherent mental model, and integration connects this organized model with prior knowledge or other knowledge units to support deeper learning. While Mayer originally developed the SOI framework for knowledge construction while learning from textual resources, in this study, we extended its applicability to online mathematical discussions. In mathematics learning, these processes manifest in domain-specific ways. For example, when solving an algebraic word problem in a discussion forum, a student may select key quantities and relationships from others' posts or shared problem descriptions (e.g., recognizing that "the rate of change" refers to slope). The student may then organize this information by linking it to relevant formulas or mathematical structures (e.g., representing the situation as a linear equation). Finally, through integration, the student connects this newly structured model with prior knowledge (e.g., the difference between constant and variable rates) to draw inferences or explain the solution to peers. Similarly, in discussions about geometric proofs, students may build on others' ideas, reorganize problem conditions into visual or logical sequences, and relate new reasoning steps to previously learned theorems. Therefore, we adopted the SOI framework as the theoretical foundation to systematically analyze students' knowledge structures by evaluating the extent to which SOI are reflected in their KGs.

Students' selection, organization, and integration of information and knowledge during learning have been empirically documented to varying degrees and are positively correlated with learning outcomes. Given the model's origination, most studies in this area have focused on learning from textual resources, often employing think-aloud protocols alongside analyses of students' writing to assess these cognitive processes. Research indicates that students are generally proficient in selecting relevant information from textual materials (Lyu et al., 2023). For example, in a think-aloud study by Anmarkrud et al. (2013), the researchers found that students could effectively differentiate between relevant and irrelevant information while processing a text, with their judgments aligning closely with expert ratings of information relevance. Beyond selection, students' organization of information is often reflected in the structural coherence of their post-learning writing. Elements such as hierarchy, connectivity, and transitions between ideas, concepts, and arguments serve as indicators of organizational structure and are frequently incorporated into rubrics for evaluating writing quality (Anmarkrud et al., 2013). Additionally, students engage in various integration processes during learning (McCrudden et al., 2021). For instance, Du and List (2020) analyzed students' notes from a reading task and found that writing performance was significantly correlated with the variety and depth of information integration, including connections drawn from multiple sources.

The present study extends the investigation of students' knowledge SOI to online mathematical discussions using graph theory metrics derived from LLM-generated

KGs. Knowledge selection captures how many unique concepts students identify and how many of those concepts are meaningfully connected in their KGs. Knowledge organization focuses on the structural complexity of the KGs, specifically the diversity of node connections as reflected by entropy. Knowledge integration examines how deeply and broadly students link ideas, represented by metrics such as distribution depth and breadth. These metrics capture students' mathematical concept selection, organization, breadth, and depth to examine how students' participation roles relate to their knowledge structures in online mathematical discussions. A KG with a high selection metric indicates that a student activates a wide range of relevant mathematical concepts, demonstrating strong conceptual recall and awareness of the ideas needed to understand the problem. A KG with high organizational complexity, such as greater entropy, suggests that the student not only identifies concepts but also understands how they relate to one another, reflecting a more coherent form of mathematical knowledge. Finally, a KG with high integration metrics, including greater depth or breadth, indicates how deeply and extensively students can traverse and combine these connections. Higher integration metrics indicate the ability to form multi-step relational chains, synthesize definitions and procedures, and link concepts across representational or procedural steps.

METHODS

Dataset

We conducted this study within Mation Nation (MN), an online math learning platform used by over one million students across the United States each year. We utilized the online discussion data focusing on Algebra I from the MN platform spanning 2013 to 2021. One unique characteristic of the MN discussion environment is that interactions occurred not only between students and their peers but also with paid tutors who were professionally trained to scaffold students' mathematical thinking. These tutors would deliberately shape students' reasoning processes and provide targeted support. This expert-guided dialogue offers a rich context for examining how students select, organize, and integrate mathematical ideas in response to structured guidance. It presents a valuable opportunity to analyze students' knowledge structures based on how they interact with both peers and experts in a large-scale, authentic, and naturalistic learning environment.

After excluding posts that did not receive any replies, our dataset comprised 237,671 top-level posts (i.e., the initial content created by a user to start a discussion) and 2,010,667 replies (i.e., responses made by users to a top-level post), involving 52,150 MN students and teachers (i.e., tutors). On average, each post received 7.51

replies ($SD = 10.17$). The discussions on MN involved two main groups: students (self and peers) and tutors (hired professionals or teachers), with tutors appointed to assist students with their questions. Within the dataset, there were 51,902 students (99.5%) and 248 tutors (0.5%). Students contributed 190,409 posts (80%) and 1,459,383 replies (73%), while tutors contributed 47,262 posts (20%) and 551,284 replies (27%). Most students provided demographic information during registration, with 20,850 identifying as female, 25,765 as male, and 5,287 not specifying their gender. However, such demographic information was not available for tutors.

Data Analysis

The data analysis consisted of five steps. First, we employed a human-in-the-loop (HITL) approach to review and refine 1,400 KGs, each representing a complete discussion thread involving students, peers, and tutors. Of these, 900 graphs were used to create a fine-tuning dataset, while the remaining 500 served as an evaluation set for assessing model performance. Second, using the full dataset, we identified core, peripheral, and x-peripheral students based on their social interaction in the MN discussion forum. Third, we randomly sampled 1,200 students, each of whom had created at least five top-level posts during the period from 2018-2019. The sample included 400 students from each of the core, periphery, and x-periphery groups. Collectively, these 1,200 students generated 12,435 top-level posts and 40,451 replies to their own posts, and were connected to 83,608 replies by 7,730 peers and 103 tutors. Then, we used a fine-tuned LLM to generate KGs for each student from the random sample, assessing their knowledge structures during the discussions. Finally, we examined the relationship between students' core-periphery roles and their knowledge structures in the discussions.

Core, periphery, and x-periphery detection

Core-periphery detection differs from traditional community detection methods such as modularity-based techniques (Chen et al., 2014). Traditional methods focus on strong internal connections within sub-communities and weaker ties between them, whereas core-periphery detection reveals a hierarchical structure: core members connect strongly both with each other and peripheral members, while peripheral members mainly interact with the core (Rombach et al., 2017). Historically, core-periphery models have classified nodes as core or periphery based on interaction breadth, often neglecting depth. Our study introduced an extra-periphery (x-periphery) category to capture the depth of connections through the presence of dyadic relationships. We defined a dyadic relationship as a reciprocal, two-way interaction. For instance, if a student responded to another but did not stimulate further dialogue, the interaction was not considered dyadic. Conversely, when a student posed a question and engaged in sustained interaction with respondents, this reciprocal exchange qualified as a dyadic relationship. Such relationships are linked to stronger, sustained interactions in online learning communities (Luo et al., 2020; Poquet et al., 2017).

To classify students into core, periphery, and x-periphery groups, we used the Surprise algorithm (van Lidth de Jeude et al., 2019), which effectively detects core-periphery structures based on statistical significance. The algorithm operates under the null hypothesis that nodes are randomly connected, measuring the extent to which the observed network partition deviates from the expected properties under this hypothesis. Appendix A shows the pseudocode of Surprise-based network partitioning. Specifically, we first applied the Surprise method to identify statistically significant core-periphery structures within student communities, grouping the analysis by academic year (e.g., 2013-2014, 2014-2015). We then refined this classification by introducing the x-periphery category for students who did not establish dyadic relationships. In cases where no dyadic interaction was observed, students initially classified as core were reassigned to the periphery, and those in the periphery were further categorized into the x-periphery group. To examine how core, peripheral, and x-peripheral students participate in online mathematical discussions, we analyzed their differences in top-level posts, total replies, self replies, peer replies, and tutor replies by conducting a series of ANOVAs, with the core-periphery structure as the independent variable.

Knowledge graph construction

Motivation. A KG is typically represented as a collection of "triplets," where an entity (e.g., a mathematical concept) is connected to another entity by a predicate that defines their relationship. Building a KG involves the extraction of entities and relationships to form these triplets. Traditionally, this process has relied on lexical and rule-based methods, such as regular expressions and hand-crafted association rules, or statistical machine learning approaches such as similarity using bag-of-words and probabilistic graphical models (see the review by Al-Moslmi et al., 2020). However, more recent studies have focused on leveraging deep neural networks, including LSTM and BERT models, to capture the semantic meaning and latent features within candidate documents, resulting in improved performance in entity and relationship recognition (Chen et al., 2018; Su & Zhang, 2020). For instance, Su and Zhang (2020) employed deep learning models to extract entities and relationships from educational materials, such as course syllabi, lesson plans, and textbooks, enabling the automatic and effective construction of a knowledge graph to support computer science learning.

The aforementioned approaches to KG construction often rely on extensive datasets for training or fine-tuning, which are necessary to achieve high accuracy in entity recognition but frequently fall short in identifying relationships accurately (Al-Moslmi et al., 2020; Dagdelen et al., 2024). In contrast, LLMs, with their advanced capabilities in natural language understanding, offer an effective alternative for KG building, requiring much fewer training examples or leveraging few-shot prompting to achieve alignment with human expectations (Dagdelen et al., 2024; Hu et al., 2024; Keloth et al., 2024). In this study, we leveraged supervised fine-tuning to better align LLMs' KG triplet extraction with our expectations. We developed seven key relationships in math learning for KG construction, guided by Bloom's taxonomy: Remember (defining meaning, identifying properties), Understand (structural relationships, sequential relationships), Analyze (differentiating, connecting), and Apply (applying knowledge). Given the research context of Math Nation, we adapted its expert-vetted, standards-aligned glossary of Algebra 1 terms (Algebra Nation, 2019), which includes 60 key entities such as *variable*, *constant*, and *coefficient*. Notably, Math Nation serves as a core curriculum in Florida and is fully aligned with state learning standards.

Human-in-the-Loop Preparation. We implemented a HITL pipeline to generate and refine KGs representing students' algebra knowledge structures in Math Nation discussions. A total of four non-overlapping random samples of Algebra I discussion threads were drawn: Sample 1 (S1, n = 300), S2 (n = 300), S3 (n = 300), and a held-out evaluation set S4 (n = 500). For each sample, KGs were initially generated by Gemini 2.0 Flash, using prompts constrained by a predefined algebra glossary and relation set, and output in a structured JSON schema that identified entities and relationships embedded in discussions (Figure 1a). To ensure quality, each generated KG underwent human validation and revision by two trained graduate annotators using Label Studio. Annotators corrected entity spans and labels, defined or adjusted relationships, added missing concepts, and removed irrelevant or erroneous items (Figure 1b). Annotator training was conducted on a separate set of 100 discussion threads, resulting in robust inter-rater reliability ($\kappa = 0.82$ for entities; $\kappa = 0.87$ for relations). Annotators discussed and resolved disagreements until full consensus was reached on all labels. The set of 100 annotated discussions was then used as a validation set during fine-tuning to guide early stopping and prevent overfitting. This HITL pipeline followed a sequential refinement process:

1. For Sample 1, model-generated KGs were fully prompt-based, and the human-corrected annotations were then used to fine-tune the generation model.

2. The updated model was then used to produce draft KGs using Sample 2, which again underwent human vetting before contributing to a second round of fine-tuning.
3. This process was repeated for Sample 3, allowing cumulative incorporation of human corrections.
4. The KGs for Sample 4 were generated using the model fine-tuned on Samples 1-3, but S4 was withheld from all training phases to serve as a final held-out evaluation set for benchmarking model performance.

Benchmarking. To avoid potential bias from self-evaluation, Gemini was excluded from comparative benchmarking. Instead, we evaluated three widely adopted and representative foundation models: GPT-4.1, InternLM2.5-20B (Wu et al., 2024), and LLaMA-3.1-8B (Grattafiori et al., 2024). These models were chosen for their complementary strengths in language understanding, multilingual robustness, and open-source accessibility. All models were trained and evaluated under three incremental training regimes (i.e., S1-only, S1+S2, and S1+S2+S3) with evaluation performed exclusively on the held-out S4 set to ensure unbiased comparison. In the generative setting, prompts explicitly defined the KG schema, and structured output was applied with HuggingFace to enforce well-formed JSON outputs. In the multitask setting, we implemented a two-stage pipeline: entities and their spans were extracted, and relation classification was performed over all valid entity pairs using a supervised classifier.

Metrics. We evaluated model performance using *precision, recall,* and *F1* score for two key tasks: (a) named entity extraction (NER), where we assessed whether models correctly identified and labeled complete concept terms and (b) relation extraction (RE), where models had to correctly identify the head and tail concepts and assign the correct relation type between them. To capture the quality of entity boundaries more flexibly, we also calculated the average *Intersection over Union* (IoU), a continuous measure that compares how closely the predicted entity spans align with human-annotated (gold) spans. Figure 2 illustrates the experimental setup for model preparation, finetuning, and evaluation.

Accuracy of LLM-Powered KGs. The HITL process led to substantial gains in annotation efficiency across rounds, with annotation time decreasing as model output quality improved through iterative fine-tuning. Annotators spent 40 hours and 23 minutes in the first round due to low-quality zero-shot outputs (averaging 2.42 entities and 0.70 relations per thread), but by the fourth round, total annotation time had dropped to 5 hours and 37 minutes (1.46 entities and 0.44 relations on average). Model evaluation results further demonstrate the effectiveness of this process, showing consistent performance gains as additional supervised data were incorporated. Although the magnitude of improvement varied across models, all benefited from fine-tuning. GPT-4.1 consistently achieved the highest overall performance across training regimes. Under the S1+S2+S3 condition, GPT-4.1 obtained the strongest results in both entity recognition (precision = 0.75, recall = 0.75, F1 = 0.73, IoU= 0.79) and relation extraction (precision = 0.86, recall = 0.84, F1 = 0.84), outperforming all other models.

Knowledge Graph Generation. We randomly sampled 1,200 students who had contributed at least five top-level posts. For each student, we applied the best-performing fine-tuned model to extract KG triplets from all of their top-level posts along with their corresponding replies. Each resulting KG was represented as a directed cyclic graph. To assess students' knowledge construction in terms of selection, organization, and integration, we used six structural metrics, which are described in Table 1.

Figure 1. Example data of KG construction by LLMs and the human-in-the-loop interface used for reviewing and revising entity and relation annotations.

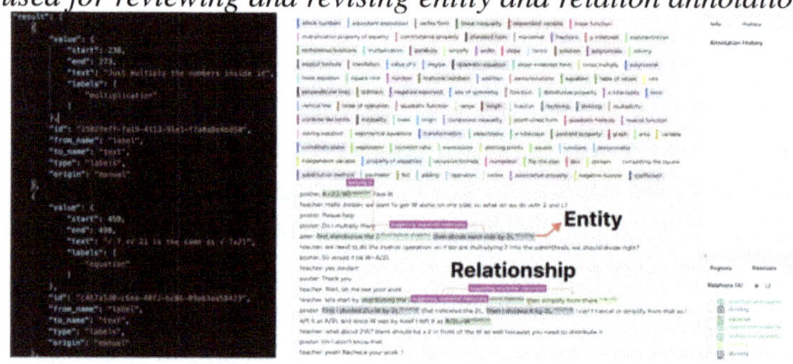

(a) Example data for draft KGs (b) Label Studio interface for human-in-the-loop vetting

Figure 2. Experimental setup for KG generation for human-in-the-loop annotation, LLM benchmarking, and evaluation.

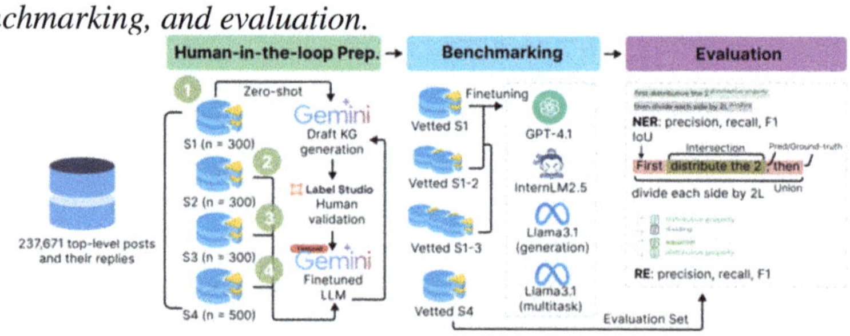

Table 1. Metrics to evaluate students' knowledge graphs.

Category	Metric	Definition
Knowledge Selection	Total Entities	The total number of unique entities (also referred to as nodes) recognized by LLMs.
	Initiated Entities	A subset of total entities, the total number of unique entities that are connected to other entities.
Knowledge Organization	Knowledge Complexity	Shannon entropy of degree distribution measures network heterogeneity; higher entropy indicates greater diversity in node degrees, suggesting a more complex structure.
	Knowledge Distribution	Degree distribution index based on the importance of nodes in a network, incorporating the degree of each node and logarithmic scaling. Higher values indicate more evenly distributed node degrees, while lower values suggest a skewed distribution.
Knowledge Integration	Depth	The longest chain of relationships or edges from a starting node to a leaf node.
	Breadth	The greatest number of immediate neighbors of a node at any depth.

Relationship between students' core-periphery roles and their knowledge structures

We examined the relationship between students' core-periphery roles and their knowledge structures in two ways. First, we assessed how core-periphery roles (i.e., inter-group differences) predicted knowledge structures while controlling for discussion participation patterns. We conducted six ordinary least squares (OLS) regression models, using each knowledge structure indicator as the dependent variable. Core-periphery roles were dummy coded, with the core role as the reference group, and models controlled for top-level posts, self-replies, peer replies, and tutor replies. Second, we investigated whether core-periphery roles moderated the relationship between participation patterns and knowledge structures (i.e., intra-group differences). We ran separate OLS regression models for core, peripheral, and x-peripheral students, using each knowledge structure indicator as the dependent variable and participation patterns as predictors. All key assumptions, including no multicollinearity and homoscedasticity, were checked and met.

RESULTS

RQ1: Associating Social Roles with Participation Patterns

Figure 3 shows the histogram of students' dyadic interactions. Most students had between 16 (2^4) and 128 (2^7) dyadic interactions, with an average of 14.86

($SD = 95.39$). Figure 4 presents the distribution of discussion activities across core, peripheral, and x-peripheral students at both the post and reply levels. Among all discussion activities, peripheral students contributed the most (57.09%, $n = 746{,}859$), followed by core students (35.37%, $n = 462{,}715$) and x-peripheral students (7.54%, $n = 98{,}639$). Notably, 92.99% of core students' discussion activities were replies to others, compared to 86.6% for peripheral students.

The core, periphery, and x-periphery detection identified 5,215 core students, 18,436 peripheral students, and 28,499 x-peripheral students from the dataset. Figure 5 shows their interaction descriptives and examples. By randomly sampling 1,200 students, with 400 from each of the three roles, and running ANOVAs using this sample, significant differences among core, peripheral, and x-peripheral students were revealed in top-level posts, $F(2, 1192) = 25.98$, $\eta^2 = .04$; self replies, $F(2, 1192) = 20.39$, $\eta^2 = .03$; peer replies, $F(2, 1192) = 36.03$, $\eta^2 = .06$; and tutor replies, $F(2, 1192) = 21.73$, $\eta^2 = .04$. Specifically, core students generated more top-level posts and received more total replies, self replies, and tutor replies than peripheral and x-peripheral students, with x-peripheral students producing the fewest posts and receiving the fewest replies. However, no significant difference was identified between core and peripheral students in the number of peer replies, although both groups received more peer replies than x-peripheral students.

Figure 3. Distributions of students' dyadic interactions.

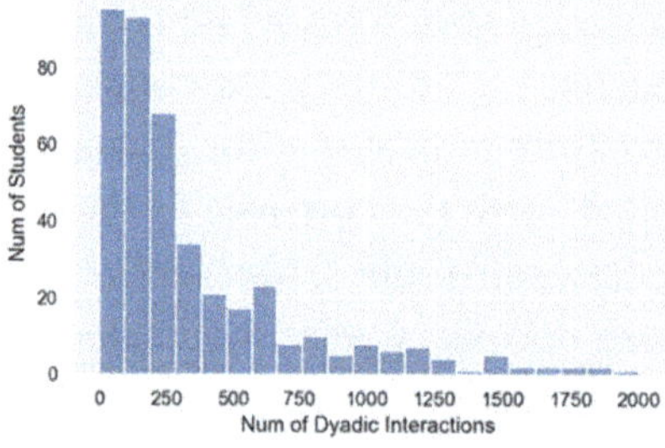

(a)

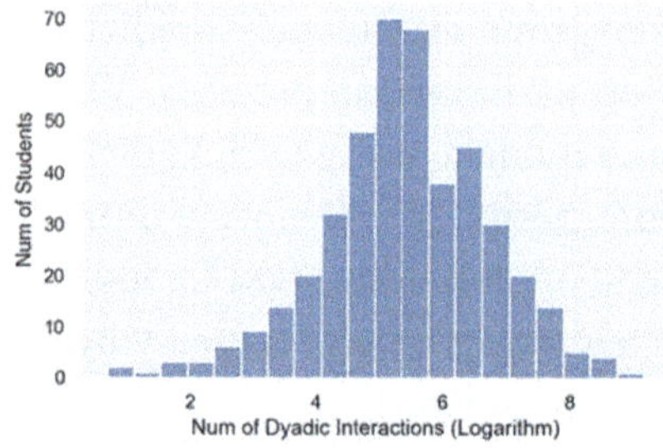

(b)

Figure 4. Core-peripheral students' discussion activities at post- and reply-levels. Darker colors indicate a greater number of activities.

	Top-level Posts	Replies	Total
Core	2.48%	32.89%	35.37%
Periphery	7.65%	49.44%	57.09%
X-periphery	2.5%	5.04%	7.54%

Figure 5. Core-peripheral student interactions at the global reply level (percentages add up to 100%), with arrow and circle sizes proportional to interaction frequency.

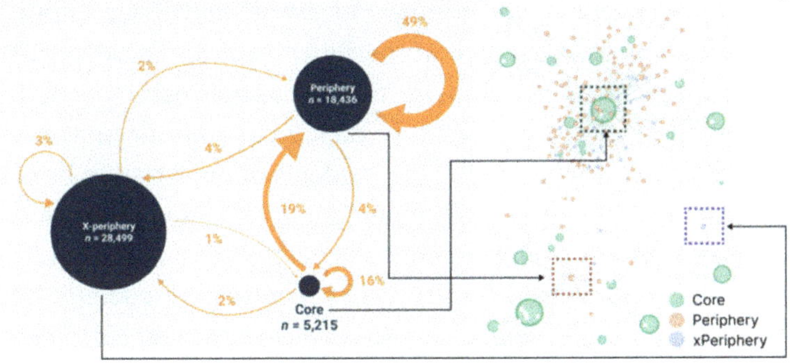

RQ2: Predicting Knowledge Structure from Social Roles and Participation Patterns

As shown in Table 2, while controlling for top-level posts, self replies, peer replies, and tutor replies, no significant differences were found between core and peripheral students regarding knowledge SOI. However, significant differences emerged between core and x-peripheral students. Specifically, core students discussed a greater number of entities overall (total entities), and these entities were more likely to make connections with one another (initiated entities). Additionally, core students demonstrated greater heterogeneity in the importance of these entities (knowledge complexity) and more extensive integration of them (knowledge depth and breadth) compared to x-peripheral students. This pattern suggests that even when students initiate the same number of top-level posts and receive similar levels of interaction, core students activate more mathematical concepts and organize them into a more hierarchical, heterogeneous, and integrated knowledge structure, whereas x-peripheral students activate fewer concepts, rely on more uniform structures, and show less integration.

In addition to the relationship between students' core-periphery roles and knowledge structures, the number of top-level posts significantly predicted knowledge selection, organization, and integration, after controlling for other predictors. Students who posted more top-level posts engaged in deeper levels of knowledge SOI. Furthermore, an increase in tutor replies was associated with greater activation and deeper integration of knowledge entities during discussions. On the other hand, peer replies showed mixed effects on students' knowledge organization. While more peer replies likely encourage students to explore and emphasize different mathematical concepts, leading to a more heterogeneous (diverse) knowledge structure (knowledge complexity), they are not necessarily linking these concepts together in a meaningful way (knowledge distribution). Finally, self replies were positively associated with heterogeneity in the importance of knowledge entities. Figure 6 shows students' example KGs of core-periphery roles. These results highlight that (1) students' structural positions in the discussion network, particularly the distinction between core and x-periphery roles, map onto meaningful differences in mathematical understanding, with core students demonstrating broader concept activation, more coherent conceptual organization, and more integrated mathematical reasoning; and (2) active engagement, especially initiating top-level posts and receiving tutor feedback, plays a critical role in strengthening students' mathematical understanding by supporting their ability to activate and synthesize interconnected mathematical ideas.

Table 2. Regression Models Predicting Knowledge Structure (Inter-Group).

Graph Components	Dependent Variables	Peri.	X-peri.	Posts	Self rep.	Peer rep.	Tutor rep.
Knowledge Selection	Total Entities, $R^2 = .65$	.00	-0.07***	0.78***	0.04	0.01	0.13***
	Initiated Entities, $R^2 = .63$	.00	-0.07**	0.76***	0.04	0.01	0.14***
Knowledge Organization	Knowledge Complexity, $R^2 = .43$	0.04	-0.23***	0.53***	0.09**	-0.06*	0.12***
	Knowledge Distribution, $R^2 = .40$	.00	0.04	0.64***	-0.02	0.05*	0.11**
Knowledge Integration	Knowledge Depth, $R^2 = .45$	0.02	-0.16***	0.59***	0.05	-0.03	0.15***
	Knowledge Breadth, $R^2 = .26$	0.02	-0.07*	0.48***	-0.01	0.02	0.07

Notes. Peri. = Periphery, Posts = Top-level Posts, and Rep. = Replies. * $p < .05$, ** $p < .01$, *** $p < .001$. Values reflect standardized regression coefficients. R^2 indicates the model fit for each dependent variable.

Figure 6. Example KGs of students in core, periphery, and x-periphery roles. Clear examples can be accessed at this anonymous folder[1]*. Nodes of the same color represent entities extracted from a shared community using Louvain community detection. Node size corresponds to centrality, as determined by the PageRank algorithm. Blue edges indicate connections between entities within the same community, while red edges denote links between entities across different communities.*

(a) Core (b) Periphery (c) x-Periphery

RQ3: Predicting Knowledge Structure from Participation Patterns Within Each Social Role

As presented in Table 3, the number of top-level posts was significantly associated with knowledge SOI across core, peripheral, and x-peripheral students. After controlling for the number of top-level posts, self replies, and peer replies, tutor replies were positively associated with knowledge selection and organization for core and peripheral students; however, this pattern was not observed for x-peripheral students. Additionally, peer replies were negatively associated with knowledge complexity. Lastly, while neither peer replies nor tutor replies were significantly related to x-peripheral students' knowledge structures, self replies had a positive effect on their knowledge organization, particularly in terms of their knowledge complexity. These findings reveal two important insights. First, the effects of participation behaviors on mathematical knowledge structures are not uniform across social roles: core and peripheral students appear more responsive to tutor replies, whereas x-peripheral students rely more heavily on self-directed engagement to build conceptual organization. Second, initiating top-level posts emerges as a consistent predictor of richer mathematical understanding across all roles, suggesting that opportunities to articulate initial ideas may play a central role in facilitating the activation, organization, and refinement of mathematical knowledge.

Table 3. Regression Models Predicting Knowledge Structure (Intra-Group).

Groups	Dependent Variables	Top-level posts	Self replies	Peer replies	Tutor replies
Core	Total Entities, $R^2 = .70$	.82***	.03	.02	.14**
	Initiated Entities, $R^2 = .68$	.81***	.03	.02	.15***
	Knowledge Complexity, $R^2 = .49$	.65***	.09	-0.07	.14*
	Knowledge Distribution, $R^2 = .44$	.67***	-0.01	.72	.10
	Knowledge Depth, $R^2 = .54$	.70***	.04	-0.03	.18***
	Knowledge Breadth, $R^2 = .31$	.57***	-0.05	.05	.06
Periphery	Total Entities, $R^2 = .66$	.76***	.02	-0.06	.24***
	Initiated Entities, $R^2 = .64$	.75***	.02	-0.06	.25***
	Knowledge Complexity, $R^2 = .41$	.58***	.05	-0.11*	.21***
	Knowledge Distribution, $R^2 = .40$	.62***	-0.05	.04	.16**
	Knowledge Depth, $R^2 = .40$	.58***	.04	-0.09	.21***
	Knowledge Breadth, $R^2 = .31$	.56***	-0.01	.05	.01
X-periphery	Total Entities, $R^2 = .34$	.58***	.09	.07	.06
	Initiated Entities, $R^2 = .34$	.58***	.08	.07	.06
	Knowledge Complexity, $R^2 = .12$	.30***	.18*	.03	.02
	Knowledge Distribution, $R^2 = .29$	.54***	.00	.08	.08
	Knowledge Depth, $R^2 = .14$	.35***	.07	.05	.12
	Knowledge Breadth, $R^2 = .02$	.08	.05	.03	.09

DISCUSSION

This study investigated how students' participation roles in online mathematical discussions relate to their knowledge structures, with a focus on the structural qualities of their KGs. Grounded in the SOI framework, we developed a HITL pipeline to generate and validate KGs from a large dataset of Algebra I discussions on the MN platform. Using iterative fine-tuning and evaluation of multiple large language models, we selected the best-performing model to extract KGs from 1,200 students' discussion threads. We then analyzed how students' roles within discussion networks, particularly core, periphery, and x-periphery roles, shaped the selection, organization, and integration of their knowledge structures. Our findings show that core students (a small, highly engaged subset) exhibited distinct participation patterns and tended to build more complex, integrated knowledge structures than their less engaged peers, and feedback from tutors and peers was differentially associated with students' knowledge structures across the core, periphery, and x-periphery groups.

RQ1: Social Roles and Participation Patterns

We first explored how students in core, peripheral, and x-peripheral positions differ in their discussion participation. Distinct participation patterns emerged that reflect well-documented stratification dynamics in online learning environments. A small proportion of students occupied core roles, yet this group contributed disproportionately to overall discourse activity. Core students initiated significantly more top-level posts and received substantially more replies, particularly from tutors, compared to their peripheral and x-peripheral peers. They also engaged more frequently in self-replies, suggesting sustained cognitive engagement and active monitoring of their own learning threads. In contrast, x-peripheral students showed minimal involvement, initiating the fewest posts and receiving the least feedback. Peripheral students exhibited intermediate levels of participation but remained less interactive than core students across multiple dimensions.

These patterns align with prior research on online learning communities, which has consistently shown that a small subset of central participants often generates the bulk of content and interaction, while the majority of learners remain on the margins (e.g., Introne et al., 2016; Safadi et al., 2021; Xing et al., 2025). For example, Introne et al. (2016) found that core contributors in online help forums drove the discourse and knowledge exchange, whereas peripheral users had limited engagement and weaker ties. Our findings mirror this dynamic in a math learning context, illustrating that core students not only led discussions but also engaged more robustly with tutors, highlighting the role of expert-guided interaction in guiding learning opportunities. Notably, we found no significant difference between core and peripheral students in the number of peer replies received, suggesting that tutor engagement, rather than peer support alone, differentiated core participants. This reflects broader findings in educational research that students who are more socially central are also more likely to receive instructor scaffolding, which in turn can foster deeper conceptual learning (Ouyang & Scharber, 2017; Poquet et al., 2017; Wang & Liu, 2020). Overall, these results underscore the importance of considering students' positionality within online discussion networks, as it can profoundly shape their exposure to ideas, the nature of feedback received, and ultimately, their learning trajectories.

RQ2-3: Social Roles, Participation Patterns, and Knowledge Structures

Our findings revealed that core students, who exhibited sustained and multi-directional engagement in discussions, constructed more coherent and complex knowledge structures compared to their x-peripheral counterparts, after controlling for their participation volume. Core students' KGs featured more idea units, more heterogeneous patterns of importance, and higher levels of connectivity, reflecting broader activation of mathematical concepts and more flexible, integrated knowledge structures. Such graph patterns indicate deeper mathematical understanding, where students can activate and relate definitions, procedures, and principles across multiple steps. This aligns with constructivist and sociocognitive theories of learning, which posit that active and social engagement supports deeper integration of new information into existing mental models (Vygotsky, 1978). Notably, knowledge structure differences between core and peripheral students were not observed when participation quantity was accounted for, which suggests that it is not centrality but students' actual engagement levels that primarily shape the richness of their knowledge structures. Peripheral students, who maintained at least one meaningful dimension of interaction (either breadth or depth), were able to achieve knowledge structures comparable to core students when equally engaged, underscoring that sufficient embeddedness in the discussion network supports knowledge development even outside the core (Safadi et al., 2021) and that some peripheral students may also engage deeply within fewer discussion threads, a pattern consistent with Bereiter's (2005) notion of 'progressive discourse.' However, x-peripheral students, who lacked both interaction breadth and depth, consistently developed flatter, less integrated knowledge structures. This distinction echoes research by Traxler et al. (2018), which found that students' structural positioning in online discourse networks influences their exposure to diverse ideas and scaffolding opportunities.

Further analysis revealed that the source and nature of feedback matter significantly, particularly in relation to students' social roles. Tutor replies predicted stronger knowledge structuring for core and peripheral students, suggesting that expert scaffolding, when embedded in active discourse, can facilitate better knowledge organization and integration, reflecting students' stronger conceptual coherence and their ability to coordinate different knowledge units during mathematical reasoning. This mirrors findings by Lee and Recker (2022), who showed that teacher feedback in online discussions enhances students' conceptual clarity and transferability. In contrast, tutor replies had no measurable effect for x-peripheral students, who likely failed to capitalize on these opportunities due to minimal engagement, a finding consistent with Vygotsky's (1978) notion that instructional support is most effective within a learner's zone of proximal development when social participation is sufficient to activate it. Interestingly, self-replies emerged as the only positive predictor for x-peripheral students, highlighting that even limited self-reflection can support knowledge organization when social input is sparse. However, this reflection lacked the integrative power observed among students engaged in richer dialogues. Furthermore, an unexpected trend appeared among peripheral students: more peer replies correlated with lower heterogeneity in concept importance, suggesting that, in some cases, peer input might simplify or even constrain the development of nuanced knowledge structures. Such patterns imply that peer interactions may reinforce surface-level understandings or narrow students' focus to familiar ideas, resulting in KGs that lack the complexity associated with deeper mathematical comprehension.This supports prior research cautioning that unguided peer feedback can vary in quality and may not always foster deep conceptual growth (Gielen et al., 2010; Nelson & Schunn, 2009). In contrast, core students who received diverse input from both tutors and peers may have developed strategies to triangulate and validate ideas, thereby mitigating the risk of being misled by lower-quality peer contributions.

Implications

This study offers a methodological advance for educational research by demonstrating how LLMs, guided through a HITL approach, can be used to construct meaningful KGs from naturalistic online math discussions. By aligning the resulting KGs with the Selection-Organization-Integration framework, we move beyond traditional participation metrics or post-level discourse coding and provide a scalable method to trace how students structure and integrate mathematical concepts through interaction. This opens promising avenues for researchers to investigate conceptual growth longitudinally, identify knowledge fragmentation, or compare student-generated structures with expert models (Sun et al., 2024). Additionally, the integration of social network analysis with cognitive indicators such as KG complexity affirms the need for a more unified analytical framework that considers both the relational positioning of learners and their cognitive outcomes. Future work might expand this approach to other domains or explore more nuanced social configurations (e.g., knowledge brokers or boundary spanners), particularly in forums where roles evolve over time.

For classroom teachers, the findings clarify how students' participation roles are related to meaningful differences in mathematical understanding. Core students' KGs demonstrated broader concept activation, richer connectivity, and deeper integration, indicating that their core status is not simply a structural position but a marker of high-quality learning behaviors. These students' sustained, multi-directional engagement enabled them to build more coherent and relational mathematical schemas. This highlights an important implication for teachers: core-like learning behaviors can be cultivated. Instructional designs that encourage students to initiate top-level posts and communicate with tutors may help more students engage in mathematical reasoning that leads to integrated mathematical understanding. At the same time, teachers should provide targeted scaffolding for x-peripheral students, who may lack opportunities to form integrated knowledge structures without structured prompts or guided reasoning support. Leveraging knowledge-graph visualizations as formative tools can further help teachers identify conceptual gaps and tailor scaffolding to promote deeper, more connected mathematical thinking.

For platform designer, the results underscore the need for platforms that actively support equitable and cognitively productive participation. System-level designs should include adaptive nudges that encourage x-peripheral users to contribute and embedded AI feedback mechanisms that offer accessible, just-in-time guidance. Because peer responses do not always promote deeper knowledge structures, designers should consider features that promote explanation quality, such as elaboration prompts, accountability cues, or automated feedback on conceptual clarity. Additionally, integrating real-time knowledge-graph analytics could help platforms detect fragmentation in users' conceptual networks, identify those at risk of marginalization, and provide personalized participation pathways.

For educational policymakers, the study highlights structural inequities in online participation that can lead to disparities in students' mathematical understanding. Policymakers and administrators should prioritize resources and training that help institutions adopt discussion systems capable of supporting role-sensitive interventions and data-informed instruction. Policies that encourage the integration of AI-enhanced scaffolding, structured discourse routines, and learning-analytics dashboards can help ensure that all students, not only the most active participants, benefit from online discussions. Furthermore, conceptual growth indicators such as KGs offer an alternative to purely behavioral metrics, supporting more holistic and equitable evaluation frameworks.

Limitations and Future Research Directions

Several avenues for future research warrant exploration. First, this study did not examine the specific relationships between knowledge entities within KGs across core, peripheral, and x-peripheral students. Future research should explore how students in different social roles identify and represent these relationships. Second, while the SOI framework emphasizes integrating new and prior knowledge, this study did not explicitly address this aspect. Distinguishing prior knowledge entities from new learning content could provide insights into how students activate, organize, and integrate knowledge. Third, because the dataset consisted of secondary discussion records without external assessments of mathematical learning, we were unable to directly evaluate whether KG-based knowledge structures correspond to actual learning gains. Future research should triangulate KG metrics with independent learning outcomes to establish stronger evidence linking students' knowledge structures to measurable improvements in mathematical understanding. Finally, core-periphery detection and KG construction were conducted post hoc; longitudinal designs would enable researchers to examine how participation roles and knowledge structures evolve and interact over time.

CONCLUSIONS

This study investigated how students' social positions in online mathematics discussions (i.e., core, peripheral, or x-peripheral roles) relate to the quality of their knowledge structures, as captured through KGs generated by LLMs within a HITL framework. By combining social network analysis with KG-based modeling grounded in the Selection-Organization-Integration theory, we introduced a novel methodology for analyzing student learning at scale in real-world educational environments. Our findings reveal that core students engage more frequently and deeply than peripheral and x-peripheral students, benefit more from tutor feedback, and develop richer, more integrated knowledge structures compared to their x-peripheral peers. Peripheral students, while less embedded than core students, can still construct complex and highly integrated knowledge structures through sustained participation, meaningful interactions, and tutor feedback. In contrast, x-peripheral students, who receive minimal feedback and exhibit limited interaction breadth and depth, face substantial challenges in developing integrated mathematical understanding. More broadly, this work demonstrates the feasibility and value of using LLM-powered KGs as a scalable analytic lens for understanding the cognitive outcomes of social participation in education. It highlights how discourse patterns and social positioning jointly shape knowledge construction in online learning. Importantly, the study calls for more nuanced and role-sensitive support systems in digital learning platforms to ensure equitable cognitive opportunities for all students, regardless of how central or peripheral they are to the conversation. As educational technologies continue to scale, tools like those developed here offer a pathway toward more personalized, data-informed, and socially aware learning environments.

REFERENCES

Al-Moslmi, T., Gallofré Ocaña, M., Opdahl, A. L., & Veres, C. (2020). Named entity extraction for knowledge graphs: A literature overview. *IEEE Access : Practical Innovations, Open Solutions, 8*, 32862–32881. DOI: 10.1109/ACCESS.2020.2973928

Albreiki, B., Habuza, T., Palakkal, N., & Zaki, N. (2024). Clustering-based knowledge graphs and entity-relation representation improves the detection of at risk students. *Education and Information Technologies, 29*(6), 6791–6820. DOI: 10.1007/s10639-023-11938-8

Anderson, R. C. (1984). Some reflections on the acquisition of knowledge. *Educational Researcher, 13*(9), 5–10. DOI: 10.3102/0013189X013009005

Anmarkrud, Ø., McCrudden, M. T., Bråten, I., & Strømsø, H. I. (2013). Task-oriented reading of multiple documents: Online comprehension processes and offline products. *Instructional Science, 41*(5), 873–894. DOI: 10.1007/s11251-013-9263-8

Bereiter, C. (2005). *Education and mind in the knowledge age*. Routledge. DOI: 10.4324/9781410612182

Bransford, J. D., Brown, A. L., & Cocking, R. R. (2000). *How people learn* (Vol. 11). National academy press.

Chen, M., Kuzmin, K., & Szymanski, B. K. (2014). Community detection via maximization of modularity and its variants. *IEEE Transactions on Computational Social Systems, 1*(1), 46–65. DOI: 10.1109/TCSS.2014.2307458

Chen, P., Lu, Y., Zheng, V. W., Chen, X., & Yang, B. (2018). KnowEdu: A system to construct knowledge graph for education. *IEEE Access : Practical Innovations, Open Solutions, 6*, 31553–31563. DOI: 10.1109/ACCESS.2018.2839607

Cheng, R., & Hill, B. M. (2022). Many destinations, many pathways: A quantitative analysis of legitimate peripheral participation in scratch. *Proc. ACM Hum.-Comput. Interact., 6*(CSCW2), 381:1-381:26. DOI: 10.1145/3555106

Dagdelen, J., Dunn, A., Lee, S., Walker, N., Rosen, A. S., Ceder, G., Persson, K. A., & Jain, A. (2024). Structured information extraction from scientific text with large language models. *Nature Communications, 15*(1), 1418. DOI: 10.1038/s41467-024-45563-x PMID: 38360817

DiSessa, A. A., & Sherin, B. L. (1998). What changes in conceptual change? *International Journal of Science Education, 20*(10), 1155–1191. DOI: 10.1080/0950069980201002

Du, H., & List, A. (2020). Researching and writing based on multiple texts. *Learning and Instruction*, *66*, 101297. DOI: 10.1016/j.learninstruc.2019.101297

Gielen, S., Peeters, E., Dochy, F., Onghena, P., & Struyven, K. (2010). Improving the effectiveness of peer feedback for learning. *Learning and Instruction*, *20*(4), 304–315. DOI: 10.1016/j.learninstruc.2009.08.007

Grattafiori, A., Dubey, A., Jauhri, A., Pandey, A., Kadian, A., Al-Dahle, A., Letman, A., Mathur, A., Schelten, A., Vaughan, A., Yang, A., Fan, A., Goyal, A., Hartshorn, A., Yang, A., Mitra, A., Sravankumar, A., Korenev, A., Hinsvark, A., . . . Ma, Z. (2024). *The llama 3 herd of models* (No. arXiv:2407.21783). arXiv. https://doi.org// arXiv.2407.21783DOI: 10.48550

Hu, Y., Chen, Q., Du, J., Peng, X., Keloth, V. K., Zuo, X., Zhou, Y., Li, Z., Jiang, X., Lu, Z., Roberts, K., & Xu, H. (2024). Improving large language models for clinical named entity recognition via prompt engineering. *Journal of the American Medical Informatics Association : JAMIA*, *31*(9), ocad259. DOI: 10.1093/jamia/ ocad259 PMID: 38281112

Ifenthaler, D. (2010). Relational, structural, and semantic analysis of graphical representations and concept maps. *Educational Technology Research and Development*, *58*(1), 81–97. DOI: 10.1007/s11423-008-9087-4

Ifenthaler, D., Masduki, I., & Seel, N. M. (2011). The mystery of cognitive structure and how we can detect it: Tracking the development of cognitive structures over time. *Instructional Science*, *39*(1), 41–61. DOI: 10.1007/s11251-009-9097-6

Introne, J., Semaan, B., & Goggins, S. (2016). A sociotechnical mechanism for online support provision. In *Proceedings of the 2016 CHI Conference on Human Factors in Computing Systems* (pp. 3559–3571). DOI: 10.1145/2858036.2858582

Keloth, V. K., Hu, Y., Xie, Q., Peng, X., Wang, Y., Zheng, A., Selek, M., Raja, K., Wei, C. H., Jin, Q., Lu, Z., Chen, Q., & Xu, H. (2024). Advancing entity recognition in biomedicine via instruction tuning of large language models. *Bioinformatics (Oxford, England)*, *40*(4), btae163. DOI: 10.1093/bioinformatics/btae163 PMID: 38514400

Kizilcec, R. F., Piech, C., & Schneider, E. (2013). *Deconstructing disengagement: Analyzing learner subpopulations in massive open online courses*. 170–179.

Koubek, R. J., Clarkston, T. P., & Calvez, V. (1994). The training of knowledge structures for manufacturing tasks: An empirical study. *Ergonomics*, *37*(4), 765–780. DOI: 10.1080/00140139408963687

Lave, J., & Wenger, E. (1991). *Situated learning: Legitimate peripheral participation*. Cambridge university press. DOI: 10.1017/CBO9780511815355

Lee, J.-E., & Recker, M. (2022). Predicting student performance by modeling participation in asynchronous discussions in university online introductory mathematical courses. *Educational Technology Research and Development*, *70*(6), 1993–2015. DOI: 10.1007/s11423-022-10153-5

Leite, W. L., Xing, W., Fish, G., & Li, C. (2024). Teacher strategies to use virtual learning environments to facilitate algebra learning during school closures. *Journal of Research on Technology in Education*, *56*(2), 95–109. DOI: 10.1080/15391523.2022.2110335

Li, N., Shen, Q., Song, R., Chi, Y., & Xu, H. (2022). MEduKG: A deep-learning-based approach for multi-modal educational knowledge graph construction. *Information (Basel)*, *13*(2), 91. DOI: 10.3390/info13020091

Lin, F., & Chan, C. K. (2018). Examining the role of computer-supported knowledge-building discourse in epistemic and conceptual understanding. *Journal of Computer Assisted Learning*, *34*(5), 567–579. DOI: 10.1111/jcal.12261

Liu, W., Sidhu, A., Beacom, A. M., & Valente, T. W. (2017). Social network theory. *The international encyclopedia of media effects*, *1*, 1-12.

Luebeck, J. L., & Bice, L. R. (2005). Online discussion as a mechanism of conceptual change among mathematics and science teachers. *International Journal of E-Learning & Distance Education/Revue internationale du e-learning et la formation à distance*, *20*(2), 21–39.

Luo, X., Gao, L., Li, J., Lin, Y., Zhao, J., & Li, Q. (2020). A critical literature review of dyadic web-based interventions to support cancer patients and their caregivers, and directions for future research. *Psycho-Oncology*, *29*(1), 38–48. DOI: 10.1002/pon.5278 PMID: 31702839

Lyu, B., Grossnickle Peterson, E., & List, A. (2023). Using PowerPoints to assess students' learning from multiple resources. *Contemporary Educational Psychology*, *74*, 102204. DOI: 10.1016/j.cedpsych.2023.102204

Lyu, B., Li, C., Li, H., & Xing, W. (2026). Exploring students' participation in online mathematical discussions using educational big data: A communicative ecology perspective. *Journal of Educational Technology & Society*, *29*(2), 171–190.

Lyu, B., Li, C., Li, H., Zhu, W., & Xing, W. (2024). Explaining technical, social, and discursive participation in online mathematical discussions. *Distance Education*, •••, 1–24.

Mayer, R. E. (1996). Learning strategies for making sense out of expository text: The SOI model for guiding three cognitive processes in knowledge construction. *Educational Psychology Review*, *8*(4), 357–371. DOI: 10.1007/BF01463939

McCrudden, M. T., Huynh, L., Lyu, B., & Kulikowich, J. M. (2021). Bridging inferences and learning from multiple complementary texts. *Discourse Processes*, *58*(5–6), 529–548. DOI: 10.1080/0163853X.2021.1924586

Nation, A. (2019, August). Glossary of terms: Algebra 1 (English version) [PDF]. Retrieved from https://youllneverwalkalonebms.wordpress.com/wp-content/uploads/2019/08/algebra-nation-glossary-of-terms-algebra-1-english-version.pdf

Nelson, M. M., & Schunn, C. D. (2009). The nature of feedback: How different types of peer feedback affect writing performance. *Instructional Science*, *37*(4), 375–401. DOI: 10.1007/s11251-008-9053-x

Nesbit, J. C., & Adesope, O. O. (2006). Learning with concept and knowledge maps: A meta-analysis. *Review of Educational Research*, *76*(3), 413–448. DOI: 10.3102/00346543076003413

Novak, J. D., & Cañas, A. J. (2006). The theory underlying concept maps and how to construct them. *Florida Institute for Human and Machine Cognition, 1*(1), 1–31.

Ouyang, F., & Scharber, C. (2017). The influences of an experienced instructor's discussion design and facilitation on an online learning community development: A social network analysis study. *The Internet and Higher Education*, *35*, 34–47. DOI: 10.1016/j.iheduc.2017.07.002

Pan, S., Luo, L., Wang, Y., Chen, C., Wang, J., & Wu, X. (2024). Unifying large language models and knowledge graphs: A roadmap. *IEEE Transactions on Knowledge and Data Engineering*, *36*(7), 3580–3599. DOI: 10.1109/TKDE.2024.3352100

Piaget, J. (1952). *The origins of intelligence in children.* International University. DOI: 10.1037/11494-000

Poquet, O., Dawson, S., & Dowell, N. (2017). *How effective is your facilitation? Group-level analytics of MOOC forums*. 208–217.

Poquet, O., Dawson, S., & Dowell, N. (2017). How effective is your facilitation? Group-level analytics of MOOC forums. In *Proceedings of the Seventh International Learning Analytics & Knowledge Conference* (pp. 208–217). DOI: 10.1145/3027385.3027404

Reif, F., & Heller, J. I. (1982). Knowledge structure and problem solving in physics. *Educational Psychologist*, *17*(2), 102–127. DOI: 10.1080/00461528209529248

Rombach, P., Porter, M. A., Fowler, J. H., & Mucha, P. J. (2017). Core-periphery structure in networks (revisited). *SIAM Review*, *59*(3), 619–646. DOI: 10.1137/17M1130046

Rumelhart, D. E., Smolensky, P., McClelland, J. L., & Hinton, G. (1986). Sequential thought processes in PDP models. *Parallel Distributed Processing: Explorations in the Microstructures of Cognition*, *2*, 3–57.

Safadi, H., Johnson, S. L., & Faraj, S. (2021). Who contributes knowledge? Core-periphery tension in online innovation communities. *Organization Science*, *32*(3), 752–775. DOI: 10.1287/orsc.2020.1364

Saleem, F., Ullah, Z., Fakieh, B., & Kateb, F. (2021). Intelligent decision support system for predicting student's e-learning performance using ensemble machine learning. *Mathematics*, *9*(17), 2078. DOI: 10.3390/math9172078

Siemens, G. (2006). *Knowing knowledge*. Lulu. com.

Siqin, T., & Chu, S. K. W. (2021). How students take collective responsibility for productive collaboration: An empirical examination of online discourse. *Interactive Learning Environments*, *29*(7), 1076–1089. DOI: 10.1080/10494820.2019.1636081

Smith, M. (Peg), & Stein, M. K. (2018). *5 Practices for orchestrating productive mathematics discussion*. National Council of Teachers of Mathematics.

Song, Y., Li, C., Ma, Y., Lyu, B., Zhu, W., Li, H., & Xing, W. (2025). Exploring effective tutoring strategies in asynchronous online mathematical discussions: Insights from ordered network analysis. *Journal of Science Education and Technology*, *34*(5), 1–21. DOI: 10.1007/s10956-025-10233-0

Su, Y., & Zhang, Y. (2020). Automatic construction of subject knowledge graph based on educational big data. In *Proceedings of the 2020 3rd International Conference on Big Data and Education* (pp. 30–36). DOI: 10.1145/3396452.3396458

Sudiarta, I. G. P., Sukajaya, I. N., & Suharta, I. G. P. (2018). Investigation on students' mathematical online discussion: A case study in grade 8 SMPN 1 Denpasar. [). IOP Publishing.]. *Journal of Physics: Conference Series*, *1040*, 012031. DOI: 10.1088/1742-6596/1040/1/012031

Sun, J., Zhang, Z., & He, X. (2024). Llm4edukg: Llm for automatic construction of educational knowledge graph. In *2024 International Conference on Networking and Network Applications (NaNA)* (pp. 269-275). IEEE. DOI: 10.1109/NaNA63151.2024.00051

Traxler, A., Gavrin, A., & Lindell, R. (2018). Networks identify productive forum discussions. *Physical Review. Physics Education Research, 14*(2), 20107. DOI: 10.1103/PhysRevPhysEducRes.14.020107

van Lidth de Jeude, J., Caldarelli, G., & Squartini, T. (2019). Detecting core-periphery structures by surprise. *Europhysics Letters, 125*(6), 68001. DOI: 10.1209/0295-5075/125/68001

Vygotsky, L. S. (1978). *Mind in society: The development of higher psychological processes* (Vol. 86). Harvard University Press.

Wang, Y., & Liu, Q. (2020). Effects of online teaching presence on students' interactions and collaborative knowledge construction. *Journal of Computer Assisted Learning, 36*(3), 370–382. DOI: 10.1111/jcal.12408

Wilkerson, D. A. (2016). Lurking behavior in online psychosocial discussion forums: Theoretical perspectives and implications for practice. *Journal of Technology in Human Services, 34*(3), 256–266. DOI: 10.1080/15228835.2016.1193456

Wise, A. F., Cui, Y., Jin, W., & Vytasek, J. (2017). Mining for gold: Identifying content-related MOOC discussion threads across domains through linguistic modeling. *The Internet and Higher Education, 32*, 11–28. DOI: 10.1016/j.iheduc.2016.08.001

Wu, Z., Huang, S., Zhou, Z., Ying, H., Wang, J., Lin, D., & Chen, K. (2024). *Intern-LM2.5-StepProver: Advancing automated theorem proving via expert iteration on large-scale LEAN problems* (No. arXiv:2410.15700). arXiv. https://doi.org//arXiv .2410.15700DOI: 10.48550

Xing, W., Li, H., Kim, T., Zhu, W., & Song, Y. (2025). Investigating the behaviors of core and periphery students in an asynchronous online discussion community using network analysis and topic modeling. *Education and Information Technologies, 30*(5), 5561–5588. DOI: 10.1007/s10639-024-13038-7

Zheng, L., Long, M., Chen, B., & Fan, Y. (2023). Promoting knowledge elaboration, socially shared regulation, and group performance in collaborative learning: An automated assessment and feedback approach based on knowledge graphs. *International Journal of Educational Technology in Higher Education, 20*(1), 46. DOI: 10.1186/s41239-023-00415-4 PMID: 37032738

Zou, W., Hu, X., Pan, Z., Li, C., Cai, Y., & Liu, M. (2021). Exploring the relationship between social presence and learners' prestige in MOOC discussion forums using automated content analysis and social network analysis. *Computers in Human Behavior, 115*, 106582. DOI: 10.1016/j.chb.2020.106582

KEY TERMS AND DEFINITIONS

Human-in-the-Loop (HITL): A design approach in which human expertise is incorporated into automated systems to guide, correct, or refine machine-generated outputs. In this study, HITL refers specifically to the process of reviewing, correcting, and refining knowledge graphs automatically generated by large language models (LLMs), with these human-validated KGs subsequently used to iteratively fine-tune and improve the model.

Knowledge Graph (KG): A structured representation of knowledge that models relationships among entities. Similar to concept maps in cognitive science, KGs encode concept-relation-concept connections, typically formalized as 'triplets,' where one entity is linked to another through a predicate specifying their relationship.

Knowledge Integration: The process of linking and synthesizing mathematical ideas to form a more unified understanding. In this study, knowledge integration is measured using KG metrics such as depth and breadth, which reflect how extensively and deeply students traverse and combine conceptual connections. Higher integration indicates the ability to form multi-step relational chains, coordinate multiple knowledge units, and connect new understanding with prior mathematical knowledge.

Knowledge Oganization: The structuring of selected mathematical ideas into a coherent representation. Within this study, knowledge organization is assessed through graph-theoretic indicators of structural complexity, particularly the diversity and distribution of connections among concepts (e.g., entropy). Higher organizational complexity suggests that a learner not only recognizes relevant concepts but also understands how these concepts relate to one another within a mathematical framework.

Knowledge Selection: The process by which students identify and activate relevant knowledge during learning. In this study, knowledge selection is operationalized through KG metrics that capture the number of unique entities represented in a student's KG and the extent to which these selected entities are meaningfully connected. Higher selection reflects broader knowledge activation and greater sensitivity to key mathematical ideas within a discussion.

Knowledge Structure: A structured representation of how students connect mathematical concepts, procedures, and ideas within a domain. Here, knowledge structures are operationalized through the graph-theoretic properties of students' knowledge graphs, capturing the extent to which concepts are selected, organized, and integrated.

Participation Patterns: The measurable behaviors through which students contribute to online mathematical discussions, including initiating top-level posts, replying to their own posts, responding to peers, and receiving tutor feedback. In this study, participation patterns capture the frequency and direction of these interactions and serve as indicators of how students engage in mathematical reasoning and discourse.

Social Role: A learner's position within the online discussion community, defined by both the nature of their participation behaviors and their relational embeddedness in the interaction network. In this study, social roles reflect the breadth and depth of students' social ties, capturing how central or peripheral they are within the discussion structure.

ENDNOTE

1 https://drive.google.com/drive/folders/1GzcTkWv1zaNgFEQISSEoHbXJM3jQoH5-

APPENDIX

Figure 7. Pseudocode of implementing Surprise for core-periphery detection.

```
Algorithm: Surprise-Based Partition Refinement
while partition has changed in the previous iteration do
    for each community C in the current partition do
        // --- Phase 1: Boundary Optimization ---
        for each node n in C do
            for each neighbor u of n do
                if community(u) ≠ C then
                    attempt to MERGE communities C and community(u)
                    if merge fails then
                        attempt to EXCHANGE node n with node u
                    end if
                end if
            end for
        end for
        // --- Phase 2: Element Extraction ---
        while extraction of a single node from C is successful do
            perform extraction
        end while
        // --- Phase 3: Subcommunity Extraction ---
        while extraction of a subcommunity from C is successful do
            perform subcommunity extraction
        end while
        // --- Phase 4: Subcommunity Relocation ---
        while relocation is successful do
            for each other community X in the partition do
                attempt to RELOCATE a subcommunity from C to X
            end for
        end while
    end for
end while
```

Notes. An operation is considered successful when it increases the Surprise value of the current partition.

Chapter 7
AI-Supported Emotion Detection in Interdisciplinary Distance Education:
Group Composition and Affectively-Informed Instructional Design

H. Tugba Ozturk
https://orcid.org/0000-0002-9614-5452
Ankara University, Turkey

Gulgun Afacan
https://orcid.org/0000-0002-0832-1808
University of Cambridge, UK

M. Bahadirhan
https://orcid.org/0000-0002-0788-1408
Ankara University, Turkey

ABSTRACT

This study explores positive emotional expressions in interdisciplinary distance education (DE) by examining how happiness emerges in relation to group composition through AI-supported emotion detection in multimodal data. Within interdisciplinary educational settings, diverse learner backgrounds give rise to a range of affective responses that shape collaborative experiences. The research focuses on how such emotions unfold in both homogeneous and heterogeneous student groups

DOI: 10.4018/979-8-3373-2927-7.ch007

with different group compositions. Sixteen participants engaged in a 10-week interdisciplinary DE course. By integrating facial emotion recognition with text mining, this study offers a holistic analysis of video- and text-based interactions. Findings revealed that happiness was most frequently linked to three socio-emotional factors: the familiarity effect, the process of establishing oneself, and a sense of ontological security. These insights inform affectively responsive instructional design and support the integration of AI in fostering emotionally attuned learning environments.

INTRODUCTION

As distance education becomes increasingly interdisciplinary and incorporates various modalities—such as video conferencing and text-based communication—understanding how positive emotions emerge within diverse group formations, an inherent characteristic of interdisciplinary settings, requires AI-driven techniques capable of capturing the affective complexity of multimodal online collaboration. However, the affective dimensions of learning—particularly sentimental reactions and positive emotional expressions—remain underexplored in the literature, and existing AI tools are usually limited to a single data modality (text-based or video-based), indicating a lack of a holistic perspective to inform instructional design, especially in interdisciplinary educational settings where diverse learner backgrounds give rise to affective responses that shape collaboration.

A closer examination of the affective aspects of students' learning experiences in interdisciplinary studies shows a lack of sufficient research in the literature. Usually, types of knowledge which are shared among group members, social network analysis and types of interactions (e.g. Haythornthwaite, 2006); collaborative models and practices (Orchard et al., 2005) are examined. From a different perspective, although some studies have examined sentimental reactions through interdisciplinary lenses—such as linguistics and media studies (e.g., Mandl et al., 2023)—the affective dimension of learning, particularly emotional experiences, remains largely underexplored.

At the intersection of an interdisciplinary study and DE environment, socio-emotional responses play a key role in shaping the affective framework. Socio-emotional aspects refer to how individuals initiate, build, and respond to relationships with others, whether these relationships are brief or long-term (Mentor, 2015). These aspects involve interacting and communicating with both familiar and unfamiliar people, managing stress, and forming positive peer connections. In this sense, socio-emotional skills are similar to interpersonal abilities that help individuals maintain and develop relationships (Mentor, 2015). The socio-emotional aspect becomes even more important in distance education because the physical separation related to social presence and lack of non-verbal cues (Garrison et al., 1999) can lead to feelings of isolation, anxiety, and a weakened sense of community, which are significant barriers to student engagement and success.

Socio-emotional factors play a critical role because emotions are contagious in online environments, demonstrating that learners influence one another both socially and emotionally through their interactions. For example, in an experimental study on social media, researchers (Kramer et al., 2014) investigate whether emotional contagion can occur beyond face-to-face interactions by decreasing the emotional content in the News Feed. They find out that when positive expressions were minimized, individuals generated fewer positive posts and more negative posts. Conversely, reducing negative expressions led to the opposite pattern.These findings demonstrate that emotions expressed by others on a social network significantly impact our own emotions, providing experimental proof of widespread emotional contagion through social networks. A further study (Stieglitz & Dang-Xuan, 2013) looks at the relationship between emotion loaded messages and their diffusion on the network. At the end of the study, they report that emotionally charged messages tend to be re-shared more frequently and more quickly compared to neutral ones. Therefore, it is possible to conclude that emotions are dynamic and powerful in group's learning cycle. Similarly, sentiments are associated with successful collaborative learning (Zheng & Huang, 2016). Hence, making the positive sentiments and emotions explicit would help the instructional designers and practitioners regulate learning environments in a productive way.

On taking a closer look at interdisciplinary distance education from the perspective of socio-emotional factors in different modalities such as via video-conference or text-based communication, learners' affective responses are shaped by multiple elements of the learning context, including technological tools (e.g., video conferencing platforms) as the primary medium for distance interaction, instructional content (especially interdisciplinary content, which can increase complexity), and interactions with peers and tutors (Lee & Branch, 2022; Patel, Addicott, & Buelow, 2023).

This demonstrate that affective factors about socio-emotional dynamics are shaped by a variety of contexts. However, given the collaborative nature of interdisciplinary work, this research focuses specifically on the critical role of group composition in distance education. The literature indicates that homogeneity or heterogeneity within a group directly influences the strength of socio-emotional bonds and positive reactions—such as hope, affection, and cohesion. These bonds are essential for mitigating the isolation inherent in transactional distance (Lieberman et al., 2005) and social presence (Garrison, 2022), a connection that will be elaborated on in the following section.

Group Composition (Homogeneous And Heterogeneous) And Emotional Reactions İn Interdisciplinary Distance Education

In the literature, group composition—whether homogeneous or heterogeneous in terms of shared characteristics such as age, background, or concerns—is discussed in relation to how groups produce sentimental and emotional reactions. For instance, Lieberman et al. (2005) compare homogeneous and heterogeneous online support groups and find that homogeneous groups exhibit stronger sentimental reactions toward the group. Members of homogeneous groups expressed more positive emotions, hope, affection, and used more inclusive language (e.g., "we," "our"), demonstrating higher commitment and group cohesion. Additionally, homogeneous groups showed more positive outcomes over time, while heterogeneous groups demonstrated weaker emotional bonding. These findings suggest that homogeneous group composition facilitates stronger socio-emotional attachment and more positive sentimental reactions within online collaborative settings.

Wilkinson and Fung (2002) also find similar results as homogeneous groups tend to create a normative social atmosphere shaped by shared expectations and behaviors, which can strengthen group cohesion and emotional alignment. However, heterogeneous groups foster richer interaction and exchange of perspectives as could be expected from interdisciplinary studies. In heterogeneous groups, learning benefits arise from interactional processes such as dialogue, cognitive restructuring, and problem solving, which are stimulated by diversity within the group. According to their study results, group composition contributes to learning outcomes, illustrating that both emotional climate (in homogeneous groups) and interpersonal interaction (in heterogeneous groups) shape students' affective and cognitive experiences.

Therefore, it is possible to say that group formation is also important in interdisciplinary environments because actors in each discipline rely on interdependence, collective ownership of goals, and reflection on the process as key components of collaboration (Bronstein, 2003). These components are connected to emergence of sentimental reactions as these reactions are cornerstone of building such relationships. Accordingly, shared sentiments, which are more commonly observed in homogeneous groups, have the potential to bring members of different disciplines into closer proximity and on this point, Ju et al. (2016; p.3) remark that close proximity in interdisciplinary studies "helps collaborators make connections, transfer information and knowledge, and trigger processes".

On the other hand, in heterogenous groups, a number of fundamental epistemological challenges arising from differences between disciplines can be observed in interdisciplinary distance education. Furthermore, learners' social presence (Garrison, 2022) may become an obstacle to establishing oneself within the socio-emotional atmosphere, which can function as a slippery slope in interdisciplinary environments.

In line with this, Moirano et al. (2023) note that in order to obtain creative results in interdisciplinary studies, some aspects of "psychology, socio-cultural and management" are essential and here, sentimental reactions such as emotions and opinions of the learners become crucial. In a view of disciplines as institutions with particular epistemic and organizational aspects, identities facilitate the intentional and psychological background leading to the emergence of disciplinary emotions (Salmela & Mäki, 2018).

In interdisciplinary studies, the main focus is on diversity of the participants and this is mainly related to profiles of the disciplinary group members. However, demographics (i.e. age, gender, major) on sentiments such as emotions, positive and negative reactions and opinions has mostly remained unaddressed and there is a need to fulfil this gap (Zhou & Yeu, 2023). On a closer look at the studies, Neumann and Linzmayer (2021) perform Sentimental Analysis (SA) while considering students' gender, and ethnicity. They note that students from different sex and ethnicity (Hispanic, Asian etc.) differ in emotions. Therefore, it is observed that sentimental reactions might depend on the background of the students and the group composition (homogeneous or heterogeneous) plays an important role in showing sentimental reactions.

Against this background, the present study aims to investigate how productive interdisciplinary emotional reactions emerge and when positive emotions as happiness occur in a variety of group composition (e.g. heterogenous and homogenous groups) in interdisciplinary DE. Group composition in giving emotional and sentimental reactions is critical as Vanslambrouck et al. (2018) remark, online and blended learning environments allow students to work together from diverse background, resulting in heterogeneous groups with diverse goals, motivations and "this makes understanding the motivation and values of students a challenging task" (p. 33). Here, it is seen that group composition is effective in sentimental reactions. Therefore, it is possible to conclude that there is a need for research examining the emotions and sentimental reactions of interdisciplinary groups in DE, based on group composition (such as homogeneous and heterogeneous groups) and the diversity of students' demographic backgrounds.

Artificial Intelligence (AI) In Detecting Positive Emotional Expressions In Distance Education

In the literature, there is a gap in research regarding how educators can quantitatively assess and modify course design and delivery in response to learners' emotional reactions (Stanworth et al., 2023; Vanslambrouck et al., 2018). Approaches to measuring sentimental reactions are relatively recent, and the socio-emotional dimensions of computer-supported argumentation remain underexplored, particularly in learning groups composed of students from diverse backgrounds (Polo et al., 2016).

In this context, to understand how these affective dynamics can be observed and analyzed, emerging AI tools offer promising solutions. There are mainly two approaches to adopting AI in detecting emotions and sentiments: the first concerns video-based data, such as online lecturing, where facial recognition is used; the second involves text-based data, where text mining as an AI approach is applied, for instance, in asynchronous discussion forums on a Learning Management System (LMS).

On a closer look at the two approaches, and in terms of video-based data, recent studies (e.g., Gómez-Ríos et al., 2025; Lawpanom et al., 2024) indicate that AI facial recognition systems can be used to detect and quantify learners' emotional expressions in real time. This approach is important given that live video lectures are a very common mode of course delivery in distance education.

In analyzing text based data such as the data obtained from asynchronous discussions, in their review of sentiment analysis research in distance education, Dalipi, Zdravkova, and Ahlgren (2021, p. 9) note that, beginning in 2019, researchers increasingly shifted from traditional supervised learning methods toward deep learning models for analyzing sentiments in MOOC environments. In addition to machine learning and natural language processing techniques (Hew et al., 2020), newer approaches—such as CNN, LSTM, BERT, and RNN—have shown improved performance in detecting and classifying emotional expressions in student-generated content (Capuano & Caballé, 2020; Capuano et al., 2020). In addition to these deep learning methods, other analytical techniques, such as epistemic network analysis (Yu, 2025), are also used to examine how emotions appear and evolve in online learning discussions.

AI used in both video-based and text-based data techniques offers promising avenues for the systematic analysis of learners' affective responses, enabling researchers and instructional designers to identify patterns and inform emotionally responsive instructional design. As Vistorte et al. (2024) report these technologies show potential for informing instructional decisions and supporting adaptive learning experiences that respond to students' emotional needs. Advancing our understanding of these aspects could further strengthen how AI is applied to emotion assessment in educational contexts.

Drawing on these discussions, the present research contributes to the literature by using an AI facial recognition tool for video-based data obtained from online video lectures and by analyzing text-based data through text analysis to capture and understand how happiness, as a positive sentimental reaction, occurs.

To sum up, this study aims to develop an affective framework and investigates the role of group composition in AI-supported interdisciplinary DE through the lens of AI-assisted facial recognition technologies and text mining analysis.

Against this background, the research questions are formulated as follows. In homogeneous and heterogeneous groups during interdisciplinary DE:

1. How does happiness, as a positive emotional expression, emerge in both video-based (synchronous) and text-based (asynchronous) learning interactions?
2. Which socio-emotional factors explain the emergence of happiness as a positive sentimental reaction during collaborative activities?

METHODOLOGY

This study adopts a mixed-methods approach. Quantitative analysis is conducted using AI-based emotion detection tools, and a grounded theory–informed qualitative analysis is then applied to interpret emotional moments and reveal socio-emotional patterns related to the emergence of positive sentimental reactions as happiness during collaborative activities.

Context

This study was conducted with a group of postgraduate students enrolled in the Interdisciplinary Science, Technology, Engineering, and Mathematics (STEM) program at the Institute of Education at a public university in Türkiye. The program prepares students to apply practical STEM knowledge in interdisciplinary settings. They learn to foster critical thinking, creativity, and problem-solving by creating learning environments and guiding hands-on projects such as robotics and coding.

The participants, who were practicing teachers, took part in a 10-week distance education (DE) course titled *Computational Thinking and Coding*. The course was designed to foster collaborative learning and included both homogeneous and heterogeneous group compositions. Instruction was delivered primarily via synchronous video conferencing, supplemented by asynchronous collaborative tasks. Accordingly, multimodal data were collected from video and text sources to enable a comprehensive analysis of the learning dynamics.

In the study, it is aimed to target how positive emotions emerged in different group compositions in interdisciplinary work. In this scope, 16 participants took part in group asynchronous discussions (text data) and seven participants joined video conference meetings (video data).

Prior to the main study, a demographic questionnaire was administered to assign participants into homogeneous and heterogeneous groups. The questionnaire collected information on age, gender, discipline (subject), teaching level, prior acquaintance with other participants, and location (city of work and residence). Below in Table 1 are demographic characteristics of participants.

Table 1. Demographic characteristics of learners

Demographic characteristics		**Frequency**
Age	24- 27	4
	28- 31	2
	32- 35	3
	36- 39	4
	40 and over	3
Total		**16**
Sex	Female	11
	Male	5
Total		**16**
Discipline	Biology	3
	English	3
	Preschool	2
	ICT (Information &Communication Technologies)	2
	Primary Education	1
	Visual art	1
	Mathematics	2
	Science	2
Total		**16**

The study involved a total of 16 participants with diverse backgrounds in terms of age, gender, and disciplinary fields. The age distribution was relatively balanced, ranging from 24 to over 40 years old, with the majority falling between 24 and 39, suggesting a mix of early to mid-career professionals.

Gender representation was predominantly female, with 11 female and 5 male participants, indicating a gender-skewed sample.

Participants came from a wide range of disciplinary backgrounds, including Biology (3), English (3), Preschool Education (2), ICT (2), Primary School Education (1), Visual Arts (1), Mathematics (2), and Science (2).

The study group is diverse in age, gender, and disciplinary background, making it suited for interdisciplinary education studies, particularly those exploring affective responses. The variation supports robust qualitative insights, particularly when exploring emotional engagement and social interactions.

Collaborative Tasks

In asynchronous discussions, since interdisciplinary work is investigated from the perspective of group composition, the groups are designed as two ways in two different tasks:

1. Homogenous groups were formed: members of the groups were chosen from the teachers working in the same or similar disciplines such as pre-school and class teachers were assigned to the first group; science, biology, maths and ICT teachers were assigned to the second group, teachers working at the same school were assigned to the third group. It is important to note that teaching levels are different in this grouping because pre-school and class teachers are the only teachers in their classes without any involvement of branch teachers. Therefore, there was no overlap between the groups in terms of teaching specialization or role.
2. Heterogeneous groups were formed: members of the groups were chosen from the teachers working in different disciplines such as art and science teachers were assigned to the first group; English and maths teachers were assigned to the second group and so on. Teachers working at the high school and pre-school teachers were assigned to the third group. Although some educational institutions involve cross-disciplinary teaching roles, participants in heterogeneous groups were assigned based on their primary teaching discipline and level, ensuring that group memberships were mutually exclusive.

The following tasks were allocated to the groups in asynchronous discussion forum in different weeks of the course:

1. For any of the mathematics units in the curriculum regardless of the grade, please design a lesson plan based on computational thinking (heterogeneous group).
2. Using the asynchronous discussion, as a group, create a drama script to teach programming (homogenous group).
3. Do you think teaching coding must be included in the curriculum? Please discuss by taking into account of your group members' ideas (heterogenous group).

In the video conference sessions, there are two groups:

Group 1 is the homogenous group consisting of students from Visual Art teaching, English teaching and Classroom teaching. The group is homogenous in terms of age, school level, gender and their history. Accordingly, their age ranges from 40 to 45. There are three male students. They teach at the similar level at school (primary and secondary school) and finally, they know each other as they work at the same School in the same city.

Group 2 is the heterogenous group consisting of four students from biology, preschool education, ICT and English subjects. Their age ranges from 30 to 45. Their teaching level ranges from preschool education to high school, and they live or work in different schools and cities; most of them do not know each other.

It is important to note that in assigning based on the subjects, educational disciplines are often categorized based on the dominant skill set or subject focus they require. Broadly, verbal-oriented (humanities/social science) fields emphasize language, communication, and social studies skills, whereas numerical-oriented (science/technical) fields emphasize mathematics and positive scientific reasoning. This distinction is reflected in how university departments are grouped and how students are selected for admission. For example, Kaşıkçı and İzmirli (2024) note that in one university system, departments like Early Childhood Education, Special Education, Social Sciences Education, Geography Education, and Turkish Language Education are classified under the *"verbal" field*, while departments such as Biology/Science Education, Computer Education and Instructional Technology (CEIT), Chemistry Education, and Mathematics Education fall under the *"numerical" field*. This means the former group of programs centers on verbal and social subject matter, and the latter group focuses on quantitative and scientific content. Such classifications are not unique – Artuvan Korkmaz et al. (2019) similarly refer to *"verbal" vs. "quantitative" programs* when comparing students in humanities-oriented majors to those in science-oriented majors, indicating that higher education tracks are often divided along these lines in different contexts (p. 266).

This is also related to STEM and working interdisciplinary. Students strong in literature, history, and language tend to pursue humanities or education majors (e.g. language teaching, social studies, early childhood teaching), whereas students strong in mathematics and science pursue STEM-related majors (e.g. engineering, biology, ICT) (Kaşıkçı & İzmirli, 2024). However, in pedagogical approaches—not necessarily in professional occupations—STEM is increasingly applied across multiple disciplines. In this study, the emergence of interdisciplinary educational practices, particularly in distance education, is examined through different group compositions, including participants from arts and language disciplines.

The task given to the students is "Design an interdisciplinary question to evaluate students' computational thinking skills". In the first group, the video lasts 40:20 minutes and in the second group, the video lasts 45:17 minutes. The participants in Group 1 are coded as G1A, G1B, G1C and the participants in Group 2 are coded as G2A, G2B, G2C and G2D.

Data Collection and Data Analysis

Data were collected through asynchronous discussions were obtained from Moodle discussion forums. Also, videos recorded while participants were performing collaborative tasks in groups.

In analysing video-based data (online meetings), a face recognition tool called MorphCast was used. It operates within the domain of affective computing, a field where AI interprets human emotions. MorphCast is informed by AI through its use of facial recognition, emotion detection, real-time analysis, and adaptive interaction, all of which rely on machine learning models and affective computing principles.

In order to understand the learning situations which happiness is emerged, when happiness is overly experienced than any other emotion types (anger, disgust, fear, sadness, and surprise) by the participants according to the emotion graphic (Please see Figure 1 as example) produced by MorphCast, the time stamp was noted and learning situation experienced in that time slot was qualitatively analysed to understand the emergence of happiness as a positive sentimental reaction.

Figure 1. Example of an emotion graphic produced by MorhCast. The yellow line represents happiness.

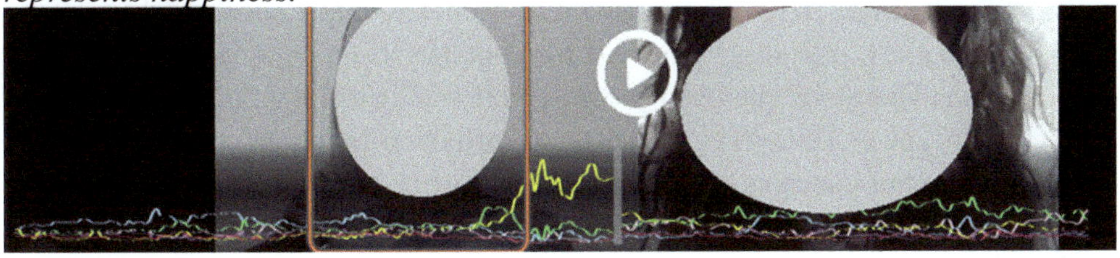

In analysing asynchronous discussions -text based data-, a sequential analysis method was used. Sequential analysis refers to "the examination of whether one behavior (e.g., teacher instruction) increases or decreases the probability of another behavior (e.g., self-injury) occurring within a specified number of coded behaviors or time units." (Yoder &Tapp, 2004, p. 228). Sequential analysis was employed because this method allows to predict the emergence of emotions in a chronological order. In other words, it helps uncover how emotions, such as happiness, spread and manifest as positive sentiments. As explained in detail by Ozturk et al. (2014), the sequential analysis method is conducted using a transitional probability matrix, which represents the likelihood of two messages occurring consecutively.

Each message in a discussion is coded according to its function—for example:

Code P1: Affirmative reaction,
Code P2: Positive attitude, etc.

These coded interactions are then analyzed pairwise to calculate the probability that a particular type of message (e.g., P1) follows another type (e.g., P2).

The resulting transitional probability matrix shows these probabilities. For instance, after a message coded as P2, there's a 50% probability the next message will be P1 or from P1 to P3, there's a 56% transition probability. In online discussions, the matrix helps identify patterns such as: Whether discussions are advancing (e.g., moving toward solutions), Or stuck in loops (e.g., same type of messages repeated). The study also uses adjusted residuals (Z-scores) to determine if the transitions are statistically significant (i.e., not due to chance). Sequential analysis provides an analytical framework for AI research due to its predictive capabilities.

In explaining socio-emotional factors for the emergence of happiness as a positive sentimental reaction during collaborative activities, this study is inspried by grounded theory provides an openness to all possible theoretical understandings. Furthermore, grounded theory provides a way to explain underlying reasons from an interpretive perspective. By repeatedly questioning the data and the concepts that emerge during analysis, researchers are able to move from descriptive accounts toward higher levels of abstraction and develop broader theoretical insights (Charmaz, 2005; Charmaz, 2010). Grounded theory aims to explore concepts that emerge from the data itself, including those that may not have been previously identified in the literature. Therefore, the term "socio-emotional" was intentionally used as an umbrella concept, as it allows us to investigate influential components that contribute to positive emotions such as happiness, and pre-defined coding categories were not imposed on the data; the concept only provided guidance.

Briefly, in explaining the question of *how*, qualitative research methods were employed, as they allow for an in-depth exploration of the nature and dynamics of relationships, actions, and contexts. Rather than measuring the effects of predetermined variables—and without imposing predefined coding categories—this study adopted grounded theory to guide the data analysis. In this way, qualitative inquiry prioritized a holistic and detailed description of what occurs within a particular setting or process (Fraenkel & Wallen, 2006).

The data analysis was carried out in two main stages, as outlined by Charmaz (2010, p. 188).

1) Line by line coding,
2) Constant comparison,
   a. Comparing different people (such as their views, situations, actions, accounts, and experiences)
   b. Comparing data from the same individuals with themselves at different points in time,
   c. Comparing incident by incident,
   d. Comparing data with category, and
   e. Comparing a category with other categories"

Table 2 presents an example of the themes (socio-emotional factors) and one of the sub-themes (the familiarity effect) that emerged during the coding process.

Table 2. Example of a thematic framework of socio-emotional factors explaining the emergence of happiness as a positive emotional response (based on the data and literature)

Quotation	Code	Sub-themes	Themes	Interpretation
oh sorry, last time (in asynchronous discussion) I addressed you with your name as I thought you were very young (they both smile)	Happiness (detected by AI)	Familiarity effect (Literature: Carr et al., 2017)	Socio-emotional factors	In Group 2, the first happiness emotion was seen when the group member got to know each other. Their age difference was significant, and they did not know each other. When they first saw each other online, G2A said G2B that "oh sorry, last time (in asynchronous discussion) I addressed you with your name as I thought you were very young". After this conversation, they both smiled at each other and this is how they first produced the emotion of happiness.

Table 2 illustrates how socio-emotional factors—informed by grounded theory analysis—explain the emergence of happiness as a positive sentimental reaction during collaborative activities. Grounded theory allowed for openness to emergent concepts; thus, no predefined coding categories were imposed on the data. Instead, "socio-emotional" was used as an umbrella concept to guide interpretation while allowing patterns to emerge naturally from participants' interactions. The analysis followed Charmaz's (2010) two-stage process of line-by-line coding and constant comparison, moving from descriptive coding toward conceptual abstraction. The familiarity effect shown in this example demonstrates how initial socio-emotional connection—such as recognizing personal characteristics during interaction—triggered happiness, as detected through AI-based emotion recognition. MAXQDA software was used to analyze the qualitative data.

Validity and Reliability

In analysing emotions, the machine learning method is considered as more reliable than other approaches as "the expression and interpretation of emotions can be culturally specific" (MorphCast, 2024a) and this is why it is important to adopt objective recognition of the emotions; thus, this is why in the present study an AI based approach was adopted. Also, numerous studies have indicated that emotion recognition technology exhibits greater accuracy in identifying certain emotions (e.g., happiness, anger) compared to others (e.g., sadness, surprise) (MorphCast, 2024b). In analysing the video data, the AI JS HTML5 SDK by MorphCast was used. Morphcast's (2023) AI SKD is an emotion reader based on Deep Neural Network AI, able to analyse spontaneous facial expressions. According to a comparative study conducted by Dupré et al. (2019), the software's accuracy level is reliable. To confirm the accuracy of the emotions identified by MorphCast, the researcher in this study reviewed the results generated by MorphCast and eliminated instances where happiness was misidentified.

Sequential analysis will be used to assess interaction patterns during the learning sessions. To ensure statistical validity, transitional probability matrices will be computed, and the significance of transition patterns will be evaluated using Z-scores. Transitions exceeding a Z-score of ± 1.96 will be considered statistically significant at the 0.05 level ($p < 0.05$), ensuring the robustness of identified behavioral sequences. This statistical rigor supports the internal validity of the observed patterns in student interactions.

While video-based data facilitated the identification and capture of participants' emotional expressions, the text-based data generated through discussions arising from collaborative tasks provided insights into the underlying reasons and processes behind these affective responses.

In terms of validity, the participant selection and research setting were deliberately designed to explore how affective responses emerge in both homogeneous and heterogeneous student groups. The sample included individuals from diverse disciplinary backgrounds (e.g., biology, English, ICT, preschool education), varied age groups, and differing gender identities, allowing for natural variation in group composition. This diversity supports the investigation of how emotional expressions—particularly positive affect such as happiness—manifest differently across group types.

The study was conducted in an AI-supported DE environment, incorporating both synchronous (video conferencing) and asynchronous (forum-based) activities. This setting enabled the collection of multimodal data (e.g., facial emotion recognition, text analysis, visual outputs), which is foundational for developing an affective framework that considers the role of group composition in interdisciplinary online learning. The methodological design thus aligns with the broader aim of informing emotionally responsive instructional strategies in digitally mediated education.

Limitations of The Data Analysis

As could happen in distance education video conferencing sessions, two of the participants in the present study turned on and off the camera for a few times and rarely some of the participant's screens were frozen due to technical problems. In these times, some data were lost to analyse their faces to recognize the emotions.

FINDINGS

In this section, the learning situations in which happiness emerges within different group compositions—homogeneous and heterogeneous learning groups—in interdisciplinary distance education are presented. These results are derived from analyses conducted using facial emotion recognition technologies and text mining methods. Based on the data analysis, the findings are reported to address the following research questions: (1) How does happiness, as a positive emotional expression, emerge in both video-based (synchronous) and text-based (asynchronous) learning interactions? (2) Which socio-emotional factors explain the emergence of happiness as a positive emotional reaction during collaborative activities?

Happiness in Video-Based Data

The video was recorded while online collaborative learning tasks were performed by two learning groups. The critical changes were identified according to the modes of the participants below:

Group 1 - The homogeneous group

Group 1 is the homogeneous group. Throughout their online video conference session, the participants' happiness was observed over the other emotions for 40 times. During the initial minutes of the argumentation, an ice-breaking activity occurred, allowing the participants to *establish themselves* and shift their mood to happiness. This activity is important especially in interdisciplinary studies before group members present their perspectives from different angles.

On looking at the times of the emotional change, the happiness was seen when the course tutor was involved in to contribute to their discussions. The participants were in interdisciplinary conversation as:

G1A: I am a teacher of visual art. You know how to formulate a question better than me (by addressing the Class Teacher).
G1B: I am just confused in between Word, Whats app and screensharing. This is a question I use in the classroom but is it OK for computational thinking?
Tutor: I think you are going well. The question is almost ready if you paint the pencils in different colours in the question.

While the participants were stressed with using different platforms at the same time, working interdisciplinary and also in an area which they both do know - computational thinking-, the tutor's critical involvement to finalize their task makes them demonstrate happiness emotion. According to the emotion graph, the longer tutor spent time in the discussion, the longer time the participants' demonstrated happiness compared to other emotional states. This may be related to the feeling of *ontological security*, "a sense of order and continuity in regard to an individual's experiences" as described by Anhtony Giddens. In other words, the presence of the tutor and her positive feedback on the group work may have led the members to feel that they were on the right track, fostering continuity in their intellectual engagement.

A further occasion when the happiness emerged according to Morphcast analysis was the time when the participants were complying with each other as the dialogue below shows:

G1A: How many (computational thinking) dimensions are there?
G1C: Do you think we need to add more?
G1A: I mean I could only write with mathematics terms.
G1C: OK, OK. No problem, go on like that.

This shows that group members depend on one another to achieve a shared goal and recognize that their success is interconnected which could be explained by positive interdependence. Positive interdependence refers to the belief that collaboration holds intrinsic value, and that both individual learning outcomes and collective products are enhanced when tasks are approached cooperatively (Laal, 2013).

However, conflict within collaborative virtual groups can serve as a productive force, particularly in democratic learning environments, where the exchange of arguments and counter-arguments facilitates knowledge construction. The resulting chaos about ambiguity or disruption should be viewed not as a barrier but as an integral and expected part of the learning process (Ozturk, 2011).

Very similar to the asynchronous communication occurred in this study, Stegmann et al. (2007) highlight the role of conflict arising from contrasting arguments within the process of social knowledge construction. An argument is defined as a series of statements that convey opinions or knowledge supporting a particular proposition, while a counter-argument challenges that proposition by presenting an opposing perspective. For example, the statement *"Tablet PCs seem like a good idea. If we also use a microphone, then it becomes a Smartclass"* illustrates an argument in favor of integrating technology. This can be countered by a concern about feasibility, as in: *"But it is very expensive; tablet PCs are not feasible due to cost."* Such divergent views give rise to interpersonal conflict, which is central to collaborative learning. Through this exchange of arguments and counter-arguments, students engage in critical reflection and construct knowledge about the use of tablet PCs as an educational technology by evaluating both its advantages and limitations.

Therefore, AI-based tools should not only support affirmative interactions but also monitor whether argumentation within discussions leads to disengagement or results in unproductive and repetitive exchanges.

Group 2 - The heterogenous group

Group 2 is the heterogenous group. Throughout their online video conference session, their happiness emotions were observed over the other emotions for 54 times. The number of emotional states are higher than the Group 1 which consists of only male participants and whose ages range between 30 and 40.

In Group 2, the first happiness emotion was seen when the group member got to know each other. Their age difference was significant, and they did not know each other. When they first saw each other online, G2A said G2B that "oh sorry, last time (in asynchronous discussion) I addressed you with your name as I thought you were very young". After this conversation, they both smiled at each other, and this is how they first produced the emotion of happiness. This could be related to *familiarity effect*; the more they know each other or make themselves familiar with the characteristics of each other, they tend to "exhibit" happiness. According to a study conducted by Carr, Brady and Winkielman (2017), familiar faces appear happier than novel faces because familiarity selectively enhances the impact of positive stimulus features.

Then, the participant G2D joint the group meeting later than the others and as of her engagement with the group discussions, emotions were produced more frequently. This shows that as discussed earlier, sometimes emotions are contagious in a group. The conversations evolved around her unawareness about the course content as she was coming from Biology background which is not closely linked to their task on computational thinking according to her. It is interesting to note that despite being unaware of the course content, the group members laughed at each other, leading to the emergence of happiness. In the later of the group discussions, G2D said "I am still adapting myself to the course, I cannot add anything new" (she says by smiling and produces happiness) and others had sympathy with her, they smiled too by producing happiness.

In the process of producing an outcome, the happiness did not emerge frequently, the members remained serious but when a group member took a responsibility to present their findings and when others supported her with their potential contribution to her presentation from the perspectives of their own disciplines, the group produced happiness emotion. The dialogue among the members was in the form of 'you can do it' and 'no, I cannot do it', as they *established themselves* within the group.

Towards the end of the online session, the group could fulfilled the task and happiness emerged again but it is noteworthy that the happiness emerged in the group were more about getting to know each other or having fun over a member who does not relate herself to the course than the happiness in the production of the learning outcome.

Emotions in Text-Based Data

During online course, asynchronous discussions also took place. The emotions which were examined are as follow: sadness, happiness, fear, anger and surprise. The emotions are coded respectively as P1, P2, P3, P4 and P5.

In the heterogenous group, happiness and fear come forth as shown in Graphic 1 below.

Figure 2. Emotions in the text data (asynchronous discussion) of the heterogenous group

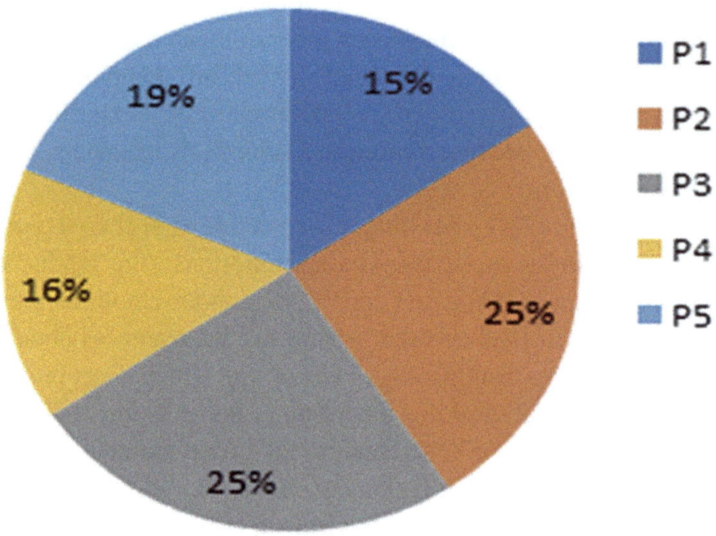

A sample of a heterogenous group discussion was used for the Transitional probabilities matrix (Table 3). Transitional probabilities matrix represents the possibilities for consecutiveness of two emotions.

Table 3. Transitional Probabilities Matrix of a Sample of Heterogenous Group Discussion

	P1	P2	P3	P4	P5
P1	,00	,00	,00	,00	,00
P2	,00	,50	,50	,00	,00
P3	,00	,00	,50	,00	,50
P4	,00	,00	,00	,00	,00
P5	,00	,00	,00	,00	,00

*Sadness (P1), happiness (P2), fear (P3), anger (P4) and surprise (P5).

In the transitional probabilities matrix, 50% of the messages containing happiness (P2) were replied with happiness (P2) and 50% of the messages containing happiness (P2) were replied with fear (P3) emotions. Likewise, fearful messages (P3) were replied 50% with fear (P3) and were replied 50% with surprise (P5).

In homogenous groups, usually "happiness" emotion was seen. In the sample group, there was not explicit "sadness" and "fear" as shown in Graph 2 below. Happiness is the dominant emotion. A further point is that in the homogenous group, there is less emotion of "surprise" compared to the heterogenous group.

Figure 3. Emotions in the text data (asynchronous discussion) of the homogenous group

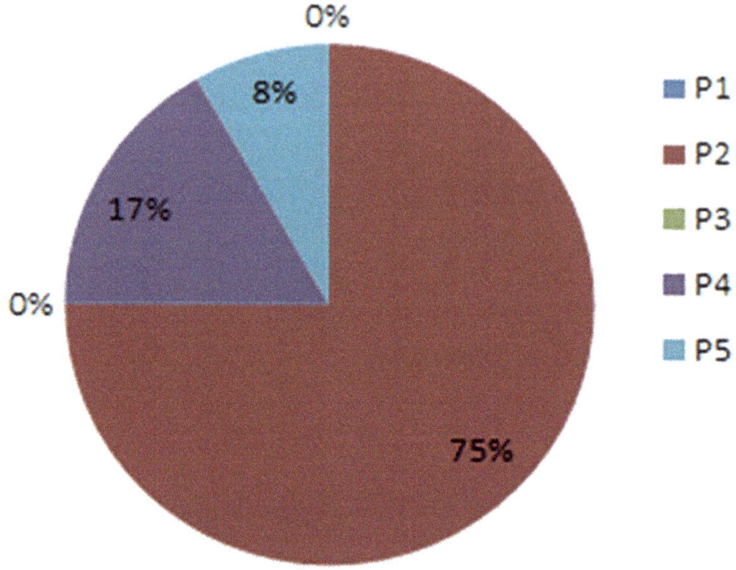

On looking at the transitional probabilities matrix (Table 4), it is seen that usually happiness follows happiness but once the flow is broken, it is not likely to change the emotion.

Table 4. Transitional Probabilities Matrix of a Sample of Homogenous Group Discussion

	P1	P2	P3	P4	P5
P1	0	0	0	0	0
P2	0	0,75	0	0,1	0,12
P3	0	0	0	0	0
P4	0	0	0	1	0
P5	0	0	0	0	0

*Sadness (P1), happiness (P2), fear (P3), anger (P4) and surprise (P5).

Accordingly, P2 (happiness) is likely to be followed by P2. Also, P4 (anger) is repeatedly seen in the subsequent messages. So, as seen in the Table 4, fragile emotions such as "anger" keeps on with the messages constituted of "anger" in a loop.

DISCUSSIONS AND CONCLUSION

The present study examined positive emotional expressions by investigating how happiness emerges in interdisciplinary distance education through AI-based analysis of multimodal data, focusing on the role of group composition—specifically, homogeneous and heterogeneous learning groups—which is critical in interdisciplinary contexts. It contributes to the literature by utilizing both video and text data for AI analysis and cross-referencing them, reflecting the increasingly multimodal structure of distance education shaped by socio-emotional group dynamics that support positive learning outcomes.

The integration of AI, particularly facial emotion recognition, provided objective and nuanced insights into learner emotions that enriched the analysis. While "students' emotional states are a potential first step toward more adaptive learning" (El Bahri et al., 2025, p. 1), the AI system in this study captured real-time emotional indicators of engagement by automatically detecting facial expressions from video—insights that would be difficult to obtain otherwise. This contributed to deeper analysis; for example, if instructional designers or tutors identify patterns where certain emotions correlate with better or worse outcomes, it aligns with recent findings that students' facially expressed emotions strongly correlate with academic performance—positive emotions tend to accompany success, while negative ones often signal difficulties. In their study, El Bahri et al. (2025) developed an AI tool called *LearnerEmotions* with a similar motivation to the present study and found comparable results. This online tool uses machine vision to detect students' emotions in real time via facial expressions, supporting both in-person and remote learning. In a study with 65 students and over 9 million data points, positive emotions like joy and surprise were strongly linked to better academic performance and attendance, while negative emotions correlated with poorer outcomes. These findings emphasize the potential of emotion-aware technologies like *LearnerEmotions* to enhance adaptive learning and real-time pedagogical support. This also highlights that, as a central motivation of the present study, AI tools for emotion detection are rapidly advancing, underscoring the need for continued research in this area. In the present study, AI tools were used to generate findings that suggest new pedagogical approaches, which are summarized below to inform practitioners and guide future research.

The results indicate that, within a socio-emotional context, happiness was associated with the *familiarity effect, the process of establishing oneself, and a sense of ontological security* in shaping group emotional dynamics. In terms of familiarity effect, the video-based findings showed that in homogeneous groups, the happiness was observed especially when the tutor involved in their discussion. As they already know each other, someone from outer circle might have triggered their emotion of happiness. Likewise, heterogeneous groups exhibited happiness more frequently as they got familiar with each other, which could be related to "familiarity effect". Thus, the members in the homogenous group may not have needed to "exhibit" happiness as they already are familiar with each other and perceive the happiness from each other's face. On the other hand, the socio-emotional dynamics of heterogeneous group may require the group members to engage in "interpersonal regulatory processes" (Heinim¨aki et al., 2021) and may need to take control of many surrounding variables than a learner in homogenous group. Hence, in order to supress the stress deriving of unfamiliarity leading to interpersonal regulatory process, they tend to "exhibit" happiness. These results in collaborative groups are consistent with Forsyth's (2014) findings that group dynamics are mostly related to socio-emotional dynamics or tasks.

In terms of *establishing oneself*, in both groups, at the beginning of video conferences, the happiness was identified when the students were involved in ice-breaking activities regardless of homogeneity or heterogeneity of the group form. This is consistent with the literature [e.g. Dixon, Crooks & Henry (2006); Maduretno (2021)] stressing the importance of ice-breaking activities in producing positive sentimental reactions. In the video data where Group 2 exhibited happiness, the group members had discussions on getting to know each other. In terms of expressing themselves, it was observed that one member joined the video conference later during the discussions. Following her participation, happiness was exhibited more frequently with her introducing herself to the group. Since the beginning of her participation as an ice-breaking event, she wore a smiley face. The group made jokes on her contribution, and they had smiling faces throughout the conversation. The finding on contagiousness of an emotion is consistent with the literature as discussed previously.

In terms of *ontological security*, it was observed that in both groups, happiness was recognised when the tutor involved in their discussions. It is suggested that the tutor's presence may influence the group members' sense of control; regardless of the homogeneity or heterogeneity of the group, and their sense of unity as a single group (identity). Thus, ontological security in collaborative e-learning groups can be central to the effective work of the groups (McConnell, 2005). In our study, the tutor's participation appeared to reinforce such a safe climate, thus bolstering positive emotional engagement in the group.

Finally, it was observed that in Group 2 which consists of female participants, the group exhibited more happiness than the Group 1 consisting of male participants. However, it is not appropriate to generalize happiness in gender in a qualitative study with limited number of participants. Also, the literature shows a variety of results. For instance, in a study conducted by Zweig (2015, p. 515), she works with big data and concludes that "women are either happier than men or that there is no significant difference between women and men ...when comparing men and women with the same life circumstances, women are happier than men in nearly a quarter of the (73) countries". However, a recent study conducted in the UK shows that men now are happier than women (Blanchflower & Bryson, 2024). Therefore, it is possible to conclude that the happiness in gender depends on complex conditions and cultural variables.

Unlike the video-based data, which showed that heterogeneous groups demonstrated happiness more frequently than the homogenous group, the text-based analysis revealed that fear and happiness were prominent emotions in heterogeneous groups, while homogeneous groups primarily showed happiness. Moreover, the transitional probabilities matrix indicated that in heterogeneous groups, happiness messages were often followed by happiness and fear messages, while fearful messages received responses with fear and surprise emotions. This finding is parallel with the findings of the study done by Huang et al. (2019), who revealed that positive sentiments are followed by positive ones (and vice versa) during the interaction of online student groups.

The findings suggest that, with intentional facilitation, diverse groups can achieve emotional convergence over time—as reflected in a growing alignment of positive emotions such as shared happiness—which complements their cognitive collaboration. This outcome contributes to the growing body of research that highlights the need to explore the emotional impact of group diversity and learner backgrounds in online learning environments (Stanworth et al., 2023; Vanslambrouck et al., 2018).

In homogenous groups, happiness was frequently followed by happiness, and there was a recurring pattern of anger in subsequent messages containing anger. Prior studies on SA generally focused on positive and negative sentiments of participants involved in the learning process (Zhou & Ye, 2023). It is important to note that positive sentiments result in expected level of interaction in the groups. However, negative sentiments should be managed well for the success of the learners (D'Mello & Calvo, 2013).

Practical Implications

In their study, Hachey et al. (2015) emphasize the need for research on support services for online STEM students, as reflected in the present study. The findings reveal that tutor presence, familiarity among participants, and the process of establishing oneself are important aspects of a course within a STEM program. Therefore, in doing learning design, ice-breaking activities, tutor's inference and giving time and space for establishing oneself are important issues in interdisciplinary DE education.

In terms of implications for AI supported learning, Karandish (2021) reports that it is estimated that AI will be embedded in 47% of learning management systems in the next three years. Thus, it is important to reflect on the outcomes of learning experiences interpreted with AI informed data.

AI tools equipped with facial emotion recognition and natural language processing can detect emotional states such as happiness, fear, or frustration during both synchronous (video-based) and asynchronous (text-based) interactions. This can provide instructors and learning designers with real-time insights into student engagement, enabling timely pedagogical interventions.

Moreover, text sentiment analysis (e.g., analyzing written feedback or forum posts) is a form of AI, specifically a Natural Language Processing (NLP) technique. For instance, Dake and Bada (2023) used machine-learning-based sentiment analysis in Moodle to predict student sentiments. While lag sequential analysis is a more traditional statistical method (not a learning algorithm itself), it complements AI by predicting student emotions, sentimental reactions and behaviors over time. As the technology has rapidly evolved in recent years such as AI (NLP), its integration in education should align with instructional design principles. This study is therefore significant, as it offers insights that can inform and support the ongoing development of such technologies. In summary, AI contributed by uncovering hidden patterns and relationships – facial emotion AI pinpointed engagement signals, sentiment analysis gauged textual attitudes, and sequential patterns showed how these unfold over time – all of which strengthen the depth and credibility of the research findings. Therefore, it can be suggested that, in addition to identifying emotions, AI tools should be enhanced with techniques that capture how emotions evolve over time, as sequential analysis techniques demonstrate. As shown in this research, happiness messages were often followed by happiness and fear messages, whereas fear-related messages tended to elicit responses expressing fear or surprise. Thus, monitoring emotional sequences—not only identifying isolated emotions—would contribute to instructional design by supporting productive learning processes and helping prevent vicious circles that hinder learning.

Incorporating affective indicators (e.g., frequency of happiness, transitions from fear to joy) into learning management systems can support emotion-aware analytics, helping tutors and instructional designers better understand the socio-emotional climate of the course. These indicators can inform decisions related to pacing, content delivery, or peer group formation. Recent learning analytics studies adopt hybrid methods (clustering, sequential pattern analysis, and NLP) to process LMS data, including click logs and emotional inputs, as part of AI-driven engagement analysis (Rodríguez-Ortiz et al., 2025). This suggests that use of sequential and sentiment analysis, even if not AI algorithms by themselves, is very much in line with modern AI-enhanced analytics especially for LMS settings. AI components demonstrate the potential of affect-aware, analytics-driven DE.

The study highlights that heterogeneous groups often exhibit a need for interpersonal emotional regulation. AI systems could be designed to monitor emotional transitions (e.g. from fear to happiness) and suggest targeted micro-interventions such as prompts, peer matching, or tutor engagement to support group cohesion and trust-building.

Since familiarity and the process of establishing oneself are key factors in eliciting positive emotions, AI can be used to customize ice-breaking activities by analyzing early emotional responses. Systems can be designed to suggest when to introduce tutor presence or modify group compositions based on emotional dynamics.

The findings indicate that the expression of happiness was associated with three key socio-emotional dimensions: the *familiarity effect*, the *process of establishing oneself*, and *the sense of ontological security*.

To address the familiarity effect, an AI-based *Familiarity Index Tracker* could be developed to analyze the frequency and quality of peer interactions, detect emotional improvement patterns as group familiarity increases, and generate a "familiarity score" based on interaction dynamics and emotional convergence.

To address the dimension of *establishing oneself*, particularly when the Familiarity Index score is low, the system could prompt the instructor to initiate an ice-breaking activity at the outset. Furthermore, sequential analysis methods could be employed to determine whether a student's presence is being acknowledged by peers or if the student is primarily engaged in self-oriented efforts to gain recognition within the group.

To foster a sense of *ontological security*, it is essential to ensure that learners feel supported by the institutional structure and do not experience emotional isolation. An AI-based system could be developed to alert instructors when emotional stability declines (e.g., signs of stress or confusion) or when discussions stagnate. This could be achieved through sequential analysis, which is effective in predicting the evolution of interactions and identifying potential patterns of unproductive or cyclical discourse. For instance, in this study, the transitional probabilities matrix revealed that happiness typically follows happiness; however, once this emotional flow is disrupted, it is unlikely to recover spontaneously. In such cases, AI-based tools, informed by sequential analysis, could be designed to make timely interventions to help restore or sustain positive emotional engagement.

To sum up, in this study, sequential method was used as a potential tool for AI based implications. It was used to measure affective responses over time (e.g., when and why "happiness" increases in a collaborative learning task). However, this method is not well-supported with AI software or platforms whereas the method can help instructional designers:

- Train models to predict future behaviors (e.g., dropout risk, emotional states);

- Analyze chat or forum conversations to detect learning paths or collaboration quality;
- Study the flow of facial expressions, gestures, or emotional states in synchronous video learning (e.g., through facial emotion recognition);
- Support adaptive learning systems that react to learner behavior sequences. A sequential analysis might reveal that helping behavior often leads to increased emotional engagement and could guide how AI systems adapt to support collaboration. However, this requires a software development process, as the existing platforms are not sufficiently developed.

Although productive collaborative learning has long been a subject of educational research, there is now an increasing need to integrate AI-driven tools capable of providing real-time, data-informed feedback to both instructors and instructional designers. Finally, according to Rajkumar (2023), emotions are shaped by cultural values and norms. Therefore, in the future research, the emotions could be analyzed in different cultures.

REFERENCES

Artuvan Korkmaz, H., Güldenoğlu, B., & Kalaycıoğlu, C. (2019). Investigation of word decoding strategies of university students from quantitative and verbal graduate programs. *Ahi Evran Üniversitesi Sosyal Bilimler Enstitüsü Dergisi*, *5*(2), 266–283. DOI: 10.31592/aeusbed.589093

Blanchflower, D. G., & Bryson, A. (2024). The female happiness paradox. *Journal of Population Economics*, *37*(1), 16. DOI: 10.1007/s00148-024-00981-5

Bronstein, L. R. (2003). A model for interdisciplinary collaboration. *Social Work*, *48*(3), 297–306. DOI: 10.1093/sw/48.3.297 PMID: 12899277

Carr, E. W., Brady, T. F., & Winkielman, P. (2017). Are You Smiling, or Have I Seen You Before? Familiarity Makes Faces Look Happier. *Psychological Science*, *28*(8), 1087–1102. DOI: 10.1177/0956797617702003 PMID: 28594281

Charmaz, K. (2005). Grounded Theory in the 21st Century. In Denzin, N. K., & Lincoln, Y. S. (Eds.), *The SAGE Handbook of Qualitative Research* (pp. 507–535). SAGE Publications.

Charmaz, K. (2010). Grounded Theory: Objectivist and Constructivist Methods. In Luttrell, W. (Ed.), *Qualitative Educational Research. Readings in Reflexive Methodology and Transformative Practice* (pp. 183–207). Routledge.

D'Mello, S., & Calvo, R. A. (2013). Beyond the basic emotions: What should affective computing compute? *CHI '13 extended abstracts on human factors in Computing systems* on - CHI EA '13, 2287. DOI: 10.1145/2468356.2468751

Dake, D. K., & Bada, G. K. (2023). Unveiling learner emotions: Sentiment analysis of Moodle-based online assessments using machine learning. *Journal of Information Technology Education: Innovations in Practice*, *22*, 109–132. DOI: 10.28945/5174

Dalipi, F., Zdravkova, K., & Ahlgren, F. (2021). Sentiment Analysis of Students' Feedback in MOOCs: A Systematic Literature Review. *Frontiers in Artificial Intelligence*, *4*, 728708. DOI: 10.3389/frai.2021.728708 PMID: 34568815

Dixon, J., Crooks, H., & Henry, K. (2006). Breaking the ice: Supporting collaboration and the development of community online. *Canadian Journal of Learning and Technology*, *32*(2), 1–14. DOI: 10.21432/T25S3M

El Bahri, N., Itahriouan, Z., & Ouazzani Jamil, M. (2025). Emotion-Aware Education Through Affective Computing and Learning Analytics: Insights from a Moroccan University Case Study. *Digital*, *5*(3), 45. DOI: 10.3390/digital5030045

Forsyth, D. R. (2014). *Group dynamics*. Wadsworth Cengage Learning.

Fraenkel, J. R., & Wallen, N. E. (2006). *How to design and evaluate research in education* (International Edition). McGraw-Hill.

Garrison, D. R. (2022). Motivation and the CoI framework. *The Community of Inquiry*. https://www.thecommunityofinquiry.org/editorial37

Garrison, D. R., Anderson, T., & Archer, W. (1999). Critical inquiry in a text-based environment: Computer conferencing in higher education. *The Internet and Higher Education*, *2*(2-3), 87–105. DOI: 10.1016/S1096-7516(00)00016-6

Giddens, A. (1991). *Modernity and self-identity: self and society in the late modern age*. Polity Press.

Gómez-Ríos, M., Paredes-Velasco, M., Velázquez-Iturbide, J. Á., & Martínez, M. Á. Q. (2025). Augmented Reality for Learning Algorithms: Evaluation of its Impact on Students' Emotions Using Artificial Intelligence. *Applied Sciences (Basel, Switzerland)*, *15*(14), 7745. DOI: 10.3390/app15147745

Hachey, A. C., Wladis, C., & Conway, K. (2015). Prior online course experience and G.P.A. as predictors of subsequent online STEM course outcomes. *The Internet and Higher Education*, *25*, 11–17. DOI: 10.1016/j.iheduc.2014.10.003

Haythornthwaite, C. (2006). Learning and knowledge networks in interdisciplinary collaborations. *Journal of the American Society for Information Science and Technology*, *57*(8), 1079–1092. DOI: 10.1002/asi.20371

Heinim¨aki, O.-P., Volet, S., Jones, C., Laakkonen, E., & Vauras, M. (2021). Student participatory role profiles in collaborative science learning: Relation of within-group configurations of role profiles and achievement. *Learning, Culture and Social Interaction*, *30*, 1–15. DOI: 10.1016/j.lcsi.2021.100539

Hew, K. F., Hu, X., Qiao, C., & Tang, Y. (2020). What Predicts Student Satisfaction with MOOCs: A Gradient Boosting Trees Supervised Machine Learning and Sentiment Analysis Approach. *Computers & Education*, *145*, 103724. Advance online publication. DOI: 10.1016/j.compedu.2019.103724

Huang, C. Q., Han, Z. M., Li, M. X., Jong, M. S. Y., & Tsai, C. C. (2019). Investigating students' interaction patterns and dynamic learning sentiments in online discussions. *Computers & Education*, *140*, 103589. DOI: 10.1016/j.compedu.2019.05.015

Ju, B., Jin, T., & Stewart, J. B. (2016). Investigating communication hindrance in interdisciplinary collaboration: A grounded theory approach. *Proceedings of the Association for Information Science and Technology*, *53*(1), 1–4. DOI: 10.1002/pra2.2016.14505301113

Karandish, D. (2021). 7 Benefits of AI in Education. *The Journal* https://thejournal.com/articles/2021/06/23/7-benefits-of-ai-in-education.aspx

Kaşıkçı, E. B., & İzmirli, S. (2024). Unpacking the relationship between online student engagement and online self-regulation in higher education. *Participatory Educational Research*, *11*(4), 198–214. DOI: 10.17275/per.24.56.11.4

Kramer, A., Guillory, J. E., & Hancock, J. T. (2014). Experimental evidence of massive-scale emotional contagion through social networks. *Proceedings of the National Academy of Sciences*. DOI: 10.1073/pnas.1320040111

Laal, M. (2013). Positive Interdependence in Collaborative Learning. *Procedia: Social and Behavioral Sciences*, *93*, 1433–1437. DOI: 10.1016/j.sbspro.2013.10.058

Lawpanom, R., Songpan, W., & Kaewyotha, J. (2024). Advancing Facial Expression Recognition in Online Learning Education Using a Homogeneous Ensemble Convolutional Neural Network Approach. *Applied Sciences (Basel, Switzerland)*, *14*(3), 1156. DOI: 10.3390/app14031156

Lee, S. J., & Branch, R. M. (2022). Students' Reactions to a Student-Centered Learning Environment in Relation to Their Beliefs about Teaching and Learning. *International Journal on Teaching and Learning in Higher Education*, *33*(3), 298–305.

Lieberman, M. A., Wizlenberg, A., Golant, M., & Di Minno, M. (2005). The impact of group composition on Internet support groups: Homogeneous versus heterogeneous Parkinson's groups. *Group Dynamics*, *9*(4), 239–250. DOI: 10.1037/1089-2699.9.4.239

Maduretno, T. W. (2021). Online Learning Solution: Ice Breaking Application to Increase Student Motivation. [EST]. *Journal of Educational Science and Technology*, *07*(01), 117–125.

Mandl, T., Jaki, S., Mitera, H., & Schmidt, F. (2023). Interdisciplinary analysis of science communication on social media during the Covid-19 crisis. *Knowledge (Beverly Hills, Calif.)*, *3*(1), 97–112. DOI: 10.3390/knowledge3010008

Mentor, D. (2015). *Mobile Phone Use Enhances Social Connectedness*. IGI Publishing., DOI: 10.4018/978-1-4666-8239-9.ch056

Moirano, R., Sánchez, M. A., & Štěpánek, L. (2023). Creative interdisciplinary collaboration: A systematic literature review. *Thinking Skills and Creativity*, *35*, 100626. Advance online publication. DOI: 10.1016/j.tsc.2019.100626

MorphCast. (2023). *How our Emotion AI works*. Retrieved from https://www.morphcast.com/responsibility-transparency-clarity/

MorphCast. (2024a). *A guide to interpret data generated by Emotion AI*. Retrieved from https://www.morphcast.com/how-to-interpret-the-emotion-ai-output-data/

MorphCast. (2024b). *Beyond the Algorithm: Building Trustworthy Emotion AI at MorphCast*. https://www.morphcast.com/responsibility-transparency-clarity/

Neumann, M., & Linzmayer, R. (2021). Capturing student feedback and emotions in large computing courses: A sentiment analysis approach. *In Proceedings of the 52nd ACM Technical Symposium on Computer Science Education* (pp. 541-547). DOI: 10.1145/3408877.3432403

Orchard, C. A., Curran, V., & Kabene, S. (2005). Creating a culture for interdisciplinary collaborative professional practice. *Medical Education Online*, *10*(1), 1–13. DOI: 10.3402/meo.v10i.4387 PMID: 28253153

Ozturk, H. (2011). Conflict in Virtual Learning Communities in the Context of a Democratic Pedagogy. *Unpublished PhD Thesis*. Lancaster University, UK.

Ozturk, H. T., Deryakulu, D., Ozcinar, H., & Atal, D. (2014). Advancing Learning Analytics in Online Learning Environments through the Method of Sequential Analysis. *The 4th International Conference on Multimedia Computing and Systems (ICMCS'14)*. April 14-16 2014, Marrakesh, Morocco.

Patel, A., Addicott, C., & Buelow, J. (2023). Instructors' emotional intelligence and learning engagement of online students. *European Journal of Open. Distance and E-Learning*, *25*(1), 129–135. DOI: 10.2478/eurodl-2023-0010

Polo, C., Lund, K., Plantin, C., & Niccolai, G. P. (2016). Group emotions: The social and cognitive functions of emotions in argumentation. *International Journal of Computer-Supported Collaborative Learning*, *11*(2), 123–156. DOI: 10.1007/s11412-016-9232-8

Rajkumar, R. P. (2023). Cultural values and changes in happiness in 78 countries during the COVID-19 pandemic: An analysis of data from the World Happiness Reports. *Frontiers in Psychology*, *14*, 1090340. Advance online publication. DOI: 10.3389/fpsyg.2023.1090340 PMID: 36818129

Rodríguez-Ortiz, M. Á., Santana-Mancilla, P. C., & Anido-Rifón, L. E. (2025). Machine Learning and Generative AI in Learning Analytics for Higher Education: A Systematic Review of Models, Trends, and Challenges. *Applied Sciences (Basel, Switzerland)*, *15*(15), 8679. DOI: 10.3390/app15158679

Salmela, M., & Mäki, U. (2018). Disciplinary emotions in imperialistic interdisciplinarity. In Mäki, Uskali; Fernández Pinto, Manuela & Walsh, Adrian (Eds.) (2018). *Scientific Imperialism: Exploring the Boundaries of Interdisciplinarity* (pp. 31-50). Routledge, Abingdon.

Stanworth, J. O., Yen, W. H., & Warden, C. A. (2023). Conflicted about online learning?: Using sentiment analysis to explore learner approach-avoidance motivation. *Online Information Review*, *47*(2), 356–370. DOI: 10.1108/OIR-09-2021-0463

Stegmann, K., Weinberger, A., & Fischer, F. (2007). Facilitating argumentative knowledge construction with computer-supported collaboration scripts. *International Journal of Computer-Supported Collaborative Learning*, *2*(4), 421–447. DOI: 10.1007/s11412-007-9028-y

Stieglitz, S., & Dang-Xuan, L. (2013). Emotions and information diffusion in social media—Sentiment of microblogs and sharing behavior. *Journal of Management Information Systems*, *29*(4), 217–248. DOI: 10.2753/MIS0742-1222290408

Vanslambrouck, S., Zhu, C., Lombaerts, K., Philipsen, B., & Tondeur, J. (2018). Students' motivation and subjective task value of participating in online and blended learning environments. *The Internet and Higher Education*, *36*, 33–40. DOI: 10.1016/j.iheduc.2017.09.002

Vistorte, A. O. R., Deroncele-Acosta, A., Martín Ayala, J. L., Barrasa, A., Lopez-Granero, C., & Martí-Gonzalez, M. (2024). Integrating artificial intelligence to assess emotions in learning environments: A systematic literature review. *Frontiers in Psychology*, *15*, 1387089. Advance online publication. DOI: 10.3389/fpsyg.2024.1387089 PMID: 38966729

Wilkinson, I. A. G., & Fung, I. Y. Y. (2002). Small-group composition and peer effects. *International Journal of Educational Research*, *37*(5), 425–447. DOI: 10.1016/S0883-0355(03)00014-4

Yoder, P. J., & Tapp, J. (2004). Empirical guidance for time-window sequential analysis of single cases. *Journal of Behavioral Education*, *13*(4), 227–246. DOI: 10.1023/B:JOBE.0000044733.03220.a9

Yu, J. (2025). Analyzing Learning Sentiments on a MOOC Discussion Forum Through Epistemic Network Analysis. *International Review of Research in Open and Distance Learning*, *26*(1), 197–215. DOI: 10.19173/irrodl.v26i1.7965

Zheng, L., & Huang, R. (2016). The effects of sentiments and co-regulation on group performance in computer supported collaborative learning. *The Internet and Higher Education*, *28*, 59–67. DOI: 10.1016/j.iheduc.2015.10.001

Zweig, J. S. (2015). Are Women Happier than Men? Evidence from the Gallup World Poll. *Journal of Happiness Studies*, *16*(2), 515–554. DOI: 10.1007/s10902-014-9521-8

KEY TERMS AND DEFINITIONS

Adaptive Learning: An educational approach that adjusts the pace, difficulty, or type of content based on each learner's progress and needs.

Affectively-Informed Instructional Design: An approach to designing learning activities that incorporates students' emotional experiences.

Facial Emotion Recognition: A technological process in which software or a tool detects and interprets human facial expressions to infer emotional states.

Group Composition: How individuals are arranged or selected to form a working group. It may take into account characteristics such as skills, background knowledge, experience, gender, or personality traits to create an effective team.

Interdisciplinary Collaboration: A process in which individuals from different academic or professional fields work together toward a shared goal.

Learning Management System: A digital platform that supports both content delivery and administrative functions.

Sentimental Analysis: An analytical method used to detect and categorize emotions, attitudes, or opinions expressed in written or spoken language.

Sequential Analysis: A technique that examines how behaviors, actions, or events unfold over time.

Chapter 8
AI-Driven Personalized Learning:
Enhancing Student Development Through Adaptive Technologies

Rashid Hashmi
https://orcid.org/0009-0006-3232-0705
Sharda University, India

ABSTRACT

The application of Artificial Intelligence (AI) in the educational field is changing the process of learning to offer an individualised learning experience, benefiting students with cognitive and affective needs. This chapter discusses the point of AI and student growth, adaptive learning technologies, intelligent tutoring systems, and emotion-aware intelligent AI models that increase engagement and knowledge retention. Increasing student achievements in academic and socio-emotional development, the AI-driven insights provide teachers with the possibility to develop dynamic curricula and cater to specific learning styles. The chapter further analyses issues of ethical concern, including algorithmic bias and data privacy, and policy systems to implement AI responsibility in education. Case studies and empirical studies help analyse in the chapter the manner in which AI-based personalisation is transforming pedagogical methods to achieve equal access to quality education.

INTRODUCTION

Artificial Intelligence (AI) has emerged as one of the most transforming dynamic forces in education in the twenty-first century. Neither is it of the future, awaited somewhere or another in science fiction or the distant recesses of research

DOI: 10.4018/979-8-3373-2927-7.ch008

laboratories-it has gradually but surely been made available in classrooms, learning management systems and digital learning networks all over the world. The last 2 of decades were a period of technological progress, and the transformation also encompassed the emergence of intelligent tutoring systems (ITS), adaptive learning systems, learning analytics, and emotion-cognizant models of artificial intelligence. These are the gadgets that are changing the experience of delivering, receiving and assessing education. The area enabled by the AI enables institutions to deliver content, speed and feedback at a pace that is tailored to both the individual learning profile of each student, as the demands imposed by the process of diversifying and digitalising the classroom become increasingly visible as the reality on the ground.

The integration of AI in the realm of education is accompanied by the overall shift towards the individualisation, inclusivity and equity of the learning process, which currently permeates the realm of pedagogy and the learning theory. Even the traditional models of education, in which one-size-fits-all has historically ruled, are being challenged by new studies that champion the differentiated way of instruction, competency-based learning, and learner-centred models. AI provides a chance to scale these principles to the next level. Data-driven personalisation helps students to get real-time feedback, have access to curated information, and adopt flexible courses of study, all of which were challenging to introduce in the past without the extensive involvement of people. Chen, Chen, and Lin (2020) list the following functions of AI in education: intelligent assessment, automated tutoring, personalised provision of content, and predictive analytics, which are aimed at maximising the results of the educational process and assisting human teachers and not displacing them.

The concept of individualised learning, however, does not belong to the present day. It is grounded in the ideas of educational theorists like John Dewey and Benjamin Bloom, who placed a high price on student-centred teaching as well as mastery learning. His famous "2 Sigma Problem" revealed that students who received tutoring individually increased their performance by two standard deviations as compared to their peers in the traditional classes. In the past, the difficulty lay in scalability. Personal tutoring has always been effective, but it could never work with individual students having a personal tutor. It is now AI that fills that gap, and provides scalable, individualised instruction that replicates many of the advantages of individual instruction. Zawacki-Richter et al. (2019) also note that AI-based technologies have enabled the transformation of educational experience with the possibility to develop unique interventions according to the ways students perform, behave, and learn. The AI has the capabilities to monitor the progress and detect the gaps to provide the learners with the learning content that suits the exact level of knowledge, thereby enabling prolonged and independent learning.

In the last ten years, schools, colleges, and universities have resorted to educational platforms based on machine learning to meet the demands of flexible and personalised education. The use of AI is already everywhere: there are automated grading systems and chatbot tutors, adaptive quizzes, and learning analytics dashboards. According to Papamitsiou, Economides, and Muñoz Merino (2021), the emergence of learning analytics can be cited as an important development in this regard. Analysing massive amounts of data produced by the learners, like quiz grades, time spent performing a task, used in a forum, and clickstreams, educators and AI systems may match the needs of learners and adapt the learning environment accordingly. The use of learning analytics is thus one of the foundations of AI-based personalisation, providing information that can be used to adjust the current instruction and adjust the system in real time.

The other great game changer based on AI in education is the development of affective computing and emotion-sensitive systems. These tools not only monitor the level of cognitive performance, but further examine, based on learner reports, their emotional state, also known as frustration, boredom, and engagement, more personalise the experience. Despite their novelty, these technologies can be regarded as a paradigm shift in the traditional paradigm of cognitive-only education towards more humanistic and holistic education. The authors (Pane et al., 2017) emphasise in their famous work dedicated to the implementation of personalised learning that the models of the successful implementation guarantee that the process of rewards-based personalisation should focus not only on academic accomplishments but also on the socio-emotional development.

Figure 1. Evolution of AI in Education from 2000 to 2025

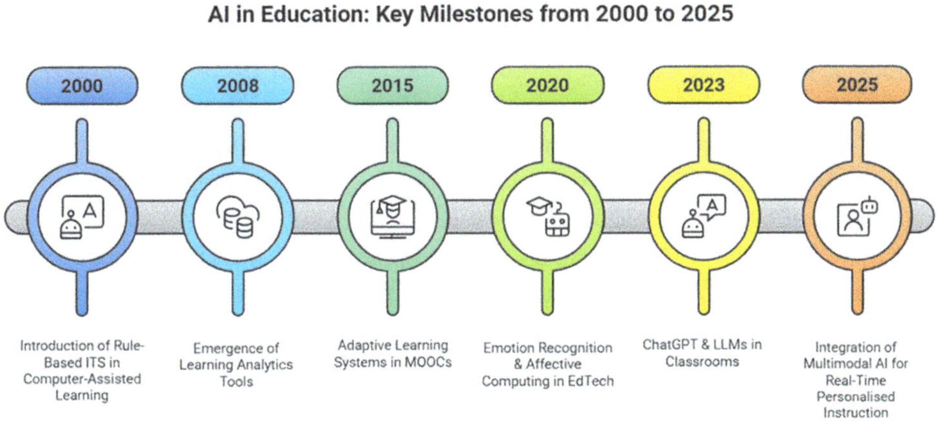

BACKGROUND

Artificial Intelligence has ceased to be a novelty in the academic field, but has become a key aspect of educational innovation. As they do not comprehend the extent of its influence on personalised learning, it is prudent to consider the conceptual and technical framework of AI applications in the field of education. In this section, the three basic domains are described in detail, namely adaptive learning, intelligent tutoring systems (ITS), and affective computing. All these have a distinct influence on the contemporary digital pedagogy. Combined, they assist in closing the gap that has always existed between a standardised teaching approach and the necessity of learner-oriented models. To create a meaningful context for AI-enabled personalised learning, this section will present definitions, historical progress, and state-of-the-art models that are currently influencing classroom practices across the world.

Definitions and Evolution of AI in Education

Artificial Intelligence in Education (AIEd) The term (AIEd) Artificial Intelligence in education is used to refer to the use of machine-based technologies in instructional systems with the intention of matching, amplifying, or complementing human intellectual competencies in teaching and learning practices. These systems tend to employ complex algorithms and make autonomous decisions about the received data about interactions of the learners. Its basic idea is to enhance learning results through decision-making in changes in real time in the delivery of material, providing feedback, and interaction processes. Although today AI in education is widely discussed, it has a long history that dates back several decades. Early attempts to use computers in computer-assisted learning in the 1960s and 1970s were largely of a rule-based nature, and thus, they were narrow in their applicability. The intelligent tutoring systems and adaptive testing platforms started to stir up some interest only in the 1990s and early 2000s, especially in such fields as computer science and language learning (Woolf, 2020).

The development of AI in education is symptomatic of the greater pedagogical trend to take the approach out of fixed or uniform learning content and shift towards dynamic and customised or individualised learning processes. In previous models, teachers were the only ones to pass control and knowledge. Nevertheless, the digital era brought new technologies that have the possibility to collect the data produced by the learners, assess their performance, and drive instruction based on the data. As data-driven instruction appeared, AI systems started to provide an extent of personalisation that can only be achieved by human tutoring. The technology built on simple drill-and-practice software has matured into the use of real-time diagnostic assessment, learning analytics dashboards, and chatbots that use AI. These advancements have contributed to the development of a feedback-laden atmosphere within which students learn at their own pace while still getting guidance and assistance. More particularly, intelligent systems are already able to track the state of knowledge of individual learners, infer learning performance trajectories, and suggest individualised content with little input on the part of the teacher. Liu, Latif, and Zhai (2025) mention that the advanced AI-based tutoring systems, in addition to offering personalised repetition of instructions, also simulate human-like communication that adapts to the mind of a learner.

Adaptive Learning and Intelligent Tutoring Systems (ITS)

Adaptive learning is the practice of technology response-based on learning practice that covers the presentation of material based on student performance, interest, and involvement. This method is in striking contrast with the ever-static e-learning frameworks offering identical content and layout to all learners. Adaptive learning not only strives to respond to right and wrong answers, but to anticipate the needs of learners and model their learning paths towards them. This flexibility usually goes on by way of student modelling, a procedural manipulate that creates a character of each student and his or her knowledge, misconceptions, and preferences as more study goes on. The system proceeds to use these profiles in selecting instructional strategies.

The most sophisticated adaptive learning technology is the Intelligent Tutoring Systems (ITS). ITs are made to resemble the decision-making structures of human tutors and, in this regard, are in contrast to simple forms of branching tutorials or quizzes. They analyse the responses of students, predict their knowledge, and help them through immediate feedback involving pedagogical principles. In her seminal work on intelligent interactive tutors, Woolf (2020) describes that major elements of ITS are the domain model (or model of subject knowledge), the student model (or model of learner progress), and the pedagogical model (or information about how to deliver content). These systems are rather self-sufficient, but also very responsive as they provide hints, explain some things, and even motivate.

The use of ITS in the STEM subjects is constantly growing, as the learning paths might be well-controlled and quantified. The use of ITS in physics, mathematics, and even programming courses has been reported in the journal Smart Learning Environments (2025) based on its capacity to enable immediate and contextualised feedback, which hastens the learning process. The report further claimed that ITS not only enhances the exam scores but also assists in lowering the dropout rates because it is able to keep the students interested through individual attention. They are not only being applied in formal education, but they are also in use in corporate training, military training, and lifelong learning. Yang, Flanagan, and Ogata

(2022) further describe adaptive formative assessment systems that incorporate principles of learning, memory cycles, and computerised adaptive testing. These insights build on Bloom's taxonomy and the spaced repetition theory, providing a more cognitive-scientific approach to personalised education. Bystrenina and Nikitin (2022) support this with research on adaptive knowledge control in digital learning environments. Their work indicates that systems that continuously update their instructional logic based on learner interaction data have a higher impact on knowledge retention and transfer.

Affective Computing and Emotion-Aware AI

To be able to personalise the learning process as an instructor, cognitive adaptation is considered a must; recent studies also note the importance of knowing and being able to respond to the emotional state of the learners. A recent and emerging broader field, affective computing, an interdisciplinary discipline between psychology and computer science, concerns itself with building systems that are sensitive to and understand human emotion, simulating human emotions. Applied in the field of education, affective computing enables platforms to understand when a student is bored, lost, or upset, and modify the learning process so that it fits the given situation.

The use of multimodal affect detection was pioneered by such authors as D Mello and Graesser (2013) in academic settings. Their study showed that the mood of a student might be derived based on the conversation signals, body language, facial expressions and such physiological information as the pulse rate. This capability brings about a feedback loop not only to the performance level, but also the motivation level and ability to cope emotionally as well when it is used as a component of the learning platform. As an example, a student exhibiting the symptoms of boredom can be assigned an interactive simulation as an alternative to text-heavy materials, whereas a confused student can be given a more straightforward explanation from another group.

There are increasing real-life usages of emotion-aware AI in education. Webcam-based monitoring to outline facial expressions is implemented in some of the platforms now, and others track the mouse, typing speed, and voice tone. AI algorithms are used to synthesize these multimodal data points to provide real-time emotional profiles. When the student is constantly frustrated, the system may either notify the instructor or change the learning course in a more systematic way to avoid mental overload. This type of emotional insight is all the more important in high-stakes, or asynchronous, settings--that is, online testing or MOOCs. Liu, Latif, and Zhai (2025) affirm that future ITS models will need to embed emotional awareness as a standard feature rather than an add-on.

Table 1. Comparison of Traditional vs. AI-Driven Personalised Learning Systems

Criteria	Traditional Learning	AI-Driven Personalised Learning
Content Delivery	Uniform for all students	Customised to individual learner needs
Feedback Timing	Delayed	Real-time
Assessment	Summative	Formative and adaptive
Emotional Monitoring	Absent	Emotion-aware interfaces
Pace of Learning	Fixed	Self-regulated and adaptive
Teacher Workload	High manual intervention	Assisted through intelligent systems

It is important to understand the essential building blocks of adaptive learning, ITS, and affective computing so that one can understand how AI is transforming the education field. They represent a heavy pedagogical and technological transformation, moving away in favour of a learner-centred teaching, a generalised approach to a personalised approach, and away one of content delivery and towards human development.

FOCUS OF THE ARTICLE

To achieve the trend of AI-based personalisation, tools or systems cannot be described technically adequately. It requires a rationalised vision of the intersection of the different teaching lines of educational theory, cognitive psychology and instructional design, in the wise learning setting. This section is therefore a transition to the theoretical background of the previous section of the chapter and the practical applications that were to be covered subsequently. It details how adaptive learning models, intelligent tutoring systems, as well as emotion-conscious kinds of platforms, impact cognitive and affective development of a learner. Through it, it also exhibits how AI-enabled personalisation is growing into a more conventional intellectual paradigm on the premise of mastery learning, constructivism, motivation theory, and universal design principles, contrary to being among the products of technological innovation.

In much the same way that Section 2 established the historical and theoretical basis of AI in education, this section now shifts into the operational sphere where the said notions are operationalised. Personalisation using AI is not a standalone mechanism but an ecosystem that consists of interdependent processes, unlimited assessment, real-time feedback, strategic intervention, emotion detection, and a repeated sequence of content. All these factors are grounded on fundamental assumptions concerning the manner in which individuals learn, the rationale behind disengagement, as well as the types of instructional choices that can support their development. To understand the functionality of these processes in practice, it is good to discuss how AI systems process learner data, how they interpret such data and convert the interpretations of these interpretations into individualised responses of the instruction, and how those responses affect the cognitive, motivational, and emotional conditions of students.

The next subsections are transporting models to mechanisms to, at last, living examples. Section 3.1 presents the overall design of AI-personalised learning with special consideration of how data streams and circles aid the progress of the learner. Intelligent tutoring systems are then looked at in greater detail in section 3.2, and how they imitate human tutoring by experts. Section 3.3 moves to recognition and involvement of emotions - a field that is being increasingly accepted to be critical to meaningful personalisation. In section 3.4, these ideas are placed within a broader context of case studies based on the comparison of various countries and educational settings. Thanks to all these elements, AI transforms the learning experience on many levels and on a wide level.

AI Personalised Learning Models

At the heart of the AI-based personalisation, there is a cyclic mechanism relying on a continuous diagnosis and adaptation. Instead of offering a preliminary collection of activities or tools, a system based on AI monitors a learner and utilises such observations to form the following step in the learning process. This active responsiveness can be compared with the point by Bloom that the process of learning speeds up astronomically when the directions are tailored to the immediate demands of the learner. Practically, this is much less than the scale and granularity of such adaptation as can be effectively done by human teachers with large, heterogeneous groups. AI thus acts more as a means to augment the instructional capacity of humans since it can have specialised approaches without necessarily having to engage each student in specific instructional time.

The majority of AI-personalised systems are driven by three interrelated steps, namely, input collection, data interpretation, and feedback generation. The initial phase, i.e., input collection, takes place each time a learner arrives at an online service. Going through a simulation, filling in a quiz, editing an essay, or maybe sitting there and unsure of an answer, all become data points. Other systems also receive multimodal data like voice tone, speech pauses, typing patterns or facial expressions; however, these modalities are also infantile and are used sparingly in practice.

The second phase of data interpretation is the one where machine learning and rule-based models can collaborate to find patterns in the behaviour of the learner. In this case, the system tries to get to know the levels of mastery, misconceptions, preferred modalities, or cognitive load appearances. According to Faber, Luyten, and Visscher (2024), the increasing integration of natural language processing, AI can process open-ended student answers better, providing them with information on how students understand concepts in the problem-solving process, their attitude, and even the methods they use to solve problems.

Lastly, the third step is the feedback generation, which gives the action to the interpretations. The system can also manage the difficulty of the following task, give a hint, note a concept to revise, suggest an additional resource, or determine that human help is required. This feedback is deliberately direct, as it is common for learners they need redirection or correction on an issue on the fly instead of after an assignment has been marked. According to Zhou (2025), this responsiveness enhances engagement because the learners do not waste long periods of time dwelling in stance of confusion or committing the same errors.

The term of deep learning would require an important explanation. The concept of deep learning can be used in the field of cognitive psychology, which deals with analytical thinking, concept integration, and meaning-making. In artificial intelligence, deep learning denotes neural network structures that process complicated information. This chapter distinguishes between the concepts of cognitive form and deep cognitive processing so that the neural network used in deep thinking does not become confused with deep learning models, which are algorithmic models. The latter point is particularly notable in Section 3, in which the two concepts play a role in comprehending the way AI derives cognitive states.

When based on these mechanisms, personalisation models go beyond content adjustments to induce metacognitive development. Numerous AI boards show evidence of progress that students should consider their strategy, speed or trends of success and failure. This is in line with the theoretical focus on self-regulation, motivation and mastery orientation, which relates the technological model to the learning sciences.

Intelligent Tutoring Systems in Action

One of the most obvious and well-researched manifestations of AI-personalised learning is Intelligent Tutoring Systems (ITS). They do not only seek to automate teaching, but to estimate the decision-making schemes of expert human tutors. As has been demonstrated by researchers like Woolf (2020), successful tutoring requires the careful diagnosis of misconceptions, providing context-sensitive hints, and adjusting the learning rate according to the readiness shown by the particular learner. The principles are arranged in ITS platforms in a model of computation that evolves with each interaction among learners.

In most contemporary ITS systems, the behaviour of the system is directed by three basic parts: the domain model (what is to be learned), the student model (what the student already knows) and the pedagogical model (how to teach stuff). The student model is movable: every reaction causes an adjustment of the framework of the estimate of mastery, motivation or error patterns of the learner. Yang, Flanagan, and Ogata (2022) demonstrate that adaptive assessment systems developed on the principles not only change the level of difficulty but also the time interventions depending upon memory retention cycles. This cyclical tracking helps reinforce learning using evidence-informed interval strategies.

To illustrate how ITS functions in practice, consider a learner working through algebraic equations. If the system notices repeated errors in isolating variables, it may present a scaffolded problem that breaks the process into smaller steps. Sajja, Sermet, and Cikmaz (2023) describe how intelligent assistants now blend ITS features with conversational interfaces, supporting not only academic tasks but also time management and emotional regulation. The convergence of tutoring logic with predictive analytics allows these systems to identify at-risk learners even before performance declines. Bystrenina and Nikitin (2022) further argue that adaptive knowledge control models—particularly those using Bayesian or neural-network-based updating—strengthen long-term retention by continuously aligning challenges with learner trajectories.

Through such interactions, ITS tools foster an environment where students are neither overwhelmed nor under-challenged. They also relieve teachers from constant monitoring of individual difficulties, giving educators more flexibility to focus on conceptual clarification and human-directed guidance.

Engagement and Emotion Recognition Tools

Though cognitive adaptation continues to be one of the foundation blocks of individualised learning, studies have begun highlighting the focal position of emotion in the determination of engagement, persistence, and understanding. Students enter the digital worlds with differing levels of emotions, curiosity, anxiety, boredom, or frustration, and these tendencies tend to have a larger impact on performance than cognitive ability alone. Emotion-aware AI thus takes personalisation a step further into the realm of affectivity so that systems can become sensitive to individual feelings in order of adapt instruction.

The modern emotion recognition platforms are inspired by multimodal data, which includes facial expressions, posture variations, voice alteration, or interaction rhythms. Zhou (2025) illustrates the ability of deep learning models to compare micro-expressions or look-away behaviour in order to categorise emotional states with a high degree of accuracy. On the same note, Ilyas, Umar, Razi and Tariq (2025) point out that there are strong correlations between emotion-sensitive adaptation and increased levels of engagement within virtual classrooms.

Relating all these mechanisms to theory, the affective learning frameworks suggest that emotions do shape the choice of cognitive approaches, the readiness to persist, and the general value of tasks. Overwhelmed students will be narrow-minded or not interested at all. Students who develop curiosity or confidence, on the other hand, will have a higher probability of putting in long-term investments. Emotion-sensitive AI is consistent with these principles as it identifies the signs of cognitive overload and the decrease in motivation early enough. As an illustration, the system might simplify the task, alternate modalities, or add an element of interactivity to refocus attention when it notices that the person is guessing rapidly or taking a long time to respond.

One of the most obvious benefits of such tools appears in remote or asynchronous learning setups where the teachers are not able to observe the effect of students visually. Liu, Latif, and Zhai (2025) point out that emotional awareness will be considered as a key attribute of next-generation ITS, which will not be an optional addition or a side-by-side feature. Such developments are a departure of the history of cognitive tutoring to the holistic learning systems that can detect intellectual and emotional obstacles.

Case Studies

Even though AI-personalised learning is a topic that is frequently presented either theoretically or technically, its applicability is more tangible when it is examined in the context of actual educational experience. Both case studies below illustrate the variability of the benefits of AI not just globally, but also the factors of its context that determine its success, i.e. its accessibility, the competency of the teachers, and culture-related demands. Such instances can be used to describe the way in which personalisation can take shape in various continents, curricula, and among various learner populations.

Case study 1: Aula Inteligente (Colombia)

In a handful of Colombian under-resourced schools in the secondary grade, Aula Inteligente ITS platform was introduced with an aim to enhance teaching mathematics and science. The adaptive sequencing of the content used was informed by the diagnostic quizzes to students aged between 12 and 16 years. Dashboards allowed the teachers to monitor misconceptions and have small-group support. The results of Fletscher, Mercado, Gomez and Mendoza Cardenas (2025) demonstrate how much better student performance was in terms of increasing standardised tests results by 18 percent in a year. Notably, educators noted that the system would assist them in capturing the attention of quiet students who were unable to attract attention before. The observation highlights the importance of ITS in facilitating equity in the classroom setting in schools with low teacher-to-student ratios.

Case study 2: LearnMatch (Finland)

A different scenario is in Finland, where multilingual primary classes give the learners in diverse language backgrounds an opportunity to learn together. The all-natural language processor-based platform, LearnMatch was used to practice grammar, vocabulary and pronunciation. According to Faber et al. (2024), the system was analysing written samples to deliver individual feedback, retelling writing to the user in addition to offering pronunciation guidance in the form of audio-based correction. This was especially advantageous to multilingual learners who could feel confident in their expressive and receptive capacities. Teachers claimed that students began to do it out of class voluntarily, which can be interpreted to mean that they were more motivated to study since they were encouraged to study through real-time, non-judgmental feedback.

Case study 3: Bangladesh adaptive cloud platform.

The adaptive learning platform was applied to the urban and rural government schools in Bangladesh to control student interaction and recognise the disengagement early warnings. According to Talukder and Ahsan (2025), the use of the patterns of login, time-on-task, and quizzes enabled educators to identify the risk of falling behind within the learner. The suggestions on the platform enabled schools to come up with intervention classes that are specific. Pass rates increased steadily in schools taking part, and the project also pointed out structural issues that affected the long-term scalability of the system, including inequitable access to devices.

Case study 4: Turkey's national LMS during the pandemic

When lockdowns were implemented due to the COVID-19 pandemic, Turkey incorporated emotion-sensitive analytics into its national learning management system. According to Taskin (2025), the ability to closely monitor the engagement of learners gave the teachers the chance to identify an inactive learner and contact them through other means of communication. The emotional detection features of the system assisted the struggling learners who feel isolated or anxious by modifying the difficulty and speed of accessing the lessons. These interventions were extremely important in ensuring continuity of learning in case of intensive school closure.

Synthesis of Section 3

Through these models and tools, as well as case studies, one can find a universality: personalisation is not a mere technical compromise or a standardised approach to instruction. It is an interactive experience of cognitive, emotional, contextual and pedagogical. This game is reinforced through AI to be visible, quantifiable, and real-time functional. Regardless of recognising any false beliefs, modifying the content, understanding the emotional conditions, or helping designate the actions of the teacher, AI acts as the reinforcer of good teaching, not the substitute of it.

In this section, it has been revealed how AI-personalised learning can generalise the existing theories into computational systems and how the latter influence the experiences of learners in different environments. The next section, 4, shifts to practical implications, i.e., technological frameworks, ethical considerations, institutional policies and implementation strategies that should go hand in hand with any responsible adoption of AI-driven personalisation.

SOLUTIONS AND RECOMMENDATIONS

Although the above sections of this chapter have discussed the history, processes, and international uses of AI in personalised learning, it is also important to translate such knowledge into practical measures. Solutions do not just exist in theory; they have to deal with the practical part according to the real-life institutional context in addition to following the tricky landscape of ethics, privacy, policy, and pedagogy. In this part, elaborate solutions and recommendations to the education stakeholders, such as the policymakers, institutional heads, curriculum developers, technologists and educators are outlined. The guidelines are positioned within four major conjectures, including technological frameworks, AI tools, ethical considerations, and systemic policy integration. The insights will focus on enabling the AI to make learning purposeful and inclusive without contributing to the existing inequalities in education.

Technology Frameworks for Implementation

The incorporation of AI into the education system must not start with tools; it must start with frameworks that can be used to select technology, scale, data governance and instruction alignment. An effective, high-quality framework of implementation of AI should be sensitive and it should be adaptable to various educational levels; it should be congruent with the aspirations of the institutions. Gupta, Kumar, Roy, and Saini (2024) stress the need to structure AI frameworks that not only can be technically viable but also pedagogically purposeful. They suggest a layered architecture in their article on AI-based adaptive learning systems in which learning analytics, cognitive modelling, and adaptive feedback will run concurrently.

The implementation framework needs to start with a definitive diagnosis of the infrastructure and current pedagogical models in place. All these aspects should be evaluated by the institutions, such as available bandwidth, availability of devices to be used, digital literacy of professors and system interoperability. Such audits should only then be followed by AI component additions. Research Corridor (2025) adds that the precondition is that the foundational digital infrastructure issues, like cloud-based data storage, Learning Management Systems (LMS), and the training modules of the teachers, have been put in place adequately before AI tools are added to the educational stack.

Institutions must realise the implementation of AI in a modular way in terms of pilot projects, after establishing the current state of infrastructure. The detailed evaluation matrix also evaluates effectiveness, student engagement, teacher support, and ethical compliance should be included in the work done by these pilots. As an example, the use of an adaptive quiz platform in one department and a chatbot support system in the other enables the institutions to learn by iteration and expand in a responsible manner. According to Wired (2024), small educational institutions that can develop slowly based on proven outcomes have better chances to integrate AI sustainably in the long run. The inclusion of students and teachers in the design and evaluation phase is critical. It not only fosters trust but also leads to more context-appropriate solutions.

AI Tools for Personalised Learning: LMS, ITS, Chatbots

The environment of AI tools is big and continuously changing. Nevertheless, there are certain types of tools that have been found particularly effective in the provision of personalised learning. The most common are Learning Management Systems (LMS), Intelligent Tutoring Systems (ITS) and chatbots powered by AI. All these tools are assigned a specific role in the personalisation ecosystem.

The platform of LMS has evolved beyond the domain of a pure course repository to an active environment consisting of content modules that can adjust to a learner, produce analytics on learning activities and enable learning event interactions in real-time. By blending the abilities of AI into LMS systems, including intelligent suggestions and project area prediction, Gupta et al. (2024) prove that such opportunities can contribute to improved autonomy and motivation levels of the learners. One of the methods through which personalisation occurs in LMS is through AI agents reviewing the actions of the learners to recommend specific material, the best way to learn, or similar.

The most pedagogically intricate type of AI application is ITS tools, as discussed in the previous sections. Such systems will be suitable when skills-based subjects are studied, and competency learning is important. This makes them customised tutors who adapt the learning material according to the assessment in real time and according to the pace of learners. The researchers (Ellikkal and Rajamohan, 2024) investigating the AI-based individualised learning process in management students noticed an objective improvement in the achievement, student engagement, and efficiency of time-on-task with the incorporation of ITS modules into curricula. When appropriately incorporated into the current course formats, such systems do not supplement course structure, but co-educate.

AI chatbots, in turn, play a meaningful role in providing administrative and academic scaffolding. Taught domain expertise and pedagogical rules, chatbots will be able to respond to requests, assign tasks, give micro-feedback, and even motivate students between classes. They are available 24 / 7 to keep up the support of the students even when they are in class. As analysed by Panagopoulou, Parpoula, and Karpouzis (2023), the generative chatbots such as ChatGPT are obviously beneficial in an academic and institutional context, especially when they use domain-relevant corpora in training. However, they also caution against uncritical adoption, stressing the importance of guardrails to prevent misinformation and misuse.

The effectiveness of these tools increases when they are interoperable—able to exchange data with one another—and when faculty are trained not just in their operation but in their pedagogical implications. Institutional support for professional development, sandbox experimentation, and technical assistance is non-negotiable. AI tools are only as effective as the ecosystem into which they are embedded.

Ethical AI: Bias, Fairness & Data Privacy

Along with the advantages of AI in education, the institutions that adopt it have to face its ethical dilemmas as well. AI is not going to decrease inequities when it is not thoughtfully designed and supported by clear policies. Algorithm bias is one of the most important issues. When the input on which AI systems are being trained harbours biases about society, in race, gender or socioeconomic status, one is likely to get an output that propagates the same bias. Mehmood (2025) provides an ethical system of AI integration which involves bias audit, model openness, explainability policy and stakeholder audit. Any policy to adopt AI should make such frameworks a requirement.

The other emerging issue is predictive privacy. Artificial intelligence systems account for and process large volumes of student data and tend to anticipate behaviour, emotions, or student performance. Although such predictive potential can help in learning, there are serious concerns with regard to privacy. Muhlich (2021) suggests the notion of predictive privacy to refer to the ethical crisis with systems that not only disclose information concerning individuals but also their likely futures as well. Educational institutions must ensure that their AI vendors comply with strict data protection standards. Consent protocols must be transparent, revocable, and written in accessible language for all learners, particularly minors. Panagopoulou et al. (2023) further stress that institutions must differentiate between formative analytics (used to support learning) and summative surveillance (used for control or discipline).

Policy and Curriculum Recommendations

To make the personalisation of AI succeed system-wide, it is necessary to introduce supportive policies and change the curriculum. Ad-hoc implementation is a possible solution to disconnected classrooms, but improving the education field at large requires consistency between country-wide plans, institutional ideals, and the daily educational actions. This part highlights salient recommendations to be taken by policymakers and curriculum developers to enable the introduction of equitable, effective AI.

At the policy level, the national education ministries will have to introduce guidelines on the proper use of artificial intelligence, the requirements of teachers to be trained, and interoperability requirements of the educational technologies. Such guidelines must be formulated through the consultations of multiple stakeholders that include technologists, educators, ethicists, and learners themselves. Regulatory bodies that will audit AI tools to ensure they achieve the standards of pedagogical and ethical desiderata before deploying the tools to classrooms should also be established by governments.

Curriculum designers will have to redesign the structure of courses to comply with AI-driven learning. This is the switching of rigid syllabi to competency-based, chunked curricula enabling self-paced progression. Formative assessment tools and learning assessment dashboards should be built into the courses to allow the timely interventions. Gupta et al. (2024) state that it is important to stop making AI a subject and view it as an infrastructure embedded in every subject. An example can be a history course, which can have AI-powered content visualisation, and a science course including equally capable simulations of laboratory experiments.

The most pressing need within the curricular area is probably teacher education. Technical training is only one aspect of the needed professional development programs, and they should also cover ethical reasoning, data literacy, and the assistance of students in an AI-mediated environment. The notion that the younger teachers will somehow adjust themselves to technology has been distorted; both the new and old teachers need to go through a specific training process. In addition, assessment policies will have to be changed as well. Conventional exams cannot necessarily reflect the skills that can be developed using AI. Scoring new rubrics designed on mastery, creativity and collaboration should be piloted and deployed.

Table 2. Comparative Analysis of AI Tools Used in K–12, Higher Ed & Corporate Training

AI Tool	K–12 Application	Higher Education Use Case	Corporate Training Use Case
LMS	Adaptive reading platforms	Performance dashboards, modular content	Skill-based microlearning platforms
ITS	Math and science tutoring	Domain-specific cognitive modelling	Certification and upskilling simulations
Chatbots	Homework help, scheduling	FAQ assistance, academic advising	HR onboarding, workflow automation
Emotion AI	Engagement detection in classrooms	Learning fatigue prediction and response	Customer service training simulations
Learning Analytics	Student performance forecasting	Predictive dropout risk detection	Employee productivity monitoring

Figure 2. Ethical AI Integration Framework for Educational Institutions

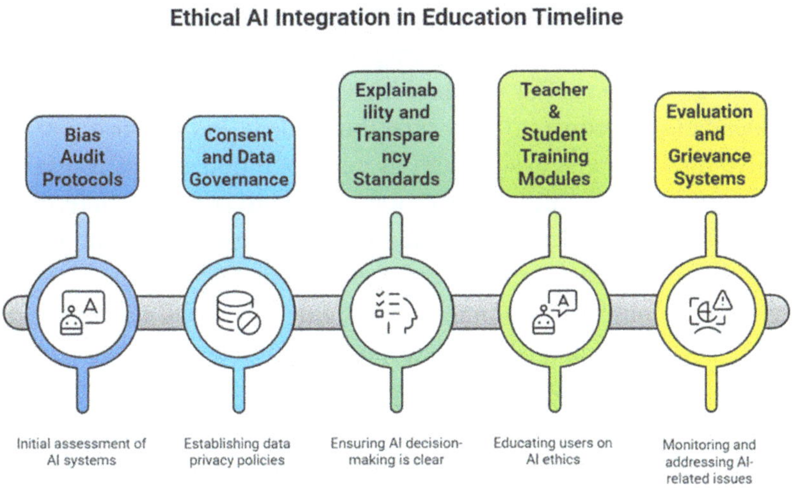

This section underscores that personalised learning through AI is not an automatic benefit of digitisation. It requires structured frameworks, thoughtfully selected tools, ethically guided practices, and systemic curricular reform.

FUTURE RESEARCH DIRECTIONS

In a world where AI is constantly changing the face of education, it becomes growingly clear that determining new trends and crucial research gaps that are going to characterise the next decade of educational innovation should be a priority concern. The application of AI to personalised learning environments has already changed the dynamics of the classroom, delivery of the contents, and assessment methods. Nevertheless, the pace of technological developments requires that the research should be in the leading edge, not responding to the current trends and practices, but extrapolating possible novelties of the paradigms of cognitive and emotional development with the help of intelligent technologies. This chapter describes five such areas that are therefore in need of immediate academic attention: general intelligence in education, explainable AI, large language models, cognitive analytics, and longitudinal study of personalised learning impact.

Artificial General Intelligence and Multimodal Learning Futures

Although it is currently only in the theoretical realm, Artificial General Intelligence (AGI) would be expected to overcome the constraints of the task-specificity of the narrow AI systems in use today. This development promised to bring AI tutors in the field of education that would be able not only to adjust to the needs of learners but also reason and transfer knowledge and interpret multimodal inputs, and create new pedagogical interventions. According to Latif et al. (2023), the potential of AGI in learning will be similar to a legitimate co-teacher-they themselves will be able to understand the context, history of the student, his or her emotional state, and cognitive direction and assist them in metacognition and reflective thinking. But all that remains is a rather loose vision, and there is further, interdisciplinary research that should be conducted into the practicability, risk potential and ethical considerations of this vision in the context of formal education.

Future studies could be conducted to examine how AGI can be merged with project-based curriculum with interdisciplinary studies, no longer along the lines of linear presentation of content, but more of a constructivist learning system. Suddenly, teacher autonomy and agency and the humanisation of learning also get questioned in the advent of AGI-based pedagogical agents. Research will have to investigate the technical competence, as well as social acceptability, cultural adaptability, and psychological security in the AGI- AGI-facilitated learning.

Explainable AI (XAI) for Trust and Transparency

With AI systems having an increased instructional power, learners, educators and administrators should be capable of comprehending and trusting their decisions. This will be the point at which explainable AI (XAI) will be crucial. Although it might be very efficient, educational tools acting like an enigma are not up to the test of transparency, which is an essential aspect in a learning environment. Lakkaraju et al. (2024) mention that explainability is not a unique technical capability but rather an ethical requirement. In cases of classification, grading, or intervention recommendation by AI systems on students, a possibility to track and describe their reasoning needs to be available.

Future studies should examine the ways of integrating the explanation models in Intelligent Tutoring Systems (ITS), Learning Management Systems (LMS) and AI (artificial intelligence) based feedback engines. This involves the examination of user-centred designs of explanations, e.g. visual dashboards, explaining choices to teachers, rationale trees explaining actions to students, and regulatory logs to enable institutional control. The urgency to come up with more age-specific explanation protocols, particularly with K-12 settings where a cognitive maturity of the student may constrain the process of system output interrogation, is also extremely significant. Moreover, empirical research must be conducted to determine the relationship between explainability and learner confidence, motivation as well as self-regulated learning.

The issue is that to a trade-off between performance and interpretability. Most of the better and more accurate models of AI, especially deep learning pairings, are notoriously explain. Hybrid models, which learn interpretable rules and also learn a powerful pattern recognition front-end, should thus be the focus of research, but the ways to make them scale and resource-efficient in low-tech educational settings should be considered.

Large Language Models (LLMs) in Personalised Learning

The emergence of large language models (LLMs), including ChatGPT, Gemini, and Claude has already started to affect the instructional ecosystem. Their abilities to understand natural language, answer questions, as well as to create generative content introduce possibilities of personalised learning. But these capabilities are neither coherent to the educational standards, the curriculum objectives, nor the needs of the learners. According to Yan et al. (2023), LLMs are both a great pedagogical tool and a potential misinformation or bias device. This is a challenge and an opportunity for them.

Due to the finetuning of LLMs on specific educational corpora, research should look at finetuning. This is not just content in a textbook, but all learner-created content, formative assessment feedback and teacher feedback. The contextual tuning will enable LLMs to be more reliable and pedagogically oriented tools. Moreover, researchers should conduct studies on how students can use such models in unmonitored environments and what impact such student dependency on generative answers has on critical thinking, creativity, and learning of the content.

A third promising thing is conversational learning, in which LLMs are used to engage in a Socratic dialogue to scaffold learning. Although anecdotal evidence has promise, high-fidelity experimental designs are necessary to determine the efficacy of the intervention on various subjects, age ranges, and learning styles. Also, the limits of ethical use of LLM, in particular, in assessment situations, should be distinct and analysed by using classroom observations in the long run.

Cognitive Analytics and Individualised Learning Trajectories

The future of personalisation lies not only in content recommendation or emotion detection but in the nuanced mapping of cognitive processes. Cognitive analytics refers to the analysis of data related to attention span, memory retention, error patterns, metacognitive awareness, and transfer of learning. Katiyar et al. (2024) argue that cognitive analytics, when combined with AI, allows for a deeper personalisation that goes beyond surface-level adaptation. Rather than simply suggesting easier or harder questions, systems can begin to understand *how* a student thinks, learns, and solves problems.

Longitudinal and Cross-Cultural Studies

While short-term studies offer immediate insights into the effectiveness of AI tools, the true impact of personalised AI in education can only be understood through longitudinal and cross-cultural research. Tlili et al. (2025), in their meta-analysis of AI in education, have noted the lack of studies that track learners across months or years, especially in diverse geographical and linguistic contexts. Longitudinal studies are critical for evaluating not only academic outcomes but also socio-emotional development, digital resilience, and adaptability in AI-rich environments. Research should aim to answer critical questions: Do personalised learning systems narrow or widen achievement gaps over time? How do students' relationships with learning change after years of AI-supported instruction? What impact does AI have on lifelong learning dispositions, such as curiosity, grit, and self-efficacy? These are not questions that can be answered through semester-long interventions—they require sustained funding, institutional collaboration, and ethical commitment. Similarly, cross-cultural studies are essential to ensure that AI tools are inclusive and equitable.

CONCLUSION

The incorporation of Artificial Intelligence in personalised learning systems denotes one of the greatest transitions in history. The question of whether adaptive technologies, intelligent tutoring systems, emotion-aware AI and learning analytics cannot simply transform the gears of teaching and learning but totally reshape the very bond between student and knowledge has been covered in this chapter. With televisions and computers moving into the classrooms, the essence of the whole process should be personal based on the development of the learner, their feelings, and their individual courses of evolution. AI applications need not be limited to making traditional processes more automated and faster, but to assist in a more humane, multicultural, and fair educational paradigm.

The key to such transformation is a central insight: AI that can enhance the field of education is at its best when it can augment the human intellect and emotional intuition of teachers. In this chapter, instances have been provided showing how the intelligent tutoring systems can provide feedback in real time, how generative models can be used to support student writing and how the affective computing tools can be deployed to respond to student disengagement sensitively. Such capabilities should not, however, be regarded as ways of replacing educators. Instead, it is best used as a co-pilot- to aid teachers in ways to make the classroom more individualised, to take care of a large classroom, to identify students at risk of learning deficits, and even to assist them in ways where it is logistically impossible. The role of a teacher, however, rather than being reduced, turns out to be much more demanding in terms of interpreting data, selecting resources and guiding students via individual pathways.

This view of cooperation between artificial intelligence and humans is not a recipe. Moderating between global case study and local context-specific studies establishes a demonstration that personalised learning technological practices develop successful results depending on their adaptation to the local scene of culture, infrastructure, and pedagogy. An example of this would be that a recommendation algorithm used in a school district in the United States might be ineffective in a small classroom in the rural region of South Asia, where access to devices, languages, and anticipated educational outcomes are extremely different. This reinforces the importance of contextual design—AI models and learning platforms must be sensitive not only to individual learner differences but also to regional, linguistic, and socio-economic nuances.

REFERENCES

Bystrenina, I., & Nikitin, P. (2022). Adaptive knowledge control in digital learning. *Education Sciences*, *12*(10), 638. DOI: 10.3390/educsci12100638

Chen, L., Chen, P., & Lin, Z. (2020). Artificial intelligence in education: A review. *IEEE Access : Practical Innovations, Open Solutions*, *8*, 75264–75278. DOI: 10.1109/ACCESS.2020.2988510

D'Mello, S. K., & Graesser, A. (2013). Multimodal semi-automated affect detection from conversational cues, gross body language, and physiology. *IEEE Transactions on Affective Computing*.

Faber, J. M., Luyten, H., & Visscher, A. J. (2024). NLP for improved personalization in adaptive learning. *Educational Technology Research and Development*.

Fletscher, L., Mercado, J., Gómez, A., & Mendoza Cárdenas, C. (2025). Innovating personalized learning in virtual education. *Multimodal Technologies and Interaction*, *9*(7), 69. DOI: 10.3390/mti9070069

Gupta, T., Kumar, A., Roy, B. K., & Saini, S. (2024). Adaptive learning systems: Harnessing AI to personalize educational outcomes. *International Journal for Research in Applied Science and Engineering Technology*, *12*(11), 458–464. Advance online publication. DOI: 10.22214/ijraset.2024.65088

Ilyas, S., Umar, M., Riaz, K., & Tariq, Z. (2025). *Emotion recognition in AI-powered classrooms impacts on student engagement and learning outcomes*. Critical Review of Social Sciences Studies., DOI: 10.59075/x1wkpx78

Katiyar, N., Srivastava, D., Sharma, P., & Trivedi, R. (2024). AI-driven personalized learning systems: Enhancing educational effectiveness. *Educational Administration: Theory and Practice*. https://kuey.org/

Lakkaraju, K., Rao, A., & Jha, M. (2024). Trust and ethical considerations in a multimodal, explainable AI-driven chatbot tutoring system. *arXiv Preprint*. https://arxiv.org/abs/2401.01234

Latif, E., Chen, Y., Zhai, X., & Liu, V. (2023). AGI: Artificial general intelligence for education. *arXiv Preprint*. https://arxiv.org/

Liu, V., Latif, E., & Zhai, X. (2025). Advancing education through tutoring systems: A systematic literature review. *arXiv Preprint*. https://arxiv.org/

Mehmood, T. (2025). Ethical AI in education: Addressing bias, privacy, and equity in AI-driven learning systems. *Journal of AI Integration in Education*. https://www.researchcorridor.org/

Panagopoulou, F., Parpoula, C., & Karpouzis, K. (2023). Legal and ethical considerations regarding the use of ChatGPT in education. *arXiv Preprint*. https://arxiv.org/abs/2302.01987 DOI: 10.31235/osf.io/c5hf3

Pane, J. F., Steiner, E. D., Baird, M. D., & Hamilton, L. S. (2017). *Informing progress: Insights on personalized learning implementation and effects*. RAND Corporation.

Papamitsiou, Z., & Economides, A. A. (2021). Deep learning analytics for adaptive systems. In *Proceedings of the 21st IEEE ICALT Conference*.

Papamitsiou, Z., Economides, A. A., & Muñoz Merino, P. J. (2021). Learning analytics and adaptive learning technologies: A systematic review. *Computers & Education: Artificial Intelligence*, *2*, 100033. DOI: 10.1016/j.caeai.2021.100033

Sajja, R., Sermet, Y., Cikmaz, M., & Arslan, A. (2023). Artificial intelligence–enabled intelligent assistant for personalized and adaptive learning in higher education. *arXiv Preprint*. https://arxiv.org/

Smart Learning Environments. (2025). *Adaptive intelligent tutoring systems for STEM education: Real-time feedback and deep learning models*. Smart Learning Environments., DOI: 10.1186/s40561-025-00389-y

Talukder, N. M., & Bin Ahsan, W. (2025). AI's impact on student engagement in virtual learning in Bangladesh. *Journal of Teaching & Learning*, *1*(1). Advance online publication. DOI: 10.58947/journal.jtgx34

Tlili, A., Saqer, K., Salha, S., & Huang, R. (2025). Effect of AIEd on achievement: Meta analysis. *Information Development*. Advance online publication. DOI: 10.1177/02666669241304407

Wired Staff. (2024). AI can't replace teaching, but it can make it better. *WIRED Magazine*. https://www.wired.com/story/ai-in-classrooms/

Woolf, B. P. (2020). *Building intelligent interactive tutors*. Morgan Kaufmann.

Yan, L., Sha, L., Zhang, X., & Chen, Y. (2023). Practical and ethical challenges of large language models in education. *arXiv Preprint*. https://arxiv.org/abs/2310.04210

Yang, A. C. M., Flanagan, B., & Ogata, H. (2022). Adaptive formative assessment system based on computerized adaptive testing and learning memory cycle. *Computers & Education: Artificial Intelligence*, *3*, 100104. DOI: 10.1016/j.caeai.2022.100104

Zawacki-Richter, O., Marín, V. I., Bond, M., & Gouverneur, F. (2019). Systematic review of AI applications in higher education – Where are the educators? *International Journal of Educational Technology in Higher Education, 16*(39). Advance online publication. DOI: 10.1186/s41239-019-0171-0

Zhou, F. (2025). *Emotion recognition in AI-powered classrooms: Using deep learning to detect student engagement.* Smart Learning Environments., DOI: 10.1186/s40561-025-00374-5

ADDITIONAL READING

Baker, R. S. J. d., & Inventado, P. S. (2014). Educational data mining and learning analytics. In *Learning Analytics* (pp. 61–75). Springer. DOI: 10.1007/978-1-4614-3305-7_4

Benjamins, R., Barbieri, M., & Rossi, F. (2020). Responsible AI: From principles to practice. *AI and Ethics, 1*, 3–12. DOI: 10.1007/s43681-020-00002-3

Heffernan, N. T., & Heffernan, C. L. (2014). The ASSISTments ecosystem: Building a platform that brings scientists and teachers together for minimally invasive research on human learning and teaching. *International Journal of Artificial Intelligence in Education, 24*(4), 470–497. DOI: 10.1007/s40593-014-0024-x

Holstein, K., Wortman Vaughan, J., Daumé, H.III, Dudik, M., & Wallach, H. (2019). Improving fairness in machine learning systems: What do industry practitioners need? *Proceedings of the 2019 CHI Conference on Human Factors in Computing Systems*, 1–16. https://doi.org/DOI: 10.1145/3290605.3300830

Luckin, R., Holmes, W., Griffiths, M., & Forcier, L. B. (2016). *Intelligence Unleashed: An Argument for AI in Education*. Pearson Education. A foundational report explaining the scope, benefits, and implications of AI in education for multiple stakeholders, including educators and policymakers.

KEY TERMS AND DEFINITIONS

Adaptive Learning: Adaptive learning refers to an instructional approach where educational content and experiences are dynamically adjusted in response to an individual learner's progress, behaviour, and preferences. Using real-time data, adaptive learning systems tailor pathways, pace, and difficulty levels to optimise student performance and engagement. It leverages technologies like machine learning and learner modelling to make instruction more effective and personalised.

Affective Computing: Affective computing is a field of study focused on the design of systems that can recognise, interpret, and simulate human emotions. In educational contexts, affective computing enables learning platforms to detect emotional states—such as frustration, boredom, or excitement—through facial expressions, tone of voice, or physiological signals, and respond appropriately to support cognitive and emotional development.

Emotion Recognition: Emotion recognition is the process of identifying and interpreting learners' emotional states through visual, vocal, or physiological signals. In AI-enhanced learning environments, this ability allows systems to adjust content delivery or intervention strategies to improve engagement and well-being.

Explainable AI (XAI): Explainable AI refers to systems that offer transparency in their decision-making processes. In education, XAI is critical for building trust among students, educators, and parents by clearly showing how recommendations, assessments, or feedback are generated. It promotes ethical use and accountability in AI-powered educational tools.

Intelligent Tutoring System (ITS): An Intelligent Tutoring System is an AI-powered software application that delivers personalised instruction by simulating one-on-one human tutoring. ITS continuously analyses student inputs, progress, and misconceptions to adapt learning materials, offer hints, and provide feedback, often in real-time. These systems are widely used in STEM education and are designed to promote mastery learning.

Learning Analytics: Learning Analytics refers to the collection and analysis of student data—such as performance patterns, engagement levels, and learning behaviours—to improve teaching and learning outcomes. It helps educators make data-driven decisions and personalise instruction based on actionable insights.

Multimodal Learning: Multimodal Learning integrates multiple forms of input—such as text, audio, video, gestures, and interactions—to enhance comprehension and engagement. By leveraging varied sensory channels, it supports deeper learning and accommodates diverse learning styles.

Student Modeling: Student Modeling is the process of creating a digital profile of a learner's knowledge, skills, preferences, and learning progress. It enables adaptive systems to predict learning needs and deliver customized educational pathways.

Chapter 9
Engaging Students in Deep Learning With AI: An ICAP Theory Perspective

Robert Z. Zheng
https://orcid.org/0000-0003-0507-3340
University of Utah, USA

Jeffrey Wallace
Millersville University, USA

Natalia Melissa Soto
University of Utah, USA

W. Jordan Charles
https://orcid.org/0009-0000-7527-3589
University of Utah, USA

ABSTRACT

This chapter aims to explore the potential of artificial intelligence (AI)-supported tools in improving learners' complex learning. The chapter is focused on the pedagogical aspects of integrating AI tools by examining the relationship between student learning and the theoretical models of learning that include cognitive load theory, self-determined theory and the ICAP approach. A proof of concept study was conducted by taking into account learners' cognitive and affective behaviors in AI-supported complex learning. It was found that the learners demonstrated differently in terms of their cognitive and affective performance when engaged across a variety of learning activities, i.e., active, constructive, and interactive. The results highlight the importance of pedagogy in implementing AI technology in education.

DOI: 10.4018/979-8-3373-2927-7.ch009

Discussions based on the findings were made pertaining to future research in an effort to provide guidance for professionals (e.g., researchers, practitioners, learners) who are interested in integrating AI in learning.

INTRODUCTION

With the advent of Artificial Intelligence (AI), the field of education is experiencing a quick and significant change that transforms traditional classrooms into dynamic, data-driven learning environments. This chapter explores the ways in which AI engages and supports students' deep learning in terms of integrating AI tools, including generative AI, chatbots, virtual tutors, intelligent recommendation systems, and adaptive learning platforms, to enhance learners' cognitive processes at a deeper level.

The challenges associated with technology-based learning, whether it be multimedia, web-based learning, or virtual reality, have traditionally revolved around the issues of (a) the role of technology in learning, (b) the relationship between the design of learning and the technology, and (c) effective approaches in technology-integrated learning.

Early in the 1990s, Clark and Kozma initiated a "media debate" focusing on the role of media and learning (Clark, 1983; 1994; Kozma 1994; Reiser 1994). Clark (1983) questioned the role of media in learning and called for a reconsideration of research on learning from media. He challenged the educational community to reexamine its research design and results, claiming that most media research was confounded, and concluded that there were no significant differences among various media. Instead, he insisted that research on media should focus on the design of learning, such as method, aptitude, and task variables of instruction, rather than the media themselves.

Kozma (1994) countered that research should be grounded in a theory that defines media in ways that are compatible and complementary with the cognitive and social processes by which knowledge is constructed. Kosma urged researchers and practitioners to understand the dynamic relationships between media and learning, the reciprocal interaction between the learner's cognitive processes and the unique characteristics of media. Reiser (1994) concurred with Kozma's view on media and pointed out that certain media attributes facilitate certain types of learning outcomes for particular types of learners. Zheng and colleagues (Zheng, 2007; Zheng et al., 2009) agreed with Reiser's view by noting the cognitive functionality of technology and media in complex learning, such as problem solving. The outcomes of this debate are positive. It (a) raised the awareness of the role of technology/media in learning, (b) identified the distinct functionality of technology in supporting learners during their learning, and (c) promoted renewed interest in the relationship between media and learning. The debate contributed to the surge of research on technology and learning that marked the eras of the Internet, educational games, virtual reality (VR), augmented reality (AR), interactive 3D, wearable technology, all the way to intelligent tutoring, machine learning (ML), and Artificial Intelligence (AI). By exploring the role of technology and its involvement in the learners' cognitive and affective processes, this line of research has unveiled the underlying cognitive and affective mechanisms that lead to learners' deep learning through learning technologies. It also provided useful guidance for both researchers and practitioners in terms of effective implementation of technology in teaching and learning (Afify 2020, Amin & Ikhsan 2021, Boldbaatar & Sendurur 2019, Mayer & Anderson 1991, Zheng 2022; Zheng et al. 2015).

As discussed earlier, research on media has led to a significant understanding of the relationship between the role of technology and the design of learning. Many scholars in the field agree to the complementary role of learning technology (Chang et al., 2017; Kee et al., 2024; Ramsey & West, 2023; Reiser, 1994; Zheng, 2007). However, much remains to be explored in regards to the extent that the learning technology can facilitate learners' deep learning in terms of applying, creating, and discovering new knowledge, specifically how new digital technologies like AI can promote learners' deep-level cognitive processes such as synthesizing and evaluating information, making inferences, and developing innovative solutions while engaging in complex problem solving. The current chapter tries to answer these questions by (1) identifying the factors that contribute to the effective cognitive and affective processes in learning and (2) proposing a cognitive framework for deep learning with AI.

Motivation to Promote Cognitive Engagement

Research in cognitive and affective learning illuminates the relationship between motivation and cognitive engagement in learning. Metwally and colleagues (2024) examined learners' intrinsic motivation and engagement in a game-based learning. They found that a gameful experience increases learners' motivation, promotes cognitive engagement, and facilitates deep thinking in gamifying online learning activities and tasks. The authors concluded that the gameful design approaches provide motivational affordances that result in behavior change and task completion. In a separate study, Ng et al. (2024) explored the motivational factors (e.g., competitiveness, meaningful and supportive visuals, etc.) in a gamified learning environment. The results of the study revealed motivational factors enhanced affective and cognitive support, fostered understanding, and solidified students' higher cognitive skills. The authors suggest that the development of technology-based learning (e.g., game-based learning) should consider affective and cognitive domains to make learning meaningful and engaging for learners. An early study by Walker et al. (Walker et al., 2006) also confirmed the directional correlation among motivation, self-efficacy, and cognitive engagement in learning.

While the existing research has pointed to a positive correlation between motivation and cognitive engagement (Aslam et al., 2020; Venn et al., 2023), the theoretical underpinnings that explain the connection between the two have not been clearly identified. In this chapter, the authors attempt to illuminate their underlying relationship based on three theories, namely cognitive load theory (CLT) (Sweller, 2018; Sweller et al., 1998), Deci's self-determination theory (SDT) (Bong et al., 2023; Deci et al., 2001), and Chi's ***Interactive*** engagement, ***Constructive*** engagement, ***Active*** and ***Passive*** (ICAP) cognitive engagement theory (Chi et al., 2018).

Cognitive Load Theory (CLT)

The cognitive load theory proposes that three types of cognitive load can significantly influence learners' learning. They are intrinsic, extraneous, and germane cognitive load. Intrinsic cognitive load refers to the load associated with the difficulty of the content materials, specifically, the level of element interactivity within the content that requires learners' mental effort during information process (Sweller, 1988). Take the following arithmetic problems as an example:

Problem 1. *5 + 6 =*

Problem 2. (2+3) + (3+3) =

Problem 3. (2+3) + (3 * 2) =

In Problem 1, the level of element interactivity involves 2 digits (5, 6) and 2 mathematical symbols (+, =). The mathematical process consists of one step, that is, adding digits *5* and *6*.

In Problem 2, the level of element interactivity increases to 4 digits (2, 3, 3, 3) with a new mathematical symbol of *parenthesis* "()" added, introducing the concept of sub-steps in calculation. Accordingly, the mathematical process increases from one step to two steps:

Step 1: adding 2 and 3 (sub-step 1); adding 3 and 3 (sub-step 2)
Step 2: adding the sums of sub-steps in Step 1.

In Problem 3, the level of element interactivity still involves 4 digits (2, 3, 3, 2,) but a new mathematical symbol "*" is added, introducing the concept of multiplication. The mathematical process thus involves two different operations: addition and multiplication.

Step 1: adding 2 and 3 (sub-step 1); multiplying 3 and 2 (sub-step 2)
Step 2: adding the production of sub-steps in Step 1.

Evidently, the level of element interactivity becomes incrementally complicated as the learner works on the arithmetic problems from Problem 1 to Problem 3. The complexity of the problems is determined by the level of element interactivity, which imposes varying levels of cognitive load on learners. This type of cognitive load is often described as intrinsic cognitive load.

Different from intrinsic cognitive load, extraneous cognitive load is caused by inappropriate instructional design. In a situation where the learner had to spend unnecessary mental effort in dealing with content irrelevant to learning, extraneous cognitive load is imposed. Figure 1 shows an example of inappropriate design in instruction. Figure 1 shows an online instructional site where learners practice arithmetic problems. Instead of simply presenting the written math problem for practice, the instructional designer added a video to the page, asking the learners to count the number of construction workers. Rather than focusing their attention directly on solving the math problem, the learners spent extra cognitive resources engaging in an activity that did not teach them the new skill of adding 5 to 6, but reinforced the previously learned skills of counting. This creates a redundancy in learning and imposes an unnecessary cognitive burden on the learners that can hurt their learning.

Figure 1. Example of Inappropriate Design in Instruction.

Of three types of cognitive load, the one that is relevant to the current chapter and discussion is germane cognitive load. Germane cognitive load represents the connection between motivation and cognitive effort. According to Sweller et al. (1998), germane cognitive load is related to the mental effort associated with problem solving or new knowledge acquisition during learning. While both intrinsic and extraneous cognitive loads can have a negative impact on learners' learning, germane cognitive load is a type of cognitive load that needs to be encouraged and nurtured during learning. Studies have demonstrated that motivation and cognitive effort are closely related (Fehrmann, 2025; Gupta & Zheng, 2020). In their study on students' problem solving in mathematical problems, Gupta and Zheng (2020) noticed that germane cognitive load and motivation were positively correlated, leading to higher achievement outcomes in math problem solving. Similar findings were obtained showing a positive relationship between cognitive effort and motivation (Woo, 2014; Zeithofer et al., 2024).

Cognitive Load Theory hypothesizes that three types of cognitive load, i.e., intrinsic, extraneous, and germane cognitive load, together make the overall cognitive load in working memory, and they are additive to each other (Cook et al., 2009; Greenburg & Zheng, 2023; Sweller, 2010). In any learning or instructional situation, the three cognitive loads should not exceed the overall working memory. The additive hypothesis of cognitive load theory stipulates that in the process of learning (a) learners' extraneous load must be low if their intrinsic load is high, (b) both learners' intrinsic and extraneous load cannot be high at the same time, and (c) for learners' germane load to be high, intrinsic load must be high and extraneous load must be low. The last stipulation explicates the relation between intrinsic and germane load. Kalyuga (2011) points out that learners become more motivated in learning when the content gets challenging. In other words, effortful learning (associated with germane cognitive load) occurs when learners face challenging, complex content (indication of intrinsic cognitive load). Kalyuga thus concludes that germane cognitive load ebbs and flows with intrinsic cognitive load. Greenburg and Zheng (2023) examined the relationship among motivation, intrinsic, and germane cognitive load. They found that learners became motivated when facing challenging problems, which consequently resulted in higher germane cognitive load as manifested by a higher level of effort in learning.

In summary, the above discussion has unveiled the relationship between motivation and cognitive effort through the lens of germane cognitive load, which reflects the learner's desire to engage in the tasks on one hand and their cognitive effort to accomplish the tasks on the other. Further, germane cognitive load is associated with and solicited by the difficulty of the tasks (Kalyuga, 2011). Because of its unique role at the intersection of motivation and cognitive effort, determining how to develop instructional conditions so that germane cognitive load can be nurtured and solicited becomes an area of interest in instructional design, particularly in digital technology-rich learning like AI learning (Zheng, 2025).

Deci's Self-Determination Theory (SDT) to Explain Cognitive Engagement

Although intrinsic load could lead to an increase of germane load (Kalyuga, 2011), it is still unclear why, under certain circumstances, learners who learn challenging content (an increase in intrinsic load) fail to demonstrate motivation to learn (an increase in germane load). Jang and colleagues (2016, also see Bong et al., 2023) examined the process of learner engagement and disengagement based on Deci's (2001) self-determination theory (SDT). According to Deci's SDT, people's psychological needs (i.e., autonomy, competence, and relatedness) are inherent motivational aspects that, when supported, facilitate optimal functioning and psychological well-being (Ryan & Deci, 2000). SDT defines self-autonomy as the need to experience a sense of control and volition in one's behavior/action. Competence refers to the need to feel competent with tasks and activities. Finally, relatedness is the need to experience a sense of belonging, community, and feel connected with and cared for by others.

Research has demonstrated that learners' cognitive engagement is related to competence need satisfaction and perceived autonomy support (Bong et al., 2023; Jang et al., 2016). Jang et al. (2016) observed that in a traditional face-to-face classroom, the teacher's supportive role in terms of facilitating learners' competence, need satisfaction, and self-autonomy can lead to success in academic performance. They pointed out the importance of nurturing students' self-autonomy and competence-need satisfaction in learning. Bong et al. (2023) conducted a study that empirically supports Jang et al.'s observation. Using structural equation modelling (SEM), the authors found that perceived self-autonomous support has a direct correlation with competence-need satisfaction ($R^2 = .77, \beta = .58, p < .001$), which further positively correlates with cognitive engagement ($R^2 = .89, \beta = .81, p < .001$). It is worth noting that in Bong et al.'s study, the need satisfaction is positively correlated with cognitive engagement. They claimed that "perceived competence support was the primary predictor of cognitive engagement" (Bong et al., 2023, p. 1024). In other words, learners' cognitive engagement, in any learning situation, is influenced by their perceived need satisfaction. It should be noted that the learners' need satisfaction in both Bong et al.'s study and SDT refers to a social support construct (e.g., "I feel connected with people"). In the current chapter, which focuses on AI learning, we argue that it can be extended to include the support of AI tools that can potentially boost learners' need satisfaction.

As discussed earlier, cognitive engagement can be proxied by the level of germane cognitive load. Since germane cognitive load ebbs and flows with intrinsic cognitive load (i.e., content difficulty), it can be presumed that a relationship may exist among germane load, intrinsic load, and cognitive engagement. About deep learning, Chi's ICAP theory (2018) provides useful perspectives on identifying intrinsic cognitive load and cognitive engagement associated with varying deep learning activities (Chi et al., 2009; Chi & VanLehn, 2012).

Chi's ICAP Theory of Cognitive Engagement

Chi (Chi, 2018; Chi & VanLehn, 2012) studied the types of learning to determine learners' engagement in deep learning and proposed the ICAP theory in deep engagement. ICAP stands for several types of learning, including ***Interactive*** engagement, ***Constructive*** engagement, ***Active*** and ***Passive*** engagement. According to Chi (2018), interactive engagement represents the highest level of engagement, which is superior to constructive engagement. Both interactive and constructive engagements would exceed the benefits of active or passive engagement.

Active learning means learners participate and are involved in the learning which include searching a term in the Internet, looking at a picture on a website, underlining a sentence in a textbook, repeating verbatim a line from a play, copying and pasting a paragraph into a composition, pointing to a 3D object in a multimedia tutorial, recording actions cumulatively, etc. By actively doing something, the learner becomes engaged in the content he/she is learning. However, as Chi points out, being active in learning does not necessarily guarantee that the learner is processing information deeply. In other words, active learning is not equivalent to deep learning. One can repeat verbatim lines from a play, but it does not indicate that one understands the lines. Thus, Chi argues that being active in learning is necessary but not sufficient to guarantee that deep cognitive learning occurs. On the other hand, constructive learning activities provide sufficient steps for deep learning to occur.

Constructive learning involves deep-level thinking processes such as comparison, categorization, hypothesizing, making inferences, etc. with outcomes demonstrating learners' deep understanding associated with the discovery of new knowledge, rules, and principles. According to Chi (2018), *being constructive* is different from *being active*. The former relates to the act of producing content-relevant new ideas beyond what was given, whereas the latter shows the act of doing something related to the content. Examples of constructive learning include (1) explaining a problem-solving process, (2) proposing a new solution to a problem, and (3) solidifying facts to arrive at a new conclusion. Constructive learning facilitates a process in which the learner not only gains a deep understanding of the content but also sees new information that was not explicitly presented in the content.

Interactive learning involves direct communication among learners in a group or community. This includes discussing an academic problem, responding to a cognitive agent in an intelligent tutoring system, or interacting with a video game. The interaction reflects a deep-level cognitive process where students engaged in problem-solving by collectively searching for solutions. Chi argues that for interaction to be meaningful and cognitively beneficial, learners within a group should make substantial contributions to the interaction with equivalent intellectual and cognitive engagement. She recommends two types of interaction: joint interaction and interaction with expert. Joint interaction means two or more students contribute substantially to the interaction process as measured by intellectual contribution. The interaction with the expert refers to the learner interacting with an expert (e.g., instructor, subject matter expert, etc.). The benefit of interacting with an expert is that the expert can monitor the student's learning process and lead the interaction by asking questions, giving explanations, providing feedback, and guiding their learning path.

Following Chi's ICAP framework, Zheng (2022) examined the roles of three types of learning: active, constructive, and interactive, in a game-based learning environment. The author investigated the learner behavior in association with cognitive processing in terms of fostering transversal skills across game-based learning. Zheng observed that active learning, which denotes learners' activity at the surface level, such as manipulating objects and locating information, involves low-level cognitive processes like remembering and understanding. In contrast, constructive and interactive learning, which promote discovery learning and innovative thinking, support deeper-level cognitive processing, such as analysis, synthesis, application, and evaluation, where the learner explores the content to discover new knowledge, rules, and principles. Zheng asserted that the active, constructive, and interactive types of learning in Chi's ICAP framework correspond well to levels of cognitive processes as defined by Bloom's Taxonomy of Learning (Bloom, 1956). Table 1 lists the relationship between levels of processing and types of learning.

Table 1. Relationship between levels of processing and types of learning

	Remembering	**Understanding**	**Applying**	**Analyzing**	**Evaluating**	**Creating**
Active	*shallow*	*shallow*				
Constructive			*deep*	*deep*	*deep*	*deep*
Interactive			*deep*	*deep*	*deep*	*deep*

With permission from R. Zheng (2022), *Foster transversal skills in game-based learning: A deep learning approach.* Hershey, PA: IGI Global Publishing.

Given the level of process and mental effort associated with levels of cognitive processing, it can be reasonably presumed that the intrinsic cognitive load associated with active learning is lower, whereas the intrinsic cognitive load associated with constructive and interactive learning will be higher. Since intrinsic cognitive load is positively related to germane cognitive load, it can be further assumed that there is an increase in cognitive engagement from active learning to constructive and interactive learning. This is because the increase in intrinsic cognitive load across the learning activities will bring in an increase in germane cognitive load.

Moreover, since cognitive engagement is related to competence need satisfaction and perceived autonomy support (Bong et al., 2023; Jang et al., 2016) and the idea that learners become increasingly engaged in deep processing as they move from active to constructive and to interactive learning activities due to increases in intrinsic and germane cognitive load, their cognitive engagement will increase and their need satisfaction also increase with the placement of AI support tools. Figure 2 presents a theoretical framework for the current study where different theories, i.e., cognitive load theory, SDT, and ICAP, overlap.

Figure 2. Summary of the relationship among intrinsic, germane cognitive load, ICAP, and SDT theories.

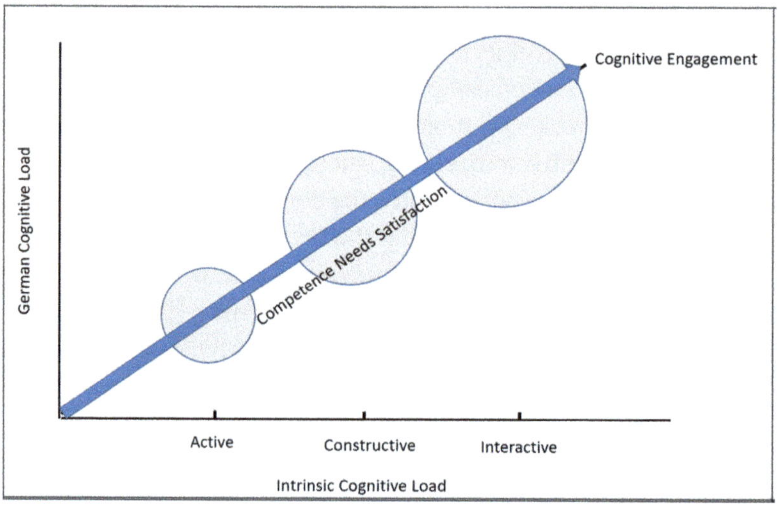

As indicated in Figure 2, a positive correlation is perceived to influence learners' competence needs satisfaction, which in turn influences their cognitive engagement. This is because an increase in intrinsic cognitive load in association with various learning activities (i.e., active, constructive, and interactive) will lead to a corresponding increase in germane cognitive load (Kalyuga, 2011). Further, Self-

Determined Theory (SDT) asserts that people's psychological needs (i.e., autonomy, competence, and relatedness) facilitate learners' optimal functioning and psychological well-being in learning (Ryan & Deci, 2000). That is, as learners' germane cognitive load increases due to the increase of intrinsic cognitive load through learning activities, they begin to develop a sense of self-confidence in terms of self-autonomy, competence and relatedness, which are interpreted and represented as cognitive engagement. Given the theoretical relationship between germane and intrinsic cognitive load (CLT), learning activities (ICAP), and factors associated with learners' competence needs and satisfaction (SDT), the study aims to achieve its goals by focusing on the following hypotheses to understand the relationship and impact of cognitive load, learning activities and cognitive engagement in AI supported learning:

H1. There is a positive correlation between intrinsic cognitive load, germane cognitive load, and student achievement scores.
H2. The intrinsic and germane cognitive loads increase correspondingly with the types of learning, from active to constructive, to interactive learning.
H3. Learners' need satisfaction will increase incrementally due to the optimal design for AI supported learning in each stage.
H4. The increase in need satisfaction will lead to an increase in cognitive engagement, resulting in higher performance in tasks.

METHOD

The Context of Study

The current study is a proof-of-concept study that tested Hypotheses 1 and 2 by examining the relationship (1) between intrinsic, germane cognitive load and student achievement scores, and (2) between intrinsic and germane cognitive load and types of learning. Hypotheses 3 and 4 will be explored in future studies. Therefore, the current study reports the findings of Hypotheses 1 and 2 with suggestions for future research (Hypotheses 3 and 4).

Participants and Design

The participants consisted of undergraduate students (*N*=45) recruited from a teaching university in the Eastern U.S. The participants first signed the voluntary consent form for voluntary participation in the study and were randomly assigned to one of the learning conditions. The study material covers polar bonds and ionic bonds in organic chemistry.

Three learning conditions were created for the study: active, constructive, and interactive learning conditions.

Active learning condition. Learners in the active learning condition were introduced to the study materials and prompted to (1) find the definition of chemical terminology and (2) record the number of terms with the support of an AI tool named Chatbot that is powered by ChatGPT. In the active learning condition, the learners were actively engaged in surface level activities such as searching for term definitions and recording searches. The role of AI in active learning was to serve as a just-in-time resource for students to get information on tasks.

Constructive learning condition. The learners in the constructive learning condition were asked to search the terminologies using Chatbot, compare them, and present what they understood based on the course material and information found from the resources (e.g., Chatbot). For example, the learners were asked to summarize in their own words the reaction between sodium and chlorine in chemical ionization. Figure 3 provides an example of the course content in chemical ionization. Similar to active learning, the role of AI in constructive learning was to provide just-in-time information for learners as they engaged in deeper learning.

Figure 3. Organic chemistry course sample.

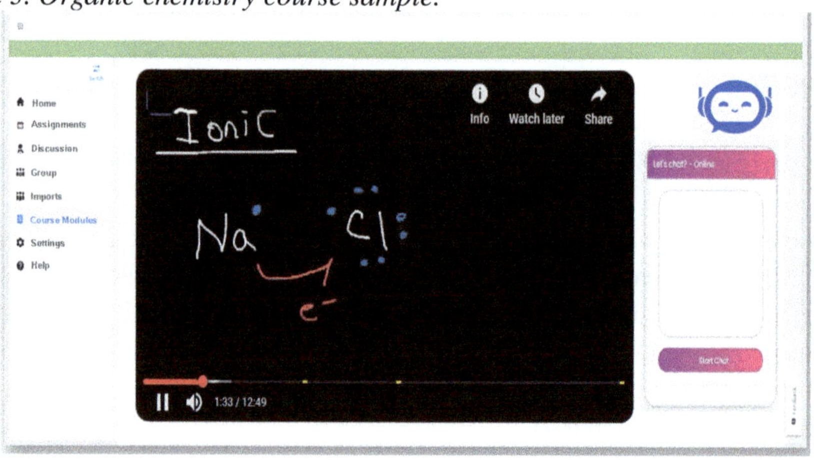

Interactive learning condition. The learners in interactive learning condition worked in pairs to study the chemical materials in a simulation environment and presented what they found about the chemical reaction, that is, the electrostatic attraction between the oppositely charged ions in the formation of sodium chloride -- an ionic compound (Figure 4). Similar to active and constructive learning, the AI

Chatbot is available in interactive learning, where learners seek information through Chatbot based on task requirements and needs.

Figure 4. Organic chemistry course simulation sample.

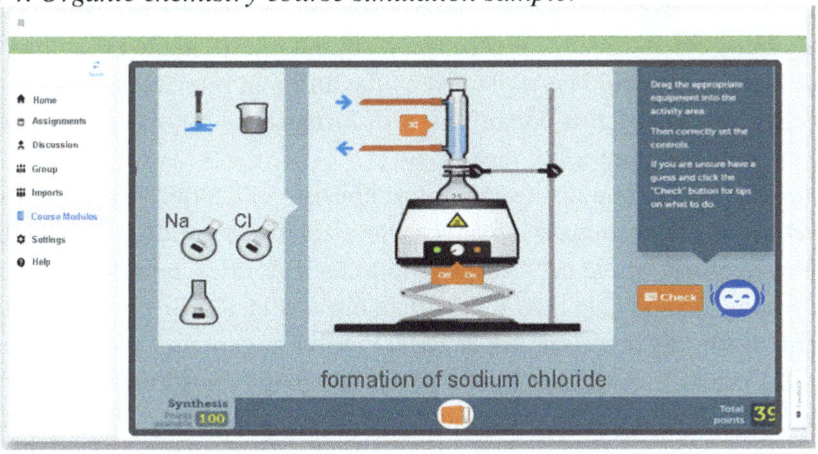

After the learning phase, the learners were asked to complete the Cognitive Load Questionnaire (CLQ) (Leppink et al. 2013) and an achievement test on chemical ionization.

Predictions of hypotheses. As mentioned earlier, the current study is a proof-of-concept study that tested Hypotheses 1 and 2. Regarding Hypothesis 1, it is predicted that there would be a positive correlation between germane and intrinsic cognitive load. The increase in challenging content would bring more effort on the part of learners to learn and solve the problems. In regard to Hypothesis 2, it is predicted that the learners would experience lower intrinsic load with active learning since it simply requires search and recording actions, but would experience higher intrinsic load with constructive and interactive learning as both require learners to engage in analytical and critical thinking, which involves deep level thinking in terms of knowledge association, synthesis and application (Zheng, 2022).

Instrumentation

Cognitive load questionnaire. The self-report questionnaire consisted of 10 questions presented on an 11-point Likert scale. Examples of questions are: "The topic covered in the video was very complex," "The instructions and/or explanations during the video were very unclear," and "The video really enhanced my understanding of the content covered." The questionnaire was adopted from Leppink et al. (2013) to measure three types of cognitive load, i.e., intrinsic, extraneous, and germane cognitive load. The instrument reported medium to high reliabilities based on the 2013 study, with three questions for intrinsic load $\alpha = 0.81$, three for extraneous load $\alpha = 0.75$, and four questions on germane load $\alpha = 0.82$. The internal consistency in the current study for the cognitive load questionnaire was $\alpha = 0.88$ for intrinsic load, $\alpha = 0.67$ for extraneous load, and $\alpha = 0.84$ for germane load, which suggests good reliability for intrinsic and germane load, but questionable reliability for extraneous load which could be explained by the different interfaces between *active/constructive* and *interactive* conditions with former as a text-based interface and the latter a simulation interface design.

Achievement test. The achievement test consists of 15 questions, of which 10 answer conceptual questions and 5 are problem-solving questions. An example of a conceptual question would be, "Negative ions like chlorides, bromides, and iodides involve adding (1) and (2)." [Ans. (1) dilute nitric acid, (2) silver nitrate solution]. The problem-solving questions ask learners to solve or explain a particular problem in chemical reaction. An example of a problem-solving question would be, "Weak acids and bases do not ionize completely. Please explain with an example the common error in assuming 100% ionization for a weak acid like HF." The total possible score a learner can attain on the achievement test is 35 points.

RESULTS

The study explored (1) whether there is a positive correlation between intrinsic cognitive load, germane cognitive load, and student achievement scores, and (2) whether intrinsic and germane cognitive load increase correspondingly with the types of learning from active to constructive, to interactive learning. Since the cognitive load questionnaire differs in the number of response items for the types of cognitive load measure (intrinsic load = 3, extraneous load = 3, germane load = 4), the raw scores for each cognitive load were summed and converted to Z scores. Table 2 presents the descriptive data of the study.

Table 2. Descriptive data

	Group	Mean	Std. Deviation	N
Intrinsic Load	Active	-1.31	.28	12
	Constructive	.38	.25	15
	Interactive	.93	.19	15
	Total	-.00	.99	45
Germane Load	Active	-1.37	.16	12

continued on following page

Table 2. Continued

	Group	Mean	Std. Deviation	N
	Constructive	.59	.16	15
	Interactive	.77	.18	15
	Total	-.00	1.00	45
Achievement	Active	18.00	3.16	12
	Constructive	24.66	3.51	15
	Interactive	30.00	3.27	15
	Total	24.22	5.93	45

To test Hypothesis 1, the correlation analysis was performed. Results showed positive correlations among intrinsic, germane cognitive load, and student achievement scores. Intrinsic cognitive load is highly correlated with germane cognitive load, Pearson $r = .955, p < .01$ and achievement scores Pearson $r = .828, p < .01$. At the same time, germane cognitive load is positively correlated with intrinsic cognitive load Pearson $r = .955, p < .01$ and achievement scores Pearson $r = .788$, $p < .01$ (Table 3).

Table 3. Correlation among intrinsic, germane cognitive load, and student achievement scores.

		Intrinsic Load	Germain Load	Achievement
Intrinsic Load	Pearson Correlation	1	.955**	.828**
	Sig. (2-tailed)		<.001	<.001
	N	45	45	45
Germain Load	Pearson Correlation	.955**	1	.788**
	Sig. (2-tailed)	<.001		<.001
	N	45	45	45
Achievement	Pearson Correlation	.828**	.788**	1
	Sig. (2-tailed)	<.001	<.001	
	N	45	45	45

** Correlation is significant at the 0.01 level (2-tailed).

Based on the results of Hypothesis 1, we further explored whether there was a variation among the correlated variables across types of learning. That is, with intrinsic and germane cognitive load positively correlated, would such correlation vary across different learning activities?

To test Hypothesis 2, multivariate tests were performed with *groups* (active, constructive, and interactive) as independent variables and intrinsic, germane cognitive load, and *achievement* as dependent variables. The results demonstrate significant difference among the groups, Wilk's Lambda $\lambda = .015$, $F_{(3, 42)} = 96.127$, $p < .001$, $\eta^2 = .87$. The tests of between-subjects effects further indicate that there was significant difference among the groups (i.e., active, constructive and interactive) in terms of intrinsic load $F = 335.75$, $p < .001$, $\eta^2 = .94$, germane load $F = 729.55$, $p < .001$, $\eta^2 = .97$, and achievement $F = 49.15$, $p < .001$, $\eta^2 = .70$. Figure 5 shows the relationship between intrinsic and germane cognitive load across three learning activities, i.e., active, constructive and interactive.

Figure 5. The relationship between intrinsic and germane cognitive load across three learning activities.

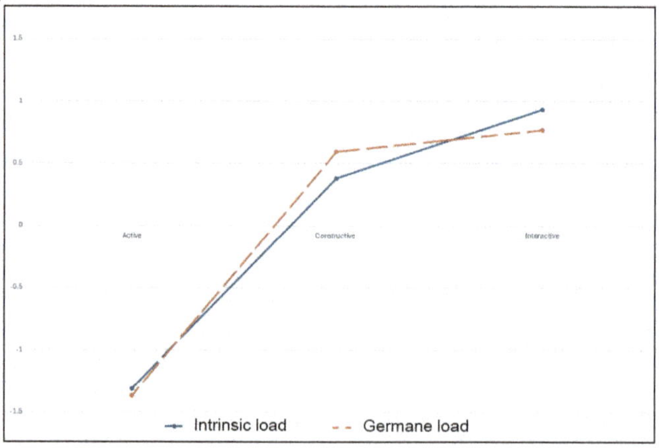

There was an uptrend for intrinsic and germane cognitive from active to constructive learning. As the content continued to increase in its difficulty, the germane cognitive load appears to reach its plateau. There was no significant difference in germane cognitive load between constructive and interactive learning. Interestingly, germane cognitive load was higher than intrinsic cognitive load in constructive learning but was lower than intrinsic cognitive load in interactive learning, forming a trend of interaction (non-significant). However, when adding achievement to the analysis, learners in the interactive learning condition showed the highest gain regardless of their low germane load (Figure 6).

Figure 6. Cognitive loads and achievement scores across three learning activities.

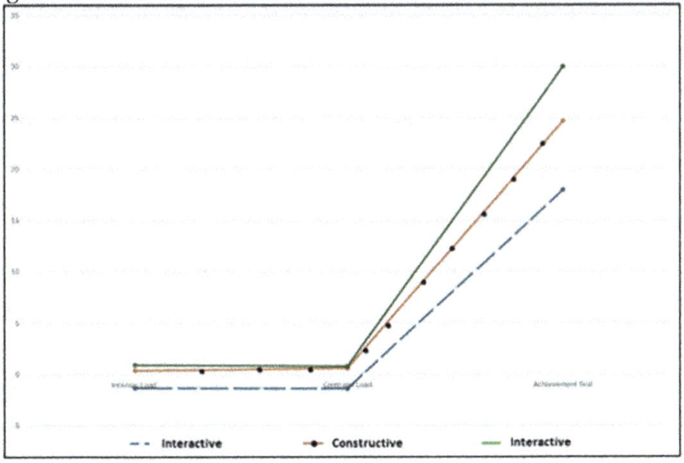

DISCUSSION

The current study aimed to understand how learners' mental effort is associated with different learning activities, i.e., active, constructive, and interactive, when engaging in difficult content. The study also explored the relationship among germane load, intrinsic load, and achievement performance. The following discussion will revolve around the two hypotheses proposed earlier.

H1. There is a positive correlation among intrinsic cognitive load, germane cognitive load and student achievement scores. The results of the study showed that the learners' intrinsic cognitive load is related to the learning activities. There was an increase in intrinsic cognitive load when learners engaged in learning activities from active to constructive to interactive. As the intrinsic cognitive load increased, the germane cognitive load also increased from active to constructive, but reached a plateau after the constructive learning condition (Figure 5). In the meantime, learners' achievement performance paralleled the increases of germane and intrinsic cognitive loads. This result is consistent with the literature that the intrinsic cognitive load can simultaneously solicit germane cognitive load (Kalyuga, 2011). What is puzzling is that in the interactive learning condition, intrinsic cognitive load did not result in higher germane cognitive load, yet the learners still showed high performance. One explanation could be that with the support of AI and socially paired work, learners' competence need satisfaction and perceived autonomy support were met (Bong et al., 2023; Jang et al., 2016). However, the need satisfaction and perceived autonomy may not necessarily be captured by the germane cognitive load measures. Hence the learners' low germane load and high achievement performance.

Another explanation could be that it is related to a possible time gap between intrinsic and germane cognitive load for the participants. Since both intrinsic and germane loads were self-reported, the learners might have experienced the difficult content (high intrinsic cognitive load) first, but could have been undecided as to which approach to take to solve the problem (low germane load). In other words, the germane cognitive load may have come late after the initial onset of high intrinsic cognitive load and was therefore under-reported in germane load measures.

H2. The intrinsic and germane cognitive load increases correspondingly with the types of learning, from active to constructive, to interactive learning. Hypothesis 2 was partially supported. There was a positive correlation between intrinsic cognitive load and achievement. With the increase of intrinsic cognitive load, the learners' performance increases across three learning activities, i.e., from active to constructive, to interactive. The intrinsic cognitive load trend reflected an increase in the content difficulty from active to constructive to interactive learning activities. The germane cognitive load showed a positive trajectory from active to constructive learning activities. It reaches a plateau from constructive to interactive learning activities (See Figure 5). Regardless, the learners maintained a strong uptick trend in performance. Even when the germane load was below the intrinsic load at interactive learning, the learners' performance was strong. As explained previously, the measures of germane load may not be able to capture learners' motivational efforts such as need satisfaction and perceived autonomy (Deci et al., 2001). Thus, even when the germane load was low, the learners were still able to perform at a higher level, being potentially motivated by other factors like need satisfaction and perceived autonomy.

The results of current study confirmed the hypotheses pertaining to the relationship between cognitive load, learning activities and achievement. What can be inferred from the study given the results? The following discussion will focus on cognitive processes, learners' perceived autonomy and self-competence in AI supported learning.

Cognitive processes in AI supported learning. There is no direct link of AI to learners' performance across the three learning activities. However, by looking at the upstick trend of germane cognitive load from active to constructive and interactive learning, it can be inferred that AI may play a specific role in each learning in supporting learning. For example, AI may help achieve the goal of effectively identifying information needed during active learning. It may also support the learners to develop deep level thinking in comparing, categorizing and evaluating the information by feeding AI with targeted questions while engaging in constructive learning. Finally, it may facilitate the social dynamics in interactive learning as the learners use the AI to engage in meaningful and innovative conversations. All these AI roles are possible while engaging in active, constructive and interactive learning. However, without direct empirical evidence, there is limitation in what we can actually presume. We propose that future research includes a scale to measure the various roles of AI in learning activities, which would provide insight into how AI may impact learners' cognitive processes.

AI and psychological needs. According to Deci's SDT, psychological needs like autonomy, competence, and relatedness are crucial to learners' success in learning. Judging by the results, it appears that learners became positively connected with the content and were emotionally engaged, particularly by showing an uptrend of germane cognitive load across three activies and positive correlations with achievement scores (Figures 5 and 6). In other words, learners may have developed a strong self-autonomy, a sense of competence and a feel of relatedness accompanied by a growing germane cognitive load and higher performance in each learning activity. The notion that the learners may have developed self-autonomy, competence and relatedness is evident in the fact that the learners demonstrated high performance even when germane load was low in interactive learning. While the preliminary results of the current study suggest some connections between SDT factors and learner performance, they are yet to be empirically proved. Future studies should include a scale of SDT factor measure to determine the relationship between the two.

In summary, the current study explored the cognitive and affective aspects that explain learners' deep processes during AI learning. The frameworks of ICAP and cognitive load theory were employed to inform the study. The results indicate a positive relationship between types of cognitive load (germane and intrinsic) and learner performance across three learning conditions, i.e., active, constructive, and interactive, suggesting learners' cognitive processes can be significantly influenced by the types of learning activities employed, which supports Chi's ICAP learning activity theory. The study overall supports Kalyuga's theory on the positive relationship between intrinsic and germane cognitive load.

CONCLUSION

AI as an educational tool has demonstrated its potential in learning. The current study examines the role of AI in supporting learners' deep learning. Three theoretical frameworks were employed to inform the study. They are Sweller's Cognitive Load Theory (CLT), Chi's ICAP, and Deci's Self-Determination Theory (SDT). Each theory contributes to the understanding of (1) how learners' mental effort affects their performance, (2) what types of learning activity or activities may influence learners' deep-level cognitive processes, and (3) how mental efforts and learning activities may be regulated by motivational factors.

One of the theoretical contributions of the current study is that it supports the positive relationship between germane and intrinsic cognitive load. Moreover, it further demonstrates the connection between cognitive load and types of learning activities. That is, the positive relationship between germane and intrinsic cognitive load is further influenced by the learning activities the learner engages in. The results of the study showed learners' intrinsic and germane cognitive load increased from active to constructive and to interactive learning. The finding supports Kalyuga's assumption that germane cognitive load ebbs and flows with intrinsic cognitive load and that learners become motivated when they face challenging content. The second contribution of the current study is its discovery of the low germane load and high performance in interactive learning. The finding of the study seems to suggest that the germane load may not necessarily explain higher performance. Instead, other factors like need satisfaction and perceived autonomy may be better factors to explain learners' performance.

Limitations of the Study

Although AI (Chatbot) was integrated in all three learning activities, it is unclear whether variation in learners' cognitive load and performance was due to AI or due to the specific design of the learning activity, or even other unknown factors. Future research should focus on the discrimination of unique features of AI and the design of learning activities to account for the factors that influence learners' performance and deep cognitive processes. Another area of improvement for future study is to include measures of additional motivational factors that germane cognitive load fails to capture. A correlational study could be conducted between motivational factors and germane cognitive load items to show how effortful learning (germane cognitive load) is related to and explained by the motivational efforts.

Future Research

As discussed previously, one of the limitations of the study is that the measures of germane cognitive load fail to capture motivational factors and therefore, were unable to explain why learners still showed high performance when germane cognitive load was low. Future research should investigate the relationship between need satisfaction and cognitive engagement as measured by germane cognitive load in AI-supported learning (Hypothesis 3). Further investigation should be made to examine the relationship among need satisfaction, cognitive engagement, and performance (Hypothesis 4). Research on how to optimally utilize AI tools to support learners' deep processing should be conducted in the context of activity design related to AI tools. The research should help improve understanding of (1) the cognitive functionality of AI tools, (2) the role of design activity to bring the AI tools to their fullest potential, and (3) cultural and social aspects in AI-supported learning. Future research should include a diverse population so the findings can be generalized to a broader educational community and a larger population.

REFERENCES

Afify, M. K. (2020). Effect of interactive video length within E-Learning environments on cognitive load, cognitive achievement and retention of learning. *Turkish Online Journal of Distance Education, 21*(4), 68–89. DOI: 10.17718/tojde.803360

Amin, D. I., & Ikhsan, J. (2021). Improving higher order thinking skills via semi Second Life. *European Journal of Educational Research, 10*(1), 261–274. DOI: 10.12973/eu-jer.10.1.261

Aslam, S., Anwer, M., & Yousaf, M. (2020). Effect of motivational strategies on science students' cognitive engagement. *Journal of Educational and Social Research, 7*(1), 1–13.

Bloom, B. S. (1956). *Taxonomy of Educational Objectives, Handbook: The Cognitive Domain*. David McKay.

Boldbaatar, N., & Sendurur, E. (2019). Developing educational 3D games with StarLogo: The role of backwards fading in the transfer of programming experience. *Journal of Educational Computing Research, 57*(6), 1468–1494. DOI: 10.1177/0735633118806747

Bong, J. Y., Cho, K., Liu, Z., & He, D. (2023). A dual-process motivation mediation model to explain female high school students' cognitive engagement and disengagement in emergency remote teaching and online learning in South Korea. *British Journal of Educational Technology, 55*(3), 1020–1040. DOI: 10.1111/bjet.13415

Chang, C., Liang, C., Chou, P., & Lin, G. (2017). Is game-based learning better in flow experience and various types of cognitive load than non-game-based learning? Perspective from multimedia and media richness. *Computers in Human Behavior, 71*, 218–227. DOI: 10.1016/j.chb.2017.01.031

Chi, M., Adams, J., Bogusch, E. B., Bruchok, C., Kang, S., Lancaster, M., Levy, R., Li, N., McEldoon, K. L., Stump, G. S., Wylie, R., Xu, D., & Yaghmourian, D. L. (2018). Translating the ICAP theory of cognitive engagement into practice. *Cognitive Science, 42*(6), 1777–1832. DOI: 10.1111/cogs.12626 PMID: 29954048

Chi, M., & VanLehn, K. A. (2012). Seeing deep structure from the interactions of surface features. *Educational Psychologist, 47*(3), 177–188. DOI: 10.1080/00461520.2012.695709

Clark, R. (1983). Reconsidering research on learning from media. *Review of Educational Research, 53*(4), 445–459. DOI: 10.3102/00346543053004445

Clark, R. E. (1994). Media will never influence learning. *Educational Technology Research and Development*, *42*(2), 21–29. DOI: 10.1007/BF02299088

Cook, A., Zheng, R., & Blaz, J. W. (2009). Measurement of cognitive load during multimedia learning activities. In Zheng, R. (Ed.), *Cognitive effects of multimedia learning* (pp. 34–50). Information Science Reference/IGI Global Publishing. DOI: 10.4018/978-1-60566-158-2.ch003

Deci, E. L., Ryan, R. M., Gagné, M., Leone, D. R., Usunov, J., & Kornazheva, B. P. (2001). Need satisfaction, motivation, and well-being in the work organizations of a former Eastern Bloc country. Personality and Social Psychology Bulletin, 27, 930e942.

Fehrmann, R. (2025). Implementing augmented reality models in the classroom environment using merge cubes: A quantitative study of the effects on students' cognitive load and motivation. *Education Sciences*, *15*(4), 414–432. DOI: 10.3390/educsci15040414

Gupta, U., & Zheng, R. (2020). Cognitive load in solving mathematics problems: Validating the role of motivation and the interaction among worked examples, task difficulty, and prior knowledge. *European Journal of STEM Education*, *5*(1), 05.

Jang, H., Kim, E. J., & Reeve, J. (2016). Why students become more engaged or more disengaged during the semester: A self-determination theory dual-process model. *Learning and Instruction*, *43*, 27–38. DOI: 10.1016/j.learninstruc.2016.01.002

Kalyuga, S. (2011). Cognitive load theory: How many types of load does it really need? *Educational Psychology Review*, *23*(1), 1–19. DOI: 10.1007/s10648-010-9150-7

Kee, T., Zhang, H., & King, R. B. (2024). An empirical study on immersive technology in synchronous hybrid learning in design education. *International Journal of Technology and Design Education*, *34*(3), 1243–1273. DOI: 10.1007/s10798-023-09855-5

Kozma, R. B. (1994). Will media influence learning? Reframing the debate. *Educational Technology Research and Development*, *42*(2), 7–19. DOI: 10.1007/BF02299087

Leppink, J., Paas, F., van der Vleuten, P. M., van Gog, T., & Van Merriënboer, J. J. G. (2013). Development of an instrument for measuring different types of cognitive load. *Behavior Research Methods*, *45*(4), 1058–1072. DOI: 10.3758/s13428-013-0334-1 PMID: 23572251

Mayer, R. E., & Anderson, R. (1991). Animations and narrations: An experimental test of a dual-coding hypothesis. *Journal of Educational Psychology*, *83*(4), 484–490. DOI: 10.1037/0022-0663.83.4.484

Metwally, A. H. S., Huang, R., Palomino, P. T., & Yousef, A. M. F. (2024). The effect of micro gamified online homework on gameful experience, intrinsic motivation, engagement, and cognitive load. *Education and Information Technologies*, *29*(18), 24489–24523. DOI: 10.1007/s10639-024-12750-8

Ng, D. T. K., Chen, X., Leung, J. K. L., & Chu, S. K. W. (2024). Fostering students' AI literacy development through educational games: AI knowledge, affective and cognitive engagement. *Journal of Computer Assisted Learning*, *40*(5), 2049–2064. DOI: 10.1111/jcal.13009

Ramsey, J. L., & West, R. E. (2023). A recent history of learning design and technology. *TechTrends*, *67*(5), 781–791. DOI: 10.1007/s11528-023-00883-5

Reiser, R. (1994). Clark's invitation to the dance: An instructional designer's response. *Educational Technology Research and Development*, *42*(2), 45–48. DOI: 10.1007/BF02299091

Ryan, R. M., & Deci, E. L. (2000). Self-determination theory and the facilitation of intrinsic motivation, social development, and well-being. *The American Psychologist*, *55*(1), 68–78. DOI: 10.1037/0003-066X.55.1.68 PMID: 11392867

Sweller, J. (1988). Cognitive load during problem solving: Effects of on learning. *Cognitive Science*, *12*(2), 257–285. DOI: 10.1207/s15516709cog1202_4

Sweller, J. (2010). Element interactivity and intrinsic, extraneous, and germane cognitive load. *Educational Psychology Review*, *22*(2), 123–138. DOI: 10.1007/s10648-010-9128-5

Sweller, J. (2018). The role of independent measures of load in cognitive load theory. In Zheng, R. (Ed.). (2018). *Cognitive load measurement and application: A theoretical framework for meaningful research and practice* (pp. 1-8). New York, NY: Routledge.

Sweller, J., van Merrienboer, J. J., & Paas, F. (1998). Cognitive architecture and instructional design. *Educational Psychology Review*, *10*(3), 251–296. DOI: 10.1023/A:1022193728205

Venn, E., Park, J., Andersen, L. P., & Hejmadi, M. (2023). How do learning technologies impact on undergraduates' emotional and cognitive engagement with their learning? *Teaching in Higher Education*, *28*(4), 822–839. DOI: 10.1080/13562517.2020.1863349

Walker, C., Greene, B., & Mansell, R. (2006). Identification with academics, intrinsic/extrinsic motivation, and self-efficacy as predictors of cognitive engagement. *Learning and Individual Differences*, *16*(1), 1–12. DOI: 10.1016/j.lindif.2005.06.004

Woo, J.-C. (2014). Digital game-based learning supports student motivation, cognitive success, and performance outcomes. *Journal of Educational Technology & Society*, *17*(3), 291–307.

Zeithofer, I., Zumbach, J., Schweppe, J. (2024). Complexity affects performance, cognitive load, and awareness. Learning & instruction, 94, pN.PAG-N.PAG. Doi:-DOI: 10.1016/j.learninstruc.2024.102001

Zheng, R. (2007). Cognitive functionality of multimedia in problem solving. In Kidd, T., & Song, H. (Eds.), *Handbook of Research on Instructional Systems and Technology* (pp. 230–246). Information Science Reference/IGI Global Publishing. DOI: 10.4018/978-1-59904-865-9.ch017

Zheng, R. (2022). Foster transversal skills in game-based learning: A deep learning approach. In Rivera-Trigueros, I., López-Alcarria, A., Ruiz-Padillo, D., Olvera-Lobo, M., & Gutiérrez-Pérez, J. (Eds.), *Using disruptive methodologies and game-based learning to foster transversal skills* (pp. 106–130). IGI Global Publishing. DOI: 10.4018/978-1-7998-8645-7.ch006

Zheng, R. (2024). Considerations on human cognitive processes in AI learning: an individual difference perspective. Poster presentation at *the 23rd International Conference on WWW/Internet 2024*. Zagreb, Coatia.

Zheng, R., McAlack, M., Wilmes, B., Kohler-Evans, P., & Williamson, J. (2009). Effects of multimedia on cognitive load, self-efficacy, and multiple rule-based problem solving. *British Journal of Educational Technology*, *40*(5), 790–803. DOI: 10.1111/j.1467-8535.2008.00859.x

Zheng, R., Spears, J., Luptak, M., & Wilby, F. (2015). Understanding older adults' perceptions of Internet use: An exploratory factor analysis. *Educational Gerontology*, *41*(7), 504–518. DOI: 10.1080/03601277.2014.1003495

KEY TERMS AND DEFINITIONS

Cognitive Load: Cognitive load refers to mental effort (otherwise called mental load) that the learner experiences during learning. There are three types of cognitive load: intrinsic, extraneous and germane cognitive load. Each represents a particular mental state pertains to learning.

Extraneous Cognitive Load: Extraneous cognitive load pertains to the mental load that the learner experiences in learning. Extraneous cognitive load is caused by the improper design in instruction that requires additional cognitive resource of the learner to process information. Such process imposes cognitive load on learners and is deemed unnecessary in learning.

Germane Cognitive Load: Germane cognitive load is related to the learner's effort in learning new knowledge and solving problems. It is considered a healthy cognitive load and should be nurtured and encouraged.

ICAP Framework: Proposed by M. Chi who distinguished four types of learning activities: **I**nteractive, **C**onstructive, **A**ctive and **P**assive (ICAP). Chi argues that active learning is different from constructive and interactive learning with latter engages the learner in deeper and more creative type of processes.

Intrinsic Cognitive Load: Intrinsic cognitive load is a type of cognitive load that relates to the complexity of the content. It is defined by the level of element interactivity of the content. The higher the elemen interactivity, the higher the intrinsic cognitive load. Educators and instructional designers work to develop instructional strategies to reduce the intrinsic cognitive load to optimize learning for learners.

Self-Determination Theory (SDT): SDT is proposed by Daci and colleagues to explain the relationship between affective aspects of learning and achievement. The theory focuses on psychological needs that drive learner's learning, which include autonomy, needs, competence and relatedness.

Working Memory: Working memory refers to the cognitive mechanism in the brain that stores and processes information for us. It mainly consists of three key components: visual-spatial sketch pad, phonological loop, and central executive. Working memory is limited. Its function can be affected when overloaded with too much information.

Chapter 10
Design and Development Effective Learning AI Education:
Navigating Deskilling in the Age of Intelligent Automation

Hanh Le
https://orcid.org/0009-0007-8172-0809
University of the Cumberlands, USA

ABSTRACT

The rapid integration of artificial intelligence (AI) into education and professional practice has brought about transformative opportunities and pressing ethical challenges. This chapter examines the principles, guidelines, and responsibilities that students must understand and follow when interacting with AI technologies. This chapter examines key topics, including academic integrity, data privacy, algorithmic bias, intellectual property, and the responsible use of generative AI tools such as ChatGPT and GitHub Copilot. Through real-world case studies, theoretical frameworks, and practical scenarios, the chapter fosters critical thinking and ethical reasoning among computer science students. It also provides educators with strategies for promoting ethical awareness and decision-making in AI-assisted learning environments. By grounding technical education in strong ethical foundations, this chapter aims to prepare future programmers and engineers to contribute to a trustworthy and socially responsible AI landscape.

DOI: 10.4018/979-8-3373-2927-7.ch010

INTRODUCTION

Artificial Intelligence (AI) is rapidly transforming the field of computer science, shaping how students learn, how software is developed, and the overall impact of technology on society. With coding assistants, AI has become a central component of how computer science students learn and prepare for their careers. As these technologies become more accessible and powerful, students must not only acquire technical skills but also develop a strong understanding of the ethical responsibilities that come with their use.

The rise of generative AI tools, such as ChatGPT and GitHub Copilot, with code completion capabilities, has introduced new opportunities for learning, collaboration, and productivity. However, it has also raised significant ethical questions about academic honesty, authorship, data privacy, fairness, and accountability. Without clear guidance and critical awareness, students may unintentionally misuse AI tools, negatively affect their learning outcomes, or participate in practices that conflict with professional and academic standards.

This chapter employs deskilling theory (Braverman, 1974) as a theoretical framework to examine how excessive reliance on AI may erode students' fundamental skills and diminish their ownership of their work. Deskilling theory highlights how automation can shift responsibility away from the human operator to an automated system. Applying this perspective, the chapter examines the tension between efficiency and deep learning, raising significant ethical and educational concerns about the long-term implications of AI-assisted education. The chapter also introduces the principles of fairness, transparency, responsibility, and respect for human dignity. Each section is designed to help students reflect on real-world dilemmas, evaluate their decisions, and act with integrity in an increasingly AI-driven environment.

By blending theoretical insights, case studies, and practical strategies, the chapter encourages computer students to think beyond coding to consider the societal impact of their work. Whether in the classroom, lab, or industry, ethical competence is no longer optional; it is essential for building trustworthy systems with the assistance of AI and shaping a digital future.

This chapter contributes to the literature by explicitly linking deskilling theory with AI-assisted education, offering a multidimensional framework for understanding the ethical, motivational, and behavioral impacts of generative AI on computer science students, and providing guidance for responsible curriculum design and professional practice.

The following Research Questions guide this study:

1. RQ1: How do programmers perceive and navigate challenges related to user experience in AI chatbot development?

2. RQ2: How do programmers address user interactions and feedback challenges during AI chatbot development?
3. RQ3: Considering technological advancements, how do programmers envision a future collaboration between humans and AI chatbots?

This chapter is organized as follows: Section 2 establishes the conceptual groundwork by presenting the theoretical frameworks that support the analysis. Section 3 offers a review of the existing literature on software development, the phenomenon of deskilling, and the integration of generative AI in programming practices. Section 4 outlines the qualitative research methodology employed to investigate these themes. Section 5 presents the study's principal findings, supported by illustrative case studies, and engages with their broader implications. The chapter concludes with Section 6, which addresses the study's limitations and outlines potential opportunities for future research.

BACKGROUND AND THEORETICAL FRAMEWORKS

This section lays the foundation for the study by first examining key developments in AI-assisted programming and exploring their implications for the field of computer science in software engineering practices. The rise of generative AI in coding education is part of a broader trend, aligning with longstanding theories that explain how technology influences work, skills, and human behavior. To better understand how AI tools are affecting students' learning experiences and educators' expectations, this chapter draws upon three theoretical perspectives: the Deskilling of Jobs Theory (DJT), Job Characteristics Theory (JCT), and Technology Threat Avoidance Theory (TTAT). These frameworks explore how generative AI transforms student' learning skills, changes their critical thinking strategies, and triggers behavioral responses in academic environments.

The integration of AI-powered coding tools into software development is gaining significant momentum worldwide. Daigle (2024) conducted a survey involving 2,000 software development professionals from enterprise teams in the United States, Brazil, India, and Germany, focusing on their experiences with AI tools in professional settings. The findings reveal that while AI adoption is on the rise, its usage is primarily confined to the workplace for a notable portion of developers. Between 17% and 27% of respondents indicated that they had only used AI tools at work, challenging the common assumption that developers are widely experimenting with these technologies outside of professional environments. Participants also reported perceived improvements in code quality due to the use of AI tools, as 90% of respondents in the U.S. and 81% in India observed an enhancement in code quality, with similar sentiments expressed by 61% in Brazil and 60% in Germany. These figures suggest that the benefits of AI-assisted programming are recognized across diverse regions.

Expectations regarding AI's potential were also high among those who had integrated such tools into their workflow. Many respondents, ranging from 61% in Germany to 73% in the U.S., believed that AI coding tools could significantly improve their ability to meet customer requirements. This optimism was shared across industries, reflecting a broad and growing confidence in the value that generative AI brings to software development in general, as well as to computer science students in the classroom (Daigle, 2024).

Deskilling of Jobs Theory

The Deskilling of Jobs Theory, grounded in Marxist labor critique and later advanced by scholar Harry Braverman (1974), argues that technological advancement can lead to the erosion of workers' autonomy, discretion, and craftsmanship. Braverman documented how machinery and automation fragmented skilled labor, shifting control from workers to systems. Applied to education, particularly programming education, deskilling theory suggests that generative AI tools may similarly displace essential cognitive processes by automating problem-solving and coding tasks.

Rather than utilizing knowledge through traditional debugging and coding skills, students who use AI tools might over-depend on system-generated code without fully understanding the fundamentals of software development. This reliance has implications not only for long-term skill retention but also for identity formation within the discipline; students may graduate with fewer problem-solving capabilities and reduced confidence in their ability to perform without AI assistance. In this way, generative AI may contribute to an academic parallel of the labor deskilling process, automating away the very skills that education aims to build and help students for the future.

Job Characteristics Theory

While deskilling theory highlights the erosion of skills and autonomy, Job Characteristics Theory, proposed by Hackman and Oldham (1976), offers an overview for evaluating the motivational and psychological effects of work design, including learning tasks. According to this theory, five core job dimensions — skill variety, task identity, task significance, autonomy, and feedback — determine critical psychological states that influence the motivation, satisfaction, and performance of workers dealing with technology.

Within the academic environment, the design of assignments and learning environments shapes how students experience these dimensions. For example, the use of AI tools may increase feedback immediacy, offering real-time corrections and explanations for students doing programming tasks. However, such tools may simultaneously reduce autonomy and task identity, as students rely on AI suggestions rather than initiating and completing code independently. Similarly, skill variety may diminish when learners consistently use AI-generated templates or solutions, minimizing exposure to diverse coding practices and problem types (Avila-Chauvet et al., 2023).

By mapping these job characteristics into the educational process, instructors and curriculum designers can more effectively evaluate the impact of AI tools. If AI tools make tasks so easy that students become disengaged, it can weaken the motivation needed for deep, meaningful learning. However, when used thoughtfully, AI has the potential to enrich the learning experience by increasing task variety, providing helpful feedback, and supporting student autonomy. This approach encourages learners to engage actively with AI as partners in the learning process, rather than relying on it as a source of ready-made answers (Khurana et al., 2024).

Technology Threat Avoidance Theory

While the previous two theories emphasize skill formation and work design, the Technology Threat Avoidance Theory (TTAT) focuses on how individuals perceive and respond to threats posed by emerging technologies. Initially developed by Liang and Xue (2009) to study cybersecurity behavior, TTAT suggests that users engage in protective or avoidant behaviors based on the perceived severity of threats, their vulnerability, and the efficacy of available safeguards.

In education, TTAT can help explain both student and faculty behavior in response to the adoption of generative AI. Some educators view AI tools as a threat to academic integrity and academic norms, prompting the adoption of restrictive policies or a complete avoidance of them. Likewise, students who fear being accused of plagiarism or who lack confidence in using AI responsibly may avoid these tools altogether. On the other hand, some users downplay the potential risks associated with overreliance on AI or overlooking possible ethical concerns.

TTAT also emphasizes the importance of safeguarding the effectiveness of institutional guidelines, training, and ethical education that enable students to use AI responsibly. When learners are equipped with the knowledge to critically evaluate AI outputs, understand their limitations, and integrate them appropriately into their work, the perceived threat diminishes, and constructive engagement becomes more likely. Without such structures, however, students may experience anxiety, misuse the tools, or avoid them entirely, hindering the potential benefits of AI-augmented learning.

MAIN FOCUS OF THE CHAPTER

Together, these three frameworks — Deskilling Theory, Job Characteristics Theory, and Technology Threat Avoidance Theory — provide a multidimensional perspective on how generative AI intersects with the educational environment. Deskilling theory emphasizes the loss of critical competencies when automation supplants human cognitive abilities. Job Characteristics Theory explains how AI alters students' motivational and psychological experiences during learning. TTAT reveals the behavioral responses to perceived risks, emphasizing the need for proactive guidance and ethical scaffolding. By applying these lenses throughout the chapter, we aim to unpack the nuanced impacts of generative AI and propose balanced approaches for its responsible integration in programming education.

Table 1. Mapping interview questions to research questions and theoretical Frameworks

Interview Question	Mapped RQ	Theoretical Framework(s)	Explanation
Q1. Please introduce yourself, including your background and experience in AI chatbot development.	N/A	N/A	Establishes participant context; not directly mapped to RQs or frameworks.
Q2. Do you use AI chatbots in your daily life? For example, ChatGPT or GitHub Copilot?	N/A	N/A	Background usage supports contextual understanding.
Q3. Do you use AI chatbots on your job? If so, how exactly? Please give an example.	N/A	N/A	Gathers descriptive data; helps frame participant relevance.
Q4. Can you describe the specific challenges you face as a programmer in a world dominated by AI and chatbots?	RQ1	JCT, DJT, TTAT	Examines how AI influences perceptions of skill erosion, task complexity, and perceived threats to skills.
Q5. How has the emergence of AI and chatbots impacted your day-to-day work and responsibilities?	RQ1	DJT	Focuses on automation and potential deskilling in routine programming tasks.
Q6. Can you share a specific instance where you encountered a challenge related to integrating or collaborating with AI technologies?	RQ1	DJT	Identifies concrete impacts of AI on job complexity and cognitive effort.

continued on following page

Table 1. Continued

Interview Question	Mapped RQ	Theoretical Framework(s)	Explanation
Q7. How do you incorporate user interactions and feedback into the development cycle of an AI chatbot?	RQ2	TTAT	Examines how developers perceive and respond to risks or limitations in feedback design.
Q8. What strategies have you adopted to adapt to the evolving programming landscape with the rise of AI and chatbots? How do you stay updated on the latest developments? Provide examples of adaptation or innovation.	RQ2	DJT, JCT, TTAT	Explores adaptation behaviors, proactive learning, and responses to perceived technological threats.
Q9. What tools or methodologies effectively address user interaction and feedback challenges during AI chatbot development?	RQ2	DJT, JCT, TTAT	Investigate the perceived efficacy of tools, their alignment with job enrichment, and the framing of AI as a threat or an opportunity.
Q10. In what direction do you foresee your job field evolving, with AI potentially playing a distinct role?	RQ3	JCT, DJT	Look at projected role shifts, deskilling risks, and the future of job satisfaction.
Q11. Which skills will become crucial for an IT specialist in your field over the next five years?	RQ3	JCT	Highlights expected skills aligned with autonomy, skill variety, and task significance.

LITERATURE REVIEW

The ethical implications of AI in education and software development have attracted significant scholarly attention in recent years. Researchers have explored how generative AI tools such as ChatGPT and GitHub Copilot are reshaping learning environments, software engineering practices, and the professional identity of programmers. Much of this discourse is anchored in broader concerns about automation, integrity, and the future of work.

In the context of AI in education, Rinta-Kahila et al. (2023) and Crowston and Bolici (2025) apply deskilling theory to explore how persistent dependence on AI may undermine students' development of core competencies such as critical thinking, problem-solving, and hands-on coding proficiency. Their studies reveal that when students routinely rely on AI-generated outputs, without fully engaging in the underlying processes, there is a noticeable risk of skill wasting. Learners may become increasingly reliant on automated guidance, resulting in a shallow understanding of concepts and a weakened ability to transfer knowledge across tasks.

These studies collectively underscore the core premise of deskilling theory in the era of AI. While intelligent systems offer powerful support, their unchecked use can reconfigure the roles of learners and practitioners, shifting them from active problem-solvers to passive consumers of automated output. This shift has implications not only for educational quality but also for the long-term resilience and adaptability of the future workforce. As AI continues to evolve, integrating it responsibly into learning environments will require thoughtful instructional design, scaffolding strategies, and ongoing evaluation to ensure that human expertise remains central to the learning process.

Avila-Chauvet et al. (2023) explore the use of ChatGPT as a support tool for online behavioral task programming. Their study demonstrates that ChatGPT can assist students in understanding and constructing experimental tasks in behavioral research, particularly by providing real-time guidance and code generation. While the tool enhances efficiency and reduces programming barriers, the authors also caution against overreliance, emphasizing the need for critical engagement and foundational skill development to ensure meaningful learning outcomes.

Automation and the Deskilling Debate

The rise of automation has raised the debate in labor and educational research: Does technological advancement empower workers and learners by augmenting their skills, or does it undermine human expertise by replacing cognitive labor with machine capabilities? This tension lies at the heart of deskilling theory. Generative AI systems such as GitHub Copilot and ChatGPT offer real-time code generation, debugging suggestions, and language explanations that significantly reduce the cognitive load on students. While this can enhance productivity and accessibility, it also poses the risk of cognitive offloading, wherein learners begin to rely on external tools instead of understanding the concepts and building their problem-solving capabilities. This shift reflects a core concern of the deskilling theory. When a machine assumes a task once performed by a human, the human's capacity to accomplish that task independently may gradually reduce.

Recent studies underscore these concerns. Crowston and Bolici (2025) found that programmers who relied heavily on AI assistance developed lower confidence in their coding abilities and showed reduced initiative in solving unfamiliar problems. Similarly, Rinta-Kahila et al. (2023) observed that AI-assisted software developers often experience a narrowing of their skill set, relying on tool-generated solutions instead of critically evaluating multiple approaches. In education, this AI-assisted system is particularly alarming, as students are still developing foundational competencies.

The deskilling debate is further complicated by contrasting arguments in favor of skill augmentation. Some researchers argue that AI can serve as a learning companion, providing real-time feedback, exposing students to industry-relevant practices, and enabling learners to tackle more complex tasks earlier in their development. From this perspective, automation is not inherently deskilling; rather, it depends on how the technology is used and what pedagogical structures support its integration. When students are taught to critically engage with AI outputs—rather than unquestioningly accept them—their learning may be enhanced, not hindered.

Nevertheless, the deskilling framework remains a critical lens through which to interrogate the ethical and developmental risks of automation in education. Instructors and institutions must consider whether their use of AI tools promotes deep learning or passive dependence and how curricular choices either reinforce or resist the erosion of human expertise. Without thoughtful design and intentional safeguards, the conveniences of automation may come at the cost of long-term competence, creativity, and professional agency.

Generative AI in Computer Science Education

The integration of generative AI tools into computer science education is reshaping how students learn, practice, and apply programming concepts. Tools such as ChatGPT, GitHub Copilot, and similar large language models (LLMs) are now widely accessible and capable of generating code snippets, offering real-time explanations, and solving complex programming problems in natural language. These tools are increasingly embedded in classroom environments, coding assignments, and self-directed learning, prompting both enthusiasm and concern from educators and researchers.

Moreover, generative AI can support creative problem-solving by suggesting multiple solutions and enabling experimentation with code structures that students may not have considered on their own. This new support aligns with constructivist learning principles, where learners build knowledge through exploration and iteration. AI can thus be positioned as a partner in learning, expanding the range of programming experiences and introducing students to industry-relevant development practices early in their education.

There are also unresolved issues around authorship and academic integrity. When a student uses AI-generated content in coursework, questions arise about the originality of the work and the appropriate way to attribute such assistance. Many institutions have yet to establish clear policies regarding the acceptable use of AI tools, leaving students uncertain about what constitutes ethical practice.

From a broader curricular perspective, the presence of generative AI is prompting educators to rethink assessment design. Traditional programming exercises may no longer be sufficient to measure authentic learning if students can easily generate answers with minimal effort. In response, some instructors are adopting AI-aware assessments, such as asking students to critique or improve AI-generated code, document their problem-solving process, or reflect on the decisions they made during the development process.

In summary, generative AI is rapidly transforming computer science education by providing support, feedback, and automation. While it has the potential to enhance learning, it also demands a recalibration of pedagogy, policy, and ethical guidance. To ensure responsible integration, educators must not only teach students how to use these tools but also why, when, and under what conditions their use is appropriate. Without such guidance, the benefits of generative AI may be overshadowed by diminished learning outcomes and increased ethical ambiguity.

Ethical Implications of AI Use in Academia

The widespread adoption of generative AI in academic environments, particularly within computer science education, has introduced complex ethical challenges that educators and institutions are only beginning to address fully. As tools like ChatGPT, GitHub Copilot, and other AI-powered assistants become common in classrooms, the boundaries between legitimate learning support and academic misconduct are becoming increasingly blurred.

One of the most pressing concerns is the erosion of academic integrity. AI tools can generate entire code solutions, essays, and explanations with minimal human input. While these outputs can be used ethically, for example, as learning aids or sources of inspiration, students may also submit AI-generated content as their work without proper understanding or attribution. This helper raises serious questions about plagiarism, authorship, and originality, especially in coursework that traditionally relies on individual effort and problem-solving.

Another ethical implication involves transparency and disclosure. Should students be required to report when and how they use AI tools in their assignments? Should AI usage be considered similar to citing a source, or is it fundamentally different due to the collaborative and interactive nature of the technology? These questions remain largely unresolved, and institutional policies vary widely. In many cases, the absence of formal guidelines creates uncertainty for both students and instructors, increasing the likelihood of unintentional ethical violations.

Beyond academic honesty, the use of AI in academia raises concerns about equity and access. Students from well-resourced backgrounds may have more consistent access to advanced AI tools, while others may rely on outdated systems or lack internet connectivity. This digital divide can exacerbate existing educational inequalities, creating unfair advantages for some students. Additionally, AI systems themselves may reproduce biases embedded in training data, leading to misleading outputs, particularly when applied to natural language tasks or code involving culturally sensitive variables.

There is also the issue of data privacy. Some AI platforms collect data from users to improve their models, raising ethical questions about how student interactions are stored, analyzed, and potentially used without informed consent. In educational settings, where students may unknowingly input sensitive or identifiable information into AI tools, clear data governance policies are crucial for safeguarding their privacy.

In response to these concerns, many scholars and institutions are calling for the development of ethical frameworks and usage guidelines tailored to academic contexts. These include promoting transparency, encouraging reflective use of AI, and establishing clear expectations around attribution and collaboration. Ethics education is increasingly recognized as a vital component of technical training, enabling students to understand not only how to utilize AI tools but also how to evaluate their impact on fairness, trust, and personal responsibility.

Stefaniak and Moore (2024) examine how generative AI can be utilized to facilitate inclusive design and collaborative decision-making in online instruction. Their study emphasizes the potential of AI tools to encourage broader participation in instructional design processes, enhance accessibility, and promote learner-centered practices. The authors also address ethical considerations and the importance of intentional implementation to avoid reinforcing existing biases or inequities.

In summary, the ethical implications of AI in academia extend far beyond simple misconduct. They encompass issues of authentic learning, institutional trust, digital equity, and professional development. As generative AI continues to evolve, educational institutions must take a proactive role in shaping ethical norms and ensuring that students are equipped to navigate this complex technological landscape with integrity and awareness.

Student Perceptions and Behavioral Shifts

As generative AI tools become increasingly integrated into academic workflows, understanding how students perceive and interact with these technologies is essential to evaluating their broader impact on learning, ethics, and professional development. Student perceptions not only shape how AI is used in practice but also influence behavioral patterns that may lead to long-term shifts in skill acquisition, academic integrity, and identity formation within the discipline of computer science.

However, this positive perception is accompanied by behavioral shifts that raise pedagogical and ethical concerns. A growing number of students report using AI tools to complete entire assignments, sometimes without fully understanding the generated solutions. In such cases, AI becomes less of a learning aid and more of a shortcut, facilitating task completion without skill mastery. This behavior aligns with the concerns outlined in deskilling theory, which posits that automation reduces the need for deep engagement, practice, and independent problem-solving.

Moreover, student behavior often reflects a lack of clarity around academic boundaries. In the absence of clear guidelines, some students rationalize the use of AI as equivalent to using a search engine or collaborating with a peer, blurring the lines between acceptable and unethical behavior. This ambiguity can lead to inconsistent application of academic standards, both among students and across institutions. Some students express concern about being penalized for using tools they believe are commonly accepted, while others deliberately conceal their use to avoid accusations of misconduct.

Importantly, student perceptions are not static. Exposure to ethics education, instructor expectations, and peer norms can all influence how learners approach AI. When ethical considerations are embedded into the curriculum, such as requiring students to document how AI tools were used or reflect on the reasoning behind their solutions, students tend to become more thoughtful and intentional in their behavior. This behavior suggests that institutional culture plays a critical role in shaping student attitudes and fostering responsible use.

Additionally, students are starting to express nuanced concerns about the long-term effects of AI dependence. Some worry that overreliance on AI tools may leave them underprepared for job interviews, technical assessments, or real-world coding scenarios that require a solid foundation in knowledge and skills. Others recognize a tension between speed and depth, acknowledging that while AI may help them complete tasks more quickly, it does not necessarily lead to a deeper understanding of the subject matter.

Finally, the use of AI is influencing students' emerging professional identities. In some cases, students begin to see themselves more as system integrators or AI supervisors than as traditional coders. While this shift can be seen as an adaptation to new technological realities, it also raises questions about what it means to be a competent and ethical software developer in an age of intelligent automation.

Barke et al. (2023) investigate how programmers interact with code-generating models, such as GitHub Copilot, in real-world development settings. Through an empirical study, they identify that while these tools accelerate coding and reduce syntactic effort, they also introduce new challenges related to code comprehension, debugging, and maintaining developer engagement. The authors emphasize the need for thoughtful integration of AI tools to ensure that productivity gains do not come at the expense of deeper understanding and developer agency.

In summary, student perceptions of AI tools are shaped by a complex mix of enthusiasm, ambiguity, and self-reflection. These perceptions drive behavioral shifts that can both support and hinder learning outcomes. To foster ethical, meaningful engagement with AI, educational institutions must provide clear guidance, embed reflective practices, and ensure that students understand not only how to use AI but also why and when its use aligns with both academic values and professional expectations.

Academic Integrity Frameworks in AI-Mediated Environments

The rapid adoption of AI tools in software development and education has prompted renewed attention to academic integrity and ethical practice. Studies have shown that reliance on AI assistants, such as ChatGPT and code-generating models, can inadvertently encourage cognitive offloading and skill erosion, potentially compromising learning outcomes and ethical standards (Barke et al., 2023; Crowston & Bolici, 2025; Rinta-Kahila et al., 2023). In programming education, AI tools may unintentionally enable students to bypass critical thinking and problem-solving steps, raising concerns about academic honesty and the acquisition of meaningful skills (Avila-Chauvet et al., 2023; Kuhail et al., 2023).

To address these challenges, researchers have highlighted the need for institutional frameworks that combine policy, pedagogy, and assessment strategies. Explicit guidance on AI use, scaffolded assignments, and reflective exercises can help students internalize responsible AI practices while maintaining core programming competencies (Khurana et al., 2024; Stefaniak & Moore, 2024). For example, structured activities that require students to annotate AI-generated code, compare alternative solutions, or justify modifications foster critical engagement and reinforce ethical decision-making.

Moreover, aligning classroom interventions with institutional policies enhances their effectiveness. When educators provide clear guidance and ethical scaffolding, students are better equipped to navigate AI tools responsibly and avoid misuse (Daigle, 2024; Liang & Xue, 2009). Conversely, limited oversight or ambiguous policies may lead to over-reliance on automated solutions, contributing to skill erosion and ethical lapses (Braverman, 1974; Hackman & Oldham, 1976).

Ultimately, cross-cultural and contextual factors influence the adoption of AI-mediated learning and integrity frameworks. Research suggests that institutions must consider local norms, available resources, and curricular expectations when implementing AI-integrity policies to ensure broad applicability and effectiveness (Riazi et al., 2023). By integrating comprehensive academic integrity frameworks, educational programs can strike a balance between innovation and ethical responsibility, thereby fostering both technical competence and the principled use of AI tools.

Institutional and Educational Responses

As generative AI becomes an everyday presence in computer science programs, colleges and universities are developing multifaceted responses that combine policy, curriculum redesign, faculty development, and student support. These efforts aim to harness the benefits of AI while safeguarding academic integrity and preserving the depth of learning.

Policy formation and clarity

Most institutions now recognize that vague "don't plagiarize" statements are insufficient in an AI-rich environment. Forward-thinking universities have issued explicit guidelines that:

- **Define acceptable versus unacceptable AI use** (e.g., brainstorming ideas vs. submitting unedited AI-generated code).
- **Require disclosure**—students must indicate when and how AI tools were used in assignments, akin to citing a source.
- **Outline penalties** for undisclosed or excessive reliance on AI output.

Where policies are co-created with faculty and student representatives, compliance and ethical awareness rise markedly, reducing unintentional misconduct.

AI-aware assessment design

Tools like Copilot easily solve traditional auto-graded programming problems. In response, instructors are:

- Shifting from output-based grading to process-based evaluation, students submit design rationales, debugging logs, or code reviews that reveal their thinking.
- Embedding reflection prompts ("Explain why you accepted or rejected the AI's suggestion").
- Adopting oral defenses or live coding interviews to verify individual understanding.

These strategies align with Job Characteristics Theory by restoring task identity and meaningful feedback, discouraging superficial copying.

Curriculum integration of ethics and metacognition

Rather than banning AI, many programs teach "AI literacy", how large language models work, their limitations, and ethical pitfalls. Typical interventions include:

- Module-level ethics mini-lectures tied to real coding labs (e.g., bias in training data, licensing issues for generated code).
- Metacognitive checklists prompt students to question the accuracy of AI output, its security implications, and the long-term impact on their skills.
- Team projects where one role is the "AI skeptic," responsible for auditing tool suggestions.

Early evidence suggests that incorporating these elements enhances students' critical engagement without diminishing their enthusiasm for AI.

Faculty professional development

Many instructors initially felt ill-equipped to supervise AI use. Successful departments now offer:

- Hands-on workshops demonstrating AI capabilities and failure modes.
- Shared rubrics and exemplars that illustrate how to grade AI-augmented work fairly.
- Cross-disciplinary faculty learning communities where educators compare strategies across writing, design, and computing courses.

By normalizing experimentation and reflection, these programs help faculty model the ethical, inquisitive mindset they want students to adopt.

Supportive infrastructure and detection tools

Some universities deploy AI detection and provenance systems, but they are moving toward "trust-and-verify" models rather than relying solely on punitive surveillance. Complementary measures include:

- Version-control mandates (e.g., Git commits showing incremental development).
- Secure coding sandboxes that log AI interactions for later review and analysis.
- Open-source exemplars that demonstrate how to integrate AI responsibly, giving students positive templates to emulate.

Synthesis

Institutional and pedagogical responses reveal an emerging consensus: outright prohibition is neither practical nor desirable. Instead, success lies in transparent policies, process-oriented assessment, ethics-infused curricula, and well-supported faculty. When these elements align, AI becomes a catalyst for deeper learning, rather than a shortcut to superficial completion, addressing concerns about deskilling while preserving the creative and intellectual growth central to computer science education.

Gaps in Literature and Future Directions

Despite a growing body of research on the ethical implications of AI in computer science education, several critical gaps remain. These gaps limit our understanding of how AI tools are truly affecting student learning, ethical behavior, and long-term professional development. Addressing these areas is crucial for developing a more comprehensive, inclusive, and forward-looking framework for the moral integration of AI.

Lack of longitudinal studies on skill retention

Most existing studies provide short-term snapshots of how students use AI tools; however, there is a lack of longitudinal evidence on how this usage impacts long-term skill development. For example, it remains unclear whether frequent reliance on tools like ChatGPT or GitHub Copilot weakens students' ability to code independently over time. Longitudinal research is necessary to determine whether learners assisted by AI develop into equally competent and adaptable professionals as those trained through traditional, manual learning methods.

Underrepresentation of student voices and ethical reasoning

While many studies focus on teacher perspectives or institutional policies, few deeply explore how students themselves perceive the ethical use of AI. Research rarely addresses how students form their ethical frameworks, how they navigate ambiguous situations involving AI-generated content, or how their sense of professional identity evolves. Future work should adopt student-centered qualitative approaches, such as interviews or narrative inquiry, to gain a deeper understanding of how learners experience and rationalize the use of AI.

Limited cross-cultural and global perspectives

Much of the research on AI ethics in education has been conducted in North America and Europe, often overlooking the influence of cultural values, educational norms, and regulatory environments on attitudes toward AI use in other regions. As AI becomes increasingly accessible globally, it is crucial to examine how students in diverse cultural and institutional contexts interpret concepts such as academic integrity, authorship, and fairness. Comparative studies across regions can enrich ethical guidelines with culturally sensitive insights.

Inadequate focus on institutional policy design and enforcement

While ethical frameworks are frequently discussed in theoretical terms, there is a lack of empirical research on how universities craft and enforce policies related to AI use in coursework. Questions remain about how clear, consistent, and effective these policies are in practice. Additionally, little is known about how faculty are trained to address AI-related misconduct or how students are taught to navigate these policies. Future research should evaluate institutional strategies and their impact on ethical outcomes.

Need for educational innovation grounded in theory

Although some educators are experimenting with AI-integrated assignments and assessments, there is a lack of theory-driven instructional models for teaching the ethical use of AI. Few approaches intentionally align with frameworks such as deskilling theory or job characteristics theory to ensure that educational design supports both ethical reasoning and skill retention. Future work should focus on developing and testing curriculum models that apply these theories to bridge the gap between ethics and practice.

To address these gaps, researchers, educators, and institutions should consider the following directions:

- Design mixed-methods studies to assess both learning outcomes and ethical development over time.
- Incorporate student voices through participatory research, ethnography, or digital diaries that capture their lived experiences with AI.
- Expand research to underrepresented regions and educational systems, particularly in Asia, Africa, and Latin America.
- Develop and evaluate institutional frameworks for AI use that are enforceable, transparent, and adaptable to emerging tools.

- Create open-source, theory-informed teaching materials that guide ethical AI engagement across the curriculum.

By following these directions, the academic community can better prepare computer science students not only to use AI effectively but also to contribute meaningfully to the development of ethical and responsible technologies.

Summary of Key Insights

The literature on generative AI in computer science education reveals a rapidly evolving landscape that is both promising and perilous. On the one hand, AI tools like ChatGPT and GitHub Copilot offer significant educational benefits, enhancing accessibility, providing real-time feedback, and accelerating skill acquisition. On the other hand, these tools raise critical concerns about academic integrity, authorship, student dependency, and the erosion of long-term skills.

Through the lens of deskilling theory, scholars have cautioned that overreliance on automation can undermine the very learning outcomes that educational institutions aim to foster. Complementary frameworks such as job characteristics theory and technology threat avoidance theory further illuminate how students interact with AI, the motivational factors at play, and the psychological and ethical tensions that arise in AI-rich learning environments.

Research findings consistently show that student perceptions are mixed, shaped by convenience, uncertainty, and evolving norms. Behavioral shifts, toward shortcut-based task completion, diminished self-efficacy, and ambiguity about what constitutes fair use are emerging as key concerns. In response, institutions are developing policies and pedagogical approaches aimed at striking a balance: allowing students to benefit from AI tools while maintaining ethical standards and preserving deep learning.

Despite these advances, the literature also reveals several persistent gaps. These include a lack of longitudinal data on skill retention, insufficient student-centered research on ethical reasoning, and a need for more global and cross-cultural perspectives. Moreover, the development of coherent, theory-driven pedagogical models that integrate AI responsibly remains limited.

In summary, the literature underscores the urgent need for ethics of AI integration tools in computer science education. As the field continues to evolve, future research must not only monitor outcomes but also shape the values, practices, and institutional cultures that guide the use of AI in the classroom and beyond.

METHODOLOGY

This study adhered to established best practices in qualitative research, employing a phenomenological approach to explore how individuals experience the integration of generative AI into programming education. Phenomenology, as defined by Peoples (2021), aims to understand the essence of lived experiences, distinguishing it from other qualitative methods by its deep focus on personal meaning and perception.

Semi-structured, open-ended research questions were employed to guide the inquiry, providing participants with the flexibility to share detailed reflections while maintaining consistency across interviews. Triangulation was applied by comparing data from participants with diverse roles, backgrounds, and experiences to enhance the credibility of the findings.

Member checking was conducted with selected participants, who were invited to review preliminary interpretations of their responses. This process helped ensure the accuracy and trustworthiness of the data analysis (Riazi et al., 2023). Additionally, the researcher engaged in reflexive journaling throughout the study to record analytical decisions, reflect on personal assumptions, and minimize potential bias.

Ethical standards were consistently upheld throughout the research process. Participant confidentiality was maintained by removing identifying information from transcripts, and all data were securely stored on password-protected devices. Transparency and respect for participant autonomy were central to the study's design, ensuring informed consent and voluntary participation.

Research Design

This study employed a qualitative research design centered on in-depth, semi-structured interviews to investigate how programmers and students experience the integration of generative AI in software development and coding education. The research approach was qualitative, designed to capture rich, contextualized insights and personal narratives. The goal was not to generalize findings to a broad population but to uncover nuanced patterns, perceptions, and meaning-making processes that emerge from individual engagement with AI tools in real-world settings.

Participant Selection

Participants were recruited using purposive sampling, targeting individuals with direct experience in programming and the development of AI chatbots. The sample consisted of fifteen participants, comprising undergraduate and graduate computer science students, as well as professional software developers. This diversity of perspectives enabled a deeper understanding of how generative AI is perceived and applied across different levels of expertise and contexts. All participants reported some level of interaction with tools such as ChatGPT, GitHub Copilot, or similar large language model-based systems.

Participants were invited through academic networks, professional contacts, and university listservs. Before each interview, participants were informed of the consent process and assured of confidentiality, with the option to withdraw at any time. No financial compensation was offered.

Data Collection

Semi-structured, in-depth data were collected through interviews conducted via Zoom between 45 and 75 minutes. The interview protocol was designed to elicit reflections on several core topics, including experiences with AI-assisted coding, perceptions of skill development and task ownership, ethical considerations, strategies for adapting to AI in the workplace or classroom, and visions for future human-AI collaboration.

Interviews followed a flexible structure, allowing participants to expand on issues that were most salient to them. This format enabled the researcher to probe deeper into emergent themes while maintaining consistency across interviews. All sessions were recorded with participant consent and subsequently transcribed verbatim for analysis.

Analytical Approach

Data analysis followed a thematic coding approach, combining both inductive and deductive strategies. Transcripts were first reviewed holistically to identify recurring concepts, language patterns, and points of emphasis. Initial codes were generated based on both participant responses and the theoretical frameworks guiding this study, namely, Deskilling Theory, Job Characteristics Theory, and Technology Threat Avoidance Theory.

Subsequent rounds of coding involved grouping similar responses, identifying contradictions or tensions, and mapping findings to the three research questions:

- RQ1: How do programmers perceive and navigate challenges related to user experience in AI chatbot development?
- RQ2: How do programmers address user interactions and feedback challenges during AI chatbot development?
- RQ3: Considering technological advancements, how do programmers envision a future collaboration between humans and AI chatbots?

Coding and organization of thematic categories were conducted using qualitative data analysis software (MaxQDA), which facilitated data visualization and ensured consistency in identifying themes across interviews.

Trustworthiness

This study followed several best practices in qualitative research. Triangulation was employed by comparing data across participants with varied roles and experiences. Member checking was conducted with select participants who reviewed preliminary interpretations of their responses to confirm accuracy. Additionally, the researcher employed reflexive journaling to document analytical decisions and mitigate potential bias in the interpretation of data.

The study also upheld ethical research principles, including confidentiality, transparency, and respect for participant autonomy. All data were stored on password-protected devices, and identifiers were removed from transcripts during analysis.

Ethical Considerations

The study received ethical clearance from the relevant Institutional Review Board (IRB). All participants provided informed consent, and confidentiality was maintained through the use of pseudonyms and secure data storage. Participants were informed of their right to withdraw from the study at any time without penalty or consequence.

SOLUTIONS AND RECOMMENDATIONS

This section presents the study's significant findings, organized by the three research questions. Drawing on participants' interviews, institutional perspectives, and theoretical frameworks, including deskilling theory, job characteristics theory, and technology threat avoidance theory, each subsection discusses how programmers navigate the technical, ethical, and human-centered dimensions of AI chatbot development.

RQ1: How Do Programmers Perceive and Navigate Challenges Related to User Experience in AI Chatbot Development?

Job Characteristics Theory and Deskilling Theory primarily inform this question. Job Characteristics Theory helps frame how programmers experience task significance, skill variety, and autonomy when designing chatbot interactions. Meanwhile,

Deskilling Theory highlights the risk that automation may reduce opportunities for human-centered problem solving. Together, these frameworks shape the analysis of programmers' struggles with balancing technical efficiency against empathy, inclusivity, and ethical considerations in AI chatbot development.

Theme 1: Tension between automation and empathy

Programmers struggle to design chatbot responses that feel human, especially in emotionally sensitive contexts. They recognize the limits of AI in understanding tone, nuance, and cultural sensitivity.

Theme 2: Limitations of training data and inclusivity

Participants expressed concern that AI models are only as good as the data on which they are trained. Biases or narrow datasets can lead to exclusionary or inaccurate responses, creating ethical and UX challenges.

Theme 3: Balancing efficiency with ethical design

While pre-built frameworks and APIs improve development speed, they often restrict the ability to tailor the chatbot to specific user needs, leading some developers to feel ethically constrained or deskilled.

Practical Implications for Educators

Educators can design learning experiences that simulate real-world UX challenges with AI tools. For example, students can be asked to evaluate AI-generated responses for cultural sensitivity, inclusivity, or ethical appropriateness, then propose modifications. Case-based assignments or reflective exercises can help learners recognize the limits of AI while practicing human-centered design principles. This approach reinforces ethical reasoning, empathy, and critical thinking in the context of AI-assisted development.

RQ2: How Do Programmers Address User Interactions and Feedback Challenges During AI Chatbot Development?

This question is guided by Technology Threat Avoidance Theory (TTAT), which emphasizes how individuals perceive and respond to potential risks in digital environments. In the context of AI chatbots, TTAT highlights how programmers assess threats related to security, misuse, and ethical responsibility. By applying this framework, the findings demonstrate how developers strike a balance between the pressures of rapid deployment and the obligation to anticipate and mitigate risks, such as bias, misinformation, and user harm, while also incorporating structured feedback from instructors and peers to inform decision-making.

Theme 1: Educator influence and guidance

While student perspectives dominated the data, participants frequently referenced guidance from instructors. Structured feedback and ethical guidance from educators helped programmers critically evaluate AI outputs, mitigate over-reliance on automated suggestions, and refine interaction designs. Conversely, limited instructor involvement left some students unsure about the appropriate use of AI, highlighting the need for explicit guidance. These insights suggest actionable strategies such as incorporating instructor-led code reviews, scenario-based feedback exercises, and reflective assignments to reinforce responsible AI practices.

Theme 2: Cross-cultural and global considerations

Programmers highlighted that AI adoption and usage norms vary across cultural and educational contexts. Some have noted that students in regions with limited access to AI tools tend to rely more on traditional coding skills. In contrast, others benefit from exposure to AI in structured environments. These differences suggest that actionable strategies—such as modular training modules, culturally contextualized datasets, and peer mentoring—can support broader adoption while maintaining ethical standards.

Theme 3: Scaling AI integration

Participants discussed strategies for integrating AI at scale, including modular curriculum design, peer learning support, and institution-wide adoption of AI-aware platforms. By embedding feedback loops, scenario-based exercises, and collaborative problem-solving activities, developers can maintain skill development while expanding AI integration across teams or classrooms.

Practical Implications for Educators

To translate these insights into actionable practice, programmers and educators can design scaffolded activities, reflective assignments, and exercises that encourage critical evaluation of AI-generated outputs. For example, students might annotate or critique code suggestions from ChatGPT or GitHub Copilot, compare alternative

AI-generated solutions, or document reasoning behind accepting or modifying AI recommendations. Such interventions reinforce foundational programming skills, foster ethical reasoning, and help maintain cognitive engagement, while providing a structured approach to integrating AI at scale.

RQ3: Considering Technological Advancements, How Do Programmers Envision A Future Collaboration Between Humans and AI Chatbots?

This question draws on both Deskilling Theory and Job Characteristics Theory. Deskilling Theory foregrounds the concern that excessive reliance on AI could erode core programming and problem-solving skills. At the same time, Job Characteristics Theory sheds light on how the design of AI-supported tasks influences autonomy, feedback, and opportunities for skill development. Together, these frameworks highlight the tension programmers face between immediate productivity gains and long-term professional growth.

Theme 1: AI as a support tool, not a decision-maker

Most participants favored a hybrid model where chatbots assist but do not replace human decision-making, especially in high-stakes or morally complex environments.

Theme 2: Fear of deskilling and loss of human oversight

While developers appreciated AI's convenience, many worried that overreliance could erode critical thinking, reduce coding skills, or displace human expertise in the long term.

Theme 3: Redefining the programmer's role

Participants envisioned a shift from writing all logic by hand to curating, auditing, and ethically supervising AI behavior, embracing roles like product managers or code verifiers after receiving responses from AI.

Practical Implications for Educators

Instructors can create assignments that require iterative interaction with AI tools, prompting students to evaluate outputs critically, collaborate on debugging, and document their problem-solving processes. Peer-review sessions and group projects can reinforce collaboration, ethical decision-making, and skill retention. These strategies strike a balance between the efficiency gains from AI and opportunities for active learning, preserving foundational programming skills while encouraging strategic use of AI.

Summary of Findings and Case Studies

This study examined how programmers engage with ethical challenges, user interaction complexities, and future visions of human-AI collaboration in the context of AI chatbot development. Guided by deskilling theory, job characteristics theory, and technology threat avoidance theory, the research identified nuanced behavioral patterns, ethical tensions, and shifting professional roles. The findings are organized by research question and supported by illustrative case studies.

RQ1: User Experience Challenges in AI Chatbot Development

Programmers reported difficulty designing chatbots that maintain empathy, clarity, and contextual sensitivity. Many expressed frustrations with the limitations of pre-trained models and biased datasets, which hindered their ability to create inclusive and emotionally intelligent bots. Developers also felt ethically constrained by frameworks that prioritized speed and automation over customization and user care.

Themes:

1. Tension Between Automation and Empathy
2. Limitations of Training Data and Inclusivity
3. Balancing Efficiency with Ethical Design

Case study 1:

A participant, a graduate student working in a hospital environment as a software developer, struggled with generating responses that were emotionally appropriate. Although the AI could mimic specific therapeutic phrases, it lacked the nuance needed to avoid sounding dismissive or robotic. Linh eventually collaborated with psychology students to craft training prompts, demonstrating a human-centered approach that enhanced the chatbot's empathy while preserving technical efficiency.

RQ2: User Interaction and Feedback Integration

Participants described having limited access to formal user feedback systems, often relying on bug reports or negative reviews as their primary source of input. Without clear feedback loops, ethical blind spots emerged, especially when users encountered misinformation or felt misunderstood. However, some developers actively sought interdisciplinary collaboration to address these gaps, improving both product quality and ethical awareness.

Themes:

1. Lack of Structured Feedback Mechanisms
2. Ethical Accountability in Real-Time Systems
3. Cross-Disciplinary Collaboration as a Learning Opportunity

Case study 2:

A first-year computer science student noted that users often abandoned the chatbot mid-conversation. After analyzing logs, he discovered that the bot frequently misinterpreted questions from non-native English speakers. The participant proposed a feedback button and multilingual prompts, working closely with UX designers. The chatbot's engagement and satisfaction scores improved, and the team adopted this model for future iterations.

RQ3: Future Collaboration Between Humans and AI Chatbots

Programmers largely viewed AI as a complementary force that should support, rather than replace, human expertise. While optimistic about the productivity gains from generative AI, many also voiced concern about deskilling, loss of critical thinking, and over-automation. Participants envisioned future roles that combine technical development with ethical stewardship, curation, and user advocacy.

Themes:

1. AI as a Support Tool, not a Decision-Maker
2. Fear of Deskilling and Loss of Human Oversight
3. Redefining the Programmer's Role

Case study 3:

A senior computer science student, although the AI performed well, the participant expressed a fear of using AI, as she was uncertain about her job prospects after graduation, given that AI can outperform UI/UI, which is her area of focus in her senior year.

These findings suggest a pressing need for curriculum reform, the development of institutional policies, and collaboration between industry and academia that promotes both ethical literacy and sustainable human-AI design practices.

FUTURE RESEARCH DIRECTIONS

While this study offers valuable insights into the ethical, experiential, and professional aspects of AI chatbot development among computer science students and practitioners, several limitations must be acknowledged. First, the study was limited by a small sample size drawn from a limited number of academic institutions and development contexts. This small sample size restricts the generalizability of the findings, as they may not adequately represent the diverse perspectives of programmers from different regions, levels of expertise, or organizational settings. Second, the research employed an exploratory qualitative approach that prioritized depth over breadth. While this method yielded rich narrative and thematic insights, the findings cannot be statistically generalized without complementary quantitative studies. Third, the data were primarily self-reported through interviews and participant reflections, making it susceptible to biases such as social desirability or retrospective distortion; participants may have underreported unethical behaviors or overstated their engagement with ethical principles. Fourth, the study primarily focused on students and early-career developers, which, while valuable, limits insight into how experienced professionals and organizational leaders approach AI ethics in chatbot development at scale. Ultimately, the rapid evolution of generative AI technology poses a challenge for drawing long-term conclusions. New tools, regulations, and ethical concerns may arise that were not fully captured during the research. Building on these limitations, future research and practice can advance this field in several important ways:

Longitudinal and Mixed-Methods Research

Future studies should track participants over time to explore how their skills, ethical awareness, and AI usage evolve in academic and professional settings. Incorporating surveys and performance assessments would also complement qualitative insights.

Broader and More Diverse Sampling

Expanding participant demographics to include professionals from various industries, cultures, and seniority levels can provide a more comprehensive understanding of how ethical standards are understood and practiced across contexts.

Comparative Cross-Institutional Studies

Research comparing how different universities or training programs approach AI ethics could help identify best practices, challenges, and the effectiveness of various curriculum models in promoting ethical reasoning.

Integration of AI Ethics into Technical Curriculum

Future work should focus on developing and evaluating curriculum models that integrate AI ethics into coding, UX design, and systems development courses. These models should be co-developed with students, educators, and industry partners to ensure relevance and sustainability.

Exploration of New Professional Roles

As AI-human collaboration evolves, research should examine emerging roles such as prompt engineers, AI ethics officers, and human-in-the-loop designers. Understanding the skills and values these roles require can help reshape education and workforce development in ethical and forward-looking ways.

By acknowledging these limitations and pursuing targeted future directions, researchers and educators can better support the development of responsible AI practices in computer science education. Equipping students and professionals with both technical and ethical literacy is essential for sustaining meaningful human agency in an increasingly automated world.

CONCLUSION

The increasing integration of generative AI in software development, especially with the help of AI chatbots, presents both promising opportunities and complex ethical challenges. This chapter explored how students and programmers perceive and navigate user experience issues, address feedback and interaction complexities, and envision the future of collaboration between humans and AI systems. Grounded in deskilling theory, job characteristics theory, and technology threat avoidance theory, the findings highlight critical tensions between efficiency and ethical responsibility, automation and agency, and innovation and integrity.

Across all three research questions, participants demonstrated a growing awareness of their ethical responsibilities in shaping AI behavior, particularly in contexts where chatbots interact with users in emotionally or socially sensitive ways. While AI tools improve productivity and streamline development, they also risk displacing fundamental skills and distancing programmers from the social consequences of their work. Students and professionals alike are now operating in a space where they must balance technical proficiency with ethical discernment, often in the absence of clear institutional policies or pedagogical frameworks.

The study revealed an emerging redefinition of the programmer's role. No longer solely viewed as technical coders, programmers increasingly see themselves as content manager to evaluate code and accept the correct code for assignments or the working environment. This shift signals the need for educational institutions and industry stakeholders to adapt, redesigning curricula, assessment practices, and mentorship models that emphasize ethical reasoning, user-centered design, and responsible innovation.

This chapter demonstrates how generative AI tools influence skill development, ethical reasoning, and pedagogical practices in computer science education. By linking Deskilling Theory and Technology Threat Avoidance Theory with student experiences, it highlights the tensions between automation and critical learning. The findings underscore the importance of educator guidance, institutional policies, and scaffolded interventions in mitigating skill erosion and promoting the ethical use of AI. Practical strategies, such as reflective assignments, AI-generated code critique, and curriculum integration, translate insights into actionable teaching practice. Collectively, the chapter contributes a multidimensional framework for understanding AI's impact on learning while offering tangible guidance for educators, administrators, and policymakers.

REFERENCES

Avila-Chauvet, L., Mejía, D., & Acosta Quiroz, C. (2023). CHATGPT as a support tool for online behavioral task programming. *SSRN*. Obtenido de https://ssrn.com/abstract=4329020

Barke, S., James, M., & Polikarpova, N. (2023). Grounded Copilot: How programmers interact with code-generating models. *Proceedings of the ACM on Programming Languages, 7*(OOPSLA1), 85-111. DOI: 10.1145/3586030

Braverman, H. (1974). *Labor and monopoly capital*. Monthly Review Press. DOI: 10.14452/MR-026-03-1974-07_1

Crowston, K., & Bolici, F. (2025). Deskilling and upskilling with AI Systems. *nformation Research an International Electronic Journal, 30*(iConf), 1009-1023. DOI: 10.47989/ir30iConf47143

Daigle, K. (2024). *Survey: The AI wave continues to grow on software development teams*. Obtenido de https://github.blog/author/kdaigle/

Hackman, J. R., & Oldham, G. R. (1976). Motivation through the design of work: Test of a theory. *Organizational Behavior and Human Performance, 16*(2), 250–279. DOI: 10.1016/0030-5073(76)90016-7

Khurana, A., Subramonyam, H., & Chilana, P. K. (2024). Why and when llm-based assistants can go wrong: Investigating the effectiveness of prompt-based interactions for software help-seeking. *arXiv.org*. Obtenido de /arxiv.2402.08030DOI: 10.1145/3640543.3645200

Kuhail, M. A., Mathew, S. S., Khalil, A., Khalil, A., & Shah, S. J. (2023). "Will I be replaced?" Assessing ChatGPT's effect on software development and programmer perceptions of AI tools. *arXiv.org*. Obtenido de DOI: 10.2139/ssrn.4571482

Liang, H., & Xue, Y. (2009). Avoidance of information technology threats: A theoretical perspective. *Management Information Systems Quarterly, 33*(1), 71–90. DOI: 10.2307/20650279

Peoples, K. (2021). *How to write a phenomenological dissertation: A step-by-step guide* (Vol. 56). SAGE.

Riazi, M., Rezvani, R., & Ghanbar, H. (2023). Trustworthiness in L2 writing research: A review and analysis of qualitative articles in the Journal of Second Language Writing. *Research Methods in Applied Linguistics, 2*(3), 100065. Advance online publication. DOI: 10.1016/j.rmal.2023.100065

Rinta-Kahila, T., Penttinen, E., Salovaara, A., Soliman, W., & Ruissalo, J. (2023). The vicious circles of skill erosion: A case study of cognitive automation. *Journal of the Association for Information Systems*, *24*(5), 1378–1412. DOI: 10.17705/1jais.00829

Stefaniak, J., & Moore, S. (2024). The Use of Generative AI to Support Inclusivity and Design Deliberation for Online Instruction. *Online Learning : the Official Journal of the Online Learning Consortium*, *28*(3), 181–205. DOI: 10.24059/olj.v28i3.4458

KEY TERMS AND DEFINITIONS

Academic Integrity: Commitment to honesty, trust, fairness, respect, and responsibility in educational work. It includes the avoidance of plagiarism, cheating, and unauthorized assistance, as well as the proper use of AI-generated content.

Artificial Intelligence (AI): A field of computer science focused on creating systems capable of performing tasks that typically require human intelligence, such as reasoning, learning, problem-solving, and language understanding.

Bias in AI: Systematic and unfair discrimination that occurs in AI outputs due to biased training data, algorithms, or system design, often affecting marginalized groups disproportionately.

Chatbot: An AI-powered program designed to simulate human conversation through text or voice. Chatbots are commonly used in customer service, education, and healthcare applications.

Deskilling: A process by which automation or technological tools reduce the need for human skills, often leading to diminished expertise, confidence, or ownership over work processes.

Ethical AI Use: The responsible and informed use of AI tools that align with moral principles, institutional policies, and social values. It includes fairness, accountability, transparency, and respect for privacy and user well-being.

Ethics-by-Design: An approach to system development in which ethical principles are embedded into the design process from the outset, ensuring that technology aligns with human values and social good.

Generative AI: A subset of AI technologies that can generate content—including text, code, images, or audio—based on input prompts. Examples include ChatGPT, GitHub Copilot, and other large language models (LLMs).

Job Characteristics Theory: A psychological framework that explains how the design of work affects motivation and performance. Key dimensions include skill variety, task identity, task significance, autonomy, and feedback.

Prompt Engineering: The practice of crafting effective input prompts to optimize the responses generated by AI models, especially in natural language and code generation contexts.

Technology Threat Avoidance Theory: A theory that explains how individuals assess and respond to potential threats posed by technology, often leading to avoidance behavior when perceived risks outweigh benefits.

Chapter 11
The Transformative Impact of AI on Student Development and Learning

Sam Ramaila
https://orcid.org/0000-0002-7351-477X
University of Johannesburg, South Africa

ABSTRACT

Artificial Intelligence (AI) is revolutionizing education by transforming how students learn, engage, and develop. AI technologies, such as adaptive learning platforms, intelligent tutoring systems, and automated assessment tools, enable personalized learning experiences and provide valuable data-driven insights to enhance academic success. This chapter explores AI's transformative impact on student development, focusing on its role in fostering personalized instruction, increasing student engagement, and improving assessment and feedback practices. It also addresses the ethical concerns, challenges, and future opportunities associated with AI integration in education. By combining AI innovations with human-centred pedagogical approaches, educators can create more inclusive and effective learning environments that cater to diverse student needs, ensuring that AI serves as a tool to empower all learners while preserving essential human interaction in the educational process.

INTRODUCTION

Artificial intelligence (AI) has rapidly become a cornerstone in the transformation of education, significantly altering traditional teaching and learning paradigms.

DOI: 10.4018/979-8-3373-2927-7.ch011

From adaptive learning systems and AI-driven assessments to personalized tutoring and intelligent content creation, AI is reshaping how education is delivered and experienced. The integration of AI technologies into educational settings is enabling greater personalization, efficiency, and accessibility, creating new opportunities for both students and educators (Lampou, 2023). AI's growing influence in education is not merely a trend, but rather a profound shift that is expanding the potential for innovation in how knowledge is imparted and how students engage with learning content (Wang et al., 2024).

In this evolving educational landscape, the concept of student development is undergoing a fundamental shift. Traditionally, student development has been centred around cognitive growth, academic performance, and the mastery of core subjects (Wang, 2023). However, in the context of AI-driven learning, student development now encompasses a broader spectrum of skills, competencies, and dispositions (Sasikala & Ravichandran, 2024). AI technologies, with their ability to deliver personalized learning experiences, provide immediate feedback, and track individual progress, are contributing to the development of not only academic knowledge but also critical thinking, creativity, self-regulation, problem-solving, and socio-emotional skills (Xu, 2024). AI-driven learning environments are becoming more than just platforms for acquiring knowledge—they are interactive spaces that foster holistic student development and prepare learners for the challenges of the future (Onyebuchi et al., 2024).

The purpose of this chapter is to explore the transformative impact of AI on student development and learning. By analyzing the intersection of AI technologies and student growth, the chapter seeks to provide a comprehensive understanding of how AI is influencing cognitive, emotional, and social development in learners. Additionally, the chapter will highlight the opportunities and challenges that arise from incorporating AI into educational settings, considering both the potential benefits and the ethical considerations that must be addressed. Through an examination of case studies, research findings, and expert insights, this chapter aims to provide a clear picture of how AI is not only changing the educational landscape but also enriching the ways in which students learn, grow, and develop essential competencies for success in an increasingly digital world.

The scope of this chapter includes a discussion of the various AI technologies currently being utilized in education, the impact of these technologies on student development across multiple domains, and a critical exploration of the implications for educational practice. Furthermore, the chapter will examine the broader societal and ethical considerations associated with AI in education, such as data privacy, algorithmic bias, and equity in access to technology. By addressing these topics, the chapter will provide a holistic perspective on the role of AI in shaping the future of student development and learning.

BACKGROUND

The rapid advancements in artificial intelligence (AI) have catalyzed a transformative shift across various sectors, and education is no exception. Over the past decade, AI has begun to reshape how educators approach teaching and how students engage with learning. This technological revolution is not only altering the methods and tools used in classrooms but is also redefining the very nature of student development, engagement, and achievement. AI's integration into educational settings has opened new possibilities for personalized learning, offering tailored experiences that meet individual needs and preferences (Naseer et al., 2024). Furthermore, AI technologies have facilitated the development of intelligent systems that can support students throughout their academic journeys, promoting better learning outcomes and preparing them for the demands of a rapidly changing world (Zhang & Aslan, 2021). The growing presence of AI in education is not limited to its application in administrative functions or content delivery. AI-driven platforms and tools are fundamentally altering the way students interact with learning materials and engage in problem-solving, critical thinking, and collaboration (Walter, 2024). From adaptive learning systems to intelligent tutoring platforms, AI offers personalized pathways that can enhance a student's learning experience, providing real-time support and feedback tailored to their unique abilities, learning styles, and progress (Kabudi, Pappas & Olsen, 2021).

In addition to academic performance, AI is playing a significant role in shaping students' socio-emotional development. With tools that integrate AI-powered chatbots, virtual assistants, and gamified learning experiences, students are receiving support not just for their intellectual growth but also for their motivation, emotional well-being, and overall academic self-efficacy (Aslam, 2023). These AI-driven technologies create immersive, interactive environments that foster a sense of agency, ownership, and intrinsic motivation—critical components of effective student development (Mohebbi, 2024). However, the integration of AI into education also presents significant challenges and ethical considerations. Issues such as data privacy, algorithmic bias, and the digital divide require careful attention. The increasing reliance on AI tools necessitates a balanced approach that ensures technology enhances, rather than replaces, the human-centred aspects of education (Markauskaite et al., 2022). While AI offers immense potential to revolutionize education, it is essential to consider its ethical implications and ensure that these technologies are designed and deployed responsibly (Xiao et al., 2025).

This chapter seeks to explore the multifaceted impact of AI on student development and learning. It delves into the ways AI is enhancing personalized learning, student engagement, and motivation, as well as its role in assessment and feedback. The chapter also examines the ethical challenges that come with AI adoption in educational settings and offers recommendations for ensuring equitable access and responsible use of AI technologies. Ultimately, the goal is to provide a comprehensive understanding of how AI is reshaping the student experience, both academically and personally, while addressing the broader implications for educators, policymakers, and society at large.

Issues, Controversies, and Problems in the Transformative Impact of AI on Student Development and Learning

The integration of artificial intelligence (AI) into education offers significant opportunities to enhance student development and learning outcomes, yet it is not without its share of challenges, controversies, and ethical concerns. While AI technologies promise to revolutionize education by offering personalized learning experiences, improving assessment practices, and enhancing student engagement, they also raise complex issues that must be addressed to ensure that AI's potential is fully realized without compromising fairness, equity, or the human aspects of education.

Data privacy and security concerns

One of the primary concerns surrounding the use of AI in education is the collection, storage, and use of student data. AI systems rely heavily on data to provide personalized learning experiences, track student progress, and predict future performance (Xu, 2024). However, this reliance on data raises significant questions about data privacy and security. In many educational settings, sensitive student information—ranging from academic performance to behavioural data—is being collected and analyzed by AI systems (Huang, 2023). Without proper safeguards in place, there is a risk that this data could be misused, hacked, or improperly shared. Furthermore, many AI-powered platforms are operated by private companies that may not adhere to the same standards of privacy and data protection as public educational institutions (Devineni, 2024). This raises concerns about the potential for exploitation, surveillance, and loss of control over student information. Students, particularly minors, should be protected from such risks, and strict regulations need to be enforced to ensure that data is handled ethically and securely.

Algorithmic bias and fairness

AI systems are only as good as the data they are trained on, and if the data used to develop these systems is biased, the resulting AI tools can perpetuate and even amplify these biases. In educational contexts, this means that AI-powered tools could unintentionally favour certain groups of students over others, leading to inequities in learning outcomes (Adewale et al., 2024). For example, an AI system trained on predominantly data from a certain demographic (e.g., based on gender, race, or socioeconomic status) may produce recommendations or assessments that are not applicable or fair for students from underrepresented groups. This algorithmic bias can lead to significant disparities in how students are treated and assessed, reinforcing existing educational inequities (Idowu, Koshiyama & Treleaven, 2024). Additionally, biased AI systems could affect students' academic self-concept and motivation, especially if they are continually subjected to inaccurate or unfair assessments (Adewale et al., 2024). There is a pressing need for transparency in the development of AI systems to ensure that they are designed to be fair, inclusive, and representative of diverse student populations.

Digital divide and access to technology

AI-driven learning tools have the potential to enhance educational opportunities, but they also risk exacerbating the digital divide, which refers to the gap between students who have access to modern technologies and those who do not (Adewale et al., 2024). While AI-powered platforms promise personalized learning, students from disadvantaged backgrounds, particularly in low-income areas or developing countries, may lack the necessary resources to fully benefit from these advancements (Wang, 2024). Access to high-speed internet, computers, and AI-enabled devices is a critical prerequisite for engaging with AI-driven learning tools, and disparities in access to these technologies can result in unequal learning opportunities (Rashid & Kausik, 2024). Moreover, schools in rural or underserved communities may face challenges in integrating AI technologies due to limited infrastructure, financial constraints, or lack of trained personnel to implement and manage AI systems effectively (Mustafa, Nguyen & Gao, 2024). Without concerted efforts to bridge this digital divide, AI risks further entrenching educational inequalities rather than promoting inclusivity.

Dependence on technology and loss of human element

Another concern associated with AI in education is the growing reliance on technology at the expense of the human elements that are fundamental to effective teaching and learning. While AI can offer personalized learning experiences and data-driven insights, it cannot replace the role of human educators in fostering critical thinking, emotional intelligence, and social skills (Guizani et al., 2025). Teachers play a crucial role in creating a positive, supportive learning environment, encouraging collaboration, and guiding students through complex, subjective problem-solving scenarios (Ibarra, 2022). As AI tools become more embedded in educational practices, there is a risk that the human connection between teachers and students may be diminished. This could lead to a more mechanized and impersonal learning experience, where students interact more with machines than with people. The key challenge lies in striking a balance between utilizing AI to enhance learning and preserving the essential human touch in education that promotes well-rounded student development.

Ethical implications and accountability

The ethical implications of AI in education are far-reaching and multifaceted. With AI systems playing an increasing role in decision-making—such as providing assessments, recommending learning materials, or predicting student performance—the question of accountability becomes more complex. When an AI system makes a mistake or produces an inaccurate recommendation, who is responsible? Is it the educators who implemented the system, the developers who created the algorithms, or the institutions that adopted the technology? In addition, as AI systems become more autonomous, there are concerns about the lack of transparency in their decision-making processes (Balasubramaniam et al., 2023). Some AI systems operate as "black boxes," meaning their reasoning and decision-making processes are not easily understood or explainable by humans. This lack of transparency can create distrust among students, teachers, and parents, particularly when AI systems are used to assess student performance or provide feedback.

Teacher roles and professional development

The integration of AI into education also brings challenges regarding the evolving roles of teachers. While AI can automate administrative tasks and provide insights into student progress, it cannot replace the nuanced, adaptive decision-making that teachers engage in daily (Thu & Tien, 2024). The growing use of AI may raise concerns among educators about their role in the classroom and their professional autonomy. Teachers may worry that AI-driven systems could undermine their authority or expertise (Ghamrawi, Shal & Ghamrawi, 2023). To ensure that AI complements the teaching profession rather than undermining it, ongoing professional development is necessary. Teachers must be equipped with the skills and knowledge to effectively integrate AI tools into their pedagogical practices while maintaining their central role as facilitators of learning. Professional development programs should focus on enhancing teachers' digital literacy and their ability to use AI systems in ways that enhance, rather than replace, their teaching practices.

While AI holds great promise for enhancing student development and learning, its integration into education comes with significant issues, controversies, and challenges that must be carefully addressed. These include concerns about data privacy, algorithmic bias, the digital divide, the potential for over-reliance on technology, and the ethical implications of AI decision-making (Min, 2023). As AI continues to shape the future of education, it is essential for educators, policymakers, technologists, and society at large to work collaboratively to address these issues. By developing responsible, ethical AI systems, ensuring equitable access to technology, and balancing the role of AI with human-centred pedagogy, we can maximize the potential of AI in fostering positive student development while mitigating its risks and challenges.

CHAPTER OBJECTIVES

The primary objective of this chapter is to explore the transformative role that artificial intelligence (AI) plays in reshaping student development and learning within modern educational contexts. As AI continues to gain prominence across diverse sectors, its integration into education promises to bring about significant shifts in how students engage with learning, develop academic skills, and grow personally. Through an in-depth examination of various AI technologies, the chapter aims to provide a comprehensive understanding of the multifaceted impact AI has on the student experience. The following key objectives guide this exploration:

Examine the Role of AI in Enhancing Personalized Learning

A central objective of this chapter is to investigate how AI-powered adaptive learning systems are revolutionizing personalized learning experiences for students. By tailoring learning content, resources, and pace to everyone's needs, abilities, and learning preferences, AI creates an environment where students can thrive at their own pace. The chapter will delve into the specific ways AI-driven platforms support differentiated instruction, address learning gaps, and enable more effective individualized learning pathways. The chapter will also address how AI facilitates greater accessibility for diverse learners, including those with disabilities or learning challenges.

Understand AI's Influence on Student Engagement and Motivation

Student engagement and motivation are essential components of academic success and long-term educational outcomes. One of the key objectives of this chapter is to explore how AI can be leveraged to enhance student engagement through interactive, gamified learning environments and real-time support. The chapter will discuss AI technologies, such as intelligent tutoring systems, virtual assistants, and immersive augmented and virtual reality tools, that foster deeper student involvement in the learning process. By understanding how AI tools motivate students through personalized, dynamic experiences, the chapter will highlight the potential of these technologies in maintaining students' intrinsic motivation and academic perseverance.

Explore AI's Impact on Assessment and Feedback

A critical aspect of student development is the continuous process of assessment and feedback, which guides learners' academic growth. This chapter will aim to explore how AI is transforming assessment models, including the development of formative and summative assessments that provide real-time, tailored feedback. The use of Natural Language Processing (NLP) for grading, predictive analytics for identifying learning gaps, and AI-driven feedback mechanisms will be discussed in depth. By analyzing the effectiveness and limitations of these AI-assisted models, the chapter will assess how AI can enhance the efficiency, accuracy, and timeliness of feedback, ultimately contributing to more informed and responsive teaching practices.

Address Ethical Considerations in AI Integration

As AI becomes more ingrained in education, it is essential to address the ethical concerns that arise with its adoption. One of the key objectives of this chapter is to examine the ethical implications of using AI in student development. This includes issues such as data privacy, security, algorithmic bias, and the potential for unequal access to AI-driven resources. By discussing these challenges, the chapter aims to raise awareness about the ethical considerations that must be considered when implementing AI technologies in educational settings. Additionally, the chapter will explore strategies for mitigating these risks and ensuring that AI tools are used responsibly and equitably.

Investigate the Future Trajectories of AI in Education

The chapter also aims to look toward the future and explore the emerging trends in AI technologies that are likely to shape the next generation of educational tools. This includes the potential of emotion-aware AI, AI mentors, and advancements in machine learning algorithms to support students in increasingly sophisticated ways. By reflecting on how these technologies might further enhance student development and learning, the chapter will provide insights into the future role of AI in fostering lifelong learning, developing 21st-century skills, and preparing students for the challenges of a rapidly evolving global landscape.

Promote a Balanced Approach to AI and Human-Centred Pedagogy

While AI has the potential to revolutionize education, this chapter aims to emphasize the importance of balancing AI integration with human-centred pedagogical practices. AI should not replace educators but rather complement their roles in facilitating student growth and development. The chapter will discuss the importance of teacher-student relationships, social-emotional learning, and the development of critical thinking and collaboration skills, which are difficult to replicate through technology alone. By highlighting the complementary relationship between AI and human-centred teaching, the chapter aims to advocate for an approach that maximizes the benefits of both.

Provide Recommendations for Responsible AI Implementation in Education

The chapter will also seek to offer practical recommendations for educators, policymakers, and stakeholders on how to integrate AI responsibly within educational contexts. This includes creating equitable access to AI tools, ensuring transparency in AI decision-making processes, and fostering an inclusive environment that supports all learners. The objective is to ensure that AI is used as a tool for empowerment, providing students with the resources they need to succeed while addressing potential inequalities in access, quality, and opportunities. Through the pursuit of these objectives, this chapter seeks to provide a thorough and insightful examination of AI's transformative impact on student development and learning. By exploring the opportunities, challenges, and ethical considerations associated with AI in education, the chapter will contribute to a deeper understanding of how AI can shape the educational experience of students today and in the future. Ultimately, the aim is to present a balanced perspective on the potential and limitations of AI in education, offering valuable insights for educators, researchers, and policymakers committed to the responsible integration of technology in student development.

AI IN PERSONALIZED LEARNING

Artificial Intelligence (AI) has introduced a new era in personalized learning, allowing for highly tailored educational experiences that cater to the unique needs, preferences, and abilities of individual students. One of the most significant innovations in this area is the development of AI-powered adaptive learning systems, which have revolutionized how content is delivered and how students engage with learning material (Moya & Camacho, 2024). These systems use algorithms to assess each learner's progress, strengths, and weaknesses, dynamically adjusting the pace and difficulty of tasks to ensure that each student is challenged appropriately without feeling overwhelmed. By continuously analyzing a student's performance, these systems provide real-time feedback and adapt content to suit their evolving needs, offering an individualized learning path that maximizes both engagement and comprehension.

The ability of AI-powered adaptive learning systems to personalize instruction has far-reaching implications for educational outcomes. These systems can identify patterns in student behaviour, pinpoint areas of difficulty, and recommend targeted interventions to address gaps in understanding (Adewale et al., 2024). For example, if a student is struggling with a particular concept, the system may adjust the curriculum to present additional explanations, interactive exercises, or supplementary resources that cater to the student's specific learning style. This approach not only enhances the learning experience but also fosters greater student autonomy, as learners can take ownership of their progress and access tailored support as needed. AI-powered learning environments, therefore, provide a more efficient and effective means of delivering personalized instruction, offering each student the opportunity to achieve their full potential (Onyebuchi et al., 2024).

Intelligent tutoring systems (ITS) are another key application of AI in personalized learning. These systems simulate the role of a tutor by offering one-on-one assistance to students, helping them navigate difficult concepts and providing immediate, context-specific feedback (Rizvi, 2023). Unlike traditional tutoring methods, ITS can be available at any time, offering flexible and convenient support for students outside of classroom hours. These systems are designed to provide personalized guidance based on a student's individual needs, using advanced algorithms to assess responses, detect errors, and suggest corrections. By mimicking the individualized attention of a human tutor, ITS ensures that each student receives the support they need to master new concepts, while also promoting active learning through interactive tasks and problem-solving exercises.

AI-driven recommendations also play a crucial role in personalizing learning experiences. These recommendations are powered by machine learning algorithms that analyze vast amounts of data to suggest relevant resources, courses, or activities tailored to a student's academic interests and goals (Xu, 2024). For instance, if a student excels in a particular subject area, the system might recommend advanced learning materials or projects that build on their existing knowledge, encouraging further exploration. Similarly, for students who need additional practice, AI can recommend exercises or tutorials that reinforce fundamental concepts. This continuous, data-driven feedback loop not only enhances student engagement but also allows educators to provide more targeted support, addressing the specific needs of each learner.

One of the most powerful aspects of AI in personalized learning is its potential to support a diverse range of learners, including students with disabilities. AI technologies can be customized to accommodate a variety of learning needs, helping to create more inclusive educational environments (Song et al., 2024). For students with visual impairments, for example, AI can provide text-to-speech capabilities, allowing them to access written content through auditory means. Similarly, AI-powered tools can support students with dyslexia by offering text-to-speech and speech-to-text functions, as well as providing real-time feedback on spelling and grammar (Iyer et al., 2023). For students with autism spectrum disorder (ASD), AI-driven systems can be tailored to offer social-emotional learning opportunities that are sensitive to their needs, helping them develop important social skills in a safe, supportive environment (Wankhede et al., 2024).

In addition to supporting students with disabilities, AI can help bridge educational gaps for students from diverse cultural and linguistic backgrounds (Garg & Sharma, 2020). AI-driven language translation tools, for instance, can break down language barriers, enabling students to engage with learning materials in their native language while still participating in the classroom. Similarly, AI-based systems that track student progress across various subjects can identify students who are struggling academically, offering personalized support and ensuring that no learner is left behind. AI-powered personalized learning systems, therefore, have the potential to enhance inclusivity and equity in education (Rahiman & Kodikal, 2023). By offering tailored learning experiences that meet the diverse needs of all students, AI ensures that each learner, regardless of their background, abilities, or challenges, could succeed (Langelaan et al., 2024). As AI technologies continue to evolve, their role in supporting personalized learning will only grow, further transforming the educational landscape and promoting a more inclusive, effective, and individualized approach to student development.

ENHANCING STUDENT ENGAGEMENT AND MOTIVATION

Student engagement and motivation are crucial elements for fostering effective learning, and AI technologies are playing a pivotal role in transforming the ways educators engage students and sustain their motivation. Through AI-driven gamification, interactive learning environments, chatbots, virtual assistants, and immersive augmented and virtual reality (AR/VR) applications, educational experiences are becoming more dynamic, personalized, and motivating. These innovations aim to create a learning experience that not only keeps students engaged but also makes the process of learning more enjoyable, accessible, and rewarding.

AI-driven gamification is one of the most exciting developments in education, as it combines game elements with learning to enhance student engagement. By integrating elements such as rewards, challenges, levels, and points systems into educational content, AI-powered gamification creates an environment where learning becomes a fun and interactive experience (Wulan et al., 2024). These systems can track a student's progress and offer personalized challenges tailored to their current skill level, providing immediate feedback and encouragement to keep students motivated (Rizvi, 2023). For example, students might earn badges for completing tasks, unlock new levels for mastering concepts, or receive personalized rewards for showing improvement. This not only makes the learning process more engaging but also provides a sense of accomplishment that motivates students to continue their academic journey. AI's ability to analyze student performance ensures that the gamified experience remains challenging yet achievable, fostering a growth mindset and promoting a deeper connection with the material (Sasikala & Ravichandran, 2024).

In addition to gamification, AI-powered interactive learning environments further enhance student engagement by creating dynamic, responsive spaces for exploration and learning (Yaseen et al., 2025). These environments are designed to adapt in real-time to students' inputs and actions, providing instant feedback and adjusting the learning experience based on individual needs (El-Sabagh, 2021). For example, AI can offer instant quizzes, simulations, and problem-solving exercises that adjust based on the learner's understanding of the subject matter. As a result, students are not merely passive recipients of information but active participants in their own learning. This hands-on approach boosts motivation by allowing students to engage in meaningful, real-world applications of the concepts they are learning. Whether through interactive case studies, adaptive quizzes, or personalized learning pathways, AI-driven interactive environments empower students to take ownership of their learning, creating a more immersive and engaging experience (Abbes, Bennani & Maalel, 2024).

Another key tool for enhancing student engagement and motivation is the use of AI-driven chatbots and virtual assistants. These tools serve as on-demand academic support, offering students personalized assistance whenever they need it. Chatbots can answer frequently asked questions, provide explanations for difficult concepts, and guide students through assignments and assessments (Okonkwo & Ade-Ibijola, 2021). By providing instant access to information and resources, chatbots ensure that students do not feel isolated or lost in their learning process, especially outside of traditional classroom hours (Laun & Wolff, 2025). Virtual assistants, which can be integrated into AI-powered learning platforms, take this a step further by offering more advanced, conversational support (Alier et al., 2025). Students can interact with virtual assistants to receive personalized study recommendations, reminders for deadlines, or tailored feedback on their progress (Yaseen et al., 2025). These tools provide a sense of continual support, enabling students to feel more confident in their learning and better equipped to tackle challenges. The personalized nature of chatbots and virtual assistants makes them particularly effective in fostering student motivation, as students feel that their individual needs and concerns are being addressed in real-time (Looi & Jia, 2025).

Augmented and virtual reality (AR/VR) applications offer an entirely new dimension for enhancing student engagement by creating immersive, interactive learning experiences. Through AR and VR, students can explore virtual worlds, interact with 3D models, and participate in simulations that would be impossible in a traditional classroom setting (Mansour et al., 2024). For example, students studying biology might use VR to explore the human body in 3D, while those studying history can virtually visit ancient civilizations. These immersive environments engage students' senses, allowing them to learn by doing rather than passively absorbing information. The hands-on nature of AR and VR makes learning more enjoyable and deeply memorable, fostering both engagement and motivation (Siricharoen, 2023). Additionally, these technologies can help contextualize abstract concepts, making them more tangible and easier to understand (Micallef & Newton, 2024). For instance, students learning about physics can use VR to conduct virtual experiments, providing them with a safe space to explore complex principles in a hands-on way.

The ability of AR and VR applications to create real-world experiences in a virtual space is particularly beneficial in fields that rely on practical, experiential learning. Whether it's engineering, medicine, or architecture, AR/VR applications enable students to simulate real-life scenarios and refine their skills in a risk-free environment (Al-Ansi et al., 2023). This type of immersive learning not only enhances engagement but also fosters a deeper understanding of the subject matter, motivating students to continue exploring and refining their knowledge (Mebert et al., 2020). The integration of AI in gamification, interactive environments, chatbots, virtual assistants, and AR/VR applications represents a powerful shift in how educational experiences are designed. These technologies not only improve student engagement by making learning more interactive and fun but also help sustain motivation by providing personalized, supportive, and immersive experiences. By leveraging AI to create dynamic, responsive learning environments, educators can foster a deeper connection with their students, motivating them to engage with the content more meaningfully and persist in their academic pursuits (Moya & Camacho, 2024). As AI technologies continue to evolve, they will undoubtedly play an even more integral role in creating learning experiences that are not only more engaging but also more effective in promoting long-term academic success.

AI IN ASSESSMENT AND FEEDBACK

The role of assessment and feedback in education has long been a cornerstone of the learning process, offering students insights into their strengths and areas for improvement. Traditional models of assessment, while valuable, often suffer from limitations such as time constraints, grading inconsistencies, and the inability to provide immediate or individualized feedback (O'Neill & Padden, 2021). In contrast, AI technologies are transforming how assessments are conducted and how feedback is delivered, making these processes more efficient, personalized, and data-driven (Yaseen et al., 2025). Through AI-assisted formative and summative assessments, the integration of Natural Language Processing (NLP) for grading and feedback, and the use of predictive analytics to identify learning gaps, AI is reshaping the landscape of educational evaluation.

AI-assisted formative and summative assessment models represent a significant shift from traditional assessment practices. Formative assessments, which are intended to monitor student progress and provide ongoing feedback during the learning process, are now being augmented with AI tools that offer real-time, personalized insights. AI systems can track student performance across various learning tasks, identifying patterns in their responses and progress (Adewale et al., 2024). This enables teachers to gain a deeper understanding of each student's learning journey and intervene when necessary. For example, AI systems can analyze a student's response to a series of questions or tasks and adjust the difficulty of subsequent tasks based on the student's demonstrated abilities. These systems can also suggest additional resources or targeted activities to help the student master a particular concept. By continuously adapting to the student's needs, AI-powered formative assessments ensure that learners receive timely feedback and support that is tailored to their unique challenges (Onyebuchi, Unachukwu & Osawaru, 2024).

Similarly, summative assessments, which are typically used to evaluate a student's overall achievement at the end of a learning unit or course, are benefiting from AI technologies that streamline the grading process and provide richer insights into student performance. AI can assist in grading large volumes of assignments, essays, or exams in a fraction of the time it would take a human instructor (Li et al., 2025). This efficiency not only frees up educators to focus on more meaningful interactions with students but also ensures that grading is consistent and objective, reducing the potential for bias or human error. AI-powered summative assessments also offer the advantage of providing more detailed and data-driven feedback, allowing students to better understand their strengths and weaknesses in relation to specific learning outcomes (van den Berg & Papadopoulos, 2024). With AI, summative assessments can become more dynamic, offering students not only a final grade but also an in-depth analysis of their performance across different areas of the curriculum (Memarian & Doleck, 2024).

One of the most transformative ways AI is enhancing assessment and feedback is using Natural Language Processing (NLP). NLP allows AI systems to understand and interpret human language, enabling them to assess written responses, essays, and other forms of open-ended student work. By applying advanced NLP algorithms, AI can not only grade written content but also provide detailed feedback on areas such as grammar, sentence structure, coherence, and even the depth of analysis (Zhao, 2024). This opens new possibilities for providing personalized feedback on assignments that would traditionally require significant time and effort to evaluate manually. For example, an AI system might assess the quality of a student's argument in an essay, highlighting areas where the argument could be strengthened, or suggest improvements in clarity and flow. Such detailed, real-time feedback enhances the learning experience, allowing students to make immediate revisions and learn from their mistakes without waiting for a teacher's manual input. NLP-driven systems can also evaluate the originality of students' work, checking for plagiarism or inconsistencies in citation (Nwohiri, Joda & Ajayi, 2021). This further supports academic integrity while offering constructive feedback on how to improve research skills and referencing. Additionally, by leveraging NLP, AI can provide feedback in a more conversational manner, mimicking the type of guidance that students might receive in a one-on-one tutorial session. This level of personalized, written feedback at scale is a powerful tool for improving student learning outcomes.

Predictive analytics is another key area in which AI is revolutionizing assessment and feedback. Through the analysis of vast amounts of student data, AI can identify patterns that predict future performance, highlight potential learning gaps, and suggest timely interventions (Shoaib et al., 2024). For example, predictive models can analyze factors such as a student's past grades, engagement with learning materials, and completion rates for assignments to forecast how they might perform on future assessments. If a student's data suggests they are at risk of underperforming, predictive analytics can prompt early interventions, such as personalized study plans, targeted resources, or additional support from tutors. This proactive approach to assessment helps ensure that learning gaps are addressed before they become major obstacles to student success. By identifying students who may be struggling with specific concepts or who show signs of disengagement, AI-powered predictive analytics allow educators to intervene early, potentially preventing dropout or failure (Embarak & Hawarna, 2024). Additionally, predictive models can offer insights into larger trends across a cohort or institution, helping educational leaders make data-driven decisions about curriculum design, resource allocation, and support services (Adesina, Iyelolu & Okpeke, 2024). For instance, if a particular group of students is consistently underperforming in a specific area, the data can indicate where curricular adjustments may be needed, or where additional support structures could be implemented to help students succeed.

The ability to continuously monitor student progress through AI-powered formative assessments, offer personalized and timely feedback through NLP, and predict learning challenges through predictive analytics offers a holistic, data-driven approach to student evaluation (Xu, 2024). AI's role in assessment and feedback not only improves the efficiency and objectivity of grading but also empowers students with immediate, actionable insights that help them improve and stay motivated (Sasikala & Ravichandran, 2024). By providing more personalized, real-time, and data-informed feedback, AI ensures that the assessment process is more than just a measure of performance; it becomes an integral part of the learning journey, promoting growth, improvement, and deeper understanding. As AI continues to evolve, its integration into assessment and feedback will play a key role in creating more personalized and effective learning environments for students across the globe.

HARNESSING INTELLIGENT EDUCATIONAL TECHNOLOGIES FOR PERSONALIZED, DATA-DRIVEN, AND IMMERSIVE LEARNING

The advancement of educational technologies has significantly reshaped contemporary teaching and learning, enabling highly personalized, data-driven, and immersive learning experiences. Among the most transformative innovations are Intelligent Tutoring Systems (ITS), predictive analytics, chatbots, and Virtual Reality (VR). Together, these technologies not only enhance the efficacy of instruction but also support the development of higher-order cognitive skills essential for the 21st-century learner.

Intelligent Tutoring Systems (ITS) represent a paradigm shift from traditional, teacher-centred instruction to adaptive, learner-centred approaches. Drawing on artificial intelligence and cognitive modelling, ITS dynamically monitors students' knowledge states, identifies misconceptions, and delivers tailored instructional scaffolds (VanLehn, 2011). This adaptive functionality aligns with Vygotsky's (1978) notion of the zone of proximal development, whereby learners benefit most from guidance that is responsive to their current understanding. ITS thus fosters mastery learning by ensuring that learners only progress once conceptual understanding has been achieved, promoting both cognitive and metacognitive growth.

The integration of predictive analytics into educational platforms extends the capacity for personalized support by leveraging large-scale learning data to forecast performance outcomes and engagement patterns. Predictive models can identify students at risk of academic underachievement or disengagement, facilitating timely and targeted interventions (Bienkowski, Feng, & Means, 2012). Beyond individual learning trajectories, predictive analytics can inform curriculum design, resource allocation, and institutional policies, enabling evidence-based decision-making that enhances systemic educational effectiveness.

Chatbots, as AI-powered conversational agents, provide interactive and immediate support, simulating human dialogue to assist learners with queries, content review, and procedural guidance. The scalability and accessibility of chatbots address persistent challenges of educational equity, ensuring learners can receive consistent support irrespective of time or location (Fryer et al., 2017). In higher education contexts, chatbots can enhance engagement by complementing instructor feedback and fostering autonomous learning habits, thereby reinforcing the self-regulated learning framework (Zimmerman, 2002).

Virtual Reality (VR) introduces immersive, experiential learning opportunities that bridge theoretical knowledge and practical application. By situating learners within interactive simulations, VR enables experimentation, exploration, and problem-solving in safe, controlled environments (Makransky & Petersen, 2021). This aligns with experiential learning theories (Kolb, 1984), emphasizing learning through active engagement and reflection. In disciplines such as science, engineering, and healthcare, VR facilitates the development of procedural skills, spatial reasoning, and collaborative competencies that are difficult to cultivate through conventional classroom methods.

The convergence of ITS, predictive analytics, chatbots, and VR establishes a comprehensive, technology-enhanced learning ecosystem. ITS provides adaptive instruction, predictive analytics informs anticipatory support, chatbots ensure continuous guidance, and VR promotes experiential engagement. Collectively, these tools operationalize principles of personalized, active, and equitable learning, equipping students with the cognitive, metacognitive, and socio-emotional competencies required in increasingly complex and digitalized societies. Importantly, their implementation underscores the necessity for educators to adopt integrative pedagogical frameworks, ensuring that technological affordances translate into meaningful learning outcomes.

In summary, the synergistic application of ITS, predictive analytics, chatbots, and VR exemplifies the potential of educational technology to transform learning experiences. By aligning technological innovation with evidence-based pedagogy, institutions can foster environments that are adaptive, engaging, and inclusive, ultimately preparing learners for the demands of the 21st century.

EMPIRICAL EVIDENCE OF ARTIFICIAL INTELLIGENCE TRANSFORMING LEARNING OUTCOMES AND ENGAGEMENT

The integration of artificial intelligence (AI) into education has transcended theoretical potential, yielding measurable impacts across diverse learning contexts. Empirical studies demonstrate that AI technologies, ranging from Intelligent Tutoring Systems (ITS) and adaptive learning platforms to chatbots and predictive analytics, enhance learning outcomes, engagement, and personalized instruction.

One of the most widely studied applications is Intelligent Tutoring Systems (ITS). For example, VanLehn (2011) conducted a meta-analysis of ITS implementations across mathematics and science subjects, demonstrating that students using ITS achieved learning gains comparable to one-on-one human tutoring. A notable case is the Cognitive Tutor system in high school algebra, which adaptively sequences problems based on individual student performance. Research indicates that students using Cognitive Tutor showed a 15–20% increase in problem-solving proficiency compared to peers receiving traditional instruction (Koedinger et al., 2013). This empirical evidence highlights AI's capacity to provide targeted scaffolding, address misconceptions in real time, and promote mastery learning.

Predictive analytics, powered by AI, has also shown significant impact in higher education. For instance, a study by Arnold and Pistilli (2012) at Purdue University employed the Course Signals predictive analytics system to monitor students' engagement and performance. The system analyzed interaction patterns, assignment submissions, and grades to identify at-risk students. As a result, students who received proactive interventions from instructors guided by predictive alerts demonstrated higher course completion rates and improved academic performance. This empirical example underscores AI's role in enabling data-driven, proactive educational support.

Chatbots represent another empirically supported application of AI in education. Winkler and Söllner (2018) examined the deployment of an AI-driven chatbot for university students, providing 24/7 assistance on administrative and course-related queries. The study reported a substantial reduction in response times and increased student satisfaction, while also enhancing engagement by encouraging learners to access resources more frequently. Similarly, in STEM education, chatbots have been used to guide students through complex problem-solving exercises, resulting in measurable improvements in both conceptual understanding and persistence on challenging tasks (Fryer et al., 2017).

Virtual Reality (VR) integrated with AI has also provided empirical evidence of enhanced learning outcomes. Makransky and Petersen (2021) investigated the use of immersive VR simulations for chemistry experiments. When combined with AI-driven adaptive prompts and scaffolding, students demonstrated higher retention of conceptual knowledge and greater engagement compared to those in traditional laboratory settings. These findings indicate that AI not only personalizes learning within immersive environments but also amplifies the pedagogical benefits of experiential learning.

Beyond specific platforms, AI's impact is evident in broader systemic applications. For example, studies in MOOCs (Massive Open Online Courses) have leveraged AI for automated grading, adaptive content recommendations, and discussion moderation. Empirical results from courses using AI-driven recommendation systems indicate increased course completion rates and improved learning satisfaction, particularly for learners who might otherwise struggle in self-directed environments (Xing et al., 2020).

Collectively, these empirical examples illustrate that AI in education can:

a. Enhance personalized learning through adaptive tutoring and scaffolding.
b. Improve predictive support by identifying at-risk students and guiding timely interventions.
c. Increase accessibility and engagement via chatbots and AI-mediated communication.
d. Enrich experiential learning when combined with immersive technologies like VR.

These findings underscore the transformative potential of AI when implemented thoughtfully, combining robust pedagogical frameworks with data-driven adaptability. As educational institutions increasingly adopt AI solutions, ongoing empirical research remains critical to optimizing design, evaluating efficacy, and ensuring equitable access for diverse learner populations.

ETHICAL CONSIDERATIONS AND CHALLENGES

As AI continues to play an increasingly central role in shaping the future of education, it is crucial to address the ethical considerations and challenges that arise from its widespread integration into learning environments. These concerns, which encompass issues of data privacy and security, algorithmic bias, and equity in access to technology, must be carefully considered to ensure that AI-driven educational tools serve to enhance learning without compromising the rights or well-being of students. While the potential of AI in education is vast, its ethical implications require transparent, responsible, and inclusive approaches to ensure that all learners benefit fairly from these innovations.

Data Privacy, Security, and Ethical Concerns in AI-Powered Learning

The use of AI in education necessitates the collection and processing of vast amounts of data about students, including personal information, learning behaviours, academic performance, and engagement metrics. While this data is essential for providing personalized learning experiences and insights, it raises significant concerns regarding privacy and security (Huang, 2023). Data breaches or unauthorized access to sensitive student information could have severe consequences, ranging from identity theft to misuse of personal data, making the safeguarding of student privacy paramount (Huang, 2023). Ethical concerns also arise in relation to how data is used and for what purposes. It is crucial that students and educators are informed about the type of data being collected, how it is being used, and who has access to it. Furthermore, there must be strict protocols in place to protect this data from cyber threats and ensure that it is used solely for educational purposes. Institutions must implement robust data encryption methods, secure storage systems, and regular audits to ensure that data privacy is maintained. Additionally, educational institutions and technology developers must adhere to local and international data protection laws, such as the General Data Protection Regulation (GDPR) in Europe, which outlines stringent requirements for data processing and protection. Equally important is the transparency with which AI tools operate. Students should have clear visibility into how their data is influencing the recommendations and feedback they receive. When AI tools make decisions about a student's learning path, assessment results, or support needs, these processes must be explainable and understandable. This transparency helps build trust between students, educators, and the AI systems, ensuring that the educational experience remains equitable and just.

Algorithmic Bias and Issues of Fairness in AI-Driven Educational Tools

While AI has the potential to offer personalized and tailored learning experiences, it is not immune to biases. The algorithms that power AI systems are often trained on historical data, which may reflect societal biases or inequities (Bircan & Özbilgin, 2025). For instance, if AI systems are trained on datasets that contain biased representations of certain groups—whether based on gender, race, socioeconomic status, or other factors—the tools could perpetuate and even amplify these biases in their decision-making processes. This can result in unfair outcomes, such as certain groups of students receiving suboptimal learning resources or being disproportionately identified as struggling, while others may be overrepresented as excelling. Algorithmic bias is a pressing issue, especially in educational settings where AI tools are used for high-stakes assessments or to determine personalized learning interventions (Boateng & Boateng, 2025). If AI systems display biases, they can inadvertently reinforce existing inequalities in education, disadvantaging students from marginalized communities or those with learning differences (Min, 2023). For example, an AI-powered tutoring system trained primarily on data from affluent students may fail to recognize the needs of students from lower-income backgrounds, potentially offering less effective or irrelevant recommendations to these learners. To mitigate the risk of bias, it is critical that AI systems are developed using diverse, representative datasets that account for the various backgrounds, experiences, and needs of all students. Moreover, these systems must undergo regular audits for fairness, with an emphasis on ensuring that they do not unintentionally favour one group over another. Educators and developers must also consider implementing fairness algorithms that actively correct for any biases detected, ensuring that AI tools operate in a way that is equitable and inclusive for all learners.

Addressing the Digital Divide and Ensuring Equitable AI Access

The digital divide—the gap between those who have access to modern technology and those who do not—poses a significant challenge to the equitable implementation of AI in education (Lythreatis, Singh & El-Kassar, 2022). In many parts of the world, particularly in rural or economically disadvantaged areas, students may not have reliable access to the internet, computers, or smartphones, which are necessary for AI-powered learning tools to function effectively (Mustafa, Nguyen & Gao, 2024). This lack of access can hinder students' ability to benefit from the personalized learning experiences that AI offers, deepening educational inequities between different socioeconomic groups (Hussain, Qureshi & Malik, 2024). To address this challenge, it is crucial that policymakers, educational institutions, and technology developers work together to ensure that AI-driven educational tools are accessible to all students, regardless of their economic or geographical circumstances. This could include providing affordable or subsidized technology to underserved communities, offering offline or low-bandwidth solutions that still leverage the power of AI, and ensuring that AI platforms are compatible with a wide range of devices.

Additionally, internet infrastructure in underserved regions must be improved to enable all students to access AI-enhanced learning tools.

Equitable access to AI also involves considering the diverse needs of students with disabilities. AI technologies must be designed to be accessible to learners with a wide range of disabilities, including those who are visually impaired, hearing impaired, or have learning disabilities. AI-powered tools can offer features such as text-to-speech, speech-to-text, and personalized support for students with special educational needs. However, these features must be thoughtfully integrated to ensure they meet the specific requirements of these learners and are easy to use. Beyond physical access, it is equally important to consider the digital literacy of both educators and students. Training and professional development programs for teachers are necessary to ensure they can effectively integrate AI into their classrooms (Huang et al., 2024). Students, too, should be equipped with the digital skills needed to navigate AI-powered learning platforms confidently. By addressing these barriers, educational institutions can ensure that AI-driven learning tools are used in a way that promotes equity and inclusivity for all students.

The integration of AI into education offers transformative possibilities for improving learning outcomes, but it also brings with it a host of ethical considerations and challenges. Ensuring data privacy and security, mitigating algorithmic bias, and addressing the digital divide are critical to realizing the full potential of AI while safeguarding the rights and well-being of students (Min, 2023). As AI continues to shape the educational landscape, it is essential that its development and deployment are guided by principles of fairness, transparency, and inclusivity. By addressing these ethical concerns proactively, we can create a future where AI serves as a powerful tool for all students, regardless of their background, ensuring that the benefits of AI-enhanced education are equitably distributed.

FUTURE OF AI IN STUDENT DEVELOPMENT

As artificial intelligence (AI) continues to evolve, its role in student development is set to expand in profound and transformative ways. The future of AI in education holds exciting possibilities, not only in how students learn but also in how they develop the skills necessary to thrive in an increasingly complex and interconnected world. Emerging AI technologies are poised to create dynamic, responsive learning environments that support the holistic development of students, preparing them for success in their academic, professional, and personal lives. In this context, the future of AI in student development will encompass innovative trends, the promotion of lifelong learning, and the adoption of responsible policies to guide its integration into educational systems.

Emerging AI Trends in Education

The future of AI in education is characterized by several emerging trends that promise to revolutionize the way students engage with learning and their development. One of the most exciting of these trends is the rise of *emotion-aware AI*, systems that can detect and respond to students' emotional states (Gamage et al., 2024). By analyzing facial expressions, voice tones, and even physiological cues, emotion-aware AI can tailor learning experiences based on students' emotional needs (Kumar & Kumar, 2025). For instance, if a student is feeling frustrated or disengaged, the system could adjust the difficulty level of the content or offer encouraging feedback to help the student re-engage with the material. This ability to understand and adapt to the emotional context of students presents a significant advancement in creating more empathetic and supportive learning environments, enhancing both academic outcomes and well-being.

Another trend gaining traction is the development of *AI mentors*. These virtual mentors can guide students through their learning journeys, offering personalized advice, support, and encouragement. Unlike traditional tutoring systems, AI mentors can provide more than academic assistance—they can also help students navigate the broader aspects of personal and professional development, such as goal setting, time management, and career planning (Rizvi, 2023). AI mentors can offer 24/7 support, helping students stay on track with their studies and providing ongoing motivation. These mentors could also serve as a valuable resource for students who lack access to human mentors or counsellors, creating more equitable learning opportunities for all. In addition, AI is enabling the creation of increasingly sophisticated learning environments that can integrate various forms of media, adapt in real-time to students' progress, and offer personalized pathways (Onyebuchi, Unachukwu & Osawaru, 2024). These intelligent, adaptive systems can present content in a way that aligns with a student's unique learning style, ensuring that each learner receives the most effective and engaging educational experience.

AI's Role in Fostering Lifelong Learning and 21st-Century Skills

AI's role in education extends beyond the classroom, especially as it relates to the cultivation of *lifelong learning* and essential *21st-century skills* such as critical thinking, creativity, collaboration, and digital literacy. In an era marked by rapid technological advancement, the ability to adapt and continuously learn new skills has become more important than ever. AI has the potential to support students in developing these competencies by offering personalized learning experiences that are tailored to individual needs and interests, fostering a mindset of continuous growth and curiosity (Xu, 2024). Through AI-driven platforms, students can access a wide array of learning materials, courses, and resources that can be revisited at any time, facilitating learning beyond formal education (Josué et al., 2023). These platforms can also identify gaps in knowledge and recommend additional resources or courses, encouraging students to continue expanding their skill sets throughout their lives. AI's ability to offer personalized learning paths ensures that students can learn at their own pace, deepening their understanding of specific subjects or acquiring entirely new competencies in areas such as coding, data analysis, or digital marketing (Xu, 2024).

Furthermore, AI has the potential to play a critical role in the development of *soft skills*—skills that are increasingly recognized as essential in today's workplace. These include communication, emotional intelligence, adaptability, and teamwork. AI tools that simulate real-world scenarios, such as virtual collaborative projects or communication exercises, can help students hone these skills in a safe, controlled environment (Borge, Smith & Aldemir, 2024). AI-powered feedback systems can also provide real-time assessments of students' progress in these areas, offering valuable insights into areas of strength and opportunities for growth (Yaseen et al., 2025). In this way, AI supports the development of the *21st-century skills* necessary to navigate the complexities of modern life and work. Whether through adaptive learning platforms, virtual mentors, or collaborative simulations, AI is poised to empower students to become lifelong learners who can thrive in an ever-changing world.

Policy Implications and Best Practices for Responsible AI Integration

As the potential for AI in education grows, so too does the need for thoughtful and responsible integration into educational systems. The rapid advancement of AI technology presents both opportunities and challenges for policymakers, educators, and developers. To ensure that AI is used effectively and ethically, several policy implications and best practices must be considered. One key area for policy focus is *data governance*. As AI systems increasingly rely on vast amounts of student data, it is essential that clear and comprehensive guidelines are in place regarding data privacy, security, and ethical use. Policies should mandate the responsible collection and storage of data, ensuring that students' privacy is always protected. Additionally, AI systems must be designed with transparency in mind, allowing students and educators to understand how data is being used to personalize learning experiences.

Another crucial policy consideration is *equity*. AI's potential to personalize learning can bridge educational gaps, but only if all students have equal access to these tools (Adewale et al., 2024). Policymakers must address issues of the *digital divide*, ensuring that students from underserved communities or with limited access to technology are not left behind. This may involve initiatives to provide affordable devices, internet access, and digital literacy programs to ensure that every student can benefit from AI-driven learning. Furthermore, efforts must be made to ensure that AI tools are inclusive and cater to the diverse needs of all learners, including those with disabilities or learning differences.

In terms of best practices, one recommendation is the *collaboration between educators, technologists, and policymakers* in the development and deployment of AI tools. By involving a broad range of stakeholders in the design process, we can ensure that AI systems are grounded in educational best practices and aligned with the needs of students and educators. Regular training and professional development opportunities for educators are also essential to help them effectively integrate AI into their classrooms (Ventista & Brown, 2023). This will empower teachers to use AI not just as a tool for content delivery, but to enhance student engagement, motivation, and development. Finally, *continuous evaluation* of AI systems is crucial to ensure that they are meeting the educational goals and ethical standards set by educational institutions and policymakers. Regular audits, feedback loops, and assessments of AI tools can help identify and address any issues that arise, such as algorithmic bias or unintended consequences (Li & Goel, 2024).

The future of AI in student development is promising, with the potential to revolutionize how students learn, engage, and develop the skills necessary for success in the 21st century. Emerging trends, such as emotion-aware AI and AI mentors, will help create more personalized, supportive, and dynamic learning experiences. At the same time, AI's role in fostering lifelong learning and essential skills will enable students to adapt to a rapidly changing world. However, as AI becomes increasingly integrated into education, it is essential that policymakers, educators, and developers work together to ensure its responsible use. By focusing on data governance, equity, and collaboration, we can harness the full potential of AI to create an educational ecosystem that is inclusive, ethical, and empowering for all learners.

CONCLUSION

The transformative role of artificial intelligence (AI) in student development is increasingly evident as AI technologies continue to reshape educational landscapes. From personalized learning experiences to enhanced engagement, AI is revolutionizing how students interact with content, assess their learning progress, and receive tailored feedback. AI's ability to analyze vast amounts of data, adapt to individual needs, and provide continuous support has opened new avenues for student growth, particularly in fostering personalized instruction, lifelong learning, and essential 21st-century skills. However, the integration of AI into education is not without its challenges, and as its use becomes more widespread, it is essential to address the complex balance between technological advancements and human-centred pedagogy.

AI has proven to be a powerful tool in enhancing the student learning experience by facilitating personalized, adaptive learning environments. Through AI-driven platforms, students are offered customized content that aligns with their individual learning styles, pace, and preferences. Whether it's through intelligent tutoring systems, AI-powered feedback, or virtual mentors, students can access tailored resources and support that help them overcome academic challenges and achieve their full potential. These advancements in AI have also contributed to improving student engagement and motivation, creating dynamic learning environments that encourage active participation and deep learning. Moreover, AI has played a pivotal role in bridging educational gaps by providing tools that support diverse learners, including those with disabilities or unique learning needs. Through applications such as speech recognition, text-to-speech tools, and emotion-aware AI, learning can become more inclusive, addressing the diverse requirements of students and promoting equity in education.

As AI continues to transform educational practices, its potential extends beyond academic achievement. AI is also contributing to the development of critical soft skills such as emotional intelligence, communication, and collaboration—skills that are essential for success in both the workforce and personal life. By facilitating immersive learning experiences, AI enables students to interact with complex scenarios and collaborate in real-time, helping them build competencies that will serve them well beyond the classroom. While AI's role in education has brought remarkable advancements, it is crucial to strike a balance between technology and human-centred pedagogy. AI can significantly enhance the learning experience, but it cannot replace the human touch that educators bring to the classroom. The role of teachers remains vital in providing emotional support, fostering a sense of belonging, and nurturing critical thinking and creativity. Educators can leverage AI as a powerful tool to augment their teaching strategies and reach a broader range of students, but it is the human element that ensures the social, emotional, and ethical development of students.

Human-centred pedagogy emphasizes the importance of empathy, social interaction, and authentic relationships, which are crucial for holistic student development. Teachers can use AI to automate routine tasks such as grading and data analysis, allowing them to devote more time to meaningful interactions with students. In doing so, they can focus on encouraging intellectual curiosity, fostering collaborative problem-solving, and inspiring students to take ownership of their learning. The combination of AI's efficiency and the irreplaceable qualities of human educators can create an optimal learning environment that supports both cognitive and socio-emotional growth. As AI continues to evolve, it is essential that educators receive training on how to effectively integrate AI tools into their teaching practices, ensuring that they maintain a student-centred approach. Professional development programs should emphasize the complementary roles of AI and human pedagogy, enabling educators to use AI to enhance their teaching while still upholding the values of empathy, inclusion, and personalized attention.

Final Thoughts on Sustainable and Ethical AI Use in Education

Looking ahead, the future of AI in education hinges on its sustainable and ethical implementation. While AI offers tremendous potential, it also raises important questions regarding data privacy, equity, and fairness. As AI technologies collect and analyze vast amounts of student data, it is essential that schools and institutions implement robust policies to ensure data security and protect students' privacy. Ethical considerations must also extend to the design of AI systems, with an emphasis on mitigating algorithmic bias and ensuring that AI tools serve all students equitably, regardless of socioeconomic background, ability, or identity. To ensure AI's positive impact on education, it is vital that policymakers, educators, technologists, and other stakeholders collaborate on creating frameworks that promote responsible AI use. This includes establishing guidelines for data governance, transparency in AI decision-making processes, and measures to ensure that AI does not inadvertently perpetuate inequality. Moreover, educational systems should strive for inclusivity, ensuring that all students have equal access to the benefits of AI-powered learning tools, regardless of geographic location or access to technology.

Finally, a sustainable approach to AI in education requires continuous evaluation and adaptation. As AI technologies continue to evolve, so too should our strategies for integrating them into educational systems. Regular feedback from students, educators, and other stakeholders can help identify areas for improvement, ensuring that AI remains a force for good in the development of future generations. By approaching AI in education with a mindset of innovation, responsibility, and inclusivity, we can create a learning environment that is not only enhanced by technology but also shaped by the values that will guide the next generation of learners.

In conclusion, AI is undeniably transforming student development, offering unprecedented opportunities for personalized learning, skill development, and lifelong education. However, the integration of AI in education must be done thoughtfully, with a commitment to balancing technological advancements with the core values of human-centred pedagogy. By prioritizing ethical considerations and ensuring equitable access, we can create a future where AI and education work together to nurture students' intellectual, emotional, and social growth.

REFERENCES

Abbes, F., Bennani, S., & Maalel, A. (2024). Generative AI and gamification for personalized learning: Literature review and future challenges. *SN Computer Science*, *5*(8), 1154. DOI: 10.1007/s42979-024-03491-z

Adesina, A. A., Iyelolu, T. V., & Okpeke, P. P.Abayomi Abraham AdesinaToluwalase Vanessa IyeloluPatience Okpeke Paul. (2024). Leveraging predictive analytics for strategic decision-making: Enhancing business performance through data-driven insights. *World Journal of Advanced Research and Reviews*, *22*(3), 1927–1934. DOI: 10.30574/wjarr.2024.22.3.1961

Adewale, U. D., Azeta, A., Abayomi-Alli, A., & Sambo-Magaji, A. (2024). Impact of artificial intelligence adoption on students' academic performance in open and distance learning: A systematic literature review. *Heliyon*, *10*(22), e40025. DOI: 10.1016/j.heliyon.2024.e40025

Al-Ansi, A. M., Jaboob, M., Garad, A., & Al-Ansi, A. (2023). Analyzing augmented reality (AR) and virtual reality (VR) recent development in education. *Social Sciences & Humanities Open*, *8*(1), 100532. DOI: 10.1016/j.ssaho.2023.100532

Alier, M., Pereira, J., García-Peñalvo, F. J., Casañ, M. J., & Cabré, J. (2025). LAMB: An open-source software framework to create artificial intelligence assistants deployed and integrated into learning management systems. *Computer Standards & Interfaces*, *92*, 103940. DOI: 10.1016/j.csi.2024.103940

Arnold, K. E., & Pistilli, M. D. (2012). Course signals at Purdue: Using learning analytics to increase student success. *Proceedings of the 2nd International Conference on Learning Analytics and Knowledge*, 267–270. DOI: 10.1145/2330601.2330666

Aslam, F. (2023). The impact of artificial intelligence on chatbot technology: A study on the current advancements and leading innovations. *European Journal of Technology*, *7*(3), 62–72. DOI: 10.47672/ejt.1561

Balasubramaniam, N., Kauppinen, M., Rannisto, A., Hiekkanen, K., & Kujala, S. (2023). Transparency and explainability of AI systems: From ethical guidelines to requirements. *Information and Software Technology*, *159*, 107197. DOI: 10.1016/j.infsof.2023.107197

Bienkowski, M., Feng, M., & Means, B. (2012). *Enhancing teaching and learning through educational data mining and learning analytics: An issue brief.* U.S. Department of Education.

Bircan, T., & Özbilgin, M. F. (2025). Unmasking inequalities of the code: Disentangling the nexus of AI and inequality. *Technological Forecasting and Social Change*, *211*, 123925. DOI: 10.1016/j.techfore.2024.123925

Boateng, O., & Boateng, B. (2025). Algorithmic bias in educational systems: Examining the impact of AI-driven decision making in modern education. *World Journal of Advanced Research and Reviews*, *25*(1), 2012–2017. DOI: 10.30574/wjarr.2025.25.1.0253

Borge, M., Smith, B. K., & Aldemir, T. (2024). Using generative AI as a simulation to support higher-order thinking. *International Journal of Computer-Supported Collaborative Learning*, *19*(4), 479–532. DOI: 10.1007/s11412-024-09437-0

Devineni, S. K. (2024). AI in data privacy and security. *International Journal of Artificial Intelligence and Machine Learning*, *3*(1), 35–49.

El-Sabagh, H. A. (2021). Adaptive e-learning environment based on learning styles and its impact on development students' engagement. *International Journal of Educational Technology in Higher Education*, *18*(53), 1–24. DOI: 10.1186/s41239-021-00289-4

Embarak, O. H., & Hawarna, S. (2024). Automated AI-driven system for early detection of at-risk students. *Procedia Computer Science*, *231*, 151–160. DOI: 10.1016/j.procs.2023.12.187

Fryer, L. K., Ainley, M., Thompson, A., Gibson, A., & Sherlock, Z. (2017). Stimulating and sustaining interest in a language course: An experimental comparison of chatbot and human task partners. *Computers in Human Behavior*, *75*, 461–468. DOI: 10.1016/j.chb.2017.05.045

Gamage, G., De Silva, D., Mills, N., Alahakoon, D., & Manic, M. (2024). Emotion AWARE: An artificial intelligence framework for adaptable, robust, explainable, and multi-granular emotion analysis. *Journal of Big Data*, *11*(1), 93. DOI: 10.1186/s40537-024-00953-2

Garg, S., & Sharma, S. (2020). Impact of artificial intelligence in special need education to promote inclusive pedagogy. *International Journal of Information and Education Technology (IJIET)*, *10*(7), 523–527. DOI: 10.18178/ijiet.2020.10.7.1418

Ghamrawi, N., Shal, T., & Ghamrawi, N. A. R. (2023). Exploring the impact of AI on teacher leadership: Regressing or expanding? *Education and Information Technologies*, *29*(7), 1–19. DOI: 10.1007/s10639-023-12174-w

Guizani, S., Mazhar, T., Shahzad, T., Ahmad, W., Bibi, A., & Hamam, H. (2025). A systematic literature review to implement large language model in higher education: Issues and solutions. *Discover Education*, *4*(1), 35. DOI: 10.1007/s44217-025-00424-7

Huang, L. (2023). Ethics of artificial intelligence in education: Student privacy and data protection. *Science Insights Education Frontiers*, *16*(2), 2577–2587. DOI: 10.15354/sief.23.re202

Huang, L., Liang, M., Xiong, Y., Wu, X., & Lim, C. P. (2024). A systematic review of technology-enabled teacher professional development during COVID-19 pandemic. *Computers & Education*, *223*, 105168. DOI: 10.1016/j.compedu.2024.105168

Hussain, M., Qureshi, Z. M., & Malik, S. (2024). The impact of educational technologies on modern education: Navigating opportunities and challenges. *Global Educational Studies Review*, *IX*(III), 21–30. DOI: 10.31703/gesr.2024(IX-III).03

Ibarra, B. (2022). Understanding SEL to create a sense of belonging: The role teachers play in addressing students' social and emotional well-being. *Current Issues in Education (Tempe, Ariz.)*, *23*(2), 1–15. DOI: 10.14507/cie.vol23iss2.2049

Idowu, J. A., Koshiyama, A. S., & Treleaven, P. (2024). Investigating algorithmic bias in student progress monitoring. *Computers and Education: Artificial Intelligence*, *7*, 100267. DOI: 10.1016/j.caeai.2024.100267

Iyer, L. S., Chakraborty, T., Reddy, K. N., Krishnaswami, M., & Iyer, L. S. (2023). AI-assisted models for dyslexia and dysgraphia: Revolutionizing language learning for children. In AI-assisted special education for students with exceptional needs (Chapter 8). DOI: 10.4018/979-8-3693-0378-8.ch008

Josué, A., Bedoya-Flores, M. C., Mosquera-Quiñonez, E. F., Mesías-Simisterra, Á. E., & Bautista-Sánchez, J. V. (2023). Educational platforms: Digital tools for the teaching-learning process in education. *Ibero-American Journal of Education & Society Research*, *3*(1), 259–263. DOI: 10.56183/iberoeds.v3i1.626

Kabudi, T., Pappas, I., & Olsen, D. H. (2021). AI-enabled adaptive learning systems: A systematic mapping of the literature. *Computers and Education: Artificial Intelligence*, *2*, 100017. DOI: 10.1016/j.caeai.2021.100017

Koedinger, K. R., Booth, J. L., & Klahr, D. (2013). Instructional complexity and the science to constrain it. *Science*, *342*(6161), 935–937. DOI: 10.1126/science.1238056

Kolb, D. A. (1984). *Experiential learning: Experience as the source of learning and development*. Prentice Hall.

Kumar, A., & Kumar, A. (2025). Human emotion recognition using machine learning techniques based on the physiological signal. Biomedical Signal Processing and Control, 100(Part A), 107039. DOI: 10.1016/j.bspc.2024.107039

Lampou, R. (2023). The integration of artificial intelligence in education: Opportunities and challenges. *Review of Artificial Intelligence in Education, 4*(00), e015. DOI: 10.37497/rev.artif.intell.educ.v4i00.15

Langelaan, B. N., Gaikhorst, L., Smets, W., & Oostdam, R. J. (2024). Differentiating instruction: Understanding the key elements for successful teacher preparation and development. *Teaching and Teacher Education, 140*, 104464. DOI: 10.1016/j.tate.2023.104464

Laun, M., & Wolff, F. (2025). Chatbots in education: Hype or help? A meta-analysis. *Learning and Individual Differences, 119*, 102646. DOI: 10.1016/j.lindif.2025.102646

Li, Y., & Goel, S. (2024). Making it possible for the auditing of AI: A systematic review of AI audits and AI auditability. *Information Systems Frontiers*. Advance online publication. DOI: 10.1007/s10796-024-10508-8

Li, Y., Raković, M., Srivastava, N., Li, X., Guan, Q., Gašević, D., & Chen, G. (2025). Can AI support human grading? Examining machine attention and confidence in short answer scoring. *Computers & Education, 228*, 105244. DOI: 10.1016/j.compedu.2025.105244

Looi, C. K., & Jia, F. (2025). Personalization capabilities of current technology chatbots in a learning environment: An analysis of student-tutor bot interactions. *Education and Information Technologies, 10639*(10), 13369. DOI: 10.1007/s10639-025-13369-z

Lythreatis, S., Singh, S. K., & El-Kassar, A. N. (2022). The digital divide: A review and future research agenda. *Technological Forecasting and Social Change, 175*, 121359. DOI: 10.1016/j.techfore.2021.121359

Makransky, G., & Petersen, G. B. (2021). The cognitive affective model of immersive learning (CAMIL): A theoretical research-based model of learning in immersive virtual reality. *Educational Psychology Review, 33*(3), 937–958. DOI: 10.1007/s10648-020-09586-2

Mansour, N., Aras, C., & Staarman, J. K.. (2024). Embodied learning of science concepts through augmented reality technology. *Educational Technology & Information, 10639*, 13120. DOI: 10.1007/s10639-024-13120-0

Markauskaite, L., Marrone, R., Poquet, O., Knight, S., Martinez-Maldonado, R., Howard, S., Tondeur, J., De Laat, M., Buckingham Shum, S., Gašević, D., & Siemens, G. (2022). Rethinking the entwinement between artificial intelligence and human learning: What capabilities do learners need for a world with AI? *Computers and Education: Artificial Intelligence*, *3*, 100056. DOI: 10.1016/j.caeai.2022.100056

Mebert, L., Barnes, R., Dalley, J., Gawarecki, L., Ghazi-Nezami, F., Shafer, G., Slater, J., & Yezbick, E. (2020). Fostering student engagement through a real-world, collaborative project across disciplines and institutions. *Higher Education Pedagogies*, *5*(1), 30–51. DOI: 10.1080/23752696.2020.1750306

Memarian, B., & Doleck, T. (2024). A review of assessment for learning with artificial intelligence. *Computers in Human Behavior: Artificial Humans*, *2*(1), 100040. DOI: 10.1016/j.chbah.2023.100040

Micallef, A., & Newton, P. M. (2024). The use of concrete examples enhances the learning of abstract concepts: A replication study. *Teaching of Psychology*, *51*(1), 22–29. DOI: 10.1177/00986283211058069

Min, A. (2023). Artificial intelligence and bias: Challenges, implications, and remedies. *Journal of Social Research*, *2*(11), 3808–3817. DOI: 10.55324/josr.v2i11.1477

Mohebbi, A. (2024). Enabling learner independence and self-regulation in language education using AI tools: A systematic review. *Cogent Education*, *12*(1), 2433814. DOI: 10.1080/2331186X.2024.2433814

Moya, S., & Camacho, M. (2024). Leveraging AI-powered mobile learning: A pedagogically informed framework. *Computers and Education: Artificial Intelligence*, *7*, 100276. DOI: 10.1016/j.caeai.2024.100276

Mustafa, F., Nguyen, H. T. M., & Gao, X. A. (2024). The challenges and solutions of technology integration in rural schools: A systematic literature review. *International Journal of Educational Research*, *126*, 102380. DOI: 10.1016/j.ijer.2024.102380

Naseer, F., Khan, M. N., Tahir, M., Addas, A., & Aejaz, S. M. H. (2024). Integrating deep learning techniques for personalized learning pathways in higher education. *Heliyon*, *10*(11), e32628. DOI: 10.1016/j.heliyon.2024.e32628

Nwohiri, A., Joda, O., & Ajayi, O. (2021). AI-powered plagiarism detection: Leveraging forensic linguistics and natural language processing. *FUDMA Journal of Sciences*, *5*(3), 207–218. DOI: 10.33003/fjs-2021-0503-700

O'Neill, G., & Padden, L. (2021). Diversifying assessment methods: Barriers, benefits and enablers. *Innovations in Education and Teaching International*, *59*(4), 398–409. DOI: 10.1080/14703297.2021.1880462

Okonkwo, C. W., & Ade-Ibijola, A. (2021). Chatbots applications in education: A systematic review. *Computers and Education: Artificial Intelligence*, *2*, 100033. DOI: 10.1016/j.caeai.2021.100033

Onyebuchi, N., Onyebuchi, N., Unachukwu, C. C., & Osawaru, B. (2024). Review of AI in education: Transforming learning environments in Africa. *International Journal of Applied Research in Social Sciences*, *5*(10), 637–654. DOI: 10.51594/ijarss.v5i10.725

Onyebuchi, N., Unachukwu, C. C., & Osawaru, B. (2024). Review of AI in education: Transforming learning environments in Africa. *International Journal of Applied Research in Social Sciences*, *5*(10), 637–654. DOI: 10.51594/ijarss.v5i10.725

Rahiman, H. U., & Kodikal, R. (2023). Revolutionizing education: Artificial intelligence empowered learning in higher education. *Cogent Education*, *11*(1), 2293431. DOI: 10.1080/2331186X.2023.2293431

Rashid, A. B., & Kausik, M. A. K. (2024). AI revolutionizing industries worldwide: A comprehensive overview of its diverse applications. *Hybrid Advances*, *7*, 100277. DOI: 10.1016/j.hybadv.2024.100277

Rizvi, M. (2023). Investigating AI-powered tutoring systems that adapt to individual student needs, providing personalized guidance and assessments. *The Eurasia Proceedings of Educational and Social Sciences*, *31*, 67–73. DOI: 10.55549/epess.1381518

Sasikala, P., & Ravichandran, R. (2024). Study on the impact of artificial intelligence on student learning outcomes. *Journal of Digital Learning and Education*, *4*(2), 145–155. DOI: 10.52562/jdle.v4i2.1234

Shoaib, M., Sayed, N., Singh, J., Shafi, J., Khan, S., & Ali, F. (2024). AI student success predictor: Enhancing personalized learning in campus management systems. *Computers in Human Behavior*, *158*, 108301. DOI: 10.1016/j.chb.2024.108301

Siricharoen, W. V. (2023). AR and VR enhances learning. In C. Anutariya, D. Liu, K. Kinshuk, A. Tlili, J. Yang, & M. Chang (Eds.), Smart learning for a sustainable society: ICSLE 2023 (pp. 1–10). Lecture Notes in Educational Technology. Springer. DOI: 10.1007/978-981-99-5961-7_27

Song, Y., Weisberg, L. R., Zhang, S., Tian, X., Boyer, K. E., & Israel, M. (2024). A framework for inclusive AI learning design for diverse learners. *Computers and Education: Artificial Intelligence*, *6*, 100212. DOI: 10.1016/j.caeai.2024.100212

Thu , P. B., & Tien, P. D. (2024). AI-powered administration: The role of intelligent tutoring systems in education. *International Journal of Religion*, *5*(10), 4560–4569. DOI: 10.61707/sqwrjn32

van den Berg, S., & Papadopoulos, P. M. (2024). Summative assessment with Artificial Intelligence: Qualitative analysis and comparison of technology acceptance in student and teacher populations. *Innovations in Education and Teaching International*, •••, 1–16. DOI: 10.1080/14703297.2024.2436613

VanLehn, K. (2011). The relative effectiveness of human tutoring, intelligent tutoring systems, and other tutoring systems. *Educational Psychologist*, *46*(4), 197–221. DOI: 10.1080/00461520.2011.611369

Ventista, O. M., & Brown, C. (2023). Teachers' professional learning and its impact on students' learning outcomes: Findings from a systematic review. *Social Sciences & Humanities Open*, *8*(1), 100565. DOI: 10.1016/j.ssaho.2023.100565

Vygotsky, L. S. (1978). *Mind in society: The development of higher psychological processes*. Harvard University Press.

Walter, Y. (2024). Embracing the future of artificial intelligence in the classroom: The relevance of AI literacy, prompt engineering, and critical thinking in modern education. *International Journal of Educational Technology in Higher Education*, *21*(1), 15. DOI: 10.1186/s41239-024-00448-3

Wang, H., Wang, F., Zhu, Z., Wang, J., Tran, T., & Du, Z. (2024). Artificial intelligence in education: A systematic literature review. Expert Systems with Applications, 252(Part A), 124167. DOI: 10.1016/j.eswa.2024.124167

Wang, L. (2023). The impact of student-centered learning on academic motivation and achievement: A comparative research between traditional instruction and student-centered approach. *Journal of Education Humanities and Social Sciences*, *22*, 346–353. DOI: 10.54097/ehss.v22i.12463

Wang, Y. (2024). The impact of AI application in education on students. *Journal of Education Humanities and Social Sciences*, *45*, 116–122. DOI: 10.54097/gg1d3q19

Wankhede, N., Kale, M., Shukla, M., Nathiya, D. R., Roopashree, K., Kaur, P., Goyanka, B., Rahangdale, S., Taksande, B., Upaganlawar, A., Khalid, M., Chigurupati, S., Umekar, M., Kopalli, S. R., & Koppula, S. (2024). Leveraging AI for the diagnosis and treatment of autism spectrum disorder: Current trends and future prospects. *Asian Journal of Psychiatry*, *101*, 104241. DOI: 10.1016/j.ajp.2024.104241

Winkler, R., & Söllner, M. (2018). Unleashing the potential of chatbots in education: A state-of-the-art analysis. *eLearning Papers*, 62, 1–14.

Wulan, D. R., Nainggolan, D. M., Hidayat, Y., Rohman, T., & Fiyul, A. Y. (2024). Exploring the benefits and challenges of gamification in enhancing student learning outcomes. *Global International Journal of Innovative Research*, *2*(7), 1657–1674. DOI: 10.59613/global.v2i7.238

Xiao, N., Pei, Y., Yuan, C., Bu, Y., & Xua, Z. (2025). Transforming education with artificial intelligence: A comprehensive review of applications, challenges, and future directions. *International Theory and Practice in Humanities and Social Sciences*, *2*(1), 337–356. DOI: 10.70693/itphss.v2i1.211

Xing, W., Chen, X., Stein, J., & Marcinkowski, M. (2020). Temporal prediction of dropouts in MOOCs: Reaching the low-hanging fruit. *IEEE Transactions on Learning Technologies*, *13*(4), 789–801.

Xu, Z. (2024). AI in education: Enhancing learning experiences and student outcomes. *Applied and Computational Engineering*, *51*(1), 104–111. DOI: 10.54254/2755-2721/51/20241187

Yaseen, H., Mohammad, A. S., Ashal, N., Abusaimeh, H., Ali, A., & Sharabati, A. A. A. (2025). The impact of adaptive learning technologies, personalized feedback, and interactive AI tools on student engagement: The moderating role of digital literacy. *Sustainability (Basel)*, *17*(3), 1133. DOI: 10.3390/su17031133

Zhang, K., & Aslan, A. B. (2021). AI technologies for education: Recent research & future directions. *Computers and Education: Artificial Intelligence*, *2*, 100025. DOI: 10.1016/j.caeai.2021.100025

Zhao, D. (2024). The impact of AI-enhanced natural language processing tools on writing proficiency: An analysis of language precision, content summarization, and creative writing facilitation. *Education and Information Technologies*. Advance online publication. DOI: 10.1007/s10639-024-13145-5

Zimmerman, B. J. (2002). Becoming a self-regulated learner: An overview. *Theory into Practice*, *41*(2), 64–70. DOI: 10.1207/s15430421tip4102_2

KEY TERMS AND DEFINITIONS

21st-Century Skills: A set of competencies—including critical thinking, creativity, collaboration, communication, and digital literacy—that are essential for success in the modern world. AI technologies play a vital role in developing these skills through interactive and adaptive learning environments.

Adaptive Learning Systems: AI-powered educational platforms that adjust the presentation of material and learning pace according to individual learners' needs, performance, and preferences, thereby enabling personalized instruction and optimized learning outcomes.

AI-Driven Assessment: Evaluation processes enhanced or automated by AI technologies, including automated grading, predictive analytics, and real-time feedback mechanisms that inform teaching and learning decisions.

Algorithmic Bias: A systematic error that occurs when AI systems produce unfair outcomes due to biased training data or flawed design. In education, this can result in unequal treatment or inaccurate assessments of certain student groups.

Artificial Intelligence (AI): A branch of computer science focused on creating systems capable of performing tasks that typically require human intelligence, such as reasoning, learning, problem-solving, and decision-making. In education, AI supports personalized learning, automated assessment, and adaptive instruction.

Data Privacy and Security: The protection of personal and academic data collected through AI systems from unauthorized access, misuse, or disclosure. Ensuring data privacy is essential for maintaining trust and safeguarding student rights.

Data-Driven Decision-Making: An educational practice where teachers and administrators use data collected from AI tools and learning platforms to make informed decisions about instruction, assessment, and student support strategies.

Digital Divide: The disparity between individuals or communities that have access to digital technologies, such as AI-enabled learning tools and high-speed internet, and those that do not—often resulting in unequal educational opportunities.

Emotion-Aware AI: Emerging AI systems that can detect and respond to learners' emotional states through analysis of facial expressions, speech, or behaviour to provide more empathetic and adaptive learning experiences.

Ethical AI in Education: A framework ensuring that AI technologies are used responsibly and transparently in educational settings, addressing issues such as data privacy, informed consent, accountability, and equitable access.

Gamification in Education: The application of game design elements—such as points, badges, and leaderboards—in educational contexts to increase student motivation, engagement, and enjoyment in learning.

Human-Centred Pedagogy: An educational approach that prioritizes human interaction, empathy, and social-emotional development while leveraging AI as a supportive tool rather than a replacement for teachers.

Intelligent Tutoring Systems (ITS): Computer-based systems that use AI to simulate one-on-one tutoring by providing customized instruction, feedback, and guidance to learners. ITS can diagnose learning difficulties and adapt content delivery in real time.

Natural Language Processing (NLP): A subfield of AI that enables computers to understand and generate human language. In education, NLP is used for automated essay scoring, intelligent chatbots, and real-time feedback systems.

Personalized Learning: An educational approach that tailors learning experiences to individual students' strengths, needs, interests, and pace, often facilitated by AI technologies that analyze learning data to inform instruction.

Predictive Analytics: The use of AI and statistical techniques to analyze historical learning data and predict future student performance, enabling early identification of learning challenges and targeted interventions.

Socio-Emotional Learning (SEL): The process through which students develop essential emotional and social skills such as self-awareness, empathy, and collaboration. AI tools can support SEL by offering feedback and simulations that foster emotional intelligence.

Student Engagement: The level of interest, motivation, and active participation that students demonstrate in the learning process. AI enhances engagement through interactive, gamified platforms and personalized feedback mechanisms.

Teacher Professional Development in AI: Ongoing training and capacity-building initiatives aimed at equipping educators with the skills and knowledge required to integrate AI tools effectively into teaching and learning practices.

Chapter 12
Use of ChatGPT in Higher Education:
Development and Validation of Questionnaire

Aisha Naz Ansari
https://orcid.org/0000-0003-0938-8980
Institute for Educational Development, Aga Khan University, Karachi, Pakistan

Sohail Ahmad
https://orcid.org/0000-0001-7344-0566
Institute for Educational Development, Aga Khan University, Karachi, Pakistan

Sadia Muzaffar Bhutta
https://orcid.org/0000-0003-0343-8932
Institute for Educational Development, Aga Khan University, Karachi, Pakistan

ABSTRACT

Advancements in AI, such as ChatGPT, have garnered significant interest within higher education. In response, policymakers and practitioners are striving to develop evidence-based strategies for its integration. Generating valid and reliable evidence requires robust tools to explore students' use of ChatGPT in higher education. This paper discusses the development and validation of a questionnaire designed to assess the perceived Knowledge, Will, Skill, Technological Support, and Use (KWSTU) of ChatGPT. The questionnaire was grounded in the theoretical foundation of the Will-Skill-Tool (WST) model and underwent rigorous content and construct validation. Confirmatory Factor Analysis validated five distinct factors comprising 30 items, with statistical evidence indicating good model-fit indices. Moreover, path analysis was employed to investigate the factors influencing ChatGPT use among university

DOI: 10.4018/979-8-3373-2927-7.ch012

students in Pakistan. This study provides a validated instrument and empirical insights that have significant implications for policy, practice, and research to make informed decisions.

INTRODUCTION

The advancement of technology has long remained a central concern in the domain of education, shaping how knowledge is created, accessed, and shared (Collins & Halverson, 2018). In recent years, the rapid progression of artificial intelligence (AI) has emerged as a transformative force, stimulating extensive debate about its potential implications for teaching and learning (Bahroun et al., 2023; Pham & Sampson, 2022; Tahiru, 2021; Zhai et al., 2021). Among these AI innovations, the launch of ChatGPT by OpenAI has drawn unprecedented attention from educators and researchers worldwide (Neumann et al., 2023). As a generative AI chatbot capable of producing human-like responses across diverse topics, ChatGPT represents both a promising pedagogical tool and a source of concern. The discourse surrounding its use is multifaceted, ranging from optimism about its potential to facilitate learning to apprehension about its implications for academic integrity (Ansari et al., 2024; Dalalah & Dalalah, 2023; Labadze et al., 2023).

Despite the growing body of literature, a notable concern arises when examining the nature of evidence available for improving teaching and learning practices, which often lacks robust empirical grounding (Ansari et al., 2024). Current discussions around ChatGPT are diverse and sometimes conflicting. On one hand, it is viewed as a powerful tool for enhancing students' writing, critical thinking, and personalized learning experiences. On the other, concerns have been raised about academic integrity, overreliance on technology, and the pedagogical implications of AI-generated content (Ansari et al., 2025; Dalalah & Dalalah, 2023; Labadze et al., 2023). Despite these expanding debates, much of the existing literature remains conceptual or exploratory. The empirical evidence explaining *how* students use ChatGPT for academic purposes and *what factors* influence its adoption is still limited and fragmented.

This gap in empirical understanding highlights the need for systematic research that measures the use of ChatGPT and identifies its key predictors within higher education contexts. Although a growing number of studies have begun to examine ChatGPT's educational applications, few have employed validated instruments to assess its use, particularly in developing contexts. Addressing this gap, the present study focuses on developing and validating a questionnaire to examine university students' use of ChatGPT through a theoretically grounded model.

Drawing upon an extensive review of technology adoption frameworks, the well-established Will, Skill, Tool (WST) model proposed by Knezek and Christensen (2000) was adapted as the foundational framework. Recognising that knowledge of ChatGPT is likely a prerequisite for its meaningful use, a new construct *Knowledge* was incorporated prior to *Will* in the model. Furthermore, as the study aimed to explore both the determinants and extent of ChatGPT use, a *Use* construct was also introduced. These modifications resulted in the Knowledge, Will, Skill, Technological Support, Use (KWSTU) model. The term *Tool* was replaced with *Technological Support* to more accurately capture the enabling conditions and access that facilitate the use of ChatGPT in university settings.

Accordingly, this paper presents the development and validation of the KWSTU Questionnaire. The questionnaire is based on the adapted theoretical model of technology integration, Will, Skill, Tool (WST). The KWSTU questionnaire is a self-reported survey that assesses the following domains: a) Knowledge, b) Will, c) Skill, d) Technological support, and e) Use of ChatGPT. It was developed using a rigorous process that included item generation, content validity, construct validity, reliability, and path analysis. By doing so, the study contributes to the growing body of empirical research on AI in education and provides a foundation for future investigations into technology integration in teaching and learning.

LITERATURE REVIEW

Artificial intelligence is a multidisciplinary field focused on creating systems capable of performing tasks that typically require human intelligence, such as learning, reasoning, problem-solving, perception, and decision-making (Mitchell, 2019). It encompasses various techniques, including machine learning, which allows systems to learn from data and improve over time (Sarker, 2021). AI can simulate human cognitive functions and perform tasks beyond human capabilities, such as large-scale computations (Zhu et al., 2023).

AI is increasingly integrated into education to enhance learning experiences, streamline administrative processes, and provide personalised learning opportunities (Ahmad et al., 2024; Pedro et al., 2019; Zawacki-Richter et al., 2019). Key applications include tutoring which provide tailored instruction and feedback, allowing students to learn at their own pace (Létourneau et al., 2025); automated grading, which enables efficient assessment of assignments and exams while freeing teachers to focus on interactive and creative teaching tasks (Jonäll, 2024); and predictive analytics, which identifies students at risk of falling behind and enables timely interventions (Crompton & Burke, 2022). AI also facilitates personalised learning, adapting instructional materials and experiences to individual student needs, preferences, and performance levels (Bhutta et al., 2025; Tapalova & Zhiyenbayeva, 2022), and supports administrative functions, including enrolment management, data handling, and resource allocation, thereby improving institutional efficiency.

In K-12 education, AI tools such as intelligent tutoring systems and educational games enhance personalised learning and automate routine tasks, while also assisting teachers in monitoring progress, forming and moderating groups, and making data-driven decisions (Crompton & Burke, 2022; Létourneau et al., 2025). However, challenges such as privacy concerns, algorithmic biases, and limited digital literacy among students and teachers can hinder effective implementation (Karan & Angadi, 2023). Similarly, in higher education, AI is employed to improve teaching, learning, and administrative processes. It personalises learning by analysing student performance and providing customised learning materials, automates grading and administrative tasks, and identifies at-risk students to provide targeted support and reduce dropout rates (Pedro et al., 2019; Jonäll, 2024; Téllez et al., 2024). Nevertheless, ethical concerns, data privacy issues, and unequal access to technology remain important challenges that must be addressed for effective integration (Dhirani et al., 2023).

In the early 21st century, Knezek et al. (2000) embarked on a successful initiative to develop a structural model of technology integration. According to this model, the successful integration of technology relies on a teacher's positive attitude (*Will*), competency in task performance (*Skills*), and access to technological tools (*Tools*). The *Will* factor encompasses positive attitudes, including confidence and openness to change which plays a crucial role in emotional and perceptual levels (Knezek et al., 2000, 2003; Knezek & Christensen, 2016). Similarly, the *Skill* factor focuses on the ability and experience that results in accepting the need for digital technologies (Knezek et al., 2000, 2003; Knezek & Christensen, 2016). Likewise, the *Tool* factor centres on access to digital technologies, including the use of specific tools like Microsoft Teams, Moodle, and Skype (Knezek et al., 2000, 2003; Knezek & Christensen, 2016).

This model is based on principles from educational psychology, specifically identifying key variables that influence the school learning environment (Klausmeier & Goodwin, 1975). It explores the interconnections among teachers' attitudes toward digital technologies, their technological competence, and the availability of digital resources. Knezek et al. (2000; 2003) assert that these three constructs are critical for incorporating any technological tools into educational practices. This is because positive attitudes, corresponding competencies, and sufficient technical infrastructures are deemed imperative for technology integration (Agyei & Voogt, 2011; Buabeng-Andoh, 2012).

WST model was adapted based on empirical studies that rigorously tested its validity, reliability, and explanatory power in the variance of technology integration in the classroom (Agyei & Voogt, 2011; Grant, 2019; Knezek et al., 2003; Petko, 2012;

Scully et al., 2021; Velazquez, 2007). While examining the predictive power of the WST model, Knezek et al. (2003) analysed data collected between 1999 and 2001 and found that the model could explain 70% to 84% of the variance in technology integration in classrooms. This indicates that the constructs of Will, Skill, and Tool are strong predictors of how effectively technology is incorporated into teaching practices. Subsequently, Morales et al. (2005) examined that teacher samples spanning 2001-2005, finding that WST accounted for 64-83% of the variance in technology integration. Morales (2006) expanded the study internationally, concluding that 90% to 96% of classroom technology integration could be attributed to WST measures for teachers in Mexico and the USA. The model consistently explained more than 90% of the variance in all samples, with Skill being the strongest predictor in the USA, while Tool was the primary predictor in Mexico (Morales & Knezek, 2007).

While these three constructs provide the foundation, the model was further enriched by adding two constructs: *Knowledge* about the newly launched AI tool and the pattern of its *Usage*. These additions resulted in a modified model, labelled KWSTU, which served as the basis for the development and validation of the questionnaire used in this study. The three original constructs adapted from Knezek et al. (2000) remained largely unchanged, except for a minor modification in terminology, where *Tool* was replaced with *Technological Support*.

The *Knowledge* construct encompasses respondents' understanding and awareness of the features and functionalities of the AI tool, while the *Usage* construct captures how frequently and in what ways the tool is applied in educational practice. The items for these constructs were derived through a rigorous review of relevant literature and guided by intellectual reasoning, ensuring conceptual alignment and practical relevance. For example, an item under Knowledge asks respondents to indicate their familiarity with AI-assisted learning methods, while an item under Usage asks about the frequency of incorporating the AI tool in learning activities. These illustrative items clarify the operationalisation of the new constructs prior to expert review.

This validated model of WST has commonly been used to assess teachers' integration of technology into educational practices, however, in the current era of technological advancements and artificial intelligence, students themselves play an active role in integrating technological tools for their learning. An exemplary case is the use of ChatGPT in education, which has been widely used by university students (Ansari et al., 2024; Turner, 2023). These university students are inherently self-reliant in their learning endeavours, often demonstrating a frequent integration of technological tools. Considering this, the WST model was adapted (see figure 1) with the inclusion of *knowledge* and the *use* of technological tools like ChatGPT by university students.

Figure 1. Theoretical framework for studying KWSTU of ChatGPT

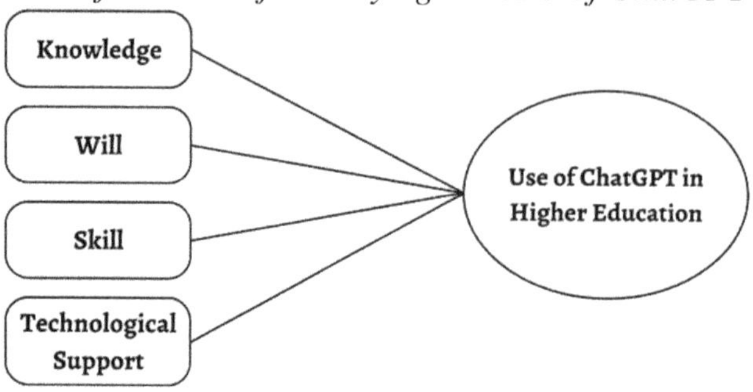

The adapted model is KWSTU, encompassing knowledge, will, skill, technological tools, and use, to predict the use of ChatGPT in higher education by students. This paper is guided by the following research questions.

- **Research Question 1:** How valid and reliable is the KWSTU questionnaire for assessing perceived knowledge, will, skills, technological support, and use of ChatGPT among higher education students?
- **Research Question 2:** How do the factors (knowledge, will, skills, and technological support) interact to influence the use of ChatGPT among students of higher education?

METHODS

Initially, an exhaustive literature review was conducted to identify factors predicting the integration of technology in education. The WST theoretical model was adapted and introduced ChatGPT knowledge as a factor influencing the use of ChatGPT, with the Use of ChatGPT as a separate factor within the same questionnaire. Thus, KWSTU ChatGPT has five factors, namely Knowledge, Will, Skill, Technological Support, and Use of ChatGPT. Additionally, existing instruments developed based on the WST model were examined for item generation. Distinct statistical models including Confirmatory Factor Analysis (CFA) and Structural Equation Modelling (SEM) were used to generate psychometric findings in response to the two research questions developed for the study.

KWSTU Questionnaire: Validity and Reliability

Questionnaire development

Following the standard criteria for developing a valid and reliable questionnaire (Kishore et al., 2021), the process began with an extensive review of the literature on factors predicting the use and integration of technology in education. Keeping in mind that the KWSTU framework served as a foundation for initiating item generation, guiding decisions on the scale, and aiding in the formulation of questionnaire items, the researchers systematically developed the questionnaire to ensure conceptual alignment with each construct. The existing questionnaires based on the WST model were examined to determine appropriate measurement approaches, which indicated that WST factors could be better assessed using a Likert-type scale (Batterton & Hale, 2017). After reviewing prior instruments and considering the study's aim to capture the degree of perceived knowledge, will, skill, technological support, and use of ChatGPT, the researchers adopted a 4-point Likert scale (Not at all = 1; To some extent = 2; To a moderate extent = 3; To a great extent = 4) for the KWSTU questionnaire. The 4-point format was intentionally chosen to encourage respondents to make a clear judgment about the extent of their knowledge, will, skill, technological support, and use of ChatGPT without the option of a neutral midpoint. This approach is particularly useful in attitudinal and self-perception measures, where a forced-choice scale can reduce central tendency bias and yield more discriminating responses (Brown, 2010).

The questionnaire encompassed these five constructs, namely i) Knowledge of ChatGPT, ii) Willingness to use ChatGPT, iii) Skill to use ChatGPT, iv) Technological Support to use ChatGPT, and v) the actual Use of ChatGPT. During the process of items development, specifically for the *use* construct, researchers consulted literature (Ansari et al., 2024) as well as currently enrolled university students. Informal discussions were conducted with a number of students from public and private universities in order to understand the various uses of ChatGPT. Based on possible uses, items were added into the construct of use. The initial pool of items in the KWSTU questionnaire was comprised of 43 items. Furthermore, some demographic questions were also added in order to capture the background information of the respondents.

The guidelines on the general features of a questionnaire (Morales, 2006) were meticulously followed. The questionnaire commenced with an informative cover page to acquaint respondents with the purpose of data collection, details about the questionnaire's structure, instructions for responding to it, and a reassurance that the questionnaire was not a test with correct or incorrect answers. This was to emphasise the significance of forthright and honest responses; the cover page underscored the ethical dimensions of voluntary participation and confidentiality.

This questionnaire, consisting of 43 items, underwent two rounds of review. First, it was evaluated by language experts to assess clarity, redundancy, and readability (Lawshe, 1975; Morales, 2006). Based on their feedback, two items were removed from the technological support construct due to redundancy and overlap. Subsequently, the revised questionnaire, now with 41 items, was reviewed by technology experts with experience in teaching and researching technology in education. They assessed the accuracy of terms, alignment with technology, and redundancy (Lawshe, 1975; Morales, 2006). This review led to the removal of seven additional items from the use construct due to the repetition of ChatGPT-related uses. As a result, the final questionnaire comprised 34 items.

Establishing content validity

The participants for content validation process brought a rich diversity of academic expertise, with a wide range of teaching and research experience. Representing institutions from across the globe, including the Aga Khan University, University of Eastern Finland, National University of Lesotho, and the University of Ibadan, each participant contributed a unique perspective. Their teaching experience spanned from four to 23 years, while their research experience ranged from two to 23 years. This combination of seasoned lecturers and researchers, from varied disciplines and geographical contexts, ensured a robust and well-rounded evaluation of the content's validity, providing valuable insights from both established and emerging academic perspectives.

The questionnaire in English as well as Urdu language underwent expert review for content validation using Lawshe's (1975) approach to estimating the Content Validity Index (CVI). The questionnaire was sent out to nine experts who have expertise in education technology and research. The reviewers were asked to rate each item for its relevance and clarity to the construct on a three-point scale (irrelevant=1; moderately relevant=2; relevant=3; ambiguous=1; moderately clear=2; clear=3). Alongside, the reviewers were asked to provide qualitative feedback, if there is any at the item level as well as construct level.

Establishing construct validity

The sample for construct validation comprised 1,218 students from six universities in the province of Sindh, Pakistan, with an equal distribution of public (n=3) and private (n=3) universities which were selected using a multi-stage sampling technique (Bryman, 2012). In the first stage of sampling, two out of seven divisions were strategically selected considering the availability of both public and private universities alongside offering multidisciplinary courses to students along with having an education department. In the second stage, public and private sector universities were selected with the criteria of having both undergraduate and graduate programmes. To maintain a balanced representation, three public and three private universities were chosen.

Data collection began after obtaining approval from the institutional Ethics Review Committee (ERC) and authorisation from university administrators. A comprehensive research information sheet and consent forms were distributed. The data were collected using a hybrid approach, combining both direct and virtual administration. For virtual survey administration, the online platform Survey Monkey was utilised. Conversely, for direct administration, the same Survey Monkey link was used to generate a QR code. For this purpose, research assistants were hired for a short duration to facilitate the research team in data collection from the selected universities.

The collected data were directly imported into SPSS version 25 from Survey Monkey. To minimise the likelihood of errors, the data underwent cleaning through frequency analysis. This cleaned dataset in SPSS was imported into Jamovi (version 2.3) for conducting Confirmatory Factor Analysis. CFA was used to validate the compatibility of the factors involved in the questionnaire. The criteria included model fit of internal structure and overall model fit indices. For the internal structure of the model, the main criterion for validating this compatibility is to look at the factor loadings of each item that should be greater than or equal to 0.50 (factor loading $\geq$ 0.50) to confirm a satisfactory fit (Bagozzi & Yi, 1988; Fornell & Larcker, 1981; Kline, 2023; Netemeyer et al., 2003). The other criteria proposed for this fit are model fitness indices which include Chi-square, RMSEA, SRMR, CFI, TLI, and NFI. These model fit indices are classified as Absolute fit indices [i.e., X2, X2/df, root mean square error of approximation (RMSEA), and standard root mean square residual (SRMR)] and Comparative indices [i.e., Comparative Fit Index (CFI), Ticker-Lewis Index (TLI), Normed Fit Index (NFI)]. The Chi-square measures the significance of unexplained covariance that is not accounted for in the model (Bentler & Bonett, 1980; Cole, 1987). However, if the ratio of Chi-square divided by its degrees of freedom (X2/df) is smaller than 3, it indicates an acceptable fit (Schreiber, 2008). Furthermore, the RMSEA and SRMR belong to residuals-based measures. RMSEA and SRMR values should be less than or equal to 0.08 (RMSEA & SRMR $\leq$ 0.08) in order to confirm the acceptable fit of the model (Bentler, 1990; Browne, 1993; Byrne, 2013; Hu & Bentler, 1999). Moreover, CFI, TLI, and NFI compare a hypothesis model to a baseline model to see how well a model fits vis-a-vis the baseline model (Bentler & Bonett, 1980). The values for CFI, TLI, and NFI greater than or equal to 0.90 indicate a very good model fit (Bentler, 1990; Hu & Bentler, 1999; Jackson et al., 2009; Schreiber, 2008).

Establishing reliability

The internal consistency among items within each factor was assessed using Cronbach's Alpha, Omega, and AVE (average variance extracted) were computed to generate varied evidence for reliability. The acceptable range for internal consistency for Cronbach's Alpha as well as Omega should be ≥ 0.70 and the average variance extracted (AVE) should be ≥ 0.50 (Bagozzi & Yi, 1988; Fornell & Larcker, 1981; Kline, 2023; Netemeyer et al., 2003).

PATH ANALYSIS OF FACTORS PREDICTING THE USE OF CHATGPT

Path analysis was conducted using Jamovi (version 2.3), an open-access software. For this analysis, the mean of each construct was computed using SPSS version 25. The SPSS data were imported into Jamovi, where path analysis under the framework of structural equation modelling was performed. In SEM, exogenous variables refer to independent variables that are not influenced by other variables in the model, whereas endogenous variables are dependent variables whose values are explained or predicted by other constructs within the model. In this study, three constructs including Will, Skill, and Use of ChatGPT, were considered endogenous variables, while Knowledge and Technological Support were treated as exogenous variables. The path analysis helped identify and validate the relationships through which Knowledge, Will, Skill, and Technological Support predict the Use of ChatGPT in higher education. Moreover, the results of the path analysis were also used to validate the KWSTU model alongside the WST model of technology integration in the adoption of ChatGPT by higher education students.

Results

This section presents the results of KWSTU questionnaire validation both for content and construct validation and reliability. Alongside this, it presents the path analysis to demonstrate the path that predicts the use of ChatGPT among university students. In addition to this, the results of path analysis are used to validate the WST model of technology integration in the adoption of ChatGPT by university students in Pakistan.

Validation of KWSTU

This section presents results to assess validity of KWSTU questionnaire using distinct models including content validation and factor structure.

Content validation

The Content Validity Index (CVI) evaluates the degree to which an instrument incorporates appropriate items that accurately represent the content domain within the examined construct (Newman et al., 2013). Content validity was assessed for both the relevance and clarity of each item (I-CVI) and for the entire questionnaire or scale (S-CVI). Experts were assigned a scale of 1 to 3 for both relevance and clarity. I-CVI and S-CVI were calculated using a dichotomous scale, where 1 was considered irrelevant or unclear, and 2 and 3 were merged as relevant or clear (Lawshe, 1975). The I-CVI indicates the proportion of agreement on the relevance and clarity of each item, while the S-CVI expresses the proportion of total items judged for content validity which ranges from zero to one (Beck & Gable, 2001; Lynn, 1986). The results are presented in table 1.

Table 1. Content validation of KWSTU questionnaire

S-CVI	Value	Remarks
Relevance	1	Excellent
Clarity	0.963	Excellent

Of the total 34 items, the relevance of all items was computed as I-CVI, which was found to be exactly 1 for the 30 items whereas only four items received an I-CVI of 0.78, which shows that the experts considered these items valid in terms of relevance to the construct. These four items were retained because their I-CVI value was in the acceptable range (Lawshe, 1095). The overall S-CVI was found to be 1, confirming the complete relevance of the entire items to their respective constructs.

For clarity, most of the items were rated 1 by the reviewers (I-CVI=1) indicating the clarity of the language in each item. However, six items were considered less clear (I-CVI=0.78) which were further modified as per the reviewers' suggestions and were sent to language experts for double check. Additionally, the S-CVI was computed, resulting in a value of 1 for relevance and 0.968 for clarity. All these values indicated an excellent level of content validity of the KWSTU questionnaire (Cicchetti & Sparrow, 1981; Lawshe, 1975).

Construct validation

CFA was conducted in three iterations to ensure good model fit and appropriate factors loading in each construct.

First and Second Iterations of CFA: In the first iteration, the model was not fitted (X^2/df= 12.15, p<0.001; CFI = 0.949; TLI = 0.945; NFI = 0.945; RMSEA = 0.096; SRMR = 0.091). Of the total 34 items, the loading value for two items, one from the construct of 'will' (W6=0.380) and the other from the construct of 'technological support' (T4=0.311) was found below 0.50; hence, these were removed. The summary of the first iteration is presented in table 2.

The second iteration yielded improved model fit indices (X^2/df= 9.92, p<0.001; CFI=0.964; TLI=0.961; NFI=0.960; RMSEA=0.086; SRMR=0.078). However, the second iteration led to the exclusion of two items from the construct of 'Use' due to low factor loadings (U1=0.44; U2=0.47). This again improved the model fit indices. The summary of the second iteration is presented in table 2.

Table 2. Summary of first and second iterations of CFA for KWSTU questionnaire

S. No.	Item	Iteration 1: Factor loadings	Iteration 2: Factor loadings
1	I know ChatGPT as an AI tool.	0.78	0.78
2	I know ChatGPT is pre-trained language model with existing information to generate responses.	0.76	0.74
3	I know ChatGPT has the potential to utilise information/ data provided by the users.	0.66	0.68
4	I know how to use ChatGPT.	0.62	0.67
5	I know ChatGPT performs various tasks (e.g., text generation, Q/A, translation).	0.69	0.71
6	I know the limitations of ChatGPT in providing reliable information.	0.63	0.68
7	I know about the ethical considerations surrounding the use of ChatGPT.	0.62	0.67
8	I know that ChatGPT will promote copy-paste culture in assignments.	0.53	0.55
9	I feel comfortable interacting with ChatGPT for educational purposes.	0.62	0.69
10	I feel enthusiastic to explore ChatGPT, for my learning.	0.72	0.75
11	I feel that ChatGPT allows me to learn at my own pace.	0.74	0.79
12	I feel optimistic to adapt my learning habits to get the maximum benefits of ChatGPT.	0.71	0.74
13	I feel that ChatGPT will improve my higher-order thinking skills.	0.68	0.67

continued on following page

Table 2. Continued

S. No.	Item	Iteration 1: Factor loadings	Iteration 2: Factor loadings
14	I feel that my teachers encourage the use of ChatGPT.	0.38	Removed
15	My university updates us on artificial intelligence tools.	0.84	0.75
16	My university provides training on the effective use of ChatGPT.	0.79	0.82
17	My university invests in technology by purchasing updated versions of AI tools (e.g., ChatGPT).	0.70	0.74
18	I have encountered accessibility issues to ChatGPT within the university.	0.31	Removed
19	I have necessary technical skills (e.g., giving accurate prompt) to interact with ChatGPT.	0.64	0.69
20	I have ability to utilise the features of ChatGPT.	0.73	0.71
21	I have ability to critically evaluate the responses generated by ChatGPT.	0.70	0.75
22	I have ability to modify information generated by ChatGPT for my tasks to avoid plagiarism.	0.73	0.76
23	I have proficiency in troubleshooting technical issues that may arise when using ChatGPT.	0.62	0.67
24	I use ChatGPT for educational purposes.	0.50	0.44
25	I use ChatGPT for learning different concepts.	0.50	0.47
26	I use ChatGPT to participate in activities inside the classroom.	0.67	0.72
27	I use ChatGPT to get ideas for my assignments.	0.68	0.73
28	I use ChatGPT to paraphrase and rewrite copied text for my written assignment.	0.68	0.71
29	I use ChatGPT to proofread and refine my written assignment.	0.71	0.76
30	I use ChatGPT for research purposes (e.g., developing data collection tools, analysing data, and reporting findings).	0.63	0.74
31	I use ChatGPT to practice language for effective written communication.	0.67	0.74
32	I use ChatGPT to read summaries of books.	0.68	0.71
33	I use ChatGPT to scan and skim my academic readings.	0.73	0.76
34	I use ChatGPT to write my complete assignments.	0.69	0.71

Final iteration: The final model was generated in the third iteration which revealed good model indices with no factor loading less than 0.50, as presented in Figure 2.

Figure 2. Five factor model in CFA

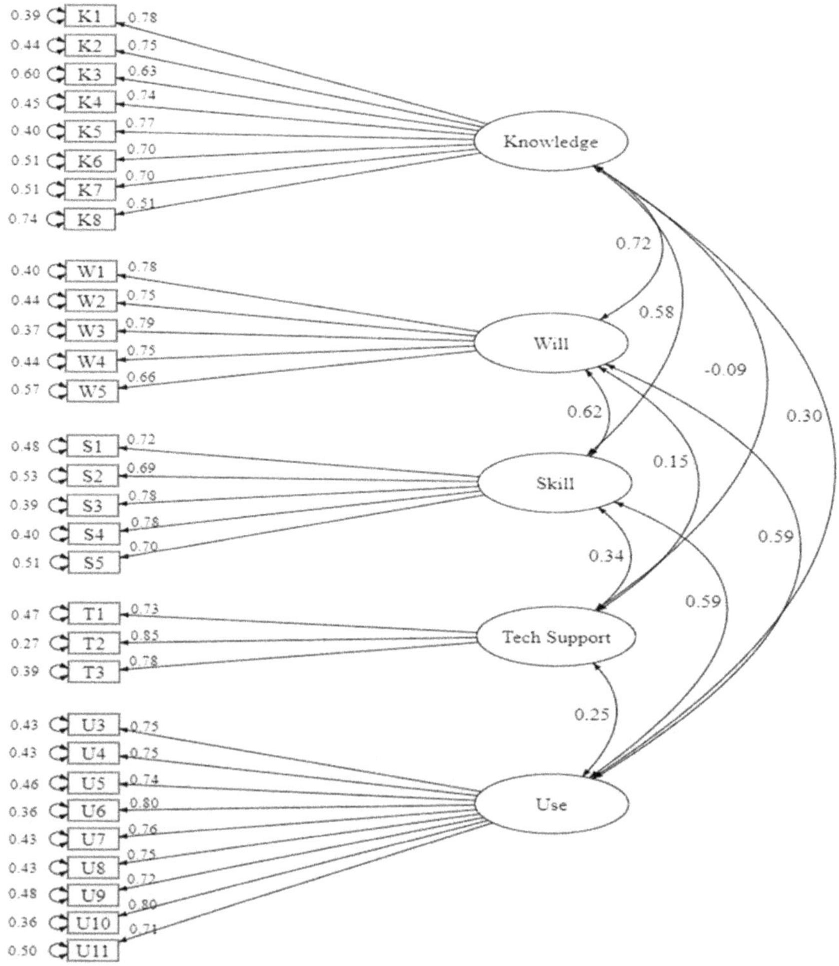

Moreover, the overall model fit indices reveal acceptable values as determined in the criteria (X^2/df = 7.50, p<0.001; CFI = 0.973; TLI = 0.970; NFI = 0.968; RMSEA = 0.077; SRMR = 0.069) expect Chi-square. Because Chi-square test is sensitive to sample size specifically with large samples (Babyak & Green, 2010). This confirms the construct validity of the five factors in the KWSTU questionnaire for assessing perceived knowledge, will, skills, technological support, and use of ChatGPT in higher education. Furthermore, the model also shows inter-correlation among the constructs.

Reliability of KWSTU

The internal consistency among items within each factor was assessed using Cronbach's Alpha. Furthermore, Omega and AVE (average variance extracted) were also computed to generate additional evidence for reliability. KWSTU ChatGPT questionnaire model has revealed acceptable values for composite reliability and AVE for each factor in the model as presented in table 3. The evidence of internal consistency in each construct estimated through Cronbach's alpha and Omega revealed similar estimates and both confirm good internal consistency (Hayes & Coutts, 2020). Amongst these, knowledge construct demonstrates marginally low value for AVE (<0.50); however, the other two measures were in the acceptable range.

Table 3. Reliability indices of five constructs

Factors	No. of items	Cronbach's Alpha	Omega	AVE
Knowledge	8	0.840	0.866	0.494
Will	5	0.814	0.834	0.556
Skill	5	0.813	0.824	0.539
Technological Support	3	0.757	0.781	0.624
Use	9	0.893	0.916	0.568

Path Analysis: Interaction among KWSTU factors

The results of the path analysis revealed that the model fit well (CFI = 0.995; TLI = 0.957; RMSEA = 0.080; SRMR = 0.012) in terms of how these constructs estimate the use of ChatGPT in higher education. The estimated model accounted for 35% of the variance in will, 33.5% in skill, and 39% in the use of ChatGPT. The direct effect of the four factors (knowledge, will, skills, and technological support) on the use of ChatGPT is presented in figure 3.

Figure 3. Direct effects in Path analysis

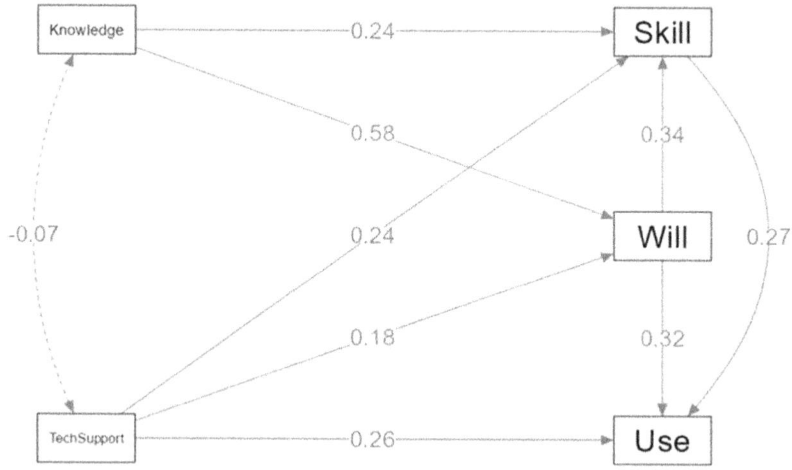

Among these, the path from '*knowledge*' to '*will*' emerged as relatively stronger, with a direct effect (β=0.58, p<0.001). This indicates that those who have more *knowledge* of ChatGPT would tend to have a more positive attitude to use ChatGPT. The path from 'knowledge' to 'skill' and 'technological support' to 'skill' revealed the same predictive power (β=0.24, p<0.001 for both) indicating that both exogenous factors affect the skills of students to use ChatGPT. Technological support was also found to be a significant predictor of 'will' (β=0.18, p<0.001). Interestingly, technological support was found to be a significant predictor of the 'use of ChatGPT' (β=0.26, p<0.001), but knowledge was not. Finally, the path 'will' to 'use' exhibited stronger prediction (β=0.32, p<0.001) in comparison with 'skill' to 'use' (β=0.27, p<0.001).

Table 4. Indirect effects in Path analysis

Path	**β**
Technological Support ⇒ Will ⇒ Use	0.057***
Technological Support ⇒ Will ⇒ Skill ⇒ Use	0.016***
Technological Support ⇒ Skill ⇒ Use	0.066***
Will ⇒ Skill ⇒ Use	0.092***
Knowledge ⇒ Will ⇒ Use	0.183***

continued on following page

Table 4. Continued

Path	β
Knowledge ⇒ Will ⇒ Skill ⇒ Use	0.053***
Knowledge ⇒ Skill ⇒ Use	0.064***

*** = p<0.001

As presented in Table 4, the examination of indirect effects demonstrates significant prediction of all the paths towards the use of ChatGPT. All seven possible paths demonstrated significant contribution (p<0.001 for all) to the outcome variable (use of ChatGPT). Amongst these, the path of "knowledge through 'will' to 'use' of ChatGPT" has shown relatively strong prediction (β=0.18) followed by the path of 'will through the skill to use of ChatGPT' (β=0.09). Furthermore, the paths through the skill to use ChatGPT either from technological support (β=0.07) or knowledge (β=0.06) and the path of 'technological support through will' (β=0.06) have demonstrated almost equal contribution. Interestingly, the paths developed through three variables [i.e., technological support ⇒ will ⇒ skill ⇒ use (β=0.02); knowledge ⇒ will ⇒ skill ⇒ use (β=0.05)] to predict the use of ChatGPT have revealed relatively weak contribution. This suggests that knowledge significantly contributes to users' will, ultimately influencing the utilisation of ChatGPT.

The path analysis highlighted that the estimation power of the paths in the *will, skill, and technological support* (WST) model is significant for using ChatGPT. This finding underscores the importance of these three constructs as interdependent and foundational pillars for adoption of technological tools. The results validate the WST model of technology integration, emphasising its relevance in contemporary educational contexts, particularly for tools like ChatGPT that require both user competence and supportive infrastructure. Interestingly, the analysis reveals that the path involving knowledge, will, and skill exerts a relatively stronger influence than the traditional WST model. This deviation could be attributed to the widespread accessibility of technological resources among students. Nearly all participants reported having access to either a computer, laptop, or smartphone, suggesting that the provision of resources - typically an important factor in adoption of technological tools - does not serve as a substantial barrier in this context. Instead, students' knowledge about ChatGPT and its practical applications appear to play a more prominent role in shaping their usage patterns. This finding highlights a paradigm shift where mere access to technology is no longer a primary concern; rather, users' understanding, inclination, and capabilities are becoming the central focus.

Furthermore, the constancy of *will* and *skill* across both scenarios indicates their central role in the adoption of technological tools. This consistency suggests that regardless of the specific technology or its tools under consideration, the willingness to engage with technology and the requisite skills to use it effectively remain essential. For teachers, fostering a positive attitude and developing technical competence is essential for integrating technology into their teaching practices. Similarly, for students, cultivating the motivation to explore technological tools and acquiring the necessary skills to use them effectively are key factors in leveraging technology for academic purposes. Therefore, the findings suggest that while infrastructure and resource availability are foundational, they are insufficient alone. The behavioural dimensions of technology use - *will* and *skill* - emerge as primary drivers of adoption and integration.

DISCUSSION

The launch and adoption of ChatGPT have garnered significant attention from stakeholders in higher education which highlights the need for empirical evidence to explore its practical use in academic contexts. For a newly introduced technological tool like ChatGPT, it is crucial to examine students' perceived knowledge, will, skill, and technological support, as these factors are likely to play a decisive role in its adoption. This can be effectively investigated through a self-reported questionnaire. This study addresses this need by offering a robust and reliable instrument to assess these critical aspects associated with ChatGPT's use in higher education.

To achieve this, we adapted the widely recognised WST model of technology integration in education to explore ChatGPT usage and related factors in higher education. Drawing on the WST model and relevant literature, we developed a conceptual framework, the *KWSTU* model, for the questionnaire. The questionnaire was created using a standardised tool-development approach, and its psychometric properties were rigorously tested. The results confirmed five constructs consisting of 30 items in the KWSTU questionnaire. Each item loaded significantly onto its relevant construct, and each construct loaded significantly onto a common factor, validating KWSTU as a multidimensional tool comprising five distinct constructs. Confirmatory factor analysis further demonstrated strong construct validity among university students, confirming that the KWSTU questionnaire is both reliable and valid for assessing the perceived knowledge, will, skill, technological support, and use of ChatGPT in higher education.

Each construct in the KWSTU model sheds light on critical aspects of ChatGPT adoption. The knowledge construct measures students' perceived knowledge of ChatGPT, including technical aspects (e.g., its nature as an AI tool, pre-trained language model, and data usage) and application knowledge (e.g., task capabilities, ethical considerations, and limitations). Knowledge is foundational to understanding ChatGPT's purpose and functionality. Without adequate knowledge, effective use is unlikely. Empirical studies (e.g., Taimalu & Luik, 2019) support the significant role of technological knowledge in integration. Additionally, perceived knowledge positively influences students' *will* (attitude) to adopt ChatGPT (Liu & Ma, 2023), further justifying its inclusion in the WST model. Similarly, the construct of will is derived from the WST model, this construct captures students' attitudes and confidence toward ChatGPT. It includes positive emotions (e.g., enthusiasm, comfort, and optimism in learning) and self-assurance (e.g., personalisation and learning improvement). As McCombs and Marzano (1990) conceptualised, *will* represents an intentional, self-generated motivation to engage with technology. Likewise, the construct of skill assesses students' perceived competence in using ChatGPT, including technical (e.g., interaction and troubleshooting) and evaluative (e.g., customising and critically assessing outputs) skills. Technological competence enables effective navigation and utilization of ChatGPT (Bizami et al., 2023). In the same way, the construct of technological support was adapted from the original WST model's *tool* construct, this measures the accessibility of ChatGPT at universities, including institutional updates, training, and availability. Previous studies (e.g., Sasota et al., 2021) highlight that technological support is crucial for successful technology integration in education. At last, the construct of use explores various applications of ChatGPT in higher education, such as classroom participation, idea generation, research, writing, paraphrasing, and proofreading.

Path analysis revealed both direct and indirect effects of the four constructs, including knowledge, will, skill, and technological support, on ChatGPT use in higher education. The analysis extended the utility of the WST model by demonstrating its applicability to ChatGPT adoption. Specifically, *will*, *skill*, and *technological support* were shown to have a direct positive impact on ChatGPT use, aligning with previous findings on technology integration in education (e.g., Taimalu & Luik, 2019; Velazquez, 2007; Liu & Ma, 2023).

Interestingly, the assumption that *knowledge* directly predicts ChatGPT use was not statistically supported. Instead, knowledge influenced usage indirectly through its association with *will* and *skill*. Among these paths, the contribution of knowledge through *will* was found to be the strongest predictor. This finding suggests that knowledge's impact is mediated by students' attitudes and motivations which highlights the intricate interplay of behavioural and cognitive factors in adopting cutting-edge technologies.

CONCLUSION

The rapid emergence of ChatGPT has introduced transformative opportunities and challenges in higher education which necessitate empirical research to understand its adoption and use. This study addressed this gap by developing and validating the KWSTU questionnaire, a robust and reliable tool designed to assess perceived levels of knowledge, will, skill, technological support, and the use of ChatGPT. It also offers the interconnected nature of these critical factors that influence the use of ChatGPT. The findings contribute to the existing body of knowledge by extending the WST model of technology integration, demonstrating its relevance in studying ChatGPT adoption, and highlighting the intertwined interplay between behavioural, cognitive, and infrastructural dimensions which students consider prior to adoption of a new technological tool.

A key insight from the study is that while skill, will, and technological support directly predict ChatGPT use, knowledge exerts an indirect influence through its impact on skill and will. This underscores the importance of fostering not only technical competence but also positive attitudes and intrinsic motivation among students for effective adoption of technological tools. Furthermore, the constancy of skill and will across the model reaffirms their essential role in technology adoption which emphasises the need for educational interventions that build these capacities.

The KWSTU questionnaire offers a robust framework for generating valid and reliable insights, providing a valuable tool for policymakers and practitioners to inform strategies for ChatGPT adoption. The multidimensional KWSTU framework offers significant implications for institutions to go beyond providing technological resources, focusing instead on creating an ecosystem that enhances students' understanding, confidence, and capabilities to engage with tools like ChatGPT. Future research could expand on this framework to explore other AI tools, refine the *knowledge* construct, and examine alternative paths of influence. Additionally, educational institutions should consider complementing technological infrastructure with targeted interventions, such as training and awareness programs, to enhance students' knowledge, will, and skill in using emerging technologies like ChatGPT.

In conclusion, this study provides a validated instrument and actionable insights to guide the integration of ChatGPT in higher education. The KWSTU questionnaire holds potential for broader application across diverse contexts, offering a pathway for future research to explore the role of emerging AI tools in shaping educational practices. By addressing the interconnections between knowledge, will, skill, and technological support, this study contributes to a deeper understanding of how technological innovations can be effectively leveraged to enhance learning experiences.

REFERENCES

Agyei, D. D., & Voogt, J. M. (2011). Exploring the potential of the will, skill, tool model in Ghana: Predicting prospective and practicing teachers' use of technology. *Computers & Education*, *56*(1), 91–100. DOI: 10.1016/j.compedu.2010.08.017

Ahmad, S., Ahmed, A., Bhutta, S. M., & Ansari, A. N. (2024). Transforming teaching learning with chatbots in higher education: Quest, opportunities and challenges for quality enhancement. *The Evolution of Artificial Intelligence in Higher Education*, 111-127.

Ansari, A. N., Ahmad, S., & Bhutta, S. M. (2024). Mapping the global evidence around the use of ChatGPT in higher education: A systematic scoping review. *Education and Information Technologies*, *29*(9), 11281–11321. Advance online publication. DOI: 10.1007/s10639-023-12223-4

Ansari, A. N., Panjwani, F., Ahmad, S., & Bhutta, S. M. (2025). Malaise of Artificial Intelligence in Education: A reflective stance. In *Examining AI Disruption in Educational Settings: Challenges and Opportunities* (pp. 359-380). IGI Global Scientific Publishing. DOI: 10.4018/979-8-3693-7873-1.ch013

Babyak, M. A., & Green, S. B. (2010). Confirmatory factor analysis: An introduction for psychosomatic medicine researchers. *Psychosomatic Medicine*, *72*(6), 587–597. DOI: 10.1097/PSY.0b013e3181de3f8a PMID: 20467001

Bagozzi, R. P., & Yi, Y. (1988). On the evaluation of structural equation models. *Journal of the Academy of Marketing Science*, *16*(1), 74–94. DOI: 10.1007/BF02723327

Bahroun, Z., Anane, C., Ahmed, V., & Zacca, A. (2023). Transforming education: A comprehensive review of generative artificial intelligence in educational settings through bibliometric and content analysis. *Sustainability (Basel)*, *15*(17), 12983. DOI: 10.3390/su151712983

Batterton, K. A., & Hale, K. N. (2017). The Likert scale: What it is and how to use it. *Phalanx*, *50*(2), 32–39.

Beck, C. T., & Gable, R. K. (2001). Ensuring content validity: An illustration of the process. *Journal of Nursing Measurement*, *9*(2), 201–215. DOI: 10.1891/1061-3749.9.2.201 PMID: 11696942

Bentler, P. M. (1990). Comparative fit indexes in structural models. *Psychological Bulletin*, *107*(2), 238–246. DOI: 10.1037/0033-2909.107.2.238 PMID: 2320703

Bentler, P. M., & Bonett, D. G. (1980). Significance tests and goodness of fit in the analysis of covariance structures. *Psychological Bulletin*, *88*(3), 588–606. DOI: 10.1037/0033-2909.88.3.588

Bhutta, S. M., Ahmad, S., Ansari, A. N., Ahmed, A., & Ali, K. Q. (2025). Exploring knowledge, will, skills, technological support, and use of ChatGPT in higher education: A cross-sectional survey. In *AI Adoption and Diffusion in Education* (pp. 359–382). IGI Global Scientific Publishing. DOI: 10.4018/979-8-3693-7949-3.ch013

Bizami, N. A., Tasir, Z., & Kew, S. N. (2023). Innovative pedagogical principles and technological tools capabilities for immersive blended learning: A systematic literature review. *Education and Information Technologies*, *28*(2), 1373–1425. DOI: 10.1007/s10639-022-11243-w PMID: 35919874

Brown, A. (2010). *Personality assessment, forced-choice*. Elsevier.

Browne, M. W. (1993). Alternative ways of assessing model fit. In Bollen, K. A., & Long, J. S. (Eds.), *Testing structural equation models* (pp. 136–162). Sage Publications.

Buabeng-Andoh, C. (2012). Factors influencing teachers' adoption and integration of information and communication technology into teaching: A review of the literature. *International Journal of Education and Development Using ICT*, *8*(1), 135–155.

Byrne, B. M. (2013). *Structural equation modeling with Mplus: Basic concepts, applications, and programming*. Routledge. DOI: 10.4324/9780203807644

Cicchetti, D. V., & Sparrow, S. A. (1981). Developing criteria for establishing interrater reliability of specific items: Applications to assessment of adaptive behavior. *American Journal of Mental Deficiency*, *86*(2), 127–137. PMID: 7315877

Cole, D. A. (1987). Utility of confirmatory factor analysis in test validation research. *Journal of Consulting and Clinical Psychology*, *55*(4), 584–594. DOI: 10.1037/0022-006X.55.4.584 PMID: 3624616

Collins, A., & Halverson, R. (2018). *Rethinking education in the age of technology: The digital revolution and schooling in America*. Teachers College Press.

Crompton, H., & Burke, D. (2022). Artificial intelligence in K–12 education. *SN Social Sciences*, *2*(7), 113. DOI: 10.1007/s43545-022-00425-5

Dalalah, D., & Dalalah, O. M. (2023). The false positives and false negatives of generative AI detection tools in education and academic research: The case of ChatGPT. *International Journal of Management Education*, *21*(2), 100822. DOI: 10.1016/j.ijme.2023.100822

Dhirani, L. L., Mukhtiar, N., Chowdhry, B. S., & Newe, T. (2023). Ethical dilemmas and privacy issues in emerging technologies: A review. *Sensors (Basel)*, *23*(3), 1151. DOI: 10.3390/s23031151 PMID: 36772190

Fornell, C., & Larcker, D. F. (1981). Evaluating structural equation models with unobservable variables and measurement error. *JMR, Journal of Marketing Research*, *18*(1), 39–50. DOI: 10.1177/002224378101800104

Grant, D. G. (2019). Predicting Web 2.0 use among US teens — Expanding the power of the skill, will and tool model. *British Journal of Educational Technology*, *50*(6), 3405–3419. DOI: 10.1111/bjet.12745

Hu, L. T., & Bentler, P. M. (1999). Cutoff criteria for fit indexes in covariance structure analysis: Conventional criteria versus new alternatives. *Structural Equation Modeling*, *6*(1), 1–55. DOI: 10.1080/10705519909540118

Jackson, D. L., Gillaspy, J. A.Jr, & Purc-Stephenson, R. (2009). Reporting practices in confirmatory factor analysis: An overview and some recommendations. *Psychological Methods*, *14*(1), 6–23. DOI: 10.1037/a0014694 PMID: 19271845

Jonäll, K. (2024). Artificial intelligence in academic grading: A mixed-methods study. *Computers & Education*, *210*, 105912. DOI: 10.1016/j.compedu.2024.105912

Karan, B., & Angadi, G. R. (2023). Potential risks of artificial intelligence integration into school education: A systematic review. *Bulletin of Science, Technology & Society*, *43*(3–4), 67–85. DOI: 10.1177/02704676231224705

Kishore, K., Jaswal, V., Kulkarni, V., & De, D. (2021). Practical guidelines to develop and evaluate a questionnaire. *Indian Dermatology Online Journal*, *12*(2), 266–275. DOI: 10.4103/idoj.IDOJ_674_20 PMID: 33959523

Klausmeier, H. J., & Goodwin, W. (1975). *Learning and human abilities: Educational psychology* (4th ed.). Harper & Row.

Kline, R. B. (2023). *Principles and practice of structural equation modeling* (5th ed.). Guilford Press.

Knezek, G., & Christensen, R. (2016). Extending the will, skill, tool model of technology integration: Adding pedagogy as a new model construct. *Journal of Computing in Higher Education*, *28*(3), 307–325. DOI: 10.1007/s12528-016-9120-2

Knezek, G., Christensen, R., & Fluke, R. (2003). *Testing a will, skill, tool model of technology integration.* ERIC. https://files.eric.ed.gov/fulltext/ED475762.pdf

Knezek, G., Christensen, R., Miyashita, K., & Ropp, M. (2000). *Instruments for assessing educator progress in technology integration.* University of North Texas. https://iittl.unt.edu/sites/default/files/Instruments/InstrumentsforAssessingEducatorProgressinTechnologyIntegration_0.pdf

Labadze, L., Grigolia, M., & Machaidze, L. (2023). Role of AI chatbots in education: Systematic literature review. *International Journal of Educational Technology in Higher Education, 20*(1), 1–25. DOI: 10.1186/s41239-023-00426-1

Létourneau, A., Deslandes Martineau, M., Charland, P., Karran, J. A., Boasen, J., & Léger, P. M. (2025). A systematic review of AI-driven intelligent tutoring systems (ITS) in K–12 education. *npj Science of Learning, 10*(1), 29. https://doi.org/DOI: 10.1038/s41539-025-00217-3

Liu, G., & Ma, C. (2023). Measuring EFL learners' use of ChatGPT in informal digital learning of English based on the technology acceptance model. *Innovation in Language Learning and Teaching*, •••, 1–14. DOI: 10.1080/17501229.2023.2289377

Lynn, M. R. (1986). Determination and quantification of content validity. *Nursing Research, 35*(6), 382–386. DOI: 10.1097/00006199-198611000-00017 PMID: 3640358

Mitchell, M. (2019). *Artificial intelligence: A guide for thinking humans.*

Morales, C. (2006). *Cross-cultural validation of the will, skill, tool model of technology integration* [Doctoral dissertation, University of North Texas]. UNT Digital Library. https://digital.library.unt.edu/ark:/67531/metadc5256

Morales, C., Knezek, G., Christensen, R., & Avila, P. (Eds.). (2005). *The will, skill, tool model of technology integration: A conceptual approach to teaching and learning with technology.* ICLE.

Netemeyer, R. G., Bearden, W. O., & Sharma, S. (2003). *Scaling procedures: Issues and applications.* Sage Publications. DOI: 10.4135/9781412985772

Neumann, M., Rauschenberger, M., & Schön, E. (2023). "We need to talk about ChatGPT": The future of AI and higher education. In *2023 IEEE/ACM 5th International Workshop on Software Engineering Education for the Next Generation (SEENG)* (pp. 10–17). IEEE. https://doi.org/DOI: 10.1109/SEENG59157.2023.00010

Newman, I., Lim, J., & Pineda, F. (2013). Content validity using a mixed methods approach. *Journal of Mixed Methods Research, 7*(3), 243–260. DOI: 10.1177/1558689813476922

Pedro, F., Subosa, M., Rivas, A., & Valverde, P. (2019). *Artificial intelligence in education: Challenges and opportunities for sustainable development*. UNESCO.

Petko, D. (2012). Teachers' pedagogical beliefs and their use of digital media in classrooms: Sharpening the focus of the "will, skill, tool" model and integrating teachers' constructivist orientations. *Computers & Education*, *58*(4), 1351–1359. DOI: 10.1016/j.compedu.2011.12.013

Pham, S. T., & Sampson, P. M. (2022). The development of artificial intelligence in education: A review in context. *Journal of Computer Assisted Learning*, *38*(5), 1408–1421. DOI: 10.1111/jcal.12687

Sarker, I. H. (2021). Machine learning: Algorithms, real-world applications and research directions. *SN Computer Science*, *2*(3), 160. DOI: 10.1007/s42979-021-00592-x PMID: 33778771

Sasota, R. S., Cristobal, R. R., Sario, I. S., Biyo, J. T., & Magadia, J. C. (2021). Will–skill–tool (WST) model of technology integration in teaching science and mathematics in the Philippines. *Journal of Computers in Education*, *8*(3), 443–464. DOI: 10.1007/s40692-021-00185-w

Schreiber, J. B. (2008). Core reporting practices in structural equation modeling. *Research in Social & Administrative Pharmacy*, *4*(2), 83–97. DOI: 10.1016/j.sapharm.2007.04.003 PMID: 18555963

Scully, D., Lehane, P., & Scully, C. (2021). "It is no longer scary": Digital learning before and during the COVID-19 pandemic in Irish secondary schools. *Technology, Pedagogy and Education*, *30*(1), 159–181. DOI: 10.1080/1475939X.2020.1854844

Tahiru, F. (2021). AI in education: A systematic literature review. *Journal of Cases on Information Technology*, *23*(1), 1–20. DOI: 10.4018/JCIT.2021010101

Taimalu, M., & Luik, P. (2019). The impact of beliefs and knowledge on the integration of technology among teacher educators: A path analysis. *Teaching and Teacher Education*, *79*, 101–110. DOI: 10.1016/j.tate.2018.12.012

Tapalova, O., & Zhiyenbayeva, N. (2022). Artificial intelligence in education: AIEd for personalised learning pathways. *Electronic Journal of e-Learning*, *20*(5), 639–653. DOI: 10.34190/ejel.20.5.2597

Téllez, A. R., Ortiz, L. M. F., & Domínguez, F. C. T. (2024). Artificial intelligence in university administration: An overview of its uses and applications. *Revista Interamericana de Bibliotecología*, *47*(2), 1–12. DOI: 10.17533/udea.rib.v47n2a05

Turner, A. (2023, June 7). ChatGPT number of users & market size statistics. *BankMyCell.* https://www.bankmycell.com/blog/chatgpt-number-of-users

Velazquez, C. M. (2007). Testing predictive models of technology integration in Mexico and the United States. *Computers in the Schools, 24*(3–4), 153–173. DOI: 10.1300/J025v24n03_11

Zawacki-Richter, O., Marín, V. I., Bond, M., & Gouverneur, F. (2019). Systematic review of research on artificial intelligence applications in higher education—Where are the educators? *International Journal of Educational Technology in Higher Education, 16*(1), 1–27. DOI: 10.1186/s41239-019-0171-0

Zhai, X., Chu, X., Chai, C. S., Jong, M. S. Y., Istenic, A., Spector, M., & Li, Y. (2021). A review of artificial intelligence (AI) in education from 2010 to 2020. *Complexity, 2021*(1), 8812542. DOI: 10.1155/2021/8812542

Zhu, S., Yu, T., Xu, T., Chen, H., Dustdar, S., Gigan, S., & Pan, Y. (2023). Intelligent computing: The latest advances, challenges, and future. *Intelligent Computing, 2*, 0006. https://doi.org/DOI: 10.34133/icomputing.0006

KEYWORDS AND DEFINITIONS

Adoption of ChatGPT: It refers to the processes and factors which influence university students to begin using ChatGPT for academic tasks within higher education settings.

KWSTU ChatGPT Questionnaire: It refers to a validated instrument designed to measure students' perceived Knowledge, Will, Skill, Technological Support, and Use (KWSTU) of ChatGPT in higher education.

KWSTU Development: It refers to the systematic process of designing and constructing the KWSTU questionnaire from conceptual grounding to generating item and revising in light of the expert review.

KWSTU Path Analysis: It refers to a statistical modelling employed to examine the direct and indirect relationships among the KWSTU constructs to identify factors and paths of those factors which influence the use of ChatGPT.

KWSTU Validation: It refers to the empirical procedures used to establish the reliability and validity of the KWSTU questionnaire through content validation, construct validation using CVI and confirmatory factor analysis, respectively.

Use of ChatGPT: It refers to the extent and manner in which university students employ ChatGPT for academic tasks.

Compilation of References

Abbas, I., & Ganesan, S. (2025, May). Exploring the feasibility of AI-driven educational robots in simulation environments for early childhood learning: A pilot study. In *2025 IEEE International Conference on Electro Information Technology (eIT)* (pp. 1-9). IEEE. DOI: 10.1109/eIT64391.2025.11103623

Abbes, F., Bennani, S., & Maalel, A. (2024). Generative AI and gamification for personalized learning: Literature review and future challenges. *SN Computer Science*, *5*(8), 1154. DOI: 10.1007/s42979-024-03491-z

Adeoye, M. A., & Sabela, W. (2024). Navigating the future of education: Integrating AI and collaborative learning in teacher professional development. *International Journal of Technology. Education and Social Humanities*, *2*(2), 41–60.

Adesina, A. A., Iyelolu, T. V., & Okpeke, P. P.Abayomi Abraham AdesinaToluwalase Vanessa IyeloluPatience Okpeke Paul. (2024). Leveraging predictive analytics for strategic decision-making: Enhancing business performance through data-driven insights. *World Journal of Advanced Research and Reviews*, *22*(3), 1927–1934. DOI: 10.30574/wjarr.2024.22.3.1961

Adewale, U. D., Azeta, A., Abayomi-Alli, A., & Sambo-Magaji, A. (2024). Impact of artificial intelligence adoption on students' academic performance in open and distance learning: A systematic literature review. *Heliyon*, *10*(22), e40025. DOI: 10.1016/j.heliyon.2024.e40025

Afify, M. K. (2020). Effect of interactive video length within E-Learning environments on cognitive load, cognitive achievement and retention of learning. *Turkish Online Journal of Distance Education*, *21*(4), 68–89. DOI: 10.17718/tojde.803360

Agyei, D. D., & Voogt, J. M. (2011). Exploring the potential of the will, skill, tool model in Ghana: Predicting prospective and practicing teachers' use of technology. *Computers & Education*, *56*(1), 91–100. DOI: 10.1016/j.compedu.2010.08.017

Ahmad, S., Ahmed, A., Bhutta, S. M., & Ansari, A. N. (2024). Transforming teaching learning with chatbots in higher education: Quest, opportunities and challenges for quality enhancement. *The Evolution of Artificial Intelligence in Higher Education*, 111-127.

Akinsemolu, A. A., & Onyeaka, H. (2025). The role of artificial intelligence in transforming language learning: Opportunities and ethical considerations. *Journal of Language and Education, 11*(1), 148–152. DOI: 10.17323/jle.2025.22118

Al-Ansi, A. M., Jaboob, M., Garad, A., & Al-Ansi, A. (2023). Analyzing augmented reality (AR) and virtual reality (VR) recent development in education. *Social Sciences & Humanities Open*, *8*(1), 100532. DOI: 10.1016/j.ssaho.2023.100532

Al-Badi, A., Khan, A., & Eid-Alotaibi, . (2022). Perceptions of learners and instructors towards artificial intelligence in personalized learning. *Procedia Computer Science*, *201*, 445–451. DOI: 10.1016/j.procs.2022.03.058

Albreiki, B., Habuza, T., Palakkal, N., & Zaki, N. (2024). Clustering-based knowledge graphs and entity-relation representation improves the detection of at risk students. *Education and Information Technologies*, *29*(6), 6791–6820. DOI: 10.1007/s10639-023-11938-8

Alcivar, D., Macias, M., & Vera, A. (2024). *Integration of artificial intelligence in English teaching*. CID - Centro de Investigación y Desarrollo., DOI: 10.37811/cli_w1046

Aldawsari, M. M., & Almohish, R. I. (2024). Treats and opportunities of students' use of AI-integrated technology (ChatGPT) in online higher education: Saudi Arabian educational technologists' perspectives. *International Review of Research in Open and Distance Learning*, *25*(3), 19–36. DOI: 10.19173/irrodl.v25i3.7642

Alenezi, A., & Alenezi, A. (2025). Evaluating the effectiveness of chatbot-assisted learning in enhancing English conversational skills among secondary school students. *Education Sciences*, *15*(9), 1–15. DOI: 10.3390/educsci15091136

Alhalangy, A., & AbdAlgane, M. (2023). Exploring the impact of AI on the EFL context: A case study of Saudi universities. *Journal of Intercultural Communication*, 41–49. DOI: 10.36923/jicc.v23i2.125

Alier, M., Pereira, J., García-Peñalvo, F. J., Casañ, M. J., & Cabré, J. (2025). LAMB: An open-source software framework to create artificial intelligence assistants deployed and integrated into learning management systems. *Computer Standards & Interfaces*, *92*, 103940. DOI: 10.1016/j.csi.2024.103940

Al-Moslmi, T., Gallofré Ocaña, M., Opdahl, A. L., & Veres, C. (2020). Named entity extraction for knowledge graphs: A literature overview. *IEEE Access : Practical Innovations, Open Solutions*, *8*, 32862–32881. DOI: 10.1109/ACCESS.2020.2973928

Alrajhi, A. S. (2023). Genre effect on Google Translate–assisted L2 writing output quality. *ReCALL, 35*(3), 305–320. DOI: 10.1017/S0958344022000143

Altınay, G., & Aydın, S. (2025). Automated feedback effect on foreign language writing motivation and anxiety. In *AI's Role in Language Learning and Communication* (pp. 27–64). IGI Global Publishing., DOI: 10.4018/979-8-3373-5681-5.ch002

American Council on the Teaching of Foreign Languages. (2024). ACTFL proficiency guidelines. https://www.actfl.org/uploads/files/general/Resources-Publications/ACTFL_Proficiency_Guidelines_2024.pdf

Amin, E. (2024). EFL students' perception of using AI text-to-speech apps in learning pronunciation. SSRN *Electronic Journal, 21*(3), 887–903. DOI: 10.2139/ssrn.4746800

Amin, D. I., & Ikhsan, J. (2021). Improving higher order thinking skills via semi Second Life. *European Journal of Educational Research, 10*(1), 261–274. DOI: 10.12973/eu-jer.10.1.261

Anderson, R. C. (1984). Some reflections on the acquisition of knowledge. *Educational Researcher, 13*(9), 5–10. DOI: 10.3102/0013189X013009005

Anderson, T., & Elloumi, F. (2004). *Theory and practice of online learning*. Athabasca University.

Anmarkrud, Ø., McCrudden, M. T., Bråten, I., & Strømsø, H. I. (2013). Task-oriented reading of multiple documents: Online comprehension processes and offline products. *Instructional Science*, *41*(5), 873–894. DOI: 10.1007/s11251-013-9263-8

Anoir, L., Khaldi, M., & Erradi, M. (2024). Intelligent tutor systems and the personalization of pedagogical objects in adaptive e-Learning. In *Interactive media with next-gen technologies and their usability evaluation* (1st ed., pp. 185–196). Chapman and Hall/CRC. DOI: 10.1201/9781032664828-14

An, P., Holstein, K., d'Anjou, B., Eggen, B., & Bakker, S. (2020, April). The TA framework: Designing real-time teaching augmentation for K-12 classrooms. In *Proceedings of the 2020 CHI Conference on Human Factors in Computing Systems* (pp. 1-17). Association for Computing Machinery. DOI: 10.1145/3313831.3376277

Ansari, A. N., Panjwani, F., Ahmad, S., & Bhutta, S. M. (2025). Malaise of Artificial Intelligence in Education: A reflective stance. In *Examining AI Disruption in Educational Settings: Challenges and Opportunities* (pp. 359-380). IGI Global Scientific Publishing. DOI: 10.4018/979-8-3693-7873-1.ch013

Ansari, A. N., Ahmad, S., & Bhutta, S. M. (2024). Mapping the global evidence around the use of ChatGPT in higher education: A systematic scoping review. *Education and Information Technologies*, *29*(9), 11281–11321. Advance online publication. DOI: 10.1007/s10639-023-12223-4

An, X., Chai, C., Li, Y., Zhou, Y., & Yang, B. (2023). Modeling students' perceptions of artificial intelligence assisted language learning. *Computer Assisted Language Learning*, •••, 1–22. DOI: 10.1080/09588221.2023.2246519

Arefian, M. H., Çomoğlu, I., & Dikilitaş, K. (2024). Understanding EFL teachers' experiences of ChatGPT-driven collaborative reflective practice through a community of practice lens. *Innovation in Language Learning and Teaching*, 1–16. DOI: 10.1080/17501229.2024.2412769

Arnold, K. E., & Pistilli, M. D. (2012). Course signals at Purdue: Using learning analytics to increase student success. *Proceedings of the 2nd International Conference on Learning Analytics and Knowledge*, 267–270. DOI: 10.1145/2330601.2330666

Arsenault, T. L., Powell, S. R., Hebert, M. A., King, S. G., Lin, X., & Lang, D. (2022). Influence of writing ability and computation skills on mathematics. *Reading and Writing*, *36*, 2025–2053. DOI: 10.1007/s11145-022-10375-2

Artuvan Korkmaz, H., Güldenoğlu, B., & Kalaycıoğlu, C. (2019). Investigation of word decoding strategies of university students from quantitative and verbal graduate programs. *Ahi Evran Üniversitesi Sosyal Bilimler Enstitüsü Dergisi*, *5*(2), 266–283. DOI: 10.31592/aeusbed.589093

Aslam, F. (2023). The impact of artificial intelligence on chatbot technology: A study on the current advancements and leading innovations. *European Journal of Technology*, *7*(3), 62–72. DOI: 10.47672/ejt.1561

Aslam, S., Anwer, M., & Yousaf, M. (2020). Effect of motivational strategies on science students' cognitive engagement. *Journal of Educational and Social Research*, *7*(1), 1–13.

Avila-Chauvet, L., Mejía, D., & Acosta Quiroz, C. (2023). CHATGPT as a support tool for online behavioral task programming. *SSRN*. Obtenido de https://ssrn.com/abstract=4329020

Aydın, S. (2023). Teachers' perceptions of the use of the Metaverse in foreign language teaching and learning. In G. Durak & S. ÇAnkaya (Eds.), *Shaping the Future of Online Learning: Education in the Metaverse* (pp. 201–219). DOI: 10.4018/978-1-6684-6513-4.ch011

Aydın, S. (2024). Construction and validation of the Perceptions of AI Usage Scale in a foreign language learning context. *Unpublished Research Paper.*

Aydın, S. (2025). Using AI in foreign language teaching. *Paper Presented at GLO-TECH 2025: Redefining Language Learning and Translation in the Digital Age.*

Aydın, S. (2020). Affective states and learning outcomes in EFL education. In Celik, S. (Ed.), *Preparing teachers for a changing world: Contemporary issues in EFL education* (pp. 153–164). Vizetek.

Aydın, S. (2022). The Metaverse in foreign language learning: A theoretical framework. *Innovational Research in ELT, 3*(2), 12–19. DOI: 10.29329/irelt.2022.505.2

Aydın, S., & Altınay, G. (2026). Artificial intelligence in education: An evaluation of four decades. In Bozkurt, A. (Ed.), *Rethinking Education and Agency in the Age of Human-Generative AI Interaction* (pp. 19–94). IGI Global Scientific Publishing., DOI: 10.4018/979-8-3373-1195-1.ch002

Aydın, S., & Tekin, I. (2023). Positive psychology and language learning: A systematic scoping review. *Review of Education, 11*(3), 1–27. DOI: 10.1002/rev3.3420

Aydın, S., & Zeinolabedini, M. (2024). Integrating artificial intelligence into foreign language learning: Learners' perspectives. *11th EJER Congress.*

Ayres, P. (2018). Subjective measures of cognitive load: What can they reliably measure? In Zheng, R. (Ed.), *Cognitive load measurement and application: A theoretical framework for meaningful research and practice* (pp. 9–28). Routledge.

Babyak, M. A., & Green, S. B. (2010). Confirmatory factor analysis: An introduction for psychosomatic medicine researchers. *Psychosomatic Medicine, 72*(6), 587–597. DOI: 10.1097/PSY.0b013e3181de3f8a PMID: 20467001

Baddeley, A. (2012). Working memory: Theories, models, and controversies. *Annual Review of Psychology, 63*(1), 1–29. DOI: 10.1146/annurev-psych-120710-100422 PMID: 21961947

Bagozzi, R. P., & Yi, Y. (1988). On the evaluation of structural equation models. *Journal of the Academy of Marketing Science, 16*(1), 74–94. DOI: 10.1007/BF02723327

Bahari, A., Han, F., & Strzelecki, A. (2025). Integrating CALL and AIALL for an interactive pedagogical model of language learning. *Education and Information Technologies, 30*(10), 14305–14333. Advance online publication. DOI: 10.1007/s10639-025-13388-w

Bahroun, Z., Anane, C., Ahmed, V., & Zacca, A. (2023). Transforming education: A comprehensive review of generative artificial intelligence in educational settings through bibliometric and content analysis. *Sustainability (Basel), 15*(17), 12983. DOI: 10.3390/su151712983

Balasubramaniam, N., Kauppinen, M., Rannisto, A., Hiekkanen, K., & Kujala, S. (2023). Transparency and explainability of AI systems: From ethical guidelines to requirements. *Information and Software Technology, 159*, 107197. DOI: 10.1016/j.infsof.2023.107197

Ballıdağ, M., & Aydın, S. (2025). *A comparison of the effects of AI-based chatbots and peer interactions on speaking anxiety among EFL learners*. Future in Educational Research., DOI: 10.1002/fer3.70005

Bandura, A. (1986). *Social foundations of thought and action: A social cognitive theory*. Prentice-Hall.

Bangert-Drowns, R. L., Hurley, M. M., & Wilkinson, B. (2004). The effects of school-based writing-to-learn interventions on academic achievement: A meta-analysis. *Review of Educational Research, 74*(1), 29–58. DOI: 10.3102/00346543074001029

Barke, S., James, M., & Polikarpova, N. (2023). Grounded Copilot: How programmers interact with code-generating models. *Proceedings of the ACM on Programming Languages, 7*(OOPSLA1), 85-111. DOI: 10.1145/3586030

Baskara, F. R. (2023). Integrating ChatGPT into EFL writing instruction: Benefits and challenges. *International Journal on E-Learning, 5*(1), 44–55. DOI: 10.31763/ijele.v5i1.858

Baskara, R., & Mukarto, M. (2023). Exploring the implications of ChatGPT for language learning in higher education. *Indonesian Journal of English Language Teaching and Applied Linguistics, 7*(2), 343–358. DOI: 10.21093/ijeltal.v7i2.1387

Batterton, K. A., & Hale, K. N. (2017). The Likert scale: What it is and how to use it. *Phalanx, 50*(2), 32–39.

Bayne, S. (2015). Posthumanism and research in digital education. In Haythornthwaite, C., Andrews, R., Fransman, J., & Meyers, E. M. (Eds.), *SAGE handbook of e-learning research* (pp. 82–89). SAGE.

Beck, C. T., & Gable, R. K. (2001). Ensuring content validity: An illustration of the process. *Journal of Nursing Measurement*, *9*(2), 201–215. DOI: 10.1891/1061-3749.9.2.201 PMID: 11696942

Belda-Medina, J., & Kokošková, V. (2024). ChatGPT for language learning: Assessing teacher candidates' skills and perceptions using the Technology Acceptance Model (TAM). *Innovation in Language Learning and Teaching*, 1–16. DOI: 10.1080/17501229.2024.2435900

Benbya, H., Davenport, T. H., & Pachidi, S. (2020). Artificial intelligence in organizations: Current state and future opportunities. *MIS Quarterly Executive*, *19*(4), 9–21.

Bentler, P. M. (1990). Comparative fit indexes in structural models. *Psychological Bulletin*, *107*(2), 238–246. DOI: 10.1037/0033-2909.107.2.238 PMID: 2320703

Bentler, P. M., & Bonett, D. G. (1980). Significance tests and goodness of fit in the analysis of covariance structures. *Psychological Bulletin*, *88*(3), 588–606. DOI: 10.1037/0033-2909.88.3.588

Bereiter, C. (2005). *Education and mind in the knowledge age*. Routledge. DOI: 10.4324/9781410612182

Berk, E. H., & Aydın, S. (2025). The impact of artificial intelligence-powered writing assistance systems on metacognitive writing strategies. In *Transformations in Digital Learning and Educational Technologies* (pp. 241–274). IGI Global., DOI: 10.4018/979-8-3373-3678-7.ch011

Bernstein, D., Nash, P., Clarke-Stewart, A., Penner, L., & Roy, E. (2008). *Essentials of psychology* (4th ed.). Houghton Mifflin Company.

Berrezueta-Guzman, S., Dolón-Poza, M., & Wagner, S. (2025). Supporting preschool emotional development with AI-powered robots. In *Proceedings of the 24th Interaction Design and Children* (pp. 1134–1139). arXiv preprint. https://doi.org// DOI: 10.1145/3713043.3731548

Bertelsen, O., & Bødker, S. (2003). Activity Theory. In Carroll, C. (Ed.), *HCI models, theories, and frameworks: Toward a multidisciplinary science* (pp. 291–324). Elsevier., DOI: 10.1016/B978-155860808-5/50011-3

Bhutta, S. M., Ahmad, S., Ansari, A. N., Ahmed, A., & Ali, K. Q. (2025). Exploring knowledge, will, skills, technological support, and use of ChatGPT in higher education: A cross-sectional survey. In *AI Adoption and Diffusion in Education* (pp. 359–382). IGI Global Scientific Publishing. DOI: 10.4018/979-8-3693-7949-3.ch013

Bienkowski, M., Feng, M., & Means, B. (2012). *Enhancing teaching and learning through educational data mining and learning analytics: An issue brief.* U.S. Department of Education.

Bircan, T., & Özbilgin, M. F. (2025). Unmasking inequalities of the code: Disentangling the nexus of AI and inequality. *Technological Forecasting and Social Change*, *211*, 123925. DOI: 10.1016/j.techfore.2024.123925

Bitchener, J. (2012). A reflection on 'the language learning potential of written corrective feedback. *Journal of Second Language Writing*, *21*(4), 348–363. DOI: 10.1016/j.jslw.2012.09.006

Bizami, N. A., Tasir, Z., & Kew, S. N. (2023). Innovative pedagogical principles and technological tools capabilities for immersive blended learning: A systematic literature review. *Education and Information Technologies*, *28*(2), 1373–1425. DOI: 10.1007/s10639-022-11243-w PMID: 35919874

Blanchflower, D. G., & Bryson, A. (2024). The female happiness paradox. *Journal of Population Economics*, *37*(1), 16. DOI: 10.1007/s00148-024-00981-5

Bloom, B. S. (1956). *Taxonomy of Educational Objectives, Handbook: The Cognitive Domain*. David McKay.

Boateng, O., & Boateng, B. (2025). Algorithmic bias in educational systems: Examining the impact of AI-driven decision making in modern education. *World Journal of Advanced Research and Reviews*, *25*(1), 2012–2017. DOI: 10.30574/wjarr.2025.25.1.0253

Boldbaatar, N., & Sendurur, E. (2019). Developing educational 3D games with StarLogo: The role of backwards fading in the transfer of programming experience. *Journal of Educational Computing Research*, *57*(6), 1468–1494. DOI: 10.1177/0735633118806747

Bong, J. Y., Cho, K., Liu, Z., & He, D. (2023). A dual-process motivation mediation model to explain female high school students' cognitive engagement and disengagement in emergency remote teaching and online learning in South Korea. *British Journal of Educational Technology*, *55*(3), 1020–1040. DOI: 10.1111/bjet.13415

Borge, M., Smith, B. K., & Aldemir, T. (2024). Using generative AI as a simulation to support higher-order thinking. *International Journal of Computer-Supported Collaborative Learning*, *19*(4), 479–532. DOI: 10.1007/s11412-024-09437-0

Bransford, J. D., Brown, A. L., & Cocking, R. R. (2000). *How people learn* (Vol. 11). National academy press.

Braverman, H. (1974). *Labor and monopoly capital.* Monthly Review Press. DOI: 10.14452/MR-026-03-1974-07_1

Bronstein, L. R. (2003). A model for interdisciplinary collaboration. *Social Work, 48*(3), 297–306. DOI: 10.1093/sw/48.3.297 PMID: 12899277

Brown, A. (2010). *Personality assessment, forced-choice.* Elsevier.

Browne, M. W. (1993). Alternative ways of assessing model fit. In Bollen, K. A., & Long, J. S. (Eds.), *Testing structural equation models* (pp. 136–162). Sage Publications.

Bruner, J. (1957). On perceptual readiness. *Psychological Review, 64*(2), 123–152. DOI: 10.1037/h0043805 PMID: 13420288

Bryant, S., Forte, A., & Bruckman, A. (2005). Becoming Wikipedian. *Proceedings of the 2005 International ACM SIGGROUP Conference on Supporting Group Work - GROUP '05*, 1–10. DOI: 10.1145/1099203.1099205

Buabeng-Andoh, C. (2012). Factors influencing teachers' adoption and integration of information and communication technology into teaching: A review of the literature. *International Journal of Education and Development Using ICT, 8*(1), 135–155.

Buendgens-Kosten, J. (2024). "Just a pocket knife, not a machete": Large language models in TEFL teacher education & digital text sovereignty. *Technology in Language Teaching & Learning, 6*(1), 1192–1192. DOI: 10.29140/tltl.v6n1.1192

Bundock, K., Hawken, L. S., Kiuhara, S. A., O'Keeffe, B. V., O'Neill, R. E., & Cummings, M. B. (2021). Teaching rate of change and problem solving to high school students with high incidence disabilities at tier 3. *Learning Disability Quarterly, 44*(1), 35–49. DOI: 10.1177/0731948719887341

Business Wire. (2020, August 25). Worldwide spending on artificial intelligence is expected to double in four years, reaching $110 billion in 2024. https://www.businesswire.com/news/home/20200825005099/en/Worldwide-Spending-on-Artificial-Intelligence-Is-Expected-to-Double-in-Four-Years-Reaching-%24110-Billion-in-2024-According-to-New-IDC-Spending-Guide

Butler, Y. G., & Jiang, S. (2025). How do pre-service language teachers perceive generative AIs' affordance?: A case of ChatGPT. *System, 129*, 1–17. DOI: 10.1016/j.system.2025.103606

Byram, M. (2012). Language awareness and (critical) cultural awareness – relationships, comparisons and contrasts. *Language Awareness, 21*(1–2), 5–13. DOI: 10.1080/09658416.2011.639887

Byrne, B. M. (2013). *Structural equation modeling with Mplus: Basic concepts, applications, and programming*. Routledge. DOI: 10.4324/9780203807644

Bystrenina, I., & Nikitin, P. (2022). Adaptive knowledge control in digital learning. *Education Sciences*, *12*(10), 638. DOI: 10.3390/educsci12100638

Carr, E. W., Brady, T. F., & Winkielman, P. (2017). Are You Smiling, or Have I Seen You Before? Familiarity Makes Faces Look Happier. *Psychological Science*, *28*(8), 1087–1102. DOI: 10.1177/0956797617702003 PMID: 28594281

Case, R., Liu, L., & Mintz, J. (2025). Integrating AI technology into language teacher education: Challenges, potentials, and assumptions. *Computers in the Schools*, *42*(2), 93–99. DOI: 10.1080/07380569.2025.2458950

Celik, I. (2023). Towards Intelligent-TPACK: An empirical study on teachers' professional knowledge to ethically integrate artificial intelligence (AI)-based tools into education. *Computers in Human Behavior*, *138*, 1–12. DOI: 10.1016/j.chb.2022.107468

Celik, I., Dindar, M., Muukkonen, H., & Järvelä, S. (2022). The promises and challenges of artificial intelligence for teachers: A systematic review of research. *TechTrends*, *66*(4), 616–630. DOI: 10.1007/s11528-022-00715-y

Chang, C., Liang, C., Chou, P., & Lin, G. (2017). Is game-based learning better in flow experience and various types of cognitive load than non-game-based learning? Perspective from multimedia and media richness. *Computers in Human Behavior*, *71*, 218–227. DOI: 10.1016/j.chb.2017.01.031

Chapelle, C. A. (2001). *Computer Applications in Second Language Acquisition*. Cambridge University Press. DOI: 10.1017/CBO9781139524681

Charmaz, K. (2005). Grounded Theory in the 21st Century. In Denzin, N. K., & Lincoln, Y. S. (Eds.), *The SAGE Handbook of Qualitative Research* (pp. 507–535). SAGE Publications.

Charmaz, K. (2010). Grounded Theory: Objectivist and Constructivist Methods. In Luttrell, W. (Ed.), *Qualitative Educational Research. Readings in Reflexive Methodology and Transformative Practice* (pp. 183–207). Routledge.

Chaudhri, V. K. H., Lane, C., Gunning, D., & Roschelle, J. (2013). Applications of artificial intelligence to contemporary and emerging educational challenges. *Artificial Intelligence Magazine*, *34*(3), 10–12.

Cheng, R., & Hill, B. M. (2022). Many destinations, many pathways: A quantitative analysis of legitimate peripheral participation in scratch. *Proc. ACM Hum.-Comput. Interact., 6*(CSCW2), 381:1-381:26. DOI: 10.1145/3555106

Cheng, L., Croteau, E., Baral, S., Heffernan, C., & Heffernan, N. (2024). Facilitating student learning with a chatbot in an online math learning platform. *Journal of Educational Computing Research, 62*(4), 687–717. https://doi-org.dist.lib.usu.edu/10.1177/07356331241226592. DOI: 10.1177/07356331241226592

Cheng, X., Liu, Y., & Wang, C. (2023). Understanding student engagement with teacher and peer feedback in L2 writing. *System, 119*, 103176. DOI: 10.1016/j.system.2023.103176

Chen, L., Chen, P., & Lin, Z. (2020). Artificial intelligence in education: A review. *IEEE Access : Practical Innovations, Open Solutions, 8*, 75264–75278. DOI: 10.1109/ACCESS.2020.2988510

Chen, M., Kuzmin, K., & Szymanski, B. K. (2014). Community detection via maximization of modularity and its variants. *IEEE Transactions on Computational Social Systems, 1*(1), 46–65. DOI: 10.1109/TCSS.2014.2307458

Chen, P., Lu, Y., Zheng, V. W., Chen, X., & Yang, B. (2018). KnowEdu: A system to construct knowledge graph for education. *IEEE Access : Practical Innovations, Open Solutions, 6*, 31553–31563. DOI: 10.1109/ACCESS.2018.2839607

Chi, M., Adams, J., Bogusch, E. B., Bruchok, C., Kang, S., Lancaster, M., Levy, R., Li, N., McEldoon, K. L., Stump, G. S., Wylie, R., Xu, D., & Yaghmourian, D. L. (2018). Translating the ICAP theory of cognitive engagement into practice. *Cognitive Science, 42*(6), 1777–1832. DOI: 10.1111/cogs.12626 PMID: 29954048

Chi, M., & VanLehn, K. A. (2012). Seeing deep structure from the interactions of surface features. *Educational Psychologist, 47*(3), 177–188. DOI: 10.1080/00461520.2012.695709

Chiu, T. K. (2024). *Empowering K-12 education with AI: Preparing for the future of education and work.* Taylor & Francis. DOI: 10.4324/9781003498377

Chiu, T. K. F., Chen, Y., Yau, K. W., Chai, C., Meng, H., King, I., Wong, S., & Yam, Y. (2024). Developing and validating measures for AI literacy tests: From self-reported to objective measures. *Computers and Education. Artificial Intelligence, 7*, 100282. DOI: 10.1016/j.caeai.2024.100282

Choi, G. W., Kim, S. H., Lee, D., & Moon, J. (2024). Utilizing generative AI for instructional design: Exploring strengths, weaknesses, opportunities, and threats. *TechTrends, 68*(4), 832–844. DOI: 10.1007/s11528-024-00967-w

Chu, T., & Wang, W. (2024). Exploring EFL teachers' epistemic agency and its influencing factors in an AI-integrated context through the double stimulation model. *The Asia-Pacific Education Researcher, 34*, 1–9. DOI: 10.1007/s40299-024-00940-4

Cicchetti, D. V., & Sparrow, S. A. (1981). Developing criteria for establishing inter-rater reliability of specific items: Applications to assessment of adaptive behavior. *American Journal of Mental Deficiency, 86*(2), 127–137. PMID: 7315877

Clark, R. (1983). Reconsidering research on learning from media. *Review of Educational Research, 53*(4), 445–459. DOI: 10.3102/00346543053004445

Clark, R. E. (1994). Media will never influence learning. *Educational Technology Research and Development, 42*(2), 21–29. DOI: 10.1007/BF02299088

Cleary, T. J., & Callan, G. L. (2017). Assessing self-regulated learning using microanalytic methods. In Schunk, D. H., & Greene, J. (Eds.), *Handbook of Self-Regulation of Learning and Performance* (2nd ed., pp. 338–351). Routledge. DOI: 10.4324/9781315697048-22

Çobanoğullari, F. (2024). Learning and teaching with ChatGPT: Potentials and applications in education. *The EuroCALL Review, 31*(1), 4–15. DOI: 10.4995/eurocall.2024.19957

Cohn, C., Snyder, C., & Fonteles, J. H., TS, A., Montenegro, J., & Biswas, G. (2024). A multimodal approach to support teacher, researcher and AI collaboration in STEM+ C learning environments. *British Journal of Educational Technology, 56*(2), 595–620. DOI: 10.1111/bjet.13518

Cole, D. A. (1987). Utility of confirmatory factor analysis in test validation research. *Journal of Consulting and Clinical Psychology, 55*(4), 584–594. DOI: 10.1037/0022-006X.55.4.584 PMID: 3624616

Collins, A., & Halverson, R. (2018). *Rethinking education in the age of technology: The digital revolution and schooling in America*. Teachers College Press.

Compagnoni, I., Oguilve, V., & Wen, W. (2025). Ethical frontiers of AI in language pedagogy: Navigating transparency, accountability, and equity. *International Journal of Linguistics, 17*(4), 1–25. DOI: 10.5296/ijl.v17i4.22768

Confrey, J., & Smith, E. (1994). Exponential functions, rates of change, and the multiplicative unit. *Learning Mathematics,* 31–60. DOI: 10.1007/978-94-017-2057-1_2

Cook, A., Zheng, R., & Blaz, J. W. (2009). Measurement of cognitive load during multimedia learning activities. In Zheng, R. (Ed.), *Cognitive effects of multimedia learning* (pp. 34–50). Information Science Reference/IGI Global Publishing. DOI: 10.4018/978-1-60566-158-2.ch003

Cosentino, G., Anton, J., Sharma, K., Gelsomini, M., Giannakos, M., & Abrahamson, D. (2025). Hybrid teaching intelligence: Lessons learned from an embodied mathematics learning experience. *British Journal of Educational Technology*, *56*(2), 621–649. DOI: 10.1111/bjet.13525

Crompton, H., & Burke, D. (2022). Artificial intelligence in K–12 education. *SN Social Sciences*, *2*(7), 113. DOI: 10.1007/s43545-022-00425-5

Crowston, K., & Bolici, F. (2025). Deskilling and upskilling with AI Systems. *nformation Research an International Electronic Journal, 30*(iConf), 1009-1023. DOI: 10.47989/ir30iConf47143

D'Mello, S., & Calvo, R. A. (2013). Beyond the basic emotions: What should affective computing compute? *CHI '13 extended abstracts on human factors in Computing systems* on - CHI EA '13, 2287. DOI: 10.1145/2468356.2468751

D'Mello, S. K., & Graesser, A. (2013). Multimodal semi-automated affect detection from conversational cues, gross body language, and physiology. *IEEE Transactions on Affective Computing*.

Dagdelen, J., Dunn, A., Lee, S., Walker, N., Rosen, A. S., Ceder, G., Persson, K. A., & Jain, A. (2024). Structured information extraction from scientific text with large language models. *Nature Communications*, *15*(1), 1418. DOI: 10.1038/s41467-024-45563-x PMID: 38360817

Daigle, K. (2024). *Survey: The AI wave continues to grow on software development teams*. Obtenido de https://github.blog/author/kdaigle/

Dake, D. K., & Bada, G. K. (2023). Unveiling learner emotions: Sentiment analysis of Moodle-based online assessments using machine learning. *Journal of Information Technology Education: Innovations in Practice*, *22*, 109–132. DOI: 10.28945/5174

Dalalah, D., & Dalalah, O. M. (2023). The false positives and false negatives of generative AI detection tools in education and academic research: The case of ChatGPT. *International Journal of Management Education*, *21*(2), 100822. DOI: 10.1016/j.ijme.2023.100822

Dalipi, F., Zdravkova, K., & Ahlgren, F. (2021). Sentiment Analysis of Students' Feedback in MOOCs: A Systematic Literature Review. *Frontiers in Artificial Intelligence*, *4*, 728708. DOI: 10.3389/frai.2021.728708 PMID: 34568815

Dang, H. (2006). Learner-centeredness and EFL instruction in Vietnam: A case study. *International Education Journal*, *7*(4), 598–610.

Daroczy, G., Wolska, M., Meurers, W. D., & Nuerk, H.-C. (2015). Word problems: A review of linguistic and numerical factors contributing to their difficulty. *Frontiers in Psychology*, *6*. Advance online publication. DOI: 10.3389/fpsyg.2015.00348 PMID: 25883575

Darwin, R., Rusdin, D., Mukminatien, N., Suryati, N., Laksmi, E. D., & Marzuki, . (2024). Critical thinking in the AI era: An exploration of EFL students' perceptions, benefits, and limitations. *Cogent Education*, *11*(1), 1–18. DOI: 10.1080/2331186X.2023.2290342

Davoodi, A. (2024). Crafting innovative paths in non-linear professional learning for bilingual education: The role of connectivism in the age of AI. *Professional Development in Education*, *51*(3), 434–450. DOI: 10.1080/19415257.2024.2421492

Deci, E. L., Ryan, R. M., Gagné, M., Leone, D. R., Usunov, J., & Kornazheva, B. P. (2001). Need satisfaction, motivation, and well-being in the work organizations of a former Eastern Bloc country. Personality and Social Psychology Bulletin, 27, 930e942.

Delello, J. A., Watters, J. B., & Garcia-Lopez, A. (2024). Artificial intelligence in education: Transforming learning and teaching. In Delello, J. A., & McWhorter, R. R. (Eds.), *Disruptive technologies in education and workforce development* (pp. 1–26). IGI Global. DOI: 10.4018/979-8-3693-3003-6.ch001

Demir, K., & Güraksın, G. (2022). Determining middle school students' perceptions of the concept of artificial intelligence: A metaphor analysis. *Participatory Educational Research*, *9*(2), 297–312. DOI: 10.17275/per.22.41.9.2

Démuth, A. (2013). *Perception theories*. Trnava University.

Desoete, A. (2015). Language and math. In P. Aunio, R. Mononen, & A. Laine, Mathematical learning difficulties—snapshots of current European research. *LUMAT, 5*, 647–674.

Detrick, R., & Kim, J. (in press). Collaborative approaches: Bridging the gap between generative AI developers and educators. In Sabbaghan, S. (Ed.), *Navigating generative AI in higher education: Ethical, theoretical, and practical perspectives*. Edward Elgar. DOI: 10.4337/9781035337873.00018

Devineni, S. K. (2024). AI in data privacy and security. *International Journal of Artificial Intelligence and Machine Learning*, *3*(1), 35–49.

Dhirani, L. L., Mukhtiar, N., Chowdhry, B. S., & Newe, T. (2023). Ethical dilemmas and privacy issues in emerging technologies: A review. *Sensors (Basel)*, *23*(3), 1151. DOI: 10.3390/s23031151 PMID: 36772190

Dillenbourg, P., Baker, M. J., Blaye, A., & O'Malley, C. (1995). The evolution of research on collaborative learning. In Spada, H., & Reimann, P. (Eds.), *Learning in humans and machine: Towards an interdisciplinary learning science* (pp. 189–211). Elsevier.

DiSessa, A. A., & Sherin, B. L. (1998). What changes in conceptual change? *International Journal of Science Education*, *20*(10), 1155–1191. DOI: 10.1080/0950069980201002

Dixon, J., Crooks, H., & Henry, K. (2006). Breaking the ice: Supporting collaboration and the development of community online. *Canadian Journal of Learning and Technology*, *32*(2), 1–14. DOI: 10.21432/T25S3M

Dmello, V. J., Frank, D., Bidi, S. B., & Rajendran, A. (2024). Unlocking the enigma of online learning: How learning styles shape adoption intention? *E-Learning and Digital Media*, *0*(0), 1–16. DOI: 10.1177/20427530241257651

Dolapcioglu, S., & Doğanay, A. (2022). Development of critical thinking in mathematics classes via authentic learning: An action research. *International Journal of Mathematical Education in Science and Technology*, *53*(6), 1363–1386. DOI: 10.1080/0020739X.2020.1819573

Duan, H., & Zhao, W. (2024). The effects of educational artificial intelligence-powered applications on teachers' perceived autonomy, professional development for online teaching, and digital burnout. *International Review of Research in Open and Distance Learning*, *25*(3), 57–76. DOI: 10.19173/irrodl.v25i3.7659

Du, H., & List, A. (2020). Researching and writing based on multiple texts. *Learning and Instruction*, *66*, 101297. DOI: 10.1016/j.learninstruc.2019.101297

Du, M., & Qian, Y. (2022). Application of massive open online course to grammar teaching for English majors based on deep learning. *Frontiers in Psychology*, *12*, 755043. Advance online publication. DOI: 10.3389/fpsyg.2021.755043 PMID: 35069332

Duong, T., & Chen, H. (2025). An AI chatbot for EFL writing: Students' usage tendencies, writing performance, and perceptions. *Journal of Educational Computing Research*, *63*(2), 406–430. https://doi-org.dist.lib.usu.edu/10.1177/07345633124131 2363. DOI: 10.1177/07356331241312363

Ebadi, S., & Amini, A. (2022). Examining the roles of social presence and human-likeness on Iranian EFL learners' motivation using artificial intelligence technology: A case of CSIEC chatbot. *Interactive Learning Environments*, •••, 1–19. DOI: 10.1080/10494820.2022.2096638

Edson, A. J., & Sedaghat, S. (2015). Using learning progressions as a design tool for task development: The case of rate of change. *The Journal of Mathematical Behavior*, *39*, 87–100.

Eguchi, A., Okada, H., & Muto, Y. (2021). Contextualizing AI education for K-12 students to enhance their learning of AI literacy through culturally responsive approaches. *KI- Künstliche Intelligenz, 35*(2), 153–161. DOI: 10.1007/s13218-021-00737-3

El Bahri, N., Itahriouan, Z., & Ouazzani Jamil, M. (2025). Emotion-Aware Education Through Affective Computing and Learning Analytics: Insights from a Moroccan University Case Study. *Digital*, *5*(3), 45. DOI: 10.3390/digital5030045

Elia, I. (2020). Word problem solving and pictorial representations: Insights from an exploratory study in kindergarten. *ZDM Mathematics Education*, *52*(1), 17–31. DOI: 10.1007/s11858-019-01113-0

Ellis, R. (2009). Corrective feedback and teacher development. *Journal of Linguistics and Language Teaching*, *1*(1), 3–18. DOI: 10.5070/L2.V1I1.9054

El-Sabagh, H. A. (2021). Adaptive e-learning environment based on learning styles and its impact on development students' engagement. *International Journal of Educational Technology in Higher Education*, *18*(53), 1–24. DOI: 10.1186/s41239-021-00289-4

Elston, D. M. (2021). The novelty effect. *Journal of the American Academy of Dermatology*, *85*(3), 565–566. DOI: 10.1016/j.jaad.2021.06.846 PMID: 34153390

Embarak, O. H., & Hawarna, S. (2024). Automated AI-driven system for early detection of at-risk students. *Procedia Computer Science*, *231*, 151–160. DOI: 10.1016/j.procs.2023.12.187

Ercan, G. E., & Aydın, S. (2022). Flipped learning in the English as a foreign language learning context: A theoretical framework. In *The new normal of online language education* (pp. 161–180). Eğiten.

Estrada, S. (2025, August 18). MIT report: 95% of generative AI pilots at companies are failing. *Fortune*. https://fortune.com/2025/08/18/mit-report-95-percent-generative-ai-pilots-at-companies-failing-cfo/

Faber, J. M., Luyten, H., & Visscher, A. J. (2024). NLP for improved personalization in adaptive learning. *Educational Technology Research and Development.*

Fan, L., Kim, J., Detrick, R., & Li, N. (2025). Developing students' higher-order thinking skills with generative AI insights and strategies from a case study. In El-Sayary, A. (Ed.), *Prompt engineering and generative AI applications for teaching and learning* (pp. 411–428). IGI Global Scientific Publishing. DOI: 10.4018/979-8-3693-7332-3.ch024

Farida, A. N., & Rosyidi, M. I. (2019). Students' writing quality: Its coherence and cohesion. Language Circle. *Journal of Language and Literature*, *14*(1), 121–129. DOI: 10.15294/lc.v14i1.21505

Fazal, S. (2025). Attitude towards teacher-AI collaboration in academic writing instruction: Transforming future of English language teaching. In Ali, M. M., Anwar, M. N., Fazal, S., & Ayyaz, S. (Eds.), *AI applications for English language learning* (pp. 15–42). IGI Global Scientific Publishing. DOI: 10.4018/979-8-3693-9077-1.ch002

Fehrmann, R. (2025). Implementing augmented reality models in the classroom environment using merge cubes: A quantitative study of the effects on students' cognitive load and motivation. *Education Sciences*, *15*(4), 414–432. DOI: 10.3390/educsci15040414

Filiz, O., Kaya, M. H., & Adiguzel, T. (2025). Teachers and AI: Understanding the factors influencing AI integration in K-12 education. *Education and Information Technologies*, *30*(13), 1–37. DOI: 10.1007/s10639-025-13463-2

Fishbein, M., & Ajzen, I. (1975). *Belief, attitude, intention, and behavior: An introduction to theory and research.* Addison-Wesley Publishing Company.

Fisher, M., & Marshall, A. (2009). Understanding descriptive statistics. *Australian Critical Care*, *22*(2), 93–97. DOI: 10.1016/j.aucc.2008.11.003 PMID: 19150245

Fitas, R. (2025). Inclusive education with AI: Supporting special needs and tackling language barriers. *AI and Ethics*, *5*(6), 5729–5757. DOI: 10.1007/s43681-025-00824-3

Fitria, T. (2021). Grammarly as AI-powered English writing assistant: Students' alternative for writing English. *Metathesis: Journal of English Language, Literature, and Teaching*, *5*(1), 65–78. DOI: 10.31002/metathesis.v5i1.3519

Fletscher, L., Mercado, J., Gómez, A., & Mendoza Cárdenas, C. (2025). Innovating personalized learning in virtual education. *Multimodal Technologies and Interaction*, *9*(7), 69. DOI: 10.3390/mti9070069

Fong, C. J., & Schallert, D. L. (2023). Feedback to the future: Advancing motivational and emotional perspectives in feedback research. *Educational Psychologist, 58*(3), 146–161. DOI: 10.1080/00461520.2022.2134135

Fornell, C., & Larcker, D. F. (1981). Evaluating structural equation models with unobservable variables and measurement error. *JMR, Journal of Marketing Research, 18*(1), 39–50. DOI: 10.1177/002224378101800104

Forsyth, D. R. (2014). *Group dynamics*. Wadsworth Cengage Learning.

Forsyth, S. R., & Powell, S. R. (2017). Differences in the mathematics vocabulary knowledge of fifth-grade students with and without learning difficulties. *Learning Disabilities Research & Practice, 32*(4), 231–245. DOI: 10.1111/ldrp.12144

Fraenkel, J. R., & Wallen, N. E. (2006). *How to design and evaluate research in education* (International Edition). McGraw-Hill.

Fryer, L. K., Ainley, M., Thompson, A., Gibson, A., & Sherlock, Z. (2017). Stimulating and sustaining interest in a language course: An experimental comparison of chatbot and human task partners. *Computers in Human Behavior, 75*, 461–468. DOI: 10.1016/j.chb.2017.05.045

Fuchs, K. (2023). Exploring the opportunities and challenges of NLP models in higher education: Is Chat GPT a blessing or a curse? *Frontiers in Education, 8*, 1–4. DOI: 10.3389/feduc.2023.1166682

Gamage, G., De Silva, D., Mills, N., Alahakoon, D., & Manic, M. (2024). Emotion AWARE: An artificial intelligence framework for adaptable, robust, explainable, and multi-granular emotion analysis. *Journal of Big Data, 11*(1), 93. DOI: 10.1186/s40537-024-00953-2

Garg, S., & Sharma, S. (2020). Impact of artificial intelligence in special need education to promote inclusive pedagogy. *International Journal of Information and Education Technology (IJIET), 10*(7), 523–527. DOI: 10.18178/ijiet.2020.10.7.1418

Garrison, D. R. (2022). Motivation and the CoI framework. *The Community of Inquiry*. https://www.thecommunityofinquiry.org/editorial37

Garrison, D. R., Anderson, T., & Archer, W. (1999). Critical inquiry in a text-based environment: Computer conferencing in higher education. *The Internet and Higher Education, 2*(2-3), 87–105. DOI: 10.1016/S1096-7516(00)00016-6

Gašević, D., Siemens, G., & Sadiq, S. (2023). Empowering learners for the age of artificial intelligence. *Computers and Education: Artificial Intelligence, 4*, 100130. DOI: 10.1016/j.caeai.2023.100130

Gayed, J. M., Carlon, M. K. J., Oriola, A. M., & Cross, J. S. (2022). Exploring an ai-based writing assistant's impact on English language learners. *Computer Education: Artificial Intelligence*, *3*, 100055. DOI: 10.1016/j.caeai.2022.100055

Geary, D. C., Boykin, A. W., Embretson, S., Reyna, V., Siegler, R., Berch, D. B., & Graban, J. (2008). Chapter 4: Report of the task group on learning processes. In U.S. Department of Education (Ed.), *The final report of the National Mathematics Advisory Panel* (pp. 4-xi–4-221). Washington, DC: U.S. Department of Education. http://www.ed.gov/ about/bdscomm/list/mathpanel/report/learning-processes.pdf

Geary, D. C. (2004). Mathematics and learning disabilities. *Journal of Learning Disabilities*, *37*(1), 4–15. DOI: 10.1177/00222194040370010201 PMID: 15493463

Geary, D. C. (2011). Consequences, characteristics, and causes of mathematical learning disabilities and persistent low achievement in mathematics. *Journal of Developmental and Behavioral Pediatrics*, *32*(3), 250–263. DOI: 10.1097/DBP.0b013e318209edef PMID: 21285895

George, A. S. (2023). Preparing students for an AI-driven world: Rethinking curriculum and pedagogy in the age of artificial intelligence. *Partners Universal Innovative Research Publication*, *1*(2), 112–136. DOI: 10.5281/zenodo.10245675

Ghamrawi, N., Shal, T., & Ghamrawi, N. A. R. (2023). Exploring the impact of AI on teacher leadership: Regressing or expanding? *Education and Information Technologies*, *29*(7), 1–19. DOI: 10.1007/s10639-023-12174-w

Ghosh, S. S. (2025). Assessing the efficacy of intelligent tutoring systems in language teacher education: A quantitative study. *Computers in the Schools*, *42*(2), 121–144. DOI: 10.1080/07380569.2024.2435308

Giddens, A. (1991). *Modernity and self-identity: self and society in the late modern age*. Polity Press.

Gielen, S., Peeters, E., Dochy, F., Onghena, P., & Struyven, K. (2010). Improving the effectiveness of peer feedback for learning. *Learning and Instruction*, *20*(4), 304–315. DOI: 10.1016/j.learninstruc.2009.08.007

Gillespie, A., & Graham, S. (2014). A meta-analysis of writing interventions for students with learning disabilities. *Exceptional Children*, *80*(4), 454–473. DOI: 10.1177/0014402914527238

Glisan, E. W., & Donato, R. (2021). *Enacting the work of language instruction: High-leverage teaching practices* (Vol. 2). ACTFL.

Gómez-Ríos, M., Paredes-Velasco, M., Velázquez-Iturbide, J. Á., & Martínez, M. Á. Q. (2025). Augmented Reality for Learning Algorithms: Evaluation of its Impact on Students' Emotions Using Artificial Intelligence. *Applied Sciences (Basel, Switzerland)*, *15*(14), 7745. DOI: 10.3390/app15147745

Graham, S., & Harris, K. R. (2018). An examination of the design principles underlying a self-regulated strategy development study. *Journal of Writing Research*, *10*(2), 139–187. DOI: 10.17239/jowr-2018.10.02.02

Graham, S., Harris, K. R., & McKeown, D. (2014). The writing of students with learning disabilities, meta-analysis of self-regulated strategy development writing intervention studies, and future directions: Redux. In Swanson, H. L., Harris, K. R., & Graham, S. (Eds.), *Handbook of learning disabilities* (2nd ed., pp. 405–438). The Guilford Press.

Graham, S., Hebert, M., & Harris, K. R. (2015). Formative assessment and writing: A meta-analysis. *The Elementary School Journal*, *115*(4), 523–547. DOI: 10.1086/681947

Graham, S., Kiuhara, S. A., & MacKay, M. (2020). The effects of writing on learning in science, social studies, and mathematics: A meta-analysis. *Review of Educational Research*, *90*(2), 179–226. DOI: 10.3102/0034654320914744

Graham, S., McKeown, D., Kiuhara, S. A., & Harris, K. R. (2012). A meta-analysis of writing instruction for students in the elementary grades. *Journal of Educational Psychology*, *104*(4), 879–896. DOI: 10.1037/a0029185

Grant, D. G. (2019). Predicting Web 2.0 use among US teens — Expanding the power of the skill, will and tool model. *British Journal of Educational Technology*, *50*(6), 3405–3419. DOI: 10.1111/bjet.12745

Greenberg, K., & Zheng, R. (2023). Revisiting the debate on germane cognitive load versus germane resources. *Journal of Cognitive Psychology*, *35*(3), 295–314. DOI: 10.1080/20445911.2022.2159416

Gregory, R. (2015). *Eye and brain: The psychology of seeing*. Princeton University Press. DOI: 10.2307/j.ctvc77h66

Guggemos, J., & Seufert, S. (2021). Teaching with and teaching about technology - Evidence for professional development of in-service teachers. *Computers in Human Behavior*, *115*, 1–11. DOI: 10.1016/j.chb.2020.106613

Guizani, S., Mazhar, T., Shahzad, T., Ahmad, W., Bibi, A., & Hamam, H. (2025). A systematic literature review to implement large language model in higher education: Issues and solutions. *Discover Education*, *4*(1), 35. DOI: 10.1007/s44217-025-00424-7

Guo, K., & Wang, D. (2023). To resist it or to embrace it? Examining ChatGPT's potential to support teacher feedback in EFL writing. *Education and Information Technologies*, *29*(7), 8435–8463. DOI: 10.1007/s10639-023-12146-0

Guo, K., Wang, J., & Chu, S. K. W. (2022). Using chatbots to scaffold EFL students' argumentative writing. *Assessing Writing*, *54*, 100666. DOI: 10.1016/j.asw.2022.100666

Gupta, U., & Zheng, R. (2020). Cognitive load in solving mathematics problems: Validating the role of motivation and the interaction among worked examples, task difficulty, and prior knowledge. *European Journal of STEM Education, 5*(1), 05.

Gupta, T., Kumar, A., Roy, B. K., & Saini, S. (2024). Adaptive learning systems: Harnessing AI to personalize educational outcomes. *International Journal for Research in Applied Science and Engineering Technology*, *12*(11), 458–464. Advance online publication. DOI: 10.22214/ijraset.2024.65088

Hachey, A. C., Wladis, C., & Conway, K. (2015). Prior online course experience and G.P.A. as predictors of subsequent online STEM course outcomes. *The Internet and Higher Education*, *25*, 11–17. DOI: 10.1016/j.iheduc.2014.10.003

Hacker, D. J., Kiuhara, S. A., & Levin, J. R. (2019). A metacognitive intervention for teaching fractions to students with or at-risk for learning disabilities in mathematics. Special issue on metacognition in mathematics education. *ZDM Mathematics Education*, *51*(4), 601–612. DOI: 10.1007/s11858-019-01040-0

Hackman, J. R., & Oldham, G. R. (1976). Motivation through the design of work: Test of a theory. *Organizational Behavior and Human Performance*, *16*(2), 250–279. DOI: 10.1016/0030-5073(76)90016-7

Hallet, D., Nunes, T., & Bryant, P. (2010). Individual differences in conceptual and procedural knowledge when learning fractions. *Journal of Educational Psychology*, *102*(2), 395–406. DOI: 10.1037/a0017486

Hammerschmidt, T., Stolz, K., & Posegga, O. (2025). Bridging the gap: Inequalities that divide those who can and cannot create sustainable outcomes with AI. *Behaviour & Information Technology*, •••, 1–30. DOI: 10.1080/0144929X.2025.2500451

Han, A. (2024). *StoryAI: Designing, developing, and evaluating generative AI-Powered story-authoring platform for young learners*. University of California.

Harmer, J. (2003). Popular culture, methods, and context. *ELT Journal*, *57*(3), 288–294. DOI: 10.1093/elt/57.3.288

Harris, K. R., & Graham, S. (2009). Self-regulated strategy development in writing: Premises, evolution, and the future. *British Journal of Educational Psychology* Monograph Series II: No. 6. Teaching and Learning Writing (pp. 113–135). *British Psychological Society., 422542*. Advance online publication. DOI: 10. 1348/978185409X

Harris, K. R., Graham, S., Mason, L., & Friedlander, B. (2008). *Powerful writing strategies for all students*. Brookes.

Hartshorne, J. K., Tenenbaum, J. B., & Pinker, S. (2018). A critical period for second language acquisition: Evidence from 2/3 million English speakers. *Cognition*, *177*, 263–277. DOI: 10.1016/j.cognition.2018.04.007 PMID: 29729947

Hattikudor, S., Alibali, M. W., Prather, R. W., Knuth, E. J., Asquith, P., & Nathan, M. (2012). Constructing graphical representations: Middle schoolers' intuitions and developing knowledge about slope and y-intercept. *School Science and Mathematics*, *112*(4), 230–240. DOI: 10.1111/j.1949-8594.2012.00138.x

Haythornthwaite, C. (2006). Learning and knowledge networks in interdisciplinary collaborations. *Journal of the American Society for Information Science and Technology*, *57*(8), 1079–1092. DOI: 10.1002/asi.20371

Hazaymeh, W., Bouzenoun, A., & Remache, A. (2024). EFL instructors' perspective on using AI applications in English as a foreign language teaching and learning. *Emerging Science Journal*, *8*, 73–87. DOI: 10.28991/ESJ-2024-SIED1-05

Hebert, M. A., Bohaty, J., Roehling, J., & Powell, S. R. (2019). Piloting a mathematics-writing intervention with late elementary students at-risk for learning difficulties. *Learning Disabilities Research & Practice*, *34*(3), 144–157. DOI: 10.1111/ldrp.12202

Heinim¨aki, O.-P., Volet, S., Jones, C., Laakkonen, E., & Vauras, M. (2021). Student participatory role profiles in collaborative science learning: Relation of within-group configurations of role profiles and achievement. *Learning, Culture and Social Interaction*, *30*, 1–15. DOI: 10.1016/j.lcsi.2021.100539

Henson, R. K. (2001). Understanding internal consistency reliability estimates: A conceptual primer on coefficient alpha. *Measurement & Evaluation in Counseling & Development*, *34*(3), 177–189. DOI: 10.1080/07481756.2002.12069034

Hew, K. F., Hu, X., Qiao, C., & Tang, Y. (2020). What Predicts Student Satisfaction with MOOCs: A Gradient Boosting Trees Supervised Machine Learning and Sentiment Analysis Approach. *Computers & Education*, *145*, 103724. Advance online publication. DOI: 10.1016/j.compedu.2019.103724

Hieu, H. H., & Thao, L. T. (2024). Exploring the impact of AI in language education: Vietnamese EFL teachers' views on using ChatGPT for fairy tale retelling tasks. *International Journal of Learning. Teaching and Educational Research*, *23*(3), 486–503. DOI: 10.26803/ijlter.23.3.24

Hildebrandt, S. A., & Swanson, P. (2016). *Understanding the world language edTPA: Research-based policy and practice*. Information Age Publishing.

Hmelo-Silver, C. E., & Barrows, H. S. (2008). Facilitating collaborative knowledge building. *Cognition and Instruction*, *26*(1), 48–94. DOI: 10.1080/07370000701798495

Hockly, N. (2018). Blended learning. *ELT Journal*, *72*(1), 97–101. DOI: 10.1093/elt/ccx058

Hoi, V. N. (2020). Understanding higher education learners' acceptance and use of mobile devices for language learning: A Rasch-based path modeling approach. *Computers & Education*, *146*, 103761. DOI: 10.1016/j.compedu.2019.103761

Hong Kong Education City. (2021). *AI education for future-ready generations.* Go AI Scheme. https://www.edcity.hk/ai/en

Hong, X. Q., & Guo, L. (2025). Effects of AI-enhanced multi-display language teaching systems on learning motivation, cognitive load management, and learner autonomy. *Education and Information Technologies*, *30*(12), 17155–17189. DOI: 10.1007/s10639-025-13472-1

Hopfield, J. J. (1982). Neural networks and physical systems with emergent collective computational abilities. *Proceedings of the National Academy of Sciences*. DOI: 10.1073/pnas.79.8.2554

Horner, R. H., Carr, E. G., McGee, G., Odom, S., & Wolery, M. (2005). The use of single-subject research to identify evidence-based practice in special education. *Exceptional Children*, *71*(2), 165–179. DOI: 10.1177/001440290507100203

Hoşer, S., & Aydın, S. (2026). The impact of AI-enhanced gamification on vocabulary learning in a foreign language context. In *AI-Powered Solutions for Bilingual Proficiency and Communication* (pp. 249–278). IGI Global Scientific Publishing., DOI: 10.4018/979-8-3373-0275-1.ch008

Hott, B. L., Morano, S., Peltier, C., Pulos, J., & Peltier, T. (2020). Are students with mathematics learning disabilities receiving FAPE?: Insights from a descriptive review of Individualized Education Programs. *Learning Disabilities Research & Practice*, *35*(4), 170–179. DOI: 10.1111/ldrp.12231

Huang, C. Q., Han, Z. M., Li, M. X., Jong, M. S. Y., & Tsai, C. C. (2019). Investigating students' interaction patterns and dynamic learning sentiments in online discussions. *Computers & Education, 140*, 103589. DOI: 10.1016/j.compedu.2019.05.015

Huang, F., Wang, Y., & Zhang, H. (2024). Modelling generative AI acceptance, perceived teachers' enthusiasm and self-efficacy to English as a foreign language learners' well-being in the digital era. *European Journal of Education, 59*(4), e12770. DOI: 10.1111/ejed.12770

Huang, L. (2023). Ethics of artificial intelligence in education: Student privacy and data protection. *Science Insights Education Frontiers, 16*(2), 2577–2587. DOI: 10.15354/sief.23.re202

Huang, L., Liang, M., Xiong, Y., Wu, X., & Lim, C. P. (2024). A systematic review of technology-enabled teacher professional development during COVID-19 pandemic. *Computers & Education, 223*, 105168. DOI: 10.1016/j.compedu.2024.105168

Huang, M. (2025). Student engagement and speaking performance in AI-assisted learning environments: A mixed-methods study from Chinese middle schools. *Education and Information Technologies, 30*(6), 7143–7165. DOI: 10.1007/s10639-024-12989-1

Huang, W., Hew, K. F., & Fryer, L. K. (2022). Chatbots for language learning—Are they really useful? A systematic review of chatbot-supported language learning. *Journal of Computer Assisted Learning, 38*(1), 237–257. DOI: 10.1111/jcal.12610

Huang, X., Zou, D., Cheng, G., Chen, X., & Xie, H. (2023). Trends, research issues and applications of artificial intelligence in language education. *Journal of Educational Technology & Society, 26*(1), 112–131.

Hua, S., Jin, S., & Jiang, S. (2024). The limitations and ethical considerations of ChatGPT. *Data Intelligence, 6*(1), 201–239. DOI: 10.1162/dint_a_00243

Huawei, S., & Aryadoust, V. (2022). A systematic review of automated writing evaluation systems. *Education and Information Technologies, 28*(1), 771–795. DOI: 10.1007/s10639-022-11200-7

Hughes, E. M., & Lee, J. (2020). Effects of a mathematical writing intervention on middle school students' performance. *Reading & Writing Quarterly, 36*(2), 176–192. DOI: 10.1080/10573569.2019.1677537

Hughes, E. M., Riccomini, P. J., & Lee, J. (2020). Investigating written expressions of mathematical reasoning for students with learning disabilities. *The Journal of Mathematical Behavior, 58*, 1–14. DOI: 10.1016/j.jmathb.2020.100775

Hu, L. T., & Bentler, P. M. (1999). Cutoff criteria for fit indexes in covariance structure analysis: Conventional criteria versus new alternatives. *Structural Equation Modeling*, *6*(1), 1–55. DOI: 10.1080/10705519909540118

Hurst, A., Lerer, A., Goucher, A. P., Perelman, A., Ramesh, A., Clark, A., . . . Kivlichan, I. (2024). *Gpt-4o system card. arXiv.* https://doi.org//arXiv.2410.21276DOI: 10.48550

Hussain, M., Qureshi, Z. M., & Malik, S. (2024). The impact of educational technologies on modern education: Navigating opportunities and challenges. *Global Educational Studies Review*, *IX*(III), 21–30. DOI: 10.31703/gesr.2024(IX-III).03

Hutchins, E. (2000). Distributed cognition. International encyclopedia of the social and behavioral sciences, 138(1), 1-10. https://arl.human.cornell.edu/linked%20docs/Hutchins_Distributed_Cognition.pdf

Hu, Y., Chen, Q., Du, J., Peng, X., Keloth, V. K., Zuo, X., Zhou, Y., Li, Z., Jiang, X., Lu, Z., Roberts, K., & Xu, H. (2024). Improving large language models for clinical named entity recognition via prompt engineering. *Journal of the American Medical Informatics Association : JAMIA*, *31*(9), ocad259. DOI: 10.1093/jamia/ocad259 PMID: 38281112

Hwang, G. J., Sung, H. Y., Chang, S. C., & Huang, X. C. (2020). A fuzzy expert system-based adaptive learning approach to improving students' learning performances by considering affective and cognitive factors. *Computers and Education: Artificial Intelligence*, *1*, 100003. DOI: 10.1016/j.caeai.2020.100003

Hwang, J., & Riccomini, P. J. (2016). Enhancing mathematical problem solving for secondary students with or at risk of learning disabilities: A literature review. *Learning Disabilities Research & Practice*, *31*(3), 169–181. DOI: 10.1111/ldrp.12105

Hwang, Y., & Levin, J. R. (2022). Demonstration of single-case two-sample randomization-test procedures: Underperforming children's implementation of an effective memory strategy. *Journal of Education for Students Placed at Risk*, *28*(3), 294–305. DOI: 10.1080/10824669.2022.2081167

Hyland, K. (2016). Teaching and researching writing. (2017). *Journal of Writing Research*, *8*(3), 531–533. DOI: 10.17239/jowr-2017.08.03.05

Hyland, K., & Hyland, F. (Eds.). (2006). *Feedback in second language writing: Contexts and issues*. Cambridge University Press. DOI: 10.1017/CBO9781139524742

Ibarra, B. (2022). Understanding SEL to create a sense of belonging: The role teachers play in addressing students' social and emotional well-being. *Current Issues in Education (Tempe, Ariz.)*, *23*(2), 1–15. DOI: 10.14507/cie.vol23iss2.2049

Ibrahim, H., Liu, F., Asim, R., Battu, B., Benabderrahmane, S., Alhafni, B., Adnan, W., Alhanai, T., AlShebli, B., Baghdadi, R., Bélanger, J., Beretta, E., Celik, K., Chaqfeh, M., Daqaq, M., Bernoussi, Z., Fougnie, D., Garcia de Soto, B., Gandolfi, A., & Zaki, Y. (2023). Perception, performance, and detectability of conversational artificial intelligence across 32 university courses. *Scientific Reports*, *13*(1), 1–13. DOI: 10.1038/s41598-023-38964-3 PMID: 36593249

Idowu, J. A., Koshiyama, A. S., & Treleaven, P. (2024). Investigating algorithmic bias in student progress monitoring. *Computers and Education: Artificial Intelligence*, *7*, 100267. DOI: 10.1016/j.caeai.2024.100267

Ifenthaler, D. (2010). Relational, structural, and semantic analysis of graphical representations and concept maps. *Educational Technology Research and Development*, *58*(1), 81–97. DOI: 10.1007/s11423-008-9087-4

Ifenthaler, D., Masduki, I., & Seel, N. M. (2011). The mystery of cognitive structure and how we can detect it: Tracking the development of cognitive structures over time. *Instructional Science*, *39*(1), 41–61. DOI: 10.1007/s11251-009-9097-6

Ilkka, T. (2018). The impact of artificial intelligence on learning, teaching, and education. *European Union.*

Ilyas, S., Umar, M., Riaz, K., & Tariq, Z. (2025). *Emotion recognition in AI-powered classrooms impacts on student engagement and learning outcomes*. Critical Review of Social Sciences Studies., DOI: 10.59075/x1wkpx78

Introne, J., Semaan, B., & Goggins, S. (2016). A sociotechnical mechanism for online support provision. In *Proceedings of the 2016 CHI Conference on Human Factors in Computing Systems* (pp. 3559–3571). DOI: 10.1145/2858036.2858582

Iyer, L. S., Chakraborty, T., Reddy, K. N., Krishnaswami, M., & Iyer, L. S. (2023). AI-assisted models for dyslexia and dysgraphia: Revolutionizing language learning for children. In AI-assisted special education for students with exceptional needs (Chapter 8). DOI: 10.4018/979-8-3693-0378-8.ch008

Jackson, D. L., Gillaspy, J. A.Jr, & Purc-Stephenson, R. (2009). Reporting practices in confirmatory factor analysis: An overview and some recommendations. *Psychological Methods*, *14*(1), 6–23. DOI: 10.1037/a0014694 PMID: 19271845

Jang, H., Kim, E. J., & Reeve, J. (2016). Why students become more engaged or more disengaged during the semester: A self-determination theory dual-process model. *Learning and Instruction*, *43*, 27–38. DOI: 10.1016/j.learninstruc.2016.01.002

Jeon, J., Lee, S., & Choi, S. (2023). A systematic review of research on speech-recognition chatbots for language learning: Implications for future directions in the era of large language models. *Interactive Learning Environments*, *32*(8), 4613–4631. DOI: 10.1080/10494820.2023.2204343

Jeon, M. (2023). *Developing middle schoolers' artificial intelligence literacy through project-based learning: Investigating cognitive & affective dimensions of learning about AI*. Indiana University.

Jiang, C., & Pang, Y. (2023). Enhancing design thinking in engineering students with project-based learning. *Computer Applications in Engineering Education*, *31*(4), 814–830. DOI: 10.1002/cae.22608

Jiang, J., & Yang, Y. (2025). GymBuddy and Elomia, AI-integrated applications, effects on the mental health of the students with psychological disorders. *BMC Psychology*, *13*(1), 1–9. DOI: 10.1186/s40359-025-02640-0 PMID: 40200376

Jiang, T., Sun, Z., Fu, S., & Lv, Y. (2024). Human-AI interaction research agenda: A user-centered perspective. *Data and Information Management*, *8*(4), 100078. DOI: 10.1016/j.dim.2024.100078

Jitendra, A. K., Harwell, M. R., Dupuis, D. N., & Karl, S. R. (2017). A randomized trial of the effects of schema-based instruction on proportional problem-solving for students with mathematics problem-solving difficulties. *Journal of Learning Disabilities*, *50*(3), 322–336. DOI: 10.1177/0022219416629646 PMID: 26968809

Jonäll, K. (2024). Artificial intelligence in academic grading: A mixed-methods study. *Computers & Education*, *210*, 105912. DOI: 10.1016/j.compedu.2024.105912

Josué, A., Bedoya-Flores, M. C., Mosquera-Quiñonez, E. F., Mesías-Simisterra, Á. E., & Bautista-Sánchez, J. V. (2023). Educational platforms: Digital tools for the teaching-learning process in education. *Ibero-American Journal of Education & Society Research*, *3*(1), 259–263. DOI: 10.56183/iberoeds.v3i1.626

Ju, B., Jin, T., & Stewart, J. B. (2016). Investigating communication hindrance in interdisciplinary collaboration: A grounded theory approach. *Proceedings of the Association for Information Science and Technology*, *53*(1), 1–4. DOI: 10.1002/pra2.2016.14505301113

Kabudi, T., Pappas, I., & Olsen, D. H. (2021). AI-enabled adaptive learning systems: A systematic mapping of the literature. *Computers and Education: Artificial Intelligence*, *2*, 100017. DOI: 10.1016/j.caeai.2021.100017

Kalyuga, S. (2011). Cognitive load theory: How many types of load does it really need? *Educational Psychology Review*, *23*(1), 1–19. DOI: 10.1007/s10648-010-9150-7

Kammer, J., & Hays, L. (2023). *Digital literacy made simple: Strategies for building skills across the curriculum*. International Society for Technology in Education.

Kanero, J., Geçkin, V., Oranç, C., Mamus, E., Küntay, A., & Göksun, T. (2018). Social robots for early language learning: Current evidence and future directions. *Child Development Perspectives, 12*(3), 146–151. DOI: 10.1111/cdep.12277

Kannan, J., & Munday, P. (2018). New trends in second language learning and teaching through the lens of ICT, networked learning, and artificial intelligence. *Círculo de Lingüística Aplicada a la Comunicación, 76*, 13–30. DOI: 10.5209/CLAC.62495

Karalekas, G., Vologiannidis, S., & Kalomiros, J. (2023). Teaching machine learning in K–12 using robotics. *Education Sciences, 13*(1), 67. DOI: 10.3390/educsci13010067

Karan, B., & Angadi, G. R. (2023). Potential risks of artificial intelligence integration into school education: A systematic review. *Bulletin of Science, Technology & Society, 43*(3–4), 67–85. DOI: 10.1177/02704676231224705

Karandish, D. (2021). 7 Benefits of AI in Education. *The Journal* https://thejournal.com/articles/2021/06/23/7-benefits-of-ai-in-education.aspx

Kartal, G. (2024). The influence of ChatGPT on thinking skills and creativity of EFL student teachers: A narrative inquiry. *Journal of Education for Teaching, 50*(4), 627–642. DOI: 10.1080/02607476.2024.2326502

Kartal, O. Y., Yazgan, A. D., Temelli, D., & Yavuz Kartal, M. (2024). The impact of epistemological beliefs and school climate on the sustainability of critical thinking dispositions in middle school students. *Sustainability (Basel), 16*(20), 8786. DOI: 10.3390/su16208786

Kaşıkçı, E. B., & İzmirli, S. (2024). Unpacking the relationship between online student engagement and online self-regulation in higher education. *Participatory Educational Research, 11*(4), 198–214. DOI: 10.17275/per.24.56.11.4

Kasneci, E., Seßler, K., Küchemann, S., Bannert, M., Dementieva, D., Fischer, F., Gasser, U., Groh, G., Günnemann, S., Hüllermeier, E., Krusche, S., Kutyniok, G., Michaeli, T., Nerdel, C., Pfeffer, J., Poquet, O., Sailer, M., Schmidt, A., Seidel, T., & Kasneci, G. (2023). ChatGPT for good? On opportunities and challenges of large language models for education. *Learning and Individual Differences, 103*, 102274. Advance online publication. DOI: 10.1016/j.lindif.2023.102274

Katiyar, N., Srivastava, D., Sharma, P., & Trivedi, R. (2024). AI-driven personalized learning systems: Enhancing educational effectiveness. *Educational Administration: Theory and Practice*. https://kuey.org/

Kee, T., Zhang, H., & King, R. B. (2024). An empirical study on immersive technology in synchronous hybrid learning in design education. *International Journal of Technology and Design Education*, *34*(3), 1243–1273. DOI: 10.1007/s10798-023-09855-5

Kellogg, R. T., & Raulerson, B. A. (2007). Improving the writing skills of college students. *Psychonomic Bulletin & Review*, *14*(2), 237–242. DOI: 10.3758/BF03194058 PMID: 17694907

Keloth, V. K., Hu, Y., Xie, Q., Peng, X., Wang, Y., Zheng, A., Selek, M., Raja, K., Wei, C. H., Jin, Q., Lu, Z., Chen, Q., & Xu, H. (2024). Advancing entity recognition in biomedicine via instruction tuning of large language models. *Bioinformatics (Oxford, England)*, *40*(4), btae163. DOI: 10.1093/bioinformatics/btae163 PMID: 38514400

Kennedy, T. (2006). Language learning and its impact on the brain: Connecting language learning with the mind through content-based instruction. *Foreign Language Annals*, *39*(3), 471–486. DOI: 10.1111/j.1944-9720.2006.tb02900.x

Khajavi, Y., & Ezhdehakosh, M. (2025). Enhancing language teacher education: Exploring the integration of AI-powered tools in preservice teacher education. *Journal of Research in Applied Linguistics*, *16*(1), 174–191. DOI: 10.22055/RALS.2024.48226.3405

Khurana, A., Subramonyam, H., & Chilana, P. K. (2024). Why and when llm-based assistants can go wrong: Investigating the effectiveness of prompt-based interactions for software help-seeking. *arXiv.org*. Obtenido de /arxiv.2402.08030DOI: 10.1145/3640543.3645200

Kieran, C. (2004). Algebraic thinking in the early grades: What is it? *The Mathematics Educator*, *8*, 139–151.

Kim, H., Shin, D., Yang, H., & Lee, J. H. (2019). A study of AI chatbot as an assistant tool for school English curriculum. *Korean Association for Learner-Centered Curriculum and Instruction*, *19*(1), 89–110. DOI: 10.22251/jlcci.2019.19.1.89

Kim, J. (2024a). Leading teachers' perspective on teacher-AI collaboration in education. *Education and Information Technologies*, *29*(7), 8693–8724. DOI: 10.1007/s10639-023-12109-5

Kim, J. (2024b). Types of teacher-AI collaboration in K-12 classroom instruction: Chinese teachers' perspective. *Education and Information Technologies*, *29*(13), 17433–17465. DOI: 10.1007/s10639-024-12523-3

Kim, J. (2025). Artificial intelligence in achieving sustainable development: Expectations of undergraduate students. *TechTrends*, *69*(1), 138–148. DOI: 10.1007/s11528-024-01025-1

Kim, J., & Cho, Y. H. (2023). My teammate is AI: Understanding students' perceptions of student-AI collaboration in drawing tasks. *Asia Pacific Journal of Education*, *45*(3), 1013–1027. DOI: 10.1080/02188791.2023.2286206

Kim, J., Detrick, R., Yu, S., Song, Y., Bol, L., & Li, N. (2025). Socially shared regulation of learning and artificial intelligence: Opportunities to support socially shared regulation. *Education and Information Technologies*, *30*(9), 1–39. DOI: 10.1007/s10639-024-13187-9

Kim, J., Lee, H., & Cho, Y. H. (2022). Learning design to support student-AI collaboration: Perspectives of leading teachers for AI in education. *Education and Information Technologies*, *27*(5), 6069–6104. DOI: 10.1007/s10639-021-10831-6

Kim, J., & Lee, S. S. (2023). Are two heads better than one?: The effect of student-AI collaboration on students' learning task performance. *TechTrends*, *67*(2), 365–375. DOI: 10.1007/s11528-022-00788-9 PMID: 36258920

Kim, J., Yu, S., Detrick, R., & Li, N. (2025). Exploring students' perspectives on generative AI-assisted academic writing. *Education and Information Technologies*, *30*(1), 1265–1300. DOI: 10.1007/s10639-024-12878-7

Kim, J., Yu, S., Lee, S. S., & Detrick, R. (2025). Students' prompt patterns and its effects in AI-assisted academic writing: Focusing on students' level of AI literacy. *Journal of Research on Technology in Education*, 1–18. DOI: 10.1080/15391523.2025.2456043

Kishore, K., Jaswal, V., Kulkarni, V., & De, D. (2021). Practical guidelines to develop and evaluate a questionnaire. *Indian Dermatology Online Journal*, *12*(2), 266–275. DOI: 10.4103/idoj.IDOJ_674_20 PMID: 33959523

Kiuhara, S. A., Li, C., Bundock, K., Levin, J. R., Smith, S., & Zheng, R. (2025). SRSD and AI? Effects of algebraic thinking through writing for high school students with a mathematics learning disability [Manuscript in preparation]. Department of Special Education, University of Utah

Kiuhara, S. A., Gillespie Rouse, A., Dai, T., Witzel, B., Morphy, P., & Unker, B. (2020). Constructing Written Arguments to Develop Fraction Knowledge. *Journal of Educational Psychology*, *112*(3), 584–607. DOI: 10.1037/edu0000391

Kiuhara, S. A., Levin, J. R., Tolbert, M., O'Keeffe, B. V., O'Neill, R. E., & Jameson, M. J. (2023). Teaching argument writing in math class: Challenges and solutions to improve the performance of 4th and 5th graders with disabilities. Special issue on teaching writing. *Reading and Writing*. Advance online publication. DOI: 10.1007/s11145-023-10459-7 PMID: 37359030

Kizilcec, R. F., Piech, C., & Schneider, E. (2013). *Deconstructing disengagement: Analyzing learner subpopulations in massive open online courses*. 170–179.

Klausmeier, H. J., & Goodwin, W. (1975). *Learning and human abilities: Educational psychology* (4th ed.). Harper & Row.

Klimova, B., Pikhart, M., & Al-Obaydi, L. H. (2024). Exploring the potential of ChatGPT for foreign language education at the university level. *Frontiers in Psychology, 15*, 1269319. DOI: 10.3389/fpsyg.2024.1269319 PMID: 38655215

Kline, R. B. (2023). *Principles and practice of structural equation modeling* (5th ed.). Guilford Press.

Knezek, G., Christensen, R., & Fluke, R. (2003). *Testing a will, skill, tool model of technology integration.* ERIC. https://files.eric.ed.gov/fulltext/ED475762.pdf

Knezek, G., Christensen, R., Miyashita, K., & Ropp, M. (2000). *Instruments for assessing educator progress in technology integration.* University of North Texas. https://iittl.unt.edu/sites/default/files/Instruments/InstrumentsforAssessingEducatorProgressinTechnologyIntegration_0.pdf

Knezek, G., & Christensen, R. (2016). Extending the will, skill, tool model of technology integration: Adding pedagogy as a new model construct. *Journal of Computing in Higher Education, 28*(3), 307–325. DOI: 10.1007/s12528-016-9120-2

Koedinger, K. R., Booth, J. L., & Klahr, D. (2013). Instructional complexity and the science to constrain it. *Science, 342*(6161), 935–937. DOI: 10.1126/science.1238056

Koh, J., Cowling, M., Jha, M., & Sim, K. N. (2023). The human teacher, the AI teacher and the AIED-teacher relationship. *Journal of Higher Education Theory and Practice, 23*(17), 199–211. DOI: 10.33423/jhetp.v23i17.6543

Kohnke, L. (2024). Enhancing teacher professional development with AI. In Kohnke, L. (Ed.), *Optimizing digital competence through microlearning: Flexible approaches to teacher professional development* (pp. 55–66). Springer Nature Singapore., DOI: 10.1007/978-981-97-8839-2_6

Kohnke, L., Zou, D., Ou, A. W., & Gu, M. M. (2025). Preparing future educators for AI enhanced classrooms: Insights into AI literacy and integration. *Computers and Education: Artificial Intelligence*, *8*, 1–9. DOI: 10.1016/j.caeai.2025.100398

Kolb, D. A. (1984). *Experiential learning: Experience as the source of learning and development*. Prentice Hall.

Könez, S., & Aydin, S. (2026). Empowering learner autonomy for developing writing skills through AI-enhanced reflective journals. In *Harnessing AI's Potential to Support Student Success and Teaching Excellence* (pp. 217–244). DOI: 10.4018/979-8-3373-1122-7.ch008

Korhonen, J., Linnanmaki, K., & Aunio, P. (2012). Language and mathematical performance: A comparison of lower secondary school students with different level of mathematical skills. *Scandinavian Journal of Educational Research, 56*(3), 333–334. DOI: 10.1080/00313831.2011.599423

Korteling, J., van de Boer-Visschedijk, G., Blankendaal, R., Boonekamp, R., & Eikelboom, A. (2021). Human- versus artificial intelligence. *Frontiers in Artificial Intelligence*, *4*, 622364. Advance online publication. DOI: 10.3389/frai.2021.622364 PMID: 33981990

Koubek, R. J., Clarkston, T. P., & Calvez, V. (1994). The training of knowledge structures for manufacturing tasks: An empirical study. *Ergonomics*, *37*(4), 765–780. DOI: 10.1080/00140139408963687

Kozma, R. B. (1994). Will media influence learning? Reframing the debate. *Educational Technology Research and Development*, *42*(2), 7–19. DOI: 10.1007/BF02299087

Kramer, A., Guillory, J. E., & Hancock, J. T. (2014). Experimental evidence of massive-scale emotional contagion through social networks. *Proceedings of the National Academy of Sciences*. DOI: 10.1073/pnas.1320040111

Krashen, S. D. (1982). *Principles and practice in second language acquisition*. Pergamon Press.

Krowka, S. K., & Fuchs, L. S. (2017). Cognitive profiles associated with responsiveness to fraction intervention. *Learning Disabilities Research & Practice*, *32*(4), 216–230. DOI: 10.1111/ldrp.12146 PMID: 29123333

Kuhail, M. A., Mathew, S. S., Khalil, A., Khalil, A., & Shah, S. J. (2023). "Will I be replaced?" Assessing ChatGPT's effect on software development and programmer perceptions of AI tools. *arXiv.org*. Obtenido de DOI: 10.2139/ssrn.4571482

Kumar, A., & Kumar, A. (2025). Human emotion recognition using machine learning techniques based on the physiological signal. Biomedical Signal Processing and Control, 100(Part A), 107039. DOI: 10.1016/j.bspc.2024.107039

Kumar, J. A., Zhuang, M., & Thomas, S. (2024). ChatGPT for natural sciences course design: Insights from a strengths, weaknesses, opportunities, and threats analysis. *Natural Sciences Education*, *53*(2), e70003. DOI: 10.1002/nse2.70003

Kung, F. Y., Kwok, N., & Brown, D. J. (2018). Are attention check questions a threat to scale validity? *Applied Psychology*, *67*(2), 264–283. DOI: 10.1111/apps.12108

Kurt, G., & Kurt, Y. (2024). Enhancing L2 writing skills: ChatGPT as an automated feedback tool. *Journal of Information Technology Education*, *23*(24), 2–17. DOI: 10.28945/5370

Laal, M. (2013). Positive Interdependence in Collaborative Learning. *Procedia: Social and Behavioral Sciences*, *93*, 1433–1437. DOI: 10.1016/j.sbspro.2013.10.058

Labadze, L., Grigolia, M., & Machaidze, L. (2023). Role of AI chatbots in education: Systematic literature review. *International Journal of Educational Technology in Higher Education*, *20*(1), 1–25. DOI: 10.1186/s41239-023-00426-1

Lakkaraju, K., Rao, A., & Jha, M. (2024). Trust and ethical considerations in a multimodal, explainable AI-driven chatbot tutoring system. *arXiv Preprint*. https://arxiv.org/abs/2401.01234

Laksana, F. S., & Fiangga, S. (2022). The development of web-based chatbot as a mathematics learning media on system of linear equations in three variables. *Jurnal Mathedunesa*, *11*(1), 145–154. DOI: 10.26740/mathedunesa.v11n1.p145-154

Lampou, R. (2023). The integration of artificial intelligence in education: Opportunities and challenges. *Review of Artificial Intelligence in Education*, *4*(00), e015. DOI: 10.37497/rev.artif.intell.educ.v4i00.15

Landis, J. R., & Koch, G. G. (1977). The Measurement of Observer Agreement for Categorical Data. *Biometrics*, *33*(1), 159–174. DOI: 10.2307/2529310 PMID: 843571

Langelaan, B. N., Gaikhorst, L., Smets, W., & Oostdam, R. J. (2024). Differentiating instruction: Understanding the key elements for successful teacher preparation and development. *Teaching and Teacher Education*, *140*, 104464. DOI: 10.1016/j.tate.2023.104464

Lan, Y. (2024). Through tensions to identity-based motivations: Exploring teacher professional identity in Artificial Intelligence-enhanced teacher training. *Teaching and Teacher Education*, *151*, 1–15. DOI: 10.1016/j.tate.2024.104736

Laoha, R., Chomthong, W., & Pongpanich, W. (2025). Artificial intelligence and English as a foreign language (EFL) teachers' competency: A systematic review. *Higher Education Studies, 15*(3), 262. DOI: 10.5539/hes.v15n3p262

Latif, E., Chen, Y., Zhai, X., & Liu, V. (2023). AGI: Artificial general intelligence for education. *arXiv Preprint*. https://arxiv.org/

Laun, M., & Wolff, F. (2025). Chatbots in education: Hype or help? A meta-analysis. *Learning and Individual Differences, 119*, 102646. DOI: 10.1016/j.lindif.2025.102646

Lave, J., & Wenger, E. (1991). *Situated learning: Legitimate peripheral participation*. Cambridge university press. DOI: 10.1017/CBO9780511815355

Lawpanom, R., Songpan, W., & Kaewyotha, J. (2024). Advancing Facial Expression Recognition in Online Learning Education Using a Homogeneous Ensemble Convolutional Neural Network Approach. *Applied Sciences (Basel, Switzerland), 14*(3), 1156. DOI: 10.3390/app14031156

LeCun, Y., Bengio, Y., & Hinton, G. (2015). Deep learning. *Nature, 521*(7553), 436–444. DOI: 10.1038/nature14539 PMID: 26017442

Lee, D., & Yeo, S. (2022). Developing an AI-based chatbot for practicing responsive teaching in mathematics. *Computers & Education, 191*, 104646. Advance online publication. DOI: 10.1016/j.compedu.2022.104646

Lee, J.-E., & Recker, M. (2022). Predicting student performance by modeling participation in asynchronous discussions in university online introductory mathematical courses. *Educational Technology Research and Development, 70*(6), 1993–2015. DOI: 10.1007/s11423-022-10153-5

Lee, S. J., & Branch, R. M. (2022). Students' Reactions to a Student-Centered Learning Environment in Relation to Their Beliefs about Teaching and Learning. *International Journal on Teaching and Learning in Higher Education, 33*(3), 298–305.

Lee, S., Jeon, J., & Choe, H. (2025a). Enhancing pre-service teachers' global Englishes awareness with technology: A focus on AI chatbots in 3D metaverse environments. *TESOL Quarterly, 59*(1), 49–74. DOI: 10.1002/tesq.3300

Lee, S., Jeon, J., & Choe, H. (2025b). Generative AI (GenAI) and pre-service teacher agency in ELT. *ELT Journal, 79*(2), 287–296. DOI: 10.1093/elt/ccaf005

Lee, Y., Davis, R., & Lee, S. (2024). University students' perceptions of artificial intelligence-based tools for English writing courses. *Online Journal of Communication and Media Technologies, 14*(1), e202412. Advance online publication. DOI: 10.30935/ojcmt/14195

Leite, W. L., Xing, W., Fish, G., & Li, C. (2024). Teacher strategies to use virtual learning environments to facilitate algebra learning during school closures. *Journal of Research on Technology in Education, 56*(2), 95–109. DOI: 10.1080/15391523.2022.2110335

Leppink, J., Paas, F., van der Vleuten, P. M., van Gog, T., & Van Merriënboer, J. J. G. (2013). Development of an instrument for measuring different types of cognitive load. *Behavior Research Methods, 45*(4), 1058–1072. DOI: 10.3758/s13428-013-0334-1 PMID: 23572251

Létourneau, A., Deslandes Martineau, M., Charland, P., Karran, J. A., Boasen, J., & Léger, P. M. (2025). A systematic review of AI-driven intelligent tutoring systems (ITS) in K–12 education. *npj Science of Learning, 10*(1), 29. https://doi.org/DOI: 10.1038/s41539-025-00217-3

Levy, M. (1997). *CALL: Context and conceptualization*. Oxford University Press.

Liang, H., & Xue, Y. (2009). Avoidance of information technology threats: A theoretical perspective. *Management Information Systems Quarterly, 33*(1), 71–90. DOI: 10.2307/20650279

Liang, J., Hwang, G., Chen, M., & Darmawansah, D. (2023). Roles and research foci of artificial intelligence in language education: An integrated bibliographic analysis and systematic review approach. *Interactive Learning Environments, 31*(7), 4270–4296. DOI: 10.1080/10494820.2021.1958348

Liang, W., & Fung, D. (2021). Fostering critical thinking in English-as-a-second-language classrooms: Challenges and opportunities. *Thinking Skills and Creativity, 39*, 1–12. DOI: 10.1016/j.tsc.2020.100769

Lieberman, M. A., Wizlenberg, A., Golant, M., & Di Minno, M. (2005). The impact of group composition on Internet support groups: Homogeneous versus heterogeneous Parkinson's groups. *Group Dynamics, 9*(4), 239–250. DOI: 10.1037/1089-2699.9.4.239

Lightbown, P. M., & Spada, N. (2013). *How languages are learned* (4th ed.). Oxford University Press.

Lima, E. F., & Wallace, L. (2024, September 12). Technology innovation: Using ChatGPT to elevate pronunciation pedagogy [Conference teaching workshop]. PSLLT 2024 Conference, Ames, IA, United States. https://drive.google.com/file/d/1YS_SXSJuOMcUm_k4GZwXGsA9ozDLjYWt/edit

Li, N., Shen, Q., Song, R., Chi, Y., & Xu, H. (2022). MEduKG: A deep-learning-based approach for multi-modal educational knowledge graph construction. *Information (Basel), 13*(2), 91. DOI: 10.3390/info13020091

Lin, C. J., Lee, H. Y., Wang, W. S., Huang, Y. M., & Wu, T. T. (2025). Enhancing reflective thinking in STEM education through experiential learning: The role of generative AI as a learning aid. *Education and Information Technologies, 30*(5), 6315–6337. DOI: 10.1007/s10639-024-13072-5

Lin, F., & Chan, C. K. (2018). Examining the role of computer-supported knowledge-building discourse in epistemic and conceptual understanding. *Journal of Computer Assisted Learning, 34*(5), 567–579. DOI: 10.1111/jcal.12261

Lin, Y., Guo, J., Chen, Y., Yao, C., & Ying, F. (2020). It is your turn: Collaborative ideation with a co-creative robot through sketch. In *Proceedings of the 2020 CHI Conference on Human Factors in Computing Systems* (pp. 1-14). Association for Computing Machinery. DOI: 10.1145/3313831.3376258

Liu, V., Latif, E., & Zhai, X. (2025). Advancing education through tutoring systems: A systematic literature review. *arXiv Preprint*. https://arxiv.org/

Liu, W., Sidhu, A., Beacom, A. M., & Valente, T. W. (2017). Social network theory. *The international encyclopedia of media effects, 1*, 1-12.

Liu, G., & Ma, C. (2023). Measuring EFL learners' use of ChatGPT in informal digital learning of English based on the technology acceptance model. *Innovation in Language Learning and Teaching*, •••, 1–14. DOI: 10.1080/17501229.2023.2289377

Li, Y., & Goel, S. (2024). Making it possible for the auditing of AI: A systematic review of AI audits and AI auditability. *Information Systems Frontiers*. Advance online publication. DOI: 10.1007/s10796-024-10508-8

Li, Y., Raković, M., Srivastava, N., Li, X., Guan, Q., Gašević, D., & Chen, G. (2025). Can AI support human grading? Examining machine attention and confidence in short answer scoring. *Computers & Education, 228*, 105244. DOI: 10.1016/j.compedu.2025.105244

Looi, C. K., & Jia, F. (2025). Personalization capabilities of current technology chatbots in a learning environment: An analysis of student-tutor bot interactions. *Education and Information Technologies, 10639*(10), 13369. DOI: 10.1007/s10639-025-13369-z

Luckin, R. (2010). *Re-designing learning contexts: Technology-rich, learner-centered ecologies*. Routledge. DOI: 10.4324/9780203854754

Luebeck, J. L., & Bice, L. R. (2005). Online discussion as a mechanism of conceptual change among mathematics and science teachers. *International Journal of E-Learning & Distance Education/Revue internationale du e-learning et la formation à distance, 20*(2), 21–39.

Luo, L. J., Hu, J. M., Zheng, Y. J., & Li, C. (2025). Human vs. AI: Does AI learning assistant enhance students' innovative behavior? *Education and Information Technologies, 30*(12), 17483–17530. DOI: 10.1007/s10639-025-13474-z

Luo, X., Gao, L., Li, J., Lin, Y., Zhao, J., & Li, Q. (2020). A critical literature review of dyadic web-based interventions to support cancer patients and their caregivers, and directions for future research. *Psycho-Oncology, 29*(1), 38–48. DOI: 10.1002/pon.5278 PMID: 31702839

Lynn, M. R. (1986). Determination and quantification of content validity. *Nursing Research, 35*(6), 382–386. DOI: 10.1097/00006199-198611000-00017 PMID: 3640358

Lythreatis, S., Singh, S. K., & El-Kassar, A. N. (2022). The digital divide: A review and future research agenda. *Technological Forecasting and Social Change, 175*, 121359. DOI: 10.1016/j.techfore.2021.121359

Lyu, B., Grossnickle Peterson, E., & List, A. (2023). Using PowerPoints to assess students' learning from multiple resources. *Contemporary Educational Psychology, 74*, 102204. DOI: 10.1016/j.cedpsych.2023.102204

Lyu, B., Lai, C., & Guo, J. (2024). Effectiveness of chatbots in improving language learning: A meta-analysis of comparative studies. *International Journal of Applied Linguistics, 35*(2), 834–851. DOI: 10.1111/ijal.12668

Lyu, B., Li, C., Li, H., & Xing, W. (2026). Exploring students' participation in online mathematical discussions using educational big data: A communicative ecology perspective. *Journal of Educational Technology & Society, 29*(2), 171–190.

Lyu, B., Li, C., Li, H., Zhu, W., & Xing, W. (2024). Explaining technical, social, and discursive participation in online mathematical discussions. *Distance Education*, •••, 1–24.

Lyu, W., Zhang, S., Chung, T., Sun, Y., & Zhang, Y. (2025). Understanding the practices, perceptions, and (dis)trust of generative AI among instructors: A mixed-methods study in the U.S. higher education. *Computers and Education: Artificial Intelligence, 8*, 100383. DOI: 10.1016/j.caeai.2025.100383

MacNeil, S., Tran, A., Hellas, A., Kim, J., Sarsa, S., Denny, P., & Leinonen, J. (2023). Experiences from using code explanations generated by large language models in a web software development e-book. *SIGCSE 2023: Proceedings of the 54th ACM Technical Symposium on Computer Science Education* V. 1, 931-937. https://doi.org/DOI: 10.1145/3545945.3569785

Maduretno, T. W. (2021). Online Learning Solution: Ice Breaking Application to Increase Student Motivation. [EST]. *Journal of Educational Science and Technology, 07*(01), 117–125.

Mah, D. K., & Groß, N. (2024). Artificial intelligence in higher education: Exploring faculty use, self-efficacy, distinct profiles, and professional development needs. *International Journal of Educational Technology in Higher Education, 21*(1), 1–17. DOI: 10.1186/s41239-024-00490-1

Mahmoud, C., & Sørensen, J. (2024). Artificial intelligence in personalized learning with a focus on current developments and future prospects. *Research and Advances in Education, 3*(8), 25–31. DOI: 10.56397/RAE.2024.08.04

Makransky, G., & Petersen, G. B. (2021). The cognitive affective model of immersive learning (CAMIL): A theoretical research-based model of learning in immersive virtual reality. *Educational Psychology Review, 33*(3), 937–958. DOI: 10.1007/s10648-020-09586-2

Mandl, T., Jaki, S., Mitera, H., & Schmidt, F. (2023). Interdisciplinary analysis of science communication on social media during the Covid-19 crisis. *Knowledge (Beverly Hills, Calif.), 3*(1), 97–112. DOI: 10.3390/knowledge3010008

Mansour, N., Aras, C., & Staarman, J. K.. (2024). Embodied learning of science concepts through augmented reality technology. *Educational Technology & Information, 10639*, 13120. DOI: 10.1007/s10639-024-13120-0

Markauskaite, L., Marrone, R., Poquet, O., Knight, S., Martinez-Maldonado, R., Howard, S., Tondeur, J., De Laat, M., Buckingham Shum, S., Gašević, D., & Siemens, G. (2022). Rethinking the entwinement between artificial intelligence and human learning: What capabilities do learners need for a world with AI? *Computers and Education: Artificial Intelligence, 3*, 100056. DOI: 10.1016/j.caeai.2022.100056

Martin, G. (2009). *Focus in high school mathematics: Reasoning and sense making*. NCTM.

Mayer, R. (2001). *Multimedia learning*. Cambridge Press. DOI: 10.1017/CBO9781139164603

Mayer, R. E. (1996). Learning strategies for making sense out of expository text: The SOI model for guiding three cognitive processes in knowledge construction. *Educational Psychology Review*, *8*(4), 357–371. DOI: 10.1007/BF01463939

Mayer, R. E., & Anderson, R. (1991). Animations and narrations: An experimental test of a dual-coding hypothesis. *Journal of Educational Psychology*, *83*(4), 484–490. DOI: 10.1037/0022-0663.83.4.484

McCrudden, M. T., Huynh, L., Lyu, B., & Kulikowich, J. M. (2021). Bridging inferences and learning from multiple complementary texts. *Discourse Processes*, *58*(5–6), 529–548. DOI: 10.1080/0163853X.2021.1924586

McGrath, C., Pargman, T. C., Juth, N., & Palmgren, P. J. (2023). University teachers' perceptions of responsibility and artificial intelligence in higher education-An experimental philosophical study. *Computers and Education: Artificial Intelligence*, *4*, 1–9. DOI: 10.1016/j.caeai.2023.100139

Mebert, L., Barnes, R., Dalley, J., Gawarecki, L., Ghazi-Nezami, F., Shafer, G., Slater, J., & Yezbick, E. (2020). Fostering student engagement through a real-world, collaborative project across disciplines and institutions. *Higher Education Pedagogies*, *5*(1), 30–51. DOI: 10.1080/23752696.2020.1750306

Mehmood, T. (2025). Ethical AI in education: Addressing bias, privacy, and equity in AI-driven learning systems. *Journal of AI Integration in Education*. https://www.researchcorridor.org/

Memarian, B., & Doleck, T. (2024). A review of assessment for learning with artificial intelligence. *Computers in Human Behavior: Artificial Humans*, *2*(1), 100040. DOI: 10.1016/j.chbah.2023.100040

Memarian, B., & Doleck, T. (2024). Embodied AI in education: A review on the body, environment, and mind. *Education and Information Technologies*, *29*(1), 895–916. DOI: 10.1007/s10639-023-12346-8

Mentor, D. (2015). *Mobile Phone Use Enhances Social Connectedness*. IGI Publishing., DOI: 10.4018/978-1-4666-8239-9.ch056

Metwally, A. H. S., Huang, R., Palomino, P. T., & Yousef, A. M. F. (2024). The effect of micro gamified online homework on gameful experience, intrinsic motivation, engagement, and cognitive load. *Education and Information Technologies*, *29*(18), 24489–24523. DOI: 10.1007/s10639-024-12750-8

Meyers, M. (1993). *Teaching to diversity: Teaching and learning in the multi-ethnic classroom*. Addison-Wesley Publishing Company.

Micallef, A., & Newton, P. M. (2024). The use of concrete examples enhances the learning of abstract concepts: A replication study. *Teaching of Psychology*, *51*(1), 22–29. DOI: 10.1177/00986283211058069

Miles, M. B., & Huberman, A. M. (1994). Qualitative data analysis: An expanded sourcebook. *Sage (Atlanta, Ga.)*.

Min, A. (2023). Artificial intelligence and bias: Challenges, implications, and remedies. *Journal of Social Research*, *2*(11), 3808–3817. DOI: 10.55324/josr.v2i11.1477

Minnillo, S., Jones, L., & García, S. (2024). AI in the L2 classroom: Serving language educators through professional development. *Journal of Linguistics and Language Teaching*, *16*(1), 1–14. DOI: 10.5070/L2.21198

Mitchell, M. (2019). *Artificial intelligence: A guide for thinking humans.*

Mohammadi, M. (2024). Language teachers' assessment literacy in AI-aided adaptive learning environments. *Journal of Research in Applied Linguistics*, *15*(2), 73–88. DOI: 10.22055/rals.2024.46120.3235

Mohebbi, A. (2024). Enabling learner independence and self-regulation in language education using AI tools: A systematic review. *Cogent Education*, *12*(1), 2433814. DOI: 10.1080/2331186X.2024.2433814

Moirano, R., Sánchez, M. A., & Štěpánek, L. (2023). Creative interdisciplinary collaboration: A systematic literature review. *Thinking Skills and Creativity*, *35*, 100626. Advance online publication. DOI: 10.1016/j.tsc.2019.100626

Montague, M., Krawec, J., Enders, C., & Dietz, S. (2014). The effects cognitive strategy instruction on math problem solving of middle-school students of varying ability. *Journal of Educational Psychology*, *106*(2), 469–481. DOI: 10.1037/a0035176

Moorhouse, B. L., Ho, T. Y., Wu, C., & Wan, Y. (2025). Pre-service language teachers' task-specific Large Language Model prompting practices. *RELC Journal*, 1–22. DOI: 10.1177/00336882251313701

Moorhouse, B. L., & Kohnke, L. (2024). The effects of generative AI on initial language teacher education: The perceptions of teacher educators. *System*, *122*, 1–10. DOI: 10.1016/j.system.2024.103290

Moorhouse, B. L., Wan, Y., Wu, C., Kohnke, L., Ho, T. Y., & Kwong, T. (2024). Developing language teachers' professional generative AI competence: An intervention study in an initial language teacher education course. *System*, *125*, 1–13. DOI: 10.1016/j.system.2024.103399

Morales, C. (2006). *Cross-cultural validation of the will, skill, tool model of technology integration* [Doctoral dissertation, University of North Texas]. UNT Digital Library. https://digital.library.unt.edu/ark:/67531/metadc5256

Morales, C., Knezek, G., Christensen, R., & Avila, P. (Eds.). (2005). *The will, skill, tool model of technology integration: A conceptual approach to teaching and learning with technology*. ICLE.

MorphCast. (2023). *How our Emotion AI works*. Retrieved from https://www.morphcast.com/responsibility-transparency-clarity/

MorphCast. (2024a). *A guide to interpret data generated by Emotion AI*. Retrieved from https://www.morphcast.com/how-to-interpret-the-emotion-ai-output-data/

MorphCast. (2024b). *Beyond the Algorithm: Building Trustworthy Emotion AI at MorphCast*. https://www.morphcast.com/responsibility-transparency-clarity/

Moussalli, S., & Cardoso, W. (2020). Intelligent personal assistants: Can they understand and be understood by accented L2 learners? *Computer Assisted Language Learning*, *33*(8), 865–890. DOI: 10.1080/09588221.2019.1595664

Mouta, A., Torrecilla-Sánchez, E. M., & Pinto-Llorente, A. M. (2025). Comprehensive professional learning for teacher agency in addressing ethical challenges of AIED: Insights from educational design research. *Education and Information Technologies*, *30*(3), 3343–3387. DOI: 10.1007/s10639-024-12946-y

Moya, S., & Camacho, M. (2024). Leveraging AI-powered mobile learning: A pedagogically informed framework. *Computers and Education: Artificial Intelligence*, *7*, 100276. DOI: 10.1016/j.caeai.2024.100276

Mujiono, M. (2023). Educational collaboration: Teachers and artificial intelligence. *Jurnal Kependidikan: Jurnal Hasil Penelitian Dan Kajian Kepustakaan Di Bidang Pendidikan. Pengajaran Dan Pembelajaran*, *9*(2), 618–632. DOI: 10.33394/jk.v9i2.7801

Mustafa, F., Nguyen, H. T. M., & Gao, X. A. (2024). The challenges and solutions of technology integration in rural schools: A systematic literature review. *International Journal of Educational Research*, *126*, 102380. DOI: 10.1016/j.ijer.2024.102380

Naseer, F., Khan, M. N., Tahir, M., Addas, A., & Aejaz, S. M. H. (2024). Integrating deep learning techniques for personalized learning pathways in higher education. *Heliyon*, *10*(11), e32628. DOI: 10.1016/j.heliyon.2024.e32628

Nation, A. (2019, August). Glossary of terms: Algebra 1 (English version) [PDF]. Retrieved from https://youllneverwalkalonebms.wordpress.com/wp-content/uploads/2019/08/algebra-nation-glossary-of-terms-algebra-1-english-version.pdf

National Center for Education Statistics. (2022). [NAEP mathematics report card: National achievement-level results]. The Nation's Report Card. Retrieved from https://www.nationsreportcard.gov/mathematics/nation/achievement/?grade=8

National Center for Education Statistics. (2022). [NAEP writing report card: National achievement-level results]. The Nation's Report Card._https://nces.ed.gov/nationsreportcard/pubs/main2007/2008468.aspx

National Council of Teachers of Mathematics. (2000). *Principles and standards for school mathematics*. NCTM.

Nazaretsky, T., Bar, C., Walter, M., & Alexandron, G. (2022, March). Empowering teachers with AI: Co-designing a learning analytics tool for personalized instruction in the science classroom. *In Proceedings of the 12th international learning analytics and knowledge conference* (pp. 1–12). Association for Computing Machinery. DOI: 10.1145/3506860.3506861

Nelson, M. M., & Schunn, C. D. (2009). The nature of feedback: How different types of peer feedback affect writing performance. *Instructional Science*, *37*(4), 375–401. DOI: 10.1007/s11251-008-9053-x

Nesbit, J. C., & Adesope, O. O. (2006). Learning with concept and knowledge maps: A meta-analysis. *Review of Educational Research*, *76*(3), 413–448. DOI: 10.3102/00346543076003413

Netemeyer, R. G., Bearden, W. O., & Sharma, S. (2003). *Scaling procedures: Issues and applications*. Sage Publications. DOI: 10.4135/9781412985772

Neumann, M., Rauschenberger, M., & Schön, E. (2023). "We need to talk about ChatGPT": The future of AI and higher education. In *2023 IEEE/ACM 5th International Workshop on Software Engineering Education for the Next Generation (SEENG)* (pp. 10–17). IEEE. https://doi.org/DOI: 10.1109/SEENG59157.2023.00010

Neumann, M., & Linzmayer, R. (2021). Capturing student feedback and emotions in large computing courses: A sentiment analysis approach. *In Proceedings of the 52nd ACM Technical Symposium on Computer Science Education* (pp. 541-547). DOI: 10.1145/3408877.3432403

Newman, I., Lim, J., & Pineda, F. (2013). Content validity using a mixed methods approach. *Journal of Mixed Methods Research*, *7*(3), 243–260. DOI: 10.1177/1558689813476922

Ng, D. T. K., Chen, X., Leung, J. K. L., & Chu, S. K. W. (2024). Fostering students' AI literacy development through educational games: AI knowledge, affective and cognitive engagement. *Journal of Computer Assisted Learning*, *40*(5), 2049–2064. DOI: 10.1111/jcal.13009

Ng, D. T., Leung, J. K., Chu, S. K., & Qiao, M. S. (2021). Conceptualizing AI literacy: An exploratory review. *Computers and Education: Artificial Intelligence*, *2*, 100041. DOI: 10.1016/j.caeai.2021.100041

Nguyen, H. D., Pham, V. T., Tran, D. A., & Le, T. T. (2019). Intelligent tutoring chatbot for solving mathematical problems in high-school. *2019 11th International Conference on Knowledge and Systems Engineering (KSE),* Da Nang, Vietnam, 2019. Pp. 1-6, DOI: 10.1109/KSE.2019.8919396

Nguyen, T. (2023). EFL teachers' perspectives toward the use of ChatGPT in writing classes: A case study at Van Lang University. *International Journal of Language Instruction*, *2*(3), 1–47. DOI: 10.54855/ijli.23231

Novak, J. D., & Cañas, A. J. (2006). The theory underlying concept maps and how to construct them. *Florida Institute for Human and Machine Cognition, 1*(1), 1–31.

Novawan, A., Walker, S. A., & Ikeda, O. (2024). The new face of technology-enhanced language learning (TELL) with artificial intelligence (AI): Teacher perspectives, practices, and challenges. *Journal of English in Academic and Professional Communication*, *10*(1), 1–18. DOI: 10.25047/jeapco.v9i1.3754

Nwohiri, A., Joda, O., & Ajayi, O. (2021). AI-powered plagiarism detection: Leveraging forensic linguistics and natural language processing. *FUDMA Journal of Sciences*, *5*(3), 207–218. DOI: 10.33003/fjs-2021-0503-700

O'Neill, G., & Padden, L. (2021). Diversifying assessment methods: Barriers, benefits and enablers. *Innovations in Education and Teaching International*, *59*(4), 398–409. DOI: 10.1080/14703297.2021.1880462

Onyebuchi, N., Onyebuchi, N., Unachukwu, C. C., & Osawaru, B. (2024). Review of AI in education: Transforming learning environments in Africa. *International Journal of Applied Research in Social Sciences*, *5*(10), 637–654. DOI: 10.51594/ijarss.v5i10.725

Open A.I. (2022). *What is ChatGPT? Commonly asked questions about ChatGPT.* https://help.openai.com/en/articles/6783457-what-is-chatgpt

Orchard, C. A., Curran, V., & Kabene, S. (2005). Creating a culture for interdisciplinary collaborative professional practice. *Medical Education Online*, *10*(1), 1–13. DOI: 10.3402/meo.v10i.4387 PMID: 28253153

Ouyang, F., & Scharber, C. (2017). The influences of an experienced instructor's discussion design and facilitation on an online learning community development: A social network analysis study. *The Internet and Higher Education*, *35*, 34–47. DOI: 10.1016/j.iheduc.2017.07.002

Ozturk, H. (2011). Conflict in Virtual Learning Communities in the Context of a Democratic Pedagogy. *Unpublished PhD Thesis*. Lancaster University, UK.

Ozturk, H. T., Deryakulu, D., Ozcinar, H., & Atal, D. (2014). Advancing Learning Analytics in Online Learning Environments through the Method of Sequential Analysis. *The 4th International Conference on Multimedia Computing and Systems (ICMCS'14)*. April 14-16 2014, Marrakesh, Morocco.

Page, M. J., McKenzie, J. E., Bossuyt, P. M., Boutron, I., Hoffmann, T. C., Mulrow, C. D., Shamseer, L., Tetzlaff, J. M., Akl, E. A., Brennan, S. E., Chou, R., Glanville, J., Grimshaw, J. M., Hróbjartsson, A., Lalu, M. M., Li, T., Loder, E. W., Mayo-Wilson, E., McDonald, S., & Moher, D. (2021). The PRISMA 2020 statement: An updated guideline for reporting systematic reviews. *BMJ (Clinical Research Ed.)*, *372*(71), n71. Advance online publication. DOI: 10.1136/bmj.n71 PMID: 33782057

Palan, S., & Schitter, C. (2018). Prolific. ac—A subject pool for online experiments. *Journal of Behavioral and Experimental Finance*, *17*, 22–27. DOI: 10.1016/j.jbef.2017.12.004

Panagopoulou, F., Parpoula, C., & Karpouzis, K. (2023). Legal and ethical considerations regarding the use of ChatGPT in education. *arXiv Preprint*. https://arxiv.org/abs/2302.01987 DOI: 10.31235/osf.io/c5hf3

Pane, J. F., Steiner, E. D., Baird, M. D., & Hamilton, L. S. (2017). *Informing progress: Insights on personalized learning implementation and effects*. RAND Corporation.

Pan, S., Luo, L., Wang, Y., Chen, C., Wang, J., & Wu, X. (2024). Unifying large language models and knowledge graphs: A roadmap. *IEEE Transactions on Knowledge and Data Engineering*, *36*(7), 3580–3599. DOI: 10.1109/TKDE.2024.3352100

Papamitsiou, Z., & Economides, A. A. (2021). Deep learning analytics for adaptive systems. In *Proceedings of the 21st IEEE ICALT Conference*.

Papamitsiou, Z., Economides, A. A., & Muñoz Merino, P. J. (2021). Learning analytics and adaptive learning technologies: A systematic review. *Computers & Education: Artificial Intelligence*, *2*, 100033. DOI: 10.1016/j.caeai.2021.100033

Park, K., Mott, B., Lee, S., Gupta, A., Jantaraweragul, K., Glazewski, K., Scribner, J. A., Ottenbreit-Leftwich, A., Hmelo-Silver, C. E., & Lester, J. (2022). Investigating a visual interface for elementary students to formulate AI planning tasks. *Journal of Computer Languages*, *73*, 101157. DOI: 10.1016/j.cola.2022.101157

Patel, A., Addicott, C., & Buelow, J. (2023). Instructors' emotional intelligence and learning engagement of online students. *European Journal of Open. Distance and E-Learning*, *25*(1), 129–135. DOI: 10.2478/eurodl-2023-0010

Pazzanese (2020, October 26). Great promise but potential for peril. Harvard Gazette. https://news.harvard.edu/gazette/story/2020/10/ethical-concerns-mount-as-ai-takes-bigger-decision-making-role/

Pedro, F., Subosa, M., Rivas, A., & Valverde, P. (2019). *Artificial intelligence in education: Challenges and opportunities for sustainable development*. UNESCO.

Peer, E., Rothschild, D., Gordon, A., Evernden, Z., & Damer, E. (2022). Data quality of platforms and panels for online behavioral research. *Behavior Research Methods*, *54*(4), 1643–1662. DOI: 10.3758/s13428-021-01694-3 PMID: 34590289

Peoples, K. (2021). *How to write a phenomenological dissertation: A step-by-step guide* (Vol. 56). SAGE.

Perkins, M. (2023). Academic integrity considerations of AI Large Language Models in the post-pandemic era: ChatGPT and beyond. *Journal of University Teaching & Learning Practice*, *20*(2). Advance online publication. DOI: 10.53761/1.20.02.07

Persulessy, S., Nikijuluw, R., & Jakob, J. C. (2024). Utilizing artificial intelligence in language learning: What about engineering students' perception? *Journal of English Education Program*, *5*(1), 48–58. DOI: 10.26418/jeep.v5i1.71159

Petko, D. (2012). Teachers' pedagogical beliefs and their use of digital media in classrooms: Sharpening the focus of the "will, skill, tool" model and integrating teachers' constructivist orientations. *Computers & Education*, *58*(4), 1351–1359. DOI: 10.1016/j.compedu.2011.12.013

Pham, S. T., & Sampson, P. M. (2022). The development of artificial intelligence in education: A review in context. *Journal of Computer Assisted Learning*, *38*(5), 1408–1421. DOI: 10.1111/jcal.12687

Phan, T. (2023). Students' perceptions of the AI technology application in English writing classes. *Proceedings of the AsiaCALL International Conference, 4*, 45–62. DOI: 10.54855/paic.2344

Piaget, J. (1952). *The origins of intelligence in children*. International University. DOI: 10.1037/11494-000

Pitura, J., Kaplan-Rakowski, R., & Asotska-Wierzba, Y. (2025). The VR-AI–Assisted simulation for content knowledge application in pre-service EFL teacher training. *TechTrends*, *69*(1), 100–110. DOI: 10.1007/s11528-024-01022-4

Polo, C., Lund, K., Plantin, C., & Niccolai, G. P. (2016). Group emotions: The social and cognitive functions of emotions in argumentation. *International Journal of Computer-Supported Collaborative Learning*, *11*(2), 123–156. DOI: 10.1007/s11412-016-9232-8

Pongsakdi, N., Kajamies, A., Veermans, K., Lertola, K., Vauras, M., & Lehtinen, E. (2020). What makes mathematical word problem solving challenging? Exploring the roles of word problem characteristics, text comprehension, and arithmetic skills. *ZDM Mathematics Education*, *52*(1), 33–44. DOI: 10.1007/s11858-019-01118-9

Ponton, M., & Rhea, N. (2006). Autonomous Learning from a Social Cognitive Perspective. *New Horizons in Adult Education and Human Resource Development*, *20*(2), 38–49. DOI: 10.1002/nha3.10250

Poquet, O., Dawson, S., & Dowell, N. (2017). *How effective is your facilitation? Group-level analytics of MOOC forums*. 208–217.

Poquet, O., Dawson, S., & Dowell, N. (2017). How effective is your facilitation? Group-level analytics of MOOC forums. In *Proceedings of the Seventh International Learning Analytics & Knowledge Conference* (pp. 208–217). DOI: 10.1145/3027385.3027404

Powell, S.R., Hebert, M.A., Cohen, J.A., Casa, T.M., & Firmender, J.M. (2017). A synthesis of mathematics writing: Assessments, interventions, and surveys. *Journal of Writing Research, 8*(3), 493-526. doi:: DOI: 10.17239/jowr-2017.08.03.04

Powell, S. R., Berry, K. A., & Benz, S. A. (2020). Analyzing the word-problem performance and strategies of students. *The Journal of Mathematical Behavior*, *58*, 100759. DOI: 10.1016/j.jmathb.2020.100759

Prentice, R. (2025, April 22). Ai and the energy issue. *Ethics Unwrapped*. https://ethicsunwrapped.utexas.edu/ai-and-the-energy-issue

Prilop, C. N., Mah, D. K., Jacobsen, L. J., Hansen, R. R., & Elena, K. (2025). Generative AI in teacher education: Using AI-enhanced methods to explore teacher educators' perceptions. *Institute for Vocational Training and Lifelong Learning, 3*, 5390-6092. https://doi.org/DOI: 10.31219/osf.io/szcwb

Rahiman, H. U., & Kodikal, R. (2023). Revolutionizing education: Artificial intelligence empowered learning in higher education. *Cogent Education*, *11*(1), 2293431. DOI: 10.1080/2331186X.2023.2293431

Rahimi, A. R., & Sevilla-Pavón, A. (2025). The role of design thinking skills in artificial-intelligence language learning (DEAILL) in shaping language learners' L2 grit: The mediator and moderator role of artificial intelligence L2 motivational self-system. *Computer Assisted Language Learning*, 1–49. DOI: 10.1080/09588221.2025.2477710

Rajkumar, R. P. (2023). Cultural values and changes in happiness in 78 countries during the COVID-19 pandemic: An analysis of data from the World Happiness Reports. *Frontiers in Psychology*, *14*, 1090340. Advance online publication. DOI: 10.3389/fpsyg.2023.1090340 PMID: 36818129

Ramsey, J. L., & West, R. E. (2023). A recent history of learning design and technology. *TechTrends*, *67*(5), 781–791. DOI: 10.1007/s11528-023-00883-5

Rashid, A. B., & Kausik, M. A. K. (2024). AI revolutionizing industries worldwide: A comprehensive overview of its diverse applications. *Hybrid Advances*, *7*, 100277. DOI: 10.1016/j.hybadv.2024.100277

Reif, F., & Heller, J. I. (1982). Knowledge structure and problem solving in physics. *Educational Psychologist*, *17*(2), 102–127. DOI: 10.1080/00461528209529248

Reiser, R. (1994). Clark's invitation to the dance: An instructional designer's response. *Educational Technology Research and Development*, *42*(2), 45–48. DOI: 10.1007/BF02299091

Riazi, M., Rezvani, R., & Ghanbar, H. (2023). Trustworthiness in L2 writing research: A review and analysis of qualitative articles in the Journal of Second Language Writing. *Research Methods in Applied Linguistics*, *2*(3), 100065. Advance online publication. DOI: 10.1016/j.rmal.2023.100065

Riccomini, P. J., Hughes, E. E., Deshpande, D., Lee, J., Fiveash, L., & Lin, T. (2024). Teaching fifth-grade students with specific learning disabilities to explain their mathematical reasoning through written expression. *Learning Disability Quarterly*, *47*(2), 124–136. DOI: 10.1177/07319487241235148

Rinta-Kahila, T., Penttinen, E., Salovaara, A., Soliman, W., & Ruissalo, J. (2023). The vicious circles of skill erosion: A case study of cognitive automation. *Journal of the Association for Information Systems*, *24*(5), 1378–1412. DOI: 10.17705/1jais.00829

Rizvi, M. (2023). Investigating AI-powered tutoring systems that adapt to individual student needs, providing personalized guidance and assessments. *The Eurasia Proceedings of Educational and Social Sciences, 31*, 67–73. DOI: 10.55549/epess.1381518

Rodríguez-Ortiz, M. Á., Santana-Mancilla, P. C., & Anido-Rifón, L. E. (2025). Machine Learning and Generative AI in Learning Analytics for Higher Education: A Systematic Review of Models, Trends, and Challenges. *Applied Sciences (Basel, Switzerland), 15*(15), 8679. DOI: 10.3390/app15158679

Roll, I., & Wylie, R. (2016). Evolution and revolution in artificial intelligence in education. *International Journal of Artificial Intelligence in Education, 26*(2), 582–599. DOI: 10.1007/s40593-016-0110-3

Rombach, P., Porter, M. A., Fowler, J. H., & Mucha, P. J. (2017). Core-periphery structure in networks (revisited). *SIAM Review, 59*(3), 619–646. DOI: 10.1137/17M1130046

Romero, M., Buzón-García, O., & Touron, J. (2019). The flipped learning model in online based education for secondary teachers. *Journal of Technology and Science Education, 9*(2), 109. DOI: 10.3926/jotse.435

Rukiati, E., Wicaksono, J., Taufan, G., & Suharsono, D. (2023). AI on learning English: Application, benefit, and threat. *Journal of Language, Communication, and Tourism, 1*(2), 32–40. DOI: 10.25047/jlct.v1i2.3967

Rumelhart, D. E., Smolensky, P., McClelland, J. L., & Hinton, G. (1986). Sequential thought processes in PDP models. *Parallel Distributed Processing: Explorations in the Microstructures of Cognition, 2*, 3–57.

Rumsey, C. (2024). *Why it's important to learn English.* Studio Cambridge. https://www.studiocambridge.co.uk/why-it-is-important-to-learn-english/

Ryan, R. M., & Deci, E. L. (2000). Self-determination theory and the facilitation of intrinsic motivation, social development, and well-being. *The American Psychologist, 55*(1), 68–78. DOI: 10.1037/0003-066X.55.1.68 PMID: 11392867

Safadi, H., Johnson, S. L., & Faraj, S. (2021). Who contributes knowledge? Core-periphery tension in online innovation communities. *Organization Science, 32*(3), 752–775. DOI: 10.1287/orsc.2020.1364

Sajja, R., Sermet, Y., Cikmaz, M., & Arslan, A. (2023). Artificial intelligence–enabled intelligent assistant for personalized and adaptive learning in higher education. *arXiv Preprint.* https://arxiv.org/

Saleem, F., Ullah, Z., Fakieh, B., & Kateb, F. (2021). Intelligent decision support system for predicting student's e-learning performance using ensemble machine learning. *Mathematics*, *9*(17), 2078. DOI: 10.3390/math9172078

Salmela, M., & Mäki, U. (2018). Disciplinary emotions in imperialistic interdisciplinarity. In Mäki, Uskali; Fernández Pinto, Manuela & Walsh, Adrian (Eds.) (2018). *Scientific Imperialism: Exploring the Boundaries of Interdisciplinarity* (pp. 31-50). Routledge, Abingdon.

Sandberg, J., Maris, M., & Hoogendoorn, P. (2014). The added value of a gaming context and intelligent adaptation for a mobile learning application for vocabulary learning. *Computers & Education*, *76*, 119–130. DOI: 10.1016/j.compedu.2014.03.006

Sarker, I. (2022). AI-based modeling: Techniques, applications and research issues towards automation, intelligent and smart systems. *SN Computer Science*, *3*(2), 1–20. DOI: 10.1007/s42979-022-01043-x PMID: 35194580

Sarker, I. H. (2021). Machine learning: Algorithms, real-world applications and research directions. *SN Computer Science*, *2*(3), 160. DOI: 10.1007/s42979-021-00592-x PMID: 33778771

Sarstedt, M., & Mooi, E. (2019). *Regression Analysis*. Springer., DOI: 10.1007/978-3-662-56707-4_7

Sasikala, P., & Ravichandran, R. (2024). Study on the impact of artificial intelligence on student learning outcomes. *Journal of Digital Learning and Education*, *4*(2), 145–155. DOI: 10.52562/jdle.v4i2.1234

Sasota, R. S., Cristobal, R. R., Sario, I. S., Biyo, J. T., & Magadia, J. C. (2021). Will–skill–tool (WST) model of technology integration in teaching science and mathematics in the Philippines. *Journal of Computers in Education*, *8*(3), 443–464. DOI: 10.1007/s40692-021-00185-w

Savran Çelik, Ş., & Aydın, S. (2018). A review of research on the use of native language in EFL classes. *The Literacy Trek*, *4*(2), 1–14.

Sayici, S., & Aydın, S. (2025). Using artificial intelligence in foreign language teaching: Teachers' perspectives. *Proceedings of The World Conference on Education and Teaching, 4*(1), 1–10. DOI: 10.33422/etconf.v4i1.1016

Schacter, D., Gilbert, D., & Wegner, D. (2009). *Introducing psychology*. Macmillan.

Schleppegrell, M. J. (2007). The linguistics challenges of mathematics teaching and learning: A research review. *Reading & Writing Quarterly*, *23*(2), 139–159. DOI: 10.1080/10573560601158461

Schmidt, T., & Strasser, T. (2022). Artificial intelligence in foreign language learning and teaching: A call for intelligent practice. *Anglistik: International Journal of English Studies*, *33*(1), 165–184. DOI: 10.33675/ANGL/2022/1/14

Schreiber, J. B. (2008). Core reporting practices in structural equation modeling. *Research in Social & Administrative Pharmacy*, *4*(2), 83–97. DOI: 10.1016/j.sapharm.2007.04.003 PMID: 18555963

Scully, D., Lehane, P., & Scully, C. (2021). "It is no longer scary": Digital learning before and during the COVID-19 pandemic in Irish secondary schools. *Technology, Pedagogy and Education*, *30*(1), 159–181. DOI: 10.1080/1475939X.2020.1854844

Self, J. (1999). The defining characteristics of intelligent tutoring systems research: ITSs care, precisely. *International Journal of Artificial Intelligence in Education*, *10*, 350–364.

Seliger, H. W., & Shohamy, E. (1989). *Second language research methods*. Oxford University Press.

Seo, E., Shen, Y., & Alfaro, E. C. (2018). Adolescents' beliefs about math ability and their relations to STEM career attainment: Joint consideration of race/ethnicity and gender. *Journal of Youth and Adolescence*, *48*(2), 306–325. DOI: 10.1007/s10964-018-0911-9 PMID: 30141096

Sezer, B., & Yilmaz, R. (2019). Learning management system acceptance scale (LMSAS): A validity and reliability study. *Australasian Journal of Educational Technology*, *35*(3), 15–30. DOI: 10.14742/ajet.3959

Shabalala, N. P. (2024). Elevating STEM learning: Unleashing the power of ai in open distance eLearning. *Research om Social Sciences and Technology*, *9*(3), 269–288. DOI: 10.46303/ressat.2024.59

Shadiev, R., Wu, T., Sun, A., & Huang, Y. (2018). Applications of speech-to-text recognition and computer-aided translation for facilitating cross-cultural learning through a learning activity: Issues and their solutions. *Educational Technology Research and Development*, *66*(1), 191–214. DOI: 10.1007/s11423-017-9556-8

Shadiev, R., & Yang, M. (2020). Review of studies on technology-enhanced language learning and teaching. *Sustainability (Basel)*, *12*(2), 524. DOI: 10.3390/su12020524

Shang, H. F. (2022). Exploring online peer feedback and automated corrective feedback on efl writing performance. *Interactive Learning Environments*, *30*(1), 4–16. DOI: 10.1080/10494820.2019.1629601

Shi, H., & Aryadoust, V. (2024). A systematic review of AI-based automated written feedback research. *ReCALL, 36*(2), 187–209. DOI: 10.1017/S0958344023000265

Shi, L. (2025). Assessing teachers' generative artificial intelligence competencies: Instrument development and validation. *Education and Information Technologies, 30*(16), 23365–23384. Advance online publication. DOI: 10.1007/s10639-025-13684-5

Shirah, J. F., & Sidney, P. G. (2023). Computer-based feedback matters when relevant prior knowledge is not activated. *Learning and Instruction, 87*, 101796. DOI: 10.1016/j.learninstruc.2023.101796

Shoaib, M., Sayed, N., Singh, J., Shafi, J., Khan, S., & Ali, F. (2024). AI student success predictor: Enhancing personalized learning in campus management systems. *Computers in Human Behavior, 158*, 108301. DOI: 10.1016/j.chb.2024.108301

Shoufan, A. (2023). Exploring students' perceptions of ChatGPT: Thematic analysis and follow-up survey. *IEEE Access : Practical Innovations, Open Solutions, 11*, 38805–38818. DOI: 10.1109/ACCESS.2023.3268224

Shute, V. J., & Zapata-Rivera, D. (2010). Intelligent systems. In E. Baker, P. Peterson, & B. McGaw (Eds.), Third edition of the Formative and Stealth Assessment international encyclopedia of education (pp. 75–80). Elsevier. DOI: 10.1016/B978-0-08-044894-7.00247-5

Siemens, G. (2006). *Knowing knowledge.* Lulu. com.

Siqin, T., & Chu, S. K. W. (2021). How students take collective responsibility for productive collaboration: An empirical examination of online discourse. *Interactive Learning Environments, 29*(7), 1076–1089. DOI: 10.1080/10494820.2019.1636081

Siricharoen, W. V. (2023). AR and VR enhances learning. In C. Anutariya, D. Liu, K. Kinshuk, A. Tlili, J. Yang, & M. Chang (Eds.), Smart learning for a sustainable society: ICSLE 2023 (pp. 1–10). Lecture Notes in Educational Technology. Springer. DOI: 10.1007/978-981-99-5961-7_27

Slavuj, V., Kovačić, B., & Jugo, I. (2015, May). Intelligent tutoring systems for language learning. In *2015 38th International Convention on Information and Communication Technology, Electronics and Microelectronics (MIPRO)* (pp. 814-819). IEEE. DOI: 10.1109/MIPRO.2015.7160383

Smart Learning Environments. (2025). *Adaptive intelligent tutoring systems for STEM education: Real-time feedback and deep learning models.* Smart Learning Environments., DOI: 10.1186/s40561-025-00389-y

Smith, M. (Peg), & Stein, M. K. (2018). *5 Practices for orchestrating productive mathematics discussion*. National Council of Teachers of Mathematics.

Smith, R. A., Smith, E., & Price, M. (2024). Utilizing emergent AI chatbot technology to generate mathematical writing models for elementary students with learning disabilities. *Intervention in School and Clinic*, *59*(5), 339–346. https://doi-org.dist.lib.usu.edu/10.1177/10534512241233512. DOI: 10.1177/10534512241233512

Solyst, J., Yang, E., Xie, S., Ogan, A., Hammer, J., & Eslami, M. (2023). The potential of diverse youth as stakeholders in identifying and mitigating algorithmic bias for a future of fairer AI. In *Proceedings of the ACM on Human-Computer Interaction* (pp. 1-27). Association for Computing Machinery. DOI: 10.1145/3610213

Song, C., Shin, S. Y., & Shin, K. S. (2024). Implementing the dynamic feedback-driven learning optimization framework: A machine learning approach to personalize educational pathways. *Applied Sciences (Basel, Switzerland)*, *14*(2), 916. DOI: 10.3390/app14020916

Song, Y., Kim, J., Liu, Z., Li, C., & Xing, W. (2025a). Students' perceived roles, opportunities, and challenges of a generative AI-powered teachable agent: A case of middle school math class. *Journal of Research on Technology in Education*, 1–19. DOI: 10.1080/15391523.2024.2447727

Song, Y., Kim, J., Xing, W., Liu, Z., Li, C., & Oh, H. (2025b). Elementary school students' and teachers' perceptions toward creative mathematical writing with Generative AI. *Journal of Research on Technology in Education*, 1–23. DOI: 10.1080/15391523.2025.2455057

Song, Y., Li, C., Ma, Y., Lyu, B., Zhu, W., Li, H., & Xing, W. (2025). Exploring effective tutoring strategies in asynchronous online mathematical discussions: Insights from ordered network analysis. *Journal of Science Education and Technology*, *34*(5), 1–21. DOI: 10.1007/s10956-025-10233-0

Song, Y., Li, C., Xing, W., Lyu, B., & Zhu, W. (2025). Investigating perceived fairness of AI prediction system for math learning: A mixed-methods study with college students. *The Internet and Higher Education*, *65*, 101000. DOI: 10.1016/j.iheduc.2025.101000

Song, Y., Weisberg, L. R., Zhang, S., Tian, X., Boyer, K. E., & Israel, M. (2024). A framework for inclusive AI learning design for diverse learners. *Computers and Education: Artificial Intelligence*, *6*, 100212. DOI: 10.1016/j.caeai.2024.100212

Stahl, A. (2021, March 10). How ai will impact the future of work and life. *Forbes*. https://www.forbes.com/sites/ashleystahl/2021/03/10/how-ai-will-impact-the-future-of-work-and-life/?sh=3c5c1a5279a3

Stahl, B. C. (2021). *Artificial intelligence for a better future*. Springer. DOI: 10.1007/978-3-030-69978-9

Stanton, K., Carpenter, R. W., Nance, M., Sturgeon, T., & Villalongo Andino, M. (2022). A multisample demonstration of using the prolific platform for repeated assessment and psychometric substance use research. *Experimental and Clinical Psychopharmacology*, *30*(4), 432–443.. DOI: 10.1037/pha0000545 PMID: 35025585

Stanworth, J. O., Yen, W. H., & Warden, C. A. (2023). Conflicted about online learning?: Using sentiment analysis to explore learner approach-avoidance motivation. *Online Information Review*, *47*(2), 356–370. DOI: 10.1108/OIR-09-2021-0463

Statista. (2024). *Languages most frequently used for web content as of January 2024, by share of websites*. https://www.statista.com/statistics/262946/most-common-languages-on-the-internet/

Stefaniak, J., & Moore, S. (2024). The Use of Generative AI to Support Inclusivity and Design Deliberation for Online Instruction. *Online Learning : the Official Journal of the Online Learning Consortium*, *28*(3), 181–205. DOI: 10.24059/olj.v28i3.4458

Stegmann, K., Weinberger, A., & Fischer, F. (2007). Facilitating argumentative knowledge construction with computer-supported collaboration scripts. *International Journal of Computer-Supported Collaborative Learning*, *2*(4), 421–447. DOI: 10.1007/s11412-007-9028-y

Steinkuehler, C. A., & Squire, K. (2014). Videogames and learning. In Sawyer, K. (Ed.), *Cambridge handbook of the learning sciences* (pp. 377–394). Cambridge University Press. DOI: 10.1017/CBO9781139519526.023

Stevens, E. A., & Powell, S. R. (2016). Unpacking word problems for diverse learners: A guide to using schemas. *Childhood Education*, *92*, 86–91. DOI: 10.1080/00094056.2016.1134253

Stieglitz, S., & Dang-Xuan, L. (2013). Emotions and information diffusion in social media—Sentiment of microblogs and sharing behavior. *Journal of Management Information Systems*, *29*(4), 217–248. DOI: 10.2753/MIS0742-1222290408

Su, J., & Yang, W. (2023). Unlocking the power of ChatGPT: A framework for applying generative ai in education. *ECNU Review of Education*, 1-12. *Doi:* DOI: 10.1177/20965311231168423

Sudiarta, I. G. P., Sukajaya, I. N., & Suharta, I. G. P. (2018). Investigation on students' mathematical online discussion: A case study in grade 8 SMPN 1 Denpasar. [). IOP Publishing.]. *Journal of Physics: Conference Series*, *1040*, 012031. DOI: 10.1088/1742-6596/1040/1/012031

Su, J., Zhong, Y., & Ng, D. T. K. (2022). A meta-review of literature on educational approaches for teaching AI at the K-12 levels in the Asia-Pacific region. *Computers and Education: Artificial Intelligence*, *3*, 100065. DOI: 10.1016/j.caeai.2022.100065

Sun, J., Zhang, Z., & He, X. (2024). Llm4edukg: Llm for automatic construction of educational knowledge graph. In *2024 International Conference on Networking and Network Applications (NaNA)* (pp. 269-275). IEEE. DOI: 10.1109/NaNA63151.2024.00051

Su, Y., & Zhang, Y. (2020). Automatic construction of subject knowledge graph based on educational big data. In *Proceedings of the 2020 3rd International Conference on Big Data and Education* (pp. 30–36). DOI: 10.1145/3396452.3396458

Swanson, H. L., & Fung, W. (2016). Working memory components and problem-solving accuracy: Are there multiple pathways? *Journal of Educational Psychology*, *108*(8), 1153–1177. DOI: 10.1037/edu0000116

Sweller, J. (2018). The role of independent measures of load in cognitive load theory. In Zheng, R. (Ed.). (2018). *Cognitive load measurement and application: A theoretical framework for meaningful research and practice* (pp. 1-8). New York, NY: Routledge.

Sweller, J. (1988). Cognitive load during problem solving: Effects of on learning. *Cognitive Science*, *12*(2), 257–285. DOI: 10.1207/s15516709cog1202_4

Sweller, J. (2010). Element interactivity and intrinsic, extraneous, and germane cognitive load. *Educational Psychology Review*, *22*(2), 123–138. DOI: 10.1007/s10648-010-9128-5

Sweller, J. (2011). Cognitive load theory. In Mestre, J. P., & Ross, B. H. (Eds.), *The Psychology of Learning and Motivation: Cognition in Education* (pp. 37–76). Elsevier Academic Press., DOI: 10.1016/B978-0-12-387691-1.00002-8

Sweller, J., van Merrienboer, J. J., & Paas, F. (1998). Cognitive architecture and instructional design. *Educational Psychology Review*, *10*(3), 251–296. DOI: 10.1023/A:1022193728205

Tafazoli, D. (2024). Exploring the potential of generative AI in democratizing English language education. *Computers and Education: Artificial Intelligence*, *7*, 1–12. DOI: 10.1016/j.caeai.2024.100275

Tafazoli, D., María, E. G., & Abril, C. A. (2019). Intelligent language tutoring system: Integrating intelligent computer-assisted language learning into language education. [IJICTE]. *International Journal of Information and Communication Technology Education*, *15*(3), 60–74. DOI: 10.4018/IJICTE.2019070105

Tahiru, F. (2021). AI in education: A systematic literature review. *Journal of Cases on Information Technology*, *23*(1), 1–20. DOI: 10.4018/JCIT.2021010101

Taimalu, M., & Luik, P. (2019). The impact of beliefs and knowledge on the integration of technology among teacher educators: A path analysis. *Teaching and Teacher Education*, *79*, 101–110. DOI: 10.1016/j.tate.2018.12.012

Talukder, N. M., & Bin Ahsan, W. (2025). AI's impact on student engagement in virtual learning in Bangladesh. *Journal of Teaching & Learning*, *1*(1). Advance online publication. DOI: 10.58947/journal.jtgx34

Tan, D. Y., & Cheah, C. W. (2021). Developing a gamified AI-enabled online learning application to improve students' perception of university physics. *Computers and Education: Artificial Intelligence*, *2*, 100032. DOI: 10.1016/j.caeai.2021.100032

Tan, X., Cheng, G., & Ling, M. H. (2025). Artificial intelligence in teaching and teacher professional development: A systematic review. *Computers and Education: Artificial Intelligence*, *8*, 1–19. DOI: 10.1016/j.caeai.2024.100355

Tapalova, O., & Zhiyenbayeva, N. (2022). Artificial intelligence in education: AIEd for personalised learning pathways. *Electronic Journal of e-Learning*, *20*(5), 639–653. DOI: 10.34190/ejel.20.5.2597

Taub, M., & Azevedo, R. (2019). How does prior knowledge influence eye fixations and sequences of cognitive and metacognitive SRL processes during learning with an Intelligent Tutoring System? *International Journal of Artificial Intelligence in Education*, *29*(1), 1–28. DOI: 10.1007/s40593-018-0165-4

Téllez, A. R., Ortiz, L. M. F., & Domínguez, F. C. T. (2024). Artificial intelligence in university administration: An overview of its uses and applications. *Revista Interamericana de Bibliotecología*, *47*(2), 1–12. DOI: 10.17533/udea.rib.v47n2a05

Teuscher, D., & Reys, R. E. (2012). Rate of change: AP calculus students' understandings and misconceptions after completing different curricular paths. *School Science and Mathematics*, *112*(6), 359–376. DOI: 10.1111/j.1949-8594.2012.00150.x

Teuscher, D., Reys, R. E., Evitts, T. A., & Heinz, K. (2010). Slope, rate of change, and steepness: Do students understand these concepts? *Mathematics Teacher*, *103*(7), 519–524. DOI: 10.5951/MT.103.7.0519

Thangavel, S., K, S., & K, S. (2025). Revolutionizing education through augmented reality (AR) and virtual reality (VR): Innovations, challenges and future prospects. *Asian Journal of Interdisciplinary Research*, *8*(1), 1–28. DOI: 10.54392/ajir2511

The National Standards Collaborative Board. (2015). *World-readiness standards for learning. languages*. ACTFL.

Thu , P. B., & Tien, P. D. (2024). AI-powered administration: The role of intelligent tutoring systems in education. *International Journal of Religion*, *5*(10), 4560–4569. DOI: 10.61707/sqwrjn32

Tlili, A., Saqer, K., Salha, S., & Huang, R. (2025). Effect of AIEd on achievement: Meta analysis. *Information Development*. Advance online publication. DOI: 10.1177/02666669241304407

Traxler, A., Gavrin, A., & Lindell, R. (2018). Networks identify productive forum discussions. *Physical Review. Physics Education Research*, *14*(2), 20107. DOI: 10.1103/PhysRevPhysEducRes.14.020107

Turner, A. (2023, June 7). ChatGPT number of users & market size statistics. *BankMyCell*. https://www.bankmycell.com/blog/chatgpt-number-of-users

UNESCO. (2021). *AI and education: Guidance for policymakers*. UNESCO Publishing. https://unesco.org/en/articles/ai-and-education-guidance-policy-makers

United Nations Environment Programme. (2024). *AI has an environmental problem. Here's what the world can do about that*. https://www.unep.org/news-and-stories/story/ai-has-environmental-problem-heres-what-world-can-do-about

United States Air Force Academy. (2025). *About*. https://datausa.io/profile/geo/air-force-academy-co?redirect=true#:~:text=The%205%20largest%20ethnic%20groups,(Hispanic)%20(3.66%25)

Urazbayeva, G., Kussainova, R., Aibergen, A., Kaliyeva, A., & Kantayeva, G. (2024). Innovation off the bat: Bridging the ChatGPT gap in digital competence among english as a foreign language teachers. *Education Sciences*, *14*(9), 1–15. DOI: 10.3390/educsci14090946

Uysal, B. Ç. B., & Yüksel, İ. (2024). AI-powered lesson planning: Insights from future EFL teachers. In Pan, F. (Ed.), *AI in Language Teaching, Learning, and Assessment* (pp. 101–132). IGI Global Scientific Publishing., DOI: 10.4018/979-8-3693-0872-1.ch006 van den Berg, S., & Papadopoulos, P. M. (2024). Summative assessment with Artificial Intelligence: Qualitative analysis and comparison of technology acceptance in student and teacher populations. *Innovations in Education and Teaching International*, •••, 1–16. DOI: 10.1080/14703297.2024.2436613

van Lidth de Jeude, J., Caldarelli, G., & Squartini, T. (2019). Detecting core-periphery structures by surprise. *Europhysics Letters*, *125*(6), 68001. DOI: 10.1209/0295-5075/125/68001

VanLehn, K. (2011). The relative effectiveness of human tutoring, intelligent tutoring systems, and other tutoring systems. *Educational Psychologist*, *46*(4), 197–221. DOI: 10.1080/00461520.2011.611369

Vanslambrouck, S., Zhu, C., Lombaerts, K., Philipsen, B., & Tondeur, J. (2018). Students' motivation and subjective task value of participating in online and blended learning environments. *The Internet and Higher Education*, *36*, 33–40. DOI: 10.1016/j.iheduc.2017.09.002

Velazquez, C. M. (2007). Testing predictive models of technology integration in Mexico and the United States. *Computers in the Schools*, *24*(3–4), 153–173. DOI: 10.1300/J025v24n03_11

Venn, E., Park, J., Andersen, L. P., & Hejmadi, M. (2023). How do learning technologies impact on undergraduates' emotional and cognitive engagement with their learning? *Teaching in Higher Education*, *28*(4), 822–839. DOI: 10.1080/13562517.2020.1863349

Ventista, O. M., & Brown, C. (2023). Teachers' professional learning and its impact on students' learning outcomes: Findings from a systematic review. *Social Sciences & Humanities Open*, *8*(1), 100565. DOI: 10.1016/j.ssaho.2023.100565

Verga, L., & Kotz, S. (2013). How relevant is social interaction in second language learning? *Frontiers in Human Neuroscience*, *7*, 1–7. DOI: 10.3389/fnhum.2013.00550 PMID: 24027521

Verschaffel, L., Greer, B., & De Corte, E. (2000). *Making sense of word problems*. Swets & Zeitlinger.

Vistorte, A., Deroncele-Acosta, A., Ayala, J., Barrasa, A., López-Granero, C., & Martí-González, M. (2024). Integrating artificial intelligence to assess emotions in learning environments: A systematic literature review. *Frontiers in Psychology*, *15*, 1387089. Advance online publication. DOI: 10.3389/fpsyg.2024.1387089 PMID: 38966729

Vygotsky, L. (1978). Interaction between learning and development. In Cole, M., Steiner, V. J., Scribner, S., & Souberman, E. (Eds.), *Mind in society* (pp. 79–91). Harvard University Press.

Vygotsky, L. S. (1978). *Mind in society: The development of higher psychological processes* (Vol. 86). Harvard University Press.

Walker, C., Greene, B., & Mansell, R. (2006). Identification with academics, intrinsic/extrinsic motivation, and self-efficacy as predictors of cognitive engagement. *Learning and Individual Differences, 16*(1), 1–12. DOI: 10.1016/j.lindif.2005.06.004

Walter, Y. (2024). Embracing the future of artificial intelligence in the classroom: The relevance of AI literacy, prompt engineering, and critical thinking in modern education. *International Journal of Educational Technology in Higher Education, 21*(1), 15. Advance online publication. DOI: 10.1186/s41239-024-00448-3

Wang, H., Wang, F., Zhu, Z., Wang, J., Tran, T., & Du, Z. (2024). Artificial intelligence in education: A systematic literature review. Expert Systems with Applications, 252(Part A), 124167. DOI: 10.1016/j.eswa.2024.124167

Wang, A. Y., Fuchs, L. S., & Fuchs, D. (2016). Cognitive and linguistic predictors of mathematical word problems with and without irrelevant information. *Learning and Individual Differences*, *52*, 79–87. DOI: 10.1016/j.lindif.2016.10.015 PMID: 28190942

Wang, D., Shan, D., Ju, R., Kao, B., Zhang, C., & Chen, G. (2024). Investigating dialogic interaction in K12 online one-on-one mathematics tutoring using AI and sequence mining techniques. *Education and Information Technologies*, *30*(7), 9215–9240. DOI: 10.1007/s10639-024-13195-9

Wang, L. (2023). The impact of student-centered learning on academic motivation and achievement: A comparative research between traditional instruction and student-centered approach. *Journal of Education Humanities and Social Sciences*, *22*, 346–353. DOI: 10.54097/ehss.v22i.12463

Wang, T., & Cheng, E. C. K. (2021). An investigation of barriers to Hong Kong K-12 schools incorporating Artificial Intelligence in education. *Computers and Education: Artificial Intelligence*, *2*, 100031. DOI: 10.1016/j.caeai.2021.100031

Wang, Y. (2024). The impact of AI application in education on students. *Journal of Education Humanities and Social Sciences*, *45*, 116–122. DOI: 10.54097/gg1d3q19

Wang, Y., & Liu, Q. (2020). Effects of online teaching presence on students' interactions and collaborative knowledge construction. *Journal of Computer Assisted Learning*, *36*(3), 370–382. DOI: 10.1111/jcal.12408

Wankhede, N., Kale, M., Shukla, M., Nathiya, D. R., Roopashree, K., Kaur, P., Goyanka, B., Rahangdale, S., Taksande, B., Upaganlawar, A., Khalid, M., Chigurupati, S., Umekar, M., Kopalli, S. R., & Koppula, S. (2024). Leveraging AI for the diagnosis and treatment of autism spectrum disorder: Current trends and future prospects. *Asian Journal of Psychiatry, 101*, 104241. DOI: 10.1016/j.ajp.2024.104241

Warschauer, M., & Healey, D. (1998). Computers and language learning: An overview. *Language Teaching, 31*(2), 57–71. DOI: 10.1017/S0261444800012970

Wiggins, G. P., & McTighe, J. (2005). *Understanding by design*. Ascd.

Wilkerson, D. A. (2016). Lurking behavior in online psychosocial discussion forums: Theoretical perspectives and implications for practice. *Journal of Technology in Human Services, 34*(3), 256–266. DOI: 10.1080/15228835.2016.1193456

Wilkinson, I. A. G., & Fung, I. Y. Y. (2002). Small-group composition and peer effects. *International Journal of Educational Research, 37*(5), 425–447. DOI: 10.1016/S0883-0355(03)00014-4

Williams, A. (2024). Delivering effective student feedback in higher education: An evaluation of the challenges and best practice. *International Journal of Research in Education and Science, 10*(2), 473–501. DOI: 10.46328/ijres.3404

Wilson, J., Ahrendt, C., Fudge, E., Raiche, A., Beard, G., & MacArthur, C. (2021). Elementary teachers' perceptions of automated feedback and automated scoring: Transforming the teaching and learning of writing using automated writing evaluation. *Computers & Education, 168*, 104208. DOI: 10.1016/j.compedu.2021.104208

Wilson, J., Palermo, C., & Wibowo, A. (2024). Elementary English learners' engagement with automated feedback. *Learning and Instruction, 91*, 101890. DOI: 10.1016/j.learninstruc.2024.101890

Winkler, R., & Söllner, M. (2018). Unleashing the potential of chatbots in education: A state-of-the-art analysis. *eLearning Papers*, 62, 1–14.

Winne, P. H. (2013). Self-regulated learning viewed from models of information processing. In Zimmerman, B., & Schunk, D. (Eds.), *Self-regulated learning and academic achievement* (pp. 145–178). Routledge.

Wirantaka, A. (2022). Effective written corrective feedback on efl students' academic writing. *Eralingua: Jurnal Pendidikan Bahasa Asing dan Sastra,* 6(2), 387-399.

Wired Staff. (2024). AI can't replace teaching, but it can make it better. *WIRED Magazine*. https://www.wired.com/story/ai-in-classrooms/

Wise, A. F., Cui, Y., Jin, W., & Vytasek, J. (2017). Mining for gold: Identifying content-related MOOC discussion threads across domains through linguistic modeling. *The Internet and Higher Education*, *32*, 11–28. DOI: 10.1016/j.iheduc.2016.08.001

Wood, D., Bruner, J., & Ross, G. (1976). The role of tutoring in problem solving. *Journal of Child Psychology and Psychiatry, and Allied Disciplines*, *17*(2), 89–100. DOI: 10.1111/j.1469-7610.1976.tb00381.x PMID: 932126

Woodruff, K., Hutson, J., & Arnone, K. (2023). Perceptions and barriers to adopting artificial intelligence in K-12 education: A survey of educators in fifty states. *Faculty Scholarship,* 1–28. https://digitalcommons.lindenwood.edu/faculty-research-papers/506.

Woo, J.-C. (2014). Digital game-based learning supports student motivation, cognitive success, and performance outcomes. *Journal of Educational Technology & Society*, *17*(3), 291–307.

Woolf, B. P. (2020). *Building intelligent interactive tutors*. Morgan Kaufmann.

Woolf, B., Lane, H., Chaudhri, V., & Kolodner, J. (2013). AI grand challenges for education. *AI Magazine*, *34*(4), 66–84. DOI: 10.1609/aimag.v34i4.2490

Wu, , CLi, , YLi, , JZhang, , QWu, , F. (2021, May). Web-based platform for K-12 AI education in China. In *Proceedings of the AAAI Conference on Artificial Intelligence, 35*(17), 15687-15694. DOI: 10.1609/aaai.v35i17.17848

Wulan, D. R., Nainggolan, D. M., Hidayat, Y., Rohman, T., & Fiyul, A. Y. (2024). Exploring the benefits and challenges of gamification in enhancing student learning outcomes. *Global International Journal of Innovative Research*, *2*(7), 1657–1674. DOI: 10.59613/global.v2i7.238

Xiao, N., Pei, Y., Yuan, C., Bu, Y., & Xua, Z. (2025). Transforming education with artificial intelligence: A comprehensive review of applications, challenges, and future directions. *International Theory and Practice in Humanities and Social Sciences*, *2*(1), 337–356. DOI: 10.70693/itphss.v2i1.211

Xing, W. L., Song, Y., Li, C. L., Liu, Z. F., Zhu, W. D., & Oh, U. (2025). Development of a generative AI-powered teachable agent for middle school mathematics learning: A design-based research study. *British Journal of Educational Technology*, *56*(5), 2043–2077. https://doi-org.ezproxy.lib.utah.edu/10.1111/bjet.13586. DOI: 10.1111/bjet.13586

Xing, W., Chen, X., Stein, J., & Marcinkowski, M. (2020). Temporal prediction of dropouts in MOOCs: Reaching the low-hanging fruit. *IEEE Transactions on Learning Technologies*, *13*(4), 789–801.

Xing, W., Li, H., Kim, T., Zhu, W., & Song, Y. (2025). Investigating the behaviors of core and periphery students in an asynchronous online discussion community using network analysis and topic modeling. *Education and Information Technologies*, *30*(5), 5561–5588. DOI: 10.1007/s10639-024-13038-7

Xin, J. J. (2024). Investigating EFL teachers' use of generative AI to develop reading materials: A practice and perception study. *Language Teaching Research*, *0*(0), 1–30. DOI: 10.1177/13621688241303321

Xu, Z. (2024). AI in education: Enhancing learning experiences and student outcomes. *Applied and Computational Engineering*, *51*(1), 104–111. DOI: 10.54254/2755-2721/51/20241187

Yan, D. A. (2023). Impact of ChatGPT on learners in a l2 writing practicum: An exploratory investigation. *Education and Information Technologies*, *28*(11), 1–25. DOI: 10.1007/s10639-023-11742-4 PMID: 37361815

Yang, A. C. M., Flanagan, B., & Ogata, H. (2022). Adaptive formative assessment system based on computerized adaptive testing and learning memory cycle. *Computers & Education: Artificial Intelligence*, *3*, 100104. DOI: 10.1016/j.caeai.2022.100104

Yang, H., & Markauskaite, L. (2025). Fostering language student teachers' transformative agency for embracing GenAI: A formative intervention. *Teaching and Teacher Education*, *159*, 1–20. DOI: 10.1016/j.tate.2025.104980

Yan, L., Sha, L., Zhang, X., & Chen, Y. (2023). Practical and ethical challenges of large language models in education. *arXiv Preprint*. https://arxiv.org/abs/2310.04210

Yan, W., Nakajima, T., & Sawada, R. (2024). Benefits and challenges of collaboration between students and conversational generative artificial intelligence in programming learning: An empirical case study. *Education Sciences*, *14*(433), 1–20. DOI: 10.3390/educsci14040433

Yaseen, H., Mohammad, A. S., Ashal, N., Abusaimeh, H., Ali, A., & Sharabati, A. A. A. (2025). The impact of adaptive learning technologies, personalized feedback, and interactive AI tools on student engagement: The moderating role of digital literacy. *Sustainability (Basel)*, *17*(3), 1133. DOI: 10.3390/su17031133

Yildiz Durak, H., & Onan, A. (2025). A systematic review of AI-based feedback in educational settings. *Journal of Computational Social Science*, *8*(96), 1–40. DOI: 10.1007/s42001-025-00428-1

Yılmaz, Ö. K., & Aydın, S. (2025). The impact of the use of artificial intelligence-generated materials on reading motivation among EFL learners. *Reading Research Quarterly*, *60*(3), e70016. DOI: 10.1002/rrq.70016

Yim, I. H. Y., & Su, J. (2025). Artificial intelligence (AI) learning tools in K-12 education: A scoping review. *Journal of Computers in Education, 12*(1), 93–131. DOI: 10.1007/s40692-023-00304-9

Yin, J., Goh, T., Yang, B., & Xiaobin, Y. (2021). Conversation technology with micro-learning: The impact of chatbot-based learning on students' learning motivation and performance. *Journal of Educational Computing Research, 59*(1), 154–177. DOI: 10.1177/0735633120952067

Yoder, P. J., & Tapp, J. (2004). Empirical guidance for time-window sequential analysis of single cases. *Journal of Behavioral Education, 13*(4), 227–246. DOI: 10.1023/B:JOBE.0000044733.03220.a9

Yoon, S., Min, S., & Kang, D. (2024). Comprehensive analysis of AI-based math learning platforms for K-12 education. In C. Bonk & G. Marks (Eds.), *Proceedings of E-Learn: World Conference on E-Learning in Corporate, Government, Healthcare, and Higher Education* (pp. 113-122). Association for the Advancement of Computing in Education.

Yu, D., Zhou, Y., Li, Y., Shen, X., Tian, M., Yang, B., Su, J., & Sun, Y. (2022). A survey of English learning softwares based on TPACK framework. *The 17th Academic Annual Conference of the Information Technology Education Professional Committee of China Educational Technology Association*, 1–9.

Yu, J. (2025). Analyzing Learning Sentiments on a MOOC Discussion Forum Through Epistemic Network Analysis. *International Review of Research in Open and Distance Learning, 26*(1), 197–215. DOI: 10.19173/irrodl.v26i1.7965

Yu, S., Han, H., & Ahn, H. (2025). Mapping children's sense of belonging through multimodal composition in the classroom. *Language, Culture and Curriculum, 38*(3), 1–22. DOI: 10.1080/07908318.2025.2534382

Zall, R., & Kangavari, M. R. (2022). Comparative analytical survey on cognitive agents with emotional intelligence. *Cognitive Computation, 14*(4), 1223–1246. DOI: 10.1007/s12559-022-10007-5

Zawacki-Richter, O., Marin, V. I., Bond, M., & Gouverneur, F. (2019). Systematic review of research on artificial intelligence applications in higher education – Where are the educators? *International Journal of Educational Technology in Higher Education, 16*(39), 1–27. DOI: 10.1186/s41239-019-0171-0

Zeithofer, I., Zumbach, J., Schweppe, J. (2024). Complexity affects performance, cognitive load, and awareness. Learning & Instruction, 94, pN.PAG-N.PAG. Doi:-DOI: 10.1016/j.learninstruc.2024.102001

Zhai, X., Chu, X., Chai, C. S., Jong, M. S. Y., Istenic, A., Spector, M., & Li, Y. (2021). A review of artificial intelligence (AI) in education from 2010 to 2020. *Complexity*, *2021*(1), 8812542. DOI: 10.1155/2021/8812542

Zhai, X., Nyaaba, M., & Ma, W. (2024). Can generative AI and ChatGPT outperform humans on cognitive-demanding problem-solving tasks in science? *Science & Education*, ●●●, 1–22.

Zhang, J., & Zhang, Z. (2024). AI in teacher education: Unlocking new dimensions in teaching support, inclusive learning, and digital literacy. *Journal of Computer Assisted Learning*, *40*(4), 1871–1885. DOI: 10.1111/jcal.12988

Zhang, K., & Aslan, A. B. (2021). AI technologies for education: Recent research & future directions. *Computers and Education: Artificial Intelligence*, *2*, 100025. DOI: 10.1016/j.caeai.2021.100025

Zhang, S., Prasad, P. G., & Schroeder, N. L. (2025). Learning about AI: A systematic review of reviews on AI literacy. *Journal of Educational Computing Research*, *6*(5), 1292–1322. DOI: 10.1177/07356331251342081

Zhang, Y. (2024). Incorporating ChatGPT as an automated written corrective feedback tool into L2 writing class. *Tydskrif vir Taalonderrig*, *4*(4), 22–34. DOI: 10.54475/jlt.2024.024

Zhao, D. (2024). The impact of AI-enhanced natural language processing tools on writing proficiency: An analysis of language precision, content summarization, and creative writing facilitation. *Education and Information Technologies*. Advance online publication. DOI: 10.1007/s10639-024-13145-5

Zheng, R. (2024). Considerations on human cognitive processes in AI learning: an individual difference perspective. Poster presentation at *the 23rd International Conference on WWW/Internet 2024*. Zagreb, Coatia.

Zheng, R., & Greenberg, K. (2018). Effective design in human and machine learning: A cognitive perspective. In: Zhou, J., Chen, F. (Eds), *Human and Machine Learning*. Human – Computer Interaction Series. Springer, Cham. https://doi.org/ DOI: 10.1007/978-3-319-90403-0_4

Zheng, L., & Huang, R. (2016). The effects of sentiments and co-regulation on group performance in computer supported collaborative learning. *The Internet and Higher Education*, *28*, 59–67. DOI: 10.1016/j.iheduc.2015.10.001

Zheng, L., Long, M., Chen, B., & Fan, Y. (2023). Promoting knowledge elaboration, socially shared regulation, and group performance in collaborative learning: An automated assessment and feedback approach based on knowledge graphs. *International Journal of Educational Technology in Higher Education*, *20*(1), 46. DOI: 10.1186/s41239-023-00415-4 PMID: 37032738

Zheng, R. (2007). Cognitive functionality of multimedia in problem solving. In Kidd, T., & Song, H. (Eds.), *Handbook of Research on Instructional Systems and Technology* (pp. 230–246). Information Science Reference/IGI Global Publishing. DOI: 10.4018/978-1-59904-865-9.ch017

Zheng, R. (2022). Foster transversal skills in game-based learning: A deep learning approach. In Rivera-Trigueros, I., López-Alcarria, A., Ruiz-Padillo, D., Olvera-Lobo, M., & Gutiérrez-Pérez, J. (Eds.), *Using disruptive methodologies and game-based learning to foster transversal skills* (pp. 106–130). IGI Global Publishing. DOI: 10.4018/978-1-7998-8645-7.ch006

Zheng, R., & Gardner, M. (2020). *Memory in education*. Routledge/Taylor & Francis Group.

Zheng, R., McAlack, M., Wilmes, B., Kohler-Evans, P., & Williamson, J. (2009). Effects of multimedia on cognitive load, self-efficacy, and multiple rule-based problem solving. *British Journal of Educational Technology*, *40*(5), 790–803. DOI: 10.1111/j.1467-8535.2008.00859.x

Zheng, R., Spears, J., Luptak, M., & Wilby, F. (2015). Understanding older adults' perceptions of Internet use: An exploratory factor analysis. *Educational Gerontology*, *41*(7), 504–518. DOI: 10.1080/03601277.2014.1003495

Zhou, F. (2025). *Emotion recognition in AI-powered classrooms: Using deep learning to detect student engagement*. Smart Learning Environments., DOI: 10.1186/s40561-025-00374-5

Zhu, S., Yu, T., Xu, T., Chen, H., Dustdar, S., Gigan, S., & Pan, Y. (2023). Intelligent computing: The latest advances, challenges, and future. *Intelligent Computing, 2*, 0006. https://doi.org/DOI: 10.34133/icomputing.0006

Zhu, M., & Wang, C. (2025). A systematic review of research on AI in language education: Current status and future implications. *Language Learning & Technology*, *29*(1), 1–29. DOI: 10.64152/10125/73606

Zimmerman, B. J. (2002). Becoming a self-regulated learner: An overview. *Theory into Practice*, *41*(2), 64–70. DOI: 10.1207/s15430421tip4102_2

Zou, B., Liviero, S., Hao, M., & Wei, C. (2020). Artificial intelligence technology for EAP speaking skills: Student perceptions of opportunities and challenges. In N. Freiermuth, M., Zarrinabadi (Ed.), *Technology and the Psychology of Second Language Learners and Users. New Language Learning and Teaching Environments* (pp. 433–463). Palgrave Macmillan. DOI: 10.1007/978-3-030-34212-8_17

Zou, M., & Huang, L. (2023). The impact of ChatGPT on L2 writing and expected responses: Voice from doctoral students. *Education and Information Technologies, 29*(11), 13201–13219. DOI: 10.1007/s10639-023-12397-x

Zou, W., Hu, X., Pan, Z., Li, C., Cai, Y., & Liu, M. (2021). Exploring the relationship between social presence and learners' prestige in MOOC discussion forums using automated content analysis and social network analysis. *Computers in Human Behavior, 115*, 106582. DOI: 10.1016/j.chb.2020.106582

Zulianti, H., Hastuti, H., Nurchurifiani, E., Hastomo, T., Maximilian, A., & Ajeng, G. D. (2025). Enhancing novice EFL teachers' competency in AI-powered tools through a TPACK-based professional development program. *World Journal of English Language, 15*(3), 117–117. DOI: 10.5430/wjel.v15n3p117

Zweig, J. S. (2015). Are Women Happier than Men? Evidence from the Gallup World Poll. *Journal of Happiness Studies, 16*(2), 515–554. DOI: 10.1007/s10902-014-9521-8

About the Contributors

Robert Zheng is a professor of instructional design and educational technology in the Department of Educational Psychology at the University of Utah, USA. His research area includes multimedia and cognition, instructional design and development, web-based learning, and educational gamification. He has published over 60 refereed journal papers and book chapters. He is the editor and co-editor of 12 books published by Routledge, Nova Science, and IGI Global. He was the founding editor of the *International Journal of Cyber Behavior, Psychology and Learning* (2008-2012).

***

Gulgun Afacan Adanir is a learning technologist and researcher at Cambridge University Centre for Alternative Finance. She was previously instructor at the Ankara University. Dr. Adanır gained her PhD from Middle East Technical University (METU) Information Systems in February 2016. She holds Associate Professor degree from Turkish Higher Education Council. Her research interests include distance education, learning analytics, social media, and human-computer interaction.

Sohail Ahmad is a doctoral candidate (Education) at the University of Cambridge and the Aga Khan University Institute for Educational Development, Pakistan. Currently, he is working as Research Specialist at AKU-IED. He has experience in large-scale research through working on various nation-wide studies on science and mathematics education in Pakistan. Most of his academic work revolves around the quality of education, mainly pedagogical quality and its impact on students' learning outcomes, from school to higher education. He has published on pedagogical quality, student learning, higher education, quality assurance, and use of technology in higher education.

M. Bahadırhan Aktaş is a PhD candidate specializing in instructional technologies, with a focus on distance education. Since 2021, he has been pursuing his doctoral studies at Ankara University. In addition to his academic work, he serves as a mathematics teacher and school administrator under the Ministry of National Education of the Republic of Turkey. His research interests include distance learning, educational technologies, and intellectual property rights in education.

Aisha Naz Ansari is a Research Specialist at the Aga Khan University, Institute for Educational Development, Pakistan. She is a PhD student at School of Education, Durham University. She has contributed as a member of Evidence Synthesis Infrastructure Collaboration, managed by Cochrane. She has experience of working on Educational Technology, including Artificial Intelligence in higher education. She has published more than 30 research articles, systematic reviews, book chapters, and research blogs in international journals and prestigious forums. Her research areas include systematic reviews, educational technology, educational psychology, teacher education, public-private partnerships, education policy, and classroom teaching and learning.

Selami Aydin is a full professor in the Department of English Language Teaching at Istanbul Medeniyet University, Istanbul, Turkey. He researches on EFL writing, testing, affective states, technology use, and social media effects on language learning and teaching processes. Currently, he teaches ELT-related courses at BA and MA programs.

Sadia Bhutta is working as an Associate Professor at Aga Khan University Institute for Educational Development, Pakistan. Her research interests include classroom practice, learning outcomes, and quantitative research methods

Kaitlin Bundock is an Associate Professor of Special Education at Utah State University. Her primary area of expertise is effective instruction and intervention for students with disabilities in mathematics at the secondary level. Dr. Bundock also focuses on effective implementation of behavioral interventions and supports in secondary schools, particularly related to adaptations of Tier 2 behavior interventions to expand their application in responsive and sustainable ways. Additionally, Dr. Bundock collaboratively examines variables that impact student success and achievement more broadly, including engagement, self-regulation, inclusive education, and personnel preparation.

Cansu Candemir Özkan (Ph.D.) is a research assistant in the Department of Foreign Language Education at the Faculty of Education Sciences of Istanbul Medeniyet University. She researches on sociolinguistics, bilingualism &

multilingualism. She got her master's degree in Gazi University, Ankara-Turkey in French Language Teaching Department and she did her second master in Stendhal University, France. She got her PhD in Marmara University, Istanbul-Turkey.

Wing Sha Chan is a Ph.D. student in Instructional Technology in Education, STEM and Professional Studies at Old Dominion University's Darden College of Education & Professional Studies. Her research areas include instructional design and AI application, instructional design for second language acquisition, educational technology, game-based learning, and the metaverse. She has co-authored multiple conference proceedings and book chapters published by Routledge. She served as a co-investigator for the project "Immersive Metaverse-Based Social Learning with Audio Dialoguing: The Impact on Students' English Speaking Proficiency", funded by a seed grant.

W. Jordan Charles holds an M.Ed. in Educational Psychology from the University of Utah. As an instructional designer, he has designed courses on emerging AI applications, including a recent course for the University of Utah School of Law teaching graduate students practical applications of artificial intelligence. His research interests include identifying effective use cases for AI in learning environments and advancing responsible AI alignment to ensure AGI and ASI systems support human flourishing and societal benefit.

Derya Coşkun graduated from Foreign Language Education Department at METU in 2015 and completed her master degree at Süleyman Demirel University, Institute of Educational Sciences, at English Language Teaching Department. She received her PhD degree and is working as a research assistant. Her main research interests include teacher education, intercultural communication, critical reading, and pedagogy practices.

Rita K. Detrick is a researcher and strategist specializing in education and workforce development. As a Ph.D. candidate in Educational Psychology and Program Evaluation at Old Dominion University, she examines AI integration in education, technology-enhanced learning, and adult learning. With experience in innovation strategy across government, commercial, and nonprofit sectors, Rita connects research and practice to strengthen education and career pathways. She has co-authored publications on student-AI interactions and presented at national and international conferences, contributing to the growing understanding of technology's impact on education and workforce development.

Rashid Hashmi is a veteran broadcast journalist and seasoned media academician with an illustrious career that spans over twenty-two years in national television journalism, alongside significant contributions to higher education and institutional leadership in media studies. Currently serving as the Professor of Practice at the Sharda School of Media, Film & Entertainment, Sharda University, he brings a rare combination of editorial expertise, academic rigor, research vision, and a deep commitment to student development. Throughout his career, Prof. Hashmi has remained at the forefront of industry-academia convergence, shaping media curriculum, initiating industry collaborations, designing live projects, and enabling students to navigate the complex realities of today's multimedia landscape. Beginning his journey in the media world in the early 2000s, Prof. Hashmi has held influential editorial positions in major Indian news channels. He served as the Executive Editor and Senior Anchor at India News from 2019 to 2024, leading key prime-time broadcasts and managing critical editorial decisions during politically sensitive and nationally significant events. Prior to this, he was the Editor-in-Chief at FM News, where he not only curated the overall programming but also anchored widely followed shows like Rajdharm, Rashid vs Rajneeti, Prime Time, and Yakshprashn. His earlier editorial leadership as the Editor Output & Anchor at India News between 2008 and 2018 saw him manage newsrooms with precision, ensuring both accuracy and audience engagement. His foundational years as an Anchor-Reporter at Total News and as a Copy Editor and Reporter at ETV laid the groundwork for his on-field reporting and newsroom strategy. Prof. Hashmi's journalistic footprint includes ground-level coverage of the Batla House Encounter, Delhi serial bomb blasts, and the 26/11 Mumbai terror attacks, underscoring his ability to report under pressure and in crisis. What distinguishes Prof. Hashmi is his parallel and equally impactful journey in media education. At Sharda University, he has played a pivotal role in shaping the School of Media, Film & Entertainment as a practical, industry-oriented academic space. He spearheads the university's TV production initiatives, manages the in-house television channel Sharda TV and newspaper Sharda Samachar, and has introduced podcasting as a core media practice. His leadership extends to the Anchoring-Reporting Club, where he guides students in voice training, studio anchoring, and live reporting simulations. Prof. Hashmi has not only conceptualized and organized flagship events like the Media Fusion Summit, which brought together news anchors, film actors, and digital influencers, but also successfully conducted the Media Fest and the Global Leadership Award ceremony, giving students direct exposure to the media industry's thought leaders. An acclaimed mentor and pedagogue, Prof. Hashmi is known for integrating theoretical knowledge with practical training. His classes on anchoring, TV journalism, radio podcasting, BARC research, and digital storytelling are lauded for their interactive methods and industry relevance. He has conducted numerous practical workshops on broadcast techniques and has enabled hands-on learning by facilitating industry visits to live newsrooms, PCR, and MCR setups. He is also deeply involved in mentoring students during internships and has guided many into successful careers in media and digital communication. His previous academic roles include teaching at Jagannath Institute of Management Sciences (JIMS) and guest faculty stints at Amity University, Galgotia University, VIPS, IILM University, Maharaja Agrasen College, IAAN School of Mass Communication, and Marwah Studios. Prof. Hashmi is also a respected researcher and published author. A Ph.D. scholar at IFTM University, his research is focused on the emerging intersections of digital media and artificial intelligence, specifically examining how these technologies are transforming journalism and public communication. He has authored five book chapters with IGI Global, contributed to five national-level books, and has presented four research papers in international conferences over the past year. Two of his upcoming research works are set to appear in Scopus-indexed journals. He is presently working on two significant books—Anchoring, Reporting, and the Paradigm Shift from Traditional to Digital Media, and Indian Democracy in 25 Years of the New Century—both of which combine media critique with real-world case studies, making them valuable resources for scholars and practitioners alike. His contributions to the media field have been recognized with several prestigious accolades. Most notably, he received the ENBA Award for Best Anchor in 2022 for his coverage of the Pakistan political crisis and again in 2023 for his reportage on the Sri Lankan crisis. Over the years, he has earned more than 20 awards for excellence in television journalism. His interviews with political figures such as General V.K. Singh, Amar Singh, and Yogi Cabinet Ministers, and celebrities including Alia Bhatt, Kangana Ranaut, Sunny Leone, and Yuvraj Singh, reflect his standing as a credible and respected voice in Indian journalism. In the realm of feature and long-format journalism, his documentaries like Ayodhya Tere Kitne Ram, Shauryagatha, Sarhad Ka Aakhri Gaanv, Aakraman, and Operation Meghprahahar showcase his narrative depth and editorial sensitivity. Further reinforcing his interdisciplinary expertise, Prof. Hashmi is also an innovator and patent holder. His AI-driven system for autonomous vehicle technology (Patent No. 202441074339) addresses real-time decision-making through advanced machine learning and sensor integration. He also holds a design patent for an IoT-based solar panel energy monitoring device (Design No. 436930-001), reflecting his forward-thinking approach to sustainable technology and real-time data systems. A Gold Medalist in Mass Communication, Prof. Hashmi also holds professional diplomas in news anchoring and video editing. His strong digital presence on platforms like YouTube and Instagram allows him to stay connected with younger audiences and significantly enhances the digital outreach of the institutions he represents. Prof. Rashid Hashmi's career is a benchmark in how media professionals can seamlessly transition into academic leadership without losing their relevance in the field. His rare ability to unite broadcast excellence, media education, research, innovation, and institutional development makes him a transformative figure in the Indian media and academic ecosystem. His continuing efforts aim to equip students with not only the technical skills needed for success in journalism and media, but also the ethical, research, and creative sensibilities required to lead in a digitally disrupted world.

Jinhee Kim is an Assistant Professor in the Instructional Design and Technology (IDT) program at Old Dominion University. Her research bridges learning sciences, human-computer interaction, and instructional design, focusing on how advanced technologies foster meaningful learning. Her main research areas include AI in education, learning and teaching analytics, the design of theoretically grounded AI learning technologies, and instructional design for inclusive AI learning experiences. Her work has appeared in leading journals such as Educational Technology Research and Development, British Journal of Educational Technology, and Journal of Computing in Higher Education.

Sharlene A. Kiuhara is Associate Professor in the Department of Special Education at the University of Utah, USA. She served as an Institute of Education Sciences (IES) Post-Doctoral Fellow at Vanderbilt University in Special Education. She was nationally recognized as an Early Career Publication Award recipient by the Division for Research of the Council for Exceptional Children, an award that honors outstanding research contributions within the first five years after doctoral degree completion. Her research focuses on developing evidence-based practices for students with or at-risk for learning disabilities in the areas of self-regulation and constructing written arguments to develop mathematical reasoning.

Hanh Le is a Senior Technology Services Manager at Orange County Healthcare in California and a research scholar at the University of the Cumberlands. Her dissertation focuses on the evolving role of programmers in the age of artificial intelligence (AI), examining how AI technologies are reshaping the programming landscape. With a strong background as a full-stack software developer across diverse industries, Dr. Le brings academic expertise and practical experience to her work. Her career spans several sectors, including Point of Sale, Accounting, Retail, Healthcare, Social Services, Medical, Inventory Control, Mortgage, Return Authorization, and Law Enforcement. Dr. Le holds a Ph.D. in Information Technology and a Master of Science in Computer Science, focusing on Software Architecture, Machine Learning, and Data Mining, providing her with a robust technical foundation. Additionally, Dr. Le is certified in Data Analytics, reflecting her ability to extract actionable insights from complex datasets. She has extensive experience designing and implementing object-oriented, database-driven applications, ensuring efficient, scalable solutions. Known for her strong leadership and team-building abilities, she has successfully managed teams and projects, contributing to organizational growth and success. Dr. Le excels in both independent and team-oriented work, consistently delivering results while promoting a positive and efficient work environment.

Chenglu Li is an Assistant Professor in the Department of Educational Psychology at the University of Utah, USA. His research focuses on designing and developing responsible multimodal AI to enhance STEM learning. He serves as Managing Director of the Learning Engineering Virtual Institute, ALTER-Math, and as PI/Co-PI of multiple grants advancing responsible AI in STEM education funded by agencies such as Office of Naval Research and Gates Foundation. His work has been recognized with multiple honors, including best paper awards from ACM LAK (2023), ACM IDC (2023), EDM (2024), and AIED (2025, nomination).

Bailing Lyu is a Postdoctoral Researcher in the Department of Educational Psychology at the University of Utah and an assistant professor in Auburn University, Alabama. Her research interests include learning from multiple resources, STEM education, learning analytics, and artificial intelligence in education.

Tuğba Öztürk is a professor of educational technology at Ankara University. She earned her PhD from Lancaster University's Centre for Studies in Advanced Learning Technology. Her publications focus on distance education, inclusive education, AI-enhanced instructional design, and educational technology topics such as computational thinking. Her work bridges educational theory with data-driven approaches to support responsive and inclusive design in open and distance learning environments.

M. Ryan Richey is a senior instructor of Spanish at the United States Air Force Academy in Colorado Springs, Colorado. He serves as the program manager for the Cadet Summer Language Immersion Program and the Cadet Semester Study Abroad program. His research focuses on non-native and native teacher and heritage speaker student language teaching abilities.

İdil Sayin is currently pursuing her PhD in English Language Teaching (ELT) at Hacettepe University and is working as a research assistant at Süleyman Demirel University's ELT Department. She obtained her BA in ELT from Süleyman Demirel University in 2018 and completed her MA in ELT at the same institution in 2020. Additionally, she earned an MS in Measurement and Evaluation in Education from Hacettepe University in 2023. Her research interests include measurement and evaluation in ELT, technology in language education, and language assessment.

Natalia Soto is a graduate student in the University of Utah

Pete Swanson is Professor of Spanish and Division Chief for Spanish and Portuguese at the US Air Force Academy in Colorado, USA. He is Past President of the American Council on the Teaching of Foreign Languages. His research focuses on the world language teacher shortage, teacher effectiveness, characteristics of highly effective world language teachers, and the measurement of learner proficiency in the target language. He is an author of more than 90 peer-reviewed publications including six books in esteemed journals and publishing houses. He enjoys traveling and spending time with his family outdoors around the world.

Seongryeong Yu is an Assistant Professor in the Early Childhood and Elementary Education Program at Old Dominion University, Teaching and Learning Department. Her research explores the language and literacy practices of young children and their teachers across various cultural, virtual, and geographic contexts. Dr. Yu's work has been published in peer-reviewed journals, including the International Journal of Multicultural Education, Pedagogy, Culture & Society, Education and Information Technologies, the Journal of Research on Technology in Education, and the International Critical Childhood Policy Studies Journal.

Index

A

C

E

G

H

T

U

www.ingramcontent.com/pod-product-compliance
Ingram Content Group UK Ltd.
Pitfield, Milton Keynes, MK11 3LW, UK
UKHW050843101026
15624UKWH00018B/477

9 798337 329277